Dear Mum,
Happy Birthday Nov 2001.

Lots of love,
Val, Gopi, Natasha, Jessica.
XXXX.

INDIRA

INDIRA

The Life of
Indira Nehru Gandhi

KATHERINE FRANK

HarperCollins*Publishers*

HarperCollins*Publishers*
77–85 Fulham Palace Road,
Hammersmith, London w6 8jb

*www.***fireandwater**.*com*

Published by HarperCollins*Publishers* 2001
1 3 5 7 9 8 6 4 2

A catalogue record for this book
is available from the British Library

ISBN 0 00 255646 4

Set in PostScript Linotype Janson by
Rowland Phototypesetting Ltd, Bury St Edmunds, Suffolk

Printed and bound in Great Britain by
Clays Ltd, St Ives plc

STEPHEN RILEY

In Memory

CONTENTS

ILLUSTRATIONS

Jawaharlal and Kamala Nehru on their wedding day, 8 February 1916. (*Hulton Getty*)

Studio portrait of Indira Nehru, aged one, with her parents. (*Images of India*)

Indira (aged six) with Mahatma Gandhi in 1924. Gandhi is wan and frail from fasting, but cheerful. (*Images of India*)

The Nehru family, circa 1929. (*Images of India*)

Jawaharlal, Indira (aged thirteen) and Kamala Nehru in white khadi Congress dress in front of Anand Bhawan, 1931. (*Nehru Library*)

Swaraj Bhawan, Motilal Nehru's palatial forty-two room home where Indira Nehru was born on 19 November 1917.

Anand Bhawan, the second, smaller but still luxurious Nehru residence where Motilal Nehru moved his family in 1930.

Indira and other students surround Rabindranath Tagore at Santiniketan. (*Santiniketan archives*)

Indira with her hair bobbed, shortly after arriving in Switzerland with her ailing mother, 1935. (*Images of India*)

Nehru and Indira, very thin and with dark circles under her eyes, en route to England – where she would enrol at Somerville College – September 1937. (*Hulton Getty*)

Indira with her fellow freshers at Somerville College, Oxford. (*Somerville College*)

Photograph of Indira taken by Feroze Gandhi during their courtship. (*Indira Gandhi Memorial Trust*)

Feroze and Indira on shipboard on their way back to India from England in early 1941. (*Indira Gandhi Memorial Trust*)

The wedding of Indira Nehru and Feroze Gandhi. (*Indira Gandhi Memorial Trust*)

Indira, the radiant bride at her wedding. (Still from Norvin Hein's 1942 film of the Nehru-Gandhi wedding)

Indira with Sanjay, aged one, in 1948. (*Mahatma Gandhi Research and Media Service*)

Indira and Nehru shortly after Independence. (*Popperfoto*)

Indira and Nehru during their trek through Bhutan, September 1958. (*Topham Picturepoint*)

Indira making her acceptance speech as President of Congress, 13 February 1959. (*Popperfoto*)

Indira, Nehru and President and Jacqueline Kennedy in Washington DC, November 1961. (*Hulton Getty*)

Indira beside Nehru's body as it lies in state, May 1964. (*Popperfoto*)

'Troubled India in a Woman's Hands.' *Time* magazine cover after Indira was elected Prime Minister in January 1966. (*Time* magazine)

Indira meets President Lyndon Johnson on her first prime ministerial visit to the United States during India's 1966 food crisis. (*Corbis*)

Indira with a bandaged nose – looking in her own words, 'like Batman' – after a rock was thrown at her in Orissa during the 1967 election campaign. (*Images of India*)

Indira with her sons, Rajiv and Sanjay, at their home, 1 Safdarjung Road, in 1967. (*Hulton Getty*)

P.N. Haksar, Indira's Principal Secretary and most important adviser. (*P.N. Haksar*)

Indira at talks with Premier Kosygin and Leonid Brezhnev in Moscow, September 1971. (*Novosti*)

Indira and the Pakistani leader Zufikar Ali Bhutto during the Simla summit conference following the Indo-Pak war of December 1981. (*Hulton Getty*)

Indira with Siddhartha Shankar Ray and Sheikh Mujibur Rahman at Delhi airport. (*Siddhartha Shankar Ray*)

Formal family portrait of Indira and her family in 1974. (*Iindira Gandhi Memorial Trust*)

Indira with Sanjay, an elected MP, in Rae Bareilly after she was returned to power as Prime Minister, 1980. (*Raghu Rai/Magnum*)

Indira, her one-year-old grandson Varun, and Maneka Gandhi on the first anniversary remembrance ceremony of Sanjay Gandhi's death, 1981. (*Raghu Rai/Magnum*)

Margaret Thatcher and Indira in front of 10 Downing Street, 22 March 1982. (*Hulton Getty*)

Indira surrounded by Sikhs during a campaign tour in the 1980s. (*Raghu Rai/Magnum*)

GLOSSARY

ayah	nanny or childminder
bahu	daughter-in-law
bewa	widow
bhai	brother
bindi	the decorative mark worn by Hindu women on their foreheads
Brahmin	a Hindu from the highest, originally priestly, caste
burkha	a long, loose garment, covering the whole body, worn by Muslim women
brahmacharya	celibacy
chamchas	sycophants (literally 'spoons')
chappals	sandals
charkha	a spinning wheel
churidars	pyjama trousers worn by men
crore	ten million (one hundred *lakhs*)
dalit	a Hindu outside the caste system, also referred to as an 'untouchable'
darshan	the sight or view of a holy or important person which bestows blessing on the viewer
dhoti	a loincloth
durbar	open court held by a ruler
gherao	a protest demonstration that involves encircling and immobilizing the protesters' target
Harijan	Mohandas Gandhi's term for a *dalit*, literally the child of God
hartal	a general strike
jhuggis	shacks inhabited by the urban poor
kameez	a long tunic worn with a *salwar* or *churidars*
khadi	hand-woven cloth
lakh	a hundred thousand
lathi	a truncheon
Lok Sabha	the 'people's assembly', the lower house of Parliament elected by common suffrage every five years

maharaja	a Hindu or Sikh princely ruler
masjid	a mosque
namaste	traditional greeting or gesture of respect made by bringing the palms together before the face or chest
puja	Hindu prayer or ceremony
purdah	the veiling or seclusion of women
raja	ruler or king
Rajya Sabha	the upper house of Parliament consisting of members elected by state assemblies or nominated by the President of India
sadhu	a Hindu holy man
salwar	trousers worn by women which are loose at the top and taper to fit tightly at the ankles
sanyassi	a Hindu who renounces normal daily life for a life of religious asceticism
satyagraha	non-violent resistance (literally 'truth force')
sherwani	long formal coat
swadeshi	an indigenous product (literally 'belonging to one's country')
swami	Hindu religious teacher
swaraj	independence or self-rule
vakil	lawyer

ACKNOWLEDGEMENTS

It took six years to research and write *Indira* and I have many people to thank for help along the way.

I am especially grateful to the following institutions and their archivists. In Delhi: the Nehru Memorial Museum and Library, the India International Centre, the Indira Gandhi Memorial Trust. In Allahabad: Anand Bhawan and Swaraj Bhawan Museums. In Santiniketan: Visva-Bharati University Archives. In London: the British Library, the Friends House Library, the London Library, the School of Oriental and African Studies Library. In Bristol: Badminton School Archives. In Oxford: Somerville College and Oxford University Archives. In Switzerland: Institut La Pelouse (Bex), Leysin Municipal Archives. In the United States: Beinecke Library at Yale University.

I am grateful to Sonia Gandhi for talking to me and for allowing me to use the correspondence between Indira Nehru Gandhi and Jawaharlal Nehru.

The following people proffered assistance, information, insights, and invariably good will:

In India: Mani Shankar Aiyar, Usha Bhagat, the late Nikhil Chakravartty, Renuka Chatterjee, Ira Vakil Chaudhuri, Rupika Chawla, P.N. Chopra, Susan Clapham, Ian Copland, Ratoo Dastoor, V.N. Datta, Nonica Datta, P.N. Dhar, R.K. Dhawan, Suman Dubey, Rustom Gandhi, V. George, Santosh and Sucheta Goindi, Sarvepelli Gopal, the late P.N. Haksar, Jagmohan, the late Pupul Jayakar, Subhadra Joshi, Promilla Kalhan, Martin Kampchen, Inder Kapur, J.C. Kapur, T.N. Kaul, Anser Kidwai, Girja Kumar, Ravinder Kumar, Inder Malhotra, Sanjana Malhotra, Surjit Mansingh, Dr K.P. Mathur, Peter Mayer, R.K. Mehra, Chandralekha Mehta, Hiren Mukherjee, B.R. Nanda, Arun Nehru, B.K. and Fori Nehru, V.Y. Nehru, Yash Pal, H.Y. Sharada Prasad, N.H. Ramachandran, Siddhartha Shankar Ray, Saugata Roy, Nayantara Sahgal, Dr Vatsala Samant, Vasant Sathe, Geeti Sen, O.P. Shah,

J.P. Sharma, K. Natwar Singh, Karan Singh, Khushwant Singh, Patwant Singh, V.P. Singh, Tarakeshwari Sinha, R.N. Upadhyay, Madhu Tandan, P.D. Tandon, Alice Thorner, Uma Vasudev, Douglas Verney, Dharma Vira, N.N. Vohra, Jehanara Wasi, Mohammed Yunus. Elsewhere: Pauline Adams, Maurice André, Simon Bailey, Sita Bali, Anne Bielman, Robert Bradnock, Michael Brecher, the late Alan Campbell-Johnson, Mary C. Carras, William Dalrymple, Annie Kathleen Davies, Bertil Falk, Trevor Fishlock, Michael Foot, Francine Frankel, Patrick French, John Kenneth Galbraith, Freddy Gerber, Terry Gill, John Grigg, Norvin Hein, Richard Hobday, Lady Pamela Hicks, Mervyn Jones, Sudipta Kaviraj, James Manor, Ved Mehta, Janet Morgan, Dr John Moore-Gillon, the late Dorothy Norman, Lord Paul, Andrew Robinson, Suzanne Rollier-Chapuis, les Soeurs de St Maurice at La Pelouse, especially Sister Jacqueline and Sister Hildegarde, Jan Scarrow, Mary Thompson, the late Anne Whiteman, Geoffrey Ward.

I am grateful for the financial assistance provided by a generous Arts Council Award and a Nuffield Foundation Grant.

Thanks to Catherine Byron – friend and editor of first resort – who read the manuscript at various stages and to Michael David Anthony who read it when it was completed. Both contributed valuable criticism. I am especially grateful to Mark Tully – who witnessed and covered many of the events in this book first-hand – for reading the manuscript with great care and giving me detailed and sensitive feedback. Sunil Khilnani was also an authoritative and helpful reader. Alexander Evans scrutinized the Kashmir sections. I am also hugely indebted to Kate Johnson at HarperCollins for her inspired and tireless editing. I alone, of course, am responsible for the Indira Gandhi who emerges in this book as well as for any errors.

Profound thanks to Bruce Hunter and Ginger Barber, the best of agents, and to Michael Fishwick, my incomparable publisher at HarperCollins. Thanks as well to Caroline Hotblack at Harper-Collins, and to my American editor, Janet Silver, and her colleague at Houghton Mifflin, Wendy Holt.

For unfailing love and support I am deeply grateful to my close friends Catherine Byron (again), Pauline Elkes and Laura Kalpakian, and to my extraordinary family: Isabel and Arthur Voss, Art Voss and Nancy White, Margaret Voss-Pierce, and Justin and Vicky Frank.

Acknowledgements

Finally, I am indebted – in more ways than I can ever say – to my husband, Stephen Riley. He died before *Indira* was completed and before his own work was harvested. This book has always been for him, and is dedicated, with abiding love, to his memory.

INDIA 1931

AFGHANISTAN

JAMMU AND KASHMIR
Srinagar

N.W. FRONTIER PROVINCE

CHINA

Lahore • Amritsar

PUNJAB

TIBET

BALUCHISTAN

Delhi
Rae Bareilly

SIKKIM BHUTAN

SIND
Karachi

RAJPUTANA

UNITED PROVINCES

ASSAM

Allahabad

BENGAL

BIHAR AND ORISSA

Arabian Sea

CENTRAL PROVINCES

Calcutta

BOMBAY
Bombay
Poona

ORISSA

Bay of Bengal

HYDERABAD

MYSORE Madras

MADRAS

CEYLON

British India

Princely States

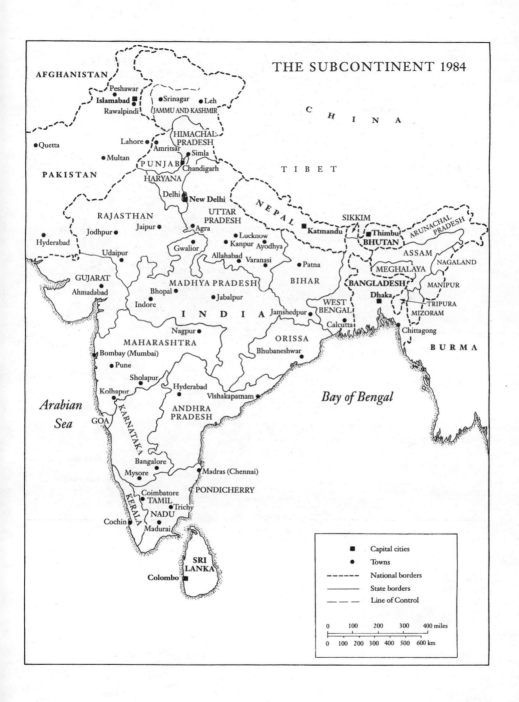

THE SUBCONTINENT 1984

Indira's Family Tree

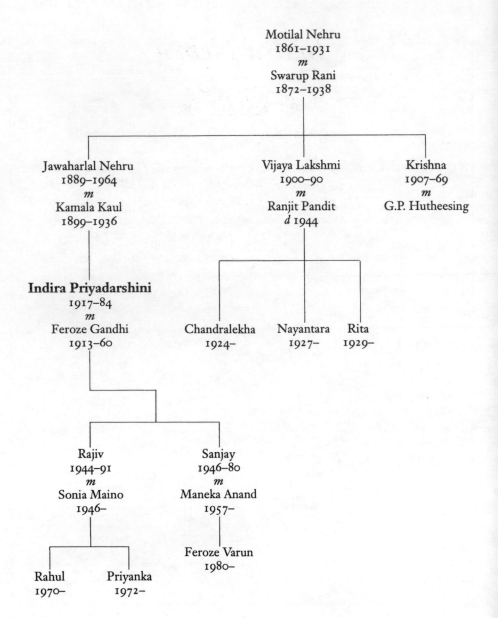

Motilal Nehru
1861–1931
m
Swarup Rani
1872–1938

Jawaharlal Nehru
1889–1964
m
Kamala Kaul
1899–1936

Vijaya Lakshmi
1900–90
m
Ranjit Pandit
d 1944

Krishna
1907–69
m
G.P. Hutheesing

Indira Priyadarshini
1917–84
m
Feroze Gandhi
1913–60

Chandralekha
1924–

Nayantara
1927–

Rita
1929–

Rajiv
1944–91
m
Sonia Maino
1946–

Sanjay
1946–80
m
Maneka Anand
1957–

Feroze Varun
1980–

Rahul
1970–

Priyanka
1972–

PART ONE

Indira Nehru

Home is where one starts from.
As we grow older the world becomes stranger,
The pattern more complicated . . .
In my end is my beginning.

T.S. Eliot, 'East Coker'
from *Four Quartets*

ONE

Descent from Kashmir

DAILY NINETY-MINUTE FLIGHTS connect Srinagar, the capital of the Indian state of Jammu and Kashmir, with Delhi. But my letter to the Kashmiri Chief Minister, Farooq Abdullah, took six weeks to reach him, and according to the date of the reply written by his 'acting assistant principal secretary', the Chief Minister's response took another five weeks to get back to me in Delhi. Had our letters languished on some functionary's desk, in a forgotten mail bag, got lost in the crush of a bustling post office? It was not going to be easy to get to Kashmir. Nevertheless, the Chief Minister's reply brought good news: Farooq Abdullah would be pleased to talk to me about the late Prime Minister Indira Gandhi. We could meet either in Delhi or Srinagar, according to my convenience.

Srinagar today – like most of the rest of Kashmir – is no longer an easy place to visit. Once the idyllic pleasure ground of the British Raj and later a tourist resort for Indian, European, American and Australian tourists and backpackers, Kashmir is now a war zone – the disputed territory fought over by two hostile nations that were once one: India and Pakistan. Those writers who go to Kashmir these days are not biographers but journalists covering an internecine conflict that rumbles, flares up, dies down and rumbles on year in and year out.

After decades of obscurity, Kashmir now makes global headlines. Several years ago, Kashmiri separatists kidnapped and murdered a group of Western climbers trekking in the Himalayas. In the spring of 1998 India and Pakistan set off nuclear devices, making Kashmir the likeliest flash point of the next nuclear holocaust. A year later, their armies were at war on the border near Kargil. In the spring of 2000, when President Clinton visited the subcontinent, a village of Sikhs was massacred –

allegedly by militants – to underscore the fact that the war still raged on.[1]

Most of the Srinagar hotels are now boarded up and derelict. Those still operating house security forces. Rows of khaki laundry flap on clothes lines in the hotel gardens. Black-booted soldiers in helmets and flak jackets patrol the streets. The traffic is mainly army jeeps and trucks. Gone are the hawkers, pavement ear-cleaners and street barbers. Ordinary life of a sort goes on here. But the atmosphere in the shops and bazaars is often tense and faces are sullen or downcast.

At the heart of Srinagar lies Dal Lake – sluggish, furry green, congealed with pollutants. From time to time, the lake belches methane gas, releasing a putrid stench into the air. No kingfishers fly overhead because no fish could live in this lake. When Indira Gandhi appointed her cousin B.K. Nehru as Governor of Kashmir in 1982 – at a time when the present conflict might still have been averted – she personally briefed him. She said not one word about the volatile political situation in the state. Instead she spoke with urgency and passion of the need to clean up Dal Lake before it was too late.[2] Nearly twenty years later, here and there, a rotting houseboat shudders on its stagnant surface.

Kashmir today is not the Kashmir Indira Gandhi knew. Kashmir today is India fouled and polluted – India lacerated – the unhealed and unhealing wound of Partition. In 1947, at independence, when British India was carved into the two sovereign nations of India and Pakistan, Kashmir, the only Muslim majority state in India, acceded to a secular India rather than an Islamic Pakistan. The Hindu Maharaja of Kashmir made this choice for his Muslim majority population. But he made it under duress – and to no one's satisfaction.

Since 1947 India and Pakistan have fought three full-scale wars over Kashmir, a place of minor material or economic importance to either country.[3] But Kashmir possesses enormous significance to Indians' and Pakistanis' conflicting, irreconcilable conceptions of the subcontinent. Kashmir has been bitterly and bloodily disputed because it has come to symbolize on the one hand, the ideal of secular democracy to Indians, and on the other, the validity of a Muslim homeland to Pakistanis. Nuclear devices, bloody skirmishes in the mountains of Kargil, village massacres, more bombs and assassinations in Srinagar – these are just the most recent chapters in a story that goes back more than half a century.

But my story – the life of Indira Gandhi – goes back even further.

It begins in a remote Himalayan fastness of snow-capped mountains, meadows carpeted with alpine wildflowers, rushing rivers that flow into tear-shaped lakes, and valleys dark with fir and pine forests where the gigantic chinar tree bursts into fiery-red blossoms every autumn until the snows come and extinguish all colour from the land.

This Kashmir – a place of beauty and transcendence – was the bedrock of Indira Gandhi's life, the thing to which she held fast, which she sought to recover again and again in the course of her long life. Kashmir was a land that nourished and solaced her. 'We were Kashmiris', Indira's father, Jawaharlal Nehru, writes on the first page of his *Autobiography*. Indira Gandhi embraced this statement and put it into the present tense – 'I am Kashmiri'. Throughout a rootless, chaotic existence, in which she never had a stable family life or owned a house of her own, Kashmir remained Indira Gandhi's anchor, her heart's home.

Her story begins – as it ends – in Kashmir.

It opens in Kashmir – but then almost immediately leaves it. Indira Gandhi's biography, like all biographies, does not begin abruptly, at the moment of birth, but rather at what seems – to the biographer – a decisive moment long before. And this moment – some two hundred years before Indira was born in November 1917 – was one of banishment – a fall or expulsion from paradise. In the opening chapter of his *Autobiography*, 'Descent from Kashmir', Nehru writes, 'over two hundred years ago, our ancestors came down from that mountain valley to seek fame and fortune in the . . . plains below'.[4] From their lofty, Edenic home in the Himalayas, Indira Gandhi's forebears were exiled to the hot, arid plains of north-central India.

The particular ancestor Nehru refers to was a Hindu Pandit – one of the Brahmin elite of Kashmir – named Raj Kaul, a Sanskrit and Persian scholar, who left Kashmir around 1716 for Delhi. Here he became a member of the court of the Mughal Emperor Farukhsiyar who granted Raj Kaul a house situated on a canal in the city. Raj Kaul's descendants came to be known as Kaul-Nehrus after *nahar*, which means canal, and in time this was shortened to Nehru.

From the beginning, the Nehru family was allied to power. First this was the power of the Mughal Emperor and when his empire declined, the might of the British. Raj Kaul's great-grandson, Lakshmi Narayan, became one of the first Indian *vakils*, or lawyers, of the East India Company in Delhi, and his son, Ganga Dar, was a police officer in the city when the Mutiny broke out in 1857. In the upheaval of the 1857 uprising, Ganga Dar fled with his family to Agra. He died four years later and three months after his death his wife gave birth to a posthumous son who was named Motilal.

Motilal Nehru – Indira Gandhi's grandfather – was raised by his elder brother, Nand Lal, and Motilal, like his brother, trained as a lawyer. Like his brother, too, Motilal married while still in his teens and had a son. But both wife and son died in childbirth before Motilal was twenty. By 1887, the year that Nand Lal died and Motilal assumed responsibility for the family as the eldest surviving son, Motilal had remarried a beautiful young woman, also of Kashmiri extraction, named Swarup Rani. The young couple moved to Allahabad, in the United Provinces (as they were then called) some 500 miles from Delhi, where Motilal pursued what quickly became a brilliant legal career.

Centuries ago Allahabad was known as the ancient city of Prayag. It features in the epic *Ramayana* and it remains a goal of pilgrimage for Hindus because it is here that the three sacred Indian rivers – the Ganges, the Jumna and the lost, subterranean, Saraswati, converge. Allahabad today is a sleepy, dusty provincial town, but at the end of the nineteenth century it was the capital of the United Provinces, seat of the High Court and home to the most distinguished university in India.

Motilal Nehru prospered both professionally and personally in Allahabad. An astute and successful lawyer, he soon became one of the wealthiest and most socially prominent citizens in the town. Fortune also smiled on him when his first child, a son named Jawaharlal – Indira Gandhi's father – was born on 14 November 1889. In the first sentence of his autobiography, Nehru states (or rather understates) in his David Copperfield fashion: 'An only son of prosperous parents is apt to be spoilt, especially in India.'[5] It is one of life's ironies – or perhaps one of fate's congruities – that this most pampered scion of an immensely rich man would grow up to be largely indifferent to and careless of material wealth.

Nehru's asceticism, however, was slow to develop which is hardly surprising given the environment in which he was raised. In 1900 Motilal Nehru moved his family to a huge, forty-two-room house on 1 Church Road in the Civil Lines (the civilian English sector) of Allahabad. He named his mansion Anand Bhawan – the 'Abode of Happiness'. It was a manorial estate on English lines and of English proportions, with spacious gardens, an orchard, a tennis court, riding ring and an indoor swimming pool. Shortly after moving in, Motilal installed electricity and running water – the first in Allahabad. After a trip to Europe in 1904, he imported a car – another Allahabad first. It may very well have been the first automobile in all of the United Provinces. Certainly it was the only one driven by an English chauffeur.

By the time Jawaharlal was sent away to public school in Harrow, England, in 1905, he had a little sister named Sarup Kumari, born in 1900. Another sister, Krishna, arrived in 1907. (A second son, born in 1905, survived only a month.) All the Nehru children had a privileged, British-style upbringing. Until he was sent to public school in England, Jawaharlal was educated by a young Irish tutor named Ferdinand T. Brooks. The girls had an English governess named Miss Lillian Hooper who gave English nicknames to all three Nehru children. In the girls' case, these lasted all their lives. Jawaharlal was 'Joe', Sarup Kumari was 'Nan', and Krishna 'Betty'.

But despite its liveried servants, dining table set with Sèvres porcelain, crystal glasses and silver cutlery, its grand piano in the sitting room and its huge library of leather-bound books, Anand Bhawan was not merely an elaborate replica of an English country estate. The Nehru household was actually bifurcated between East and West, India and Britain. Motilal Nehru wore expensive suits ordered from Savile Row tailors (though contrary to rumour his linen was not shipped back to Europe to be laundered). He eschewed religion, drank Scotch whisky, ate Western food (including meat) prepared by a Christian cook, and insisted that only English be spoken at his table. He employed British tutors and governesses to educate his children and, after Harrow, sent his son to Cambridge.

But Motilal's wife, Swarup Rani, was a traditional Kashmiri woman and a devout Hindu. She allowed her daughters to be dressed in French frocks, but she herself never wore anything other than a sari in the Kashmiri fashion. She bathed in the Ganges, performed the Hindu prayer ceremony of *puja*, was a strict vegetarian, kept her own Kashmiri cook and ate with her fingers, seated on the floor. She understood but did not speak English. The women of Anand Bhawan conversed in Hindi.

7

Two parallel worlds, then, co-existed but did not really overlap, at Anand Bhawan. This was strikingly revealed in the otherwise mundane arrangements for disposing of human waste. The adults in the family used commodes or 'thunderboxes' – European-style toilets on which one sat. The children and servants relieved themselves in the traditional Indian way at ground level. Both methods were perfectly sanitary and Anand Bhawan, like other Indian households, had 'untouchable' – or Harijan[6] – sweepers responsible for cleaning out both types of toilets, though when running water was introduced, the thunderboxes became flushable.

Most of the time, the two worlds of Anand Bhawan – Western and Indian – were respectively male and female realms. But not always. Despite the Hindu injunction against foreign travel (which brought with it a loss of caste), Swarup Rani accompanied her husband and children to Britain and Europe when Jawaharlal first went away to school in 1905. And Motilal Nehru, for all his British thinking, values, habits and attitudes, remained deeply traditional when it came to the choice of his son's career and wife.

Jawaharlal Nehru had little say in either matter. Apparently without protest, he obeyed his father's wishes and endured a seven-year exile from his family and India while he was educated in England. Then when Motilal decided that his son should follow in his steps and take up law, Jawaharlal read for the bar in London. These years abroad were not ones of great accomplishment. Jawaharlal's career at public school and university was undistinguished, and as he says in his autobiography, 'I got through the bar examinations ... with neither glory nor ignominy.' In London, he 'was vaguely attracted to the Fabians and socialistic ideas and interested in political movements of the day'. But for the most part he 'drifted' and led 'a soft and pointless existence'. This careless, hedonistic period was the one time in Nehru's life when he displayed 'expensive habits'. Often, in fact, he exceeded 'the handsome allowance' that Motilal gave him, and had to wire home for more funds.[7]

Jawaharlal entered the legal profession without demur. But he put up something of a struggle before he agreed to marry the woman his father chose for him. By the time he returned to India in 1912, England had transformed Jawaharlal. At Cambridge he mixed with a set who read Havelock Ellis and Krafft-Ebing and considered themselves 'very sophisticated and talked of sex and morality', though Nehru adds that 'in spite of our brave talk, most of us were rather timid where sex was concerned'. His own sexual knowledge, he says, was 'for many years, till after I left Cambridge . . . confined to theory'.[8]

But even this theoretical knowledge – and the Western attitudes towards romantic love and marriage associated with it – affected Nehru, and initially he rebelled not so much against his father's choice of a bride as the notion that Motilal should do the choosing for him. The selection was made before Jawaharlal even returned to India in 1912. Shortly before he was called to the bar in London, Jawaharlal received a letter from his father with the news that Motilal had decided that his son's future wife should be a twelve-year-old girl named Kamala Kaul. 'A little beauty [and] . . . very healthy', as Motilal described her, Kamala was the daughter of a conservative Kashmiri family who lived in Delhi. The contract between the two families had been drawn up and the dowry agreed on, Motilal informed his son. All Jawaharlal had to do was give his assent.

This was not immediately forthcoming. Jawaharlal responded to his father's letter with ambivalence. 'I do not, and cannot possibly, look forward with relish to the idea of marrying a girl whom I do not know,' he wrote to Motilal. 'At the same time . . . [if] you are intent on my getting engaged to the girl you mention I will have no objection . . . I shall bide by your decision.' With his mother, Swarup Rani, Jawaharlal was more outspoken. He confessed that he was frightened at the prospect of marrying 'a total stranger'. He accepted 'that any girl selected by you and father would be good in many respects', but he feared that he might 'not be able to get along with her'. And to his mother, Jawaharlal voiced his disapproval of arranged Hindu marriages: 'In my opinion, unless there is a degree of mutual understanding, marriage should not take place. I think it unjust and cruel that a life should be wasted merely in producing children.'[9]

Once back in India, Jawaharlal had several years to adjust to the prospect of marrying Kamala Kaul, for at twelve, she was far too young to wed right away. And it was not only the prospect of marriage that unsettled Jawaharlal when he was transplanted – after seven formative years abroad – back to Allahabad. As he says in his autobiography, 'the habits and ideas that had grown in me during my seven years in England did not fit in with things as I found them' back home. He was overcome with a feeling of ennui: 'a sense of the utter insipidity of life grew upon me'.[10] Nevertheless, Jawaharlal took up law, and gradually an interest in the nationalist movement for Indian home rule replaced his ennui. Whether he continued to argue with his parents over his marriage partner is unknown. Time passed and Jawaharlal's eventual marriage to Kamala became an inevitability.

In 1915, when Kamala was sixteen, she came to live in Allahabad in order to be groomed as Jawaharlal's wife. Coming from a traditional Kashmiri family Kamala was ignorant of European manners and habits. The Nehru daughters' governess, Miss Hooper, undertook Kamala's training in the use of cutlery and speaking English. It was not an easy education. Kamala was a serious, intense, highly-strung girl of great beauty, with fair skin, dark hair, and large, luminous brown eyes. But there was no warmth or gaiety in her beauty – she was shy and with-drawn, with a face that often wore the look of a stricken deer.

Nor was she as malleable and unformed as she appeared. Kamala submitted to her transformation into an acceptable bride for Jawaharlal Nehru because she had no choice. But her underlying character remained untouched, though it would take many years for others – including her own husband – to discern how strong and stubborn she could be and how committed Kamala was to her principles. Motilal Nehru doubtless believed he was acquiring a complete cipher for a daughter-in-law, and for years Motilal's wife and daughters and many other members of the household treated Kamala as such.

In fact, as time would tell, Motilal had inadvertently chosen a woman who far from being a nonentity, eventually developed with her husband what is still rare in any culture – a marriage of equals, of shared sexual intensity, of mutual respect and shared values and dreams.[11] It would take many years for Jawaharlal and Kamala Nehru to achieve this; to some extent Nehru recognized it only after Kamala had died, and after, as well, Kamala had rejected marriage at the end of her life for a religious goal she felt was higher and more precious still.

The marriage date was selected by family astrologers: 8 February 1916, which was *Basant Panchami*, the festival which heralds the coming of spring. For weeks beforehand, tailors, seamstresses and jewellers toiled at Allahabad preparing the bride's trousseau, often under Motilal's personal supervision. Gifts from all over India flooded Anand Bhawan. The wedding was to be held in Delhi and Motilal arranged for a special train to carry 300 guests – family, relations and friends of the groom – to Delhi, where a huge tented city was set up outside the walled city with a sign made of flowers announcing the 'Nehru Wedding Camp'.

One surviving wedding photograph of Kamala and Jawaharlal Nehru poignantly reveals their plight on the day they wed. They are standing carefully posed and elaborately dressed – Jawaharlal in a brocade *sherwani* (a long formal coat) and turban, and Kamala in a pearl-studded sari that had taken a team of craftsmen months of labour to produce. But the bride and groom's posture and their expressions belie their finery and the occasion. Their arms are loosely linked – they are, after all, now man and wife – but they do not stand close together and they look almost melancholy. Jawaharlal stares tentatively into the camera, dark circles under his eyes. Kamala looks off to the left, away from her husband. There is a shadow of a smile on her lips, but her dark eyes are wide with what seems to be fear.

The newlyweds honeymooned in Kashmir – just as twenty-six years later their daughter would go to Kashmir with her bridegroom. It was the first time either Jawaharlal or Kamala had been to Kashmir; the first sight they had of their homeland. What Kamala made of Kashmir we do not know. For Nehru, however, it was a haunting and nearly fatal visit.

Arriving in Srinagar, Jawaharlal left his bride to go climbing for several weeks with a cousin in the mountains of Ladakh, the remote, eastern region of Kashmir. No one seems to have thought this an odd way for a young man to spend his honeymoon. This journey into the Himalayas was, as Nehru records in his autobiography, his 'first experience of the narrow and lonely valleys, high up in the world, which lead to the Tibetan plateau'. The bleak beauty and the solitude of the mountains thrilled him: 'the loneliness grew; there were not even trees or vegetation to keep us company – only the bare rock and the snow and ice and, sometimes, very welcome flowers. Yet I found a strange satisfaction in these wild and desolate haunts of nature: I was full of energy and a feeling of exaltation.'[12]

At a place called Matayan, they were told that a famous cave, the cave of Amaranath, was only eight miles distant and they resolved to trek there, despite the fact that 'an enormous mountain' lay in their way. With a local shepherd for a guide and porters to carry their gear, they set off at four in the morning and soon crossed several glaciers. As they climbed higher, their breathing became laboured and they stopped to attach connecting ropes to their waists. Several of the heavily-laden porters started to spit blood. It began to snow and the glaciers were 'terribly slippery'. The entire party was 'fagged out, and every step' was an effort, but still they trekked on.

After twelve hours of increasingly laborious climbing, late in the afternoon they came out onto a huge ice field, surrounded by snow-covered peaks. Bathed in the dying rays of the sun, it looked 'like a diadem or an amphitheatre of the gods'. Then fresh snow and mists descended on them and obscured this celestial vision. In order to reach their goal, the Amaranath cave, they had to cross the ice field, now almost wholly obscured by the bad weather. 'It was a tricky business,' as Nehru describes it, 'as there were many crevasses and the fresh snow often covered a dangerous spot.'[13]

Suddenly Jawaharlal plummeted down one of these – a great gaping chasm, lightly overlaid by a blanket of snow that hid the 'tremendous fissure'. But the rope tied round his waist, which connected him to his companion, held fast. He was not consigned to 'the safe keeping and preservation' of future 'geological ages'. Nehru clutched the side of the crevasse and was hauled out.[14]

This narrow escape changed the course of Indian history and many individual lives, including my own some eighty-odd years later.

It also awakened in Nehru an enduring fascination with and longing for the mountains of Kashmir. The Himalayas became for him a symbol of inexpressible desire and release. Writing his autobiography in prison, nearly twenty years after his fall down the crevasse, Nehru speaks with undiminished passion of this landscape which he had not yet been able to revisit. 'I dream of the day when I shall wander about the Himalayas and cross them to reach that lake and mountain of my desire.'[15]

Historical and political imperatives determined and shaped the lives of Jawaharlal Nehru and his daughter, Indira Gandhi. Both Nehru and Indira were 'handcuffed to history'. Only death offered release. Neither feared death, but it was never far from their minds – the death of those they loved, of their dreams, of themselves. The mountains of Kashmir were sublimely indifferent to human life and death. Untouched by human sorrows, immune to human joy, their beauty and stillness existed far above the plains of human toil and struggle.

No wonder that Indira Gandhi, for all the years of her life, longed for Kashmir and thirsted for its mountains and 'their untroubled snows'.[16]

TWO

'Hua'

❦

ON 5 OCTOBER 1917, Annie Besant – a stout, white-haired, seventy-year-old Englishwoman who had been released from political imprisonment two weeks earlier – made a triumphant visit to Allahabad. Dressed in a gold-embroidered white sari, she was met at the railway station by a huge crowd, including the nationalist leaders Motilal and Jawaharlal Nehru, Sarojini Naidu and Bal Gangadhar Tilak. Her carriage was unhorsed and dragged by a team of young men through streets lined with cheering people and decorated with flags, bunting and floral arches. When the procession reached Motilal Nehru's palatial house, Anand Bhawan, Mrs Besant – founder of the Indian Home Rule League, shortly to be elected President of the Indian National Congress, world-famous Theosophist and brilliant orator – delivered an impassioned speech calling for Indian independence. Kamala Nehru, barely eighteen years old and eight months pregnant, stood on the veranda of Anand Bhawan next to her husband Jawaharlal, listening to this rousing speech. Their child-to-be was attending its first political event. She would grow up to become President of Congress, following in Annie Besant's as well as her grandfather's and father's footsteps. Forty-eight years later, also clad in a white sari and with a streak of white like a bird's wing in her dark hair, Indira Gandhi would be elected the third prime minister of an independent India.

Indira was born six weeks after Mrs Besant's visit, on the stormy night of 19 November in the northwest corner room of Anand Bhawan where all new additions to the family traditionally came into the world. Weighing scarcely four pounds, the baby's tiny body was topped by what looked, incongruously, like a finely-formed adult's head with masses of black hair, huge dark eyes, a delicate mouth and (to her lasting grief) an overgenerous nose. On the veranda outside the birth room a crowd of expectant aunts, second cousins, friends, neighbours and servants, including a new Tamil *ayah* (nanny), had been waiting impatiently all day.

Around 11 p.m. Swarup Rani Nehru, the baby's grandmother, emerged from the room onto the veranda calling for her husband who was drinking Haig's Dimple Scotch with the men in the library.

'Hua [it has happened],' Swarup Rani announced when he arrived.

'Baccha hua [it has happened]?' repeated Motilal, knowing full well that his wife used the neutral pronoun because she could not bring herself to say that a female child had been born.[1]

An unmistakable wave of deflation and disappointment swept through the crowd on the veranda. As Indira Gandhi diplomatically put it years later, 'while my family was not orthodox enough to consider the birth of a girl child a misfortune, it did regard the male child a privilege and a necessity'.[2]

No one seems to remember just where Jawaharlal Nehru was and what he said when his daughter was born. But he was probably the only person in Anand Bhawan that evening not unduly concerned about the child's sex. In his autobiography, written in prison seventeen years later, he failed to record the events of that stormy November night and his own feelings about them. What was significant to him, as he later told his daughter in a letter written on her thirteenth birthday, was that 'the very month in which you were born', saw the birth of the Russian Revolution thousands of miles away from India.[3] Nehru, the most unsentimental and unsuperstitious of men, savoured this coincidence of history and held it out to Indira as a portent throughout her childhood. She was, he said in another letter, conceived in and born to a world of 'storm and trouble' – a child who would grow up in the midst of another revolution.[4] Like many of those who have written about his daughter, Nehru often viewed her through a cloud of myth.

Indira's own earliest memories – as recalled in adulthood – were also mythic, highly political ones. In 1920, when she was just three, as part of the drive for Indian self-rule, nationalists launched a non-cooperation movement which involved boycotting British institutions, including schools and courts, and refusing to abide by the laws and regulations of the imperial government. In addition, all British and foreign goods were shunned in favour of Indian products, especially homespun *khadi* cloth. Almost overnight, the opulent Nehru home was transformed: crystal chandeliers, Spode china, sterling silver, Venetian glass, expensive carpets, carriages, Arabian horses, all vanished, and the family members (Swarup Rani, among others, protesting) donned coarse *khadi* clothes.

Indira's first memory is of a bonfire of English apparel and imported cloth on the veranda of Anand Bhawan. She saw the wood being thrown on the piles of richly-coloured satins, silks, chiffons, hand-tailored Savile Row suits and starched shirts. She watched as the fire put 'forth its first flickering tongue of flame'.[5] Even more vividly, she remembered how she spurned a French frock brought back from Paris by a relative who then pointed out that her doll, too, was a foreign product. Indu (as she was always called in the family) thought of the doll as her flesh and blood, not a treasonous object. 'For days on end – or was it weeks?' she was torn between 'love of the doll and . . . duty towards my country'. Finally, on her own one day, she took the doll up to the roof terrace of Anand Bhawan and set light to it. Afterwards she was ill with a temperature. As an adult she confessed, 'to this day I hate striking a match'.[6]

The bonfire of clothes and the doll cremation were the first two fires in a life measured out, as Hindu lives are, by ritual conflagrations: of weddings, naming ceremonies, worship and cremations, all underlaid by the idea of rebirth or reincarnation. By the time Indira Gandhi recalled these childhood memories in 1980, she knew that her life had had more than its share of these burning milestones – and comebacks. She chose its controlling metaphor of fiery destruction and resurrection.

In November 1917, however, instead of myth, there was only regret over the birth of a girl. But not devastation. Kamala Nehru, after all, was only eighteen and her husband twenty-eight; they had been married less than two years and no one suspected that this would be an only child. Motilal Nehru chose his mother's name Indrani, modified to the more modern and fashionable Indira, for the baby and Jawaharlal added the Buddhist Priyadarshini which means 'dear to the sight' and also 'one who reveals the good'. A learned Pandit drew up the baby's horoscope and no tragic – or revolutionary – configurations were forecast. A lavish naming ceremony was held. After these ripples of excitement, ordinary life at Anand Bhawan resumed.

Rather than a catastrophe, the arrival of a female child even in such a prosperous and aristocratic family as the Nehrus, was an event of little consequence except, of course, to her parents. The poet and nationalist leader, Sarojini Naidu, wrote from Madras and sent 'a kiss to the new Soul of India', but this was an allusion to one of Mrs Naidu's recent poems, not a prophecy.[7] The baby's mother, Kamala, and grandfather, Motilal (who ordered a British perambulator from Calcutta), doted on her, but for much of this huge household of nearly a hundred (counting all the servants) the infant was not an important family member. In her very earliest years, Indira was small, unobtrusive, causing little trouble, provoking little notice. Her cousin, B.K. Nehru, who grew up in Allahabad and lived in Anand Bhawan during the twenties, once asked Indira when she became Prime Minister where she had been during those years; he had no recollection of her. 'I was right there,' she answered, 'but no one ever noticed me.'[8] Yet, once she emerged from infancy, she was never excluded from the political activity that soon gripped the household. She was in the midst of things – at first underfoot and then in general view.

The year before Indira's birth Jawaharlal Nehru had met Mohandas Gandhi at the 1916 Lucknow meeting of the Indian National Congress – the party that spearheaded independence from the British. This was a decisive encounter because Gandhi had an immediate and profound impact on Jawaharlal. He focussed Jawaharlal's inchoate nationalism, radicalizing him in the process in a way that distressed the more conservative Motilal. In a sense, Gandhi soon became a rival father figure for Jawaharlal and therefore in Motilal's eyes, personally threatening as well as politically suspect. Preferring to beard this lion in his own den, Motilal invited Gandhi to Allahabad for discussions. In early March 1919 Gandhi, dressed in a flapping loincloth, arrived at Anand Bhawan and was installed in Swarup Rani's Hindu side of the house where he could eat his vegetarian meals on the floor and use the servants' Indian-style latrines. He and Motilal had private talks in the library, and after several days Gandhi counselled Jawaharlal to moderate his political activity in deference to his father and not at this stage to defy or otherwise upset him. Obviously an impasse had been reached in Motilal's book-lined library, but Gandhi was willing to bide his time. He preached patience to his young disciple.

Neither of them had to wait long. On 18 March 1919, just a few days after Gandhi left Anand Bhawan, the British imposed the Rowlatt Act which extended the wartime powers of arrest and detention of suspected subversives without trial. That night Gandhi literally dreamt up (the idea came to him in a dream) the plan of protesting this unjust and repressive act with a country-wide *hartal* – a general strike – and a day of fasting and prayer. *Satyagraha* – non-violent resistance – was publicly launched on 6 April. A week later, on the 13th, in Amritsar in the Punjab, a peaceful demonstration inside a walled garden called Jallianwala Bagh was met by hundreds of rounds of ammunition fired by soldiers under the command of Brigadier General Reginald Dyer. By the time 'order was restored', 379 unarmed and trapped men, women and children had been killed.

When the news of the Amritsar massacre – the most infamous episode in the history of British rule in India – reached Anand Bhawan, it accomplished in a moment what the eloquent and persuasive Gandhi had failed to achieve in hours of discussion: Motilal Nehru was converted to *satyagraha*. As Indira herself later put it, 'Jallianwala Bagh was a turning point ... Hesitation and doubt were swept aside ... This is when the family came much closer to Mahatma Gandhi and our whole way of life changed.'[9]

Not quite the whole family however. With the exception of Kamala, the women of Anand Bhawan were initially hostile to Gandhi and resisted his influence. Swarup Rani, in particular, could not comprehend how and why this little man in a *dhoti* with his dietary and health fads should intrude on her family and advise them on both personal and political matters. She felt, in fact, 'instinctively that [he] ... was the enemy of her home'.[10] Certainly the position Gandhi now assumed in the household was highly intimate and influential. Indira could scarcely recall a time when he was not 'an elder of the family to whom I went with difficulties and problems'.[11] No issue or difficulty was too great or too small for 'Bapu', as the Nehrus all called him, from moral dilemmas and political goals to digestive ailments and whether or not young women should wear lipstick. Gandhi dispensed advice on the whole gamut and though he was not dictatorial, for many years his word determined events in the Nehru family as well as the nationalist movement.

Motilal and Jawaharlal's closeness to Gandhi and their increasing political involvement in *satyagraha* did not go unnoticed by the British government and their intelligence apparatus in India. In May 1920 Jawaharlal took his mother, his sisters Nan and Betty, his wife, Kamala, and two-and-a-half-year-old Indira to the northern hill station of Mussoorie where it was cooler. The hot season in Allahabad is ferocious, with average temperatures of 40 degrees and higher and the Nehru women always spent their summers in the hills. An additional reason this year was that both Swarup Rani and Kamala were unwell. Swarup Rani, admittedly, had been 'delicate' for most of her adult life, and Kamala had never thrived since her arranged marriage to Jawaharlal in 1916. Letters between Jawaharlal and Motilal and also between them and Gandhi are peppered with references to Kamala's symptoms, many of which in these early years seemed to be psychosomatic. She suffered from headaches, lassitude, lack of appetite, weight loss, breathing difficulties and 'heart attacks' which were actually palpitations.

Because Kamala was relatively unsophisticated, reserved and could not speak fluent English, she was looked down upon by her mother-in-law and two sisters-in-law, especially Sarup or Nan who did nothing to hide her possessive love for her brother and her scorn for his unWesternized wife. The female household at Anand Bhawan was, in fact, rife with jealousy, hostility and resentment, and for many years Kamala suffered intensely in this atmosphere. Illness would confine her to her room and take her out of the fray. But not surprisingly, when she migrated to the hills, in the company of her mother-in-law and sisters-in-law, her health failed to improve.

When the Nehrus arrived in Mussoorie in May 1920 they took a suite of rooms at the Savoy Hotel. An Afghan delegation was also in residence at the Savoy, having come to Mussoorie to negotiate with the British following the brief Afghan war of the previous year. The eye of the British government read a dark motive in this coincidence and concluded that Jawaharlal Nehru had come to the hill station to liaise with the Afghans. The day after the Nehrus arrived, the local Superintendent of Police called on Jawaharlal and demanded that he have no contact with the Afghans. Nehru, in fact, had no intention of associating with the Afghan delegation, but on principle, he refused to comply with this command.

The following day Jawaharlal was served with an externment order stating that he must leave the district within twenty-four hours. He had no choice but to return to Allahabad, leaving his ailing mother, wife, daughter and two sisters on their own in Mussoorie. It was the first of many sudden disappearances of her father that punctuated Indira's childhood.

Motilal Nehru was enraged at his son's expulsion and prevailed on his old friend, Sir Harcourt Butler, Governor of the United Provinces, to lift 'the stupid order'. When Jawaharlal returned to Mussoorie one fine June morning, the first thing he saw in the Savoy courtyard was an Afghan minister holding Indira in his arms. The Afghans had read of the externment order in the newspaper and in Jawaharlal's absence, sent flowers and fruit to Swarup Rani and Kamala every day and taken Indira out to play each morning.[12]

In September 1920, shortly after they returned from Mussoorie, Indira, who was not yet three, travelled with her parents and grandfather to her first Congress meeting – a special session held in Calcutta. In later years, she had no memory of this historic event, but felt it was deeply significant that she had been present when Gandhi publicly launched the non-cooperation movement and called for *swaraj* – self-rule for India – within a year.

On their return to Allahabad, the bonfire at Anand Bhawan was ignited and things would never be the same again. Motilal resigned his seat on the Provincial Council, gave up his lucrative law practice (though he continued to practise intermittently when he needed the money), withdrew his youngest daughter Betty from school, disposed of horses and carriages, sold all but one of his automobiles, changed the Anand Bhawan cuisine from continental to Indian, closed the wine cellar, reduced the number of servants and had those who remained exchange their gold and wine-coloured livery for *khadi* (which Jawaharlal was later to call 'the livery of freedom'). For Indira this new austerity was the only form of existence she could remember at Anand Bhawan and it would become a lifelong habit.

It was not only the appearance and texture of life at Anand Bhawan that changed radically after the beginning of the non-cooperation move-ment. Both Motilal and Jawaharlal now devoted all their time and ener-gies to political activity. In his *Autobiography* Jawaharlal recorded how 'I became wholly absorbed and wrapt [sic] in the movement . . . I gave up all my other associations and contacts, old friends, books, even newspapers ... In spite of the strength of family bonds, I almost forgot my family, my wife, my daughter ... I lived in offices and committee meetings and crowds.'[13] Years later, when he was in prison, he was haunted by this neglect of his family, but at the time, he was so engrossed by politics that a reproachful letter from his father (who was away from home) had no effect:

> Have you had any time to attend to the poor cows in Anand Bhawan? Not that they are really cows but have been reduced to the position of cows by nothing short of culpable negligence on your part and mine – I mean your mother, your wife, your child and your sisters? I do not know with what grace and reason we can claim to be working for the good of the masses – the country at large – when we fail egregiously to minister to the most urgent requirements of our own flesh and blood and those whose flesh and blood we are.[14]

Far from attending to the 'poor cows' at Anand Bhawan, Jawaharlal removed himself from them altogether when he was sent to jail – along with Motilal himself – in December 1921. The previous month, the Prince of Wales (later King Edward VIII,) and his entourage (which included the twenty-one-year-old Louis Mountbatten) had visited Allahabad in the course of the future King-Emperor's progress through India. Instead of welcoming the Prince, Allahabad observed the country-wide *hartal* against him with empty streets and shuttered shops. In sharp contrast to the welcome given to Annie Besant four years earlier, the town was transformed into a 'city of the dead'. The Prince's procession made its regal way along the eerily silent streets 'with nobody to see it'.[15] Motilal Nehru had organized the Allahabad *hartal* against the royal visit and on December 6 he was arrested at Anand Bhawan. So, too, was his son who recorded in his prison diary that after the arrests, while the police waited for Motilal and Jawaharlal's belongings to be packed, Swarup Rani, Kamala and Nan were all composed but Indira, aged four, 'made a nuisance of herself objecting to her food and generally getting on people's nerves'.[16]

Motilal was tried the next day at Naini Jail in Allahabad and charged with being a Congress volunteer – a criminal offence because the British had outlawed the Indian National Congress. The courtroom was packed: Motilal Nehru, the leading barrister of Allahabad, now publicly rejected the British legal system he had practised and upheld for so long by refusing to accept any defence or to defend himself to the Government Advocate – an old friend and former colleague.

As all the newspapers reported, Motilal sat in the dock with Indira on his lap throughout the trial. It was her first political appearance; not only was she an observer but also a participant in this legal spectacle. Why did Motilal – apparently with Jawaharlal's and Kamala's approval – involve his young granddaughter in this way? The idea may have been to initiate her into political activity; but whether intended or not, she was also an instrument and a symbol in the courtroom: a personification of innocence which exposed what Motilal called the 'farce' of the proceedings. She may have enjoyed the attention or been transfixed by the unfamiliar surroundings; the newspapers all reported that she behaved impeccably.

Motilal was sentenced to six months imprisonment and fined 500 rupees and Jawaharlal was given a similar sentence for distributing handbills for the *hartal*. They were in good company: across India some 30,000 people were jailed by the British between December 1922 and January 1923 in what Jawaharlal called 'an orgy of arrests and convictions'.[17] Both Motilal and Jawaharlal were imprisoned at Lucknow District Prison, 140 miles northwest of Allahabad.

In court the Nehrus had refused to defend themselves; in jail they refused to pay the imposed fines with the result that the police descended on Anand Bhawan to collect what valuables remained – mostly pieces of furniture. Swarup Rani and Kamala watched this despoliation without complaint, but Indira protested with vehemence, 'expressed her strong displeasure', and nearly severed an officer's finger while brandishing a bread slicer at him.[18]

In late December 1921, just a few weeks after her father and grandfather were jailed in Lucknow, Indira made her first visit to Gandhi's ashram, Sabarmati, and her first third-class train journey. This trip was a baptism of fire for all the Nehru women: Swarup Rani, Kamala, Betty and Indira. During the long rail journey to Ahmedabad in Gujarat, the women sat on hard wooden benches in a dirty, crowded third-class carriage. As the train snaked across the flat, monotonous plains of northern India, at every station where it stopped, women and children congregated at their carriage windows and showered them with food and flowers. By now the Nehrus were almost as famous as Gandhi himself and people felt great solidarity with these women whose son, husband and father had been incarcerated by the British.

At Ahmedabad they attended the annual Congress meeting with Gandhi. Unlike the previous year, when Gandhi had launched *satyagraha*, Indira remembered this session. It was at this point that Congress took on the trappings of a mass movement. At Ahmedabad the green, white and saffron Congress flag was unfurled, everyone sat on the floor rather than chairs; Hindi was proclaimed the national language and *khadi* the national dress. The Nehru women were cheered as the representatives of the imprisoned Motilal and Jawaharlal.

Afterwards they went with Gandhi to his ashram on the banks of the Sabarmati river: a collection of low, whitewashed huts, situated in a grove of trees, surrounded by twenty acres of farmland. Below the ashram compound ran the river where the women washed laundry and the boys took the cows and buffaloes to drink. A pastoral setting, despite snakes which it was forbidden to kill, but scarcely an idyllic life. The seventy or so ashramites were all *sanyasis* – renunciates – who had vowed to be celibate (even if married), non-violent, abstemious in their eating, and not to observe untouchability. This austere existence, however, required more income than the ashram farm generated, with the result that life at Sabarmati was largely financed by Ahmedabad textile magnates and Bombay shipping barons. As Sarojini Naidu later quipped of Gandhi, it took a lot of money to keep him in poverty.

Days at the ashram began at 4 a.m. with prayers on the river bank and were regulated by a spartan routine of spinning, planting grain, fruit picking, drawing water, cooking, sweeping, washing, and latrine cleaning. Despite the supporting capital of big business, at Sabarmati, Gandhi attempted to create a self-sufficient utopia based on a lofty value system described by one of his biographers as 'truth, non-violence, moral economics, true education and an equitable social order'.[19]

Nothing, however, could have seemed less utopian to the Nehru women, with the exception of the resilient Indira and the traditional and naturally austere Kamala. They were housed in a bare hostel room, slept on the floor, rose at four in the morning with the others, ate meagre portions of unspiced food and used communal latrines in contrast to the European-style thunderboxes with enamelled pots they had at Anand Bhawan. Even Indira, a fussy eater, was hungry most of the time. Gradually, however, they adapted, especially during daily discussions with

'Bapu' in his cell-like hut. For Gandhi could charm and cajole as well as exhort. By the time they returned to Allahabad, all the Nehrus, including the reluctant Swarup Rani, had embraced *satyagraha*.

Jawaharlal was released early from Lucknow Jail on 3 March 1922, only to be rearrested and imprisoned again on 11 May and charged with 'criminal intimidation and extortion' involving the boycott of Allahabad merchants selling foreign cloth. Indira attended her father's trial just as she had her grandfather's the year before, but this time she sat with her mother, among the spectators, rather than in the dock. She was again, however, a distinct presence in the courtroom, especially, as the newspapers reported, when she piped up before the trial began and asked, 'Mummie, are they going to have a bioscope [film] show?'[20]

Jawaharlal's second prison term lasted eight months, until the end of January 1923. He was imprisoned first in Allahabad District Jail and then again at Lucknow, and in his solitude he finally had the leisure to worry about his family, especially about Indira who was far from well during most of 1922. In late May, Motilal, who had been transferred to Naini Jail from which he would soon be released, wrote to Jawaharlal that he was very concerned about Indu 'who is paying for the sins of her father and grandfather'.[21] At his last jail interview with Kamala and Indira, Motilal reported, Indu was pale, thin and listless.

She was also wilting in the extreme heat of the Allahabad summer, but both Kamala and Swarup Rani refused to go to the hills of Mussoorie while their husbands sweltered in jail. Instead, the women remained at Anand Bhawan and made the hot, dusty journey to Lucknow every month for a short interview with Jawaharlal in the prison warder's office. These awkward, far from private meetings were always observed by at least one prison official. Both Jawaharlal and his visitors – Swarup Rani, Kamala, Indira and Betty – would look forward to them eagerly and then feel frustrated and depressed afterwards because they had not been able to express themselves adequately. The time was too brief and they felt embarrassed and constrained under the guard's eye. Only five-year-old Indira was not inhibited by the unnatural situation. Jawaharlal recorded each interview in his prison diary and noted on October 23 that 'Indu [was] very thin and weak-looking after her severe illness but cheerful.'[22]

It was during this 1922 incarceration that Jawaharlal began his lifelong correspondence with Indira – a voluminous, highly revealing exchange of letters that was of great significance to both of them because for many years it was their principal means of communication. In many ways, in fact, theirs was essentially an epistolary relationship during all the years of Indira's growing up. Their letters created an extraordinary closeness between them because they were both unreserved, fluent writers. But this very spontaneity and openness could create difficulties when they were actually together. The letters created an intimacy that was often difficult, even impossible, to sustain in person.

In October 1922 Jawaharlal sent his first note to Indira from jail – in Hindi, but he switched to English as soon as she was able to read and write:

> Lots of love to dear daughter Indu from her Papu.
> Get well soon and write to Papu. Also come and see me in jail. I long very much to see you. Did you ply the new *charkha* [Gandhi-style spinning wheel] that Dadu [grandfather] has given you? Send me some of the yarn you have woven.
> Do you say your prayers every day with Mummie?
> Your Papu.[23]

A month later Jawaharlal wrote again to Indira now in Calcutta where Motilal had taken her and Kamala for homeopathic treatment:

> My dear Indu,
> How do you like Calcutta? Which do you like the better – Bombay or Calcutta? Have you seen the zoo there? What kind of animals are there? There is a very big old tree. See that also.
> Be sure you are quite fit when you return.
> Your loving father, Papu.[24]

Whether or not the Calcutta treatment was successful is unclear – as indeed is the nature of Indira's illness. Her symptoms as described in Motilal's and Jawaharlal's letters and in Jawaharlal's prison diary are, however, similar to many of those Kamala still suffered – weight loss, pallor, weakness – and like her mother's, they may have been partly psychosomatic. Jawaharlal certainly feared so; even more, he worried that Indira would develop what he called 'an invalid mentality' or hypochondria. Hence his injunction to be 'quite fit'. Throughout her childhood he worried about Indira's fitness and insisted she perform regular exercise – particularly daily running – to make her strong and healthy. He also fought Kamala's, Swarup Rani's and the *ayah*'s tendency to coddle her. Indira thus learned at an early age that her father disapproved of illness and in the future she sometimes used her health, or lack of it, as a lever in her relations with him.

In early 1923, however, when Jawaharlal was released from his second prison term, Indira was for the time being as healthy as he could wish her to be. The previous year Gandhi had called off the non-cooperation movement when twenty-two policemen were burned to death by a mob in the village of Chauri Chaura. But this did not halt political activity at Anand Bhawan. In December 1922, just before Jawaharlal was released, Motilal and a Bengali lawyer of Allahabad, C.R. Das, formed the Swaraj Party, within the Indian National Congress. The Swaraj Party diverged from Gandhi and his followers – also members of Congress – on the issue of the suspension of non-cooperation. Even more crucially, the Swarajists sought to end Congress' boycott of the legislatures. They supported council entry – political participation in the provincial legislatures as provided for by the 1919 Government of India Act – in order 'to carry the good fight into the enemy's camp'.[25]

Jawaharlal now found himself in the difficult position of disagreeing with both of his 'fathers': he strongly opposed Gandhi's suspension of non-cooperation but he no less strongly objected to the Swarajist Party plan to subvert the British system from within. The tension between Motilal and Jawaharlal was thus revived and pervaded the house. Mealtimes in particular could be silent and strained. Increasingly, Indira and Kamala ate alone together in the first-floor apartment Motilal had built for his son's family. Anand Bhawan was also the scene of incessant meetings. Indira one day rushed into a Congress Working Committee meeting in the sitting room shouting 'no admission without permission' at the top of her lungs, preaching but not practising what she had obviously been instructed.[26]

As an adult Indira sometimes breezily described her childhood as a time when she 'was surrounded by love and energy'. She denied that it was ever traumatic.[27] But in less guarded moments, she told a different story. In one candid interview she complained that she 'did not see enough' of Kamala. 'I did not see enough of anybody,' she went on, 'we hardly saw each other because people in the house left early in the morning on some sort of work or other in different directions. Sometimes we mct for meals. Mostly we did not . . . The whole house was in [such] a state of tension that nobody had a normal life.'[28]

But it was not only this continuous 'abnormal' activity, 'police raids, arrests and so on', as Indira described them, that made Anand Bhawan life fraught. In addition to the stressful atmosphere created by the ongoing political disagreement of Motilal and Jawaharlal over council entry, as she grew older, Indira became aware of her grandmother, Swarup Rani's and Swarup Rani's widowed sister's disapproval of her parents. Bibi Amma, as Indira always called her great-aunt, was the 'wicked witch' of Anand Bhawan and of Indira's childhood. Widowed at eighteen, for the rest of her long life she lived with and dominated her younger sister, Swarup Rani, and effectively ran the household. Bibi Amma was, in the words of B.K. Nehru, 'a joyless troublemaker . . . so warped that she could not bear to see anybody happy'.[29] To a child like Indira she was also frightening. She was far from attractive and like most Indian widows she wore a plain white sari, no jewellery and no *bindi* – the decorative mark worn by married Hindu women on their forehead. She adhered to the rule that widows should live in separate quarters, apart from the rest of the family, and cook and eat their own plain food privately.

For Indian women at that time, widowhood was a living death – scarcely a better alternative than throwing themselves on their husband's funeral pyres – and Bibi Amma embraced her grim fate with a vengeance. It had soured her and made her resent and disapprove of Jawaharlal and Kamala in particular. As a child Indira thought her great-aunt 'was all evil' because she overheard Bibi Amma criticizing her parents: 'I was very protective of them . . . I knew she disapproved . . . of their way of life and the whole idea of giving up of things. She thought that was very foolish. Here was a family with all the comforts and they just pushed them aside for . . . no good reason.'[30]

Unlike her sister, Bibi Amma never became a convert to *satyagraha*. As a Hindu widow she was obliged to become a *sanyasi* and renounce all material pleasures, but she could not forgive the rest of the household for voluntarily rejecting 'all the comforts'. And yet she was one of the few members of the family who wanted and had time to care for Indira. Reluctantly, Indira allowed Bibi Amma to put her to bed: 'I would say "You can come tell me stories, but I won't look at you."'[31] She also refused to eat the delicacies and treats her great-aunt prepared for her in her separate kitchen.

There was another person in the family who also distressed Indira – her aunt, Nan, who was a source of tension and heartache because of her hostility to Kamala Nehru. Nan, who was only a year younger than Kamala, adored Jawaharlal and resented her sister-in-law from the moment Kamala married him in 1916. Indira, of course, gradually became aware of this as she grew older. The jealous atmosphere at Anand Bhawan was only slightly alleviated when Nan married Ranjit Pandit in 1921.[32] The slights and insults continued – Kamala, for example, would not be invited to see an English film with the others because they said her English was too poor. Things became even worse in later years when Jawaharlal was away from home in prison much of the time, when Kamala's health deteriorated and when Indira herself became a target of her aunt's hostility. Essentially the adult women – Swarup Rani, Nan and Kamala – were competing for the restricted time, attention and affection of Jawaharlal. Kamala was the most reserved and also the proudest of the three and not surprisingly, she suffered the most – as Indira witnessed. Jawaharlal himself, for a long time at least, seems to have been too preoccupied to be aware of the volatile and unhappy relations among his mother, sister and wife.

As a small child Indira was able to escape from the charged atmosphere of Anand Bhawan when she visited her maternal grandparents at their huge traditional home, Atal House, in Sita Ram bazaar in Old Delhi. She had a close and uncomplicated relationship with her grandmother Rajpati Kaul and the whole large, extended family indulged and petted her. She was sent to kindergarten at the newly opened nationalist Modern School and taken visiting among the neighbours. One in particular, a ten-year-old boy named Parmeshwar Narain Haksar, remembered a silent, large-eyed Indu perched on a servant's shoulder being fussed over by the neighbour women who clucked 'poor thing', as they stroked her.[33] Far from being ignored and unnoticed, in Delhi, Indira was indulged by everyone including the servant who brought her fresh *puris* (deep fried bread) and hot milk each morning.

But she never stayed with her maternal grandparents for more than a month every year. Back at Anand Bhawan basic family routines continued to give some semblance of stability in the midst of change and conflict. Swarup Rani would often wake Indira at sunrise and take her to the Ganges and then to temple. If Jawaharlal was at home, there were morning readings of the Gita with both of her parents, followed by supervised runs in the large Anand Bhawan gardens. Bazaar merchants and hawkers came each day to the house to sell vegetables, fruit, soap and other necessities, as did *kulfi* (ice cream) and *chhat* (savoury snack) vendors. Tailors sat cross-legged on the veranda and stitched saris, *kurtas* (tunics), and *churidars* (pyjama trousers). From time to time various entertainers also turned up: the *bhaluwala* (bear-man) and his performing bear, the *bandarwala* (or monkey-man), acrobats, conjurors and minstrels. And every year, on her birthday, Indira was weighed against a *thali* (brass tray) of rice until the scales were balanced and then the grain was distributed to the poor. This was followed by a lavish Western-style birthday party even after the ban on foreign goods and ways had been imposed at Anand Bhawan.[34]

And then, like all children, Indira spent a great deal of her time in a fantasy world of play. Much has been made of her childhood games – the rousing political speeches to assembled Anand Bhawan servants, the freedom fighter dolls, the mock *lathi*(baton)-charges and pretend police raids – as if they foreshadowed her later political career. But far from being prophetic, Indira was simply playing at being an adult and this is what she saw those around her doing. She was, as well, undoubtedly encouraged by her family in this kind of play. Motilal gave her a *charkha* – a spinning wheel – when she was five. (Spinning yarn for homespun *khadi* cloth was enjoined on Congress members who boycotted imported British cloth.) Kamala habitually dressed Indira in a boy's *khadi* Congress volunteer uniform, including a Gandhi cap. She was, in fact, frequently taken for a boy and from very early on in her letters to her father signed herself 'Indu-boy'.

The unusual thing about Indira's games was not what she played at but the fact that they were almost always solitary. She grew up in a household with no other children and apart from the spell in kindergarten in Delhi, she was not sent to school in Allahabad until 1924 when Motilal decided to enrol her at St Cecilia's, a school run by three British spinsters named Cameron. It was an unhappy beginning to what turned out to be an erratic academic career. Indira was miserable at St Cecilia's. She was shy and tongue-tied in the midst of the other girls and acutely aware of her skinniness. She also felt freakish as the only student at the school who wore *khadi* clothes. She recalled how 'sometimes, in order not to appear in the *kurta* and be made fun of, my younger aunt [Betty] . . . would conspire with me and help me to take off my *kurta* so that I could stay in my petticoat, which passed off as a sleeveless A-shaped dress'.[35] She was also frightened of the British sergeant major who taught the girls drill and cracked a whip to keep them in line.

She was soon delivered from the purgatory of St Cecilia's by a furious row between Motilal and Jawaharlal. Jawaharlal apparently had not been consulted by his father in the choice of a school for Indira and was away from home when she was first sent there. St Cecilia's was a private, not a government institution, but Jawaharlal felt that since it was run by an entirely British staff and had mostly British pupils, Indira's attendance violated the principles of the Congress boycott of all things foreign. Thus began another episode in the by now well-established conflict between Jawaharlal and Motilal. Both of them appealed to Gandhi to mediate and a flurry of letters and telegrams flew back and forth among the three men. Jawaharlal won this round. Indira was withdrawn from St Cecilia's after several months and taught by Indian tutors at home.

This may have been politically correct, but it was far from ideal educationally. Indira's two aunts had been taught by an English governess who made sure they learned to read, write and do arithmetic competently as well as submit themselves to cold baths and inflexible bedtimes. Indira's lessons and general upbringing were more haphazard. The Pandit who taught her Hindi sometimes failed to turn up; she studied English with her mother, but here again instruction was erratic. Jawaharlal was her most gifted and enthusiastic tutor, but he was often too busy or away from home.

The household was bilingual in several senses. Indira's grandmother and great-aunt, Swarup Rani and Bibi Amma, spoke only Hindi as Kamala had done originally. (During the twenties Kamala took lessons in both English and Urdu.) Motilal and Jawaharlal were more comfortable conversing in English, but switched to a combination of Hindi and Urdu with the beginning of non-cooperation. English remained, however, the medium for virtually all their reading and writing. Indira grew up, then, in the midst of a family where Hindi was the principal language of the women and English of the men. As a result she was probably the most truly bilingual member of the household. For the most part she spoke Hindi, but she learned to write and to read English at an early age and became a lifelong compulsive and very fast reader. A great deal of her time as a child, in fact, was spent sitting in the trees in the Anand Bhawan garden, reading books. At first these were fairy tales given to her by her aunt Betty (a legacy of the English governess), but as Indira grew older she raided Motilal's library, which contained the largest private collection of books in northern India.

The mid-twenties, when Indira was seven, eight and nine, marked a lull in the nationalist movement and a time of disquiet and uncertainty for the Nehru family. Gandhi had revoked non-cooperation in 1922; later the same year he was arrested and charged with writing seditious articles for his magazine *Young India*. He was sentenced to six years imprisonment in Yeravda Central Prison, near Bombay, and, despite becoming President of Congress at the December 1924 annual Congress session, he remained largely detached from politics until 1928. During these years of relative political quiescence, Gandhi continued to play a central role in the Nehru family. In January 1924 he was released early from prison because of an acute appendicitis. In February the entire Nehru family, including Indira, travelled to Juhu, by the seaside near Bombay, where Gandhi had chosen to recuperate at the very unprison-like home of the wealthy industrialist Shantikumar Morarjee.

Inadvertently this pilgrimage to see Gandhi became a holiday – the first the Nehrus had taken apart from summer sojourns in the hills. They rented a cottage on the beach front and spent the days swimming, running and horseback riding by the sea. This, in fact, was when Jawaharlal taught Indira how to swim. But the more serious purpose of their visit was to consult Gandhi. Motilal wanted to explain the Swarajist position to him and Jawaharlal to discuss his future. Both Nehrus, however, went home disappointed. Gandhi continued to reject the Swarajist approach and 'did not resolve a single one of [Jawaharlal's] doubts'.[36] The trinity of Motilal, Jawaharlal and Gandhi – which the British called 'the Father, Son and Holy Ghost' – was, in fact, hopelessly at odds with one another.

Jawaharlal's problems at this juncture were both political and personal. In the autumn of 1923 he had been gravely ill with typhoid fever and the experience had left him with 'a strange detachment' which had 'a lasting effect' on his way of thinking.[37] By 1924, when he saw Gandhi at Juhu, he felt restless and dissatisfied. He was thirty-five – an age when he had expected his aspirations to bear some fruit. But the political cause that had obsessed him two or three years earlier now seemed spent, or rather it lay in the hands of the Swarajists with whom he could not ally himself. He could neither follow Motilal's political platform nor retreat with Gandhi into spirituality and a 'constructive programme' of social uplift.

He had also become increasingly unhappy about his financial dependence on Motilal which was harder to bear as he grew older and he and Motilal diverged politically. Motilal's accumulated capital had long run out and Motilal himself was forced to take on legal cases in order to finance the running of Anand Bhawan even on its reduced scale. But despite the suspension of the non-cooperation movement, Jawaharlal was determined not to practise law again because Indian law remained the law of the British. In his *Autobiography* he summed up his dilemma: 'The idea of my associating myself with the Government as a Minister was unthinkable ... indeed, it was hateful ... But I ... yearned for a chance to do some solid, positive, constructive work. Destruction and agitation and non-cooperation are hardly normal activities for a human being.'[38] In Juhu and in letters afterwards Gandhi suggested that Jawaharlal work as a press correspondent or a college professor. The Bombay business firm of Tata's – probably at Gandhi's instigation – also offered to employ Jawaharlal. But none of these alternatives – which can hardly have been attractive to him – came to anything.

Meanwhile, Kamala had become pregnant during their time in Juhu. She, if not Jawaharlal, must have felt that much now hung in the balance for them. It had been eight years since they married and seven since Indira was born. Kamala's position in the family, particularly in relation to her mother-in-law Swarup Rani and her sister-in-law Nan (now herself the mother of a baby girl), would be greatly enhanced if she had a male child. Not that Kamala cared overly about position, but it would be difficult for the other women to disparage and neglect her if she produced a male heir to carry on the Nehru name. Even more, of course, she desperately wanted a son for her own and Jawaharlal's sake.

A boy was, in fact, born to them in the middle of November 1924. But he was premature and died two days later. When Gandhi heard the news he sent a telegram on 28 November: 'Sorry about baby's death. God's will be done.'[39] Kamala, Jawaharlal and Indira were all devastated, but Kamala most of all.

Almost immediately she fell ill with a cough and high fever and was taken from Anand Bhawan to the European ward of Lucknow Hospital (boycotts, obviously, were suspended in such circumstances). She travelled there by ambulance, along the same road she had covered so often on her visits to Jawaharlal in prison. At Lucknow the British doctors diagnosed pulmonary tuberculosis for the first time: a judgement that sounded like a death sentence. After years of malingering, Kamala's symptoms were suddenly transformed into an illness which at that time was often fatal.

She remained at Lucknow Hospital, on a ward of mostly British women, well into the new year. Jawaharlal shuttled back and forth between Allahabad and Lucknow, but Indira was not allowed to visit her mother. In February 1925 she wrote a postcard to her in careful English handwriting: 'Love to darling Mummie from Indu.'[40] She probably wondered if her mother would die as her baby brother had. Perhaps in an attempt to distract her, Gandhi wrote to suggest that Indira form a children's spinning group in Allahabad – the Bal-Charkha Sangh, an offshoot of his own Gandhi Charkha Sangh. This she dutifully organized, but it did not allay her deep anxieties about her mother.

Despite the best possible medical care, Kamala failed to improve in Lucknow. Motilal and Jawaharlal summoned the prominent physician and nationalist leader, Dr M.A. Ansari, who found Kamala's condition so serious that he did not broach the expected alternative of a rest cure in the hills. Instead, he urged Jawaharlal to go to Switzerland to consult tuberculosis specialists in Geneva with whom Ansari was in contact.

As Jawaharlal confessed later, the proposal to leave India at this time of political stagnation and when he, Motilal and Gandhi were out of harmony, appealed to him quite apart from the imperative of seeking a cure for Kamala. But an indefinite stay in Europe would be extremely expensive; he was entirely without capital and he was reluctant to ask Motilal – who was hard-pressed in any event – to subsidize the journey. Jawaharlal now had no alternative but the distasteful one of raising the necessary money through the only skill he possessed: the law. Motilal secured a brief for him from a wealthy client and Jawaharlal was paid the hefty fee of 10,000 rupees.[41] It is unlikely that Kamala ever knew where the money for their trip came from.

Nan and her husband Ranjit Pandit had already planned a six-week European holiday in early 1926 and had booked their passage on the Lloyd liner the *Triestino* which would sail from Bombay. Motilal decided that he, Betty, Jawaharlal, Kamala and Indira should all go with the Pandits. As usual, the Nehrus preferred to travel en masse, but from Kamala's point of view this was far from ideal. Proximity to Nan always upset her, and she may have feared that Nan would blame her for the expense and trouble of her illness. To make matters worse, at the last minute Motilal and Betty had to postpone their departure, so that only the Pandits and Nehrus would sail together on 1 March 1926.

On 26 February Motilal (who was only accompanying the others to Bombay), Jawaharlal, Kamala, Indira, Nan and Ranjit Pandit boarded a first-class train carriage (for Kamala's comfort) at Allahabad's main Prayag station. For much of the journey to Bombay, Indira sat in the lap of her mother whom she had not seen for so many months. This later provoked a letter from Motilal to Jawaharlal: 'On the journey . . . to Bombay I noticed that Indu frequently kissed Kamala. This should be stopped. If possible they should avoid hugging each other in the way they do, as . . . even perspiration carries germs.'

Three days later, Motilal stood on the Bombay dock and watched the *Triestino* weigh anchor and head off into the brilliant blue waters of the Arabian Sea. On deck, a skinny child – it would have been difficult for anyone else to make out if it was a boy or a girl – waved and waved until she was merely a speck on the horizon.

THREE

Breathing with Her Heels

IN 1926 – BEFORE AEROPLANES divorced distance from time – it was
a long journey from Bombay to Venice: across the Arabian Sea, round
the Gulf of Aden, through the Suez Canal into the Mediterranean, past
Crete and the Ionian Islands and up to the very top of the Adriatic. 'A
rough voyage', is how Nehru described it in a letter to his father, both
in terms of the weather at sea and the emotional climate on board ship.[1]
Only Indira relished the electrical storms and towering waves that left
everyone else giddy and nauseated. But the tense relations between
Kamala and Nan Pandit were eased when Kamala came down with an
attack of bronchitis and was confined to her cabin. Kamala still had a
high fever when they reached Italy.

As soon as they landed, the Pandits rushed off on their six-week
European holiday, but Kamala was too ill to travel further so the Nehrus
stopped for three days in Venice – a magical place for Indira – a city
of islands, like a mirage suspended on water, where people moved about
in gondolas rather than automobiles, carriages or bullock carts. When
Kamala's temperature fell, they boarded a train that sped across northern
Italy to Geneva – a bustling city with trams, honking cars, paved and
cobblestone streets, with people in dark clothes wielding umbrellas.
Though spring, Geneva was damp and cold; mist and fog hovered over
the lake and for days there was no sign of the encircling mountains –
or the sun.

For several months they lodged in cheap pensions until they found
a two-bedroom flat at 46 Boulevard des Tranches. After the army of
servants at Anand Bhawan, a single Swiss maid was hired named Marguerite who spoke only French. Jawaharlal was determined to live as
frugally as possible. This suited Kamala's ascetic temperament, but back

in Allahabad Motilal was incensed at what he called his son's 'false economy'. 'It seems,' he wrote, that 'you have undertaken the trip merely to demonstrate how cheaply it is possible for a man, wife and child to live in a European town. It was hardly necessary to go so far afield for such a practical demonstration of domestic economy.' He criticized Jawaharlal for not purchasing an overcoat and for 'giving to Kamala some very inferior stuff' to wear outdoors.[2]

Part of the reason for Nehru's over-zealous economizing was the great expense of Kamala's treatment. He had brought enough money to last them the six or so months he expected they would stay in Europe, but he either did not calculate medical expenses or underestimated them from his vague memory of the cost of living in England fifteen years earlier.[3] Kamala consulted medical specialists at the famous Geneva Research Institute of the Swiss bacteriologist Henri Spahlinger as soon as they arrived in the city. Laboratory tests revealed TB bacilli in her sputum – confirming the Lucknow doctors' diagnosis. She then underwent a course of Spahlinger's vaccines which cost more than £200 – a large sum in 1926. This controversial vaccine was an anti-tuberculosis serum derived from the blood of horses, though its source and nature were kept secret.[4] To Jawaharlal's chagrin, he had to wire Motilal for the money for this treatment. His drive to cut corners in every other direction was obviously a way of compensating for its hefty cost. But, as Motilal argued, if at the same time Kamala was being injected with the Spahlinger serum she was also inadequately clothed, meagrely fed, and shivering in chilly, draughty lodgings, it would defeat 'the very object of your visit'.

Nehru did not, however, compromise on Indira's education in Geneva. The city was the headquarters of the League of Nations, formed in 1919 and in 1926, still 'the hope of international order [and] . . . at the height of its prestige'.[5] L'École Internationale, a multilingual (French, German and English) school, had been established for the children of those who were involved in the League. Jawaharlal and Kamala decided it would be perfect for Indira and well worth the fees. Good schools in India were invariably British-run, with a British outlook and curriculum hostile to the Nehrus' nationalism. The League of Nations school was truly international with seventy-five pupils from most of the League countries. The syllabus was neither Eurocentric nor underpinned by any political or religious dogma.

But what did Indira make of L'École Internationale? In later years, she merely said that she was happy there and that she liked her teacher Miss Hartoch. What she remembered was the distance of the school – housed in a Swiss chalet with magnificent mountain views – from their pension. To get to school Indira had to take a long walk, followed by a tram ride and then a bus ride – all negotiated four times a day. She left each morning at eight o'clock, came home for lunch at noon, went back to school at two when the children were taken by bus to the country for games, farming and nature study, and then finally returned home again at six in the evening. At first Nehru accompanied her to and fro, but this took a large chunk out of his day. So eight-and-a-half-year-old Indira began making the daily trek on her own, her satchel of exercise notebooks and primers strapped on her back. 'Indu is a wonderful little girl,' Motilal wrote from Allahabad, 'to be able to make her way in the streets of a Swiss town in the way you describe . . . it [is] a brave thing to do.'[6]

Indira, in fact, came into her own in Geneva where there were no servants, no *ayah*, grandmother or great-aunt to look after her. She helped the maid Marguerite with the housework and went shopping with her. She read to Kamala, who was largely confined to bed, and made sure she took her medicines. Jawaharlal wrote to his father of Indira's increasing autonomy and initiative to which Motilal replied, 'Dear little Indu is a marvel . . . her mental growth has been remarkable . . . Who could have imagined she would within a few months cultivate all the self-reliance she is showing?'[7]

Indira's rapid adjustment to life in Geneva was helped by the speed and ease with which she became fluent in French. Instruction at L'École Internationale was in both French and English and of course out on the streets of Geneva she spoke French. Nehru wrote to his sister how 'her English is becoming infected with her French and she talks of going *jusqu'a* the post office and it being *presque* ten o'clock. As for Hindustani, she tries to avoid talking in it.'[8] Kamala and Jawaharlal, however, feared she would forget Hindi altogether and insisted that she speak it with them.

Indira was metamorphosing in other ways too. Though Kamala wore saris the whole time she was abroad, Nehru reverted to the European dress he had worn during his years at Harrow and Cambridge and in India before the non-cooperation movement. And despite his economy drive, a new wardrobe was purchased for Indira. Instead of the scrawny little Allahabad Indu dressed in coarse *khadi*, Indira now wore starched Swiss dresses, knee socks and strapped patent leather shoes. A large hair bow was added on special occasions – when she and Nehru went, for example, to tea with the French novelist, biographer and critic Romain Rolland who lived at the eastern end of Lac Leman at Villeneuve. They also called on the German-Jewish poet and political activist Ernst Toller, and they received invitations from the large number of radical Indians living in exile in Switzerland.

Among these was an old, ailing couple named Krishnavarma. Jawaharlal took Indira to call on Shyamaji Krishnavarma and his wife who lived on the top floor of a crumbling house in Geneva – quite alone and friendless. Books and papers littered the floor; everything was covered in a thick layer of dust. Shyamaji Krishnavarma's 'pockets bulged with ancient copies of his old paper, the *Indian Sociologist*, and he would pull them out and point with some excitement to some article he had written a dozen years previously. His talk was of the old days, of India House in Hampstead, of the various persons that the British government had sent to spy on him, and how he had spotted them and outwitted them.' Shyamaji Krishnavarma had plenty of money, but would not waste it on servants and told his guests how he would walk long distances rather than spend a few centimes on the tram. 'Over the whole place,' as Nehru described it, 'there hung an atmosphere of gloom, an air of decay.'[9]

Meanwhile, far away in Delhi, thirteen-year-old Parmeshwar Narain Haksar listened one day in 1926 to a heated conversation between his mother, some other female relations and Kamala Nehru's mother Rajpati Kaul. Their discussion 'centred on her daughter's delicate state of health and how she had suffered thanks to Jawaharlal's involvement in the national struggle and his pilgrimages . . . to jails'. But Rajpati now was full of hope for Kamala because Jawaharlal had taken her to Europe. 'Why Jawaharlal should have gone to Europe was not clear' to young P. N. Haksar who sat silently in the midst of the women. Then Rajpati explained that 'the climate in Europe . . . was better than India's. But more than the climate was the importance, in her eyes, of Kamala and Jawaharlal being alone together with their child Indu.'[10]

Kamala's mother and the Haksar women understood perfectly. During those early months in Geneva – before Jawaharlal's younger sister

Betty arrived to join them in June 1926 – Indira and her parents were alone together for the first time in their lives, entirely free of the web of family, servants and political workers that bound them in Allahabad. Kamala was released from the oppressive, hostile atmosphere of her mother-in-law and sister-in-law and Jawaharlal of their smothering attention. Kamala and Indira had carved out a shared intimacy at Anand Bhawan in the midst of others, but Indira only began to experience this with her father in Geneva. She now often had his undivided attention.

Even more regularly than in Allahabad, he made her run every morning before she went to school, insisting that she not only cultivate speed but also 'elegance' and 'style'. 'It didn't matter,' Indira later recalled, 'whether I ran a long distance . . . but I must be graceful while running.'[11] Many Indian women run with their weight thrown backwards, but Indira was taught by her father to run like an athlete 'on her toes, with the weight of her body thrown forwards, running with long strides, her muscles perfectly co-ordinated, her breath in harmony with her body'. Or as Indira herself put it, 'I learnt to breathe with my heels.'[12]

Indira and Jawaharlal also went on excursions together in Geneva. One Sunday in early May he took her up a small mountain nearby called the Salève – a two-hour journey by train and funicular. The view on the top was magnificent: they could see the whole of the Mont Blanc chain, the Jura, Lake Geneva and the valleys far below dotted with villages. To Indira's delight, there was still snow – the first she had ever seen. Jawaharlal showed her how to make snowballs and he and Indira had a snowball fight.[13]

It was at Geneva, in fact, that Indira fell in love with mountains – their beauty and precipices, and the panoramic vistas they disclosed. Later she was called and called herself, 'a daughter of the mountains', because of her love – amounting to obsession – with Kashmir. But her first exposure to mountains was in Switzerland, not India, and it was only much later that she imbibed the Kashmiri belief that no mountains – including the Alps – can hold a candle to the Himalayas.

On 6 June 1926 Indira committed some sort of misdemeanour and at the age of eight-and-a-half wrote her first extant letter to her parents – while still at home with them in Geneva:

> My dear Mummie and Papu,
>   I am sorry that I wasn't good. But from today I am going to

be good. And if I am not good do not speak to me. And I will try my best to be good. And I will do whatever you tell me to do.

Love from your, Indu.[14]

Whatever her crime, it was an aberration. Indira kept her promise. Though she was an intelligent, precocious child, she was rarely assertive or 'difficult'. Indira, in fact, was a remarkably 'good girl' – docile, quiet, undemanding and obedient – not only in Switzerland but for most of her childhood. Kamala was often ill which meant that as Indira grew older she took on a nurturing role, inverting the usual parent-child relationship. Both of her parents encouraged her to be independent and then as she always said later, she felt somehow that they were vulnerable and in need of her protection. The only time Indira felt she could be needy herself as a child was if she fell ill, and in fact she succumbed to a bad bout of bronchitis – sharing many of Kamala's symptoms – in the late spring of 1926 shortly after her Aunt Betty arrived from India.

Because of the ever-present fear that Indira would develop tuberculosis, Nehru was alarmed when she came down with bronchitis. Additional funds were wired from Allahabad and he had Indira 'thoroughly overhauled by children's specialists and other doctors' in Switzerland. To his and Kamala's relief, examinations and tests revealed nothing 'organically wrong', yet, as Nehru said, 'obviously she was below par'. He began to suspect that his daughter's illnesses were psychosomatic. As a man who enjoyed robust health himself, ate sparingly, practised yoga and took regular exercise, Nehru placed great importance on physical fitness and could be intolerant of others' ill health. He complained of Indira's 'infantile weakness' and argued that she always fared much better when she was away from home.[15]

Thus Nehru decided in the summer of 1926 to send her away to school in the mountains where there would be 'suitable companions' and no 'coddling and arguing and [and no] attempt to feed up and consequent disinclination to eat'.[16] Although 'she was not very keen on going' to the new school, Indira was withdrawn from L'École Internationale. Nehru wrote to Nan Pandit that Indira 'was still remarkably weak and delicate', and that he had her vaccinated before taking her on the four-hour journey from Geneva to Chesières where the new school was located.[17] From here Indira wrote to Kamala and Jawaharlal on 27 July:

My dear Papu and Mummie,

Did you give me a new toothbrush? Ask Mummie if my skip-
ping rope is there, I cannot find it. Thank you for your letter
. . . Yesterday all the children had a swimming bath and gymnastics. Tell me all about Geneva. I will write a bigger letter next
time. Give Puphi [Betty] her letter.

Love from your loving little daughter, Indu.[18]

Before this letter reached her parents, Nehru wrote anxiously from
Geneva, 'Have you forgotten Mummie and Papu? You had promised
that you would write to us daily,' to which Indira replied on the 2nd
of August: 'My dear Mummie and Papu, Thank you for your letter. Ask
Mummie what number is my new toothbrush. Where is Rochers de
Naye? We had a lot of fun yesterday . . . How are you? Love from your
loving, Indu.'[19]

For several months Indira's letters remained as laconic as these first
two; her only anxiety apparently her toothbrush. She did not tell her
parents that she was unhappy at Chesières – a family-run school headed
by a huge man named Herr Muller with 'a heavy bull-like neck full of
protrusions'. He and his equally repellent wife treated their handful of
students like servants. They worked long hours in the garden, chopped
wood and carried about heavy pots of geraniums 'to catch the sun'. Students who misbehaved were confined indoors and fed rations of dry bread.
At Chesières, however, Indira did make a close friend, a girl from San
Salvador named Margot, and she attracted her first admirer: a nine-year-
old French boy named Claud whose adoration she did not reciprocate.[20]

Back in Geneva, by the summer Kamala had finished her expensive
course of Spahlinger vaccines. On 11 August Nehru wrote to his old
friend Syed Mahmud, 'Kamala is doing well. So is Indu who is in the
mountains. As for me, I am flourishing like the proverbial green bay
tree.'[21] But a month later, on 12 September, he reported to Mahmud
that 'Kamala I am sorry to say has not been keeping very well.' She was
running a temperature again and the doctors' verdict was that 'the
disease is present still'.[22] The specialists now advised that Kamala be
moved to Montana, a resort high in the Alps in Valais canton southeast
of Lake Geneva. In mid-October she, Nehru and Betty journeyed up
into the mountains to Montana and Dr Theodore Stephani's famous
tuberculosis sanatorium 'Le Stephani' which had been a magnet for
wealthy consumptives since it was established in the 1890s.

In November, to celebrate her ninth birthday, Indira travelled on her own from Chesières to Montana to see her parents after an absence of nearly five months. She stayed with Nehru in a small pension close to the sanatorium and visited her mother twice a day. Since the first snowfall in the mountains, she had been skiing and sledging at Chesières and now she and her father skied together. It was exhilarating, and the beauty of their surroundings – the tallest peaks in Switzerland, bathed in sunlight – sublime. Nehru wrote to Nan Pandit that he had decided that 'skiing is the finest sport going – excepting only the ever exciting game of life and revolution'. 'Indu,' he added, 'is making steady progress in skiing.'[23] For Nehru, physical exercise in the clear, cold mountain air banished doubts and anxieties, both personal and political. He felt liberatingly cut off from India. They saw very few Indians and indeed very few people at all apart from the 'little colony' in the mountain resort.

For Montana was a resort – a playground for the leisured rich as well as a refuge for the ill and dying: a strange atmosphere for Indira. On the one hand there was the sanatorium for tuberculosis patients – many of them 'advanced cases' – where her mother lay in a white-sheeted bed in a room with windows and doors opened wide to the cold mountain air. But on the other hand, there were more than a dozen fashionable hotels, full of cosmopolitan guests from all over Europe and America, who skied and skated by day and went to galas, concerts and ice ballet performances at night. Indira picked up on the tension that existed between Montana's two classes of visitors. Invalids and holiday-makers resented each other's presence, and relations between doctors and hoteliers were even less cordial. Hotels like the Palace Bellevue, l'Eden, le Royal and le Continental posted large signs announcing 'On n'accepte pas les malades.'[24]

Indira came to Montana again at Christmas and it was during this longer stay that she finally confessed how unhappy she was at Chesières. Nehru made inquiries about other schools in the region and arranged for her to move to L'École Nouvelle at Bex, only a two-hour journey away which meant she could visit her parents and ski with her father nearly every weekend. Like the League of Nations school, this was an international institution and the students – all girls between the ages of nine and eighteen – came from South America, the United States, and India as well as Europe. L'École Nouvelle was situated in a beautiful, extensive estate outside Bex called La Pelouse which had originally been built by a wealthy Russian émigré. Indira boarded in a brightly painted Swiss chalet surrounded by apple, pear and chestnut trees and vineyards. From her window she could see the snow-covered Dents du Midi across the valley. The headmistress, Mlle Lydie Hemmerlin, was an intelligent, kind fifty-year-old Swiss woman, though, in Indira's words, 'a fiend for exercise and a strict disciplinarian'.[25]

Indira's later memories of Bex scarcely mention the syllabus or her studies. Rather than the books she read and what she learned, what Indira recalled about L'École Nouvelle were things like getting up 'first thing in the morning' for 'a cold, or rather icy, shower – no matter what the weather . . . Then we ran around the garden in shorts. On Thursdays and Sundays we had a two-hour fast walk and on other days a similar gymnastics or athletics period. Windows were . . . kept open' round the clock.[26] Precisely the sort of bracing atmosphere her father wanted for her. And in fact Indira thrived at L'École Nouvelle. She even loved the farm work required of all the students in the autumn: picking apples and chestnuts and harvesting grapes in the vineyards.

Slowly Kamala improved at Dr Stephani's sanatorium and increasingly Nehru and his sister Betty were able to leave her and make brief trips to Paris, Berlin, London, and in February 1927, to Brussels for the Congress of Oppressed Nationalities which led to the formation of the League Against Imperialism. Motilal Nehru was expected in the late spring by which time Kamala felt so much better – and was so weary of the sanatorium regime – that she announced she wanted to accompany the others on the 'grand European tour' Motilal had already planned for all of them, including Indira.

Indira's summer holidays began in mid-April, but shortly after she reached Montana, a telegram arrived from India: Motilal was deferring his European trip for at least another three months. Back in Allahabad, he was embroiled in a long-standing legal case that had been subject to incessant stays and adjournments and which now further delayed him. In addition, he was in the process of building a new family home and this too was not going forward speedily. For years Jawaharlal had argued that Anand Bhawan, even on its present reduced scale, was far too large an establishment and that they should live in a smaller, simpler house. Shortly after he, Kamala and Indira left for Europe, Motilal began constructing a new home in the grounds of Anand Bhawan. And for a time at least it remained a fairly modest venture. But it was difficult for

Motilal – even in straitened financial circumstances – to do anything by half-measures. Inevitably, the new Anand Bhawan – though smaller than the original – grew into an ornate, wedding-cake-like structure of two floors and numerous apartments with an encircling veranda and extensive gardens. As a result, in May 1927, when Motilal originally planned to sail for Europe, it was not even near completion.

If they waited for Motilal to arrive, it would be September or later, by which time Indira had to be back in school. Jawaharlal felt strongly that she should at least see Paris and London before they returned to India. Kamala was restless, unhappy and eager to leave Montana. Obviously they could make an abbreviated, not-so-grand tour now, but they were hampered by scant funds. Then another wire arrived from Allahabad: Motilal urged them to begin travelling without him and sent a draft for £500. Jawaharlal, Kamala, Betty and Indira set off from Montana on 1 May.

They arrived in Paris the next day and found a cheap hotel in Mozart Gardens. It was spring with the trees in full flower on the boulevards. They went to Arc de Triomphe, Notre Dame, the Eiffel Tower and the Louvre, but what Indira later remembered most vividly were the number of amputees who had been wounded in the Great War whom she saw on the streets and also on the métro where special benches were reserved for the 'mutilés de la guerre'. In addition to the usual tourist sights, Jawaharlal took her to the Concierge prison, a forbidding place after Naini Jail in Allahabad.[27] One night they went to a sensational and much publicized performance of *Dracula*. To create the appropriate atmosphere for the play, ambulances had been stationed outside the theatre and uniformed nurses positioned inside the hall to treat members of the audience who fainted with terror. During the performance doors and windows burst open and Dracula flew in on invisible wires.[28]

The next evening they went to see George Bernard Shaw's *Saint Joan* which had a less dramatic but possibly more profound impact on Indira. Joan of Arc looms large among Indira's childhood influences – but significantly only in recollections dating from the period of Indira's prime ministership. When she was still a child Nehru wrote about Joan of Arc in several letters to his daughter and also in *Glimpses of World History*, but Indira herself never mentions her in her own letters and there is little contemporary evidence that the story and example of Joan of Arc were important to her. Krishna Nehru Hutheesing in her 1968 family memoir, *We Nehrus*, and in her biography of Indira published a year later, claims that when her niece was a child she used to stand on the verandah of Anand Bhawan, clutching a pillar with one arm while raising the other high and saying, 'I'm practising being Joan of Arc . . . some day I am going to lead my people to freedom just as [she] . . . did.'[29] But this romantic description of Indira-cum-the Maid of Orleans does not appear in Hutheesing's earlier family autobiography, *With No Regrets*, published in 1946, long before Indira became politically significant.

When she became Prime Minister Indira herself could be inconsistent about the role of Joan of Arc in her life. On the one hand she would say, 'I was fascinated by Joan of Arc because she fought the British and because being a girl, she seemed closer to me than other freedom fighters.'[30] She even told a biographer in 1967 that it was Joan's martyrdom that particularly attracted her: 'She died at the stake. This was the significant thing that I envisaged – an end like that for myself.'[31] But Joan of Arc never appears in Indira's correspondence, interviews, reminiscences and speeches during the years before she came to power. And even then, she told one woman biographer – and Indira was always more candid with women interviewers than men – that she had no memory of Joan of Arc being significant to her as a child, and she confessed that Nehru had reminded her that this was the case after she was grown up.[32] Joan of Arc seems to have been a retrospective ideal for Indira, a key ingredient in her much later mythologizing of her childhood and political development.

Far more thrilling to her in Paris in 1927, was Charles Lindbergh's epoch-making arrival at Le Bourget field on 21 May after a solo, thirty-three-and-a-half-hour transatlantic flight in the monoplane, *Spirit of St Louis*. Perched on Nehru's shoulder, Indira was part of the vast crowd that watched Lindbergh land and then cheered him wildly when he climbed out of the plane. Nehru had been fascinated by aviation ever since the Wright Brothers' 1903 Kitty Hawk flight. When he briefly became a Theosophist in his teens he began to dream of 'astral bodies and imagined [himself] flying vast distances', and 'the dream of flying high up in the air (without any appliance)' remained a recurrent one throughout his life.[33] Then, eighteen years before Lindbergh's transatlantic flight, Jawaharlal and Motilal had stood in a crowd of more than a million in Berlin to witness Count Zeppelin land in his airship.

Two months later they saw Comte de Lambert fly over Paris and circle the Eiffel Tower. All of this paled, however, beside Lindbergh's epic flight 'like a shining arrow from across the Atlantic'.[34] Indira was as excited by it as her father, and though she herself did not inherit his obsession with flying, much later both of her sons did.

As the days wore on and Nehru and Indira continued their sightseeing in Paris, Kamala increasingly stayed behind in the hotel, plagued by many of her old symptoms – headaches, 'heart attacks' as she called her palpitations, lack of appetite, faintness and fatigue. She also became deeply depressed. We know of her state of mind during the spring and summer of 1927 because she wrote a series of remarkably candid letters to Syed Mahmud during this period. Mahmud was not only an old friend of and fellow Congress worker with Jawaharlal. He had also been teaching Kamala Urdu since the early twenties, and during their lessons an emotional intimacy developed between them. Neglected by most of the adults at Anand Bhawan and with her husband often absent, Kamala had turned to Mahmud and confided in him as she might have to a brother.

In one of her early Paris letters to Mahmud, Kamala makes no pretence of being well or happy: 'A constant illness renders life unbearable . . . I am of no use to the world and am making it heavier every day by doing nothing: only eating and sleeping . . . I am a burden to everybody. I wish that my end will come soon. Your brother [Jawaharlal] cannot do his work owing to me.'[35]

And in another letter, dated 4 May, her mood is even darker: 'Death is better than such a life, but even death is frightened of me . . . I was happy when I thought that tuberculosis would relieve me of this world but I never knew that death itself would fight shy of me . . . Only the rich and healthy ought to come here [Paris]. I regard myself as a prisoner here . . . Everyone has gone out for a walk but I am alone at home.'[36]

Kamala became more and more withdrawn and silent. She and Indira were finely attuned to each other's moods so Indira was aware of Kamala's despair. Eventually Nehru was too and he urged that they go on to London.

But in England things were even worse. They had great difficulty getting hotel rooms in London, as Kamala explained in a letter to Syed Mahmud: 'We arrived in London on 1st June. I did not like London from the moment we arrived at the station. The longer I stay, the more I dislike the place . . . The question of colour is rife everywhere. Wherever you go, you got the answer that they would not accommodate a black man . . . I have grown to dislike the English intensely . . . here at almost every step we are made to realize that we are slaves.' In Switzerland, Kamala said, 'we . . . never felt we were strangers'.[37]

They went on to the fashionable seaside resort of Brighton for ten days, which they found every bit as hostile, and then returned to London for several weeks. Nehru took Indira to the Natural History Museum in South Kensington where she saw fossils, stone-age tools and huge skeletons of dinosaurs, and to the British Museum where they saw the Egyptian mummies and then on to visit the Houses of Parliament. They also called on a strange, emaciated young man with a beak-like nose and sunken eyes named V. K. Krishna Menon who talked hectically of setting up an organization to agitate for Indian independence.[38]

Back at the seedy Berkeley's Hotel, Kamala kept up her correspondence with Mahmud, a persistent theme of which was the necessity for him to educate his daughters and to liberate them and his wife from *purdah*. Kamala had obviously discussed this issue with Mahmud before she left Allahabad and in nearly every letter that she wrote from Europe she asked him what action he had taken. When he remained silent, Kamala threatened, 'Until you give me the good news that the arrangement for the education of your daughters has been made, I will not write to you about my health.'[39]

Kamala's passionate feelings about women's education were both personal and political. She told Mahmud that it was utterly inconsistent – even hypocritical – to devote himself to the independence of India while depriving his daughters of an education: 'Can you ever imagine our country free without women being educated? . . . you make them rot in purdah and . . . their minds are closed.'[40] She also morally condemned Mahmud's attitude: 'Was it your duty only to bring girls into this world and then leave them alone like animals? In my view all of you [men] are great sinners. The time is coming,' Kamala threatened, 'when women are emancipated [and] they will keep you people in purdah'.[41]

The irony of Kamala and Mahmud's ongoing debate is that he was her mentor and thus to some degree her liberator – an irony she herself grasped and pointed out to him. In pleading for him to educate his daughters, Kamala also revealed how she felt her own lack of education had blighted her life. 'When I look at my plight,' she told Mahmud, 'I think that small girls ought to be saved from wasting their lives – like me ... My life has been wrecked altogether ... The greatest pity is that I myself am not intelligent enough to instruct others. I have to suppress my passion for doing things.'[42]

Kamala's argument with Mahmud was fuelled by her own feelings of regret and worthlessness. And this is the context for her chronic worries about Indira's education. She says in one letter to Mahmud, that 'on our return [to India] Indu will face many difficulties because there is no school in Allahabad which I like'.[43] The greatest consolation of being in Europe for Kamala was that she felt Indira was at last receiving a proper education.

Although later Indira herself always denied being a feminist, her mother's feminism impressed her deeply. She understood how it was an integral part of Kamala's political commitment to *swaraj* and how it shaped the way she raised her daughter: insisting that Indira be independent from an early age and have every opportunity, expectation and demand that a male child would have had. But Kamala's was a lonely voice both in India and within her own family. Her mother-in-law Swarup Rani and Swarup Rani's widowed sister Bibi Amma were archetypal traditional Indian women, though as Kashmiris they never observed *purdah*. Nan Pandit and Betty were Westernized but scarcely feminists. Nor were they particularly well-educated. For Motilal Nehru was a classic Edwardian patriarch when his daughters were growing up in the first decade of the century. Though he spent a great deal of money on Jawaharlal at Harrow and Cambridge, he saw no point in sending Nan and Betty to school. Even after the beginning of the non-cooperation movement and Gandhi's call for the women of India to become active, Motilal resisted Betty's desire to train as a Montessori teacher until Jawaharlal intervened on her behalf.

From England the Nehrus went to Berlin and Heidelberg in early July – a relief to Kamala because as she wrote to Mahmud, 'I like every place better than London.'[44] Then Indira was sent on her own to a children's summer camp in Annecy, France, near the Swiss border, while Kamala and Jawaharlal went back to Paris. In August, to Kamala's dismay, they returned to London from which she wrote to Mahmud on the 20th, 'Jawahar ... is going to Annecy to see Indu ... Our friend wrote to us that Indu was looking much better. I hope she will get a little fat on her. She is frightfully thin. She seems quite happy there. Papaji [Motilal] is coming here in September.'[45]

Before Motilal finally arrived in early September 1927, Indira was back at school at Bex, and she remained there while Kamala, Jawaharlal, Betty and Motilal now did Motilal's 'grand tour' of European capitals, staying this time in first-class hotels (which were less reluctant to accommodate Indians – as long as they were affluent – than the cheap ones Jawaharlal had chosen) and consulting more medical specialists. In early November 1927 the Nehrus went to Moscow to celebrate the tenth anniversary of the Russian Revolution. From here Nehru wrote a postcard, dated 10 November, to Indira back at Bex: 'We are in Moscow in Russia. I shall come for you soon. Hope you are quite well. Love from Papu.'[46]

Nehru's promise to retrieve Indira was the result of his decision, after a year and nine months abroad, finally to return to India. Motilal wanted to stay longer and said he would remain on in Europe for several more months after Jawaharlal, Kamala, Indira and Betty departed in early December. Kamala was by no means fully recovered but her tuberculosis, which had brought them to Europe, seemed to be in abeyance. Jawaharlal himself was in his own words 'in good physical and mental condition'.[47] The time abroad had turned out to be more decisive for him, in fact, than his wife. It had indelibly shaped his intellectual and political thinking; he had forged important links with European intellectuals and political leaders, participated in the birth of the League Against Imperialism, and witnessed communism at first hand in Russia. All of this contributed to his sense of being recharged, even renewed. He was eager to rejoin the political fray in India.

And Indira – who had turned ten while her parents, aunt and grandfather were in Russia – how had she changed? She had grown a certain number of inches – indeed she was rapidly catching up with Kamala. She had filled out a little too and was physically stronger from all the running and skiing. She was now fluent in French and had made strides in German. She had been exposed to a foreign culture and landscape which appealed to her. She had also become remarkably independent and resilient as a result of living away from her parents and travelling about alone.

Indira, in fact, was no longer a young child when they sailed from Marseilles on 2 December 1927. Throughout her life she always felt that she was the right age at the right time – that somehow the curve of her years was linked to the trajectory of history. Now in 1927, at the age of ten, she was leaving childhood just as the political struggle back in India was also reaching a kind of fruition.

FOUR

Indu-Boy

THE NEHRUS REACHED SOUTH INDIA on Christmas Day 1927, just in time for the annual Congress meeting held that year in Madras. On 27 December Indira was in the crowded audience with Kamala when Nehru went to the platform and for the first time since the Indian National Congress was formed in 1885 moved the resolution that 'Congress declares the goal of the Indian people to be complete national independence.'[1] Delivered in his clipped, correct English accent – Madras was in the Tamil-speaking south so he did not speak in Hindi – this was nevertheless a battle cry.

And not only to the British. Both Motilal Nehru and Gandhi were reluctant to sever unconditionally India's ties with Britain. They wanted to achieve *swaraj* through dominion status within the Empire.[2] Nehru – whose political vision had been further radicalized in Europe – wanted to jettison *all* imperial links. His resolution, calling for complete independence, was passed, though soon it was modified and diluted to a kind of 'unreality', as he put it. Nevertheless, the die was cast: not merely for a struggle between Britain and India, but within the ranks of Congress, and most significantly for Indira, within her own family.

She was back in India, South India: the tropics. Even in December, Madras is hot. The sun burned overhead, palms and lush vegetation enveloped the city; cows and emaciated dogs wandered the streets. After the Congress meeting ended, Indira, Kamala and Jawaharlal boarded a train that snaked its way north up the spine of the subcontinent to Delhi and then west along the familiar track to Allahabad which they had not seen in nearly two years.

Back at Anand Bhawan, Indira needed and wanted to go to school. Despite Nehru's repudiation of Britain at the Congress session, he agreed to send her to St Mary's Convent, a school of the Institute of the Blessed Virgin Mary, established in Allahabad by the British in 1866. It consisted of several imposing red brick buildings set amidst the white colonial bungalows and broad, tree-lined streets of the Civil Lines, and was staffed by British and German nuns. The students were mostly British and Anglo-Indian, with a handful of well-to-do Indian girls.[3]

Kamala may have overcome her husband's objections to St Mary's with the same argument that she used with Syed Mahmud: it was pointless to struggle for independence while Indian women remained ignorant or ill-educated. And at this time neither she nor Nehru questioned that the best education was a Western, British one. Nehru himself, of course, knew that virtually all of the leaders of the nationalist movement – Gandhi, Vallabhbhai Patel, Rajendra Prasad, Mohammed Ali Jinnah, Subhas Chandra Bose, as well as himself – were the products of Oxbridge or the London Inns of Court.

But it is one thing to go to a Western school in the West and quite another to attend one in India. Back home, Indira shed her Swiss frocks for coarse *khadi*, and the first day at school she discovered she was the only pupil dressed in it. Kamala had also bobbed her hair and got rid of the hair bows. The few other Indian girls came from wealthy, Westernized families who supported British rule in India. Indira's clothes immediately announced her family's radical politics. She never complained to her parents, but years later admitted that she felt 'terribly alienated' at St Mary's.[4]

The British and German sisters at St Mary's knew little about India or how Indians lived and their customs. At the time of the Holi festival – when every Indian is doused with dyed waters and powders – the nuns made Indira stand on a bench all day because she could not wash off the indelible Holi colours from her face and hands.

It was such episodes that she remembered about St Mary's. She had little to say about her studies, except that they 'seemed so remote from the life we had at home that I just wasn't in the mood to take in anything ... It ... seemed that what they were trying to teach me had nothing to do with life.'[5] Her indifference was compounded by long periods when she was absent because she went to Mussoorie in the hills in the summer or travelled with her family: a pattern of disrupted schooling that encouraged what Indira later called a 'healthy or unhealthy disdain of exams . . . I never really was bothered whether I was passing or not passing.'[6]

Her grandfather supported this nonchalance. Motilal Nehru returned to Allahabad in February 1928, laden with European furniture and fittings for the new Anand Bhawan which was still under construction. It was Motilal who insisted that Indira go to Mussoorie as soon as the hot weather set in or travel with her parents despite lessons and upcoming examinations. Though he cheerfully paid the expensive St Mary's fees for the two years Indira was enrolled there, he was as indifferent to her studies as Jawaharlal and Kamala were passionately concerned about them.

Life at Anand Bhawan in 1928 may have been remote from St Mary's, but it had become a good deal less austere than during the early days of the non-cooperation movement. Motilal's epicurean tastes had revived in Europe and despite Jawaharlal's objections, Western ways started to creep back in at Anand Bhawan. When he returned from Europe, Motilal began drinking Haig's Dimple Scotch again despite the Congress ban on alcohol. He also smoked large quantities of Egyptian and Turkish cigarettes. Swarup Rani's vegetarian meals were relegated to her own kitchen and dining room. In Motilal's, European cuisine, prepared by a Christian Goan cook, was prepared, though at Jawaharlal's insistence, the menu was reduced from five to three courses.[7]

Motilal worked all day in his study or at a desk on the veranda, with short breaks for lunch or tea. In the late afternoon he would take Indira across the lawns to inspect the new Anand Bhawan and the elaborate garden he was planning all around it. Then it was back to his desk until 8.30 or 9 p.m. – just when Indira was going to bed in the room next to her mother's. She would hear Motilal bellow out '*koi hai*' to his servant Bhola, a shout also heard by Indira's desperately hungry cousin, B.K. Nehru, in his room. Nineteen-year-old Briju (as the family called him) was now a student at Allahabad University and living at Anand Bhawan. '*Koi hai*' heralded the appearance of the whisky bottle. Barristers, judges, Congress workers and the occasional British colonial officer would turn up to partake of the Scotch. Indira, who had eaten with her mother in her mother's room, was usually asleep by the time Motilal, her father if he was at home, Briju and whatever guests were on hand retired to the dining room for dinner.[8]

*   *   *

In February 1928, the same month Motilal returned from Europe, the Simon Commission, headed by Sir John Simon and including among its members the Labour MP Clement Attlee, arrived in Bombay. Their ostensible mission was to devise constitutional reforms in order to augment the 1919 Government of India Act, but as one historian has put it, the Simon Commission actually came to India 'with the remit of encouraging stagnation'.[9] Once again, the British government failed to comprehend Indian public opinion which was outraged that there was not a single Indian member on the commission. When the seven-strong party toured the country, they were met everywhere with black flags, *hartals* and angry demonstrators shouting 'Simon Go Back'. Nehru led a demonstration in Allahabad and another in Lucknow where he was battered by *lathi*-wielding police who left him – and many others – covered 'with contused wounds and marks of blows'. This beating was a rite of passage, just as going to prison had been in the early twenties. But what disturbed Nehru more than his aches and bruises, were the English sergeants' faces 'full of hate and blood-lust, almost mad'.[10]

The Simon Commission's high-handed approach to India's constitutional future provoked Congress to form a committee to produce an Indian rather than British-ordained constitution. Motilal Nehru was put in charge of this heterogeneous group composed of Muslim, Hindu, Sikh, liberal and socialist members, and Jawaharlal was made its secretary. After several months of heated debate and disagreement they would produce a document known as the Nehru Report. This document was Motilal's, rather than Jawaharlal's, brainchild; it flatly contradicted the younger Nehru's independence resolution at Madras and endorsed the political goal of dominion status within the Empire.

What all this meant for Indira was that her father and grandfather were preoccupied and inaccessible during the spring of 1928 and that there was more tension than ever before at home. As B.K. Nehru recalls, 'differences between father and son were now acute'.[11] Mealtimes had become particularly stressful. Jawaharlal tried to shun political discussions at the table. But the atmosphere was still explosive. One evening at dinner Motilal recited some Persian couplets to his guests and asked his son to translate them. Jawaharlal refused; Motilal persisted. Finally Jawaharlal mumbled an inaccurate translation and Motilal chided him for not knowing the difference between two similar-sounding Persian words. Jawaharlal retorted, 'At least I know the difference between dominion status and independence!' Enraged, Motilal jumped to his feet and tipped the dining-room table and its contents onto the floor.[12]

Indira and Kamala were not present at this performance, but they witnessed others. For Kamala this was an anxious time for another reason too. She was pregnant again and she desperately wanted the child. To her grief, however, in the late spring of 1928 she lost the baby in the third month of pregnancy. Immediately after her miscarriage she developed violent stomach pains and had to be operated upon for appendicitis.[13] When she came home from the hospital after the operation, she became depressed and ill. Gandhi sent his own medical advice to Nehru from Sabarmati Ashram. 'I utterly distrust [the] doctors' reports about Kamala ... I wish you and father and Kamala will make up your minds for her to take to the natural treatment, that means Kuhne's baths and sun baths. Sun baths are now in vogue even amongst the medical profession and very extraordinary results are claimed for them.'[14]

But Kamala kept to her room where Indira spent most of her time before and after school. B.K. Nehru was the only other regular visitor. He was shocked at the way the rest of the household neglected Kamala and seemed utterly indifferent to her poor physical and mental state.[15] When the weather got warmer, Kamala's bed was carried onto the veranda outside her room where she lay listlessly all day. B.K. would come home from his lectures in the late afternoon and go up and read Turgenev to her and Indira. Kamala's niece, Nan Pandit's daughter, also remembers Kamala lying out on the veranda – always in white, a silent, shadowy figure around whom Indira hovered protectively.[16]

In May, when temperatures soared, Kamala, Indira and the other women in the family – Swarup Rani, Bibi Amma, Betty, Nan Pandit and her little daughter, Chandralekha – accompanied by Nan's husband, Ranjit Pandit, went to Mussoorie. Here they took a suite at their usual summer headquarters, the Savoy Hotel, from which Indira wrote to her father on 16 May:

> Papu darling,
>   We arrived here at twelve o'clock. We travelled in the train till Dehra Dun, we got down at Dehra Dun and went in a car ... Then Pupha [Ranjit Pandit] and Puphi [Nan Pandit] rode on horseback while Mummie, Chand and I came on *dandis* [chair conveyances]. I wanted to ride very much but Puphi said it

would be better if I didn't because I did not have my riding clothes.

I have just had my lunch. How are you? . . . Write soon, and tell me when you are coming.

With love from your loving daughter,
Indu[17]

But Jawaharlal had been heavily involved in the work of the Nehru Committee. Unable to visit Indira in Mussoorie, he tried to sustain the intimacy they had established in Europe through letters. During the summer of 1928, while he was arguing with Motilal and the rest of the Nehru Committee, he stayed up late in the evenings and wrote a series of long letters to Indira that were published two years later in a little volume called *Letters from a Father to His Daughter*.[18] Written in the form of chapters, these letters were meant to be a corrective to the British education Indira was receiving at St Mary's. Thus Nehru opens his first letter-chapter, entitled *The Book of Nature*:

> When you and I are together you often ask me questions about many things and I try to answer them. Now that you are at Mussoorie and I am in Allahabad we cannot have these talks. I am therefore going to write to you . . . short accounts of the story of our earth and the many countries, great and small, in which it is divided. You have read a little about English history and Indian history. But England is only a small island and India, though a big country, is only a small part of the earth's surface. If we want to know something about the story of this world of ours we must think of all the countries and all the peoples that have inhabited it, and not merely of one little country . . . I . . . can . . . tell you [only a] little in these letters . . . But that little, I hope, will interest you and make you think of the world as a whole, and of other peoples in it as your brothers and sisters.[19]

In his *Letters* Nehru begins at the very beginning of time, with the origin of the earth from a burning fragment of the sun. Then he goes on to the evolution of living things, the emergence of *homo sapiens*, the ice, stone and iron ages, different races, languages and civilizations. But as well as information, Nehru wants to convey a certain vision. Discussing religion, he tells her that it 'first came as fear and anything that is done because of fear is bad . . . we see even today that people fight and break each other's heads in the name of religion. And . . . many people ... spend their time in trying to please some imaginary beings by making presents in temples and ... sacrifices of animals.'[20] While explaining different forms of government, kings and revolutions, he says, 'in India we still have many Rajas and Maharajas and Nawabs. You see them going about with fine clothes in expensive motor-cars and spending a lot of money on themselves ... While they live in luxury, their people, who work hard and give them money, starve and their children have no schools to go to.'[21] He goes on to discuss the class system and condemns the exploitation of peasants and labourers by the upper classes and nobility.

Quite apart from the moral and political ideals that lie at the heart of *Letters*, is the recurrent theme of fossils. Nehru reminds Indira of the fossils they saw in the museum in Geneva, in the Natural History Museum in London and also of the beautiful fossils of fern markings and other plants that they found on their walks in India. He is urging on her a fascination with underlying structures – that which is fundamental – and also with relics that survive the ravages of time and human history. The subtext of *Letters* encouraged Indira to look beyond the political turmoil they were living in – to take the longest possible view of time and life on earth.

Nehru himself, however, remained embroiled in politics in Allahabad. Three months after Indira, Kamala and the others returned from Mussoorie, the crisis between him and Motilal and between the heterogeneous elements within the Congress – radical, conservative and communal – came to a head at the annual All-India Congress Committee session held in Calcutta in December 1928.

The whole family travelled to Calcutta by train – a large party that included Nan Pandit's new baby Nayantara. Motilal had been elected President of Congress, and he and his entourage were treated like royalty.[22] In Calcutta they stayed at a mansion decorated with bunting, flowers and national flags, guarded by mounted Congress volunteers. They rode to the opening Congress meeting in a procession with Motilal, Jawaharlal, Kamala and Indira in a carriage drawn by thirty-four white horses, followed by mounted Congress volunteers, marching women in green and red-bordered *khadi* saris, a medical unit, and finally a fleet of motorcyclists led by the radical Bengali Congress leader Subhas Chandra Bose.[23]

One of those watching this imposing procession was an eight-year-old boy named Siddhartha Shankar Ray, a grandson of Motilal's old friend and Swaraj Party colleague the now late C.R. Das. At the 1928 Calcutta Congress Siddhartha and the other children and grandchildren of Congress delegates wanted to participate, so a hundred or so of them were organized to make large red banners with white slogans that read 'Mahatma Gandhi *Ki Jai*' (Long live Mahatma Gandhi) and 'Congress *Ki Jai*' (Victory to Congress). At the second or third meeting of the children's group, it was announced that Indira Nehru would arrive shortly. The children were eager to see what the granddaughter and daughter of their heroes Motilal and Jawaharlal Nehru would look like. Indira arrived in her loose white *khadi* clothes and they were bitterly disappointed: she looked so weak and insignificant. But several days later a rumour went around that Indira had eaten half a dozen bananas that morning at breakfast and this went a long way toward redeeming her image.[24]

On 27 December 1928, a year to the day after Nehru made his independence resolution in Madras, Gandhi moved before a closed session at Calcutta that the Nehru Report – including its endorsement of dominion status – be adopted if the British accepted the report and granted its demands within two years. Jawaharlal passionately denounced the dominion status formula which he called 'an extremely wrong and foolish act' that acquiesced to the 'psychology of imperialism'. An all-night emergency session ensued and the next day Gandhi reduced the time limit given to London to one year. Nehru was still bitterly unhappy and so was his ally Subhas Chandra Bose. But he yielded by default. Instead of voting for or against Gandhi's revised resolution, he absented himself from the proceedings. Gandhi's motion was carried by 118 votes to 45.

This culmination of the struggle between those who supported complete independence and those who favoured dominion status – a struggle that had threatened to split Congress and the Nehru family – revealed important qualities in Nehru, as one of his biographers has noted: 'his vacillation when confronted with the problem of unpleasant choice; his devotion to Gandhi and his father even at the expense of yielding on principle; and his profound conviction that party unity had the highest political priority'.[25] Still, Nehru had not really compromised. There was never a possibility, in anyone's minds – Jawaharlal's, Motilal's or Gandhi's – that the British would accept the Nehru Report and grant dominion status in one, two or even five years. Gandhi's resolution stated that civil disobedience would be reactivated if they did not. Hence Jawaharlal knew that the coming year would be one of preparation for a massive renewal of the nationalist movement.

1929, then, became a kind of time bomb, steadily ticking off, day by day, the one-year limit given to the British. For Nehru these were hectic months of readying Congress for direct action. He toured the country most of the time, and was not at home when the family moved into the finally completed new Anand Bhawan in the spring. Despite Swarup Rani's and Bibi Amma's objections, Motilal vetoed having the traditional house-moving *puja* performed. The new Anand Bhawan was smaller than the original; but it was still large, and in some ways more lavish since it was adorned with items collected by Motilal in Europe – porcelain door handles, brass light fixtures, European baths, toilets and bidets (reportedly the first bidets in India). An ornate spiral staircase connected the two storeys; wide verandas with red and white speckled stone floors encircled the house; white Mughal domes perched like stone mushrooms on the roof. Indira had a large room of her own at the back of the first floor, next to her father's dressing room and parents' bedroom. Out in the garden English roses bloomed. The day after the family moved in, the local newspaper, the *Pioneer* (edited by an Englishman named Wilson), ran a front-page photograph of the imposing new Anand Bhawan under the caption 'How our poor politicians live.'[26]

As usual, the Nehru women, including Indira, decamped to Mussoorie for the summer. When they returned in the autumn, the great political question was who would succeed Motilal as Congress President at the December 1929 Lahore annual meeting. The year of grace 'granted' to the British would then be up; whoever took over as Congress President would launch the new civil disobedience campaign. Gandhi was the obvious choice, but at the Lucknow All-India Congress Committee held in September, he emphatically refused. Instead, Gandhi warmly supported Jawaharlal as President with the result that Jawaharlal was elected, as he put it, 'not ... by the main entrance or even a side entrance; I appeared suddenly by a trap-door and bewildered the audience into acceptance'. He felt humiliated – like 'a necessary pill', bravely swallowed. But Motilal, despite all their differences, was elated that his son would succeed him.[27]

Indira had never been to the Punjab before and it was bitterly cold when she arrived in Lahore with her family in late December 1929. Instead of staying in a decorated mansion as they had the year before in Calcutta, the Nehrus went directly from the train station to a vast camp of white tents – the site of the Congress meeting – erected on the banks of the Ravi river. Here, along with some 300,000 other delegates, they ate, slept and met for the next six days.

Nehru refused to ride to the opening session in a chariot pulled by bullocks, as was urged on him. He wanted to walk unescorted, without procession, but in the end he agreed to ride a white charger through the streets of Lahore, teeming with flag-waving, cheering crowds. The number of people who waited for hours to catch a glimpse of Nehru filled the streets, roofs and trees that lined the route. Gandhi, the king-maker, captured the spirit of this ride when he described Nehru as 'a knight *sans peur et sans reproche*'.[28] A process of glorification, even deification, had begun.

At the opening session, which Indira attended, Motilal passed on the mantle of the Congress presidency to Jawaharlal, quoting a Persian couplet: '*Herche ke pidar natawanad, pesar tamam kundad*' (what the father is unable to accomplish, the son achieves).[29] These words sowed the seed of another myth – that of the Nehru (and later the Nehru-Gandhi) dynasty. This was the first time a son had succeeded his father as Congress President. Motilal's pride was boundless; Swarup Rani was 'in a sort of ecstasy'. Indira, of course, was thrilled too. Twenty-eight years later, she, in her turn, would 'inherit' the Congress Presidency, but with great ambivalence on both her own and her father's parts.

In his 1929 presidential address, Nehru boldly stated the new Congress ethos: 'independence for us means complete freedom from British dominion and British imperialism'.[30] The climax of the Congress meeting was to be the adoption of the *Purna Swaraj* (complete independence) resolution and Nehru spent hours drafting it in Lahore. Indira happened to be with him when a secretary handed Nehru the typed copy of the final draft and he immediately gave it to her and told her to read it aloud. She began haltingly; he interrupted her and told her to 'read it properly'. She started again, reading slowly and deliberately:

> We believe it is the inalienable right of the Indian people, as of any people, to have freedom and to enjoy the fruits of their toil and have the necessities of life, so that they may have full opportunities of growth. We believe also that if any government

deprives a people of these rights and oppresses them, the people have a further right to alter it or to abolish it. The British Government in India has not only deprived the Indian people of their freedom but has based itself on the exploitation of the masses, and has ruined India economically, culturally and spiritually. We believe, therefore, that India must sever the British connection and attain Purna Swaraj or complete independence . . .'[31]

When Indira finished the whole text, Nehru said to her, 'Well, now that you have read it, you are committed to it.'[32]

But it was not until Gandhi moved the resolution before the assembled Congress delegates at Lahore the next day, that Indira realized she had been the first person in India to take the pledge. Gandhi also called for the boycott of legislatures and government committees and relaunched civil disobedience. The resolution was passed at midnight on 31 December, just as the year and the decade turned, and at the hour when the one-year Congress ultimatum to the British expired. The flag of independence was unfurled on the banks of the Ravi to cries of 'Long live revolution'. All this foreshadowed another midnight hour – no one then knew how many years hence.

When the Nehrus returned to Allahabad, they were celebrities and Anand Bhawan ceased to be a private home. Jawaharlal was not merely Congress President, he was a national hero and all those close to him partook of his reflected glory. From far and near, adoring followers travelled to Anand Bhawan. 'Crowds of pilgrims', as Nehru described them, swarmed about the grounds, the verandas filled up, 'each door and window had a collection of prying eyes'. It became difficult to talk or work or eat under this intrusive scrutiny which 'was not only embarrassing,' as Nehru described the influx of admirers, but also 'annoying and irritating'. 'Yet there they were, these people looking up with shining eyes full of affection . . . pouring out their gratitude and love and asking for little in return, except fellow-feeling and sympathy.'[33] Periodically during the day Nehru would go out to meet the multitude, listen to their problems, and receive their homage – and be ashamed of his earlier impatience and exasperation.

Songs and legends about Nehru and his family circulated and were hastily printed in broadsheets and pamphlets; garish picture posters of them were sold in the bazaars. At first Nehru found this hero worship intoxicating; it gave him 'confidence and strength'. But then he realized that his 'reputation as a hero [was] entirely bogus' and based on a spurious perception of the Nehrus as aristocrats, nobility, even demi-gods. Rumours abounded that he had gone to school with the Prince of Wales in England, that he and Motilal used to send their linen weekly from India to London to be laundered. And then, so the legend went, they completely renounced luxury, position and wealth for the Indian people.[34]

In time this iconic status, like the notion of the Nehru-Gandhi dynasty, would become inveterate and damaging. But in the early days it was a source of jokes for Kamala and Nehru's sisters. Mimicking the encomiums showered on Jawaharlal, they would address him as '*Bharat Bhushan*' (Jewel of India) and '*Tyagamurti*' (Embodiment of Sacrifice).[35] For Indira, however, the fame of her father and the lack of privacy that now prevailed at Anand Bhawan were disorientating. Nor was she herself exempt from hero worship. As her banana-eating feat in Calcutta had shown, she was already aware that she represented the family and that she had a public image to maintain.

At the Lahore Congress session, 26 January was targeted as Independence Day, to be celebrated across the country. In Allahabad, on that day in 1930, Indira – as the youngest child (except for Nan Pandit's babies) – was chosen to hoist the national flag at Anand Bhawan before the assembled family members and servants. They stood on the veranda as the tricolour was raised, then recited the independence pledge and sang the national anthem – a scene re-enacted throughout the land.

In the weeks and months that followed protest and civil disobedience engulfed India, spearheaded by Gandhi's famous salt *satyagraha* to protest against the government salt tax, an especially unjust tax since salt was a basic necessity of life. In March 1930 Gandhi and seventy-eight fellow marchers walked 240 miles from Sabarmati ashram to Dandi on the coast where they made salt from the muddy sea water. This 'silly salt stunt', as the Viceroy, Lord Irwin, described it, was in fact a masterpiece of strategy that galvanized the whole country.

One of the most remarkable consequences of the salt march and the general resumption of civil disobedience in 1930 was the massive involvement of Indian women who had not played a significant political role in the twenties. In the early years of the nationalist struggle women like Annie Besant and Sarojini Naidu were anomalies – honorary men in the Congress. But now, as Nehru wrote, 'an avalanche' of women 'took not only the British government but their own menfolk by surprise ... women of the upper or middle classes, leading sheltered lives in their homes, peasant women, working-class women, rich women – pouring out in their tens of thousands in defiance of government order and police lathi'.

Among these, indeed leading them in Allahabad, were the Nehru women, especially Kamala who rose from her sick bed, put on a white *khadi* Congress volunteer uniform, and went out to picket foreign cloth and liquor stores, government schools and courts. Kamala's physical ailments and lassitude disappeared or were ignored by her. Much later Nehru realized that she had been longing 'to play her own part in the national struggle and not be merely a hanger-on and a shadow of her husband', but it was only in the early months of 1930, he said, that 'I sensed her desire and we worked together and I found in this experience a new delight.'[36]

Children, as well as women, clamoured for a role, and who better to lead them than Indira Nehru? Hence the *Vanar Sena* or monkey brigade created in March 1930. Years later Indira took all the credit, explaining that she single-handedly formed a children's contingent of Congress workers because she was told she could not join the regular volunteers until she was eighteen.[37] But the *Vanar Sena* was actually the joint idea of Kamala and Bishambar Nath Pande, one of the secretaries of the Allahabad Congress Committee who worked closely with Kamala. One day Kamala was canvassing in a poor part of the city with Pande where the street children, as usual, followed them shouting 'Kamala Nehru *ki jai*' (Victory to Kamala Nehru). An old woman standing nearby said to Kamala that the children were like the *Vanar Sena* in the *Ramayana* – where the monkey god Hanuman's army of monkeys builds a bridge between India and Lanka (Sri Lanka) in order to rescue Sita, the wife of Lord Rama. Kamala suggested to Pande that they form a *Vanar Sena* of Congress children and he proposed making twelve-year-old Indira its leader. Indira, however – according to Pande – was hesitant, and before agreeing to the plan, made sure Pande would help her. Together they drew up a programme, visited Allahabad schools and in a remarkably short time, managed to recruit nearly a thousand children.

In the spring of 1930 Congress called for a demonstration week across the country, and in Allahabad Indira led a huge procession of 15,000 children viewed by a crowd of more than 50,000 gathered on the streets of Allahabad. The procession ended with a mass meeting at Anand Bhawan where Indira addressed the sea of '*Vanar Sainiks*'. But because her voice was so weak, Pande had to function as a human loudspeaker, bellowing out her words, sentence by sentence, to the huge audience. Through Pande, Indira exhorted the crowd to collect rations for *satyagraha* camps, to distribute *satyagraha* bulletins and to collect one *paisa* each per day from every household for the *Vanar Sena* fund.[38]

Despite her initial hesitation, Indira quickly became absorbed in *Vanar Sena* activities. Originally the idea was for the children to help the adult Congress workers by doing menial jobs such as carrying messages, preparing food, sewing flags and distributing leaflets. But the children soon realized they could be useful in an intelligence capacity. They would hang around police stations playing street games and overhear arrest orders or the whereabouts of the next police raid; then they would run and warn the Congress members concerned. As Indira later put it, 'nobody bothered about an urchin hopping in and out of the police lines. Nobody thought that they could be doing anything. The boy would memorize the message and go then to the people concerned and say: "You know this is what has to be done or not done. All the police are there. So and so is going to be arrested."'[39]

As the leader of the *Vanar Sena*, Indira now became famous in her own right. She wore the male Congress volunteer uniform of *khadi* and a Congress cap. A photograph of Indira and her parents at this time appeared in newspapers across India. The three of them are in the garden of Anand Bhawan. Jawaharlal, in a white *khadi* Congress uniform, and Kamala, in a plain *khadi* sari, flank Indira clad in *kurta*, *khadi* waistcoat and cap, her hair bobbed. The photo has both a political and a quasi-religious aura: the charismatic, handsome young family, pure and austere in white *khadi*, look poised for non-violent battle. Indira no longer hovers on the periphery; she is centre stage, standing tall in her Congress uniform – Indu-boy.

It was in March 1930, the month the *Vanar Sena* was formed, that Kamala and Indira met Feroze Gandhi when they went with a band of

Congresswomen to picket the British-staffed Ewing Christian College in Allahabad. Feroze, an eighteen-year-old student at the college, was lounging with his friends on a wall watching the women demonstrators with wry amusement when Kamala fainted in the midday sun. He ran for water and a fan to revive her, and in the process of helping Kamala and taking her home, Feroze was converted to her cause – or perhaps more accurately, to Kamala herself. The next day he dropped out of Ewing Christian College, reappeared at Anand Bhawan and signed up as a Congress volunteer. Henceforward Feroze Gandhi was Kamala's shadow and disciple. Inevitably this meant that he saw a great deal of Indira too, though for a number of months Indira did not differentiate between this plump, loquacious Parsi boy and the other adoring assistants Kamala attracted.

In April 1930, the month after Feroze entered their lives, the government tried to stem the tide of civil disobedience with a country-wide crackdown. The Congress Working Committee was declared illegal and its officials rounded up. Nehru was arrested on 14 April and sentenced to six months imprisonment at Naini Jail for manufacturing salt. Gandhi was jailed on 5 May and Motilal Nehru on 30 June. With Jawaharlal and Motilal in prison across the river in Naini, the Nehru women sweated through the long hot summer in Allahabad – although Kamala could not have gone to Mussoorie because of her political work. She was now working an eighteen-hour day and had recently set up a hospital for wounded Congress demonstrators in a wing of the old Anand Bhawan, which Motilal had donated to Congress and renamed Swaraj Bhawan (Abode of Freedom).

In early September Kamala wrote to Jawaharlal that she wished she herself would be arrested and jailed, in part to escape a bad flare-up of old animosities at home. Ranjit Pandit had decided to become involved in the Swaraj Bhawan hospital yet both he and Nan Pandit, Kamala claimed, had spent the summer 'sitting comfortably indoors, behind *khas chiks* (sun blinds), under the cool breeze of a fan. They have not stirred out in the heat to work.'[40]

On 8 September Motilal was released from jail because he was seriously ill. Jawaharlal was set free on the 11th and he immediately travelled to Mussoorie with Kamala and Indira to visit Motilal, only to be rearrested on the 19th. This time he was charged with sedition, incitement to manufacture salt and non-payment of taxes, and sentenced to two-and-half years and five more months in default of fines. This severe sentence led to nationwide demonstrations on his birthday, 14 November, which was proclaimed 'Jawahar Day'. In Allahabad, Swarup Rani, Nan, Betty and Indira led a procession to the City Park where Kamala addressed the crowd and read out in its entirety the 'seditious' speech which had led to Nehru's conviction.

It had been nearly seven years since Nehru had been locked up in his 'other home', as he referred to prison in his letters. He missed Kamala and Indira acutely and meticulously recorded their fortnightly visits in his prison diary. When he was returned to Naini Jail in October 1930, with a nearly three-year sentence stretching before him, he was dismayed at the prospect of the long separation and decided to write another series of letters to Indira – a continuation of the *Letters from a Father to His Daughter*, which had been published earlier that year.

Thus on 26 October 1930 – Indira's birthday according to the Hindu calendar – Nehru began what was to become one of his most revealing and engaging works, *Glimpses of World History*, with a letter from 'Central Prison, Naini' headed 'For Indira Priyadarshini on her Thirteenth Birthday.' From the very beginning Nehru conceived of *Glimpses* as a gift or offering to Indira – 'a present', as he says, 'of the mind and the spirit'. At 196 letter-chapters and 970 densely printed pages, written over the course of the next three years, it must be one of the most protracted and voluminous birthday gifts ever created.

In his opening letter Nehru invokes Joan of Arc, reminds Indira that she was born the same month that Lenin started the Russian Revolution, and speaks of the revolution Gandhi is inspiring and leading in India. On the one hand, he thus endorses Thomas Carlyle's 'heroic' view of history – the idea that history consists of the deeds of great men. *Glimpses*, in fact, contains a pantheon of heroes: Socrates, Ashoka, Akbar, Alexander the Great, Garibaldi, Bismarck, Hitler and Franklin Roosevelt, among others. But at the same time, Nehru insists that 'real history' is 'not just a record of the doings of big men, of kings and emperors'. It concerns all 'the people who make up a nation'.[41] The other crucial theme in this opening letter and the book as a whole is that history is not something that is dead and over – in the past. History is happening, Nehru insists, *now*, all around them: 'in India today we are making history, and you and I are fortunate to see this happening before our eyes and to take . . . part ourselves in this great drama'.[42] Both the 'great men' view of history and Nehru's conviction that Indira had a historical destiny to pursue were assimilated by her much later, though not in the manner he intended.

Glimpses was also inspired by H.G. Wells's *Outline of History* which Nehru had with him in prison, along with a pile of his reading note-books. Apart from these two sources, this vast and erratically erudite book was conjured out of his extensive reading (much of it done in prison and in Europe). Unlike Wells, Nehru offers a decidedly non-Eurocentric view of the world, placing South Asia back on the historical map. *Glimpses* was meant to be an antidote to the European history Indira was being taught at St Mary's. As well as being a compelling history of the world from ancient Greece to the rise of Nazi Germany, *Glimpses* distils Nehru's political vision. Nationalist heroes like Akbar and Garibaldi are celebrated. So, too, are women leaders like Joan of Arc and the Rani of Jhansi. Nehru traces the collapse of capitalism, the negative impact of religion (except for Buddhism which fascinated and attracted him), the development of intellectual movements and ideologies such as democracy, socialism, Marxism and fascism. Nor does he neglect cultural, artistic and scientific movements though these tend to be the thinnest passages in the book.

Quite apart from providing an historical and political education for Indira, *Glimpses* sprang from deeply personal, emotional sources. When Nehru started to write these letters he effectively began to carry on two separate but parallel correspondences with his daughter: the letters which were actually posted to her from Naini Prison and the phantom correspondence of the *Glimpses* letters which were neither sent nor received. Indira, in fact, did not even know about the *Glimpses* letters until 1932, two years after Nehru began them, and she did not have access to them until the book was published in 1934.

Not surprisingly, perhaps, the long, unsent letters that formed *Glimpses* – those which Nehru says at one point 'no one sees but myself' and which he realizes Indira will only read 'months or years hence' – are the most unguarded and revealing of the two correspondences.[43] Here Nehru speaks from the heart, as if in a diary, both to Indira (who cannot hear) and to himself. He gets depressed and is upset by political and family news that filters through to him in prison – that Indira is ill, that his mother and Kamala have not been allowed to visit him. He wonders if the vast manuscript he is producing will bore Indira. On some days the letters seem simplistic; on others he does not have the heart to write. And yet he cannot let go of the book. It serves a crucial purpose to him in jail. It creates a sense of powerful and sustaining intimacy with his absent daughter and assuages his guilt at being separated from her. During the long hours he spends writing, he almost feels as if they were together. At the same time, the *Glimpses* letters are a distraction and preoccupation from personal and political doubts and anxieties. The 'solid work' of composition and the mental transport to distant times allows Nehru 'to control' his mind and 'live for a while far away from . . . present troubles'.[44]

While Nehru was locked up in Naini, writing unsent letters to his daughter, she was working hard with the *Vanar Sena*, helping to nurse patients at the Swaraj Bhawan hospital and also still attending St Mary's Convent. On 17 November, two days before Indira's thirteenth birthday, she, Kamala, Swarup Rani and Betty took Motilal to Calcutta to consult an Ayurvedic doctor, Kaviraj Shyamdas Vachaspati. Motilal, who was now sixty-nine, was suffering from a variety of ailments, including asthma, fibrosis of the lungs, high blood pressure and kidney failure, none of which was responding to conventional treatment. In prison he had lost a great deal of weight and once out, he remained weak and frail, a shadow of his former massive self.

Indira took a hefty pile of books to read in Calcutta and reported to Nehru that she had finished Maurice Maeterlinck's *The Life of the Bee* and begun his *Life of the Ant*, after which she promised to read 'the book about Garibaldi you gave me. At the present Dadu [Motilal] and Chhoti [Betty] have both begun it and none of them has read the whole of it.' She signed the letter 'From your loving Indu-boy' and added a postscript: 'My shorts have been made' – presumably for gymnastics and running.[45]

By Christmas Indira and Kamala were back in Allahabad and on the 27th they had a prison interview with Nehru at Naini Jail. On New Year's Eve they were alone in Anand Bhawan, reading Tennyson's *In Memoriam* aloud together, when the telephone rang. Indira answered and an unfamiliar voice hurriedly told her that Kamala would be arrested the next day and then hung up. Tennyson was forgotten; Indira went to pack her mother's suitcase while Kamala rang up local Congress workers and gave them instructions. Then because Kamala feared the house might be searched, she and Indira burnt piles of papers and pamphlets far into the night. Neither slept.

At 5 a.m. on New Year's Day, with Indira standing beside her, Kamala was arrested by the British police, on the steps of Anand Bhawan. The press had been alerted and reported the event. Kamala made a brief statement: 'I am happy beyond measure and proud to follow in the footsteps of my husband.'[46] Then she was driven off to Malacca Jail in Allahabad and Indira was left alone, but for the servants, in the large house.

Scarcely a mile-and-a-half away from Kamala's prison, in Naini Jail Nehru heard of her arrest within hours and wrote in his diary, 'Kamala arrested! – a good beginning to the New Year. She will be happy now and it is quite possible that she may profit by the rest in prison. Poor Indu alone – What impressions must be produced on a growing child's mind by all these events?'[47] The same day he wrote an unposted *Glimpses* letter to 'poor Indu' telling her that Kamala's arrest 'was a pleasant New Year's gift to me . . . and I have no doubt that Mummie is thoroughly happy and contented. But you must be rather lonely.'[48]

She was. Motilal, Swarup Rani and the others returned from Calcutta as soon as they heard of Kamala's arrest, but Indira still felt bereft with both of her parents in jail. After Kamala was given a six-month sentence and transferred from Allahabad to Lucknow Central Jail, she was even less accessible to Indira. From Lucknow Kamala wrote to Jawaharlal that 'when I was arrested I was worried about Induji. I wondered what she would do by herself. But I now feel somewhat reassured about her being able to look after herself. She gave me her word that she would remain cheerful and take care of herself.' As for Kamala herself, she was determined to benefit from the prison routine:

> After a cup of tea when I wake up in the morning I walk nearly a mile and a half to two miles. After prayers I read. Dinner is at 6pm and then we are locked up for the night. We sleep around 9 or 10 pm. Up again at 5 am . . . I wanted to weave a *dari* (a coarse carpet) but it takes time learning to do it. So I am concentrating on *niwar* (a thick cotton tape) making. I shall compare it with the *niwar* turned out by you. Let us see whose is better done. Jail life is strange. One runs into different types of people here and gets an opportunity as nowhere else to study

their temperaments . . . I am determined to gain strength while
in jail and fight with greater vigour when I am out.[49]

On 12 January Indira went with her grandparents to visit Nehru at
Naini Jail. The next day he wrote another unsent *Glimpses* letter that
shows how disturbing the interview had been: 'It was good to see you
all yesterday. But I had a shock when I saw Dadu. He was looking so
weak and ill . . . I could hardly speak to you yesterday. What can one
do in a short interview? I try to make up for all the interviews and talks
we have not had by writing these letters. But they are poor substitutes,
and the make-believe does not last long.'[50]

A week later Nehru received a letter from Indira reporting she had
read a great many books from the Anand Bhawan library and asking
him to suggest more. In another 'make-believe' (because unposted)
Glimpses letter he chided her for not telling him what specific books
she had read and then went on to lecture her: 'It is a good habit to read
books, but I rather suspect those who read too many books quickly. I
suspect them of not reading them properly at all, of just skimming
through them, and forgetting them the day after.'[51] Even though this
letter remained unsent, Indira's reading – her education in fact – had
clearly become a contentious subject. Nehru wanted to control her
intellectual development. Indira wanted freedom to read what she liked,
including fairy tales when she was little and romantic novels as she got
older. Nehru pressed H.G. Wells on her and books about Garibaldi.
Sometimes Indira obediently read them – with little understanding as
she confessed later – sometimes she resisted. She clearly resented the
pressure on her to read a certain kind of worthy book, and when she
complied and did read what was urged on her but could not understand
it, she felt slow and inadequate.

The third week of January Indira at last received a letter from Kamala
in Lucknow Jail:

> Love to Induji.
>   Ever since I came to prison I have no news of anyone. Your
> father's letter reached me on the 15th and I had hoped the
> packet would contain one from you too. The jail authorities
> allow letters only once a fortnight. So you can write to me, but
> how many letters I may send out I do not know . . . Let me
> know your daily routine. Please send the fortnightly reports

about your studies obtained from your teachers to your father. I hope you remember what I told you when I was leaving home. Whenever I go outside the barrack for a stroll I think of you. You too must stroll everyday. When I am released we shall go out for walks, though that will be six months away, but six months will pass without either you or I feeling it.[52]

More pressure about her studies. Her own letters were not getting through to Kamala. And Indira knew that six months would not pass quickly at all.

Fortunately she only had to wait a few days. On 26 January 1931 the British government announced that Jawaharlal, Kamala, Gandhi and the other members of the Congress Working Committee would all be immediately released from prison. Kamala and Jawaharlal returned to Anand Bhawan to find what was essentially a house of death. It was clear Motilal was extremely ill and would not last long. Jawaharlal cabled Gandhi who set off immediately from Bombay, arriving late at night in Allahabad. Motilal had lain awake waiting for him all day. He told Gandhi that he knew he would not 'be here to see Swaraj. But I know that you have won it and will soon have it.'[53]

In the following days, Motilal's face and throat swelled up and he was no longer able to speak. On 4 February he was taken to Lucknow for deep x-ray treatment, Jawaharlal, Gandhi, Swarup Rani, Betty and the Pandits – but not Indira or Kamala – accompanying him. He died in hospital there in the very early hours of 6 February 1931 with Jawaharlal and Swarup Rani at his side. Later that same day, they brought his body back by car to Allahabad.

Indira was stunned by her grandfather's death and left very much to herself in the paroxysm of grief that gripped the family – and the country. Her younger cousin, Nayantara Pandit, was one of the few to notice Indira the day of her grandfather's funeral, standing alone by the sideboard in the Anand Bhawan dining room, silently weeping.[54] P. N. Haksar, now a seventeen-year-old student at Allahabad University, was among the crowds outside the house when Motilal's body was brought out, and he noticed Indira too. He had not seen her in ten years. She was tall, painfully thin, pale as death. Her eyes were deeply shadowed and even larger than he remembered.[55]

Though it was not customary for Hindu women to participate in or even attend funeral rites, all the Nehru women – Swarup Rani, Nan

Pandit, Betty, Kamala and Indira – accompanied the Congress flag-draped body as the cortege wound its way through the streets of Allahabad – lined with crowds of mourners – to the Ganges for cremation. As Jawaharlal described it, 'as evening fell on the river bank on that winter day, the great flames leapt up and consumed that body which had meant so much to us who were close to him as well as to millions in India'.[56] Five days later Motilal's ashes were submerged at the Sangam – the holy confluence of the Ganges, the Jumna and the mythological Saraswati rivers. This was the first death in Indira's life – the first link in a lengthening chain of grief over the years.

FIVE

Enter Feroze

ON AN APRIL DAY IN 1931, Indira, her parents, a driver, maid and Jawaharlal's servant Hari Lal were travelling the road from Colombo to Kandy in Ceylon when they rounded a bend at high speed and drove into a much steeper, sharper curve. The back wheels of the car skidded to the edge of the precipice. As the driver braked and jerked the steering wheel in the opposite direction, Indira, seated beside him, opened the passenger door and leapt to safety, leaving the rest of those in the car – as her father pointed out five minutes later – to be hurled down the cliff to their deaths. The driver's quick reflexes, however, saved them. Deeply ashamed, Indira never again panicked in the face of danger.[1]

They were in Ceylon on holiday. Nehru's health had completely broken down after his father's death and what he called the 'total and unwarranted surrender' of the March 1931 Gandhi-Irwin Pact. By the terms of this truce Gandhi called off civil disobedience and agreed to work towards self-government by stages while the British released political prisoners and allowed villagers to make salt for domestic consumption. Ceylon was supposed to be an escape from grief and political compromise. Indira thought it 'very lush, green and beautiful'. Nehru likened it to lotus-eater land: 'an enchanted place . . . It is ever afternoon here . . . One forgets almost the struggle and misery of the world of action.'[2]

Yet it was far from an idyllic or private time. Even on holiday the Nehrus remained celebrities. They were public property, their every move reported by the press, their faces familiar to a huge public who had seen them on Congress placards or in newspaper photographs. At the ancient sacred city of Anuradhapura Jawaharlal, Kamala and Indira

were visited daily by 'groups of labourers, tea-garden workers and others
. . . walking many miles, bringing . . . gifts [of] . . . wild flowers, vegetables, home-made butter'.[3] As they toured the rest of Ceylon, visiting
Buddhist monuments, old fortresses, palaces and temples, they were
pursued by 'one great crowd [after] another' and embroiled in 'a whirl
of engagements, addresses, meetings, receptions'. They travelled to the
southernmost tip of the island and then to the far north by train to
Jaffna where there was also 'a heavy programme'.[4]

Yet despite this hectic schedule and the crowds, the marriage of
Jawaharlal and Kamala – now in its sixteenth year – underwent a transformation in Ceylon that profoundly moved and surprised them both.
As Nehru described it, they 'seemed to have discovered each other anew.
All the years we had passed together had been but a preparation for
this new and more intimate relationship.' Contemplating the wreck of
so many marriages, they marvelled at how they had managed to keep
'the vital spark alight'.[5] And it was not only a platonic spark. As Nehru
confessed later to Gandhi (of all people), Kamala's touch 'would always
thrill' him. Their relationship was 'often painful', but also 'electric'.

Nehru's love for his wife, he now realized, was a rare amalgam. There
had always been the fortunate accident of sexual attraction. But ever
since Kamala became politically active two years earlier this had been
heightened and intensified by Nehru's growing respect and admiration.
He was a man who could only become passionate about a woman whom
he felt was his equal. And Kamala assumed this status belatedly – when
she went out on the streets of Allahabad to demonstrate in 1930. Now
in Ceylon they shared a paradoxical sort of emotional intimacy. On the
one hand, Kamala was 'the only person who could . . . peep into' her
husband's 'lonely personal life' – the only person able to penetrate his
reserve. And yet they remained somehow fundamentally elusive and
unknowable to each other. 'She was a mystery to me and I was a mystery
to her and . . . the novelty and surprise never wore off.'[6]

How did Indira figure in her parents' new intimacy? Three, of course,
is a crowd. The Nehrus now were an asymmetrical trio in which Indira
was an onlooker, hovering on the fringes of her parents' relationship,
perhaps moved by, but also to some extent excluded from, it.

Others were puzzled by the family. At the age of forty-two, Nehru
was bald and had dark shadows under his eyes. Ten years younger,
Kamala was slender, her skin perfectly clear and smooth. She still looked

like a young girl. Indira, at nearly fourteen, had reached her full height of five foot two and was a good inch or two taller than her mother. Everyone who saw them recognized Nehru immediately, but there was confusion over Kamala and Indira. As Nehru wrote to his sister, 'Kamala has often been taken for my daughter. But what do you say to Indu being taken for the mother! This has happened repeatedly!'[7]

They returned to Allahabad via southern India and the Princely States of Travancore, Cochin, Malabar, Mysore and Hyderabad where the crowds were again 'overwhelming' and they were rushed 'from place to place and function to function with little rest and less peace'.[8] But what struck Indira most forcefully in the south was the omnipresent caste bar. She had been raised to disregard caste – an unusual upbringing in the twenties and thirties. The Nehrus had many Harijan servants at Anand Bhawan who lived and ate with them, including Hari Lal who had been Motilal's and was now Jawaharlal's personal servant. In South India, for the first time, Indira was confronted with caste prejudice everywhere they went. 'Whole streets', as she said, were barred to Harijans or 'untouchables' with large signs reading 'Brahmins only'. Hari, however, walked down them with the others.[9]

Indira's other vivid memory of their return journey was of Kamala making a speech in Hyderabad in which she urged women to come out of *purdah*. Indira was deeply impressed by her mother's performance. But she did not as yet understand Kamala's feminism, having never herself experienced any disadvantage being a girl. Nor did Indira see any oppression of women around her. Certainly not in Hyderabad where they stayed with the Congress leader Sarojini Naidu who, along with her daughters Leilamani and Padmaja, was an intelligent, forceful and charismatic woman.

Something happened shortly after the Nehrus arrived back at Allahabad in early May – one of those submerged, invisible events that nonetheless shape a life and leave scars. Indira's aunt, Nan Pandit, reportedly said that Indira was 'ugly and stupid' and the remark was repeated and overheard by her niece. Tall for her age and thin, with a large nose and skin she felt was too dark, Indira was devastated by her aunt's 'annihilating words'. She was already shy and insecure. After Nan Pandit delivered this brutal assessment, Indira became a silent, moody adolescent. For a long time she did not feel at home in or at ease with her body. More than fifty years later, her aunt's thoughtless remark 'remained fresh in [her] memory'. It had, she said, 'blighted her youth'.[10]

Many – perhaps most – women suffer similar 'blighting' experiences in adolescence. But there were few, if any, props for Indira to fall back on. And no one really to turn to. Her parents were absorbed by politics and each other. Her grandfather was dead. She had scarcely any friends and her cousins were still young children. Furthermore, she was about to be sent off to school. This had been decided before Ceylon. Jawaharlal and Kamala thought it best, given the insecurity of their position and the possibility that they would be imprisoned simultaneously again.

Thus in May 1931 Indira was exiled to the Pupils' Own School in Poona, Gujarat, run by a Parsi couple named Vakil who were close to Gandhi and had previously taught at Rabindranath Tagore's famous school at Santiniketan. Jehangir Vakil, an Oxford-educated socialist, was, like Nehru, an agnostic. His wife Coonverbai was a gifted singer and batik artist.[11] Together they ran a kindergarten and junior school for the children of Congress members which was a nationalist venture and inspired by the aesthetic ethos of Santiniketan in Bengal. The students and staff all wore *khadi*; holidays were taken when Congress leaders were arrested. Classes were held out of doors under the trees in the gardens which surrounded the Vakils' colonial-style bungalow at 3 Stavely Road in the cantonment area of Poona. The curriculum prepared the students for the matriculation examination but as was the case at Santiniketan, the arts, especially dance and music, were emphasized.

The Vakils had two daughters, the younger of whom, Ira, was at home when Indira first arrived: what she saw was a tall, skinny, nervous girl with dark circles under her eyes and lots of unruly hair. The older Vakil girl, Jai, who became Indira's close friend, glimpsed her later in the day weeping behind a tree. For a long time Indira remained miserable – desperately homesick, acutely missing her parents. There were seventy students – both boys and girls – in the school. (This number swelled to 120 over the next two years, with the influx of children of jailed political prisoners, including the Pandit daughters.) But Indira was for some time the only boarder. She was also the oldest and tallest student in the school and had by far the most famous parents. She stuck out in every way.[12]

Experimental, socialist ideas underpinned the teaching at the Pupils'

Own School, but the subjects, aside from the arts, were the conventional ones taught at British-run schools in India. Indira took history, geography, civics, physics and chemistry. Nehru also paid extra for French and Sanskrit lessons and she learned folk dancing and picked up some Gujarati. Though the school was run on a shoestring and the day students only paid 7 rupees per month, Indira's monthly fees, including extra tuition, came to 100 rupees, not a small demand on the precarious Nehru finances.

Did she profit by this expensive education? Though she was good at French, Indira was an indifferent student, perhaps because until 1932, when a Parsi girl named Shanta Gandhi (no relation of either the Mahatma or Feroze) joined the school, Indira had no peers, no one to compete or even learn with. She was the oldest student by several years and inevitably the classes were taught at the level of the younger majority. She remained unchallenged and unstretched.

But gradually she developed and progressed, especially after Nan Pandit's three small daughters (the youngest barely two) came to the school in 1932. Indira mothered her little cousins who were even more miserable and homesick than she had been. As a teenager, Indira was often 'difficult', as an adult she could be cold and remote, but from an early age she thawed before vulnerability and despite her reserve, reached out to those who needed her. When she was young it was children and animals who touched this chord in her. Later it became a great strength and asset and lay at the heart of her enormous populist appeal. The poor, the sick, the downtrodden and oppressed – the majority of the population of India – looked to her and believed she could and would help them. The most important lesson Indira learned at the Pupils' Own School was that she was good at taking care of people. As Shanta Gandhi put it, 'her maternal instinct was very powerful'.[13] Not only her cousins, but also the much younger students and the Harijan children who were admitted at the time of Gandhi's 'fast unto death' in September 1932 all thrived under her care.

The students and staff at the Vakils' school all felt great solidarity with Gandhi during his fast and not only admitted several Harijan students, but also went out to teach them in the Poona slums. According to Shanta Gandhi, who had joined the school and become a close friend of Indira's by this time, Indira became particularly attached to a little Harijan girl who refused to learn how to count. Indira bathed her, picked the lice out of her hair and showed her how to plait her hair. Then together they counted the lice they had found in her scalp and in this way Indira taught the girl her numbers.

As was so often the case in Indira's life, at the time of Gandhi's famous 1932 fast she was in the right place at the right time. In fact, she had a ringside seat. At the beginning of 1932, after the failure of the second Round Table Conference in London which Gandhi attended, and in the wake of peasant unrest in the United Provinces, Gandhi, Vallabhbhai Patel and thousands of others were arrested under the Emergency Powers Ordinances implemented by the new Viceroy, Lord Willingdon. Nehru would spend all but six months of the next four years in jail, beginning with a long term at what he came to refer to as his 'other home' of Naini Prison in Allahabad. Gandhi was incarcerated at Yeravda Prison near Poona where Indira and sometimes the little Pandit girls visited him on the weekends.

On 13 September Gandhi had announced that he was embarking on 'a fast unto death', beginning 20 September, in protest against the communal award announced by the British Prime Minister Ramsay Macdonald which provided separate electorates for Harijans. The communal award dismayed nationalists who saw it as a British tactic of divide and rule, but Gandhi's objection to separate electorates was fundamentally religious and rooted in his commitment to the abolition of untouchability. The Harijans for their part, led by a remarkable figure named Dr Bhimrao Ramji Ambedkar, initially supported the award because it would give them a political voice and identity.

Hence there was a deadlock and in Yeravda Prison Gandhi chose to respond in one of the few ways the powerless can hit back: he went on a hunger strike. Though this was not his first public fast and though fasting was an integral part of Hindu life, Gandhi's 1932 'fast unto death' had an enormous impact. Locked up in Naini Jail, Nehru wrote to Indira (in an unsent *Glimpses* letter), 'I am shaken up completely and I know not what to do. News has come, terrible news, that Bapu has determined to starve himself to death. My . . . world . . . shakes and totters and there seems to be darkness and emptiness everywhere.'[14] The British authorities, for quite different reasons, were also appalled. They did not want Gandhi to die in their hands. They tried to persuade him to go to his ashram for the duration of his fast, but Gandhi refused to be released from jail.

Day after day, with the whole of India (and Whitehall) watching, Gandhi rejected food. Despite increasing physical weakness, his spirits remained buoyant. Indira and her cousins visited him as usual on the weekend of 23/24 September and Gandhi sent a reassuring and cheerful telegram to the distraught Nehru: 'Saw Indu and Sarup's [Nan Pandit's] girls. Indu looked very happy and in possession of more flesh.'[15]

On the fifth day of the fast, by which time Gandhi was much weakened, Dr Ambedkar forestalled tragedy by agreeing with Gandhi to the Poona Pact whereby Harijans would give up their claim for separate electorates but were guaranteed a number of reserved seats from the Hindu allocation.

On 26 September Gandhi theatrically broke his fast before an audience of 200 at Yeravda Jail, amongst whom were Rabindranath Tagore, Kamala Nehru, Swarup Rani Nehru and Indira. It was Indira, in fact, who squeezed and gave to Gandhi the orange juice that was his first nourishment. The event, as she wrote to her father, made

> a great impression on me and has taught me a lesson . . . These last . . . days have been terrible . . . when I saw his condition I thought he would not survive. And from eight o'clock to twelve were some of the worst hours I have spent in my life. But now I am perfectly assured that Bapu can do the most imaginary [unimaginable or extraordinary] things.[16]

The crucial lesson Indira learned from Gandhi's fast was the power of passive resistance. Locked up in a British jail, Gandhi nevertheless wielded enormous political and moral authority. The last thing the British imperial authorities wanted or needed was a martyr. Indians, on the other hand, could not conceive of *swaraj* without Gandhi to lead them – he was indispensable. Gandhi, for all his humility, knew all of this. What Indira witnessed was the dramatic appropriation of power and control by one who is legally and physically powerless and under the control of others. By refusing to eat, by threatening to die, Gandhi coerced Dr Ambedkar into compromising his aims and triumphed.

What was fascinating about Gandhi's victory – and a valuable lesson to a teenage girl – was his ingenious means: inaction. Fasting is a common practice of Hindus and so it is perhaps not surprising that it became an oft-used tool of political protest in India. Hunger striking also has a history of proven political effectiveness. Gandhi took his cue in part from the nineteenth-century Irish Fenians, the Irish nationalists of the early twentieth century and from British suffragettes.

After Gandhi's dramatic hunger strike, Indira began to pursue another but closely related method of getting her way. The strategy of empowerment she chose was a refusal to speak rather than to eat. As a small child she chattered incessantly, often inconveniently – piping up during trials, protesting during arrests and demonstrations, monopolizing jail interviews. But when she became an adolescent she learned how to gain control of a situation by refusing to respond – verbally or in letters – to others. In time this evolved into a legendary genius for silence.

After Indira went away to the Pupils' Own School, she never again had a settled life with her parents at Anand Bhawan – or anywhere else. And for a time it seemed they might even lose the family home. In January 1932 the government took possession of Swaraj Bhawan and closed down the hospital Kamala had started there. Rumours spread that the new Anand Bhawan would also be seized because Nehru refused to pay income tax to the British. He worried about his elderly mother and certainly did not want her to be homeless, but in his autobiography he confessed that he would not have regretted losing Anand Bhawan at a time when so many of the peasantry were being dispossessed.

Kamala's health broke down again in 1932 and for most of that year she was receiving medical treatment away from home, first in Bombay and then in Calcutta where she was also initiated into the Ramakrishna religious order.[17] As her body weakened, her religious ardour grew – to the irritation of her husband who was only told of her initiation afterwards.

Meanwhile Nehru was moved from Naini to Bareilly jail and then even further away to the prison at Dehra Dun. Stranded in Poona, hundreds of miles distant from her parents, Indira missed them acutely. She read of them, of course, in the newspapers and one evening she went with the Vakils to a Congress film show in which Jawaharlal and Kamala figured prominently. Indira reported in a letter, 'both of you looked adorable'.[18]

In May of 1932, with her grandmother and mother, Indira visited Ranjit Pandit at Naini Jail, taking with her a letter from Jehangir Vakil concerning the Pandit daughters' progress at the Pupils' Own School.

The prison warden objected to Indira giving her uncle the letter whereupon Swarup Rani (who had been severely beaten during a demonstration the previous month) protested and all three Nehru women were
thrown out. The upshot of this unpleasant episode was that Nehru was
told by the authorities that he would not be allowed to have prison
interviews for a month. In response, he indignantly wrote to the Superintendent of Prisons that rather than subject his mother, wife and daughter to future insults, he would give up prison interviews entirely. This
meant that Indira did not see her father for another seven months.

In the interim, Kamala communicated by letter to Jawaharlal that Indira
was depressed over her separation from them. He promptly wrote to his
daughter 'none of us, least of all you, has any business to be depressed and
to look it. Sometimes you feel a little lonely – we all do that – but we have
to keep smiling through.' And he warned her that when they *did* meet
again she 'must not forget that Papu can stand much but he cannot stand
one thing – depression and a long face in Indu'.[19] This very British, stiff-
upper-lip advice apparently worked. Either Indira cheered up or she
became a convincing actress. When she saw her father at Dehra Dun
Prison on 12 January 1933, he wrote afterwards in his prison diary, 'I was
so exuberant and full of light-hearted laughter . . . Indu is becoming a little
woman and remarkably attractive and smart looking . . . I felt so happy
and proud to see her healthy and straight and growing up apparently without any marked inhibitions.'[20]

But such meetings were oases in the desert, and their exhilaration
soon faded. Four months later, during the school holidays, Indira went
to stay with her mother at Dehra Dun where Kamala had rented a house
to be close to Nehru. He was now permitted fortnightly interviews,
but these were unsatisfactory according to his prison diary. Under the
pressure of time (the interviews lasted only half an hour), Nehru 'held
forth', as he confessed, 'like a tap left open'. Indira reacted to her father's
outpourings, by clamming up and barely responding. Their inability to
connect was reinforced for Nehru when he finished *Glimpses of World
History* in early August in Dehra Dun Jail: 'What a mountain of letters
I have written! And what a lot of good *swadeshi* ink I have spread out
on *swadeshi* paper.' Like all the others, this final letter was not posted,
but even so with the end of his massive, imaginary correspondence with
his daughter – which had sustained him for nearly three years – Nehru
felt a vital bond had not so much snapped as dissolved.[21]

At the end of August, after Indira returned to school, Nehru was released from prison because his mother was critically ill, and he remained a free man for the next five months. In September he visited Indira in Poona (and also Gandhi in Bombay). He arrived at the Pupils' Own School loaded down with books and 'amusement kits' (mechanical models) for Indira and the other children which he spent hours constructing and demonstrating. But everyone was overawed by Nehru – second in stature only to Gandhi in the freedom struggle – and also unnerved by the horde of uniformed and plain-clothes policemen who shadowed him even on the school grounds.

In October, a month before Indira's sixteenth birthday, Feroze Gandhi proposed to her – perhaps by letter since she was at Poona, or possibly in person if Feroze had come to Bombay to visit relatives and gone on to Poona to see Indira. This proposal came like a bolt out of the blue. For Indira, Feroze was just one of any number of young men who were Congress Party fixtures back at Anand Bhawan in Allahabad. She had seen him infrequently since she had gone away to school. It is unlikely, however, that Feroze, who had become very attached to Kamala and the Nehru family, proposed impulsively. He had probably made up his mind to marry Indira quite early on in his association with the Nehru family, but bided his time until she was older.

Whatever had been his reasoning, Feroze was immediately rebuffed. Both Indira and Kamala diplomatically told him that she was still too young (it is not clear if Nehru was aware of Feroze's proposal). Not that this was a convincing reason for rejecting Feroze. Most Indian women were married by the time they were sixteen. Kamala was a bride at sixteen; Gandhi and his wife, Kasturba, were married when they were both thirteen. Teenage marriages were the norm. In fact, just a few days after Feroze proposed, Gandhi wrote to Nehru that he had found a good match for Indira.[22] 'Bapu' was more difficult to put off than Feroze, but Jawaharlal, Kamala and Indira reiterated that Indira was not old enough. Only Swarup Rani urged an early marriage for her granddaughter and she spent a good deal of time fruitlessly trying to set up suitable matches.

The only marriage that did come off – on 20 October 1933 – was Krishna or Betty Nehru's wedding to Raja Hutheesing at Anand Bhawan. It was, unusually, a civil marriage because Hutheesing was a Jain and under British law and Hindu tradition, a religious ceremony could not be performed for a couple from different castes or faiths. Betty – the most conventional member of the Nehru family – was nevertheless the first to take the radical step of marrying outside the Brahmin fold – a step that prefigured a number of contentious marriages in the family later.

By Indian standards, Betty's wedding was a muted affair, but even so a catered wedding party and trousseau had to be paid for. During his short stint of freedom in 1933 Nehru tried to sort out the family finances which had been in disarray since Motilal's death two years earlier. He himself considered money and possessions 'a burden', and 'looked forward to the time when [he] would have no money left'. But he needed money for two reasons: he did not want his mother to be destitute in her old age and he was determined to educate Indira and this involved, in his eyes, a British or European university degree. He and Kamala took stock and decided to sell all the family heirlooms and silverware – 'cartloads of odds and ends' – that had not been confiscated by the British in lieu of fines over the years.

Their most valuable asset, however, was Kamala's jewellery which was locked away in a safe deposit bank vault. Almost all of this dated from her marriage and was given to her by Motilal Nehru who had spared no expense and personally designed many of the precious pieces. In the autumn of 1933 Kamala parted with her jewels only with great reluctance, but not because she was fond of them. She had not worn jewellery in years and had never liked it – Indira later said that her mother 'hated' jewellery and thought of it as a symbol of women's enslavement. Kamala, however, wanted to keep her gold and gem-studded necklaces, bracelets, earrings and ornaments in order to bequeath them to her daughter as a secure financial legacy.[23] But nothing was destined to be secure in Indira's life. All but a few pieces of the jewellery were sold.

Early in 1934 Indira wrote to her mother from the Pupils' Own School now situated in Ville Parle in suburban Bombay where it moved when an epidemic of bubonic plague broke out in Poona in late 1933:

> Mummie darling,
>   You must be back from Calcutta by now. What did the doctors

say? Do let me know. Did you go to Santiniketan? . . . Did you
feel the earthquake at Allahabad? . . . You people might write
oftener . . . Give my love to Papu, Dolamma [Swarup Rani] and
keep lots of it for yourself.
    Your ever loving,
    Indu.[24]

On 15 January Nehru and Kamala had gone to Calcutta, again for
specialist medical treatment and also to visit Rabindranath Tagore's
school at Santiniketan, some hundred miles northwest of Calcutta. But
on the very day that they set off from Allahabad, Nehru felt the ground
pitch and shudder beneath him as he stood on the veranda of Anand
Bhawan while delivering a speech to a crowd of peasants. That night
their Calcutta-bound train travelled through the earthquake-devastated
state of Bihar where the death toll was mounting to 20,000 and more
than a million homes were destroyed. It was a horrific natural calamity,
though Gandhi insisted the earthquake was 'divine chastisement sent
by God for the sin of untouchability'. Far away in Bombay, Indira felt
anxious about her parents – her mother's health, whether they had been
affected by the earthquake – and also about her own future, for the
purpose of the Santiniketan visit was to decide whether she would go
there after taking the matriculation exam in the spring.

Her next news was a telegram from her father: 'Am going back to
my other home for a while [stop] all my love and good wishes [stop]
cheerio Papu.'[25] Nehru was arrested on 12 February in Allahabad,
charged with making seditious speeches in Calcutta and sent back to
jail where he was tried and given a two-year sentence. Kamala and her
mother-in-law migrated to Calcutta to be near him. Kamala also spent
a great deal of time in religious devotion at the Ramakrishna mission
which she visited daily. Despite soaring temperatures, she and Swarup
Rani refused to use a fan in their lodgings because Nehru did not have
one in prison. Meanwhile, on the other side of the subcontinent, Indira
was studying for her matriculation exam, which she took in April. Then
she joined Kamala in Calcutta where she spent whole days with her
mother at the Ramakrishna mission and went to the fortnightly twenty-
minute interviews with her father at Alipore Jail.

It was a bleak time. Kamala was unwell; Nehru was in prison; Indira
was anxious about her exam results, her parents and her future. The prison
visits with her father were strained and she was withdrawn and silent. To

others she appeared apathetic and low, and she showed no enthusiasm at the prospect of attending Santiniketan where it had been decided she would go if she passed her exams. Describing this period years later Indira said, 'I was an intense person, wilful and self-centred . . . This gave rise to moments of self-pity and frustration and, in adolescence, to depression.'[26]

But Nehru saw selfishness and irresponsibility in his daughter rather than loneliness and sadness. He complained in a letter to Nan Pandit that Indira scarcely wrote to her parents anymore – 'she ignores us . . . completely'. He felt that she had become 'extraordinarily self-centred . . . remarkably selfish. She lives in a world of dreams and vagaries and floats about on imaginary clouds.' It was no surprise, then, he said, that Indira 'gets on my nerves'. She seemed to him to be growing up 'into a languid, languishing type of girl!'[27] In a second letter he expanded on this theme: 'If there is one type I dislike it is the languishing type which lounges through life undecided as to what to do, but expecting everybody to minister to his or her comforts. Indu has already developed many characteristics of this type . . . she is remarkably casual and indifferent to others. This is a serious blemish . . . Indu . . . revolves around herself . . . self-centred, she hardly thinks of others.'[28]

Indira did not help matters when she wrote to her father about her boarding arrangements at Santiniketan. She claimed that Jehangir Vakil, who had taught at Santiniketan, had told her the student hostels would not be 'convenient' for her, 'specially the food'. She feared she would become ill and wondered if she could stay in a cottage near the school owned by a friend and take an Anand Bhawan servant to Santiniketan to cook and clean for her. Nehru vetoed this plan by return post: 'I dislike very much the idea of your keeping apart from the 'common herd' and requiring all manner of special attention, just as the Prince of Wales does when he goes to school . . . I am sure you will have no physical discomfort there. I think you should stay wherever the college authorities put you . . . Take the food also as it comes . . . My fear is that you will be too much looked after there, not too little. That can't be helped because you happen to belong to a notorious family.'[29]

This rebuke had almost as great an impact as Nehru's reproof when Indira hopped out of the car on the cliff edge in Ceylon. Never again would she (openly at least) request special treatment.

*   *   *

Before enrolling at Santiniketan, Indira went to Kashmir for four weeks with the Pandits – her aunt, uncle and three young cousins, Chandralekha, Nayantara and Rita, and also the children's English governess, Mrs Belcher. Ranjit Pandit had just finished translating a twelfth-century Sanskrit history of Kashmir (most of which he had done in prison) and he wanted to take some photographs for the book. They stayed in Srinagar at the home of a distant relative whose forebears had chosen not to migrate south with the rest of the clan two centuries earlier. He lived in a huge, rambling house surrounded by cherry trees with magnificent views of the Himalayas in every direction.[30]

Kashmir was a revelation. For years Indira's parents and grandparents had talked of the place and now she fell in love with it for herself. She wrote to her father that it was a 'wonderful land' where 'no matter where you are you get a lovely view of the snow-covered peaks . . . and the beautiful springs . . . Ever since I first saw the *chenar* [sic: chinar, an indigenous tree of Kashmir], I have been lost in admiration. It is a magnificent tree.'[31] The enchantment Indira found in Kashmir was real and profound. And on this very first visit she picked out the *chinar* tree as a kind of totem – a symbol of a place that came to represent peace and beauty and illumination for her.

There was clarity in Kashmir; the air was sharp and pure and you could see for miles. The streams and rivers flowed icy and swift in contrast to the turgid, polluted Ganges. The distant mountains were white, stark and massive – sublime. Indira felt wide awake and alive here. And there were so few people after the congested streets and towns and cities of the plains. Indira and the Pandit girls took long treks in the woods during which they did not see another soul for hours at a time. In the silence they could hear birdsong, the rustle of small animals, the wind in the trees, the distant chanting of Buddhist monks.

Again and again in the coming years, Indira would return to Kashmir at times of great joy, stress, danger, defeat and grief. She felt it never failed her and she became obsessive, even superstitious, in her devotion to it. Whatever religious faith she possessed was permeated by the landscape of Kashmir – her idea of paradise – one of the rare constants in her life. Kashmir was also a place that for many years politics did not seem to touch – and so it afforded solace – it was clean and clear in that sense too. Indira was never greatly attached to the United Provinces (later Uttar Pradesh), Allahabad or even Anand Bhawan. She deliberately became Pan-Indian, adopting, chameleon-like, the saris, food and languages of the diverse regions of India. This, of course, was a deliberate political stratagem, but there was a genuine impulse behind it too: Indira Gandhi did connect with *all* of India. But in her heart she was a Kashmiri. This was her great discovery in May and early June 1934.

While Indira was in Kashmir, Nehru, locked up in Dehra Dun Jail, wrote a long 'Note' to accompany her application to Santiniketan which was submitted when her matriculation marks (good in English and French but barely passing in the other subjects) arrived in June:

> From her earliest childhood Indira has had to put up with national political troubles and domestic upheavals caused by them. Her education has suffered because of these and there has been no continuity in it. For long periods there has been no peace or quiet in her home atmosphere owing to her parents' and other relatives' preoccupation with public affairs, and often because of their absence in prison. These events naturally left a strong impression on her growing mind . . .
>
> Her parents would like her later to specialize in some subject or subjects which would enable her to do some socially useful work in after life efficiently, and at the same time enable her to be economically independent, so long as the present structure of society lasts. She is not likely to have an unearned income and it is not considered desirable by her parents that she should depend for her sustenance on a husband or others...
>
> We have tried to find out what her own inclinations were but so far we have not succeeded in bringing out any marked bent. Unfortunately during the last four years I have been mostly in prison and thus cut off from her and unable to watch her development. She has a vague desire of doing social or public work, probably because she has a certain admiration for her parents' activities. This is no doubt good but it does not take one far, and special knowledge is necessary in a special subject. She will have to choose this later.
>
> Meanwhile, if she is admitted to Santiniketan, she would presumably join the Sikshabhavana or the College Department and take the Intermediate Course of the Visva Bharati. Apart from

the other compulsory subjects (such as English, History and Civics, Social Service etc) I would suggest that she might take Hindi as one of the Indian languages and French as a modern language.

Indira is fairly healthy and has grown well. Occasionally she has little troubles which are not important. Her throat is especially troublesome at times. When she was a child, about ten years ago, tonsils were removed but latterly there has again been throat trouble. Her eyes give her a little pain occasionally and she was advised last year to wear glasses when reading, but she has seldom followed this advice. These troubles usually depend on her general health. When she is otherwise fit, the troubles disappear; when she is below par they appear. At present, and for some time past, she has been fit. Absence of physical exercise usually makes her languid and seedy.[32]

Nehru also wrote less formally to Rabindranath Tagore's secretary, Anil Chanda, that 'my own ideas of education are rather peculiar . . . I dislike the education which prepares a girl to play a part in the drawing room and nowhere else. Personally . . . I would like to have my daughter work in a factory for a year, just as any other worker, as part of her education. But this I think is quite impossible at present in India.' What Nehru wanted for Indira was a rigorous education and in his mind this remained a British one. He and Kamala, he told Chanda, 'had no desire to send [Indira] . . . to official [Indian] universities. I dislike them greatly.'[33]

Much as he revered Tagore, Nehru had doubts about Santiniketan's academic standards and thought of it as a kind of educational staging post for Indira – it would have to do until they were able to send her to a European university. The irony of his attitude is that of all the schools – Indian and European – that Indira attended in her chequered career as a student, Santiniketan was the only one which had a lasting effect on her and which taught her anything that she found meaningful and rewarding.

At the beginning of July she and Kamala took the train from Calcutta northwest to the small town of Bolpur, about two miles from Santiniketan. The school was situated in the middle of a wild and beautiful region with groves of palm, sal and mango trees and red dirt roads. The land was gently rolling rather than flat, and a vast, blue sky stretched overhead. There were black-faced monkeys everywhere, hooting owls at dusk, and when night fell, hundreds of fireflies in the darkness. It would be Indira's first real experience of rural life.

Rabindranath Tagore, a Bengali poet and philosopher, had established a school at Santiniketan – which means 'the Abode of Peace' – in 1901 in a deliberate attempt to marry the best of Indian and European culture. He described it to Gandhi as the 'vessel which is carrying the cargo of my life's best treasure'. What was a 'a bare tract of land in a poverty-stricken district of Bengal became in his mind a utopia'.[34] In 1921 a university was also established at Santiniketan: Visva-Bharati, with three main departments – Fine Arts, Music and Indology. Tagore's vision involved the harmonious collaboration of students and teachers in pursuing an education that synthesized the values of East and West. Pupils – both male and female – were encouraged to work with their hands and to give full rein to their artistic impulses. Classes were held out of doors and everyone – students and staff alike – went barefoot. A romantic atmosphere of communing with nature was fundamental to Santiniketan.

Such were the ideals of Tagore's 'Abode of Peace'. The reality appeared to some quite different. In 1934, when Indira enrolled, Tagore – or Gurudev, as he was called – was seventy-three and had a huge, reverential following among both Indians and Europeans (he had been awarded the Nobel Prize for Literature in 1913 and was knighted by King George V two years later). He was viewed by many as an almost semi-divine figure. Indira remembered him as 'frail and bent . . . with his wavy hair falling softly to his shoulders and his flowing beard, his deep-set and penetrating eyes and wide forehead, he was beautiful to look at – a perfect picture of the romantic poet'.[35] This magnetism and iconic status encouraged a sycophantic ambience around the Great Man. Tagore's most recent biographers have described Santiniketan in the thirties as producing 'an insidious and repellent atmosphere of adulation, cynicism and hypocrisy'.[36] But Indira was not there long enough nor sufficiently critical to perceive this.

From the moment of her arrival on 7 July, in fact, she was entranced. She wrote enthusiastically to her father, 'Santiniketan at last! . . . Everything is so artistic and beautiful and wild.'[37] For her, the place, the school, the landscape, Tagore himself, all lived up to the name the Abode of Peace. Santiniketan became a haven and a refuge. For the first time in her life she was, as she later said, removed from 'an atmosphere of intense political living'.[38] 'I had never been in a quiet place before . . . I had always been in crowds . . . And this was . . . partly the reason for the considerable bitterness in me . . . I built up a lot of hatred and bitterness inside me, and I think it was really at Santiniketan that I washed it out.' It was the place where her 'mind and soul unfolded'.[39] The landscape, people and atmosphere – all external forces – revealed to Indira a still centre within herself where – as in Kashmir – she felt safe: 'What I learnt most at Santiniketan was the ability to live quietly within myself no matter what was happening outside. This has always helped me to survive.' The film maker Satyajit Ray, who was at the school in the early forties, responded similarly and explained, 'If Santiniketan did nothing else, it induced contemplation, a sense of wonder, in the most prosaic and earthbound of minds'.[40]

Despite her fears, Indira adapted quickly to the food and living conditions in the girls' hostel, Sri Bhawan Ashram, where she shared a white-washed, stone-floored room with three other girls.[41] They slept on mats on the floor, took cold bucket baths, and used an outdoor latrine. There was no electricity. The school bell woke the students at 4.30 in the morning. They made their beds, bathed, cooked and ate their breakfast, and swept and scrubbed the floors before a congregation of meditation and hymn-singing at 6.30 a.m. Classes began half an hour later. Indira studied history, English, Hindi, civics, chemistry, and French which was taught by a German Buddhist monk, Lama Govinda (originally Ernst Hoffman). Another German teacher on the staff was a man named Frank Oberdorf. He and Govinda were permanent staff, but there was also a stream of visiting European professors at Santiniketan, including a Hungarian art historian named Fabri against whom Indira helped to organize a boycott when he refused to remove his shoes and go barefoot like everyone else.

In Dehra Dun Jail Nehru was anxious to hear news of Indira at Santiniketan. He wrote to her on 12 July about what he considered the school's academic deficiencies: 'It does not give quite an up to date education for the modern . . . life. It concentrates too much on the artistic side.'[42] He urged her to take at least two science subjects, but she studied only chemistry and soon dropped it to avoid failing the exam. She was also poor at Hindi, taught by the distinguished scholar Hazari Prasad Dwivedy – who spent most of his lectures declaiming poetry. As Indira wrote to her father, 'I have not had any grounding in Hindi and know nothing whatsoever about grammar and the like.'[43] But Hindi, unlike chemistry, was essential so she persevered and just barely managed to pass.

Indira's favourite classes – and they became a passion – were in classical Indian dance of the ancient Manipuri school, the most lyrical and graceful of the four main schools of classical Indian dance. She progressed swiftly and was soon participating in school performances. The artistic bias at Santiniketan was the other important reason that she thrived there. With the exception of literature, the arts were not important to the Nehru family. At Santiniketan Indira was exposed not only to dance, but also to music (classical Indian and European), theatre, painting, sculpture and crafts of all sorts. She discovered her own aesthetic sensibility and responsiveness and also her own creativity. Dance was the most important of the arts for her, but they all gave her pleasure, and it was at Santiniketan, too, that Indira began to be obsessed with colour, not only in the visual arts but also the natural world and even in such a mundane context as clothing. The colours of her own clothes – usually saris – were from this time deliberately chosen by her – according to her state of mind, where she was, the season, and what was going on in the world – as if she were part of a larger work of art – an oil canvas say – with which she, as one constituent, must be in harmony. For the rest of her life, the colours Indira wore remained highly significant, changeable and revealing.

Nehru continued to look upon Indira's education at Santiniketan in narrow academic terms, and he wanted to be kept informed of her progress. He asked her to send him her examination papers 'by post direct [to Dehra Dun]. I should like to see them.'[44] And he continued to badger her about physical fitness: 'What about exercise? You do not mention any. Don't become like the much-too-ladylike Bengali girls who are so delicate and willowy and incapable of hard exercise. If you can't get anything else, have a run in the morning.'[45]

In early August, barely a month after Indira arrived at Santiniketan, a telegram came for her: Kamala had had a severe attack of pleurisy and was gravely ill with a high temperature and breathing difficulties. Indira took the next train to Calcutta and then on to Allahabad. She arrived on 9 August to find a house full of relatives, doctors and nurses in white starched uniforms. Because Kamala's condition was so critical Nehru was released from jail and arrived home two days later. Both he and Indira now realized that Kamala might not recover. Nehru later wrote of this period, 'the thought that she might leave me became an intolerable obsession', but despite their great anxiety, neither he nor Indira spoke to each other of their fears.[46]

By the following week Kamala had improved slightly; on the 23rd the British authorities informed Nehru that his compassionate leave had expired and he was sent back to Dehra Dun Prison. Several days later Indira left for Santiniketan – almost eagerly, despite her anxieties for her mother. As she later confessed, 'the reality of my life [then] was so harsh that I needed to be free for my own survival'. Anand Bhawan that August of 1934 had the same smell about it, the same oppressive atmosphere, as three years earlier when Motilal Nehru lay dying. But Indira found she could not easily leave it all behind her. Soon after she got back to Santiniketan she dreamt one night that she was floating in a vast dark sea and discovered she could not swim. The waves closed over her and she awoke.[47]

Indira was also haunted by the thought of her mother left alone and neglected in her upstairs bedroom at Anand Bhawan. She wrote to Nehru in Dehra Dun:

Do you know anything about what happens at home when you are absent? Do you know that when Mummie was in a very bad condition the house was full of people, but not one of them even went to see her or sit a while with her, that when she was in agony there was no one to help her. It was only when Madan Bhai [Kamala's cousin, a doctor named Madan Atal] came that she got a little comfort and with your release everything was changed – people flocked from all directions, came to ask about her; sat with her. Now that you have again gone and Madan Bhai cannot come as often as before, there [is] . . . some danger of Mummie being left to herself . . . As soon as Mummie is strong enough she should be removed to any place outside Allahabad.

Before closing Indira added,

'You were not looking too well yourself.' In a letter that crossed with hers, Nehru for his part complained: 'I was not at all happy to find how weak physically you were when you could not do some simple exercises ... I wish you would not allow yourself to grow limp and flabby. Not to be physically fit seems to me one of the major sins a person can be guilty of.[48]

Their anxiety over Kamala obviously coloured their perceptions of each other's health.

Nehru was alarmed by Indira's charge that Kamala was neglected at Anand Bhawan, but he was loath to point an accusing finger. Nan Pandit was, of course, the main though unspecified perpetrator of this neglect, and Nehru raised the subject with his sister, hesitantly and reluctantly, in a letter he wrote from Naini prison in early September. He said that he had observed during his recent visit 'that there is sometimes some overlapping in the nursing and attention that is paid to Kamala; at other times there appears to be under-lapping (if there is such a word)'. More generally, he was saddened by 'an occasional lack of harmony, a touch of non-cooperation ... in our household ... I should like you therefore to remove any discordant notes that might have unwittingly crept in.'[49]

Not surprisingly, life for Kamala at Anand Bhawan remained lonely and discordant. In October, Indira was summoned home once again to accompany her mother to the hill station of Bhowali where she could be treated at the British-run King Edward VII Sanatorium. Indira packed her mother's suitcase and then she, Kamala, Madan Atal, Feroze Gandhi and Nehru's servant Hari Lal all made the long journey first by train and then by car to Bhowali on 10 October. A week later Nehru was transferred from Dehra Dun to Almora Jail, close to Bhowali, so that he could visit Kamala at three-week intervals (not once or twice a week as Sir Samuel Hoare, Secretary of State for India, declared in Parliament in London).

Kamala spent the next nine months confined to her sanatorium bed in Bhowali. A radiograph showed that her left lung was badly diseased and she began to undergo artificial pneumothorax – an unpleasant and risky treatment during which a needle was inserted into the chest every few days in order to collapse the lung by injecting air into the pleural cavity. Kamala was given morphia the night before her 'gassings', and the next day she had a local anaesthetic before the doctor pierced her chest with a hollow needle and pumped in oxygen. Artificial pneumothorax did not work immediately and sometimes it did not work at all: when successful, it took five or six additional injections administered over a fortnight to collapse the lung and then it had to be maintained by regular 'refills'. Serious complications, including gas embolism, pleural shock and infection (often fatal in the days before antibiotics), were not uncommon. But despite these risks artificial pneumothorax was a popular procedure because it was thought that if the diseased lung were collapsed, it could rest and heal itself and the patient might make a full recovery.[50]

Indira stayed with her mother at Bhowali for almost a month. On 2 November she wrote to her father, 'the last few days have not been good ones for Mummie, her temperature rising . . . and she felt rather weak and low. Day before yesterday AP [artificial pneumothorax treatment] was performed for the fifth time.' But Kamala, she added, had managed to gain three pounds and now weighed eighty pounds (about six stone).[51] During this prolonged stay at Bhowali, Indira was able to make one visit to Nehru at Almora Jail. They quarrelled, but about what is not clear. Indira 'threatened not to come back [to see him] for six months', then fell silent, turned her back, and left.[52]

It was really only when she went to Bhowali with her mother and the others that Feroze Gandhi came into focus for Indira and became a part of her life, though he had by this time proposed to her at least twice. Who was the ubiquitous Feroze Gandhi – formerly a fixture at Anand Bhawan and now Kamala's attendant and companion at the hill station sanatorium? He was no relation of the Mahatma, but a Parsi with a Gujarati name, the youngest child of a marine engineer named Jehangir Faredoon Gandhi and his wife Rattimai. Jehangir Gandhi and his family lived in Bombay, but Feroze was raised for the most part in Allahabad by his unmarried aunt, a physician named Dr Shirin Commissariat, who adopted him and took all responsibility for his upbringing. Dr Commissariat was a highly qualified surgeon, and in Allahabad she was in charge of fifty-two districts under the Lady Dufferin Hospital. She also moved in the highest echelons of Allahabad society. Why, then, did she take full responsibility for her young nephew? Possibly because Feroze was actually her own child. If this was the case, a likely candidate as his father was a distinguished advocate practising at the Allahabad bar named Raj Bahadur Prasad Kakkar.[53]

The fact that no birth certificate has been found for Feroze Gandhi and the fact, too, that the records of the Parsi maternity hospital in Bombay do not register Rattimai Gandhi giving birth to a son there on 12 September 1912, suggest that Shirin Commissariat may indeed have been Feroze's real mother. Whatever Feroze's parentage, by the early twenties, Rattimai Gandhi's husband, Jehangir Gandhi, had died and she and her four children had come to live with Dr Commissariat and Feroze in Allahabad. Feroze was a student at Bidya Mandir High School and Ewing Christian College and seems to have been completely unpolitical before the Ewing College demonstration that brought him into the Nehru orbit and made of him a devoted follower of Kamala in particular.

But Feroze was more than just Kamala's acolyte. When Congress was banned by the British in 1930 he was arrested and imprisoned at Faizabad Jail along with Lal Bahadur Shastri, the President of the Allahabad District Congress Committee (and many years later Prime Minister of India for nineteen months in between Jawaharlal Nehru and Indira Gandhi). After his release, Feroze became active in the agrarian no-rent campaign in the United Provinces in the early thirties. He was jailed a second time in 1932 and again in 1933 after Nehru sent him into rural villages to see how peasants who had participated in the 1932 no-rent campaign were suffering at the hands of the authorities.[54]

Virtually all Parsis were loyal to British rule in India, and Feroze's family was extremely unhappy about his political involvement and closeness to the Nehrus. They argued that his political activities could jeopardize Dr Commissariat's government medical appointment, disqualify his brother Faredun from finishing his legal studies, and prevent his sister Tehmina from doing a master's degree at Allahabad University. When Mahatma Gandhi came to Allahabad at the time of Motilal Nehru's death, Rattimai appealed to Gandhi to persuade Feroze to get out of politics and resume his education. Gandhi's retort – delivered in Gujarati – was 'if I could get seven boys like Feroze to work for me, I [would] get *swaraj* in seven days. In the India of the future nobody will ask whether your son passed his BA or MA, but they will like to know how many times he has been interned for nationalist activities.'[55]

Personally, Feroze could not have been more unlike Jawaharlal Nehru. Their only similarity was that they were both short: Feroze just five foot six. But, unlike Nehru, he was stocky and had a thick head of dark hair. He was handsome but not at all in the refined, aristocratic manner of the Nehrus. There was nothing effete about Feroze Gandhi. He was no intellectual and like Indira, he had been an indifferent student, though he shared with her a love of classical music and flowers. Some people thought him boisterous and crude, others refreshingly frank. Certainly he was loud and passionate with a great appetite for life, including food, drink and sex.

Throughout his life Feroze was a womanizer – a fact that is hard to square with his devotion to the ethereal, austere, and by her Bhowali days, intensely religious, Kamala Nehru. What Kamala's feelings were for Feroze is far from clear. Their unlikely relationship has been explained as a spiritual, Dante-and-Beatrice one, with Feroze as the adorer of the saintly Kamala. But a Congress leader and jail mate of Nehru's named Minoo Masani (who later left Congress and was instrumental in forming the right-wing Swatantra Party) reported rumours of an affair between Kamala and Feroze, who was twelve years Kamala's junior.[56] And Masani was not the only person in Allahabad aware of these rumours. Posters, in fact, had been put up in Allahabad proclaiming an improper relationship and the instigators of this smear campaign (which enraged Nehru who was in jail at the time) were not British sympathizers but members of the Congress Party.[57]

An affair between Kamala and Feroze, however, was inconceivable given Kamala's poor health, her values and the complete lack of privacy at Anand Bhawan, though it is true that Feroze often travelled with her. It is improbable, too, that Feroze would have proposed to the daughter of a woman with whom he was involved. They were living, after all, in 1930s provincial India, not the late eighteenth-century Paris of Laclos. Yet the groundless rumours of an intimate relationship between Kamala and Feroze were never completely laid to rest.

If the rumours of an alleged affair between her mother and Feroze ever reached Indira's ears – now or later – she would not have believed them. When she first spent time alone with Feroze at Bhowali and began to take notice of him, he seemed like a vital, vibrant presence in a world of disease and death at the sanatorium. Feroze was handsome, energetic, hopeful, helpful and as devoted to Kamala as was Indira. Inevitably, they drew closer together. For Indira Feroze was a much needed ally.

*   *   *

On the night of 31 December 1934 Jawaharlal and Indira were both with Kamala (and Feroze) at Bhowali to see in the New Year. Oddly, given their circumstances – Kamala in the sanatorium and Nehru in prison – their spirits were high and they looked ahead to 1935 and beyond with hope. The next day Nehru returned to Almora Prison and wrote in his diary:

> Hardly ever before have I had such a long and comforting time with [Kamala] . . . We talked and talked about the past, present and future . . . I have left her today full of peace and goodwill . . . It really surprises me how attached we are to each other. How much she means to me and I to her . . . And Indu – she seems to get on well with the Santiniketan people. On the whole she is growing up well . . . What a brick Feroze has been! Without him it would have been a terrible job . . . She [Kamala] has few companions now – indeed only Feroze and the nurse.[58]

But when Nehru visited Kamala next, at the end of January, she had greatly changed. At first she was merely unresponsive and he thought this due to her illness, but then she told him, as he recorded, that 'she wanted to realize God and give her thoughts to this, and as a preparation for this our relations should undergo some change. Apparently I was not to come in the way of God.' Kamala told Nehru she would no longer have sexual relations with him – that she wanted to take the Hindu vow of *brahmacharya* or celibacy. He was stunned at this rejection – especially after their intimacy at the New Year. Kamala's religious commitment had 'long irritated' him, in part because he had no use for religion himself, but even more because it made him feel that 'I counted for less and less in her mental make-up. I seemed to be losing her – she was slipping away and I resented this and felt miserable.' Back in Almora Prison the next day, he wrote, 'Loneliness everywhere. Nothing to hold on to, no life-boats or planks to catch while I struggle with the rising water.' He was drowning and there was 'nothing to be done . . . except to sit in this long prison barrack, all alone, and think what a dreadful thing life can be'.[59]

Kamala's sexual rejection of Nehru could be misinterpreted as evidence that she was having an affair with Feroze, especially when during Nehru's next visit Feroze developed violent stomach pains in the evening and Nehru had to sit up with and nurse him all night rather than be

with Kamala. 'A tiring night with little sleep.'[60] But Kamala's letters to
a close woman friend at this time reveal that she was indeed undergoing
an intensification of her religious beliefs. 'He [Jawaharlal] is angry with
me. There is no one with me now except God. The world is a net and
if one is entangled in it, there is sorrow and more sorrow. I made a big
mistake by spending . . . years of my life as a housewife. If I had searched
for God during that period, I would have found him.'[61]

As she became increasingly ill and as the prospect of death became
more real to her, Kamala detached herself from the 'net' of the world.
Slowly she was letting go of the ties that bound her to life, including
those of her husband and child. Kamala was looking forward now and
she would have to leave them behind. When she died she would be
free. But Jawaharlal and Indira were still enmeshed in it and bowed
down with 'sorrow and more sorrow'.

Indira, meanwhile, was negotiating a very different sort of emotional
storm of her own at Santiniketan. Frank Oberdorf, a German who
taught French at the school, had declared himself in love with her and
Indira found herself for the first time strongly attracted to a man. This
was no adolescent crush. Indira was a mature and serious seventeen-
year-old and Oberdorf was in his mid-thirties. He had met Tagore in
South America in 1922 and come to teach at Santiniketan in 1933. He
seems to have loved Indira for herself – rather than as a member of the
Nehru family. He may have been the first person to perceive her as an
individual – as somebody in and of herself. She insisted to him that she
was an ordinary person except for the accident of 'my birth, being the
daughter of an extraordinary man and an exceptional woman' – a poig-
nant and accurate self-assessment.[62]

In March 1935, the medical superintendent at the Bhowali sanatorium
issued a report on Kamala's condition. Her weight had gone up from
seventy-seven to ninety-four pounds, her pulse down from 120 to 100
a minute, and her evening temperature had stabilized at 100 degrees.
Her appetite and digestion were both better and her paroxysms of
breathlessness had entirely abated. But there was also bad news. 'The
expectoration' still 'contains tubercle bacilli . . . and the last skiagram
of her chest . . . shows a partially collapsed left lung with multiple
adhesions in the upper part of the pleural cavity and fluid up to the level
of the fourth rib in the basal part.'[63] The adhesions made it impossible to
continue artificial pneumothorax and Kamala was switched to Nordolin

treatment and told that if she failed to improve on it, she must go to Europe for surgery.[64]

By April she was no better – she would have to go abroad. This was particularly awkward with Nehru in prison and unable to accompany her. He broached the idea of Indira going with her mother, but Indira was not eager to leave Santiniketan: 'I'm not frightfully keen on going . . . apart from the fact that I'd like to be with Mummie, specially during the operation.'[65] She did not want to leave the Abode of Peace or possibly, Frank Oberdorf, or both.

On 13 April Indira was rehearsing for her first solo appearance in a Manipuri dance performance when Tagore – who had just received a telegram from Nehru – called her to his studio to break the news that Kamala was worse and must go to Europe as soon as possible. Indira had no choice now. She immediately went to the girls' hostel and packed her things. The next day she left Santiniketan, taking the train to Calcutta and then travelling on to Bhowali. A week later Tagore wrote to Nehru that they 'bade farewell to Indira' with 'a heavy heart . . . for she was such an asset to our place . . . Her teachers, all in one voice, praise her and I know she is extremely popular with the students. I only hope things turn for the better and she will return here.'[66] But the Santiniketan chapter in Indira's life was over.

At Bhowali Indira found Feroze, of course, as well as Kamala, and Feroze told her that he was trying to arrange a way of going to Europe with them. Meanwhile, at Almora Prison, Nehru wrote 'a farewell epistle' to his daughter even though he would see her at Bhowali at the time of their departure. 'I want you to leave India in a happy and expectant frame of mind,' he wrote. 'At your time of life you should grow in happiness for otherwise your youth would be darkened with care and worry . . . I do not want you to be a quarrelsome and disgruntled specimen of humanity.'[67]

Given the circumstances, it was hardly realistic to expect Indira to feel young, hopeful and carefree as she left India. She had just been removed from the first apolitical, peaceful period in her life. She did not want to leave Santiniketan and go to Europe. Her father was in prison and her mother was gravely ill. In addition, a great deal of responsibility would be placed on Indira's shoulders even though Kamala's cousin Dr Madan Atal would also go abroad with them. As Nehru wrote to her, 'all decisions will have to be taken by you there

... I want you to take [charge of] the arrangements whether it is engaging hotel rooms [or] reserving accommodation on the railway ... You must get used to shifting for yourself.'[68]

Nehru went to Bhowali on 15 May to say goodbye to Kamala and Indira, and while sitting next to Kamala's bed he wrote up a detailed medical history for her to take to Europe for the surgeon and doctors there. This last meeting was not an intimate or even a very emotional one. Indeed it was stilted and witnessed by Swarup Rani and Betty Hutheesing who had come to Bhowali to take Kamala home. In the early afternoon, they all left by car for Allahabad. Nehru wrote in his prison diary, 'I bade goodbye to them and immediately started for Almora. I took the high road and she took the low. Will we meet again? And where?'[69]

Several days later Indira and Kamala went by train to Bombay, accompanied by Feroze who was by now actively devising a plan to get himself to Europe. In Bombay they visited Gandhi who wrote to Jawaharlal in Almora, that he had never seen Kamala with so much religious faith – scant consolation to Nehru's agnostic mind. On 23 May Kamala, Indira and Madan Atal sailed for Germany on the *Conte Rosso*. Feroze took the train back to Allahabad, determined to follow them as soon as possible.

SIX

In the Black Forest

'THE COMPANY ON BOARD isn't very encouraging,' Indira wrote to her father five days after sailing, as the *Conte Rosso* entered the Red Sea. Most of the first-class berths were occupied by wealthy Indians, 'all of whom are suffering from some disease or the other and are going to Vienna to consult ... doctors'.[1] The remainder – healthy Italians and other Europeans – kept their distance from the cargo of invalids.

Not that Indira saw a great deal of the other passengers. 'Every night we have either a cocktail dance or a cinema or something else,' she wrote, '[but] I don't go to these functions and I'm sure I don't miss much, though Mummie thinks that I am tied to the cabin because of her.'[2] When they reached the Suez Canal Indira was tempted to go to Cairo and then to visit the pyramids but decided against it because it would mean leaving her mother for a whole day and night. But she did go to Port Said for the day with Madan Atal. They set off to collect their post at Thomas Cook's, but got lost in a labyrinth of narrow, winding lanes and finally called in at an Indian shop where the Sindhi man at the counter 'recognized me and asked about Mummie & you'. He then personally led them to Cook's, took them shopping, and escorted them back to the ship where he presented them with three boxes of Turkish delight and a bouquet of roses for Kamala.[3] Even in Port Said's dusty back streets – thousands of miles from home – Indira could not be anonymous. She was a Nehru.

Among the letters they collected in Port Said were several from her father written in Almora Jail. Nehru wanted to know how Kamala and Indira were faring, of course, but he was also keen to hear what Indira thought of his just-published *Glimpses of World History*. Nehru had made sure that a brand new copy sailed with Indira from Bombay and now he asked her what parts she liked best and said he was afraid she would find his discussion of economics dull – 'it is a new subject for you and it takes time to get one's bearings'.[4] As they entered the Mediterranean, Indira wrote back to him, 'I miss you so much. There is no one to talk to or walk about with and when I'm not with Mums, I feel so lonely.'[5] But despite her loneliness and boredom on the ship, *Glimpses of World History* remained a closed book in her cabin – and later in hotel rooms, trains and pensions throughout Europe.

They landed at Trieste on 3 June. An ambulance whisked Kamala, Indira and Madan Atal to the railway station and they set off immediately on the wagon-lit for Vienna. Arriving the next morning at nine, they were met at the station by Subhas Chandra Bose – the radical Bengali Congressman – who took them to the Hotel Bristol and continued to visit Kamala daily during their stay in Vienna. Bose was often accompanied on his visits by an Indian journalist and associate named A.C.N. Nambiar (or Nanu as they called him). A good friend of the Nehrus and the brother-in-law of the nationalist leader Sarojini Naidu, Nambiar was one of a group of long-time Indian expatriates in Europe. Bose, however, had only been abroad since 1933. He had originally come to Vienna because of his own failing health, but he used his exile to agitate for Indian independence, and at this time he was busy forging alliances with German and Italian fascists.

On 10 June Indira wrote to her father that she had accompanied Kamala and Madan Atal to consult various Viennese medical specialists, but that apart from these visits had seen little of the city. She stayed in to keep Kamala company, but also because 'it is awful going out in a sari. Everybody turns round and stares and looks me up and down till I want to just sink in the ground or run back to the hotel.'[6] But Kamala insisted that Indira explore Vienna and to avoid feeling like a freak, Indira went to a dress shop and bought two dresses and then to a hairdresser and had her hair cut. Dressed in European clothes with her bobbed hair, she was no longer stared at when she went out. But both Bose and Nambiar criticized Indira for 'leaving off the sari' – despite the fact that they of course wore Western clothes abroad. Nehru, however, wrote, 'I am glad you have shed most of your hair . . . also you had better stick to frocks . . . the sari . . . is not a worker's dress, it is a lounger's costume.'[7]

Indira, however, never considered dress in purely functional terms. For her clothes were a means of disguise or display – they provided concealment or revelation. Though she was not vain, her strong aesthetic sense – her heightened sensitivity to colour and the texture and feel of cloth – meant that clothes were always deeply important to her and that she was never carelessly dressed. In Vienna she dressed and wore her hair so as to to blend in. At other times in Europe she wore saris in order to stand out. Much later, back in India, the saris she wore – their colour, material and style – evolved into a sophisticated form of personal expression and political communication.

By mid-June 1935 Indira, Kamala and Madan Atal had left Vienna for Berlin where Kamala had been advised to undergo surgery. On the 19th she was operated on by Professor Unverricht who cauterized and removed the fibroid adhesions that had formed in her lungs. Madan Atal witnessed the complicated operation and wrote a detailed account of it to Nehru who was fascinated by the advanced medical technology and wrote in his prison diary, 'an electric bulb [was] introduced through a small [incision in the chest], thus lighting up the inside – also an eye piece'.[8] It was hoped that with the removal of her lung adhesions, Kamala could again undergo artificial pneumothorax treatment which had seemed beneficial when she was at Bhowali. Professor Unverricht referred her to a sanatorium in Badenweiler in southwest Germany, for another course of 'AP', and just a week after her surgery Kamala and Madan Atal left Berlin.

Indira, however, stayed behind in order – she told her father – to have some more dresses made. In fact, she herself was ill with acute stomach pains, as Madan Atal (unbeknownst to Indira) had already written to Nehru. She was x-rayed, dosed with bismuth and told that she would have to have an appendectomy. But then, after her mother and Madan Atal's departure, Indira's stomach pains suddenly disappeared and she felt, to her surprise, perfectly fine. The appendectomy was cancelled, she checked herself into the Hotel Adlon and had a two-day holiday – shopping, visiting the zoo, wandering the streets.

But there was an ominous atmosphere in Berlin which seemed to her 'on the eve of war'. Three months earlier, Hitler and Goering had established (in defiance of the Treaty of Versailles) the Luftwaffe, and by June aircraft buzzed overhead all day long. At night 'they flew low and their sound and the searchlights made sleep difficult'.[9] The newspapers were full of Hitler's plans to annex Austria. Indira was oppressed by a sense of something dark closing in.

It was with relief that Indira left Vienna and boarded the train that would take her and Kamala far south to Badenweiler in the Black Forest, close to both the Swiss and French borders. The town – a spa with hot springs with reputed curative powers – was scarcely more than a village with a population of about 4,000, evenly divided between permanent residents and invalid visitors. The Romans had built baths here nearly 2,000 years before. In the eighteenth century the thermal springs were rediscovered and ever since Badenweiler had drawn to itself the ailing, the idle, the wealthy, the famous – and the dying. The American novelist Stephen Crane died in Badenweiler in 1900 and Chekov – one of Kamala's favourite writers – expired here in 1904.

Indira found Kamala at Badenweiler's most exclusive sanatorium, the Hans Waldeck, under the care of Dr Steffan, a nurse named Annette and a paid companion, a young, cheerful German woman named Louise Geissler. Both Kamala and Indira became very fond of Louise and soon after arriving at Badenweiler, Indira left the pension where Madan Atal was staying to share a room with her at the Pension Ehrhardt. The only disadvantage here was that Frau Ehrhardt refused to let her guests use the bathroom – 'people,' Indira quoted her landlady to Nehru, 'did not bathe at [her] place'. Fortunately, Kamala had her own private bath at the sanatorium so Indira was able to bathe there when she went to visit her.

In between twice-daily visits to her mother, she roamed about the town, past hotels and pensions, clinics and sanatoria. She walked in the gardens of the *Kurpark* where a band played daily in the open-air pavilion. And she walked, too, out into the countryside, through farms, orchards and vineyards and into the forests of pine and spruce. Badenweiler was said to be the sunniest spot in Germany; its air pristine enough for the most delicate invalids. But the woods were dark and reminded Indira of Grimm's fairy tale 'Hansel and Gretel' which she had read as a child. Badenweiler was no place for a young girl anxious about her mother and nervous about her own health. The Roman ruins and the encircling *Schwarzwald* were as ominous and forbidding in their way as the searchlights and low-flying aeroplanes of Berlin.

Nor was the social and political atmosphere pleasant. Badenweiler was so small that Indira had to go to Freiburg to shop where she saw, she said, 'how the Jews were being treated'. An elderly German couple at the pension befriended her and told her they could tell she was a 'true Aryan'.[10] Their attitude, however, was exceptional. Indira well knew that in many German minds Indians were classed with blacks and Jews. She told her father, too, that 'there is a lot of propaganda against Indians in the papers because of the foreign policy to be friends with England. Hence it is not very agreeable sometimes.'[11]

Strangely, Nehru said nothing about the European political situation in his letters to Indira at Badenweiler though he was an early and severe critic of Mussolini and Hitler in *Glimpses of World History* (which Indira still had not bothered to open). Instead, in response to Madan Atal's report on Indira's illness in Berlin, Nehru sent her another sermon on her health – the strongest he had yet delivered. 'I do not particularly fancy you hobnobbing ... with the tribe of doctors,' he wrote. He repeated his old refrain that good health is best achieved by 'forgetting the body rather than tending it carefully like a hothouse plant'. In the past Nehru had told Indira that he considered illness a 'sin'. Now he proposed that 'speaking about disease and illness, except in the case of necessity, should be forbidden by law', and he urged her to read Samuel Butler's novel *Erewhon* in which illness is 'a crime; the more serious the illness the heavier the sentence'.

Nehru also held himself up as a shining physical example to his daughter: 'during all the long years I was at Harrow, Cambridge & London I never spent a day in bed owing to illness. I paid no special attention to my health. I simply lived a normal life and looked down upon those who were often ill or who frequently complained of their bodily troubles.' Madan Atal, Nehru added at the end, had reported that Indira's German doctors 'were of the opinion that there was nothing fundamentally wrong with you'.[12]

Both Nehru and Kamala felt that Indira should not stay in the morbid atmosphere of Badenweiler, surrounded by chronic cases, with no activity other than visiting her mother and wandering about the spa and environs. And so in July she set off for Switzerland. Travelling alone, she took a series of trains from Badenweiler to Mulheim, Mulheim to

Basel and then on to Lausanne, passing the mirage-like beauty of Biel and Neuchatel lakes. After Lausanne, the track kept close to Lake Geneva as it curved east to Montreux and the Chateau de Chillon. 'Looking at the lovely lake, with the swans & seagulls and the mountain ranges and behind them the snow-covered peak of the Dents du Midi,' Indira wrote to her father, how she remembered their Swiss life together in the Alps, now nine years earlier, and 'I thought of you and Mummie and missed you.' From Montreux she went on to Bex, to visit her old school mistress, Mlle Lydie Hemmerlin whom she had not seen since she left L'École Nouvelle in 1927. Bex, too, was full of memories, and she and Mlle Hemmerlin 'talked about the old days (one would think I was at least sixty) and you & Bapu'.[13]

After Bex, Indira went on to Ascona in southern Switzerland on Lake Maggiore to attend a conference – 'Rendez-vous of East and West'. 'Many big guns from all over Europe,' she wrote to Nehru, were scheduled to speak, including several university professors with whom she wanted to discuss the possibility of enrolling in a Swiss university. Nehru, however, was opposed to this idea. He wanted her to go to Oxford and he had already written to Gandhi's close friend, C.F. Andrews, to ask him to make inquiries. Andrews had talked with Helen Darbishire, the Principal of Somerville College, who told him 'she would like so much to take Indu if she could qualify'.[14] This was the rub – *could* Indira qualify? From the time Somerville College was first broached, both she and Nehru worried about the Oxford entrance exam which Indira would have to take.

When she went to Switzerland in the summer of 1935, Indira took along her hefty copy of *Glimpses of World History*. She wrote to Nehru, however, that it was 'very inconvenient for travelling [It] . . . takes up almost half the place in a small suitcase. But I liked the parts I have read – I have not been reading from the beginning – though I suppose in a book of history that is what one should do.'[15] This rather tepid response was for a long time the only return Nehru got for all the passion and hard work he had put into his book for his daughter.

Back in Badenweiler in August, Indira was too worried about her mother to continue her desultory reading of her father's book. Kamala was 'thin and . . . and very weak', Indira wrote anxiously to Nehru; 'Mummie is always very tired and exhausted because of [her] . . . continuous high temperature and she doesn't talk and hardly listens when anyone else talks.'[16] Despite Kamala's uncommunicativeness and abstraction, Indira went to see her at the sanatorium every morning and again every evening. Walking back to her pension at night, she could 'feel the trees of the Black Forest closing in on her'. There were terrific storms in the middle of the night throughout August and when Indira got back to her room, she would sit with the curtains drawn, in a state of misery and near panic, listening to the thunder and the wind. Years later, when a violent storm broke out in Delhi one evening, she told a friend who was shocked at her fear: 'ever since Badenweiler, I cannot bear thunder and lightning and the sound of high winds in the trees . . . I was alone in the Black Forest, my mother was dying . . . I have never been able to free myself of this terror.'[17]

There was no one with whom she could share her fears. Feroze wrote that he hoped to persuade his aunt to send him to the London School of Economics, but as yet nothing was settled. Meanwhile, Frank Oberdorf surfaced in Europe – whether on leave from Santiniketan or because he had pursued Indira there is unclear. He was in touch with her, but as yet they had not met. Clearly he could not come to Badenweiler (neither Kamala nor Madan Atal knew of Oberdorf's existence) and Kamala was far too ill for Indira to leave her.

In late August, a *deus ex machina* – who would initiate the chain of events that led to Nehru's release from jail – turned up in Badenweiler in the person of Rabindranath Tagore's former secretary, Amiya Chakravartty. Chakravartty, who had met Nehru and Kamala when they came to Santiniketan, was now studying at Balliol College, Oxford. He had come to Germany on holiday and reading in the papers that Kamala was at Badenweiler, decided to visit her. He was shocked at her condition and had a frank talk with her doctors who told him that her case was 'hopeless' and that 'if her husband wanted to see her alive, he should come by the first airmail [flight]'. Chakravartty was anxious about Indira too whom he found 'in a piteous state of mind', sick with worry over her mother.

He left directly for London to consult Agatha Harrison, a fifty-year-old Quaker social worker who had twice visited India, come under Gandhi's influence and formed at his request, the Indian Conciliation Group to work for Indian independence in England. Chakravartty and Agatha Harrison cabled Dr Steffan at Badenweiler and requested that he notify the Viceroy in Delhi of the severity of Kamala's condition.

Then they wrote an urgent letter to the India Office.[18] Several days later, Agatha Harrison received a letter from Indira (whom she had not yet met) saying that Dr Steffan had cabled the Viceroy, the Secretary of State for India, Lord Zetland, and her father. Kamala, she said, was no better: 'she is still getting high temperature [sic] and is unable to take any nourishment, with the result that she is getting weaker'.[19]

After reading Indira's letter, Agatha wrote to Mahatma Gandhi about her anxieties over Kamala and Indira and then decided to go to Badenweiler herself to see if she could do anything for them. She found Kamala 'desperately ill and terribly weak' and Indira 'a pathetic figure – though young in years – old beyond her years in experience in suffering'.[20] Agatha was profoundly moved by Indira's odd mix of loneliness and self-reliance and the two women – the middle-aged, rather humourless English spinster and the shy, anxious Indian teenager – formed an enduring bond.

When Nehru received Dr Steffan's telegram at Almora Jail he wrote in his prison diary, 'So this is the end.' On 4 September the Government of India released him on compassionate grounds and he immediately began the air journey to Europe: Delhi to Karachi, Baghdad and Cairo, and then a seaplane from Alexandria to Brindisi from where he took a train to Basel. He was met at Basel by Subhas Chandra Bose and they drove together to Badenweiler, arriving in the early hours of 9 September, just five days after Nehru left Almora Jail.

As Nehru wrote to his sister, Nan Pandit, he 'was shocked to see Kamala. She had changed greatly for the worse,' since he had bade her farewell just four months earlier in Bhowali. Kamala now had a bad pleural infection and was running a temperature of 104.5 degrees. She was semi-delirious, nauseated, and scarcely able to take any nourishment. After seeing his wife, Nehru had a long talk with Dr Steffan that 'was far from encouraging'.[21]

Nehru's reunion with Indira was balm to his frayed nerves after his abrupt release from prison, his transplantation to Europe and the shock of Kamala's condition. Their reunion also soothed Indira. The next morning Agatha Harrison came upon Nehru and Indira standing together outdoors in the sun: 'Indira was holding tight to his arm, every now and then rubbing her head against his shoulder and some of the "years" that I noticed [in her] seemed to have slipped away and she was a different person.'[22]

For more than a month after Nehru's arrival in Badenweiler, Kamala remained acutely ill. In late September her temperature soared to 106 degrees. Dr Steffan began to issue bulletins on her health to Reuters news agency which cabled them on to India. A TB specialist was summoned from Freiburg who pronounced 'there was some chance of recovery despite the gravity of the case'. But as Nehru observed in a letter to his sister, though his ray of hope brought some 'relief . . . it does not take us far'.[23]

Every morning Nehru and Indira trudged from the Pension Ehrhardt to the sanatorium with a sense of foreboding. Most of the time Kamala was too weak to carry on a conversation, so Nehru would read Pearl S. Buck's *The Good Earth* out loud to her and Indira. Then father and daughter went back to their separate rooms in the pension and their separate gloomy thoughts. Nehru tried to work on revisions to his autobiography, but found himself obsessively thinking about Kamala and their marriage. Kamala began to merge in his mind with his vision of India. No longer merely an individual, she became 'a symbol of Indian woman herself . . . curiously mixed up with my ideas of India . . . so elusive and so full of mystery'.[24]

In late October Kamala suddenly 'took a turn for the better,' as Nehru wrote a friend, 'not very marked' but still cause for relief. Both he and Indira were worn down by the strain of her illness and with this partial reprieve, they decided to go to London at the end of the month for a brief trip organized by Agatha Harrison and also to visit Somerville College, Oxford. They arrived at Victoria Station to find a welcome party that included Agatha, Bertrand Russell, Horace Alexander, the Labour MP Ellen Wilkinson and Krishna Menon (who had come directly to the station from St Pancras Hospital where he was being treated for a nervous breakdown). A photograph of their reception at Victoria shows a pale, hollow-eyed Indira holding a huge bouquet of flowers and just managing a smile.

They stayed at the Mount Royal Hotel overlooking Marble Arch and immediately embarked on a hectic round of political rallies and meetings. Everywhere they went, Nehru was feted, or as he put it in a letter to Nan Pandit, 'all sorts of people crowded round me and tried to make love to me'.[25] Despite their limited time, they also managed to see four plays – *Romeo and Juliet*, *1066 and All That*, *Love on the Dole* and *Night*

LEFT Jawaharlal and Kamala Nehru on their wedding day, 8 February 1916.

BELOW Studio portrait of Indira Nehru, aged one, with her parents.

BELOW Indira (aged six) with Mahatma Gandhi in 1924. Gandhi is wan and frail from fasting, but cheerful.

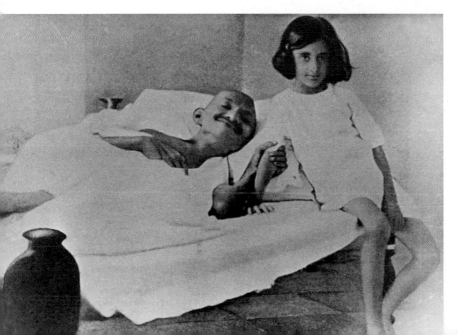

ABOVE The Nehru family, circa 1929. *Front row*: Sarup Rani, Motilal, Kamala; *second row*: Jawaharlal, Vijaya Lakshmi Pandit, Krishna, Indira, Ranjit Pandit.

LEFT Jawaharlal, Indira (aged thirteen) and Kamala Nehru in white khadi Congress dress in front of Anand Bhawan, 1931.

ABOVE Swaraj Bhawan, Motilal Nehru's palatial forty-two room home where Indira Nehru was born on 19 November 1917.

RIGHT Anand Bhawan, the second, smaller but still luxurious Nehru residence where Motilal Nehru moved his family in 1930.

ABOVE Indira (standing fifth from right) and other students surround Rabindranath Tagore at Santiniketan.

RIGHT Indira with her hair bobbed, shortly after arriving in Switzerland with her ailing mother, 1935.

Nehru and Indira, very thin and with dark circles under her eyes, en route to England –
where she would enrol at Somerville College – September 1937.

Indira (third from left in the fourth row) with her fellow freshers at Somerville College,
Oxford.

Must Fall, and also a new film version of *A Midsummer Night's Dream,* starring James Cagney and Olivia de Havilland.

On 5 November they went up to Oxford where they had a friendly meeting with the Somerville Principal, Helen Darbishire and the Dean, Vera Farnell, during which they discussed Indira's application for admission for the coming academic year beginning in October 1936. The problem of the entrance exam reared its head again, and the Principal and Dean decided, in the words of an Education Committee Meeting minute taken the next day, that 'owing to her mother's serious illness in Switzerland, Miss Nehru could not fulfil the condition that Indian students must qualify in India for Senior status. It was agreed that under the circumstances Miss Nehru should be allowed to compete in the [entrance] examination in March 1937 and she would in the meantime [i.e., from October 1936] take Modern Languages and the History General Paper.'[26] In other words, Helen Darbishire was willing to relax entrance regulations for Indira – or more accurately, for the daughter of Jawaharlal Nehru.

Even though Somerville had opened its doors to her, Indira remained deeply apprehensive about the entrance exam – especially the Latin part of it. So did Nehru. He was also worried about the toll Kamala's ill health would take on Indira's studies if she tried to prepare for the exam in the unhappy and anxious atmosphere of Badenweiler. He suggested that Indira go back to L'École Nouvelle in Switzerland – a place she loved – to prepare for Somerville.

Hence shortly after they returned to Badenweiler in late November, Indira went again to Mlle Hemmerlin's school in Bex. In theory this was a good idea, but in fact Indira immediately felt a 'misfit' there because she was considerably older than the other students but much younger than the teachers. Predictably, after travelling and living on her own in Germany and Switzerland, she found school life irksome. Her day was divided into periods for lessons and other activities; there was scarcely any free time to write letters, read or take solitary walks. And she resented what she considered wasted hours spent at compulsory singing, drawing, sewing and needlework classes. But her mood improved slightly when the snows came in December and she was able to begin skiing again – rather clumsily after a hiatus of nine years. Much more cheering, however, was news from Feroze that he hoped to arrive in Europe before the end of the year and that he would come directly to Badenweiler to see the Nehrus before going on to London.

Meanwhile, back at the sanatorium Kamala's condition deteriorated again alarmingly. Her pleural infection returned and with it, a high fever and agitated semi-delirium. The doctors removed fluid from her lungs with suction aspiration, but the procedure had little if any effect. Nehru spent most of the day and evening at her bedside. At night he sat up late at the pension revising his autobiography which Krishna Menon – who not only ran the India League in London but was also an editor at the publishers The Bodley Head – had undertaken to have published by the firm.

On 21 December Indira arrived in Badenweiler from Bex to spend Christmas with her parents. She was shocked to find her mother so weak and ill, and wrote despairingly to her headmistress, Mlle Hemmerlin back in Bex, that 'Mummy . . . is almost unconscious. She can hardly recognize anybody and speaks with great pain and it is very difficult for us to understand her, as her words are very indistinct. She has not eaten or drunk anything the last two days except for a few teaspoons of juice or tea. You cannot force her as then there is the danger of suffocation. There is nothing to do but pray.'[27] On Christmas Day Nehru wrote just as pessimistically to his old friend Syed Mahmud: 'The future outlook is dark. [Kamala] is terribly thin and emaciated and unless she can gain strength she can hardly resist the disease.'[28] Nehru and Indira 'ploughed' through 'snow and slush', wondering how many days Kamala had left. To Nehru and probably to Indira, too, 'the calm winter scene' of the Black Forest 'with its mantle of snow seemed . . . like the peace of cold death'.[29]

Nehru had his autobiography to revise and he was also keeping in close touch with political developments back in India, but Indira had nothing to distract her from what now seemed to be her mother's approaching end. Nehru urged her to go away skiing. Indira protested that she did not want to leave Kamala. Nehru insisted and then Indira surreptitiously received a letter from Frank Oberdorf. Reluctant as she was to leave her mother, she now wrote to Mlle Hemmerlin at L'École Nouvelle and asked her to send her ski equipment (which she had left behind at school) to Badenweiler. Then, with Nehru still urging her to go skiing for a few days, Indira secretly arranged to meet Frank Oberdorf at Wengen, a resort in the Jungfrau in Switzerland.

She left Badenweiler on 27 December. Two days later Feroze Gandhi turned up unannounced in Badenweiler – to Kamala's and Nehru's astonishment. On 31 December Feroze followed Indira to Wengen. What transpired when they met at Wengen after a separation of seven long months is far from clear. Did Feroze meet his mysterious rival (or indeed even knew of Oberdorf's existence)? Was there a confrontation – or explosion – with Indira? Was something between them very nearly broken or decided? All that is known for sure is that Feroze left Wengen the very same night, New Year's Eve, and that he went back to Badenweiler and remained there rather than going on to London, as he originally planned.[30]

It was after Feroze arrived unexpectedly in Badenweiler and then pursued Indira to Wengen that Kamala tried to discuss Indira's future with Nehru – a conversation that took place in the presence of A.C.N. Nambiar who had come to Badenweiler to visit Kamala and see Nehru in early January 1936. According to 'Nanu', Kamala told her husband that she was very worried about Indira's relationship with Feroze and said that she did not want Indira to marry Feroze because she was sure he was unstable. Nor did Kamala think Feroze would enter any profession and be in a position to support Indira. Nehru tried to soothe Kamala and banish her anxieties, but when he left the room, Kamala turned to Nanu and said, 'Indu will listen to no one but me. I could have guided Indu gently away from Feroze. But my end is near. Jawahar will give no guidance to Indu. She will . . . be allowed to commit the mistake of her life.'[31]

Why 'the mistake of her life?' Certainly Kamala knew Feroze better than did Nehru (and possibly Indira), and Kamala had a better grasp of his character. But there is no indication that she had shown the least disapproval of him before this outburst. Certainly, too, Kamala would have foreseen the family and wider social opposition to a 'mixed' marriage between a Kashmiri Brahmin woman and a Parsi man.

Whatever the reason or reasons behind her great anxiety over Indira and Feroze's relationship, Nehru, though he seemed to shrug it off at the time, did not forget Kamala's appeal to him.[32]

Indira woke up in Bex one Sunday morning in January 1936, as she wrote to her father, 'with a queer singing feeling in my heart'. She could not tell whether 'it indicated joy or sorrow' but 'decided it is always best to assume the feeling is one of joy'. After the numbing, lonely months of responsibility with her mother, Indira was now flooded with a powerful sensation of being intensely alive – a kind of exhilaration and heightened awareness born perhaps of the prospect of both death and love in her life. 'I lay in bed till nine,' she wrote, 'thinking all sorts of things of the past and what the years to come would bring. I thought of you and Mummie. I felt curiously peaceful . . . Since then the feeling has remained. I love everything – the horrible south wind included – and I am feeling happy and frightfully optimistic about everything.'[33]

This resurgence of happiness and peace undoubtedly derived from Feroze Gandhi's arrival in Europe. But Indira's discovery of reserves of hope and vitality during this dark time also revealed an unexpected strength in her personality. Her ability to resurrect herself – or more accurately from her point of view, to feel herself resurrected – became, in fact, an enduring pattern that rescued her in the most difficult circumstances in the years to come. Though she often appeared frail and vulnerable, there was a hard and resilient core within her: she never collapsed.

Objectively, though, there was little in the opening days of 1936 to cheer Indira, and almost no grounds for hope. Feroze would not be able to put off going to London much longer and now Nehru began to talk about returning to India. Kamala, meanwhile, remained gravely ill and her psychological state darkened as her daughter's lifted. Though she was in no condition to be moved, Kamala announced that she wanted to leave Badenweiler and go to Switzerland. The Black Forest had become a fearful place for her too, especially after the death of another patient who had befriended her – a handsome young Irishman who had sent her flowers and visited her and who was in much better health than Kamala until he suddenly collapsed and died.

But moving Kamala was medically risky and also awkward because Nehru, who was scheduled to make a brief visit to Paris and London at the end of January, would not be able to oversee the move himself. Kamala, however, prevailed, perhaps by insisting that she wanted to be closer to Indira at Bex. Nehru departed for Paris and on 31 January Kamala, her nurse Annette and Madan Atal set off by ambulance for the Clinique Sylvana in Lausanne, less than an hour away from Indira who went to visit her mother the next day. Feroze meanwhile made his way to London but within days he too was in Lausanne. Nehru returned from London to Switzerland on the eve of his and Kamala's twentieth wedding anniversary on 8 February 1936.

Then the last struggle began. In London Nehru had learned that he had been elected the new President of Congress. Reunited with Kamala in Lausanne, he was torn over whether to remain with her and refuse the Party presidency or leave her and return to India in time for the annual Congress meeting. Kamala urged him to go, saying he could always come back to Switzerland and reluctantly Nehru booked a ticket to India for 28 February. Then, when everything was arranged, he found that 'Kamala did not at all like the idea of my leaving her. And yet she would not ask me to change my plans?[34]

Indira, too, did not want him to go. She visited her parents (and Feroze) in Lausanne every weekend and wrote to them on 11 February, 'it was lovely to see both of you . . . and a week seems an awfully long time to wait [to see you again] . . . I have really got all the bad qualities of the only child and feel so dependent on you. I don't know what I'm going to do when I shall be left all alone.'[35] She came the following weekend and again on 24 February for a longer visit to say goodbye to her father who was still scheduled to leave on the 28th.

The family atmosphere was familiar but heartbreaking: the old Nehru dilemma of political duty at war with personal need, a conflict which duty always won. Soon after Indira arrived on the 24th, Kamala seemed to detach herself from those surrounding her – Indira, Nehru, Feroze. She became remote and withdrawn and barely responded to them. The only thing that roused her slightly was a letter from her Calcutta spiritual guide at the Ramakrishna Mission, Swami Abhayanandaji, which Nehru read out to her. Nehru wrote to the Swami how his letter 'gave peace and joy and a forgetfulness of pain for a while . . . but her body, after the terrible long fight it has put up with, seems to have exhausted all its strength and is deteriorating . . . One never knows what she may be capable of even now, but ordinarily speaking, there is no hope.'[36]

Kamala's temperature rose even higher; she began to hallucinate and insisted that someone was calling to her. On the advice of her doctors, Nehru cancelled his flight, but by this time Kamala was past caring.

She died at 5 a.m. on 28 February – the very day Nehru had planned to leave. Indira and Nehru were both with her when she died, and so was Feroze. His presence at the worst moment in Indira's life was decisive. Sharing her mother's death and her own overwhelming grief with him, forged the greatest possible intimacy and trust between them. As Indira said many years later, Feroze 'was always there for me'. This was a powerful reason for falling in love and for agreeing to marriage. Everyone else in Indira's life had disappeared, including now Kamala. Soon her father would be gone. But she would not be 'left all alone' with Feroze a permanent part of her life.

On the afternoon of the 28th Nehru cabled Agatha Harrison in London: 'Kamala died this morning. Nehru.' Agatha informed the British press, key political figures and Nehru's friends in Britain. Then at the end of a long day she wrote to him, 'I rely on you to call on me if there is anything [I can do] You . . . know that Indira has friends here.'[37] This was her promise that she would take care of his daughter in Europe.

Two days after she died, Kamala was cremated at the Lausanne crematorium. Feroze returned to London and Indira and Nehru went to Montreux for several 'black days', as Nehru described them, before he flew to India. He was 'broken', his 'mind did not function properly'.[38] Indira's optimism and hope were smashed. It was nearly a year since she had left home for the Black Forest and this is how that journey ended: in a lively, picturesque resort that seemed to mock her grief. Nine years earlier they had been here with Kamala – and the happy ghosts of who they were then haunted Indira too. On 5 March she and Nehru parted – with no words of when they would meet again – at Montreux Station. Indira boarded the train for Bex alone.

The next day Nehru began the air journey to India with an urn containing Kamala's ashes, feeling 'our bright dreams were also dead and turned to ashes'.[39] When the plane touched down at Baghdad, he sent a telegram to his publisher at The Bodley Head in London, which was about to publish his *Autobiography*. It was a short cable with the dedication for his book: 'To Kamala who is no more.'

SEVEN

A Veteran at Parting

ON THE MORNING OF 8 MARCH Indira turned on the wireless at La Pelouse and recognized Hitler's strident voice in mid-broadcast. Her German was just good enough for her to understand that Nazi troops were marching into the Rhineland. She wrote to Nehru that Hitler 'sounded very threatening' and that the French had already sent troops to the frontier. 'Hatred of the Germans is much in evidence . . . in Bex as well as elsewhere.'[1] Switzerland was an oasis in a Europe on the brink of war.

Once Indira had settled back at Bex, she was swamped with grief and depression. She tried to apply herself to studying for the Oxford entrance exam, but she could not concentrate. The only thing that banished thoughts of Kamala's death was a gripping book which worked, for an hour or two, like a sedative or narcotic. Indira had been a great – and very fast – reader since childhood and now she hungrily consumed book after book. Mlle Hemmerlin became alarmed. 'When I am alone,' Indira wrote to Nehru, 'it is not good for me for I mope. And books, says Mlle Hemmerlin, are depressing for me. What is to be done?'[2]

There was nothing to be done, but fortunately the entire school went on a three-week holiday to Italy in early April – to Rome, Florence, Naples, Pompeii and Sicily. Indira reported unenthusiastically to Nehru that she was 'disappointed with Rome', where the girls visited the Vatican and had an audience with the Pope, but Florence 'was a most charming place'. Everywhere they went, 'Il Duce's [Mussolini's] photographs are very much in evidence.'[3]

In Sicily some feeling began to return to Indira's grief-numbed mind. The other students were 'in an ecstasy' over the Greek temples, museums and churches while Indira saw an entirely different Sicily.

'The people are poor and the roads dirty & full of creaking carts and victorias,' she wrote to Nehru. 'There are many beggars ... The people are dark [skinned] and stare at us as at strange objects in a museum – in the villages the sight of a car seems to be rare, for as we were passing through everybody shouts to each other & rushes out to see the marvel. It reminds me so much of India – I feel terribly homesick.' And even in remote corners of Sicily 'Mussolini's sayings are printed in huge letters on village walls.'[4]

Soon after Indira returned to Bex, she set off for England in order to take the Oxford entrance exam. She travelled via Paris where she was reunited with Feroze for the first time since Kamala's death three months earlier. Then she went on to London where she stayed with Agatha Harrison before going up to Oxford at the end of June. On the 29th, the same day that Indira took the gruelling, seven-hour Oxford exam, Nehru wrote to her reassuringly from India, that 'examinations are a nuisance. All that can be said for them is that they do push us on a little ... But ... [they] are no real test of anything worthwhile.'[5]

This may have consoled Indira when she got her results and learned that she had failed, with a particularly bad performance in Latin. She had no option but to wait and resit the exam, but clearly La Pelouse – which was essentially a finishing school – could not prepare her to pass next time. Agatha Harrison suggested they consult her old friend Beatrice May Baker, the headmistress of Badminton School for girls, near Bristol. Miss Baker, an ardent admirer of Nehru, came to lunch and persuaded Indira to return to Badminton with her immediately and study Latin in their sixth form for the rest of the summer term. Indira protested that her clothes and possessions were still in Bex. On the way to Paddington Station, they stopped for her to buy two dresses for ten shillings, and then caught the next train to Bristol. And so Indira was enrolled at a pukka English public school in July 1936 – the same month the Spanish Civil War broke out.

Badminton School was light-years away from Santiniketan or any other school Indira had attended. But it was also very different from Harrow where Nehru had been a student some thirty years earlier. Fifty-eight-year-old Beatrice May Baker, with her steel-grey hair pulled back into a bun and her faith in cold baths and regular exercise, may have looked the archetypal spinster schoolmistress, but she was anything but conventional. She was a committed socialist, pacifist, feminist and vegetarian. And her staunchly-held beliefs defined the girls' school she had directed for nearly forty years. 'BMB' as she was called – though the girls, of course, addressed her as 'Miss Baker' – was passionately committed to the League of Nations, subscribed to the Left Book Club and successfully recruited a large number of foreign students. She held weekly current events discussions on the international situation, invited refugees from the Spanish Civil War to speak at Badminton, and took the students on field trips to the local Wills' cigarette factory to observe present-day working conditions. Throughout the thirties, Badminton was also a haven for German Jewish refugee girls.

But despite her unorthodox convictions, Beatrice Baker ran Badminton like an autocrat. Indira arrived at the school, set amidst rose gardens with wisteria-covered stone balustrades and clipped yew trees, to find a formidable list of regulations posted in the entrance hall of Northcote House, the eighteenth-century turreted main building:

1. Stockings must always be worn with Wellingtons for all walks.
2. During term girls must never wear mufti unless they are in their own rooms. Mufti must never be worn in Bristol.
3. No girl is to bring talcum powder back to school.
4. Sixth form girls may listen to the wireless from 6 onwards on Saturday, from 5–6 on Sunday and between 8.40 and 9 p.m. during the week.
5. Prefects and Subprefects may have baths every night if they are out by 9.45.
6. Sixth form girls may use basins in bathrooms but not baths. They must be out by 9.30.
7. Bed-times for sixth form: 9 p.m. during the week; 9.30 on Saturday.

Not surprisingly, Indira found the atmosphere stifling and complained to her father of 'all the stupid rules and regulations'.[6]

At the beginning of August she escaped what was beginning to feel like a prison camp and returned to Bex to retrieve her things, stopping en route in Paris where she spent two more days with Feroze. They visited Versailles and 'walked & walked & saw everything the American tourist sees'.[7] By the end of the month they were both back in London where Indira rented an attic room at 24 Fairfax Road near Swiss Cottage and began to have private tuition in Latin for the Oxford entrance exam in September. She wrote to Nehru how exhilarating it was to be in London, 'I . . . love the crowds, the parks & everything. Perhaps because it is the first time I was entirely on my own. A tiny little room to sleep in – the whole city to live in and no one to bother you – to go & come & do whatever you want to and just when & how you want to. Sometimes it . . . [is] lonely, but I like it.'[8]

She was being economical with the truth. Indira was far from being alone in London. Feroze lived close by and Shanta Gandhi, her old friend from the Pupils' Own School in Poona, who shared Feroze's name but was not related to him, rented a room across the hallway at the Fairfax Road boarding house. The three of them went to concerts, the theatre and opera at Covent Garden, to Hyde Park Corner to listen to the speakers, to an Indian restaurant at 12 Gower Street where Darwin had once lived, to a shop in Soho which sold imported *paan* (a mildly addictive mixture of betel nut, lime and aniseed wrapped in a leaf) at the inflated price of six shillings which they chewed slowly to make the betel last as long as possible.

Feroze was now centre stage and Shanta Gandhi knew he and Indira were in love. But Frank Oberdorf still hovered in the wings. That September Oberdorf visited Indira in London and urged her to come to Germany at Christmas. Briefly she was torn. But shortly after he left, she wrote to him that she would not come to Germany to see him because she realized she did not love him, and, she brutally added, she did not want to love him either 'even if he was the last man on earth'.[9] Feroze now had no challenger, but he confided to Shanta Gandhi that although he was determined to marry Indira, he was worried that the Nehru family would diminish him – that he would be absorbed and become a Nehru rather than Indira a Gandhi. He also worried about Indira's reserve and self-containment, her inability to give emotionally. 'She was not prepared,' he thought, 'to merge or lose her separate identity.'[10]

Indira sat the Oxford entrance exam for the second time in late September and passed in English, French and mathematics. She did not take the Latin part of the exam because she had made scant progress during her private Latin lessons in London and realized she would probably fail it again. Since she had not yet passed Latin, she could not begin at Somerville College in October as she had planned. She had no option but to return to Badminton, cram Latin, which she now positively loathed, and take the exam again in March.

In November 1936 the Spanish Civil War was entering its fourth month. On the 7th Indira wrote to her father from Badminton that the fascists were attacking Madrid. 'What is going to happen? . . . Fascism seems to be spreading almost like flames.' The next day she reported, 'Franco has entered Madrid,' and described the atmosphere at Badminton as 'terribly anti-Fascist and very pacifist . . . But on the whole, imperialism seems to be inherent in the bones of the girls . . . [though] they hate to hear you say so. They worship the King, admire Baldwin and although Eden's popularity is waning . . . he is still considered by some as the last word in cherubic innocence!'[11] When Edward VIII abdicated in December, Indira listened to his broadcast on the wireless along with the other girls. Many of them wept at the news while Indira wrote cheerfully to Nehru, 'perhaps this is the beginning of the end of the monarchy in England'.[12]

Nehru wanted Indira to feel herself part of the political events that preoccupied both of them. On a train to Multan he wrote to her how he had spotted a gate called 'Indira Gate' in a village in Sind. Indira herself now was poised at a gate in her life story. Behind her lay 'a heritage of storm and trouble' which she could not escape even if she wanted to. 'None of us,' Nehru told her, 'in this present age, can have an easy time or freedom from storm or trouble. But to some of us fall a greater share . . . and it is your lot, because of your family . . . to have to bear this heavier burden.'[13]

Indira, in fact, was eager to pass through this gate to her future, but she was stuck at Badminton. As the months passed, she felt increasingly alienated, especially from the upper-class English girls, yet she did not make friends with any foreign – including three Indian – ones. She joined no school clubs or societies. Her name was entirely absent from the school magazine while Badminton's other famous *alumna*, Iris Murdoch, shone in its pages as a prefect, student, debater, essay prize winner and editor of the literary magazine. Though Iris was not close to Indira (no one was), she realized that Indira was 'very unhappy, very lonely, intensely worried about her father and her country and thoroughly uncertain about the future'.[14]

BMB also saw all this in Indira and tried to involve her in the annual school League of Nations trip. But Indira did not want to go to back to Geneva – where she had lived with her parents – with a pack of Badminton girls. BMB was not a warm, maternal woman like Mlle Hemmerlin or Agatha Harrison, but in her own no-nonsense way, she tried to be sympathetic when she asked Indira if she was unhappy so far away from home and friends. Indira retorted, 'I don't like being away from India at this time, but I must get to know the British [in order] to fight them.'[15]

For her nineteenth birthday, Nehru sent Indira a beautiful copy of a Sanskrit poem called 'Meghaduta'. Indira told him 'you cannot imagine what joy it brought to me – the sunshine and the warmth of India in this damp & dreary land'. She ached for her mother. 'At first,' she told Nehru, 'I had not realized what had happened but with time – each day – that realization presses deeper into the heart.' She confessed she felt 'dead . . . the only word which approaches the meaning I wish to convey'.[16]

She also chafed at the separation from Feroze who was now studying at the London School of Economics. She was dismayed when BMB told her she must not go to London over Christmas but instead to Cornwall because London was unhealthy. BMB also vetoed Switzerland, where Indira and Feroze wanted to holiday together. Indira asked Nehru to intervene and write to BMB in support of London and Switzerland – 'I promise to take care of myself . . . I don't want to go to Cornwall among strangers.'[17]

She had her way – and BMB relented. In mid-December Indira went to London and stayed at the YWCA on Great Russell Street in Blooms-bury. Then she, Feroze and Shanta Gandhi travelled together to Wengen in Switzerland to ski. She wrote to Nehru that she was 'with friends', without revealing the friends' identities. It was exactly a year since Kamala lay dying in Badenweiler and Indira had gone to Wengen for the first time with Frank Oberdorf and Feroze had turned up unannounced on New Year's Eve. Now Oberdorf was off the scene and Kamala dead.

At the end of January Indira morosely returned to Badminton. She began to worry in earnest now about her upcoming Latin exam and tried to follow the Indian provincial elections (provided for by the 1935 Government of India Act) from afar in the *Manchester Guardian* and

The Times. Nehru opposed the elections which he viewed as a palliative offered by the British to forestall more radical demands. But he campaigned tirelessly throughout India, living, as he wrote to Indira, 'in a kind of moving cyclone – in trains and motors and vast gatherings'.[18]

In mid-March Indira took the train from Bristol to Oxford to be interviewed at Somerville College. Helen Darbishire, and two history dons, May McKisack and Lucy Sutherland, told her that her entrance exam essays were 'very interesting' and 'a pleasure to read', and her French excellent. But her Latin, they said, was 'abominable'.[19] With this judgement ringing in her ears, exactly a week later Indira returned to Oxford to retake the much-dreaded Latin part of the entrance exam. She was astonished, as well as ecstatic, when she passed. She could escape the prison walls of Badminton. Somerville College was now the future.[20]

But first there was India. Indira travelled by train to Amsterdam in late March and on the 31st she boarded a KLM air liner. It was the first time that she had flown in an aeroplane. Four days later she arrived home at Anand Bhawan in Allahabad where she fought back tears because everything reminded her of Kamala.[21] It had been nearly two years since she had left Santiniketan and sailed for Europe with her mother. Everything now – including Indira herself – was utterly changed. She was nineteen, much wiser and sadder, but secretly in love.

The political situation in India had changed drastically too. Congress had won impressive victories in the provincial elections in February. Both Vijaya Lakshmi Pandit and her husband, Ranjit, were elected in the United Provinces and Mrs Pandit went on to become a minister – the first woman minister in the British Empire. Nehru, however, was exhausted and depressed. During the run-up to the elections – between July 1936 and February 1937 – he had toured every province in India, covered 50,000 miles by rail, car, bullock cart and foot, addressed up to thirty meetings a day and come into contact with ten million people. Then after the elections, Congress' entry into office led to a scramble for power and created tension and division within the party, of which Nehru was again the President in 1937. Shortly before Indira arrived home, his usual robust health broke down entirely and he was bed-ridden. He needed respite – he needed, in fact, to get away from India and Indian politics. In early May, when Nehru had recovered sufficiently, he and Indira left for a 'working holiday' to Burma, Malaya and Singapore.

The month-long trip began inauspiciously when they arrived at Howrah station in Calcutta and an ardent Nehru admirer fell between the train and the platform and had his foot cut off – 'a ghastly sight', as Nehru described it, 'and yet in spite of his pain he clung to me, pleased to see me, and wanted to put his head on my feet'.[22] Then soon after they sailed from Calcutta, one of the passengers committed suicide by jumping overboard. Unlike Nehru, Indira believed in omens and astrological forecasts and tried to decode their significance. She was, of course, shocked by these two accidents, but also disturbed by what they could portend for her and her father.

After arriving in Rangoon, they spent two weeks travelling all over Burma 'in style', as Nehru reported to a friend, 'no third-class or rickety old Ford cars, [but] expensive motors or aeroplanes or air-conditioned railway cars'.[23] They visited temples and monasteries, but as was the case in Ceylon six years earlier, most of their time was taken up with 'a succession of crowds and processions and big functions'.[24] Indira wilted in the tropical heat, got chilled in air-conditioned trains and did not sleep well. By the time they sailed from Burma, her throat was bothering her and she was running a temperature.

In Malaya and Singapore, she continued to feel unwell – altogether 'keeping rather poorly', according to Nehru. It had been more than a year since Indira and her father parted in Switzerland after Kamala's death. Now they could not connect – even when abroad and removed from family and political pressures and tensions at home. They tried in vain to re-establish the intimacy of their letters when both father and daughter periodically poured out their hearts to each other. But it was no good. Indira did not breathe a word to her father about Feroze. He did not speak of his weariness of the political struggles both within Congress and against the British, or confess that he felt old and stale. After Indira returned to Europe, Nehru wrote to her of their time together in India and the Far East: 'is it not curious that during all these months we hardly had a proper conversation apart from our brief talks about day-to-day activities. I felt the gulf . . . and could not bridge it.' He added that henceforth it might be best if 'we meet infrequently'.[25]

Nehru had his own secret. Like Indira, he was in love, and this became apparent to his daughter during the spring and summer of 1937. Their estrangement was largely due to Nehru's affair with a woman named Padmaja Naidu which had begun shortly after his return to India following Kamala's death. Padmaja, the daughter of Nehru's old friend Sarojini Naidu, was just a year younger than Kamala, but apart from this closeness in age, in every other respect, Nehru's wife and mistress were utterly dissimilar. Unlike the delicate, reserved, unsophisticated and intense Kamala, Padmaja was physically large and flamboyant, well-educated, witty, vivacious and uninhibited. An ardent nationalist, she nevertheless shunned white *khadi* and always wore silk saris in brilliant greens, gold and purples and huge flowers in her hair. As one friend put it, 'there was something of the bird of paradise about her'.[26]

Indira had been close to both Padmaja and her mother, Sarojini Naidu, for years and she was to remain deeply attached to Padmaja for the rest of her life. But her realisation that Nehru was having an affair with Padmaja was deeply disturbing. It seemed, for one thing, a betrayal of her mother's memory – though Indira too had found a reprieve from grief in her relationship with Feroze. When Indira realized that she would now have to share Nehru's affection, she retreated. And so there was – as Nehru put it – 'a gulf' between them.

The affair between Nehru and Padmaja Naidu went on 'for years', according to Nan Pandit. But Nehru told his sister that he did not feel free to marry Padmaja because 'Indu had been hurt enough'. He did not want to hurt her further.[27]

Many years later Indira Gandhi was furious when her father's official biographer, Sarvepalli Gopal, published Nehru's love letters to Padmaja Naidu in Nehru's *Selected Works*.[28] These are unguarded, passionate, highly revealing letters that disclose a rare view of Nehru's vulnerability and need. He and Padmaja met erratically. Throughout 1936 Nehru was touring the country while Padmaja was usually in Hyderabad or Calcutta. Nehru had always found it easier to express himself in letters – often written late at night in a state of reverie and exhaustion. Hence the intimate, confessional mood of his 'Bebee letters' (he and Indira always called Padmaja 'Bebee'). He told her that he had 'no desire to be desireless', that behind 'the mask of [his] pale set face' there were 'all manner of desires and fantasies and urges'. Two months before Indira returned to India in the spring of 1937, Nehru wrote to Padmaja, 'You are a nineteen-year-old [she was, in fact, thirty-seven while *Indira* was actually nineteen] . . . And I? A hundred or more. Will I ever know how much you love me?'[29]

In fact, Nehru did know the extent of her love, and this became a problem. Padmaja wanted more from Nehru than he could give, for as he made clear, though he loved her in return, other things came first. 'Those I love have to suffer . . . It is not my love that wavers but another overmastering passion or obsession . . . Even while I hold the loved one in my arms my mind wanders away and forgets the present and I become a stranger . . . I look on detached.'[30]

Nehru was haunted by the pain he was causing Padmaja. In the midst of a Congress Working Committee meeting her 'picture filled' his mind, 'and your sad eyes disturbed me and I forgot what was happening around me'.[31] This worried him: the one thing Nehru was unwilling to do for any woman (including Indira) was sacrifice his work – his political and moral responsibilities – to personal desires and needs. And so he and Padmaja perforce came to a new understanding. She ceased to make demands or to ask for more than he could give, and this freed Nehru to continue their relationship with gratitude as well as love. Several days before Indira reached Allahabad in April 1937, Nehru wrote to Padmaja, 'You move me too much . . . the thought of you vitalizes me.'[32] And while he and Indira were in Malaya he wrote how 'I famish for news of you . . . how I long to see you, to hold you and to look into your eyes.'[33]

When Indira and Nehru reached Calcutta, at the close of their month-long tour to the East, she was still ailing and they consulted several doctors who told her that her sore throat was caused by badly inflamed adenoids which should be surgically removed, they said, before Indira returned to Europe. (She had already had her tonsils out as a child.) This meant she would have to postpone her departure – and reunion with Feroze. She returned to Allahabad and rested at Anand Bhawan for several weeks, and then in early August she and Nehru left for Bombay – where it had been decided the operation should be performed. After the surgery, she recuperated at her Aunt Betty Hutheesing's Bombay home on Malabar Hill.

On 11 September Indira sailed on the SS *Victory* for Europe. The ship was full of Indian students, most of them men, but there were also two other Indian women: Kamila Tyabji (bound for St Hugh's College, Oxford) and Aruna Mukherji. Kamila, who had never been separated from her family or outside of India, was astonished at the composure with which Indira parted from Nehru on Ballard Pier in Bombay. 'She was already a veteran at parting. We stood side by side [on the deck], waving, she, perfectly controlled, while I . . . did not know what to do with my tears.'[34] Years later Aruna Mukherji recalled Indira on board wearing dangling earrings with green stones and having her fortune read by one of the male students who was an amateur palmist. He predicted that Indira 'would be famous all over the world . . . [and] occupy a position of prestige and power'.[35] If this is not an apocryphal story, it was scarcely prescient of the fortune-teller to foresee future greatness for Jawaharlal Nehru's daughter. During the sea voyage, Indira herself reported prosaically that she spent at least two hours a day in the ship swimming pool wearing a bright orange bathing suit. And feeling guilty, perhaps, over the geographical as well as emotional gulf that now separated her from her father and the stoicism with which she had parted from him, she wrote to Nehru, 'I do miss you so much, darling – and I do so love you – much more than I ever did before.'[36]

After Indira landed at Marseilles she went directly to Paris to meet Feroze as they had arranged. They had not seen each other in six months; they were alone, far away from the prying eyes of friends, family and acquaintances. It was a glorious early autumn and they felt somehow outside of time. Inevitably, Feroze proposed again, but this time all seemed changed – and possible – to Indira. As she told a close friend many years later, 'it was on the steps of the [Basilica of] Sacre-Coeur that we finally and definitely decided . . . Paris was bathed in soft sunshine and her heart truly seemed to be young and gay, not only because we ourselves were young and in love but because the whole city was swarming with people who were young at heart and in a holiday mood . . . the awareness of the war to come . . . was veiled.'[37] It was not a matter of Indira at long last succumbing to Feroze; she says '*we* finally and definitely decided'.

Two weeks later, 'with piles of luggage', Indira arrived at Somerville College on a cold, rainy Thursday afternoon in October, 'feeling terribly nervous and agitated'. She was nearly two years older than the other members of the class of 1937 – and the only one from a famous family. Many of her classmates, in fact, knew in advance that they were to 'be in good company with Nehru's daughter' when they came up to Somerville. There was considerable curiosity about 'the Nehru girl', relief that she seemed as apprehensive as the rest of them, and mild surprise that she wore tweed jackets, skirts and sensible shoes just as they did.[38]

She was assigned a ground-floor room (all Somervillians had singles) in a wing of 'the Library' furnished with a bed, table and straight-backed chair. For heat there was a coal fire, and students were provided with one scuttle of coal per day which with luck could warm a room from early evening until it was time to go to bed. (Throughout her stay at Somerville, Indira was perpetually cold.) The bathroom was several doors down the hallway and consisted of one tub and one basin for the eight women on the corridor. The toilets were 'in the outer darkness' beyond the bathroom and very cold.[39]

Tutorials were scheduled to begin the following Monday. In the intervening days Indira and the other freshers put on their gowns and met individually with Helen Darbishire, and their tutors. They also went to their first Junior Common Room meeting which was attended by all the Somerville undergraduates. The JCR meeting held on 14 October 1937 was largely taken up with the controversial and unusual case of a second-year student named Mary Brignoli who had been caught *in flagrante* in her boyfriend's room by his landlady who reported the matter to the Somerville authorities. The boyfriend's fate had already been decided: he was 'rusticated', or banished for a term, after which he could return to Oxford and resume his studies. The Somerville rules and regulations stipulated for Mary Brignoli the heavier sentence of being 'sent down' – permanent dismissal from Oxford and an ignominious end to her academic career. A petition protesting against the inequality of the punishments meted out to Mary Brignoli and her boyfriend, had been drawn up and was hotly debated at the JCR meeting. No vote was taken, but at the end of the meeting most of those present signed the petition, including Indira Nehru. It was then submitted to Helen Darbishire, whom it was rumoured was sympathetic to Mary Brignoli. The Dean, Vera Farnell, however, was not. Several days later the news was out that Mary Brignoli was being sent down in disgrace.[40]

The following week Indira matriculated wearing her academic gown, cap, a white blouse, black tie and black skirt. The freshers marched in a procession from Somerville to the Sheldonian Theatre where the

Master of Balliol, A.D. Lindsay – a large, red-faced Scot with hairy legs visible at the bottom of his gown – presided over 'a most tedious & boring ceremony'.[41] Then Indira got down to work which she found gruelling: a full schedule of lectures and tutorials in the four areas she was reading for her pass moderations exam. She had history tutorials with another student named Kay Davies in the sitting room of their don, May McKisack. The first-year history course consisted of Roman, Anglo-Saxon and medieval history and each week they wrote an essay for McKisack, a constitutional historian, who would then minutely dissect their work during the course of the tutorial. 'They work us like slaves,' Indira protested to her father in mid-October, but several weeks later she reported that she was 'settling down now & find it easier to spend a whole morning solidly working'.[42]

Somerville was going to stretch her, but she gradually developed confidence that she was up to it. Indira had never been and was not now a brilliant student, but at Somerville she began to apply herself. She always prepared for and performed credibly in her tutorials. She was industrious, intelligent and could write well.[43] But she remained highly nervous about her Latin and went every week for remedial coaching with a superannuated don who was hard of hearing and had false teeth. He was the only tutor she had who did not know she was Jawaharlal Nehru's daughter, and she did not correct him when he persisted in calling her 'Miss Denver'.

Indira had to succeed in the pass moderations examination in order to move on to study for an honours degree in history, and she worried incessantly about the exam throughout that first Michaelmas term. It could be taken any time during the first year, but virtually all freshers sat for it at the first opportunity in December. In early November, when she had been at Somerville less than a month, Indira wrote to Nehru, 'P Mods is rearing its ugly head.' Several weeks later, she reported, 'Nearer and nearer comes P Mods and I am in the throes of revision.'[44]

Soon there was an endless round of social and political activities that also engrossed her – meetings, public lectures, concerts, theatre productions, plus all the distinguished members of the university community who were eager to befriend and entertain Nehru's daughter. Indira also joined the University Labour Club and the Indian Majlis – an organization of the Indian students at Oxford (about a hundred in all in 1937, only a handful of which were women). On 8 November

Indira described the previous day in a letter to her father. She had lectures and tutorials all morning, and then she went to a Labour Club meeting in the early afternoon.

> At three fifteen Basil Matthews [a distinguished Oxford scholar] and his wife came and took me for tea. I got back at six forty-five – at seven I was having supper [at the College High Table] with 'The Darb' [the Principal Helen Darbishire and the other Somerville dons] and at eight thirty I had to go to a Majlis meeting for Krishna Menon was speaking. After that I had coffee with Krishna and got home at eleven fifteen pm – just in time to be locked out! My essay on the Evolution of Parliament had to be read at a class at ten am this morning and until eleven fifteen last evening I had not even read about it! Well, I read until about twelve forty-five and then wrote until three fifteen am. It was a job getting up this morning – I missed signing the register as well as my breakfast . . . However, I got Very Good for the essay![45]

Indira was too busy to join in the casual social atmosphere of Somerville which took place at meals and in the evenings when the women popped in and out of each other's rooms to drink hot chocolate and roast chestnuts over the coal fire. The rooms in the Library had transom windows above their doors, and in the evenings Indira's transom window was invariably dark because she was out.[46] Nor did she often 'eat dinner in Hall' except when she was invited once a term, as all Somerville students were, to dine in evening dress at the high table. This could be an unnerving experience with Helen Darbishire, a Milton scholar who in social situations 'specialized in prolonged silences', and the Dean, Vera Farnell, whom Indira described as 'a tall, gaunt woman with sinister dark hollows under her eyes'. Sometimes a distinguished guest would also be present, Dorothy L. Sayers, for example, 'monolithic in black velvet', whose Somerville-set detective novel, *Gaudy Night*, had been recently published.[47] Kay Davies was the only English Somervillian who became Indira's close friend, in part because they took tutorials together. The other two students Indira mentioned with enthusiasm in her letters were a Syrian named Mary Dimishky and a blind student from Mauritius named Monique Raffray.

But Indira's most important connections were outside the College – in the Indian community and most of all, in Feroze's circle of left-wing friends in London. Indira's classmates at Somerville, in fact, sensed that she led a double life. She moved – frail, beautiful and aloof through the College, looking painfully thin in a tweed suit and white jersey or a skirt and twin-set. But her real life lay elsewhere. They glimpsed her in vibrantly-coloured silk saris sweeping out to Majlis meetings in the evening or on the Oxford station platform waiting for a train to take her down to London for an India League event.[48]

Indira remained acutely aware of her role and stature as Nehru's daughter when she was at Oxford, but she was a political presence rather than leader. When she arrived at a Majlis or Labour Club meeting, the other Indian members queued up to greet her. She only spoke once on a platform – at the India League in London at Krishna Menon's insistence – and it was a fiasco. She froze with nervousness and when she finally opened her mouth to speak and uttered an unintelligible sound, someone in the audience yelled, 'She doesn't speak, she squeaks'.[49]

But this humiliating experience did not curb Indira's activism which was motivated by a genuine commitment as well as a sense of responsibility. She reported to Nehru how Lord Zetland, the Secretary of State for India, looking 'so superior & smug', spoke to a Majlis audience on 'Please Try to Understand Us', answered the following week by the Indian Communist Palme Dutt on 'Why We Understand the British Government Too Well'. And it was not only Indian politics that engaged Indira. She enrolled volunteers for the International Brigade for Spain, auctioned one of her bracelets to raise money for the Republicans (it fetched £50), boycotted Japanese goods in Oxford after Japan attacked China, and helped organize a benefit performance by Uday Shankar to raise money for medical aid to China. Feroze was even more active. To Indira's dismay, he tried to go to Spain to fight, but British intelligence – which closely monitored all India League members, including Feroze and Indira – impounded his passport.[50] Feroze, in fact, was on the verge of dropping out of the London School of Economics in order to devote himself to the India League and other political activities full time.

On 6 December Indira began the much-dreaded pass moderations exams which lasted three days. As soon as they were over she went down to London, and then she, Feroze and Shanta Gandhi went to Garmisch Partenkirchen in Germany to ski. They also visited Innsbruck and spent

New Year's Day at Munich where they went to the Deutsches Museum. She wrote to her father that across the street from the museum there was an 'anti-Jewish exhibition' with crowds pouring into it. At the entrance and in the advertisements were enormous pictures of 'a very ugly Jew holding a bag of money in one hand, the map of the USSR & hammer & sickle in the other . . . [It] made me sick. It was absolutely revolting.'[51]

Far away in Allahabad, Indira's grandmother and great-aunt, Swarup Rani Nehru and her widowed sister Bibi Amma (the 'wicked witch' of Indira's childhood), both had fatal strokes in January 1938. Before Indira got back to Somerville from Germany and read her father's telegram, she learnt the news from the newspapers at Victoria Station in London. The blow of her grandmother's and great-aunt's deaths may have taken the sting out of the bad news awaiting her in Oxford: she had failed the pass moderations exams and would have to retake them in March.[52]

This failure oppressed Indira – nearly everyone else had passed on the first attempt. She realized now that she would really have to knuckle down. She cut back on social and political activities and stayed in her room in the evenings studying. Predictably, her spirits sank. 'Term has begun,' she wrote to Nehru in late January, 'and what a term. It is going to be most terribly heavy . . . The thrill of Oxford has worn off I am afraid and Oxford life as it really is, is not a very attractive spectacle.'[53] She became increasingly unhappy, lost weight and developed dark circles under her eyes. More and more, she took to wearing Indian rather than Western clothes. She was lonely despite her friendships with Mary Dimishky and Kay Davies. Jenifer Wayne, who did not know Indira well, remembers how students would say, 'There goes Nehru,' when they saw her 'gliding through the quad with her notebooks . . . a wand-thin, remote figure in beautiful saris . . . unknowable . . . Not unfriendly; simply apart'.[54] Indira was also anxious about her relationship with Feroze. Their engagement remained a secret, unknown to all but Shanta Gandhi. She began to worry what would happen in India, and in the Nehru family in particular, when her secret was out. She was also probably dimly aware that Feroze had other women friends in London.[55]

In March 1937 Indira sat the pass moderations exam again on the same day that Hitler invaded Austria. To her amazement, she passed in French, constitutional law and history, and political economy. But *not* in Latin. This is not surprising. Whilst other Oxford students had studied Latin for years at school before coming to university, Indira had had only seven months of cramming at Badminton. Had she had an English education – which was possible at the excellent British-run convent schools in India – she too would have passed Latin. But she had gone to Santiniketan and studied another dead language, Sanskrit, which had caused her almost as much trouble. The pass mods Latin paper lasted three hours and was based on a set medieval Latin text that Indira had now been labouriously studying for two terms. But the exam also involved translating a passage from an unseen text and this was her downfall.[56] If she wanted to stay at Somerville, she would have to take the exam again in June – for a third time – and this would be her final chance.

Meanwhile, Nehru wrote to say that he planned to come to Europe in early summer – a prospect that aroused mixed feelings in Indira. Nevertheless, she, Krishna Menon and Agatha Harrison immediately began to plan the English part of his visit. Indira was alarmed to hear that her father had been invited for a weekend at the country home of Philip Henry Kerr, the eleventh Marquess of Lothian. Lord Lothian was a journalist and statesman who had been Under-Secretary of State for India in the early thirties. He was a great admirer of Nehru with whom he had been carrying on a friendly correspondence for several years, despite their disagreement over the 1935 Government of India Act. He had favourably reviewed Nehru's *Autobiography*, and when he came to India in 1937, he and Nehru had a cordial meeting in Allahabad. Lothian, however, was a member of the 'Cliveden set' which supported Chamberlain's policy of appeasement. In fact, Lothian wrote to the Aga Khan that Germany should be appeased for otherwise it would make alliances with Italy and Japan against the British Empire which 'would exactly suit Jawaharlal Nehru'.[57]

In late April Indira wrote to Nehru about his trip to England:

> The only thing that is worrying me is your intention of staying with Lothian . . . Lothian is not just another Conservative. He is a very prominent member of the 'Cliveden Set', the set that forced Eden to resign and the set that is commonly known as 'Hitler's friends in Britain'. He is a thorough Fascist & doesn't make any bones about it. He even praised Hitler on the Austrian affair . . . Your staying with him would amount to the same as if you spent a weekend with Hitler himself or with Mussolini.

It would create a terrifically bad impression on all people in this country who are even slightly 'left' & who sympathize with India & the Congress ... After all, Lothian is against all that you stand for and believe in and the people that you are likely to meet in his house will be the same – die-hard Tories and Fascists. I am afraid I feel very strongly on the point and even if you do go – Lord Lothian will have to excuse me ... I do hope you will reconsider the matter and change your mind.[58]

This is the first episode on record of Indira blatantly disagreeing with her father and attempting to influence his behaviour. It did not go down well.

'I know about the Cliveden set and Lothian's pro-Fascist and pro-Hitler activities. I think they are dangerous,' he responded. 'But ... after careful consideration I decided to accept his invitation.' Then Nehru proceeded to put Indira in her place:

I happen to be something more than a prominent leader of a group or party. I have a special place in India and a certain international status ... I happen to know something about my work and I am not unacquainted with international affairs. I have to judge what I should do and should not do ... And I am quite clear in my own mind that I cannot say no to Lothian as far as accepting his invitation is concerned. If I am so weak as to be influenced by him then I am not much good anyway ... I feel therefore that I should accept. Indeed I have done so already. I shall be sorry if you are unable to accompany me.[59]

Indira was stung by her father's reply, but nevertheless held her ground:

Darling, I did not for a moment presume to advise you what to do or to suggest that you had not been following Lothian's tactics – of course you are the only person who can decide what is the best thing to do. I was only stating my own opinion on the matter. And, I am afraid, it is still unchanged. I shall hate being away from you for even a couple of days but I don't think I could bear to stay with Lothian. On the other hand, I don't want to seem rude to Lothian so I think the best thing for me to do ... would be to get myself invited by some friends for the weekend on which you will be at Lothian's.[60]

This is precisely what she did and then she wrote a polite note to Lord Lothian declining his invitation, only to receive by return post a

warm letter from him asking her to please postpone her prior engagement and come with her father to Lothian's Elizabethan estate, Blickling
Hall in Norfolk.

Indira was scheduled to take the pass mods on 21 June. Failure would
mean she would not be able to go on and read history and would have
to leave Oxford. Her friend Mary Dimishky – who shared Indira's Latin
lessons with the deaf, elderly don – was in the same position and did
fail in June and was subsequently sent down. Indira, however, decided
in the end not to take the exam at all. Perhaps because she was unwilling
to risk a third failure that would bring a shameful and abrupt halt to
her university career. A failure, too, and the fate of being sent down,
that would coincide with Nehru's visit to England. Indira did not consult
her father about not taking the exam, but instead merely wrote that 'life
here is very end-of-termish and exhausting. Then there is my Latin.
Between all this I am feeling like going to bed for weeks . . . I shall go
to London on Tuesday the 21st morning [the day of the Pass Mods
exam] & spend the whole day in Agatha's [Harrison] most comfortable
bed, so as to be . . . energetic to greet you.'[61]

She needed a rest. Ever since she had come back from Germany in
January, Indira had felt off colour. Her friends noticed that she was
now even thinner, the circles under her eyes darker, that she had an
unhealthy-looking, sallow complexion and nagging cough. Not that she
complained of feeling unwell. But by the late spring of 1938 she was
very run down physically and psychologically, and at the eleventh hour
she decided to absent herself from the pass mods Latin exam.[62]

Nehru arrived in Genoa on 14 June where he was met by Krishna
Menon. The next day they left for Barcelona – and the Spanish Civil
War – as guests of the Republican government. A week later they flew
to London where Nehru was reunited with Indira at Agatha Harrison's
house. They then moved into a rented flat of their own on St James's
Street which Nehru reported to Nan Pandit was 'good but expensive.
We are paying nine guineas a week for two bedrooms and a sitting
room.'[63]

Krishna Menon had scheduled a hectic programme of activities for
Nehru in London, beginning with a 'Public meeting to Welcome Jawaharlal Nehru' at Kingsway Hall with Palme Dutt, Harold Laski and

Ellen Wilkinson on the platform and a performance by the African-American actor and singer Paul Robeson. Nehru gave speeches for the Aid Spain Committee at the Royal Albert Hall and Trafalgar Square, attended a series of events at the India League, went to a Left Book Club rally, lunched with the editor of the *New Statesman* at the House of Commons, and held discussions with members of the Communist Party and also with Labour leaders, including Clement Attlee. He also spoke at Chatham House, 'a famous and noted die-hard centre,' as Nehru described it, where 'politely and quietly,' he 'laid it on thick on old Anglo-Indians and others till they grew red in the face and excessively irritated'.[64]

On their first weekend in London, Indira and Nehru made a 'pilgrimage', as Nehru put it, to have tea with the octogenarian Sidney and Beatrice Webb. Both Webbs, Nehru reported to his sister, were 'still most vigorous of mind'. Sidney Webb had 'some difficulty in talking, but Beatrice' was 'extraordinarily keen-minded' and also 'walked fast and well' when she took the Nehrus out for a walk. Nehru was entranced by his hostess and wrote to his sister 'she was beautiful when young and is beautiful still'.[65] Beatrice Webb wrote of him and Indira in her diary, 'Nehru the leader of the Indian Congress and his lovely daughter spent some hours here on Saturday . . . He is the last word of aristocratic refinement and culture, dedicated to the salvation of the underdog whether in race or class.' But Beatrice doubted whether Nehru had 'the hard stuff of a revolutionary leader'.[66]

In late June, Indira and Nehru spent several days with the Labour MP Stafford Cripps at his country house, Goodfellows, in Gloucestershire.[67] This would prove to be a far pleasanter experience than Lord Lothian's house party which took place the weekend of 9/10 July. Although Indira confided to her Somerville friend Kay Davies that she felt desperately torn over this invitation, in the end, she reluctantly agreed to accompany her father to Lothian's estate.[68] Lothian had summoned an elite gathering to meet the Nehrus, including the Conservative MP Nancy Astor (the first woman MP in the House of Commons), General William and Lady Ironside, the Oxford MP Sir Arthur Salter, and Thomas Jones, principal adviser to the Prime Minister, Stanley Baldwin. The house party fulfilled Indira's worst expectations. As she later described it, 'Lord Lothian was a gracious host but the conversation was irritating beyond words, whether it was about the atrocities on the Jews which were regarded only as a minor evil . . . or the very supercilious view taken of our struggle for freedom.' At dinner Indira sat next to Lady Astor who delivered a tirade against socialism and then turned to Indira and said, 'If only you [would] marry a Maharaja, the Indian problem will be solved.'[69]

On the eve of their European travels, Indira was famously counselled by Harold Laski (whose lectures at the LSE she sometimes attended with Feroze) that she should not accompany her father on his tour. Laski was one of the few people at this time to perceive that Nehru's stature, his intellect and forceful presence, threatened to engulf Indira. 'Look,' Laski told her, 'you're just developing your personality, and if you tag along with your father, you'll just become an appendage. So you'd better not go with him. You must strike out on your own.' It was an acute observation – and a prophetic warning – but Indira was in no mood to be dictated to. Besides, she wanted to be with her father while he was in Europe and much of the time he would be travelling. Laski was annoyed when she did not heed him and he condemned what he called her 'timid desire to submerge my personality in my father's'. He complained that he had given her a lot of his time, only to have her spurn his advice. They parted acrimoniously.[70]

Others were also disappointed with Indira. Mrs Laski thought she was 'a mousy, shy little girl who did not seem to have any political ideas', and the Labour MP Reginald Sorenson described Indira as 'the reflection of her father . . . purely her father's daughter'.[71] Christine Toller, the wife of the Jewish poet Ernst Toller, was one of the few to see anything in Indira at this time. After she came to lunch with the Tollers, Christine Toller wrote to Nehru, 'I . . . want to tell you how delighted I was to have met her. Not only that she is so beautiful, but so pure . . . She seems to me like a little flower which the wind might blow away so easily, but I think she is not afraid of the wind.'[72]

In mid-July Indira and Nehru crossed the Channel to Europe – 'a continent,' as Nehru wrote to Padmaja Naidu, 'going to the Devil with extreme rapidity'.[73] They visited France, Munich (where Nehru refused to meet with Nazi officials), Czechoslovakia and Hungary. In Paris they attended the World Peace Conference during which there was a protest against the bombing of Spanish civilians. La Pasionaria – Dolores Ibarruri, the great Spanish heroine and leader of the Communist Party in Spain – had been barred from speaking by the conference organizers and so the entire audience moved to an enormous shed and gave her 'a delirious and noisy reception'. Czechoslovakia was in a state of crisis because the Nazis were expected to invade the Sudetenland region at any time. In Prague Nehru and Indira stayed in the same hotel as the Runciman Mission sent by Neville Chamberlain. The faces of the Czechoslovakians, in Indira's words, 'bore a trapped look. Gloom was all over them . . . There was a tense grimness which gave one a feeling of chill.' Indira herself felt utterly exhausted and others told her that 'I looked terrible and I was very thin, but because the programme was so full, I just felt I couldn't fall ill.'[74]

When they got to Budapest, however, Indira collapsed and was hospitalized for two weeks with a severe attack of pleurisy – the lung disease that had been the beginning of the end for Kamala Nehru in Bhowali in 1934. At this juncture Nan Pandit (never a congenial presence for Indira) turned up in Budapest on the first leg of a European holiday. At the beginning of September Indira, Nehru and Nan Pandit flew together to London. Indira was admitted to Brentford Hospital in Middlesex on the same day – 15 September – that Neville Chamberlain flew to Berchtesgaden to urge a peace settlement on Hitler. Indira was exhausted and her weight had sunk to eighty-five pounds, but she felt well enough to worry about Chamberlain's mission: 'I can't help thinking that he is up to no good and will make a mess . . . as far as Czechoslovakia is concerned.' Six days later she wrote again to Nehru at his London hotel, 'Isn't the European situation perfectly sickening? . . . I knew Chamberlain couldn't be up to any good when he flew to Germany & I shouldn't be surprised if our friend Nancy [Astor] was the originator of the bright idea.'[75]

Events would prove Indira right. The Munich Conference and Agreement, by which Germany annexed the Sudetenland, were the outcome of the Czechoslovakian crisis. This was Chamberlain's 'last and most invidious act of appeasement' – a pact which Nehru later described as 'the rape of Czechoslovakia by Germany with England and France holding her down'.[76]

Term began at Somerville at the start of October, but Indira was too ill to go back to Oxford even if her pass mods Latin situation had been resolved – which it had not. The doctors at Brentwood Hospital had advised her to take at least one term off to recuperate in a healthy climate. This excluded London or Oxford, and Nehru pressed her to return to India with him and recover at a hill station there. She was very reluctant to be separated from Feroze, but her mother's fate also frightened her. Her own bout of pleurisy had given her a bad scare. She was young, in love and hoped to have her whole life before her. So Indira sailed from Marseilles with her father at the beginning of November, breaking the journey at Cairo in order to at last visit the pyramids. They reached Bombay on 17 November 1938, two days before Indira's twenty-first birthday.

An interval of five months followed which sometimes seemed to Indira like five days and at other times five years – the sameness of the days made time both speed up and slow down interminably. Most of it was spent in the mountains, but first Indira went to Allahabad. On her birthday, 19 November, she came of age and enrolled in the Congress Party at its headquarters, Swaraj Bhawan.

Two weeks later she went to Almora, far to the north in the United Provinces, with her aunt Krishna Hutheesing and Krishna's two little boys Harsha and Ajit. Almora is not far from Bhowali where Kamala had languished in a sanatorium before going to Europe four years earlier. Almora was also where Nehru was jailed during Kamala's last months in India. It is built on ridges and looks towards the inner Himalayas – a town of cobbled streets and intricately carved wooden houses decorated with traditional murals. In the dead of winter it was entirely cut off by the deep snows that left it clean, silent and remote.

Here, in a rented cottage called 'Snow View', Indira felt frozen in time and space. Her aunt and nephews got on her nerves; Krishna because she chattered all the time and the boys because they were noisy and whined to go back to Bombay. Indira got a bad cough and began running a temperature. She blamed this on the inefficient wood fires in the house which was even colder than her room at Somerville. Her health did not improve despite the salubrious climate and a list of instructions sent to her by Nehru (derived from his long familiarity with sanatoria regimes) which included the advice to:

1. Take your temperature morning & evening.
2. Take three hours rest in the afternoon and some rest before and after meals.
3. If you feel tired increase your rest. Also if there is any rise in your temperature.[77]

Indira suffered even more acutely from her separation from Feroze. The post was maddeningly slow and unreliable. First, Feroze's letters had to make the long ocean crossing. Then it would takes weeks or even months for them to find their way up the snow-covered mountains. When they finally arrived, Indira had to open and read them surreptitiously, away from her aunt's prying eyes. She now bitterly regretted having come back to India.

One letter which did reach Indira in late December was from Nehru who was pursuing an exhausting political schedule down on the plains. It provides a striking counterpoint to the 'heritage of storm and trouble letter' he wrote to her whilst she was at Badminton. Worn out and disillusioned, Nehru wrote on a train speeding from Bombay to Allahabad:

> I used to dream that when you grew up, you ... would play a brave part in what is called public life in India, to shoulder this heavy burden, to help putting brick upon brick in the building of the India of our dreams. And I wanted you to train and fit yourself in body and mind for this engrossing task. But I am not sure that I desire you to do this now, and to experience the heartache and the crushing of spirit that this involves ... For me there is no escape, no refuge ... But why should I encourage others who are dear to me to enter into the heartbreaking business?[78]

Indira did not respond to this letter because she expected her father to visit her in Almora in early January. Almost as soon as he arrived, she told him that she felt better and was determined to return to England as soon as possible. She insisted on going back to Allahabad with Nehru at the end of the month, and she persistently argued that she must return to Oxford in time for the summer term. Her real motive, of course, was her desire to be with Feroze. Nehru confessed to Madan Atal, Kamala's cousin and doctor, that he did not think Indira well or strong enough to go back to England and furthermore, he was extremely reluctant to allow her to return to a Europe that was 'on the brink of an abyss'. For war was now clearly inevitable. But Indira was adamant. This time she defied and overruled Nehru. In April 1939 she went to Bombay and set sail for Europe on the SS *Strathaird*.

After landing at Marseilles, Indira went to Paris where there were nightly blackouts and 'sirens . . . shrieking away'. When she arrived in London it, too, seemed poised for war and 'perfectly ugly'. 'Terrific posters' were plastered on Nelson's Column, outside cinemas, in shop windows: 'We've Got to Be Prepared', 'National Service – Enrol now', 'Have You Done Your Duty?' 'What Are You Doing For Your Country?' Air raid precautions were prominently posted in all public places.[79]

Indira took a room at the YWCA in Bloomsbury to be close to Feroze whom she saw almost daily. By now he had dropped out of the London School of Economics and was working for the London County Council and also for the Royal Institute of International Affairs. But he devoted even more time to Krishna Menon's India League – the most radical organization fighting for Indian independence in Britain. Among other things, Feroze single-handedly produced the India League's weekly magazine. Indira herself began to put in hours at the League's pokey office in the Strand, not far from the YWCA. As Nehru's daughter, her presence at the India League was felt and valued. Nevertheless, like the other women volunteers, she ended up doing tedious clerical work.

It was at this time – during the spring and early summer of 1939 – that Indira came to know Krishna Menon well. He would remain a significant character in her life for the next thirty-five years. Vengalil Krishnan Krishna Menon was born in Kerala in 1896, the eldest son in a Nair family which belonged to the Dravidian Sudra caste. Like Nehru, Menon was a Theosophist as a young man, and while he was at presidency college in Madras he became a protégé of Annie Besant who paid his passage to England, to study, in 1924. Menon's intention was to spend six months in Britain; he ended up staying twenty-eight years. In London he was one of Harold Laski's most brilliant students at the LSE, gaining a first class honours degree. Menon joined the Labour Party in 1930 and served as a councillor for the London Borough of St Pancras for more than a decade. He also read law and was called to the bar at Middle Temple in 1934, the same year that he earned a master of arts degree from University College, London.

In 1931 Menon had transformed the moribund Commonwealth of India League into the India League, and it and Indian independence became the ruling passions of his life. In order to earn money to subsidize the India League, Menon worked as an editor – first at The Bodley Head Press, which published Nehru's *Autobiography*, and then for

Penguin Books which Menon established with Allen Lane. He poured his entire salary into the India League – renting the cramped office in the Strand and buying all the office equipment and supplies. At first he even slept at the League office on a table so he did not have to spend money on lodgings. Menon's total commitment to the Indian cause was displayed when he called on the journalist Romesh Thapar. Thapar's father-in-law, 'a very formal and correct' man, answered the door, invited Menon in and politely asked what work he did for a living. Menon 'snapped back . . . "I don't work for a living. I work for India's independence." '[80]

In London Menon soon attracted his own set of disciples, radical young Indians like Feroze Gandhi, P.N. Haksar, who had studied social anthropology at the LSE under Malinowski and was now reading law at Lincoln's Inn; the journalist Nikhil Chakravartty who had just come down from Oxford; Mohan Kumaramangalam, a product of Cambridge and destined to be one of Indira Gandhi's cabinet ministers; and the slightly older Mulk Raj Anand, who had already published two remarkable novels about the 'lower depths' of Indian society, *The Untouchable* and *Coolie*. Menon was an arresting looking guru – tall, emaciated and wild-haired with hawk-like eyes. Marie Seton, an English woman who worked for the India League, described him as 'a very handsome man in a hacked out sculptural manner . . . but distinctly devilish to look at. If his hair had been red instead of black, it would have appeared as if on fire.'[81]

Menon was a fiercely intelligent and intense man, devoid of social graces. In 1935 he had a nervous breakdown when a romantic relationship with an Englishwoman named Barbara McNamera foundered. This occurred just before Nehru and Indira visited London in November, 1935. Menon, in fact, left his bed in St Pancras Hospital against medical advice in order to meet the Nehrus at Victoria Station. He recovered, but emerged a cynical, untrusting man, deeply dependent on both stimulant and sedative drugs to keep him going.

After his breakdown, Menon's life in a series of cheap boarding houses in Camden Town became even more idiosyncratic. He turned into a misogynist and vowed never to marry, though many of the women who worked for the India League, such as Marie Seton and Alice Thorner, found him highly attractive. But he was detached and impersonal, and indeed seemed to have no personal or social life whatsoever. He lived principally on black tea, chased down with warm milk, with occasional buns and biscuits. Not surprisingly, in addition to tuberculosis of the kidneys and a persistent cough, he had chronic digestive problems. His incessant activity verged on the manic and he needed very little sleep. Yet he was liable to fainting spells and for days at a time would lie prostrate in bed with migraine headaches.[82]

Throughout his life, people either adored or loathed Menon. Nehru – to the bafflement of many and to his later grief – trusted him completely, relied on him and confided in him more than anyone else, more even than Indira or Padmaja Naidu.[83] Indira had mixed feelings about him. Unlike Feroze and Menon's other acolytes, she was not awed by him and she resented his abrupt and autocratic ways. She never forgave him for the fiasco of her first political speech when she had 'squeaked' rather than spoken. She also grasped the satanic and unstable undercurrents of his personality. But she admired Menon's total commitment to Indian independence and the way he handled Nehru's affairs in England – including the financial arrangements for her own support which was largely funded by the royalties from Nehru's books.

Menon was also involved in Indira's medical treatment in the spring of 1939. He asked Dr P.C. Bhandari, an Indian physician in London who was a close friend of Nehru, to arrange a consultation for Indira with a well-known Harley Street respiratory specialist named Dr Herbert. Dr Herbert examined and x-rayed Indira, told her she had a shadow on her left lung, and said that she must be 'very careful', and x-rayed every six months. No one mentioned tuberculosis, but clearly this was feared.

Meanwhile, Helen Darbishire, learning that Indira was back in England, wrote to her in London and said that both she and Lucy Sutherland (Indira's history tutor) hoped Indira would return to Somerville for the remainder of the current term. Indira rang Dr Bhandari and 'informed him of the Darb's wishes. He just muttered "impossible".' Indira, however, did go up to Somerville for an overnight visit. The Darb was 'very affable, kissed me on both cheeks & asked which room would I like to have in October'. Then she told Indira that she and Lucy Sutherland thought that Indira should switch from the honours degree course in history to a diploma in social and public administration which would prepare her for a career in government administration or in an international organization. Significantly, too, the diploma was a non-degree course and had no Latin requirement.[84] This, then, was Helen Darbi-shire's solution to the awkward situation regarding the pass mods Latin exam which Indira had now failed twice. The Somerville authorities were clearly as reluctant to risk sending down Indira Nehru as she herself was to risk a third and final failure.

Both Dr Herbert on Harley Street and Dr Bhandari urged Indira to spend a restful summer in Switzerland before going back to Somerville in October – a prescription that delighted both Indira and Feroze. She left London on 24 May and went to a health resort at Stansstad on Lake Lucerne recommended by Bhandari. A month later she moved a short distance to Burgenstock (also highly recommended by Bhandari) where Feroze came and stayed with her at the Park Hotel. In a letter from Burgenstock, Indira told Nehru how 'terribly lonely and alone' she felt – 'so dependent upon you', but she also enclosed a 'whole heap of snaps' taken by Feroze with his Leica camera, which clearly indicated that she *was not* alone. And she described to Nehru how she and Feroze climbed to the Joch Pass at 7,303 feet above sea level and to the Jochs-tockli peak 1,303 feet beyond that.[85]

This is a very rare sighting of Feroze in Indira's letters. During the five-and-a-half years she was in Europe, Feroze was either with Indira or in constant touch with her, but he is mentioned only two or three times in her correspondence with her father. It is all the more surprising that she divulged that Feroze was in Switzerland with her because they were quite alone. Indira's guardians – Agatha Harrison and Krishna Menon in London and Helen Darbishire in Oxford – were all far away. Feroze, himself, also wrote to Nehru and enclosed more pictures in the form of colour slides. 'The photos are in technicolor,' he explained. 'To view them just hold them against the light ... It is also possible to project them on the screen.' He meticulously labelled the slides and added as a gloss on one, 'Luzern at night from Indu's window at Burgen-stock', and the information that the exposure time had been five-and-a-half hours. Clearly there was a subtext in these two letters, the photos and the slides – one which Nehru acknowledged when he wrote back to Feroze, 'They are remarkably fine pictures and if you have taken them, as I presume you have, I must congratulate you.'[86]

They stayed in Burgenstock nearly a month before returning to Eng-land in August. Indira now announced that going back to Oxford would be 'futile' and that she wanted to do some sort of war work. She went to an enlisting centre in London where they advised her to finish her studies at Somerville before taking up war work, though they also told her that if she was determined to do something immediately, she could nurse or join the Land Army or one of the services.[87] Indira *was* determined, but then she was x-rayed again by Dr Herbert on Harley Street who unequivocally vetoed war work though he said she could return to Somerville if her health remained stable. Oxford – and separation from Feroze – loomed again.

By the time this was decided, Krishna Menon and Ellen Wilkinson had arranged for Indira to spend September with the family of a Professor Macmillan who lived in Penn, a small village in Buckinghamshire. In August Germany and Russia had signed a non-aggression pact, and Britain a treaty with Poland. In the late summer of 1939 war seemed closer than ever and this was one reason why Menon, Agatha Harrison and Ellen Wilkinson were eager to get Indira out of London. In addition, the Harley Street doctor recommended Penn where 'the air . . . is decidedly better than in London', as Indira told Nehru.[88] But it is also likely that despite their best efforts to conceal it, the relationship between Indira and Feroze was now transparent, especially to Menon who worked closely with Feroze at the India League. Removing Indira from London would not only remove her from danger but from Feroze as well.

On 2 September, the day after Hitler invaded Poland and the day before Britain and France declared war on Germany, Indira wrote to Nehru from Penn that the village was already filling up with children evacuated from London. 'For the last three days I, who have always disliked the sight of needle and thread, have been sewing almost incessantly' – blackout curtains and blinds and blankets for the evacuated children.[89] Indira also volunteered for canteen duty. But she longed for more arduous and dramatic full-time war work only to have all such plans vetoed by Harley Street, Dr Bhandari and Agatha Harrison. Reluctantly, she agreed to return to Oxford to study for the social and public administration diploma. Somerville sent her a list of necessary items to bring to college when term began on 16 October: a gas mask, electric torch and blackout material for windows. By the end of September Indira had also been issued an identity card and food rationing coupons.

Early in October, two weeks before she was due back at Somerville, Indira came down with a bad cold that rapidly developed into another severe attack of pleurisy. Her fever shot up to 103 degrees, her weight dropped from ninety-two to seventy-seven pounds. Her chest was very painful and congested with fluid. Agatha Harrison arranged for Indira to be moved by ambulance from Penn to Brentford Hospital. Her return to Oxford was cancelled and Bhandari, the Harley Street specialist and the Brentford doctors all advised her to go to a sanatorium in Switzerland as soon as she was well enough to leave hospital.

No one uttered the word tuberculosis, but the feared prognosis was clear to everyone, including Indira. Agatha Harrison visited Indira at Brentford every day and wrote in confidence to Gandhi's associate, C.F. Andrews, 'Indira is ill . . . the tendency is there . . . [but] I believe that if she is taken seriously in hand now we may make a normal person of her.' In order to do this, however, Indira would have to go to Switzerland and as Agatha Harrison wrote to Nehru, 'it was no light job these days' getting a Swiss visa and a British exit permit. Feroze – whom Agatha described as 'a great help and like a faithful dog' – spent whole days at the Swiss legation while Agatha herself lobbied at the India Office and Whitehall.[90]

All of this took time, and Indira was still in Brentford Hospital on her twenty-second birthday, 19 November 1939, when she was allowed to get up and have 'a real, regular bath, the first since I fell ill five weeks ago. I wasn't allowed to stay in very long but it was grand all the same.'[91] Even when the air raid sirens went off, she was confined to bed.

Finally, at the beginning of December, Indira's passport, exit permit and Swiss visa were all in order. Nehru wanted Indira to go to Davos – where Thomas Mann's novel about a tuberculosis sanatorium, *The Magic Mountain*, is set. But Gandhi had written to Agatha Harrison and Dr Bhandari that Indira should go to Dr Auguste Rollier's sanatorium in Leysin in the French Swiss Alps. Gandhi himself had visited Rollier in Leysin in 1931 and was much impressed by his 'heliotherapy' regime for tuberculosis which entailed daily, long exposure to the sun year-round, even in the dead of winter. Gandhi had fruitlessly recommended sunbathing for Kamala, and now he again urged Nehru and Agatha Harrison to have Indira follow this regimen. And so it was decided.

Indira and Agatha flew to Paris on the morning of 14 December 1939. They rested in a hotel all day and then took the night train to Geneva. Early on the 15th they travelled on to Leysin, a small, storybook village high in the Alps. The last leg of the journey was a steep climb in a cog-wheel train, up past the timber line, towards the jagged peaks of the Dents du Midi and Mont Blanc beyond. As night was falling, they arrived in a white, frozen world of sickness and death.

EIGHT

The Magic Mountain[1]

Indira was put to bed as soon as she and Agatha Harrison arrived at Les Frênes sanatorium perched on a hill above the village of Leysin. Unlike her pokey Somerville quarters, her room there was large and airy with tall windows and a balcony that looked out on to the Alps. Next door there was a friendly Indian couple, a Mrs Nanavati and her tubercular husband from Bombay. Dr Rollier – a ruddy-cheeked man in his sixties with an impeccable bedside manner – examined Indira the next day. He told her that there was 'no disease, only a scar from the pleurisy', but he was concerned about her 'great weakness – thinness and lack of muscle'. He prescribed strict bed rest for an initial period of three months, and cheerfully pointed out that the beds at Les Frênes were all equipped with wheels so Indira would not be isolated in her room. The wide sanatorium doors and corridors had been specially built so that bedridden patients could be wheeled about to socialize.

To Agatha Harrison, in private, Rollier outlined his standard tuberculosis treatment regime that Indira was to follow: 'sun treatment, rest, exercise to develop her chest muscles and good food'. Agatha remained in Leysin for three days to settle Indira. She bought her a wireless 'to keep her in touch with the world', and suggested that she embark on a book of letters to her father – a sequel to Nehru's *Letters from a Father to His Daughter*. But on the eve of Agatha's departure Indira broke down and declared that she felt 'caught in a cage' at the sanatorium. Agatha, however, reported to Nehru that she left Indira the next day looking cheerful in bed in 'a flame-coloured wool cape she . . . knitted herself'.[2]

After Agatha left, Indira wrote contentedly enough to Nehru on 21 December:

This is not a bad place at all – very neat and comfortable rooms, very good food. I have rather an expensive room . . . [with] a balcony & a magnificent view of the Dents du Midi. This view is reflected in my mirror . . . so actually I have the Dents du Midi on both sides of me . . . You would like Dr Rollier . . . Agatha was most impressed. [with him] . . . He wants me to stay here for about three months, at the end of which time I shall be transformed into a Diana! He said to me, 'You are a perfectly good motor car whose engine & wheels and everything is quite in order but there is no petrol so it cannot run.' . . . He believes in exercises, breathing and otherwise [and] . . . says my left lung is much smaller than the right & nothing can be done until its size is increased by breathing exercises . . . he believes in the sun . . . [and] in handwork as a potent help towards better health, so it's a good thing I learnt knitting . . . I have a radio . . . So far, the acid voice of the German announcer from Bremen & Hamburg . . . and the BBC news are my only connection with the world outside.[3]

Indira's only complaint was that she was wheeled out on to her balcony for much of the day where she found it too cold to write or knit or even read a book.

In what sort of world was she now stranded? Until the end of the nineteenth century Leysin, high in the Alps above the Rhône valley, had been a tiny, isolated agricultural village. It would have remained entirely unknown but for the fact that Thomas Malthus, a hundred years earlier, had devoted six pages to Leysin's salubrious climate and the long life expectancy of its inhabitants in his *Essay on the Principle of Population*. During the first decade of the twentieth century, Leysin was transformed into a fashionable mecca for tuberculosis patients. In 1939 it had 5,698 inhabitants, 3,000 of whom were patients in its seventy clinics and sanatoria. Eighteen of these establishments were owned and run by Dr Auguste Rollier, the presiding genius of Les Frênes – his largest and most luxurious sanatorium.

In 1903, as a young surgeon, Rollier had come to Leysin with his fiancée who had pulmonary tuberculosis. Her illness was the making of him. She survived, they married and Rollier transformed himself into a tuberculosis specialist. He became a fervent advocate and hugely successful popularizer of open air and sun treatment – or heliotherapy – for TB. He prefixed 'Professor' to his name and added fashionable adjuncts to his heliotherapy treatment: breathing exercises, Margaret Morris modern dance movements (practised in bed), vegetarianism and occupational therapy, including basket weaving, knitting, needlework and typing. He promised – and claimed – a high cure rate.[4]

In reality, however, tuberculosis was still the 'white plague' in 1939 – an incurable disease which killed at least a million people a year in Europe alone.[5] A German bacteriologist named Robert Koch had isolated the tubercle bacillus in 1882, but until antibiotics were discovered in the 1940s, TB could not be prevented, palliated or healed. The poor – who were its principal victims – died of it in the squalid, crowded, unhygienic living conditions the disease thrived upon. The privileged, like Indira Nehru, migrated to mountain sanatoria, 'medically supervised refuges', where they submitted to a treatment of strict rest and over-feeding.[6] The medical rationale for this regime was that it would enable the lungs to recuperate and heal themselves. Rollier's unique contribution of heliotherapy to the treatment of tuberculosis derived from the discovery that sunlight killed the tubercle bacillus. The sun's rays could indeed alleviate and sometimes even cure tuberculosis of the skin and other exposed parts of the body. But the sun, of course, could not penetrate to the lungs, and one third of Rollier's cases were pulmonary TB patients.[7]

'The Sun Doctor', as Rollier was known, had built Les Frênes in 1911 as a model heliotherapeutic sanatorium – not that it was called a sanatorium. None were in Leysin. Most sanatoria and clinics were euphemistically designated 'hotels' (the Grand Hotel, Hotel Belvedere and Hotel Chamossaire among others), but some simply had attractive-sounding names such as Les Frênes (or 'the Ashes', the kind of tree that surrounded the clinic). Certainly Les Frênes resembled a fashion-able hotel rather than a hospital with its central hall (where films were shown and concerts and other entertainments held), dining room, ladies salon, smoking room and billiard room. The consulting rooms, laboratory, small operating theatre and radiography department were discreetly housed in one wing. The patients' luxurious rooms were in another wing. The whole sanatorium was centrally heated and had large windows through which Leysin's famous sun streamed. Most patients' rooms also had wide balconies on to which they were wheeled for hours every day and exposed to the cold alpine air and the sun's rays. On the roof of Les Frênes – accessible by an electric lift – was a huge solarium with views of the Alps in every direction. For the exorbitant sum of 25 francs a day, Indira was provided with her centrally heated room (though, in fact, Rollier insisted that rooms be kept cool and windows open most of the day), four huge meals a day, and the medical attentions of Dr Rollier and his staff. X-rays and activities such as Margaret Morris exercises and typing lessons cost extra.[8]

Les Frênes, like other TB sanatoria, was, as one historian has put it, a place of 'hope deferred'. It had a disorienting, looking-glass atmosphere where much was not as it appeared to be. Sanatoria seemed like fashionable resorts: 'one met a good class of people there . . . many stayed for years. They composed bizarre cosmopolitan assortments of mostly young adults of both sexes.'[9] But despite appearances, these people often had a leper complex. Tuberculosis was infectious and therefore stigmatized. Les Frênes, like most sanatoria, was geographically, socially and psychologically isolated from the world 'down below'.[10] And its inmates were also cut off from village life in Leysin. Patients were bedridden for months or years. They became obsessed with their temperatures (taken four times daily) and their weight (also closely monitored). Time became strangely distorted – both interminable and fleeting. Sense perceptions were heightened by fluctuating fevers. Rollier and other doctors rarely if ever articulated the dread word 'tuberculosis'. Because TB was associated with poverty, dirtiness, poor hygiene and 'bad blood' (it was thought to be inherited), it was often concealed under the cloak of less terrifying diseases – pleurisy for example – with similar symptoms.[11]

With so many sanatoria and more than half its population TB patients, 'all of Leysin was a hospital'.[12] But Les Frênes stood out for several reasons. It was the most fashionable and expensive of Leysin's treatment centres. When Mahatma Gandhi was travelling in Switzerland in 1931, he had visited Les Frênes. Gandhi was fascinated by 'nature' cures and therapies and wanted to learn about Rollier's sun treatment. Since Gandhi's visit and endorsement, Les Frênes had attracted a large number of Indian patients, including a young Indian prince who arrived with his entire entourage and rented a whole floor of the sanatorium. And finally Les Frênes was unique because it had many non-pulmonary tuberculosis cases.[13] These were patients with tuberculosis of the bones, joints, glands and limbs. Pulmonary TB sufferers were usually 'fashionably slender', with an attractive pallor heightened by a feverish flush.

But patients with non-pulmonary tuberculosis were often disfigured by crippling or unsightly lesions. Such were many of the inmates of Les Frênes, and because they followed Rollier's regime of prolonged exposure of the entire body to the sun in all weathers, they were for the most part very scantily clad and thus unable to hide their deformities.

In early January 1940, Indira wrote to Nehru that she now weighed just eighty-four pounds whereas Dr Rollier had told her she should weigh at least 110 for her height of five foot two inches. She had not got out of bed since arriving at Les Frênes and she was beginning to be discouraged: 'the more I stay in bed the weaker I feel and the less I want to do anything. The days are most frightfully monotonous, especially as there is no one to talk to.'[14] Her friendly next-door neighbours, the Nanavatis, had left for another sanatorium in Montreux and Indira kept her distance from the other patients, in part because a *Life* magazine article by John Gunther on 'Nehru of India', which included family photographs, had been circulating around the sanatorium and it made her feel self-conscious.

Rollier now prescribed breathing exercises and the *position ventrale* which had Indira lying for hours on her stomach propped up by her elbows and forearms with her chest and head raised. This was convenient for reading in bed, but neither the *position ventrale* nor the breathing exercises increased her lung capacity or eased the pain in her chest. In February she felt no better. 'There doesn't seem to be outward progress,' she wrote to Nehru on the 9th, when she had been at Les Frênes nearly two months, though she added that 'of course I know nothing of the condition of the lungs except that the pain on the left side is persistent'.[15]

Rollier did not frankly discuss Indira's case or prognosis with her. She was in a famous sanatorium, surrounded by coughing, disfigured TB patients, yet the word 'tuberculosis' was never uttered. This was deliberate, and common practice at this time. Their rationale for this medical equivocation was that doctors and nurses feared patients would lose 'the will to live' if they knew they had a potentially fatal disease. But evasion was harmful in Indira's case as well as many others. Indira knew that her mother had died of tuberculosis and that she herself had been exposed to Kamala's TB germs over a long period of time. She was also well aware of the classic tuberculosis symptoms, many of which

plagued her: weight loss, night sweats, coughing and breathing difficulties. And she realized, too, that Rollier's treatment programme was
essentially the same as that Kamala had received. In fact, Rollier actually
curtailed her sunbathing while making sure that she got great doses of
cold, fresh air. Indira wrote to her father that 'the sun is supposed even
by sun enthusiasts such as Professor Rollier, to be bad for weak lungs.
So I am allowed to sunbathe only below the hips and that for not more
than half an hour.'[16] In his famous textbook, *Heliotherapy*, Rollier stated
that the 'sun cure' was contraindicated for active cases of pulmonary
tuberculosis which involved fever and at Les Frênes Indira was often
feverish.[17]

To an extent, Indira and Nehru colluded in Rollier's deception, for
they, too, never mentioned 'tuberculosis' in all the letters they wrote
to each other while Indira was at Les Frênes. Indira almost certainly
told Feroze the truth in her letters to him, but to her father, she wrote
only of her chronic low weight and increasing depression. She wrote
to Nehru of 'the gloom and darkness of my mind'. She was weary of
lying in bed and terribly lonely. Even the dramatic landscape that she
gazed at for hours from her balcony had taken on a bleak appearance:
'roads wallowing in mud, trees so desolate and naked without their
foliage . . . worst of all the thick mists that . . . rise from the valley' and
blot out the mountains, 'clothing everything in obscurity'.[18]

Suzanne Rollier, Dr Rollier's youngest daughter who taught Indira
modern dance exercises in bed once a week, found her very reserved,
even unapproachable. They were almost exactly the same age and
Suzanne had just returned from three years of studying modern dance
at Margaret Morris's dance school in England, but she and Indira did
not become friendly. Indira was 'very troubled and sad', and also 'very
solitary'. She avoided the other patients, even the other Indians of whom
there were several after the Nanavatis left Les Frênes. Suzanne and the
nursing staff, including her sister Odette, were unaware that Indira's
mother had died of tuberculosis (though Professor Rollier must have
known this), nor did they know that she had a fiancé in England. Feroze
never visited her at Les Frênes, nor – with one or two exceptions – did
anyone else.[19]

One of Indira's rare visitors was Lydie Hemmerlin, her former headmistress at Bex, down in the valley below Leysin. Indira had very little
to read at Les Frênes because she had not been able to bring any books

out of England. She asked Mlle Hemmerlin to lend her Nehru's *Glimpses of World History* and she now began to read it 'right from the beginning' for the first time since it had been published five years earlier. She read it avidly every afternoon, while lying in the *position ventrale* in bed on her balcony; it took her outside of the claustrophobic atmosphere of Les Frênes, connecting her to the outside world, her father and India.

But her spirits remained very low. Rollier was alarmed at her continued weight loss – she was now thirty pounds underweight – and decided to help 'the process of nature' by dosing her with cod liver oil and phytic acid which Indira reported had improved her appetite slightly. Rollier also prescribed the archaic TB treatment of 'cupping' that was popular in the nineteenth century. Not surprisingly, Indira found that it did not 'seem to make the slightest difference'.[20] She was a conscientious patient: she forced herself to eat the rich meals brought to her on a tray in bed, she lay in the *position ventrale*, withstood the chilly air in her room and the cold out on her balcony, but to little avail. 'Two months in Leysin,' she wrote to her father in late February. 'Four and a half months in bed [counting her time at Brentford Hospital]. When I first arrived here, Prof Rollier himself suggested the time limit of three months . . . as being the time required to set me up on my feet strongly. I suppose the three months has been extended . . . If only I could see or feel, or that at least the doctor could see, any improvement – then staying in bed or anything else would not matter. If – if.'[21]

As time passed and there was no end in prospect, Indira worried about the great expense of her treatment. Her weekly bill was now averaging 180 francs. Nehru told her not to fret – that her treatment was an investment in her future and so priceless. But he was worried. Krishna Menon had informed him that his London publisher, The Bodley Head, had gone into receivership: there would be no future royalty payments, and Nehru's royalties had been paying the Les Frênes bills.

Nehru's response to Indira's depression was akin to his cavalier dismissal of her money worries. He posted a parcel of books to her and also suggested that he send her a *takli* or spindle so that she could spin. Like Gandhi, Nehru found spinning 'very soothing' and may have hoped it would calm Indira's anxieties about her health and money. He urged her to 'knit as you did in England. Or play about with cardboard. I hear children in the Basic Schools here make delightful boxes and other things out of cardboard. It is a fascinating pastime.' He added gratuit-ously that while Indira's weight continued to plummet, no matter how much she ate, 'I have been growing disgustingly plump . . . The other day . . . I weighed myself and I was horrified to find that I had gone up to 143 pounds . . . 3 lbs more than I have ever been.'[22]

By early March Indira was feeling marginally better and Rollier allowed her to get up and take a fifteen-minute walk late in the afternoon on the roof-top solarium and then sit in the downstairs lounge afterwards. She was also permitted to take a proper bath once a week. Her days now followed the regimented pattern of the other ambulatory patients: breakfast at 7.30 a.m.; *position ventrale* in bed wheeled out on the balcony in the morning; morning tea at eleven; dinner at one; the '*cure de silence*' from two to four, during which Indira lay motionless in bed in her room. Reading and talking were banned during the *cure de silence*, and to ensure that it *was* silent the road in front of Les Frênes was closed for two hours and the local farmers prohibited from working in the nearby fields. Afternoon tea was at 4 o'clock; then Indira took her little walk at 4.30, followed by sitting in the lounge and knitting until six. Supper was served at seven, after which she listened to the wireless. Finally a bedtime glass of milk was brought on a tray at 9 p.m. Then the corridor lights were dimmed for the night and Indira turned off her bedside lamp and tried to sleep. She had bad nights because she kept waking up terribly thirsty and hot from her fever.[23]

Very soon she found this new ambulatory routine at Les Frênes as deadening as the months spent in bed. In order to survive sanatorium life psychologically, a patient needed to become involved with the other patients and the institution – to form relationships, listen to gossip, develop strong feelings about the nurses and doctors. In short, leave behind the outside world and take sanatorium life seriously – and this Indira could not do. She was not interested in what went on at Les Frênes. She formed no close friendships there. She lived for letters – from Feroze in London and Nehru in India – and for the BBC news bulletins on the radio.

The post, however, was unpredictable and days, even weeks, could pass without anything arriving for her. But the news was broadcast several times a day and Indira followed it closely. The period of the phoney war was drawing to a close in the early spring of 1940. In November 1939, the Soviet Union, which had signed a non-aggression pact with Nazi Germany, invaded Finland and ultimately won a fiercely fought winter war in March 1940. Back in India, Nehru wrote an article for the *National Herald* which sympathized with Finland's plight. He sent the cutting to Indira. She violently disagreed with his views as she explained in a long letter. She blamed both the Russo-German pact and the war with Finland on 'eight years of British foreign policy'. She took the hardline, pro-Soviet view that the USSR still rejected both Nazism and imperialism and that its demands against Finland were justified. She condemned British arms support for Finland in contrast to Britain's earlier refusal to help Republican Spain. 'Was this [refusal to aid Spain] because, as Lady Ironside remarked at a certain [Lord Lothian's] house party . . . "But Franco is such a gentleman"?'

Indira was only warming to her main theme. She reminded Nehru of how right-wing Finnish forces led by Baron Mannerheim had suppressed a revolution following the First World War and slaughtered 15,000 communists. 'This is the democracy,' Indira wrote indignantly, 'world imperialism is aiding . . . All this talk of poor Finland makes me sick. Just because a country is small in size, do the crimes of its Government lessen also and does its repression & totalitarianism likewise become softer & more bearable?'[24]

Not only does this letter show how closely Indira had been following the increasingly volatile European situation, it boldly states an ideological stance at variance with her father. Laski and Nehru's other admirers in London had misjudged Indira. She was more than a pale reflection of her father. In this letter she takes a position considerably to the left of Nehru. This was already evident, of course, in her objections to visiting Lothian – a grievance she did not let go of as this letter's reference to Lady Ironside shows. But she not only abhorred Chamberlain; she also heaped scorn on Labourites – 'the Hugh Daltons of the world', and 'Mr Attlee'. In her eyes, imperial Britain could do nothing right and would soon drag India into war.

But just how sophisticated and considered Indira's left-wing, communist-leaning sympathies were is unclear. She was greatly influenced by Feroze and his radical circle of friends and colleagues in London, many of whom were communists. The intelligentsia's disaffection with Russia and Stalin had certainly begun by 1939, but it was not shared by all those on the left. Indira, like many in the India League circle, still looked to the Soviet Union, even in the wake of Stalin's show trials and the Nazi-Soviet Pact. If what Indira called 'world imperialism', Chamberlain and appeasement were the best that the parliamentary democracies could offer, Stalin's Soviet Union seemed the only alternative. As one historian has observed, a good many fellow-travellers and sympathizers remained loyal to the USSR, and 'the prestige – and the gullibility – of Western intellectuals were considerable assets to Stalin'.[25]

Nehru did not respond to Indira's letter about Russia and Finland, but he *did* finally write to her about her depression at Les Frênes – or rather about how helpless he felt to advise her. He said that because his life had been full of incessant activity and moving 'about in crowds . . . perhaps I understood crowds a little . . . [but] I did not understand individuals'. He had always sacrificed personal relations to political demands and felt as a consequence that he had 'failed in the hard test of life,' and 'this sense of failure has pursued me in almost all I do. With this lack of faith in myself, how can I advise anyone? . . . So my darling, I am a poor kind of person to seek advice from. Everything that I can possibly give you is yours for the asking, but do not seek advice from me, for my mind is disturbed and lacks clarity.'[26] To Krishna Menon, Nehru was even more explicit some months earlier when he confessed that he 'was very ill mentally'.[27] Indira was hurt, but even more, she was alarmed by her father's letter which took, she said, 'all the blue, clear brightness out of my sky. It filled me with a great sadness, and above all, with a great longing to be with you.'[28]

In the spring of 1940 Nehru was fifty and Indira twenty-two; he was stranded in middle age, she should have been on the brink of life but lived in a state of 'hope deferred'. The world was on the verge of war, and in India independence seemed as remote as ever as Congress leaders disagreed amongst themselves, and even more with Mohammed Ali Jinnah's Muslim League. For all these reasons, Nehru and Indira were both absorbed by their own troubles and unable to help each other – Nehru because he felt himself a failure and Indira because of their separation. Their inability to connect at this time marked a turning point: they would never again be so open, so revealing or so needy with each other. Henceforth they observed an unspoken taboo on speaking from the heart.

What of Feroze – was he able to give Indira the solace and hope that

Nehru could not? Probably he tried, but his correspondence with Indira during this period – and later – is closed and we can only speculate about the nature and extent of his support.[29] Certainly their separation was very painful for Indira and the irregularity of the post maddening. Feroze undoubtedly proffered understanding and comfort. Even with the onset of war, to an optimist like Feroze, the future seemed green and full of promise. But, realistically, the shadow of Indira's illness was a serious threat to them. The worst prospect was that Indira would die like her mother. If she survived, the illness could remain debilitating and chronic. Tuberculosis patients were told not to marry and if they were already married, not to have children. By this time, Indira passionately wanted both marriage and children. Given Feroze's devotion to Kamala in India and Switzerland, he would not have been deterred by Indira's illness from his determination to marry her. But Feroze and Indira did not live in a vacuum. In addition to doctors, there were plenty of Gandhis and Nehrus to object to the marriage who could exploit Indira's illness in their efforts to prevent it.

At the end of March, Indira had been at Leysin the three months Rollier had stipulated to 'set her on her feet', and she was as far as ever from being the Diana he had promised to make of her. She frankly assessed her 'progress' in a letter to Nehru.

> There is no doubt that I am better now than when I arrived . . .
> but not much. I look slightly better, I breathe much better. In
> weight I have gained 3 lbs, my present weight being 85 lbs. Just
> about a month ago I started getting up in the afternoons –
> starting with fifteen minutes and now [I remain out of bed] for
> two and a half hours, during which I go for a short walk. On
> the other hand, that perpetual fatigue I used to feel is still a
> faithful companion, my appetite is not improving and I eat very
> little with great effort, and I don't sleep at all well.[30]

Predictably, Rollier told Indira she merely needed another three months at Les Frênes, but when Lady Maharaj Singh (whose own tubercular son was in a sanatorium in Montana) visited Indira, Rollier confided to Lady Singh that he actually wanted Indira to remain another year at Les Frênes. Lady Singh passed this information on to Indira who was understandably appalled at the idea of being incarcerated until the spring of 1941. And even then Rollier doubted that Indira would be cured. When she finally left Switzerland, he said she would need to spend at least two years in the mountains in India. A life of invalidism stretched before her.[31]

After Lady Singh's revelation of Rollier's real prognosis, Indira began to plot to leave Les Frênes – against medical advice if necessary. She told Nehru that she had 'a very strong – almost overpowering – desire to go to India. It obsesses me.' She also suggested that her illness was largely psychosomatic: 'I think my fatigue and insomnia are due mostly to the state of my nerves.' And the state of her nerves, of course, was a product of her 'wretched months' at Les Frênes and the insufferable dullness of 'the little gossiping group of Les Frênes patients whose main topics of conversation are: food & the strangers who pass by on the road below'.[32]

Nehru gave Indira no encouragement to leave Les Frênes. He told her that the doctors must 'have the last word'. To this end, he asked both Dr Bhandari in London and Dr Jivraj Mehta – an eminent Indian doctor – to write to Rollier. Nehru felt certain that they, like Rollier, would urge Indira to 'stay [at Les Frênes] as long as you can manage it . . . It would be folly to do anything which would undo the good already done.' As for Nehru himself, 'I want so much to see you,' he wrote, 'but I am not fool enough to allow my wishes to interfere with your treatment. We absolutely must build on a firm foundation this time, and if we have to err, we must err on the safe side. You know well enough that weak lungs or pleura take a devil of a time to strengthen.'[33]

The ghost of Kamala Nehru hovered between the lines of this letter. Nehru was unwilling to take risks with Indira's health, no matter how much she wanted to leave Les Frênes, and he invoked medical authority and a string of 'musts' to drive home his case. He also insisted 'that health is not merely a physical condition. It is very much a mental affair. You complain of nerves. We are all more or less nervy but we must not be dominated by them . . . you should deliberately put worry and nerves on the shelf. It can be done, it has been done.'[34]

In late April, Dr Bhandari came to Leysin from London to see Indira and discuss her case with Dr Rollier. He and Rollier 'came to the unanimous decision', as Bhandari wrote to Nehru, that Indira should stay at Les Frênes, at least for some months longer.[35] Indira was dismayed at this verdict, and wrote protestingly to Nehru, but he misunderstood her eagerness to leave Switzerland. Though he conceded that 'sanatorium life . . . is mentally debilitating' – and even asked, 'Have you read Thomas Mann's *The Magic Mountain*?' – he thought that Indira wanted to return to India out of an exaggerated sense of duty to help and support him. This, no doubt, she did hope to do, but even more, she was desperate to be with Feroze again, whom she had not seen now in five months. Nehru also inadvertently gave her another reason to leave Les Frênes, when he conceded in the spring of 1940, that money, after all, was a problem, because the war had stopped his royalty payments. He was not even sure, in fact, how he was going to pay the next month's wages to the Anand Bhawan servants.[36]

But for Indira the most wounding thing in all this wrangling over when she should leave Les Frênes, was Nehru's failure to reach out and help her. He frankly stated his views and feelings in a letter written in early May, prefacing what he had to say with 'it is not easy to write about such matters, especially when [the] prying eyes [of censors] look through our letters'. 'It is obvious,' he said, 'that you have had to put up with a great deal of mental trouble and conflict.' But 'such conflicts,' he maintained, 'have to be faced without much help from outside. No outsider can really help. Certainly I cannot help you, howsoever I might try . . . I do not even know how your mind works, though vaguely I might sometimes guess. You told me very rightly once how blind I was. That is perfectly true . . . And so we have grown progressively more and more ignorant of each other, and even our love for each other has not brought any understanding. You are such a stranger to me, and perhaps you do not know much about me.'[37]

In April 1940 Germany invaded Denmark and Norway, and on 10 May – the same day that Winston Churchill replaced Neville Chamberlain as Prime Minister – it overran Holland, Belgium and Luxembourg. The Mediterranean sea route was now closed and ships from India had to travel to Europe via the Cape of Good Hope. This meant that mail was even slower and more erratic. 'Barriers grow,' Nehru wrote, 'and this tight little world, which flying and the rest of it had made so small and accessible, again expands . . . and you go further away from me.' Indira wrote 'a hurried line to reassure' her father on the 10th though she knew that 'this letter will be hopelessly out of date by the time it reaches you'. 'Don't worry about me, darling,' she said. She added, however, that two Swiss towns had been bombed that morning – 'they say it was a mistake'.[38]

A week later she wrote again to her father: 'Don't get agitated or worried about me . . . I shall be perfectly all right. A crisis is the one time when I do keep my head' – an accurate self-assessment. 'Here are my plans,' she went on. She would stay in Leysin 'unless and until Switzerland was involved in the war'. If that happened, she had been told that all foreigners would have to leave. She had contacted the British Consul to arrange for a transit visa through France, and when and if she had to leave Switzerland she would go directly to England and attempt to get a boat to India 'via the Cape, of course'. The only thing about which Indira was 'a little worried' was that she would run out of money and not be able to pay her last Les Frênes bill. She had written to Krishna Menon (who routinely forwarded her allowance from London), but in case she had to leave before he could send money, she would borrow to get to England.[39]

The war continued to spread like a dark stain and now threatened Switzerland's frontiers. The evacuation of British troops from Dunkirk began at the end of May. Paris fell on 14 June and on the 22nd the French signed an armistice with Germany. War, as Indira put it, had 'come right on top of England now', and indeed the Battle of Britain began on 10 July. It seemed only a matter of time before Britain too was overrun. Surrounded and trapped by the hostilities, Indira was desperate to leave for England – with or without Rollier's consent – because, as she confessed much later, 'Feroze was in London, which was being daily bombed, and I felt my place was with him.'[40]

Postal communication ceased altogether in June and July of 1940, during which Indira sent Nehru two cryptic cables – 'don't worry am alright' and 'am well'. When she was finally able to send a letter at the end of July, she described 'how poisonous is the atmosphere here nowadays. At [Les] Frênes there are two Spaniards who fought for Franco, two Frenchmen who were clamouring for a military dictatorship even before Pétain [head of the collaborationist Vichy government] formed his government . . . The *famille* Rollier is loud in its praises of imperialism – British and French. As a result I just can't open my mouth on any subject.' Indira, in fact, found the atmosphere at the sanatorium so intolerable that she almost left when a route to London via Portugal opened up. But she had 'such a horror of falling ill again that ... I didn't think I could risk that. So here I am still [in Leysin].'[41]

This letter took three months to reach Nehru in India, and in the interim Indira received no word from him. Theoretically postal communication had resumed, but a great many letters got held up or were lost. On 10 September Nehru cabled, 'No letters are reaching. The situation here [in India] is rapidly verging on crisis. Early resumption of old pilgrimage [to prison] is likely.'[42] But it was more than a month before he was arrested on 31 October 1940 for making seditious speeches. He was swiftly tried and sentenced to his eighth prison term – four years in Gorakhpur Jail.

Indira felt no less imprisoned at Les Frênes and she wanted out. At the end of October, she felt strong enough to announce to Dr Rollier that she was leaving Les Frênes against medical advice. Krishna Menon had forwarded her money, and she paid her bill and decamped to Mlle Hemmerlin's school at La Pelouse in Bex. From there Indira made herculean efforts to get to England before all the frontiers closed. The only safe route was via France, Spain and Portugal and visas were required for all these countries. Then she needed to buy a plane ticket from Lisbon to England. She waited in Bex for weeks to get the Portuguese visa. There were blackouts every night from ten until seven the next morning, and both food and clothing were rationed.

Finally, at the end of November all of Indira's papers were in order and she boarded a bus in Geneva which drove through France to the Spanish border and then on to Barcelona. Here she spent the night before getting a plane to Lisbon. When she arrived at the Lisbon aerodrome the next day, Indira was detained for 'a most unpleasant half-hour' because a police officer 'after one look at my passport photograph ... said that it was not me, and therefore the passport could not be mine' – probably an indication of how greatly she had changed since falling ill. She was stranded in Lisbon, waiting for a flight to England, for nearly two months. 'The Portuguese are very poor and very dirty' she wrote to Nehru, who had been transferred to Dehra Dun Prison. 'A lot of women & children are barefooted and there are many beggars. People spit all over the place – there is a terrific amount of shouting and many hawkers ... It is almost like being in India.'[43] Every day Indira queued at the airline office for a ticket to England and was told to come back the next day. She was tempted to go by sea, but in England Feroze,

Krishna Menon and Dr Bhandari all vetoed this idea because so many ships were being sunk. Eventually Feroze managed to obtain an air ticket for her.

On New Year's Day 1941, Indira finally flew from Lisbon to Bristol where Feroze – whom she had not seen in more than a year – was waiting to meet her. They immediately took the train to London and went straight to Feroze's one-room flat in St John's Wood. The next day Indira cabled Nehru: 'Arrived last night. Well. Plans uncertain.'[44]

In fact, she had already decided to stay with Feroze in London until they could make their way together back to India by sea. Ships now travelled by convoy; the Mediterranean remained closed and the only way to get to India was via South Africa and the Cape of Good Hope – the old route East India Company traders and missionaries used to take before the Suez Canal opened. Many ships were sunk by German submarines, but even so, there was a long waiting list to get a passage.

On the morning of 3 January, P. N. Haksar's telephone rang in his Primrose Hill flat. Feroze was on the line: 'Indu's here!' he said. 'Can you come over and cook for us?' Haksar was now a barrister in training at Lincoln's Inn, but among his friends he was valued as much for his superb Kashmiri cuisine as his intellect and radicalism. He lived just round the corner from Feroze and that evening went to Feroze's flat at 20 Abbey Road to make a delicious, rich meal. He found Indira thin and pale, but also 'radiant' and obviously overjoyed to be with Feroze. They made no pretence over where she was staying or what the sleeping arrangements were in Feroze's tiny, book-filled flat.[45]

Nehru, of course, did not know where Indira was living in London. His only communication with her now was in the form of brief, fortnightly telegrams that they sent to each other via Agatha Harrison. He probably assumed she was with Agatha or Dr Bhandari.

For Indira and Feroze it was a heady, intense time. They had been secretly engaged now for nearly four years – an engagement punctuated by anxieties and separations. Now at last they were together again, and alone, with family and most of their friends at a distance. Their intimacy was intensified by the fact that they were reunited in a world at war. In January 1941 bombs still rained down on London. One night Indira and Feroze emerged from Piccadilly underground station to find that it had been hit by a bomb just minutes before.[46] In February, the Blitz intensified, with up to 700 German aircraft attacking British cities in simultaneous raids night after night.

The photographs Feroze took of Indira in London are the most revealing and beautiful ever taken of her. They are intimate pictures taken by and of someone in love. Though Indira is too thin, far from appearing ill, she glows. In one she looks directly – even provocatively – at camera, straight at Feroze who is taking the picture, her head slightly bent down but her eyes unflinching and warm. The reserve and hesitancy so noticeable in nearly every photograph of her as a young woman and the impassive mask that she wears in so many photos taken during her mature years, are entirely absent here. No one looking at this photograph can doubt that her relationship with Feroze was a passionate one.

The uncertainty of Indira and Feroze's world – the sensation of living on a precipice – was a potent backdrop to their relationship. Indira now decided that they should get married in London, before returning to India – perhaps, in part, because she and Feroze were living together as man and wife, though she was indifferent to social conventions. Still, she was the famous daughter of a famous man and the year was 1941. The situation was awkward.

In addition, there was much to be said for arriving in India as newlyweds – their marriage a *fait accompli*. They knew that great controversy and opposition awaited them otherwise. Indira pressed hard to have an English registry wedding. Feroze pointed out that Nehru would be deeply hurt if they did so.[47] This was a strong argument. In addition, Nehru (and others) might suspect that Feroze had somehow coerced Indira into marriage in England because he was afraid she would be dissuaded from it in India. Indira, however, had resolved to have her way.

But then she fell ill and the marriage issue was suspended. In February she began running 'the usual high temperature and was scared stiff that the old trouble had started again'.[48] She consulted Dr Bhandari who detected fluid in her lungs. There is no evidence that Feroze was the least bit reluctant to marry Indira because of her uncertain health. They both knew that tuberculosis patients were told to stay single – advice that only made Indira even more determined to marry. But in early March, with Feroze still opposed to a London registry wedding, they both got last-minute berths on a steamer to India. By this time Indira's fever and other symptoms had considerably subsided and she was well enough to travel.[49] Marriage was deferred.

Feroze and Indira sailed on the *City of Paris* – a troopship in a long convoy – on 10 March. The captain gave Indira a cabin on her own because she was not yet fully recovered. The company and atmosphere on board were not congenial. In addition to the troops, there was the Governor General of British Burma and assorted government officials who denounced Indian nationalists and with whom Feroze and Indira 'had terrific quarrels'. As Indira put it later, she and Feroze 'experienced humiliation all the way' home.[50]

As they steamed down the west coast of Africa the ship dropped depth charges at regular intervals which made a deafening noise and 'shook every bone in one's body'.[51] On 20 March they crossed the equator. The heat was even more intense than it was in Indian plains in summer. The ship observed a strict blackout all night. Their cabins were too furnace-like to inhabit even after sundown, so Indira and Feroze sat up on deck, in the dark, talking and dozing far into the night.

They reached the Cape of Good Hope at the end of March and the ship docked for a day at Cape Town. Indira and Feroze went ashore and visited Parliament where they saw General Smuts who had recently proclaimed in a speech that skin colour was one's passport. The *City of Paris* then steamed on to Durban where it paused for a week.

It was in Durban that Indira inadvertently found her political voice. The large Durban Indian community gave Nehru's daughter a warm and enthusiastic welcome and arranged a formal reception in her honour at which she was asked to speak. Remembering her disastrous performance in London, Indira refused, though she agreed to sit on the platform at the reception. In the meantime, she went to a hotel room that had been rented for her and Feroze to freshen up in before touring Durban. A porter knocked on the door to say they had a visitor. Indira asked that the visitor be told to meet them in the hotel lounge which the porter, without embarrassment, said was not possible because the visitor was an Indian. Indira and Feroze were both fair, and of course, were still dressed in English clothes, but Indira bluntly asked the porter what did he think *they* were? The porter 'said he didn't care what we were

. . . we didn't *look* Indian so it was alright'. She and Feroze left the hotel hastily.[52]

Driving around Durban they were appalled to see the desperate living conditions in the squalid, segregated black ghettos. These were no worse than the slums of Calcutta or Bombay, but they were built on a foundation of racism as well as poverty. That evening, when Indira arrived at the cinema hall where a reception was being held in her honour, she was seething with indignation over what they had seen earlier in the day. She accepted the *namaste* greetings and garlands of the crowd of African Indians coldly, and to everyone's amazement, she insisted upon speaking after all.

Instead of acknowledging the chairman's speech of welcome, Indira spoke with passion about white South Africa's oppression of the black population which she likened to Hitler's persecution of the Jews. She predicted that 'it may not be today, it may be ten or twenty years, but it is they [the black Africans] who will rule this country'. She went on to condemn the servile attitude of the Indians towards white South Africans and their indifference to the plight of the black majority. This was not the speech the audience had expected, and a stunned silence – rather than applause – filled the hall when Indira sat down. During their remaining days in Durban, Indira and Feroze were shunned by the city's Indian community.[53]

Indira's speech in Durban was her first autonomous and unpremeditated political act. To everyone's surprise, including her own, it exposed an inner strength and fearlessness. As Christine Toller had observed in London three years earlier, Indira was indeed 'unafraid of the wind'. Henceforth, if she had something to say, Indira did not hesitate. If she was roused, words – sometimes passionate, fluent ones – came.

From Durban they steamed north into the Indian Ocean, past Madagascar and the Seychelles, up to the Arabian Sea, and finally reached Bombay on 16 April 1941. This time Indira was coming home to India to stay. She was young, in love and on the verge of being someone else – Indira Gandhi.

PART TWO

Indira Gandhi

*Nothing was less inevitable in modern Indian politics
than Indira Gandhi's rise to power. Yet, as often happens
in history, once it happened nothing was more decisive.
It was modern Indian history's most crucial and indelible accident.*

Sudipta Kaviraj, 'Indira Gandhi and Indian Politics'

NINE

Not a Normal, Banal, Boring Life

AS SOON AS SHE ARRIVED in Bombay, Indira received a telegram
from Mahatma Gandhi telling her to come directly to see him at his
Sevagram ashram near Wardha. Gandhi had long treated the Nehrus
as family members. He had not seen Indira since she had last been in
India two years earlier. Now he wanted to scrutinize her and assess her
health in person. But Indira defied Gandhi's summons and announced
she would first go to Allahabad with Feroze and visit Gandhi afterwards.
Then a message arrived from her father urging her to go to Bapu. She
went.

It was an awkward reunion in the parched, poverty-stricken central
plains of India. Indira swept into Gandhi's austere ashram dressed in
silk and wearing lipstick. 'The Great Soul' told her to put on *khadi* and
wash her face. Indira found the atmosphere at Sevagram sycophantic
and rife with 'petty quarrels'. Gandhi's disciples argued over who would
serve his food, who would milk his goat, who would carry his papers
or take dictation from him. One day it suddenly began to rain and
Indira dashed outside to take in the washing only to be rebuked by an
ashramite for touching Gandhi's clothes. Though Gandhi himself was,
in Indira's words, 'the same as ever', he was surrounded by a fawning
community of devotees that Indira was glad to escape when she left for
Allahabad two days later.[1]

Her return to India was widely covered in the press. When she got to
Allahabad, Indira gave several interviews to the Lucknow-based *National
Herald* which Nehru had established in 1937, and these stories were
reprinted in the national newspapers. Thus before she visited her father
at Dehra Dun Jail, Nehru – who was allowed newspapers during his prison
term – read that his daughter 'still looks weak and far from healthy'.[2]

They met in the small interview room of Dehra Dun Jail on 27 April 1941, under the watchful eye of the warder. Indira and Nehru had not seen each other since she had sailed for England in 1939. More than ever before a gulf separated them and it became all but unbridgeable when Indira told Nehru that she intended to marry Feroze as soon as possible. In his prison diary Nehru recorded how frail Indira looked and how filled with anxiety he was 'about her future'; but he recorded what happened during their interview in cryptic, oblique terms: 'Apart from health, other difficulties. I was very happy to see her and yet my mind became engrossed with these difficulties . . . it is not going to be a soft way. She has determination and self-reliance which is good. But she is . . . immature . . . Yet she must have depths . . . My mind was full of her and of life's queer ways after she left.' Ten days later, Nehru wrote in his diary, 'My mind has been troubled and uneasy – constantly thinking, brooding about various matters which chiefly revolve round Indu. Restless nights.'[3]

After their interview in late April, Indira kept aloof for nearly a month during which she wrote to her father only once to tell him she would not be visiting him again soon 'because the heat is getting me down completely – and the journey to Dehra Dun is long & very tiring'.[4] Finally, at the end of May, she sent 'an angry, agitated letter', as Nehru described it, which provoked another anguished entry in Nehru's prison diary: 'I cannot even gain the confidence of my own daughter! . . . she [has] drawn into herself – These last ten years separated her from me, till now we look at each other as strangers . . . What is to be done? What is to be done?'[5]

Why did the prospect of Indira and Feroze marrying throw Nehru into such turmoil? He would, of course, imagine the strength of family, social and even political objections to such a marriage. And to a certain extent, he agreed, for despite his egalitarian convictions, Nehru thought Feroze a poor match. It mattered little to him that Feroze was not a Kashmiri or even a Hindu. Vijaya Lakshmi Pandit's husband was a Maharashtrian and Krishna Hutheesing's a Gujarati, and Nehru had not objected to their marriages. But Ranjit Pandit and Raja Hutheesing were both Oxford-educated, professional men from wealthy families. Pandit was a barrister as well as an eminent Sanskrit scholar; Hutheesing, too, was a successful barrister. They were patrician in a recognizably British way.

Feroze, on the other hand, lacked this family and class pedigree, the associations and connections Nehru valued. Feroze did not have a university degree, a profession or even the prospect of a steady income. He knew a great deal about European classical music and art and had probably scrutinized the writings of Marx and other communist theorists. But their personalities were polar opposites. Feroze was loud, boisterous and a great user of expletives. Nehru was soft-spoken, subtle and did not swear even when enraged. Like many fathers, Nehru was also reluctant to lose Indira – and to feel himself superseded. Then there was the issue of Indira's continued poor health and the medical inadvisability of marriage and childbearing. And finally there was the painful memory of Kamala's deathbed fear that Indira would 'make the mistake of her life' by marrying Feroze. Kamala had thought Feroze unstable and unreliable. Even if he had dismissed the idea that Kamala and Feroze had had an affair, it may have occurred to him that Feroze had behaved inappropriately towards Kamala.

At this juncture, Feroze himself tried to talk to Nehru. He made the journey to Dehra Dun with Kamala's cousin, Dr Madan Atal. But when he presented himself at the jail, the prison authorities refused to grant Feroze an interview with Nehru because he was not a relative. Madan Atal, however, was allowed in in the capacity of Indira's medical adviser. Indira had just begun a course of injections and Madan wanted to talk to Nehru about her 'future treatment and programme'. All Feroze could do was send Nehru a conciliatory crate of Alphonso mangoes when he returned to Allahabad.

In order to escape the ferocious heat of the plains, Indira went in May to Mussoorie –where she rented a two-bedroom cottage with 'Lilliputian bathrooms' for the next six months. At the end of the month she visited her father again in jail. 'A long interview,' according to Nehru, 'and we seemed to come nearer to each other.'[6] They made a peace of sorts, but nothing had fundamentally changed. Indira was more determined than ever to marry Feroze. Now, as throughout her life, objections and obstacles merely strengthened her resolve.

She wanted both to reassure her father and to make her own non-negotiable position clear. But as in the past, Indira chose to do this in letter form rather than in person. 'Darling,' she wrote from Mussoorie,

'I was quite shocked to see how you had changed since I saw you last. You mustn't let these things get you down.' She went on to insist that there was nothing to worry about. On the contrary,

> I have a serene happiness surging up from within, that no one and nothing can mar or take away from me ... Most people spend their lives waiting for happiness but the cup always seems to be just a little beyond their reach and they have not the courage to stretch their arms to grasp it. I took it in my two hands and drank deep into it – and it entered into every nerve and tissue of my mind and body, and bathed me in its rich warm calmness. I have this now and forever.

Indira ignored Nehru's response when he wrote back, 'Happiness is rather a fleeting thing, a sense of fulfilment is perhaps more abiding.'[7]

And then something – just what is not clear – undermined Indira's supreme confidence and her conviction that she must shape her own future – including her marriage to Feroze. On 2 June she wrote to Nehru again, but this time 'in the throes of remorse and regret'. 'Far from being an imposition,' she now said, his advice was her 'strongest prop'. 'How much I need you – how utterly lost I am without you. I have been so arrogant and stupid. I tried to sail out on my own before I knew the rudiments of managing a boat.' At the end of the letter, Indira opened herself to Nehru as she never had before, in the process revealing the burden of being a 'great man's' daughter. 'I seem to be just beginning to have a glimpse at the beauty and the richness in you. In the past you were [not] ... an approachable being, always so immersed in your work, and ... I was rather scared of you – you seemed so high up. One feels so inferior when you are about and I suppose that unconsciously one resents it.'[8]

This unguarded, self-aware letter could have revived the intimacy that had formerly existed between father and daughter. Indira had opened a locked door, but for whatever reasons, Nehru hesitated to walk through it. If she had doubts about Feroze and the marriage, she now kept them to herself. She may have realized even this early that she and Feroze were in for a stormy journey together. Many years later, Indira was unusually frank about her marriage in an interview with the Italian journalist Oriana Fallaci. 'We quarrelled a lot,' she told Fallaci. 'It's true. We were two equally strong types, equally pigheaded – neither of us wanted to give in. And I like to think that those quarrels . . . enlivened our life, because without them we would have had a normal life, yes, but banal and boring. We didn't deserve a normal, banal and boring life.'[9]

In June Indira went to Calcutta for three weeks with Madan Atal to get 'thoroughly overhauled' by medical specialists including Dr Bidhan Chandra Roy who was a Congress leader as well as an eminent physician. When she returned to Mussoorie, her maternal grandmother, Rajpati Kaul, came from Delhi to stay with her. Indira confessed to her that she wanted to marry Feroze, and to her amazement, her grandmother raised no objections. Though Amma, as Indira called her, was an ortho-dox Hindu, she said, as Indira later related 'that since neither Feroze nor I were much concerned with religion, she did not see that it mattered what either of us were. If we were religious, then it might matter, but not being so, it did not.'[10]

Indira saw her father again at Dehra Dun Jail on 6 July and the next day Nehru wrote her a long letter full of the advice that Indira had sought the previous month, but now no longer wanted. He began by reassuring her that 'in no way will I obstruct you in following your own decisions about yourself . . . your marriage . . . [will] depend upon your own choice'. But then he went on to outline what, he said, had long been his plans for her. He had hoped that after university Indira would travel and learn languages:

> Then with this background of mental training and a wider cul-ture I expected you to return to India and discover the fascinat-ing thing that is India. In this task I wanted to help you personally and I expected you to help me somewhat also. There are very few persons in India, I think, who could give effective help not only in public life but almost for any activity . . . better than I could. Hundreds and thousands of young men and girls have wanted to serve me as secretaries or in some way to get this training. I have never encouraged anyone and have shoul-dered my burdens alone, for I had always imagined you to occupy that niche. Till you come, that niche had better be left empty. No one else could take your place. It was with this idea ever hovering in my mind that I wrote piles and piles of historical and other letters to you. I wanted gently, slowly but yet surely to train your mind in that wider understanding of life and events

that is essential for any big work. Of course I did not think of you just as a secretary to me or otherwise attached to me all the time. That would have been excessively selfish of me. I knew you would marry and I wanted you to do so and thus to live your own life. I only wanted to give you some special training which would stand you in good stead in later life. It was a training for which many people hanker and hanker in vain.[11]

But now, Nehru went on, 'our sense of values seems to differ vastly. That hurt.' Then he turned to Indira's determination to marry as soon as possible. He felt strongly that she should wait and he invoked Indira's poor health to make his case. He also clearly felt that marriage would pre-empt other, valuable experiences: 'Marriage is an important thing in life. It may make or mar one's life. And yet marriage is something smaller than life. Life is a much bigger thing . . . Your present health indicates . . . an avoidance of marriage for some time, some months at least . . . there is an element of absurd haste in your returning from Europe in failing health and suddenly marrying.'

Finally, Nehru told Indira that he wanted her to discuss the matter with other people, including Kamala's mother, Rajpati Kaul, Gandhi, Nan Pandit, Krishna Hutheesing and senior members of the family, all of whom he thought would side with him. 'Avoid . . . breaking as far as possible with old contacts and ways. You do not know what the new ones will be like and you might well be landed high and dry. I am not referring to Feroze but life's other contacts, including Feroze's family. Of course one does not marry a family; yet one cannot ignore it either and it can make itself pleasant or unpleasant. I know nothing about his family or other contacts.'[12] It was precisely to avoid all this – long letters from her father, travelling all over India to consult family members and withstanding their opposition – that Indira had wanted to marry in London.

In August Krishna Hutheesing and her two children came to stay with Indira in Mussoorie. Indira visited Nehru again on the 7th and wanted to tell him that she was in no frame of mind to discuss Feroze and marriage with her aunt, but mid-interview she and Nehru heard on the warder's wireless that Rabindranath Tagore had died, and they spent the rest of the time talking about 'Gurudev'. Krishna Hutheesing returned to Bombay in October none the wiser about Indira's wedding plans.

Indira stayed on in Mussoorie until late November. She was not well – according to Nehru's diary, she looked 'delicate and feeble'. But she was also in no hurry to return to Anand Bhawan because Nan Pandit and her family were now living there. Nehru recorded in his diary how Indira objected to her aunt's plan to throw a birthday party for her and that 'she hardly wants to stay in Anand Bhawan – wants just to pick up her clothes etc and go to Wardha and then to Bombay. Anywhere but Anand Bhawan!'[13] For Indira, old wounds never healed; nor could she forget or relinquish a grudge. Some six years after Kamala's death and more than a decade after Nan Pandit had slighted Kamala and called Indira 'ugly and stupid', Indira remained hostile and unforgiving.

When she returned to Allahabad from Mussoorie in November, Indira followed through with Nehru's request to canvass family and friends, determined all the while to get her own way. First she went to see Gandhi again at Sevagram. This meeting was as awkward as their previous one. Like Nehru, Gandhi told Indira that she should not rush into marriage, and Gandhi was not used to having his advice spurned. Indira, however, remained obdurate, and Gandhi interrogated her about her sexual feelings for Feroze and insisted that sexual attraction was no basis for a marriage. When Indira reassured him that her love for Feroze was much deeper than this, Gandhi suggested that they subscribe to his marital ideal of *brahmacharya* and remain celibate after marriage. Indira – who was irate by this point – turned his suggestion down flat, saying, 'You can tell a couple not to get married . . . but when they are married, to ask them to live a life of celibacy makes no sense. It can result only in bitterness and unhappiness.'[14]

Once he was convinced that Indira would not be dissuaded, Gandhi gave his consent to the union, but he insisted on discussing the situation with Feroze and obtained from him an assurance that they would only marry with Nehru's consent.[15] Gandhi also insisted that once this was forthcoming, Indira and Feroze should not have the small, simple wedding they both desired because, as he said to them, 'there is going to be opposition to this marriage, and if it is a quiet marriage, they will say that the family didn't want it . . . So you must invite people.'[16] Inevitably, the wedding of the daughter of Jawaharlal Nehru would be a national event and must be publicly celebrated.

After gaining Gandhi's blessing, Indira went to see her aunt, Krishna Hutheesing, in Bombay, and finally confided in her. Krishna, predictably, urged her to wait and meet more men before settling down, and also told her to try to marry someone from a similar background. Krishna Hutheesing, however, had herself married a Jain – outside the Kashmiri Brahmin fold – after a very short courtship. Indira met her aunt's objections with, 'Why? It took you only ten days to make up your mind to marry Raja Bhai and I have known Feroze for years. So why should I have to wait and why should I have to meet other young men?'[17]

Finally, Indira returned to Allahabad to confront her old opponent, Nan Pandit, who was highly conscious of her aristocratic Nehru heritage and clearly thought Feroze 'common'. Her aunt bluntly advised Indira to have an affair with Feroze rather than marry him. This suggestion incensed Indira; she felt it insulted both Feroze and herself. Life at Anand Bhawan now became particularly tense.[18]

When Indira had dutifully consulted everyone, Nehru capitulated and agreed to the marriage, but he did ask Indira and Feroze to wait until he was released from prison, and in 1941, three quarters of his prison term still lay ahead of him. Then, unexpectedly, Nehru was released by the British authorities on 4 December 1941 along with all the other imprisoned Congress leaders. It looked, at last, as though the marriage battle had been won.

This battle, however, had not been Indira and Feroze's sole preoccupation since returning from England. Both were politically active in the spring of 1941. Feroze was a member of the Friends of the Soviet Union and he organized a Soviet exhibition in Lucknow. He and Indira were also involved in the All India Students' Federation which had split into Congress and communist wings. Indira addressed the communist faction in Lucknow, and in December she attended the annual conference of the Communist United Provinces Students' Federation.[19]

In addition, both Indira and Feroze were as active as ever in the nationalist struggle. And along with other nationalists, they knew that the struggle for Indian independence was bound to be affected by a larger world now engulfed in war. On 7 December 1941 Pearl Harbor was bombed and the United States entered the war. Over the next months the Japanese army steadily advanced throughout Southeast Asia. By the end of January it had driven the British out of Malaya. On 15 February 1942 the great British imperial base of Singapore fell. Java, Sumatra and Rangoon were occupied by early March, and India lay open to invasion.

But not even these menacing developments could eclipse the Nehru marriage saga. On 21 February 1942, the main Allahabad paper, the *Leader*, ran a front-page article headlined, 'Miss Indira Nehru's Engagement', and the next day papers throughout India reported that Indira was soon to marry Feroze Gandhi. The news provoked a storm of controversy – almost all of it hostile to the marriage.

Nehru was in Calcutta when the *Leader* story broke, but as soon as he got home he issued a public statement that was published in the *Bombay Chronicle* and other papers:

> A report has appeared in the press about the engagement of my daughter Indira with Feroze Gandhi. As inquiries have been addressed to me on the subject, I should like to confirm this report. A marriage is a personal and domestic matter, affecting chiefly the two parties concerned and their families. Yet I recognize that in view of my association with public affairs, I should take my many friends and colleagues and the public generally into my confidence. I have long held the view that though parents may and should advise in the matter, the choice and ultimate decision must lie with the two parties concerned. That decision, if arrived at after mature deliberation, must be given effect to, and it is no business of parents or others to come in the way. When I was assured that Indira and Feroze wanted to marry one another, I accepted willingly their decision and told them it had my blessing. Mahatma Gandhi, whose opinion I value not only in public affairs but in private matters also, gave his blessing to the proposal. The members of my family as well as the members of my wife's family also gave their willing consent. Feroze Gandhi is a young Parsi who has been a friend and colleague of ours for many years and I expect him to serve our country and our cause efficiently and well. But on whomsoever my daughter's choice would have fallen, I would have accepted it or been false to the principles I have held. I hope and trust that this marriage will be a true comradeship in life and in the larger causes that we hold dear.... The marriage will take place in about a month's time in Allahabad.[20]

Gandhi also issued a statement of support in his paper, the *Harijan* which was reprinted in papers across the country. But even with Gandhi's blessing, the controversy over and animosity towards the 'mixed' marriage of Indira and Feroze did not die down. They were flouting two deeply held traditions of Indian marriage which remain largely intact even to this day. They were not submitting to an arranged union determined by their families, and they were marrying outside their faiths. For years the Nehru family had been the first family of India. Nehru and Kamala had been worshipped as the perfect married couple – and theirs had been an arranged marriage. It was one thing for private individuals to defy convention and quite another for public figures to do so. Indira and Feroze would be setting an unwelcome precedent.

Thousands of letters and telegrams streamed into Anand Bhawan, some abusive, most hostile, a few congratulatory. The marriage was debated in the press; various prominent citizens spoke out. As Indira recalled many years later, 'the whole country was against it'.[21]

But they went bravely ahead. After consultation with learned Pandits, 26 March was chosen for the wedding day. This was a particularly auspicious date because it was *Ram Navmi*, the birthday of Lord Rama, the hero of the *Ramayana*. But politically it was not convenient because a British delegation headed by Sir Stafford Cripps was scheduled to arrive in India on 22 March with an offer from Churchill on the 'India Question'. Nehru – as well as many of the other wedding guests – would inevitably be much preoccupied by the Cripps Mission negotiations.

Despite the public outcry against Indira's marriage, in the weeks and days before the wedding, presents arrived at Anand Bhawan from all over the country. 'Her room became a cloud of rustling tissue paper and satin ribbon from which emerged gifts of silver and crystal, and occasionally a velvet-lined casket containing a jewelled ornament. Most of these presents had to be carefully rewrapped and returned to the senders,' because they were unknown to the family.[22]

26 March dawned a sunny, cloudless morning. The wedding began early, before it became too hot. At 9 a.m. the bride came down from her room dressed, significantly, in *khadi* – hand-woven from thread spun by Nehru in prison into a sari that was tinted pink and edged with delicate silver embroidery. She wore a garland of fresh flowers and translucent, coloured glass bangles, rather than traditional, heavy gold jewellery on her wrists. Indira had never looked so beautiful, nor, in a very long time so well – tall, slender, her complexion no longer sallow but 'the golden colour of ripe wheat', her fine features like the profile on a Greek coin.[23] Feroze was dressed in the traditional white Congress

khadi sherwani and *churidar* trousers, and he, too, wore a garland of flowers.

The ceremony was held outdoors under a canopy on the ground-floor Anand Bhawan veranda which had been decorated with greenery. Indira, Nehru and Feroze sat around the traditional fire built on a slab of marble. An empty cushion next to Nehru marked Kamala's absence. The invited guests sat on carpet or chairs around the veranda, and beyond them, stretching out over the Anand Bhawan grounds hundreds of uninvited spectators stood in the morning sun. In the midst of the crowd there was a photographer from an American fashion magazine. Norvin Hein, another American who was a young teacher at Ewing Christian College, struggled to film the wedding with his 8 mm movie camera.[24]

The ceremony uniting Indira and Feroze was neither conventional nor legal. Under British imperial law in India, people of different faiths could not be married unless they renounced their own religion. Though Indira had never been a practising Hindu nor Feroze an observant Parsi, they were both reluctant to sign a declaration stating that they did not belong to any religion. Seven years earlier, Indira's cousin, B.K. Nehru, has faced the same dilemma when he married his wife Fori who was a Hungarian Jew. As usual, at the time of B.K. Nehru's marriage, Mahatma Gandhi was consulted and his advice taken. B.K. Nehru and his wife were married according to Hindu rites in a ceremony performed by Professor Kalla of Delhi University who devised a sequence of rituals which, according to him, were the original Vedic rites of marriage. Though Hindu law prohibited a Hindu from marrying a non-Hindu, Hindu rites did not require a confession of faith and this meant that a non-Hindu could go through a Hindu ceremony. But such a marriage was not recognized by either British or Hindu law. Hence the illegality of both B.K. Nehru's and Indira's marriages.[25]

Like the B.K. Nehrus' wedding, Indira and Feroze's rites were performed by Professor Kalla and followed the earlier ceremony exactly except for a Sanskrit verse which Indira chose to recite because of its political resonance in 1942: 'If there are any people in the four quarters of the earth who venture to deprive us of our freedom, mark! Here I am, sword in hand, prepared to resist them to the last! I pray for the spreading light of freedom; may it envelop us on all sides!'[26] The ceremony took about two hours – short and simple by Indian standards.

Throughout, the aroma of incense filled the air, a priest chanted; the fire sizzled as clarified butter was poured into it from a silver spoon.

At first Indira sat on the veranda beside Nehru. Then with the *Kanya Dan* – the giving away of the daughter by the father – she crossed to the other side of the fire and sat next to Feroze. Feroze presented Indira with a bundle of clothing and she fed him a morsel of food – gestures that symbolized they would care for each other's physical needs. Then their wrists were bound together with a garland of flowers. The Pandit made the fire flame up with another libation of *ghee*, and Indira and Feroze rose for the *Sapt Padi* when they walked around the sacred fire seven times, repeating Sanskrit vows dedicating themselves to each other, their community and the world.[27] Indira put her foot on a stone, vowing rock-like firmness, and the Pandit placed the red *bindi*, worn by married Hindu women, on her forehead. The union of Indira and Feroze was now irrevocable. Flower petals rained down as family and friends surged forward to embrace and congratulate them.

In most respects the wedding had closely followed Hindu ritual and practice. But under his North Indian *sherwani* Feroze wore the thread of his Parsi ancestors.[28] He may have done so to placate his mother who had objected to the marriage but nevertheless attended the wedding. (Norvin Hein was even able to capture the camera-shy Rattimai Gandhi in his film.) But then again, wearing the Parsi holy thread may also have been Feroze's first gesture towards not being absorbed by the famous family he was marrying into.

The guests milled about the gardens of Anand Bhawan throughout the afternoon and then attended a dinner in the early evening. Norvin Hein caught highlights of the dinner in his film, including the long line of seated guests eating the simple fare of *chapattis* and green vegetables. These guests not only included scores of relatives, neighbours and friends, but also most of the Congress leadership (including Sarojini Naidu and her daughter Padmaja), countless local Congress workers and, incongruously, the daughter of the famous scientist Marie Curie, Eve.

A number of key people, however, were conspicuous by their absence at Indira's marriage. Her grandmother, Rajpati Kaul, who had been corresponding with Nehru for weeks about the wedding, fell ill and could not come.[29] Nor did Mahatma Gandhi who, on 26 March, was travelling to Delhi to meet Sir Stafford Cripps. Cripps himself is often said to have been a guest at the wedding, but in fact he visited Allahabad later. On the wedding day, he was in Delhi buying light summer clothing to survive the heat and awaiting Gandhi's arrival.[30] The Congress President, Maulana Azad, also missed the wedding because his train was delayed, but he reached Anand Bhawan in time for dinner.

Even on Indira's wedding day political activity was not suspended. The Congress leadership met in the ground-floor drawing room of Anand Bhawan shortly before the wedding dinner to prepare their strategy for the Cripps Mission. In 1942 Britain was in a weak negotiating position: its armed forces had suffered serious military reversals in the Far East and Churchill was coming under increasing pressure from the Americans to settle the India Question. Churchill had therefore dispatched Stafford Cripps, now Lord Privy Seal and a member of the War Cabinet, to Delhi in a desperate move to break the deadlock with Congress in the face of what seemed an imminent Japanese invasion. Churchill's offer was that if Congress was prepared to support the British war effort, India would be granted *full* dominion status *after* the war, or 'jam tomorrow in exchange for cooperation today'.[31]

Negotiations had begun on 25 March – the day before Indira and Feroze's wedding – and dragged on for a further eighteen days. During this time, Cripps – whom Indira and Nehru remembered from England – came to stay at Anand Bhawan for several days. A strict vegetarian (a fact which endeared him to Gandhi), Cripps found himself to be the only vegetarian in the household and there being very little fruit or vegetables in the Allahabad market, the Nehrus sent all the way to Kabul for melons and to Quetta for grapes.

Despite being eagerly anticipated, the Cripps Mission would turn out to be the 'non-event of 1942'.[32] Congress turned down the British offer, after deliberations, on 9 April, and made immediate independence a necessary condition for Indian support of the war. As Gandhi put it, the Cripps Mission amounted to a 'post-dated cheque on a failing bank'.

Immediately after their wedding, Indira and Feroze moved into a small rented house at 5 Fort Road in Allahabad. Feroze did not have a job and apparently at this stage money was not a problem. (And no doubt a substantial part of the wedding gifts came in the form of cash.) But Feroze did earn some money sporadically by writing occasional illustrated articles for newspapers and magazines, drawing on his own huge collection of photographs. He also seems to have sold some insurance policies, though he was never, as he is often described, an insurance salesman.

In late May, just as the ferocious heat was setting in, Indira and Feroze set off for a belated honeymoon in Kashmir. In Srinagar they were the guests of the charismatic Kashmir leader, Sheikh Abdullah. Indira wrote to Nehru on 3 June, 'we are having a glorious time'. She and Feroze took the road to Ladakh and visited Pahalgam and Sonemarg, 'the meadow of gold', high up among the glaciers and eagles. 'I am so full of the joy of discovering Kashmir,' Indira reported in her next letter. They undertook a four-day trek on horseback to the Kolahoi glacier, and when they returned to Srinagar they spent 'three days on a house-boat. Three glorious moonlit nights.' From Mohanmarg Indira wrote:

> Truly if there is a heaven, it must be this . . . There is nothing in Switzerland to compare with these flower-filled slopes, the sweet-scented breezes . . . running water that pour[s] over the soul the anodyne of forgetfulness and peace . . . Since I cannot bottle the beauty of Mohanmarg, I am sending you two little flowers as a token – forget-me-not and edelweiss. They both grow in abundance along with anemone, buttercups, Dutch slip-pers and a host of other so-called Alpine flowers.[33]

For two months in Kashmir, Indira and Feroze had no newspapers or wireless and received few letters. They felt utterly free and cut off from the world below – the world of politics and beyond it, the world of war. Their Kashmiri honeymoon became a touchstone in their turbulent marriage: an unfading, sustaining memory. Again and again in years to come – both with Feroze and on her own – Indira would return to Kashmir and try to regain paradise.

In July 1942 the Congress Working Committee met at Gandhi's Sevag-ram ashram and passed a resolution that the British government should surrender all political power in India without further delay. If they did not 'Quit India', Indians would refuse to support the British war effort. Quit India did not mean, however, that all British citizens – or even the British army – should depart from India immediately, but rather that the government must be handed over to the Indian people. A meeting of the All-India Congress Committee (AICC) to consider the resolution was scheduled for early August. Back in London, the War Cabinet watched these developments with alarm and authorized the Viceroy, Lord Linlithgow, to arrest, if necessary, the entire Congress leadership and initiate complete repression.

As soon as Indira and Feroze returned to Allahabad, they set off for the AICC meeting in Bombay. They were present, with hundreds of others, at Gowalia Tank on the evening of 8 August when Jawaharlal Nehru moved the Quit India resolution. It was resoundingly passed and the mass struggle for freedom, led by Gandhi, recommenced. As Gandhi stated at the meeting, it was now 'Do or Die'. Nehru called it the 'zero hour of the world'.

In Bombay Nehru, Indira and Feroze all stayed at the Hutheesings' flat at Sakina Mansions on Carmichael Road. On the night of 8 August they did not get home until ten. They had a late supper and then stayed up talking until 1 a.m. Hours later, at 5.15 a.m., on 9 August, Indira walked into Nehru's bedroom, gently woke him and said, 'The police have come.' Indira packed her father's suitcase while Nehru shaved and took a bath. Then they had a leisurely breakfast after which Nehru wrote a letter to his bank giving Indira control of his account. It was only then that he went into the sitting room and confronted the police sergeant who read out the arrest warrant and ordered Nehru and his brother-in-law, Raja Hutheesing, to accompany him.

Indira, Feroze and Krishna Hutheesing followed them outside and at first stood helplessly as Nehru and Hutheesing were bundled into taxis. Then they jumped into a friend's car and followed the taxis as they drove off 'in the cool of the early morning as the great city was waking'. When they reached Bombay's Victoria Station, the taxis swept ahead whilst Indira, Feroze and Krishna were stopped at the entrance by the police. There was a great deal of traffic and it became clear that a large number of Congressmen had been arrested. There was no way Indira and the others could get a last glimpse of Nehru and Hutheesing before they were shunted onto trains for where no one knew.[34]

Nehru was taken to Ahmadnagar Fort, a sixteenth-century Mughal fortress with a moat and a drawbridge which lay in a remote corner of Bombay Province. The British had long used it for detaining state prisoners because of its maximum security. Here the entire Congress Working Committee – the party high command – Asaf Ali, Abul Kalam

Azad, Shankarrao Deo, Narendra Dev, P.C. Ghose, J.B. Kripalani, Syed Mahmud, Harekrishna Mahtab, Govind Ballabh Pant, Vallabhbhai Patel and Pattabhi Sitaramayya, was incarcerated together. This would be Nehru's final and longest prison term, lasting two years and ten months. Gandhi, his wife Kasturba, his secretary, doctor and Sarojini Naidu were taken to the Aga Khan's palace in Poona – by comparison a luxurious jail.

For six weeks following these arrests, strikes and demonstrations engulfed much of the country. India seemed on the verge of insurrection and anarchy: telegraph and telephone wires were cut, public buildings were torched, railway lines, roads and bridges were blown up. This was the most serious threat to British rule since the Great Rebellion of 1857. By the end of 1942, over 60,000 people had been arrested. The Viceroy Lord Linlithgow – a man Nehru described as 'heavy of body and slow of mind, solid as a rock and with almost a rock's lack of awareness' – overcame stolidity and cabled Churchill. Undaunted by the Quit India disturbances, Churchill proclaimed, 'I have not become the King's first minister in order to preside over the liquidation of the British Empire.'[35]

On 10 August a warrant was issued for Feroze's arrest for his activities as a well-known Congress volunteer. To evade the police, he disguised himself as an Anglo-Indian soldier in a khaki uniform. But he still feared being recognized in Allahabad, so he hitched a ride into town with a lorry full of British and Anglo-Indian soldiers. Taken in by the disguise they warned Feroze that 'the damned natives would hack him to pieces if he was caught alone and unarmed'.[36] Several days later Feroze reached Lucknow where he joined the underground movement.

Later Feroze returned to Allahabad where he stayed at various Congress workers' homes and augmented his disguise with a moustache. Indira, meanwhile, ran Quit India activities at Anand Bhawan. By this time Nan Pandit had been arrested and sent to Naini Jail. Indira was left in the house with Nan Pandit's three daughters and their Chinese governess, Mrs Chew. Also resident at Anand Bhawan was Lal Bahadur Shastri (later Prime Minister of India), who was in hiding, locked in an upstairs room where Indira brought him meals at night on a tray. The servants were told that he was an ailing Nehru relative. Next door, Swaraj Bhawan was occupied by the army which kept Anand Bhawan under close surveillance. On the last day of August the police came for eighteen-year-old Chandralekha Pandit, who had just come of age and become active in Congress demonstrations in Allahabad. She was taken to join her mother at Naini Jail.

For the next month Indira and Feroze met sporadically, usually under cover of night, at friends' houses such as that of Indira's new Allahabad doctor, a woman just a few years older than Indira, named Vatsala Samant. Because there was still a warrant for his arrest, it was too risky for Feroze to come to Anand Bhawan. He was operating an illegal wireless transmitter for the Underground Congress Radio, organizing the telegraph wire-cutting operation in Allahabad and running the local civil disobedience movement.

In early September Indira was *lathi*-charged by the police when she participated in a nationalist flag-raising ceremony at Ewing Christian College where she and Kamala had first encountered Feroze eleven years earlier. Several days later she learnt that she would soon be arrested but vowed not to go tamely. A public meeting was arranged for 11 September at the Allahabad clock tower at which Indira planned to make a speech. Feroze also attended, in disguise, at a distance. More than 3,000 people gathered at the clock tower at 5 p.m. Shortly before Indira rose to speak, a truckload of police arrived. They were armed and when a sergeant raised his weapon near Indira, Feroze charged forward, shouting at him to lower his gun. The crowd surged to come to Feroze's and Indira's defence. The police closed in, restrained Indira, Feroze and a number of others, and bundled them into a van.[37]

That same evening Nan Pandit was in the women's barracks at Naini Jail when 'a bruised and battered Indu, with some of her clothes torn, arrived'.[38] Naini Jail, the British prison where Indira had visited her father so many times in the past, had an imposing, fortress-like gate, but inside it almost resembled a colonial gymkhana club, with elaborate gardens and fountains in the well-tended, spacious grounds. The women's barracks where Indira was confined, however, were small, hot and overcrowded. Six women occupied just one room with barred windows and a curtained-off latrine at the far end. They slept on mattresses on the stone floor. There was no privacy and a great deal of noise.[39]

But uncomfortable as it was, prison was a rite of passage for Indira. Virtually everyone she knew had served a jail term. As she said many years later, she had set her heart on going to prison. It was a culmination

or fulfilment: 'without that . . . something would have been incomplete
. . . I was glad to be arrested.'[40]

On 19 September at Naini Jail Feroze was sentenced to one year's
imprisonment and fined 200 rupees, in default of which he would have
to spend an additional six months in jail. Indira, however, was not
charged but instead detained without trial under the terms of the
Defence of India Act.

For the first six weeks in prison Indira was ill and ran a fever. She
also lost weight on the diet of mouldy *dhal* and rice. Then Indira, her
aunt and her cousin were upgraded to the status of A-class prisoners
and Indira's health improved on the richer fare that included eggs and
milk. She was also granted the privilege of being able to sleep out in
the prison yard to escape the heat.

Amazingly, given the circumstances, there was little, if any, friction
between Indira and her aunt in jail. Nan Pandit had been depressed
before her daughter and Indira joined her, but she cheered up after
their arrival. Indira and Lekha Pandit named their individual tiny parts
of the barrack. Lekha named hers 'Bien Venue' because she had a slight
view of the main gate. Her mother's, which had no view at all, was
'Wall View'. Indira exotically called her small space 'Chimborazo'. A
communal area, furnished with blue bedding brought from Anand
Bhawan, they named the 'Blue Drawing Room'. In fact, Indira and
Lekha named almost everything in the barrack: the jail cat was Mehitabel
and one of her kittens was Parvati. The lantern was Lucifer, and a
bottle of hair oil that had lost its top they called Rupert the Headless
Earl.

Nan, Lekha and Indira all kept jail diaries, but Indira wrote hers in
French so 'that people couldn't peek'. Indira was granted an interview
with Feroze once a fortnight until he was transferred to Fyzabad Prison
in March, and on Indira's twenty-fifth birthday, 19 November 1942,
they had their second interview. Lekha (whom Indira had been tutoring
in French in jail) stole a look at Indira's diary while the interview was
taking place and read, 'mon mari est ici and je suis très contente'.[41]

Indira found the lack of privacy and the constant noise in the barracks
trying. She was incarcerated with six other political prisoners and just
outside the prison yard women who had been convicted of theft, prosti-
tution and murder milled about, creating a terrific din. After a month
or so in jail, Indira announced that she neither wished to speak nor to

be spoken to before 5 p.m. each day, and thus carved out a solitude of sorts for herself in the midst of others.

This was disrupted, however, when a newly-born baby girl named Sarala joined the barracks. Sarala was the daughter of a political prisoner named Kalavati Mishra who was married to a Congress worker but was herself uneducated. Nan Pandit described her as 'the vaguest person I have ever known'. Indira decided that Kalavati was an irresponsible mother and decided to take charge of the baby. Soon she became deeply attached to and wanted to adopt the child. The baby's mother was surprisingly willing to give her up to Indira, but Nan Pandit intervened saying, 'you've just got married and you'll have children of your own. How will you feel about this child when you've had your own family?'[42]

In late November Nehru received a message at Ahmadnagar Fort from the United Provinces government informing him that Indira had been examined by the Civil Surgeon at Naini Jail who stated that 'her health was indifferent on the whole'.[43] This message was the first news he had had of his daughter since she had been imprisoned. They had not been allowed to communicate with one another and had no contact with the outside world. They were therefore not aware of the famine raging in Bengal or that Gandhi had embarked on a three-week fast in prison. In the early spring of 1943 they were finally given permission to reply to letters they received, but not to initiate correspondence.

On 25 March Indira was at last given permission to write to her father and broke the seven-month silence that had been imposed on them. 'All these months I have been waiting and waiting and was finally giving up all hope of hearing from you. And all that time, miles away, you were waiting too. You behind one set of walls and I behind another.'[44] She told him of the baby Sarala (now gone, as her mother had been released) and of her reading in jail – Balzac, Rousseau, John Stuart Mill and Thomas De Quincey's *The Confessions of an English Opium Eater*, as well as other 'old books . . . one is always meaning to read but somehow keeps on postponing'.[45] She had also been reading contemporary writers such as George Bernard Shaw, Upton Sinclair and the Chinese novelist Lin Yu-tang. In a later letter she described her 'A-class' diet and how she was sleeping outside now that the hot weather had set in. It was 'thrilling to wake up at night and see the

Great Bear sprawling comfortingly and protectively overhead'.[46]

Indira and Nehru now wrote to each other once a week (the maximum allowed) until Indira's release. All these letters were read by government censors and sometimes whole pages were blacked out – particularly if there were references to prison conditions or if either of them strayed beyond personal concerns.

As time passed in prison and her health improved, Indira's spirits rose and remained buoyant even when Feroze was transferred to Fyzabad Prison and her aunt and cousin, Lekha, were released. Indira had also gained weight. In the early spring of 1943 she weighed ninety-five pounds, twenty pounds more than she had at Les Frênes. In late April she wrote to Nehru that 'On *Nauroz*, I wore a new sari and was gay all on my ownsome.'[47] She was upset, however, when she had news from Sarala's mother to the effect that Sarala had lost weight, cried a lot and clearly missed all the doting Indira had lavished on her in prison. Now Indira bitterly regretted that Nan Pandit had persuaded her not to adopt the child. Sarala, she told her father, was such a lively, intelligent baby and now Indira was sure she would grow up neglected and turn 'into just such a bovine creature as her mother'.[48]

Indira was released from Naini Jail on 13 May 1943 after 243 days of imprisonment. On the drive across the Jumna to the Civil Lines of Allahabad and Anand Bhawan she was flooded with the stimuli of the outside world. Even in the extreme heat (with temperatures up to 117 degrees), 'dusty old Allahabad' looked 'green and beautiful'. 'The worst thing about jail,' she said many years later, 'was that everything was mud-coloured. After I got out, I couldn't get enough of colours, I had to touch everything I saw. After so much roughness, I had to feel soft textures.'[49] But while her senses feasted, Indira wilted in the heat. She continued to sleep outdoors at Anand Bhawan and she sent for the family barber who cut her hair into a short bob, as she had had it styled as a teenager in Europe. 'Everyone,' she wrote to her father, 'prophesied that I would look ghastly, but I decided on comfort and coolness at all costs of looks. Actually it has not turned out at all bad.'[50]

She visited Feroze at Fyzabad Prison on 21 May and reported to Nehru that he was being kept in isolation and 'was looking pulled down'. Another prisoner's wife saw that Indira was in tears when it came time to leave. On her return to Allahabad, Indira fell ill with a fever, cough and chest pains, and her Allahabad doctor, Vatsala Samant, admitted her to hospital for four days. After she was discharged, she remained feverish and found it difficult to shake the cough. Nor did a visit from Sarala and her mother cheer her. Indira wrote Nehru that her 'worst fears' had come true: the little girl had shrunk back to her skinny smallness 'instead of getting rounder and fatter as all babies should. She didn't even look intelligent as she used to.' Indira arranged for the mother to attend a school, but had little hope that the baby would get more attention and stimulation from her.[51] Meanwhile, Indira and Nan Pandit were served with a government internment order to go to Khali, the Pandit's home in the hills near Almora, and remain there until further notice. They would have gladly gone there – where it was much cooler – if the government had not ordered it. Under the circumstances, they both refused. They were about to be rearrested when Indira was examined again by the Civil Surgeon and her arrest warrant withdrawn on the grounds of ill health. (Nan Pandit, however, was sent back to jail.) In June Indira went to Bombay where she consulted medical specialists and was x-rayed. Feroze was released from Fyzabad Jail on 10 July and immediately went to Panchganj, south of Poona, where Indira was holidaying with her former school teachers, the Vakils. Indira and Feroze spent the rest of the summer at Panchganj, returning to Allahabad in late August.

By this time Nan Pandit had been released from jail again and was living at Anand Bhawan whilst her husband Ranjit Pandit remained in prison in Bareilly. Though Nan and Indira had managed to get along in the cramped women's barrack at Naini, they found it impossible to remain on warm or easy terms in the large family home. There was constant tension and periodic flare-ups. One day, without warning, Nan Pandit announced to Indira that she planned to move house. She also wrote to Nehru of her decision. Far away in Ahmadnagar Fort, when Nehru got her letter he was 'bowled over'.[52] He entreated his sister to reconsider. 'Have we lost the capacity even to pull together and accommodate ourselves in the petty affairs of life, and if so what of the larger undertakings to which we have allied ourselves so intimately that they have become a part of our being?' Nehru felt that Nan's departure from Anand Bhawan would be a public demonstration of disharmony in the family. He invoked the memory of Motilal and the teeming household over which his father had presided. He implored his sister not to reduce Anand Bhawan to 'a symbol of emptiness'.[53]

Nehru was so upset at the prospect of his sister leaving the family home that he prevailed on Indira to write to her aunt, begging her to stay. Indira obediently sent her a note saying, 'I do wish you were not going . . . this is a plea to you to reconsider your decision, please?'[54] But Nan Pandit was adamant. In early November 1943, she moved to a small, rented house in Allahabad, leaving Indira and Feroze in possession of Anand Bhawan which they then worked hard to get 'spick and span' again and make 'alive and beautiful'. Indira cleared out, aired and repainted inside and Feroze took charge of the garden, restoring it to the glory of the days of Motilal Nehru.

In November, Nehru – still in prison – decided to make his will. Though he was now fifty-four, he had never considered doing this before, in part because his life had involved, in his own phrase 'few encumbrances', and he doubted whether 'there will be anything at all to dispose of at the time of my death'. 'For this reason also,' he explained, 'I did not at any time insure my life.'[55] Nehru's indifference to money – and his ineptness in handling it – were both ingrained in his personality. His attitude towards finances had not changed, but he was now worried about Indira's future. 'Her marriage,' as he wrote in his diary, 'which is not strictly legal under the present law, might create difficulties.'[56] He wanted to make sure that she would inherit from him. So in the will he drafted in prison Nehru stipulated that 'my daughter and only child, Indira Priyadarshini, married to Feroze Gandhi, is my sole heir and I bequeath to her all my property, assets and belongings.' Not that he had a great deal to leave her. There was only the house, Anand Bhawan, and its contents, a few investments and shares (though these had been much depleted since Motilal Nehru's death) and a small amount of capital (also greatly reduced).

Ensuring that Indira was his sole heir was the *raison d'être* for Nehru's will. Given the tension between Indira and Nan Pandit, Nehru may have feared a legal struggle between them after his death. But now that he had embarked on his will, he included other provisions, two of which later became significant. He left nothing to his sisters, but he stated that Anand Bhawan 'should always be open to' them and that they could 'stay there whenever they like and for as long as they like'. He also unequivocally stated that he was not to have a funeral involving Hindu rites: 'I do not want any religious ceremonies performed for me after my death.'[57]

On New Year's Day 1944 Indira was ill in bed. 'Nothing special,' she wrote to Nehru, 'just losing weight and looking and feeling awful.' (In fact, she was pregnant though she did not as yet know it.) A frantic trunk call came through to her from Nan Pandit in Lucknow where her husband, Ranjit, was now in hospital. He had fallen gravely ill in Bareilly Jail and the prison authorities had belatedly released him to Lucknow hospital. Indira roused herself and set off for Lucknow with Feroze the next day.

Two weeks later Ranjit Pandit died, aged forty-four. It was an unnecessary death, directly attributable to the poor conditions and treatment he had received in jail. By this time Indira and Feroze had returned to Allahabad and his widow, Nan, was left utterly on her own to cope with this catastrophe. Her two oldest daughters were now at university in America; her sister was in Bombay and Nehru was in prison. She brought Ranjit's body back to Allahabad where there was an emotional rapprochement with Indira and Feroze – both of whom were devastated by Ranjit's death. They gave up all their other activities to help and console Nan, who for once in her life, seemed utterly vulnerable and crushed. As she herself put it, without Indira and Feroze, 'I would not have been able to get through.'[58]

In the aftermath of her uncle's death and in the early months of pregnancy, Indira fell apart both physically and psychologically, and was 'on the verge of breaking down completely'. She went to bed and did not write to her father until late in February and then she found it difficult to explain her collapse: 'I can only analyse it as utter, utter weariness, so tired that my mind and my body refused to work, so tired that I could not rest, could not sleep, could not eat . . . didn't actually feel alive at all . . . It was as if a terrible blackness or nothingness had stolen over me.' It was a relief to discover that she was pregnant and ascribe at least part of her breakdown to that. She told Nehru that her doctor, Vatsala Samant, wanted her to go to Bombay and put herself under the care of Dr N.A. Purandare, a well-known gynaecologist and obstetrician, and live with Krishna Hutheesing until the baby was born in late August or early September.[59]

Ever since she had been a patient at Les Frênes, Indira was repeatedly advised not to have children. But as she said many years later, 'I always wanted to have children – if it had been up to me, I would have had eleven. It was my husband who only wanted two.' Doctors in Switzerland, London and India, however, told her 'not to have even one'. This diagnosis, she said, 'provoked me, it infuriated me'.[60] As was often the case in her life, obstruction only hardened Indira's resolve. Her instincts, with this pregnancy at any rate, were sound. After a shaky start, she sailed through it.

Nehru had used the danger of pregnancy as part of his argument against Indira's marriage. But when she told him her news, he was relatively sanguine and certainly happy for her. He wrote in his prison diary, 'I am glad she is going to have a baby, though this must involve a great strain on her and the risks are obvious . . . But she loves children and I think she has rather fretted at the possibility of her not having any because of the danger to her health . . . The risk has to be taken with all possible precautions.'[61]

In March Indira went to stay with the Hutheesings at their flat in Bombay. (Feroze remained behind in Allahabad to oversee local Congress activities and run Anand Bhawan.) When the summer heat descended on the city, Indira made extended visits with the Hutheesings and the Vakils to Matheran (a small hill station near Bombay), and Mahabaleshwar where Feroze came and joined her for a while. She also went to Poona where she saw Gandhi who had just been released from his imprisonment at the Aga Khan's Palace. Indira wrote Nehru how 'when I arrived he [Gandhi] was sitting spinning and gave me a big grin and the usual whack – only much milder. He was looking very pale and weak and tired.'[62] Gandhi's wife, Kasturba, had died just three months earlier and he himself was recovering from a severe illness. He was now almost seventy-five, weakened by his imprisonments and fasts over the years, and desolate over Kasturba's death.

During the spring of 1944, Nehru, still imprisoned in Ahmadnagar Fort, began writing what would be his last work, *The Discovery of India*. This is the one book of his that we know Indira read with care because she corrected the proofs for her father. It had begun life as a second volume of autobiography and contained a highly personal chapter about Nehru's relationship with Kamala and her death in Switzerland. But the book evolved into something less literally autobiographical and quite revealing. *The Discovery of India* is both a nationalist history of India and, as Sunil Khilnani observes, a work of 'self-making'. In it Nehru describes the voyage of discovery whereby he is transformed from a Western-educated 'man who carried with him the burden of an anglicized past' into an Indian.[63]

This process provides the underlying narrative of the book, but its significance for Indira lay in Nehru's vision of India. Though Nehru romanticized it and relied heavily on British orientalist analyses, he saw the history of India – and by implication its future – as accommodative, integrative, and inclusive: 'an ancient palimpsest on which layer upon layer of thought and reverie had been inscribed, and yet no succeeding layer has completely hidden or erased what has been written previously'. There was an 'essential unity' of India 'that no political division, no disaster or catastrophe' had ever destroyed.[64] It was this catholic conception of India and its paradoxical underlying 'oneness' that Nehru, above all, bequeathed to his daughter.

While Nehru was writing *The Discovery of India*, Indira – now six months pregnant – was working her way through a great pile of books on child care. She was particularly impressed with A.S. Neill's *The Problem Child* and his account of his famous 'free school', Summerhill, in Suffolk. Indira wrote to her father that 'the way Neill writes makes this method sound the only possible way to deal with children ... Neill says that the child if not forced to learn ... may start learning later but will learn faster and with more lasting benefit. He says the child must not have any kind of discipline thrust on it.' Nehru wrote back and disputed the suitability of Neill's method for raising children who were not difficult or troubled and urged Indira to remember that not only must a child be happy, it must also live 'as a social being who can live at peace and cooperation with others'.[65]

At the end of June Indira had her seven-month pregnancy check-up and began to investigate suitable hospitals and nursing homes in Bombay. By now she was seeing her doctor every fortnight. In between she often popped back to Poona or Mahabaleshwar to escape the summer heat. Her health was better than it had been in years; she felt energetic, happy and hopeful as the time for her confinement drew near. In the eighth month she switched to another obstetrician named Dr Vithal Nagesh Shirodkar who promised to deliver the baby himself. (Dr Purandare had refused to give this guarantee.)

Feroze came to Bombay in mid-August to be with Indira for the baby's birth. Early on the evening of the 19th, Indira began a letter to Nehru, but she was interrupted by a visitor who dropped by to chat with her and Feroze. At 3 a.m. the next morning she woke up and wanted to finish the letter to her father, but was afraid of waking Feroze, and so she lay in bed as the night ebbed, listening to her body.

By dawn, she knew the baby was on the way. She woke Feroze, and in the cool of the early morning, they and Krishna Hutheesing drove to the nearby Belle Vue Nursing Home. Dr Shirodkar was summoned by telephone. Despite being in the early stages of labour, Indira felt hungry and began eating a breakfast of toast. Then Dr Shirodkar arrived. After a remarkably easy and short labour, a six-and-a-half pound baby with a great shock of black hair, a boy (as Indira had predicted), entered the world at 8.22 a.m.

TEN

Things Fall Apart

IN PRISON, Nehru mulled over names for his grandson and sent a list of suggestions to Indira, but for a long time they could not agree on anything.[1] Thus it was 'the babe' (as everyone called him) who slept through his first audience with Gandhi in mid-September in Bombay before his parents took him home to Allahabad. He was still 'the babe' or 'the wee one' at the end of October when he was two months old. Nehru wrote to his sister, Nan Pandit, that if the family did not decide soon 'we shall have to call [him] . . . the Nameless or the One with Innumerable Names'.[2] To Indira, he suggested, 'I think you should stick to Rajiva Ratna [Indira's preference] . . . As a second name you can have Birjees if you like . . . What about adding "Nehru" as an additional name? I do not mean that he should have a double-barrelled name – Nehru-Gandhi. That sounds silly . . . But just as a separate name.'[3]

It was a revealing request, though not a 'dynastic' one. As Nehru himself put it, 'it is really a matter of sentiment' – the wish of a man without sons to see his name carried on.[4] Indira duly recorded her first-born's name in his baby book as Rajiva Ratna Birjees Nehru Gandhi. Rajiva means 'lotus' as does 'Kamala' and Ratna means 'gem' as do the first three syllables of 'Jawaharlal'.[5] Three out of five of the baby's names, then, derived from the Nehru side of the family. Birjees apparently came out of the blue. Feroze – the only person who does not seem to have had a voice in the long-drawn-out baby-naming saga – contributed, of course, the memorable surname. Almost too memorable in fact: outside of India, Indira and Rajiv Gandhi have often been referred to – even by otherwise well-informed people – as the daughter and grandson of Mahatma Gandhi.

Feroze, to his growing discomfort, was now finding himself a somewhat peripheral member of the family. Before marriage, he had worried about being absorbed by the Nehrus. During their wedding ceremony, Feroze had presented Indira with a bundle of clothing to symbolize the material care he would provide her. But he and Indira had had to give up their house at 5 Fort Road when they were imprisoned in 1942 and ever since their release the following year they had lived at Anand Bhawan. After Rajiv was born, Feroze's only employment was working for the Congress Party's legal aid committee in Allahabad and Lucknow, engaged in relief work and arranging financial and legal assistance for imprisoned Congress workers and their families. For this he received 100 rupees a month out of his father-in-law's account. Nehru also gave Indira and Feroze a gift of 1,000 rupees. But even though they were living in the Nehru family home, they still had difficulty managing financially, and Indira, at least, was uneasy about being supported by her father.

Nehru wrote reassuringly from prison, 'do not hesitate to draw upon my account whenever Feroze thinks it necessary', and again because Indira remained anxious, 'It is rather silly of you to go on worrying about money matters . . . I have told you to draw upon my account . . . and surely I have not got to repeat this on every . . . occasion.'[6] Nehru's relaxed attitude towards money was in character. Before Indira and Feroze had married, Feroze's sister, Tehmina Gandhi, had, in her own words, warned Nehru that 'we were not at all wealthy people and . . . that Feroze had no fixed income of his own and I did not know how he could support a wife'. Nehru said he was not worried about his prospective son-in-law's lack of resources. Tehmina, then, tried to warn Feroze himself. She told him 'not to live in a fool's paradise', and that before marrying, he 'should wait till he had some stable income by which he could support a wife, and specially one like Indira'.[7] But Feroze was as nonchalant about money as his father-in-law – a fact that Indira did not really grasp until after she married him.

Nehru's cavalier attitude reflected his asceticism. Feroze, however, liked to live well. He was not materialistic, but he drank and smoked, consumed good food with relish and was intrigued by expensive mechanical and electrical gadgets and cars. Good Congressman though he was, there was nothing austere about Feroze. In this his temperament was quite unlike Indira's as well as his father-in-law's. He was loud, extroverted, boastful, emotional, quick to lose his temper but equally hasty in making amends after an explosion. He had a loud booming laugh which exploded when he cracked ribald jokes. Indira, of course, was reserved, cool and a great holder of grudges. Inevitably, there was friction between them and this was exacerbated by Indira's money worries. It was clear to Indira's cousins, the Pandit daughters, that there were strains in the marriage as early as 1943.[8] And added to these, of course, was the fact that Indira and Feroze did not have a settled domestic existence. Politics invaded and disrupted their marriage just as it always had Indira's life.

On 28 March 1945 Nehru was transferred from Ahmadnagar Fort to Bareilly Central Prison in the United Provinces. He travelled, under guard, from one to the other by train via Allahabad where he was confined for a day in his 'old home' Naini Central Prison. This meant that Indira and Feroze were able to see Nehru fleetingly at the Naini prison gate. They had not laid eyes on each other in nearly three years – since the morning of 9 August 1942 when Nehru was arrested in Bombay. In his prison diary Nehru wrote, at 'Naini Gate there was Indu clad in a shalwar . . . standing some distance away! . . . I went to her – was with her a few seconds – and then had to enter the police car'.[9] The day after this brief encounter, Indira wrote to her father how overwhelmed she had been to see him again – even at a distance and despite the fact they had only been able to exchange a few words. She greatly regretted not bringing Rajiv, for Nehru had not yet seen his grandson. She also told her father how distressed she was that he looked 'so thin . . . [and] shrunken'.[10]

The following month, Indira and eight-month-old Rajiv went to Kashmir with Rajiv's *ayah* and a Danish woman named Anna Ornsholt who had been the Pandit daughters' governess and would later be the same for Indira's children. Feroze stayed behind in Allahabad to look after Anand Bhawan and continue doing Congress relief work. Indira and Rajiv stopped in Lahore for several days and then went on to Srinagar where they stayed with the Hutheesings in a house on Gupkar Road with 'a most gorgeous view of the whole snow range'. Then they settled at the family home of Indira's uncle, Brijlal Nehru (B.K. Nehru's father), who was financial adviser to the Maharaja of Kashmir.

Indira had not been to Kashmir since her honeymoon three years earlier, and as before, she immediately succumbed to its magic. Far away, on the searing plains in Bareilly Central Prison, Nehru tried to follow his daughter imaginatively to the paradise lying in the shadow of the Himalayas:

> What flowers are blooming, what fruits hang from the over-burdened branches? ... The lotus must still be in bud ... It blossoms on Dal Lake in July ... Cherries will soon be out and apricots and apples and peaches ... Is the Dal Lake much the same as ever or have the fancy boulevards made much difference? What birds chirp and sing in the trees? I think of all these scenes treasured in memory's chambers, but even more I visualize the higher valleys leading up to the snows and glaciers, with their ice-cold brooks gurgling and rushing down to the vale below.[11]

Meanwhile, down in the world below, the war was in its death throes. On the afternoon of 30 April, in his underground bunker in Berlin, Hitler put a gun in his mouth and pulled the trigger. Hitler's Indian collaborator, Subhas Chandra Bose – who had been so close to Kamala and Indira nine years earlier in Switzerland – lost the war too. On 3 May Rangoon fell and Bose's Indian National Army – recruited from Indian troops captured by the Japanese – surrendered. Bose himself and some of his followers fled to Bangkok and Formosa. On 7 May the German forces unconditionally surrendered.

In Britain the Labour Party won the general election on 26 July 1945. Clement Attlee – who had been a member of the boycotted Simon Commission that visited India in 1928 – now replaced Churchill as Prime Minister. In India there was rejoicing over the Labour victory because it was clear that a Labour government would grant independence to India with far greater alacrity than a Conservative one, though the Viceroy, Archibald Wavell, was exaggerating when he sourly predicted that Labour would 'obviously [be] bent on handing over India to their Congress friends as soon as possible'. The end of the war became inevitable when the atomic bomb was dropped on Hiroshima on 6 August. After an interval of three days the lethal mushroom cloud bloomed again over Nagasaki. Nine days later Bose died in an air crash at Taipei, shortly before Vice-Admiral Lord Louis Mountbatten accepted the surrender of the Japanese in Southeast Asia and Singapore.

But as was the case with Hitler, a myth emerged that Bose had miraculously survived, was living abroad, and that he would return and reveal himself. The reality was the war was finally over and this, in turn, spelled the end of British India.

In early June 1945 Nehru was transferred from Bareilly Prison to Almora Jail, where he had been incarcerated ten years earlier when Kamala was languishing in the Bhowali sanatorium. On the 15th he was finally released after nearly three years of imprisonment. All prominent Congress leaders across India were set free, and the day before their release Viceroy Wavell announced that a provisional government was to be formed, all members of which were to be Indians except for the Commander-in-Chief and Viceroy.

Indira was still in Kashmir when she heard on the radio, late in the afternoon on 15 June, that her father was about to be released. She booked a seat on the next train and departed almost immediately for Allahabad, leaving Rajiv in Kashmir with her uncle's wife Rameshwari Nehru. Both Indira and Feroze were at Anand Bhawan to receive Nehru when he arrived home like a modern-day Odysseus after his long imprisonment. Indira then rushed off to Bombay with her father for a Congress meeting, but shortly afterwards came down with the flu and began running a fever. When she got back to Anand Bhawan she had to spend most of the time in bed. She was not well enough to return to Kashmir until the second week of July when she was greatly upset to find that Rajiv too had been unwell and 'gone very thin' and lost all his 'sturdiness' during her absence. She immediately took him to Pahalgam where she hoped the 'lovely pine-laden air' would build up both of them.[12]

Nehru joined them in Kashmir after the first Simla Conference of nationalist leaders was held in July 1945. This summit proved an utter failure at reconciling Congress and Muslim League demands, with the result that if independence now seemed certain, an undivided India looked like a chimera. Nehru came up to Kashmir from Simla to see Indira and Rajiv, but he was not alone and he was not merely on holiday. He, Maulana Azad and the Northwest Frontier Province Congressman, Khan Abdul Ghaffar Khan, had been invited by the Kashmiri leader, Sheikh Abdullah, to attend a meeting of his political party, the National Conference, which opposed both the Muslim League and the autocratic Hindu ruler of Kashmir, Maharajah Hari Singh.

Indira had first met Sheikh Abdullah when she and Feroze stayed with him during their honeymoon in 1942, but it was only now that she came to know well the forceful, towering (six feet tall to Nehru's five feet four), 'Lion of Kashmir', as he was called. Like Nehru, Sheikh Abdullah was a socialist and a secularist. He espoused a notion of *kashmiriyat* – a common Kashmiri identity that transcended religious allegiances – and had plans for 'a new Kashmir' that incorporated radical measures such as land redistribution once the oppressive Dogra ruler, Hari Singh, had been overthrown. When Nehru arrived in Kashmir, Sheikh Abdullah arranged for Nehru, Indira, Azad and himself to participate in a magnificent river boat procession – a traditional Srinagar ceremonial. A foretaste of the troubles to come occurred, however, when hostile members of the opposition party, the Muslim Conference, staged a demonstration and at least one of Sheikh Abdullah's followers was killed.[13]

Sheikh Abdullah was also the host at baby Rajiv's naming ceremony on his first birthday, after which Indira left Rajiv again with Rameshwari Nehru while she and her father went trekking in the Kashmir mountains for ten days. Except for guides and servants, she and Nehru were finally alone together, and in the place they both loved most in the world. They were not only alone, but utterly cut off as they trekked, camped, ate simple food over an open fire and slept in tents under a sky spangled with the constellations they both used to pick out when they slept outdoors in prison.

In a letter to Nan Pandit, Nehru described how he and Indira crossed the Yamber Pass connecting the Liddar and Sindh valleys.

> We had to cross fifty yards or more of sheer precipice, covered with ice and snow, with an enormous drop of 4,000 feet if one slipped. A number of Gujars [guides] cut a way for us through the ice and we marched across. It turned out to be easier than it looked, as with most things in life. Yet when I looked back it looked formidable enough and I felt thankful that Indu and I were on the other side ... Then we watched the riding ponies and the pack ponies being led across. I turned almost sick at the sight for at every moment I expected one of them to roll down the precipice ... I wondered how I would have felt if I had to see in this way Indu or anyone else dear to me crossing that almost vertical slope. I don't think I could have stood it.

This episode recalls Nehru's nearly fatal descent into a crevasse while trekking in Kashmir on his honeymoon. The appeal of Kashmir was not merely its sublime beauty. There was also something deeply exciting in the danger one courted there. But in his letter to his sister, Nehru rounded off his account of crossing the Yamber Pass on a humorous note. 'I wish I had a camera to take a picture . . . of Indu and me crossing; that would have established our reputation as intrepid mountaineers. That reputation would have been a bogus one, but then most reputations are bogus.'[14] To Gandhi, Nehru wrote that he and Indira had covered more than a hundred miles during their Kashmiri trek, reached altitudes of up to 14,000 feet, crossed dangerous passes, camped in remote river valleys and returned 'elated over it all'.[15]

Indira and Rajiv returned to Allahabad in September. The next month she came down with the mumps and had to be isolated in a ground-floor room of Anand Bhawan. She did not see her son or husband, or anyone else bar the servants, for several weeks. She was miserable and low. She had been prone to bouts of illness – including 'the old trouble', tuberculosis – since she had returned to India in 1941. Everyone worried, yet no one talked about this. Whilst she had the mumps, she read the proofs of *The Discovery of India* for Nehru who was away campaigning across the country for the upcoming central and provincial assembly elections, to be held in each state, between November 1945 and March 1946. Nehru, in fact, was barely at home during this period.

In the elections, Congress won in every state except for Bengal in the east, and Sind and the Punjab in the west. But Jinnah's Muslim League also performed well. Britain, like Congress, wanted an undivided independent India. In early 1946, Stafford Cripps, despite the failure of the Cripps Mission four years earlier, was dispatched again to India, heading his three-man Cabinet Mission to devise a scheme for a federal India. Because of the enmity between Congress and the Muslim League, and Jinnah's intransigence, the ensuing negotiations were arduous and largely unproductive. The 'three Magi' of the Cabinet Mission, as the Viceroy called them, made numerous concessions, but as Wavell described it, 'the frankincense of goodwill, the myrrh of honeyed words, the gold of promises – have produced little. Indian politicians are not babes even if they do wear something like swaddling clothes'.[16]

In May Nehru became Congress President and there was another confrontational conference in Simla of Cabinet Mission members and Congress and Muslim League leaders. The usual suspects gathered again and behaved much as they had before. Jinnah refused to shake Maulana

Azad's hand and called him a Hindu stooge. Nehru did the negotiating for Congress, though Gandhi, who had come to Simla on a special train with 'fifteen whey-faced disciples', was a major player behind the scenes. Stafford Cripps negotiated secretly with his co-vegetarian, Gandhi, with no effect. As Wavell put it, 'I am not ... persuaded that C[ripps] ... led G[andhi] up to the altar. I believe it more likely that G has led C down the garden path.'[17] By mid-May nothing had been agreed or achieved and the futile conference ground to a halt. What was now abundantly clear was that India almost certainly would be partitioned. For Nehru and Gandhi, especially, this was a heartbreaking prospect.

Nevertheless, on 2 September 1946 the first step in the transfer of power was taken when the new Interim Government of India was sworn in, headed by Nehru, who now held all the powers of a prime minister of a dominion though his official position was vice-president of the Executive Council. Nehru also took the Foreign Affairs portfolio. Indira wrote to her father from Allahabad the day before he took the oath of office:

> Darling Papu,
>   How I long to be in Delhi at this moment to witness this, a triumph for you personally but even more so for the great organization you represent. I shall be with you in mind and spirit [on 2 September], wishing you well in this new task you have undertaken. May you be able to wipe out the many disgraceful evils existing in the government of the country, so that India may really march towards freedom and true Swaraj. *Jai Hind.*
>   With all my love to you, Indu.[18]

But fear as well as hope took hold as independence approached. The previous month, on 16 August, Jinnah had called for a Direct Action Day 'to achieve Pakistan'. A Muslim *hartal* was called in Calcutta where rioting and looting broke out. At the end of three days of chaos, at least 5,000 were left dead and 15,000 injured. The 'Great Calcutta Killings' heralded the communal carnage that would engulf India over the next two years.

During the summer of 1946, Indira discovered she was pregnant again. She and Feroze were then leading a relatively quiet existence together in Allahabad. Years later, Indira said that what she wanted most at this time was a private, domestic life with her husband and children. Independence was on the horizon and after that, she assumed, she could be unhandcuffed from history and in charge of her own destiny. For the first time also there was the prospect of financial independence and stability. Feroze had been appointed to his first real job as director of the *National Herald*, the Lucknow-based newspaper that Nehru had founded in 1937 as an organ of Congress and the freedom struggle. Rather than submit to censorship, the *Herald* had suspended publication in 1942 at the outset of the Quit India movement. It started up again in September 1946 with the establishment of the Interim Government, and Nehru arranged Feroze's appointment as managing director with a salary of 600 rupees a month.

In November, Indira and Feroze moved to Lucknow and rented a bungalow in the Huzratganj area, the only drawback of which was that it had Mutiny graves in the garden. Feroze was an expert amateur carpenter and he designed and made beautifully crafted furniture with which they furnished the house. Indira, with her subdued good taste, decorated it, and Feroze, who was also a gifted gardener, transformed the Mutiny graveyard with flowers and shrubs. Everything seemed to be in place for a perfect married life: Feroze was finally a breadwinner, they had a perfect house, one adorable child and another on the way.

The *National Herald* job had obviously been created for Feroze, and initially Nehru was happy with his son-in-law's performance. Six months after Feroze's instalment at the newspaper, Nehru reported 'there is peace in the *Herald* office and cooperation between the editorial, managerial and press departments'.[19] This state of affairs, however, did not last for long. Not everyone was as pleased with Feroze as Nehru was. Feroze was neither a journalist nor a businessman. M. Chalapathi Rau, the *Herald*'s editor, years later complained of his 'ignorance, inexperience and adventurism'. And according to Rau, Feroze ran the paper in a high-handed, impetuous way.[20]

But it was the *Herald*'s financial standing that caused the most concern. Soon after Feroze took over the *Herald*, it began to run up a large overdraft which alarmed Nehru who wrote to Feroze about it. In addition, Feroze himself apparently pocketed an interest-free loan of 200,000 rupees made to the *Herald* by Maharajah Pratap Singh of Baroda. When this became known, Feroze sent a panicky but enigmatic telegram to Nehru's secretary in Delhi: 'Please meet Laxman personally *stop* nearly rupees forty thousand locked up due to their enquiries & no confirmation *stop* you must help else sunk *stop* wire reply immediately.' Feroze never repaid the loan and when a trust was established some years later to oversee the financial management of the *Herald*, the Maharaja transferred the loan to the trust as a donation.[21]

Then there was the complicated business of a New Delhi edition of the *Herald* which Nehru was eager to see Feroze establish. Feroze ordered some expensive printing equipment from America for the projected Delhi edition with the help of the United Commercial Bank. The machinery duly arrived but remained crated up on the Bombay docks for years while demurrage and bank interest mounted. No place could be found to house the equipment in Delhi. Feroze ultimately failed to start up the Delhi edition of the *Herald*, but it was later established by the manager who succeeded him.[22] Nehru was too preoccupied with national and international matters to closely monitor Feroze's management of the *Herald*, but Indira did and it soon became a matter of great concern to her and a further source of friction in their marriage.

Just a month after moving to Lucknow with Feroze, Indira returned to Delhi to stay with her father at his government bungalow on York Road. Ostensibly she went to help Nehru set up house as head of the Interim Government and to have her baby in Delhi which had better medical facilities than Lucknow. But she also wanted to put some distance between herself and Feroze. Soon after they had settled in Lucknow, Indira began to realize that Feroze was involved with various women there. She was particularly incensed by his relationship with her younger cousin, Lekha Pandit, who was now a cub reporter on the *Herald*. Feroze, in fact, had secured the job for Lekha, and according to her sister, Nayantara, he was 'too fond' of her and Indira was 'extremely jealous'.[23] Tongues wagged and Lekha left the *Herald*. It was a painful episode for Indira and in the small, parochial atmosphere of Lucknow, something of a scandal.

But the most serious of Feroze's liaisons was with a young Muslim woman who was the daughter of a Lucknow politician named Ali Zaheer. Feroze met her in Lucknow, but she actually worked in New Delhi for All India Radio. Unlike his other affairs, before and after this one, Feroze's relationship with the Zaheer woman was serious. With his other girlfriends, Feroze remained 'unattached', and Indira – if she knew about his philandering – looked the other way. But Feroze fell in love with the Zaheer woman and told her that he wanted to divorce Indira and marry her. She loved him and informed her father of Feroze's intentions.

Ali Zaheer was a Congress Minister in the United Provinces and he wrote with alarm to Nehru, whereupon Nehru sent for Feroze. Feroze was no coward; he told Nehru that he wanted to divorce Indira and took the blame for the breakdown of their marriage. Nehru then summoned Indira and asked her what she wanted to do. Indira made it clear that she did not want to divorce. At this point, Nehru decided to do what he could to keep the marriage intact. He confided in his close friend Rafi Ahmed Kidwai and asked him to intervene and put a stop to and forestall the scandal of Feroze's affair. Kidwai dutifully went to Lucknow and first reassured Ali Zaheer that nothing would come of the relationship between Feroze Gandhi and his daughter. Kidwai then persuaded Feroze to give up the woman, which, after a struggle, Feroze very reluctantly did. And so Indira ultimately won this round. But it was a hollow victory. The affair ended and the Zaheer woman soon married someone else, but the way in which Feroze was coerced into remaining with Indira added yet more rancour to their marriage.

Not surprisingly, Indira began to spend longer and longer periods away from Lucknow. In Delhi Nehru needed her. Years later, when her biographer Dom Moraes asked her about her life as Nehru's housekeeper and hostess, Indira said, 'Obviously I had to do it because my father was doing more important work than my husband.'[24] She explained to someone else that 'I felt it was my duty to help [my father]. It was also . . . important for the country that someone look after him. And there was no one else but me.'[25] But living with Nehru in Delhi also suited Indira's own needs because it gave her a reprieve from her marital difficulties. Inevitably, Feroze felt humiliated by his wife's prolonged absences while she was living with her father. And so he sought consolation elsewhere.

It was a vicious circle. And yet for the next five years – until Feroze became an MP and moved to Delhi – Indira continued to commute between New Delhi and Lucknow with the children. Nehru obviously knew that there were strains in the marriage and though he is often accused of contributing to them by demanding Indira's presence in New Delhi, this was far from the case. In June 1947, for example, Nehru wrote to Nan Pandit that 'I want very much to see Indu settle down for the time being in Lucknow. Feroze must carry on with the *Herald*, and it is right that Indu should live there for a good part of the year.'[26] At no point in their marriage were Indira and Feroze ever officially separated, but as time passed they spent less and less time together. In the late fifties, when Nayantara Pandit Sahgal's own marriage was disintegrating, Nehru told his niece to either end or mend the situation, saying 'Don't be like Indu, leaving the issue unresolved for all time. She is neither married nor separated.'[27]

On 13 December 1946 Indira and Feroze were staying in Delhi at Nehru's York Road house because their baby was almost due. Lady Cripps dropped by late in the afternoon and asked Indira to go shopping with her to buy a Kashmiri shawl. Indira was feeling weak and exhausted, but she felt she could not disappoint Lady Cripps and they drove off to the Kashmiri craftsmen in Old Delhi. It was a chilly evening and when she returned home, Indira went directly to bed. The house was crowded because the Hutheesings and other relatives were visiting. Perhaps because she was not feeling well in the last stages of her pregnancy – or because their relations were strained – Indira and Feroze were not sharing a bedroom, and Feroze, to his annoyance, had to sleep in a tent out in the garden.[28]

At three in the next morning, Krishna Hutheesing was woken up by a maid who told her that 'Mrs Gandhi is not feeling well.' She went to Indira's room and found that labour had begun. She sent the servant to wake up Feroze in his tent and then, without waking Nehru, Krishna and Feroze drove Indira to Willingdon Nursing Home. Krishna rang Indira's English obstetrician who arrived an hour-and-a-half later in a temper at having been roused at such an ungodly hour. He disappeared into the delivery room and Feroze and Krishna paced the corridor. Hours passed. Finally, at about 9.30 that morning, the doctor emerged and said, 'Well, I saved her . . . The kid's all right but Mrs Gandhi had a terrible time and lost a lot of blood.' Then he turned on his heel, leaving Feroze and Krishna to find out from a nurse that the baby was a boy.

Indira, in fact, had suffered a massive haemorrhage and had nearly died. When Feroze and Krishna went into her room they found a white, semi-conscious figure on the bed. 'With all her blood drained away . . .

she seemed not . . . to be alive.' Krishna immediately rang Nehru who arrived shortly and the three of them sat around Indira's bed, consumed with anxiety, until she began to revive. It was several days, however, before she was declared out of danger.[29]

Sanjay Gandhi had arrived in the world. From the start, he was big trouble.

After the birth of her second son Indira stayed on in Delhi to convalesce and Feroze returned to Lucknow. Soon the other guests and relatives departed too. Nehru and Indira were now in sole possession of the house, apart from the servants and Nehru's secretary, M.O. Mathai. Mathai, a short, squat, moon-faced man from South India, had entered their lives unobtrusively the previous year, with no indication of the role he would play later. Shortly after Nehru was released from prison in the summer of 1945, Mathai (who had never met Nehru) wrote to him offering his services because he said he was 'looking for a purpose in life'.[30] They met; Nehru was impressed by Mathai's seriousness and dedication, and he agreed to take him on in a rather nebulous capacity.

At first Mathai merely dealt with Nehru's correspondence and did his typing. Then, gradually, his responsibilities became more compli- cated and extensive. Nehru, for example, put his tangled financial affairs in Mathai's hands (including Nehru's publishing arrangements), which had previously been handled by Indira. After independence, Mathai was designated personal private secretary to the Prime Minister and put in charge of several stenographers and typists. By this time, everything passed through Mathai's hands before reaching the Prime Minister.

For the next twelve years, in fact, Mathai was like a human shield surrounding Nehru: he controlled who Nehru saw, spoke to on the telephone, and everything that went into and out of his office. He decided exactly what papers Nehru saw and often attached to them notes or memos of his own. Papers Mathai considered too insignificant to show to Nehru, he acted on himself, in the Prime Minister's name. He sent Nehru memoranda on various subjects and passed on gossip. As Nehru's biographer, S. Gopal, points out, Prime Ministers 'are lonely figures . . . cut off from society'. For seventeen years Nehru never entered a shop or a bank, hailed a taxi or caught a bus. He never carried money or placed his own telephone calls. Mathai saw to everything and was invariably at Nehru's side and beck and call. Nehru relied on Mathai for information, 'for saving him from minor routine, for sheltering him from importunate friends and for warning him against intriguing colleagues'.[31] In the process Mathai was in a position to exploit Nehru's reliance, build up his own power base and acquire wealth as well as power over Nehru. It is not surprising, then, that members of the family such as Indira, Nan Pandit and her daughters and close friends like Padmaja Naidu were careful to remain on good terms with Mathai because of his omnipresence and closeness to Nehru.

Who exactly was this man? Like Krishna Menon – whom Mathai came to loathe – he attracted and repelled people in almost equal numbers. No one was indifferent to Mathai with the result that others' testimony about him is highly partisan. In addition, much of what we know about Mathai comes from his own two-volume autobiography written in the mid-1970s by which time he had become an embittered alcoholic, eager to malign those he felt had wronged him – especially Indira Gandhi.

In his autobiography Mathai does not say when he was born, but he was probably about ten years older than Indira. He was a Christian, from Kerala, who decided early in life not to marry. He claimed to hold a degree from Madras University, though Nehru's biographer says he was 'a stenographer with no education'.[32] His English was good and he was well read. During the war he had worked for the American Red Cross on the Assam-Burma border. He was paid a generous salary and when the war ended, Mathai obtained valuable surpluses from the Red Cross. He saved and invested this Red Cross money which provided him with a tidy private income. In his memoirs, Mathai boasts that he received no salary from the government or from Nehru and that he was never asked to sign a secrecy oath.[33] Therefore he felt able to disclose a range of controversial matters in his autobiography. It did not, however, entitle Mathai to make and retain in his personal possession copies of all of Nehru's papers, an activity that only came to light after Nehru's death.[34] It is also alleged Mathai was in the employ of the CIA.[35]

Whether people liked or disliked Mathai (who was called 'Mac' by those in the Nehru inner circle), in the early years everyone agreed that he was a great boon to Nehru. Mathai was efficient, tireless and clever. He was the first person in the office in the morning and the last out at night. He was on call twenty-four hours a day and could be summoned at any time from his room in Nehru's house. He travelled with Nehru and oversaw virtually all his activities – political and personal – which meant that he came into continuous, close contact with Indira. He had no family, no responsibilities, no interests – no existence, it would seem – beyond Nehru's life and needs.

Mathai's status, however, was peculiar, for he rapidly outgrew the role of general factotum. Mathai was an assertive, cunning man. When relaxed he was often vulgar though he was careful never to be crude in Nehru's presence. Nehru abhorred vulgarity, but he knew about Mathai's drinking which he overlooked.[36] After Mathai manoeuvred his way into Nehru's confidence and inner circle, he behaved as if he had attained his rightful station. Though technically he was Nehru's secretary and in the beginning at least did menial chores such as typing or arranging for Nehru's preferred brand of cigarettes (State Express 555), he had nothing of the subaltern about him. And unlike Nehru, Mathai was not immune to the intoxication of power. Even if he had possessed exemplary rectitude, his position in the Nehru household from 1946 onwards was dangerous, and Mathai was no saint.

In December 1946, when Mathai was already ensconced in the Nehru household and at just about the time that Sanjay Gandhi entered the world, in London Edwina Mountbatten made a cryptic entry in her diary, 'Possible new horror job.'[37] The new British Prime Minister, Clement Attlee, did not consider the unprepossessing Viceroy of India, Archibald Wavell, and his ponderous wife Queenie, to be the right people to oversee Britain's withdrawal from India. He therefore called upon Edwina's husband, Viscount Louis Mountbatten of Burma – or 'Dickie', as he was called by all those close to him – to take over from Wavell and thus become the last Viceroy of India.

Twenty-four years earlier, when she was a glamorous young heiress, Edwina Ashley became engaged to dashing Dickie Mountbatten on Valentine's Day 1922 in Delhi, while Mountbatten was touring India with the Prince of Wales. They were married the following July with the Prince of Wales as best man. As the historian David Cannadine has observed, 'sociologically the match was perfect: she had wealth; he had status; they both had ambition'.[38] Edwina, in fact, had inherited £2 million from her grandfather Sir Ernest Cassel; Mountbatten earned a mere £610 per annum, but he was born Prince Louis Francis Battenberg (the family name was de-Teutonized by royal decree during the First World War), and was the great-grandson of Queen Victoria. For the first twenty years of their marriage, Edwina led an idle, frivolous existence during which she took a string of lovers while her irrepressible and dynamic husband rose in the ranks of the Royal Navy.

The Second World War was the making of both the Mountbattens. Dickie became Supreme Commander of Southeast Asia, whose forces stopped the Japanese offensive into India and reconquered Burma. Meanwhile Edwina underwent a conversion experience. During the Blitz in London, Edwina continued to have weekly manicures and procure rare stores of lipstick, but she also embraced left-wing causes, became pro-Soviet, sympathetic to nationalist movements, and hostile to capitalism. She worked tirelessly for the Red Cross, the St John's Ambulance Brigade and did other valuable war relief and social work. In late 1946, Edwina was in her mid-forties and in the midst of a difficult menopause. Early the next year she had a partial hysterectomy. Physically and emotionally, the last thing she felt up to was the 'horror job' of moving to the subcontinent and helping her husband inaugurate independence in India.

Dickie was not keen to accept this difficult assignment either and laid down so many conditions that he thought Attlee would surely rescind the offer. But Attlee did not and in February 1947 Mountbatten finally agreed to succeed Wavell as Viceroy. He and Edwina planned to take their eighteen-year-old younger daughter, Pamela, with them to India. Still recovering from her hysterectomy, Edwina was harassed by the complexities of their preparations. Lady Wavell tried to be helpful in letters from Delhi: 'I found a tiara superfluous during the war . . . but have worn it several times this winter. Nice gloves are difficult to get here . . . Enid, Connaught Place, is the best dressmaker.'[39]

On 22 March 1947 Edwina, Pamela and Dickie Mountbatten arrived at Delhi airport with sixty-six pieces of personal luggage. They were driven, like royalty, in an open landau with a cavalry escort to the palatial Lutyens-designed Viceroy's House where the outgoing Wavells met them at the top of a great red-carpeted set of steps.[40] Within days, the Mountbattens caused a stir by going to a garden party at Nehru's York Road bungalow. Then Nehru, Indira and Krishna Menon were invited to lunch at the Viceroy's House, and this was just the beginning. At the Mountbattens' parties and dinners not less than 50 per cent of their guests were Indians (Dickie was a precise man), and Edwina added Indian vegetarian dishes to the menus which were served in the traditional Indian way on brass *thalis*. When Gandhi came to tea he was served goat's-milk curds in a tin bowl. Sarojini Naidu, her daughter Padmaja, Maniben Patel, Gandhi's secretary Rajkumari Amrit Kaur, among many others, partook of a more conventional tea. Such was Edwina's skill for diplomacy that when she had Nan Pandit and Fatimah Jinnah to tea together, it was the first time that Jinnah's and Nehru's sisters had spoken to each other in three years.[41] A dinner for the Jinnahs she found 'almost unbearably tedious' but the next night when Nehru, Indira and Nan Pandit dined at the Viceroy's it was, according to Edwina's diary, 'all quite charming and a joy after last night'.[42]

What did Indira make of the glamourous, socially gifted but rather brittle Edwina Mountbatten – and of the romance that eventually developed between her father and the last Vicereine? For by the time the Mountbattens left India in June 1948, Edwina and Nehru had fallen in love.[43] Eleven years earlier, Indira had been greatly upset by her father's affair with Padmaja Naidu, in part because it began so soon after Kamala Nehru's death, but also because Indira herself was reluctant to share her father's affection, and there was a real possibility Padmaja and Nehru might marry. This was never the case with Edwina and Nehru, and so Indira did not feel threatened by their relationship. In addition, Indira was herself now a married woman with two small children, and had intense emotional attachments apart from her father.

The Mountbattens first met Nehru and established an immediate rapport with him in 1946. In the spring and summer of 1947 they and their daughter, Pamela, also became close to Indira. Edwina Mountbatten – who could be difficult with attractive women like Indira – was wise enough to be diplomatic and affectionate. She knew how to unfreeze Indira's reserve, and tactfully offered advice on running the Prime Minister's household. Sometimes this was taken, sometimes not. Indira, for example, decided to abolish seating by protocol at formal dinner parties because Indian wives rarely spoke English. 'They should have a good time, too,' she told Edwina, 'so I'm going to seat people according to what language they speak, so that people from the same place will be together.' Edwina tried to dissuade her, but Indira was adamant. Worthy as her motives may have been, the plan proved a disaster. The Indian men – the husbands of the wives who were supposed 'to have fun too' – rose up and protested that they and their spouses had been insulted by the new seating arrangement.

Edwina and Pamela Mountbatten thought Indira attractive, socially adept and interesting, but they were a bit taken aback by her 'acid tongue'. Indira was quite vocal in her criticisms, decrying the Indian princes and their lifestyle, but her most scathing attacks were reserved for her aunt, Nan Pandit. When Mrs Pandit was made ambassador to Moscow by her brother, she returned to Delhi with a mink coat. This Indira loudly condemned, even though it was a gift from the Soviet government. Indira also criticized her cousins, Chandralekha and Nayantara, for attending 'finishing school' in America (it was actually Wellesley College 'while the rest of us were all fighting for independence and in prison'. The Mountbattens saw little of Feroze, although he would turn up from time to time, such as for the independence celebrations. They thought Feroze a 'nonentity', and wondered why Indira had married him and why she kept dashing to Lucknow to see him with the boys. It seemed like she 'was being dragged in two directions', and it was clear to anyone close to the family that 'there was trouble in the marriage'.[44]

In May 1947 Nehru and Krishna Menon went to Simla and Mashobra with the Mountbattens and Dickie Mountbatten impulsively showed Nehru 'Plan Balkan' – the British blueprint for a loosely federated conglomeration of Indian states. Nehru studied it late at night, after everyone had gone to bed, and was aghast at its 'picture of fragmentation and conflict and disorder'. He burst into Krishna Menon's room at 2 a.m. in a rage, and fired off a memo of protest to Mountbatten before finally going back to bed.[45] V. P. Menon, Mountbatten's Reforms Commissioner, was called in to rescue the situation, and after three hours he came up with 'the Menon Plan' for dividing India. Power would now be transferred to two central governments: India and Pakistan. Jinnah would get his Muslim homeland, but it would be a truncated, 'moth-eaten' one with both the Punjab and Bengal bifurcated. The Menon Plan was approved by the Indian leaders in Delhi on 3 June. The next day Mountbatten announced at a press conference that India and Pakistan would become independent states on 15 August 1947.

On the evening of 14 August Indira, Feroze, Nehru and Padmaja Naidu were dining at 17 York Road when a trunk call came through from Lahore. Nehru was informed that the city was in flames with rioting, looting and murder in the streets. Water supplies to the Hindu and Sikh quarters had been cut. When householders ventured out with pails in search of water they were butchered by Muslim mobs. Nehru was devastated by this news, but the independence celebrations scheduled for midnight would still go ahead.[46] V. P. Menon, who had drafted Mountbatten's partition plan, was in his Delhi sitting room when he got news of what was happening in Lahore. He told his daughter, 'Now our nightmares really start.'[47]

At one minute before midnight on 14 August 1947, Nehru stood up before the Constituent Assembly in Delhi, and said, 'Long years ago, we made a tryst with destiny and now the time comes when we shall redeem our pledge.' Though the large hall was packed, the only sound was the whirring of the ceiling fans churning the hot air. 'At the stroke of the midnight hour,' Nehru went on, 'when the world sleeps, India will awake to life and freedom. A moment comes, which comes but rarely in history, when we step out from the old to the new, when an age ends, and when the soul of a nation, long suppressed, finds utterance.'

Nehru was articulating that soul and Indira was in the audience listening to his words. Seventeen-and-a-half years earlier hers had been the first voice to utter Nehru's independence resolution after he drafted it at the December 1929 Congress meeting in Lahore. And with thousands of others, Indira had taken the pledge on the banks of the Ravi river. Her whole life had been shaped and coloured by the freedom struggle. Now it had finally come to fruition. As she said many years later, 'It was impossible to take in that after all these years something that we had thought of and dreamt of and worked for ever since I could remember, had happened. It was such a powerful experience.' Independence seemed a miracle. But in the midst of the euphoria that engulfed Delhi and most of India, Indira felt curiously 'numb': 'You know when you go to an extreme of pleasure or pain there is numbness. Freedom was just so big a thing that it could not register, it seemed to fill all of you and all your world.'[48]

The next morning – 'The Appointed Day!' as Nehru scribbled in his pocket diary – Mountbatten, now the Governor General of India (but not, to his chagrin, Pakistan because Jinnah had insisted on retaining the post himself), swore in Nehru as the first Prime Minister of an independent India. The saffron, white and green flag of a free India was raised in Princes Park before a tumultuous crowd of nearly half a million. The Mountbattens rode back to Lutyens' palace in a gilded state carriage rapturously cheered by the hordes of people that lined the way. A magnificent banquet, with turbaned, liveried bearers behind every chair, lasted until the small hours. Both Indira and Feroze attended. Radiant, in silk and some of her mother's surviving jewellery, Indira sat near to her father while Feroze was far down the table next to Mountbatten's press attaché, Alan Campbell-Johnson.[49]

The independence celebrations continued for days and juxtaposed with them, increasingly disturbing news of communal riots in the Punjab reached Delhi. Indira's 'numbness' wore off. Both the euphoria and horror of independence were sinking in. At the end of August Feroze went back to Lucknow and Indira took the two children for a short holiday to Mussoorie.

India was free, but it was in pieces.[50] Flanking the western and eastern boundaries of northern India and separated by a distance of more than 1,200 miles, were the two wings of Jinnah's Pakistan. The boundary line between Pakistan and India was drawn by a British barrister named Sir Cyril Radcliffe, who had never been east of Gibraltar before arriving in Delhi in early July 1947. He had five steamy weeks to divide three hundred million people and when he finished he wrote to his stepson, 'Oh I have sweated the whole time'.[51]

Radcliffe's most difficult task was dissecting the Punjab. Making the best of a bad job, he still left five million Sikhs and Hindus stranded in Pakistan's half of the Punjab and over five million Muslims in India's half. After Radcliffe saw Mountbatten sworn in as Governor General, he went directly to the Delhi airport and boarded the next plane for England: 'Nobody in India,' he explained, 'will love me for the award about the Punjab and Bengal and there will be roughly 80 million people with a grievance who will begin looking for me.'[52]

Mountbatten delayed the announcement of the boundary award in order, he said, not to detract from the independence celebrations in both India and Pakistan. But neither the skittish Radcliffe nor anyone else foresaw the chaos and carnage that would explode when the line dividing Pakistan and India became known on 16 August 1947. What followed was the greatest migration of populations in history. People packed up their belongings and left homes where their forebears had lived for generations, never to return – and often not to arrive at their destinations. Rich and poor, city dwellers and villagers, old men, women, infants and children, men and boys left, helter skelter, by foot, by bullock cart, by car, by lorry and by rail.

In the ensuing chaos Hindus, Muslims, and Sikhs, who had heretofore lived together largely harmoniously, now turned on each other. Whole villages were razed and their inhabitants massacred. Women and girls were raped and abducted – or threw themselves down wells or were shot by their menfolk to avoid this fate. The platforms of Lahore railway station ran with blood. Some people, however, made it onto departing trains. Hours later railway carriages of butchered corpses would arrive at the train's terminus, having been attacked en route by bands of Muslims, Sikhs or Hindus. Indian killed Indian. At least a million died. The departing British – withdrawing often in great haste – were left unmolested. The only sort of person who could travel in comparative safety in the Punjab during that autumn of 1947 was a white one.

In September 1947 communal mayhem broke out in Delhi with the huge influx of Hindu and Sikh refugees from the Punjab arriving in the city. There was widespread rioting, murder, arson, looting, and rape. The civil authorities were on the verge of losing all control. In Mussoorie, Indira heard on the radio that there were 'troubles' in Delhi and rang Feroze who had come to Delhi from Lucknow and was staying with Nehru. Feroze told Indira not to return. Food was scarce, he said, and the situation was dangerous. Indira said she would bring some sacks of potatoes, and insisted on taking the next train back with the children. When the train stopped at the Delhi suburb, Shahdara, she looked out the carriage window to see two old Muslim men pursued by a mob of Hindus. Leaving the boys in the carriage with the *ayah*, she leapt out of the train along with some other passengers and tried to intervene in the fracas. They managed to save one of the old men, but the other was too far away and there were too many people chasing him.[53]

When Indira got to Nehru's York Road house, she found large numbers of refugees there who were being fed and sheltered in tents by the household. A number of these Punjabi Hindus – including a young woman named Vimla Sindhi who had been separated from her family – were eventually taken on as clerical or domestic staff. More arrived daily and Indira talked to them every morning, individually and in groups, trying to arrange for their care. Obviously only a few could be accommodated at York Road and she saw that the others were transferred to various refugee camps in the city. Nehru himself toured Delhi in a jeep. Brandishing a stick, he often plunged into a scene of looting or violence, shouting orders at the mob. Edwina Mountbatten put on a khaki uniform and toured the refugee camps, coordinating relief operations and organizing cholera vaccines and sanitation facilities.

A peace corps – or *Shanti Dal* – was formed in Delhi by a follower of Gandhi and friend of Nehru, a Gujarati woman named Mridula Sarabhai. Sarabhai herself was preoccupied with the rescue and recovery of abducted women in the Punjab, and she put a Punjabi woman named Subhadra Datta (later the MP Subhadra Joshi), in charge of refugee relief work in Delhi. Hearing of Indira's work with refugees at York Road, Gandhi told her he wanted her to go into the city's Muslim and Hindu refugee camps where 200,000 people lived in filth and squalor. In these congested, unsanitary camps there would be two water taps for 25,000 people, mountains of uncollected rubbish and overflowing latrines because sweepers refused to enter the camps to clear them. Cholera, typhoid and other infectious diseases were rife. People were also starving because food rations had not got through to the camps. Many of the inhabitants had been wounded on their journey to Delhi and their wounds had not been cleaned or their dressings changed in weeks.

Indira joined Subhadra Datta working in the camps. At first she told her she could only come for two hours a day because Sanjay was still a baby and she was breast-feeding him. But soon she was spending eight or ten hours a day doing relief work with Subhadra Datta. Every morning, Indira would appear at the camp gates on foot, alone, because the driver who brought her from York Road was reluctant to enter the 'disturbed areas' of the city. She and Subhadra brought in cleaners and sweepers, arranged for medical supplies and food rations, listened to the refugees' grievances and requests. According to Subhadra Datta (who later became a great enemy of Indira Gandhi), Indira had the right temperament for relief work. She was fearless, decisive and a good organizer. She also knew how to talk to people in extremity. She was not emotional, but she was empathetic and tough.[54]

As Indira had told her father some years earlier, she coped best in a crisis. Partition and the communal unrest and suffering it brought to

Delhi in the autumn and winter of 1947 and 1948 was the worst national crisis ever to descend on India. Many years later the artist Satish Gujral painted a haunting picture of Indira as a Partition refugee after asking her, "'Why do you wear a mask? To hide yourself?' To which she . . . answered "One does not wear one's heart on one's sleeve."' Indira certainly did not expose her heart during relief work, but there was no doubt that she had one. It is probable that she was motivated as much by indignation and anger as by sentiment.[55]

Communal violence was just one legacy of Partition. Another was the fate of the Nehrus' homeland and Indira Gandhi's lifelong retreat, Kashmir. One of the peculiarities of British rule in India was that about a third of the Indian subcontinent consisted of 565 Princely States – ancient, hereditary kingdoms whose rulers had individually signed treaties with the British Crown. These states were anathema to Nehru who had condemned their feudal societies and despotic maharajahs and nawabs in *Glimpses of World History*. Years later, Indira Gandhi would strip the Indian princes of their privileges and emoluments. The immediate difficulty that the Princely States posed in 1947, however, was their problematical status after Indian independence. Would the Princely States be subsumed by India or Pakistan or in the case of several of the larger states such as Kashmir, become independent themselves? Fortunately, by 15 August, all but three of the states had acceded to either India or Pakistan, depending on which country's boundaries they were located within.

The state of Jammu and Kashmir (often referred to as just Kashmir) was politically the most sensitive of the three undecided Princely States because it shared borders with both India and Pakistan. Though ruled by a Hindu maharajah, about 80 per cent of the population of Kashmir was Muslim and for this reason Jinnah expected it to become part of Pakistan. Nehru, however, wanted Kashmir to remain in India, for political and strategic reasons and also because of his intense attachment to the state. Both Jinnah and Nehru were foiled when Kashmir technically became independent on 15 August because the Maharajah, Hari Singh, had not decided whether accede to India or Pakistan.

Kashmir's anomalous independence lasted only seventy-three days. At dawn on 22 October 1947 at least 3,000 Pathan tribesmen from the Northwest Frontier Province of Pakistan crossed the Jhelum river into Kashmir. Pakistan maintained that the Pathan raiders were aiding an indigenous Kashmiri uprising against the despotic rule of Hari Singh. India held that they constituted a Pakistani invasion, sanctioned at the highest level of government.

As the Pathan tribesman closed in on Srinagar, the Maharaja, Hari Singh, panicked. He appealed to Delhi for military aid to repulse the invaders and then, on 24 October he, his family, and a vast entourage (including the Maharajah's Russian jeweller Victor Rosenthal) fled from Srinagar to the Maharajah's winter palace in Jammu. Nehru and Mountbatten made Kashmir's accession to India a condition for sending in Indian forces. Hari Singh had no option but to acquiesce. On 27 October an Indian army airlift to Srinagar began and within days 35,000 troops had arrived in Kashmir. Whether or not this military intervention occurred before or after the instrument of accession was actually signed by Hari Singh is open to dispute.[56]

After Kashmir acceded to India, Nehru's friend, Sheikh Abdullah, was installed as head of the state's emergency administration government. Hari Singh did not formally abdicate, but he was exiled from Kashmir and he relinquished control in May 1949 by which time Sheikh Abdullah had become the state's Prime Minister. Hari Singh's son, Karan Singh – who forged a lasting friendship with Nehru and his daughter – never succeeded his father but rather served as Head of State or *Sadar-i-Riyasat*. But it was Sheikh Abdullah and his party, the National Conference, who actually governed Kashmir.

Though Hari Singh signed the instrument of accession, it was obvious that he did so because he desperately needed military assistance from India. Furthermore, he was the autocratic Hindu ruler of a predominantly Muslim state: his decision could not conceivably be taken as an expression of the will of the people of Jammu and Kashmir. Thus, both Mountbatten and Nehru stipulated that the ultimate fate of Kashmir should be settled 'by reference to the people', and on 2 November Nehru broadcast on All India Radio that 'we are prepared when peace and law and order have been established to have a referendum'.[57] Nehru reiterated this pledge in a telegram to the new Pakistani Prime Minister, Liaquat Ali Khan, and added 'we have agreed to an impartial international agency like the United Nations supervising any referendum'.[58]

But peace was not forthcoming. Fighting in Kashmir continued for more than a year until a United Nations cease-fire took effect on 1 January 1949. The resulting cease-fire line left approximately one-third of Kashmir under the control of Pakistan in what is known as 'Azad Kashmir' in Pakistan or Pakistan-occupied Kashmir in India. Nehru's promised referendum has never been held with the result that to this day the 'tragedy of errors' in Kashmir remains unresolved – a combustible source of ongoing hostility between India and Pakistan.

Kashmir had long been important to the Nehru family which originated there. Nehru later facetiously called himself 'the last Englishman to rule India' and Indira self-mockingly referred to herself as the 'Empress of India'. But in their hearts they felt themselves to be first and last Kashmiri Pandits, even though their forebears had migrated to the plains generations before and neither Nehru nor Indira could speak Kashmiri. With Partition, however, Kashmir took on a different kind of centrality in Nehru's and Indira's lives. It had always been a kind of geographical objective correlative for internal impulses, needs and desires. But after 1947, Kashmir became a source of pain as well as pleasure, of trouble and danger as well as solace and peace – an intractable political wound that refused to heal.

Throughout the autumn of 1947, Indira and the children were with Feroze in Lucknow, trying to make a go of things. It was an unhappy, stressful time. Indira felt isolated. Feroze was still involved with other women. Quite apart from this, Indira found Lucknow 'dreary' and 'narrow minded'. Above all, she hated provincial politics. 'What a peculiar deadness there is in our provincial towns,' she wrote to Nehru in December. 'What makes the atmosphere sickening is the corruption and the slackness, the smugness of some and the malice of others. Life here has nothing to offer.' She was also appalled at the strength in Lucknow of the revivalist Hindu organization, the Rashtriya Swayamsewak Sangh (or the RSS), a fascist communal group similar to Hitler's brown shirts.[59] Indira was not physically well in Lucknow. As the cold of winter set in, she was plagued with her old symptoms of cough, temperature and weight loss. Early in the New Year, she and the children returned to Delhi.

Soon after they re-established themselves at Nehru's York Road house, Gandhi, who was now living in Delhi at the home of the rich industrialist G.D. Birla, embarked on his sixteenth hunger strike to protest against the continued violence in the city perpetrated against

Muslims. This time Gandhi nearly died, but self-starvation was averted at the eleventh hour when leaders of the city's religious communities came to his bedside and pledged to stop the violence. Gandhi broke his fast, after six days, on 18 January. Two days later, he survived death again when an assassin's bomb exploded at his daily prayer meeting, leaving him miraculously unscathed.

Late in the afternoon of 29 January 1948 Indira, Rajiv, Nayantara Pandit (who was living with Nehru while her mother was ambassador in Moscow), Krishna Hutheesing and Padmaja Naidu visited Gandhi at Birla House. Just before leaving home, the *mali* (gardener) gave Indira a bunch of jasmine for her hair which she decided to take with her and give to Gandhi. At Birla House they sat in the garden where Gandhi was taking a sunbath in a straw hat and loincloth while eating mashed up fruit and goat's milk. Rajiv chased butterflies across the lawn and then came and sat down at Gandhi's feet and began to stick the jasmines between the old man's toes. Gandhi pulled the child's ears and told him not to 'do that. One only puts flowers around dead people's feet.'[60]

The next afternoon, Indira and Nayantara were having tea at York Road when the phone rang. Indira answered and took the urgent message: Gandhi had just been shot as he walked to his daily prayer meeting. Indira and Nayantara immediately jumped into the car and drove to Birla House to find Gandhi, unconscious, in the midst of a crowd of family and followers. He died without regaining consciousness.

As the news of Gandhi's assassination spread, first in India and then across the world, disbelief gave way to grief and then to fear. Who was the assassin? If a Muslim, communal violence would inevitably explode again and spiral out of control. It was soon established, however, that Gandhi's murderer was, in fact, a fundamentalist Hindu – a Brahmin from Poona – who had been enraged by Gandhi's fast for Muslims and blamed him for Partition. At precisely 5.03 p.m. on 30 January 1948, Gandhi had emerged from Birla House to go to his afternoon prayer meeting in the spacious grounds of the house. A crowd of nearly 300 people filled the garden, and as soon as they saw the old man, they pressed forward to greet him. Nathuram Godse, a thick-set man in his thirties, was in the forefront. He approached Gandhi and made obeisance to him, cupping in his hands an automatic 9mm Beretta. Then Godse fired three shots, at close range, into the old man's bony chest.

For a moment, everyone froze. The shots had not sounded like a revolver, but like a Chinese cracker that a child might have set off. Then a young American man in the crowd rushed forward and wrested the gun out of Godse's hand. This broke the spell and others lunged forward and overpowered the assassin. Gandhi was carried into the house while a terrible wailing lament rose from the crowd left behind. He died half an hour later.

Within minutes of the assassination thousands of people flocked to Birla House, including Nehru and the Mountbattens who arrived and entered the crowded room where Gandhi was laid out on the floor on a bare mattress. Feroze Gandhi (then visiting his wife and the children in Delhi) arrived too and quickly sought out Indira in the crowd. At the threshold of the room where Gandhi's body had been laid, there was a great pile of shoes and sandals (because footwear is not worn in the presence of the dead). The pungent smell of incense hung in the air. The room was silent except for the sound of women weeping and chanting prayers. Then the American photojournalist Margaret Bourke-White came tottering in on high heels, a camera dangling from her neck. Her shoes beat a tattoo across the floor. The sharp click click of a camera shutter was heard as she stooped in front of Gandhi's lifeless body and began snapping pictures. Feroze Gandhi leapt up, yanked the camera from her neck, snatched out the film and then led Bourke-White out of the room.[61]

Bernard Shaw said of Gandhi's assassination, 'This comes of being too good.'[62] Nehru broadcast on the radio to the Indian people, 'The light has gone out of our lives and there is darkness everywhere. I do not know what to tell you and how to say it. Our beloved leader, Bapu as we called him, the Father of the Nation, is no more.'[63] Gandhi's funeral was the first of a chain to follow in independent India: the flower-laden carriage bearing the frail, bullet-riddled body, the thousands of mourners lining the route through Delhi to Raj Ghat on the banks of the Jumna, the sandalwood pyre, the son who set fire to it, the chanting priests, the unappeasable grief at senseless, violent death.

After Gandhi's assassination Nehru's safety became a matter of grave concern. Astonishingly, the Prime Minister of India had no personal bodyguards, no security apparatus to protect him. Anyone could walk into his York Road house or his offices in the Parliament building unquestioned and unmolested. Immediately after Gandhi's funeral, the

Delhi police closed in on Nehru, much to his dismay. The York Road house and compound now looked like an armed camp with a sea of police tents surrounding it. Guards were stationed at the door and inside the house as well.

But the small bungalow could not easily accommodate all this police protection and the police themselves complained that the house had too many entrances and exits, was too close to the road and needed a surrounding high wall and police post at the end of the drive. Nehru, however, resisted all these measures. Finally, Mountbatten told him that he must move into the twenty-room Commander-in-Chief's house, which had elaborate, enclosed grounds and a secure entrance gate. Nehru refused. The last thing he wanted was to live in the grand style of a national leader. But the Home Minister, Sardar Patel, persuaded Nehru to move. Patel had been with Gandhi moments before he was shot; he helped to carry his bleeding body from the site of the assassination. Patel told Nehru how Gandhi's murder preyed upon his mind and haunted his sleep. As Nehru's long-time colleague in Congress and now his Home Minister, Patel said he could not face the prospect of another such death and he refused to take responsibility for Nehru's security at the York Road bungalow. Very reluctantly, Nehru agreed to move to the Commander-in-Chief's house, though he managed to delay it for another seven months.

During this period Indira commuted back and forth between Delhi and Lucknow, and then in May she and Feroze took the boys to Kashmir in an attempt to enjoy a family holiday and even a second honeymoon. But both they and Kashmir had changed. Srinagar and its environs were full of refugees who had flocked to the city after the Pakistani invasion of the previous year, and Indira immediately began doing relief work amongst them. Despite Sheikh Abdullah's reforms, the state had deteriorated economically. Even at the height of 'the season', there were few visitors because people felt Srinagar was no longer safe in the wake of the Pakistani invasion. The result was that hotel owners, shopkeepers, houseboat proprietors, boatmen, artisans and labourers were all suffering. Sheikh Abdullah was personally popular but his new government was not. Indira wrote to Nehru that Pakistani newspapers were 'spreading their vile propaganda'. 'The only thing,' she said, 'that can save

Kashmir for India and the Kashmiris will be an influx of visitors this summer . . . I am sure that if there had been enough publicity, people would have flocked to Srinagar. Both the Kashmir and Indian Govts should go all out to assure people that Srinagar is SAFE.'[64]

In mid-May Nehru himself made a brief visit to Srinagar. After he left Indira wrote to him again of the volatile political situation:

> There seems to be a woeful lack of political propaganda on behalf of the Kashmir Govt. The 'Azad Kashmir' radio is blaring out the most brazen lies night and day and there is nothing to counteract them. . . . Sheikh [Abdullah] should have a powerful transmitter here . . . Every day there is a fresh crop of rumours . . . Only radio can reach into the byways of Srinagar and give authentic news and contradict the ridiculous stories spread by the 'Azad Kashmir' radio. Do you know that on the day you left Srinagar, the 'Azad Kashmir' radio announced that on your arrival in Srinagar you were met by one lakh of people waving black flags & shouting 'Go Back!'!!?[65]

Indira left Srinagar in the middle of June for Delhi to attend the round of festivities connected with the Mountbattens' departure from India on 21 June and also to make arrangements (with the help of Padmaja Naidu) to move into the Commander-in-Chief's house. Nehru, Indira and the boys finally made the big move to the new Prime Minister's residence – from now on called Teen Murti House on 2 August 1948. (Teen Murti means 'three statues' and the house is named after the monument of three soldiers that stands on the roundabout at its entrance.) They moved very early in the morning – in part because Indira needed to catch an early plane to Lucknow. But also, as Nehru wrote to his sister, because of

> a sudden urge of Indu to come at the auspicious moment. A holy gentleman in Uttar Kashi, who apparently takes an interest in my career, sent word about the auspicious moment. Indu felt it would be unwise to challenge fate. So we arrived here at 6.45 in the morning . . . to find Sarojini and Leilamani [Naidu] with a big coconut in their hands. The sage at Uttar Kashi . . . sent a brief account of what is going to happen in the future. I am going to have plenty of troubles and occasionally danger, nevertheless I survive and go from height to height. In 1952 . . .

I retire from politics ... and lead some kind of world crusade. So now you know all about it.[66]

Designed by R.T. Russell for the British Commander-in-Chief and completed in 1930, Teen Murti House was a palatial residence with towering ceilings, long, echoing corridors and cavernous rooms, including a huge ballroom, formal dining room, hall-like drawing rooms, reception rooms and master bedroom suites. Dark oil portraits of imperial heroes hung on its walls and heavy curtains smothered the tall French windows. All around the house stretched finely manicured gardens and lawns.

Teen Murti was formal, chilly and wholly British in character and both Indira and Nehru had shrunk from the prospect of living in it. Before moving in, Indira had the imperial portraits crated up and sent to the Defence Ministry. She replaced them with Indian artworks, had the walls repainted eggshell white, removed the heavy drapes and put up curtains made out of raw Indian silk. She arranged Nehru's simple but elegant bedroom, with a single pallet-like bed and filled it with his favourite books and family photographs. In the opposite wing of the house – on the far side of the ballroom, on the first floor – Indira took for herself a dark, stuffy room with tiny windows up near the ceiling, which she furnished with dreary government-issue furniture. It had the bleak anonymity of a far-from-deluxe hotel room. The boys' nursery was next door, and their governess, the Danish Anna Ornsholt, had a small room next to theirs.

It was impossible to run Teen Murti informally as the York Road house had been. For one thing, by the standards of the time, there was elaborate security. Guards were posted at the main entrance and a receptionist logged in every visitor. Indira now had a complicated establishment to manage and a large number of staff and servants to oversee. Teen Murti was actually run on a smaller scale than Anand Bhawan in the old days under Motilal Nehru, but Indira could scarcely remember that time of plenty. She and Nehru now had to do a good deal of formal entertaining and Indira toiled over menus and seating arrangements. Nehru, however, refused to take advantage of the prime ministerial tax-free entertainment allowance of 500 rupees per month. The Teen Murti food was, for the most part, simple Indian fare. No alcohol was served. Nehru paid his own living expenses and those of his guests. He sent Feroze Gandhi a monthly invoice to cover the cost of maintaining Indira and the children.

Years later, Indira described these early days at Teen Murti:

> It wasn't really a choice. My father asked me to come and to set up the house for him. There was nobody else to do it. So I set up the house, but I resisted every inch of the way about becoming a hostess. I was simply terrified of the . . . social duties. Although I [had] met a large number of people, I wasn't good at 'socializing' and small talk . . . I had always hated parties . . . I used to stay [at Teen Murti] for a period of time and then go. Later it became more and more difficult to leave. My husband was . . . in Lucknow and I used to go there. But, invariably, I would get a telegram [from Nehru]: 'Important guests coming, return at once' . . . It was a real problem because, naturally Feroze didn't always appreciate my going away. I was living about half the month in Lucknow and half in Delhi.[67]

It was the custom for visiting heads of government to stay several days at Teen Murti and then go to Rashtrapati Bhawan, the President's residence. At Teen Murti there was also an endless stream of people for breakfast, lunch, tea, receptions and dinners. Indira told an interviewer: 'We [have] guests at every meal.' Though far from a relaxed hostess, she was a relentlessly conscientious one. As she put it, 'if one has to do a thing, one might as well do it well, so I grew into it'.[68] She personally checked every light bulb in the lamps and every tap in the bathrooms. She made sure tall guests had high-back chairs and small ones footrests. She was also scrupulous about providing appropriate menus for Hindus who did not eat beef, Muslims who did not eat pork, meat eaters who were vegetarians on certain days of the week, vegetarians who ate eggs and milk and those who did not.[69]

Teen Murti's best feature was that it had plenty of space for animals. The Nehrus had always had dogs – usually golden retrievers – but now they added to the canine population a Red Himalayan panda named Bhimsa (who later acquired a female partner, Pema, and had offspring), and three tiger cubs. The children also had a full quota of ducks, parrots, turtles, fish and various other small creatures. In time what amounted to a small zoo grew on the back lawns of Teen Murti.[70]

*   *   *

A month after Nehru, Indira and the children moved into Teen Murti, Jinnah died of advanced tuberculosis in Karachi, on 11 September 1948. Though he had long been a sallow, cadaverous man with a hacking cough, he kept his fatal illness a secret to the very end. History might have been different had Nehru – himself personally familiar with the deadly nature of TB – and Mountbatten known that Jinnah was tubercular. They might, then, have deferred, rather than pressed for, independence, and waited until Jinnah – the greatest obstacle to an undivided India – was out of the way.

In October 1948 Nehru went to England for the first Commonwealth Conference, visited the Mountbattens in London and spent two weekends with them at their Hampshire country house, Broadlands. Back in Delhi, Indira and the boys were bedridden with whooping cough. Feroze was in Lucknow. In January of 1949 Indira was busy with the arrangements for Nayantara Pandit's marriage to Gautam Sahgal at Anand Bhawan – the first wedding held there since Indira and Feroze's in March 1942. Three months later, Nan Pandit's other daughter, Chandralekha, married Ashok Mehta, a young Foreign Service officer, at Teen Murti. In February 1949 Edwina and Pamela Mountbatten visited India and stayed at Teen Murti – the first of a regular series of annual visits.

And so life went on. The boys started nursery school. Feroze visited Indira and the children periodically as it was increasingly difficult for her to escape her responsibilities as Nehru's hostess. The marriage continued to unravel. Nevertheless, in the late spring of 1949 Indira became pregnant.

In August and September she was much preoccupied with plans for an upcoming trip to America with her father which would be her first official visit abroad as the Prime Minister's daughter. One weekend in September Indira went to Allahabad alone and suffered a miscarriage while she was there. Nehru was in Delhi and Feroze was in Lucknow. Feroze rushed to Allahabad and brought her back to Delhi.[71] Indira soon rallied and continued her preparations for the American visit. Her Delhi doctors advised her to cancel it because she was still weak, but Indira insisted she was well and that she must and would go. Eventually, as was usually the case with her, she had her way. Feroze was the loser.

Indira's miscarriage and her determination to go abroad with her father marked the end of a turbulent, troubled phase in her marriage, and a turning point in her life. This was her last pregnancy. If the baby had survived, it is likely – or at least possible – that she would have spent more time with Feroze in Lucknow and then in Delhi when he moved there after being elected an MP. Another child might have 'saved' their marriage as many couples hope a new baby will and perhaps this indeed was Indira's motive for getting pregnant despite the fact that Feroze only wanted two children.

At this time Indira's personal hierarchy of commitments probably ran, from the top, like this: Nehru, then her children, then Feroze and finally herself. Such a ranking of responsibilities would have seemed to most women at this time like a law of nature rather than a matter of personal choice. Had Indira and Feroze had a third child, her husband and the children might have taken over the top position from Nehru and thus ended the conflict of loyalties in Indira's heart. It was a conflict, quite simply, between the needs of her father and husband. But Indira lost the baby and in a way the marriage miscarried too.

In October 1949, she got on a plane bound for America, and said goodbye to what might have been.

ELEVEN

Metamorphosis

ON 11 OCTOBER 1949 Indira and Nehru flew into Washington DC in the *Sacred Cow*, President Harry Truman's personal aircraft, which Truman had sent to London for the last leg of their journey. They had flown from Delhi to London on an ordinary scheduled flight, and Nehru had paid for Indira's airfare despite the fact that the Indian Finance Minister had approved the cost of her ticket and a daily allowance for her while abroad.[1] For Indira was accompanying her father in a semi-official capacity. Over the next decade, she would make a total of twenty-four trips abroad with Nehru. Indira was now launched on a new – and irrevocably transforming – phase of her life.

Several months before their American trip Nehru had appointed his sister, Nan Pandit, as Indian ambassador to the United States, and it was she who arranged their itinerary, beginning with a red-carpet welcome in the capital. But the old antagonism between aunt and niece was as strong as ever. To Indira's chagrin, Mrs Pandit excluded her from formal functions and effectively usurped her role during their three-week visit by accompanying Nehru everywhere, including to Princeton where Nehru met Albert Einstein.

Indira did, however, attend a number of informal gatherings with her father, especially when they went to New York. The first of these, held at their hotel, the Waldorf Astoria, was a reception hosted by the novelist Pearl S. Buck, whose *The Good Earth* they had read aloud to Kamala in Switzerland. Amongst the scores of guests Buck invited was forty-five-year-old Dorothy Norman, a wealthy, unhappily-married photographer, left-wing political activist and patron of the arts who cultivated and collected prominent writers, artists and intellectuals. Like many women, Dorothy Norman found Nehru extremely attractive. She succeeded in making an impression on him with the result that Nehru and Indira accepted her impromptu invitation to a 'literary tea' the next day.

Dorothy Norman was a great convenor of the rich and famous, and to meet Nehru she summoned W. H. Auden, Lewis Mumford and Anaïs Nin, among others, to her home on East 70th Street, filled with modern art, photographs by Alfred Stieglitz (with whom Dorothy Norman had a long love affair), oriental rugs and ethnic wall hangings. Nehru was charmed. And so was Indira who felt an immediate rapport with their hostess. They invited Dorothy to travel with them to Boston and when they returned to New York, Indira spent a great deal of time with Dorothy while Nehru attended meetings and official events with Nan Pandit.

Nehru and Indira got a warm welcome in the States but it was a difficult visit. This was their first exposure to the country and it was a shock. As Nehru remarked later, one should never go to America for the first time. They were taken aback in particular by the transparent materialism of American life and the uninhibited talk of money and 'deals'. What seemed to Nehru Americans' loud voices and unappealing accent grated on his nerves. Even more, he found the political atmosphere that would soon spawn Senator Joseph McCarthy repellent. Nehru's talks with both Truman and the Secretary of State Dean Acheson – whom he felt patronized him – 'failed to develop any cordiality or understanding'.[2] Americans seemed obsessed with the bogey of communism and it was impossible to make India's foreign policy of nonalignment understood.

Matters improved when Nehru and Indira left Washington. In Chicago, Governor Adlai Stevenson fulsomely welcomed Nehru: 'Only a tiny handful of men have influenced the implacable forces of our time. To this small company of the truly great, our guest ... belongs ... Pandit Jawaharlal Nehru belongs to the even *smaller* company of historic figures who wore a halo in their own lifetimes.' In St Louis a female journalist reported in the *St Louis Post Dispatch* that 'Nehru has departed from us, leaving behind clouds of misty-eyed women.'[3] After the midwest, Indira and Nehru went on to Canada for a brief holiday and then returned to New York where Indira made one of her few official visits with her father when they went to see Eleanor Roosevelt at Hyde Park and laid a wreath on Franklin Roosevelt's grave.

Back in New York City, Indira went to fashionable art galleries, smart restaurants, off-Broadway plays and shopping in Macy's basement with her new friend, Dorothy Norman, who being Jewish and left-wing was a member of an elite cultural world which fascinated Indira. Dorothy was also a woman who had taken charge of her life. Like Indira, she had two children, but she was in the process of extricating herself from a difficult marriage. She wrote a regular column for the *New York Post;* she was active in the American Civil Liberties Union, in 'planned parenthood' and other worthy liberal causes. She was not merely a hostess but was also a person of some consequence in her own right; not a great artist, not a leader, but someone with a creative, worthwhile life that was not submerged in the lives of others.

When Indira returned to India after their American trip, she began to write to Dorothy Norman and their correspondence, which continued on and off for the next thirty-four years, became a kind of lifeline. It also provides one of the few windows into Indira Gandhi's inner world after 1950 when her letters to her father tailed off. As Indira herself confessed in one letter to Dorothy, 'What amazes me is the way I can write to you about myself – I haven't done this to anyone ever.'[4]

Indira and Dorothy had much in common, including the fact that they were both in unhappy marriages. But Indira also felt she could open up to Dorothy because they belonged to different cultures and were geographically separated. Dorothy Norman was safe – removed from Indira's daily world, including its rumour and gossip – in a way that no one in India was. Indira told Dorothy that she felt she had no option but to subordinate her life to her father's: there being no choice 'in the sense that I *felt* my father's loneliness so intensely, and I felt also that whatever I amounted to, or whatever satisfaction I got from my own work, would not, from a wide perspective, be so useful as my "tagging along" [as Harold Laski had warned her not to do so many years before], smoothing the corners and dealing with the many details ... However, I ... must do something else as well. Write? ... Perhaps writing would bring some kind of order and clear the path to future thought and work.'[5]

Indira also wrote to Dorothy of her unhappiness with Feroze, but not with complete candour. She failed to mention his infidelities just as Dorothy had failed to tell Indira about her own husband's psychological instability and violent behaviour. A recurrent theme in Indira's letters to Dorothy was her loneliness in the midst of others in Delhi. Indira worried that she was not sufficiently interested in other people; she confessed that she became irritated with them too easily, most of all that she felt *different*. 'They amuse me and they irritate me and sometimes I find myself observing them as if I were not of the same species at all.' When the film of Robert Penn Warren's novel *All the King's Men* came to Delhi, Indira thought it excellent, but the rest of the audience she felt seemed to miss the point 'which irritates me intensely, [though] it is silly to be irritated at such trifles . . . all the same, not having anyone with similar tastes gives one a sense of loneliness and isolation which is not at all pleasant'.[6]

There was also an element of narcissism in Indira and Dorothy's relationship. They reinforced one another's self-perceptions as long-suffering, neglected, superior beings. They viewed themselves – and each other – as highly sensitive, artistic women trapped in unhappy marriages to difficult men who felt threatened by their wives' intelligence and self-sufficiency. A note of flattery colours their letters. Dorothy, for example, wrote to Indira in August 1951: 'I have often thought how badly you need to be loved and to be able to love to your fullest capacity. To be honest and open about the most delicate things. There is so much of the artist in you – in your search for form and line and color, in the way you dress, and in your use of flowers – in every way. And in the way in which you look at things.'[7]

Indira felt at home with artistic women – her closest Indian friend Pupul Jayakar and her personal assistant Usha Bhagat, among others. But Dorothy Norman was elevated to a 'soul mate'. In the mid-1950s Indira wrote to Dorothy, 'I think you know me almost better than I know myself.'[8] Years later, Dorothy Norman said they 'fell in love instantaneously'.[9] But there was nothing sexual in their friendship. It was, in fact, all quite ethereal – talk of books and art and loneliness. They perhaps fell in love less with each other than with the reflected image of themselves that they glimpsed in each other. In the early years of their friendship, Indira felt that the person Dorothy so admired was her *essential*, true self. As she grew more politically involved, however, it was eclipsed, and after she became Prime Minister, 'the Dorothy Norman Indira' survived but in a splintered off, disconnected form. Dorothy Norman may have had access to Indira's emotional and aesthetic depths, but Indira's political personality was like the dark side of the moon to her.[10]

*   *   *

After Indira returned to India in mid-November 1949, she went to Lucknow to spend time with Feroze and the boys. It was a rude shock after New York, Dorothy Norman and her artistic friends. The 'rot' and 'corruption' of Lucknow politics were as repugnant as ever, and in December Indira wrote to Nehru of how people like the Chief Minister of Uttar Pradesh, G.B. Pant, were attempting to control the *National Herald*'s editorial policy. Indira closed her letter to her father with the threat, 'if you don't call Pantji to order for interfering . . . (with the full strength of Govt machinery & personnel including District Magistrates) in the business of a newspaper, then please stop in future talking about democracy & the freedom of the press in India. With all the other ills let us not also have hypocrisy, Indu'. This was one of her few letters not signed with 'love'.

As was the case in Kashmir the year before, Indira felt strongly about a political situation and tried to influence her father. This time, however, with little, if any, effect, for Nehru merely responded with an evasive note saying that he was confident nothing 'terrible is going to happen. We must not lose our perspective.' But Indira refused to be placated. She wrote another angry letter denouncing the corruption in Lucknow, and this letter, too, she merely signed with her name. By the end of December, however, she had calmed down. Two days before Christmas she wrote, 'Darling I go off the track occasionally – small things . . . assume gigantic proportions and one is depressed and frustrated.' In early January she escaped the 'rot' and 'corruption' of Lucknow and Uttar Pradesh politics when she, Feroze and the boys went back to Teen Murti in order to participate in the celebrations on 26 January 1950 when India officially became a republic.[11]

Dorothy Norman came to Delhi for the festivities and stayed for six weeks at Teen Murti in a room just down the hall from Indira's. She was not impressed by Feroze Gandhi whom she thought 'crude', and she made little effort to hide her feelings from Indira – or from Feroze himself who was as unimpressed with Dorothy as she was with him. There was considerable tension between Dorothy and Feroze until he returned to Lucknow in early February.[12]

When Dorothy herself left in March, Indira and the children remained at Teen Murti. Sometimes they visited Feroze in Lucknow at the weekends, but their permanent base – their real home – was now the Prime Minister's residence in Delhi. In May they went to Kashmir without Feroze, returning to Delhi in July. And thus the situation remained – with Indira and the boys in Delhi and Feroze in Lucknow – until Feroze was elected to Parliament the following year.

When India's first general election was held, between October 1951 and May 1952, Congress Party workers urged Indira to stand for Parliament but she refused on the grounds that the boys were too young. Her other reason, however, was that Feroze was standing for the constituency of Rae Bareilly – a district situated mid-way between Allahabad and Lucknow in Uttar Pradesh. Indira knew that her faltering marriage could not accommodate two political careers. Instead, Indira worked hard canvassing for both her father and Feroze. Rae Bareilly, in fact, was such a large constituency that she and Feroze divided it in two and worked their individual halves. In Phulpur, Nehru's constituency, Indira virtually ran her father's campaign. She also worked tirelessly in Delhi. Nehru wrote to Edwina Mountbatten in January 1952, 'One of the surprises of this election . . . has been the very fine work done by Indira. She has worked terribly hard. In Delhi she used to go out at 8 in the morning and return about 11 at night addressing numerous small meetings and groups. She is reported to be a very effective speaker and is in great demand.'[13] And to another friend Nehru boasted: 'Indira has done a man's job during these past two months, indeed more than that. She is still wandering about [campaigning in] the villages of Allahabad and Rae Bareilly Districts.'[14] Across the country Congress swept the polls, winning 364 seats out of 499 and twenty-two out of twenty-six states.

After winning his seat, Feroze moved from Lucknow to Delhi. In addition to becoming an MP, he had also been appointed managing director of the New Delhi edition of the *Indian Express* which already had established editions in Bombay and Madras. Like all MPs, Feroze was allocated a government bungalow, but initially he only used it for meetings and to receive friends and associates. He continued to take his meals and sleep at Teen Murti, sharing Indira's dark, hotel-like room in the west wing next to the boys' nursery. But Feroze quickly found the atmosphere at the Prime Minister's residence stifling. Shanta Gandhi, Indira and Feroze's old friend from their time in London, had lunch with them one day at Teen Murti and Feroze told her privately with a 'sneer in his voice' that 'this whole place [Delhi] is going to become Chanakya Puri [a town of intrigue]'. At the lunch table, Shanta said to Indira and Feroze, 'How can you live here [in Teen Murti]? It is a museum not a house to live in.' Indira, who had worked hard to humanize the former commander-in-chief's residence, shot back 'everyone is not as lucky as you are. You have to take things as they are.'[15] It was clear to Shanta Gandhi that the marriage was under considerable strain.

And it would only worsen with time. Feroze soon found his position in the household, living in the shadow of his father-in-law, all but intolerable. Indira was at her father's beck and call. She was Nehru's hostess at formal functions to which Feroze was sometimes not even invited or if he was, he found himself placed at the table at a much lower position than his wife. When the Soviet premier Nikolai Bulganin and the then first secretary of the Soviet Communist Party, Nikita Khrushchev, addressed a public meeting during a state visit, Indira and Nehru were on the platform, while Feroze and some other MPs were refused entry by security officers. Feroze, enraged, raised the matter in Parliament and Nehru was forced to apologize to him. At an All-India Congress Committee meeting, Nehru reminded party members that their families had not been invited and admonished those who had brought along their wives and children, only to be interrupted by Feroze who declared, 'It wasn't I who brought my wife here', referring to Indira's presence on the platform next to her father. Increasingly, Feroze spent more of his time at his bungalow on Queen Victoria Road though he slept most nights at Teen Murti.

Indira stoically endured Feroze's outbursts and absences. There was much to distract her looking after her father and children and running Teen Murti. In the early fifties Rajiv and Sanjay attended an exclusive private school, *Shiv Niketan* ('the Abode of Shiva') run by a German woman named Elizabeth Gauba who was married to an Indian. (One of the teachers, Usha Bhagat, an attractive, artistic young woman from Lahore, would later become Indira's personal assistant.) Nehru had a punishing schedule and routinely worked each day from 7 a.m. to 2 a.m., with short breaks for meals and yoga. Between 1951 and 1954, in addition to being Prime Minister he was also Minister of Foreign Affairs, chairman of the Planning Commission and President of Congress. He gave speeches nearly every day, toured India extensively and regularly travelled abroad. In the early fifties he visited the United States, Canada, Indonesia, Burma, Europe and Britain nearly every year.

Although Indira's life was entirely subordinated to her father's she found time to be extremely active in social welfare and cultural work. She established Bal Bhawan, a centre for destitute children in Delhi, and Bal Sahayog where homeless street children were housed and taught a skill or craft. She was vice-chairman of the Social Welfare Board, president of the Indian Council for Child Welfare, and vice-president of the International Council for Child Welfare. She was involved in traditional arts and crafts associations and organized performances of tribal dancing at the annual Republic Day celebrations. Indira was also active in the women's section of Congress for which she travelled throughout India, establishing contact with the party rank and file.

Indira's life at this time was crowded, often hectic, but predictable and uncontroversial. Some who had known Indira in her political London days were disappointed by her low-key involvement in public affairs, and felt she was not living up to expectations. And it is true that despite her work for the women's section of Congress, in these early years, Indira's role was largely apolitical despite her position at the heart of the Prime Minister's house.

In April 1953 Indira and the two children sailed to England for the coronation of Queen Elizabeth II. Nehru was to join them later, but Feroze did not go to Britain at all: the more his wife travelled abroad, the more disinclined he was, it seemed, to leave India. Eventually he would become hostile to the point of xenophobic about foreign travel.

In London Indira, nine-year-old Rajiv, seven-year-old Sanjay and their grandfather, Nehru, stayed at Claridge's Hotel in Mayfair. They saw a good deal of Krishna Menon. And Indira met up with P.N. Haksar – Feroze and Indira's old friend from their London days – who was now a member of the Indian Foreign Service and the Indian High Commission.

In June, after the coronation celebrations, Indira travelled for the first time to the Soviet Union where she stayed until late July visiting Moscow, Leningrad, Tashkent, Samarkand, and Georgia. This was also her first solo trip as the Indian Prime Minister's daughter. She was enormously impressed with the country, especially Soviet technology and the discipline of Soviet life. And the Russians were enamoured of Indira as well. 'Everybody – the Russians – have been so sweet to me . . . I am being treated like everybody's only daughter – I shall be horribly spoilt by the time I leave' she wrote.[16] The Black Sea – where Indira swam and sunbathed ('I don't think I have had such a holiday in years'[17]) was 'like the Mediterranean' – she did not even mind its pebbled beaches and the sunburn she got. Leningrad, she wrote to her father, was 'a truly beautiful city'. She was entranced by the Hermitage Museum and delighted with her suite of rooms at the hotel – 'bedrooms, bathroom, sitting room, dining room and study. Wallowing in luxury!'[18] She reassured Nehru, however, that her visit remained a strictly private one and that she had no intention of making any sort of statement.

While she was still in the Soviet Union, Nehru – now back in India – wrote to Indira on 1 July 1953 about the trouble brewing in Kashmir. The state, he said, had become 'a cauldron of unreason and intrigue'. A month later he reported on the 'headache' of Kashmir 'where Sheikh Saheb has turned many somersaults and is bitter against India and me. The situation . . . is explosive.'[19] For the past six years Nehru had based his Kashmir policy on Sheikh Abdullah – the Prime Minister of Kashmir – and his faith in Abdullah's commitment to India and secularism. But there had been signs that Abdullah harboured a vision of an independent Kashmir – or so Nehru and many Indians feared. Particularly disturbing was the Sheikh's apparent courting of the United States. He had recently had a meeting, for example, with Adlai Stevenson, who later told the *Manchester Guardian* that Kashmir did not need to be allied to either India or Pakistan. Abdullah was also being accused of running a one-party state.

All this came to a head when Sheikh Abdullah was dismissed from office on 8 August by Karan Singh, the *Sadar-i-Riyasat*, and arrested. Nehru's biographer, S. Gopal, says the dismissal took place 'by stealth of night' and that Nehru's 'consent had been neither sought nor given for the arrest' of Abdullah. Nevertheless in the coming years Nehru's 'ultimate responsibility for the detention of Sheikh Abdullah gnawed persistently at his whole sense of public values' and also, surely, the trust implicit in private friendship.[20]

Meanwhile Indira had left Russia for Norway, Denmark and then Switzerland where she joined Rajiv and Sanjay who had spent much of the summer at the experimental Swiss school – L'École d'Humanitié' run by the famous educationalist, Paulus Gaheeb. Indira was in Zurich on 10 August 1953 when she read in the Swiss newspapers that two days earlier Sheikh Abdullah had been dismissed as Prime Minister and placed under arrest. She immediately wrote to her father, 'I am filled with a terrible and deeply penetrating sadness. I suppose one has to do some things for the greater good but it is like cutting off a part of one-self.'[21] Sheikh Abdullah had hosted Indira and Feroze on their honeymoon in 1942; he had presided at Rajiv's naming ceremony three years later. He was a close personal friend – virtually part of the family – as well as her father's political colleague. The idea of his treachery filled Indira with a kind of moral sickness – if treachery it really was, for she well knew that Abdullah had many enemies eager to malign him falsely to the central government. Equally distressing was the image of his disgrace and arrest. In the face of the news from Kashmir, Indira wanted to return to India immediately – 'I am feeling absolutely wretched and in no mood to talk to people' – but Nehru insisted she go back to London for a complete medical examination before coming home.[22]

Indira flew from Zurich to London on 11 August and two days later she entered hospital for a complete checkup and 'all kinds of disagreeable medical tests'.[23] The tests were doubtless to assess the state of her lungs and the possibility of a recurrence of tuberculosis. She now had plenty of time to think as she lay in bed all day and she decided, as she wrote to her father, that when she returned to India she wanted to 'reorganize my life and get out of all the silly committees. I am so sick of people doing social work as a step up [the] political & social-set ladder, and equally sick of the vague goodness of the so-called Gandhians.'[24] She had now been away from India for nearly five months and had been rethinking her commitments: what they had been, what she now wanted them to be. She was weary of decorative, adjunct activities.

Despite her resolve to reorganize her life, Indira realized when she got back to Delhi how little room for manoeuvre she had. Although her day-to-day domestic routine had been simplified when Rajiv and Sanjay were enrolled at the elite Doon School – the Eton of India – in Dehra Dun,[25] Indira's time was now even more taken up with government and political activities. In June 1954 the Prime Minister of China Chou En-lai and his entourage arrived in Delhi. Then in October Indira accompanied Nehru to China. The night before they left she wrote to Dorothy Norman, 'I am doing a tremendous amount of work these days but I haven't discovered my métier yet. And consequently am still looking for something in which I can put my whole heart and soul; to feel "that sense of utter exhaustion and peace that comes in dying to give something life." '[26] Exhaustion – but neither peace nor a métier – came soon enough. The Chinese tour was gruelling from the moment Nehru and Indira landed in Peking and were greeted by a million people who lined the twelve-mile route from the airport. In the coming months and years, a succession of tours with Nehru followed to Indonesia, the United States and Canada, Scandinavia, Japan, the Soviet Union, Britain and Europe.

Meanwhile, Feroze was belatedly coming into his own as a parliamentarian. For more than two years, since his election as the MP for Rae Bareilly, he had been an unprepossessing backbencher. Then quite dramatically in early 1955 he made his maiden speech in the Lok Sabha, the lower house of Parliament, attacking the nexus between insurance companies and the business community. Feroze exposed the shady deals of the Bharat Insurance Company run by a wealthy Indian businessman named Ram Krishna Dalmia. A commission of inquiry was formed; Dalmia was convicted, and ultimately Feroze's crusading led to the nationalization of the life insurance business in India. His reputation as a radical and an enemy of corruption was now made. This reputation was further enhanced the following year when he sponsored the Parliamentary Proceedings Act of 1956 which gave the Indian press the hitherto denied right to publish parliamentary proceedings without running the risk of prosecution or being held up for contempt of Parliament.

That same year Indira suddenly became a member of the Congress Working Committee (CWC), the highest policy-making body of the Congress Party.[27] She did not seek membership; her inclusion came about at the instigation of Congress President U.N. Dhebar and also Lal Bahadur Shastri. Many of her father's colleagues perceived Indira as a conduit to the Prime Minister and as a potentially useful tool. The Congress old guard sought to establish Indira as a shadow political entity: someone with stature and position but no real substance of her own. It is unlikely, however, that Indira was aware of their plans for her. Although she was modest, self-effacing and still unsure of herself at this time, she certainly did not see herself as a cipher. Indira could become a member of CWC either by being appointed by the President or by being elected by the party members. Significantly, she insisted upon being elected. She wanted both a mandate and a power base.

As a friend remarked later, Indira's election to the CWC marked 'a very sharp turning point in her life. Up to then . . . she was only regarded as . . . her father's hostess . . . a "nice girl." . . . But with the announcement, attitudes changed overnight towards her. She was instantly reclassified . . . and subjected to scrutiny as a politician.'[28] Indira wrote of her new role to Dorothy Norman, 'What a life I have made for myself! Often I seem to be standing outside myself, watching and wondering if it's all worth the trouble. . . . It's certainly true that I have grown enormously since you saw me last. I am confident of myself but still humble enough to feel acutely embarrassed when all kinds of VIPs come for advice . . . I still haven't gotten used to being on the [Congress] Working Committee . . . Can you imagine me being an "elder statesman"?'[29]

Indira shouldered political responsibility and power at this point in her life for a number of reasons. Practically, her schedule was far more flexible because the boys were away at boarding school. At thirty-seven she also felt it was high time she began to establish herself in her own right, whilst realizing that as long as her father was alive she would need to devote her work and life to his. Meanwhile, although her husband had become a political force to be reckoned with, he, unlike Nehru, did not want a consort. Feroze's soaring reputation may also have roused Indira's competitive instincts. More importantly, however, their marriage had reached what seemed a point of no return. Around this time, Indira wrote to Dorothy Norman, 'I have been and am deeply unhappy in my domestic life. Now the hurt and unpleasantness don't seem to matter so much. I am sorry, though, to have missed the most wonderful thing in life, having a complete and perfect relationship with another human being; for only thus, I feel, can one's personality fully develop and blossom.'[30]

In April 1955 Indira accompanied her father to Bandung in Indonesia – her first trip abroad since she had joined the CWC. The occasion was the Bandung Conference, an unprecedented gathering of Asian and African heads of state to mark the birth of the non-alignment movement comprising newly-independent countries unwilling to align themselves with either of the superpowers, the United States or the Soviet Union. Nehru, Indira and her cousin B.K. Nehru (now a joint secretary in the Ministry of Finance) flew to Rangoon on a chartered Air India plane.

Here they met up with Gamel Abdul Nasser of Egypt and Chou En-lai. The latter had flown to Burma secretly because Chinese intelligence had detected an assassination plot against him. The next day Nehru and Indira, Nasser and Chou En-lai flew on to Bandung together.

On this flight from Rangoon to Jakarta they learned that Chou En-lai's decoy plane had been blown up after refuelling in Hong Kong. Nehru immediately accepted the unproven surmise that the explosion was the work of British intelligence. 'He wrote out a stinking telegram to Anthony Eden which with his usual impetuosity, he got up to take to the pilot to radio immediately ... Indira ... sitting near him, held him back, had a look at the telegram ... and counselled patience. She said that he was being very hasty in assuming the guilt of the British Government. Would it not be better ... to wait till there was some proof or some other more solid evidence?' Nehru 'cooled down', and the telegram was not sent.[31]

Despite its historical momentousness, the Bandung Conference was something of an anti-climax. As B.K. Nehru observed, 'its importance did not lie in what it did; what was important was that it was held at all'.[32] Like many international conferences, it was, to Nehru's annoyance, tedious and slow-moving. Nehru 'was forever vainly and unsuccessfully trying to speed up the proceedings,' but 'the long-winded and vacuous statements of various delegations' continued despite his efforts.[33] When the Prime Minister of Ceylon, Sir John L. Kotelawala – who had close links with the United States – moved a resolution condemning 'the neo-imperialism of the communist bloc', Nehru exploded and threatened to walk out of the conference. But Indira again intervened, admonishing him sharply, 'Control yourself, Papu,' whereupon Nehru calmed down.

Just two months after returning from Bandung, Indira and Nehru toured the Soviet Union. As in 1953, Indira was greatly impressed with the Soviet system, which had inspired her father's soviet-style planning programme of industrialization and modernization for India. The trip initiated an important and long period of Indo-Soviet collaboration. The immediate stir it aroused for Indira in India, however, was due to Khrushchev's gift to her of a mink coat. Some years earlier Indira had condemned Nan Pandit for accepting the very same gift when she was ambassador in Moscow, but Indira chose to accept the mink coat from Khrushchev and indeed wore it for many years with pleasure.

Shortly after Indira returned from the Soviet Union eleven-year-old Rajiv broke his arm when he was visiting Dalhousie with Feroze during a school holiday. From Delhi, Indira wrote to Rajiv, 'one must not be afraid of being hurt. The world is full of all kinds of hurts and it is only by facing them that we can become strong and hardy ... You know how much I want ... you to be courageous in mind and body. There are millions of people in the world but most of them just drift along, afraid of death and even more afraid of life.'[34] The preaching tone of the letter echoes some of the letters Nehru wrote to Indira as a child – she herself had become a didactic parent. But far more revealing is Indira's reflection that most people 'just drift along, afraid of death and even more afraid of life'. The continued longing to take control of her life, *not* to just drift along, was still haunting her.

Perhaps as a result, Indira was becoming more outspoken – politically as well as personally – in her relationship with her father. She complained to her father's secretary, M.O. Mathai, that Nehru would never discuss political issues at meals. She told a number of people, in fact, that she wished her father confided in her more. In April 1956 she cautioned Nehru that he should not rely too heavily on the Bombay Chief Minister Morarji Desai and the South Indian Congress leader, Kamaraj, because it 'creates dissatisfaction in many and cuts at your contacts with all those who hold different views. Sorry to inflict this on you but I just had to get it off my chest.'[35]

It had come to the point where Indira clearly wanted to be more than Nehru's hostess. She had toured on his behalf, for example, in Orissa in January 1956; she discussed issues with him and served as his sounding board. Nehru had long made a habit of sending Indira out to gather information and he frequently asked her to talk to people he did not have the time or inclination to see. But he did not seek counsel from Indira or even discuss problems or issues in any depth with her. He turned to others – such as Desai and Kamaraj – for this. Nehru knew that his daughter was knowledgeable and reliable; but he saw her as an assistant rather than a confidante or adviser. Indira was becoming increasingly dissatisfied with this subordinate role.

In December 1956 Indira returned from a nine-day trip to America with Nehru utterly exhausted. In early January 1957 she wrote to

Padmaja Naidu, 'I am not feeling too good but . . . what is required is not rest so much as a course of injections . . . It is the old trouble.'[36] She went on to complain of anaemia, low blood pressure and a lack of calcium. It is likely that the 'course of injections' Indira sought out and received in 1957 was, in fact, aimed at eradicating 'the old trouble' – her long-standing tuberculosis.

During the acute phase of her illness in the late thirties, when Indira was at Rollier's Swiss sanatorium, there had been no 'cure' for TB. Rest, 'feeding up', fresh air and sun were then the only, and none too efficacious, treatments. But a decade later the powerful drugs streptomycin, paraminosalicylic acid (PAS) and isoniazid, which individually or in combination can wipe out the TB bacillus, had been discovered. By the early fifties they were in general use in Europe and North America. In 1956 the pharmacological treatment of TB arrived in India when the Tuberculosis Chemotherapy Centre was opened in Madras, under the auspices of the World Health Organization. TB patients in Madras were treated with daily injections of PAS and isoniazid for a year, and five years later 90 per cent of those who stayed the course of injections were clear of the disease.[37] The Prime Minister of India – and his daughter – inevitably would have known about the drug treatment for tuberculosis in use at the Madras TB centre.

In 1957, with India's second general election looming, Indira's life had become more politically active – and arduous – than ever before. In addition to her work on the CWC, she had just been elected to the Congress Central Election Committee which discussed applications from prospective parliamentary candidates. There was talk of her also joining the Congress Parliamentary Board and indeed by the following year she was a member. All this political work required physical robustness and stamina. And at around this time she gradually began to acquire both.

Though she later suffered from a serious kidney ailment, Indira's health had radically improved. Her figure rounded out; her colouring changed from a sallow pallor to a ruddy hue; she ceased being periodically laid low with colds, coughs and flu. Photographs of her taken in the late fifties record this dramatic transformation. Earlier in the decade she looks thin, frail, pale and hollow-eyed. By its end it is clear that Indira has gained a good stone or more; the dark circles under her eyes have disappeared, her skin is clear and fresh and her eyes bright. She exudes radiance and energy.

The remarkable metamorphosis supports the assumption that she did, in fact, receive drug treatment for TB in the fifties. Ever since childhood, Indira had been 'sickly'. But from the age of about forty – and she turned forty in 1957 – she became an unusually healthy and fit woman. This did not go unnoticed. Indira wrote to Dorothy Norman that people had told her she looked 'lit up from inside' with a new vitality. But although the change in Indira was unmistakable, no satisfactory explanations for it were forthcoming. Indira had never smoked or drunk alcohol and had always watched her diet and exercised. She had begun to practise yoga regularly, but that was the only apparent change in her lifestyle. Tuberculosis was still, of course, a taboo disease in India, highly contagious and endemic among the poor. Though it was widely known that Kamala Nehru had died of the disease, after her death in the thirties, a veil had been drawn over the private affairs of the Nehru family, including their health. There may have been speculation about it, but there was no public discussion of what was deemed a personal matter, even after Nehru suffered a debilitating stroke some years later.[38]

Despite her increased political involvement, Indira did not stand for Parliament in the general election of 1957, though she told Padmaja Naidu that the Congress President, U. N. Dhebar, and 'other mischievous people' had been spreading rumours that they could persuade her to accept a seat. She insisted to Padmaja and others that 'I have no intention of standing.'[39] And, for now at least, she did not. Instead she canvassed even more strenuously in 1957 than she had in 1952 though this time it was principally for her father rather than her husband. Indira, in fact, visited and spoke at nearly every one of the 1,100 villages in Nehru's Phulpur constituency, drawing crowds of up to 20,000 people. She also campaigned for Congress candidates in Gujarat and the Punjab. On 17 February she wrote to Nehru from Allahabad how she was out every day from 'the crack of dawn' until midnight. 'Punjab was strenuous but most exhilarating too. I had 100,000 people in Rohtak just for me – imagine that!'[40] These were the first elections since Indira had become a member of the CWC and she more than proved her organizational skills and value as a vote getter.

In the midst of all this frenetic political activity, Indira's marriage deteriorated further. To her humiliation and Nehru's embarrassment,

Feroze now openly flaunted his affairs with other women, including the MPs Tarakeshwari Sinha, known as 'the glamour-girl of the Indian Parliament', Mahmuna Sultana and Subhadra Joshi (who, as Subhadra Datta, before her marriage, had worked with Indira at the refugee camps in Delhi at the time of Partition). Feroze's other well-known girlfriends included a beautiful Nepalese woman who worked for All India Radio and a divorcee from a high-caste Kerala family.[41]

But it was also widely rumoured at this time that Indira was having an affair with none other than her father's squat and moon-faced secretary, M.O. Mathai. Admittedly it was Mathai himself who was the primary source of these rumours. He boasted openly of his liaison with Nehru's daughter, both at the time and for many years after. There is no question that Indira and Mathai were very close; that she enjoyed and spent a good deal of time in his company, that she was attached to and confided in him. They walked the dogs together every day, took the boys on outings, conferred over Nehru's schedule and the running of Teen Murti, and of course they travelled together with Nehru.

From the start, Mathai's relationship with Indira had been an ambivalent one, in part because he usurped a number of her responsibilities such as handling Nehru's dealings with his publishers. Seeing Mathai's prominent role in her father's life, Indira may have had little choice other than to cultivate him. But there was also a kind of latent competition between them – and definitely a certain attraction. According to Nehru's biographer Savrepalli Gopal, 'Indira Gandhi encouraged him beyond normal limits.'[42] Despite his unabashed misogyny and lack of good looks, Mathai had a compelling, forceful personality. He was a hot-blooded, domineering man, not unlike Feroze Gandhi. In his autobiography he says, 'I have never suffered from over-humility' and pleads guilty to 'male chauvinism' – adding, 'one of the things I hate most is to go shopping with a woman. I do not think I can ever sleep in a room at night if there is a woman in it. I cannot bear the thought of sharing a bathroom with a woman.' But such feelings merely formed 'a barrier against matrimony'.[43] They did not prevent Mathai from being intimate with women or using them for his own purposes.

He and Indira enjoyed baiting one another. Mathai, for example, relates how after his mother died, Indira and Nehru went to his room to commiserate with him, only to find him sleeping like a baby. When Indira told Mathai this, he said, ' "that shows that I have a clear conscience," to which

Indira retorted . . . "It can also mean that you have none."' Mathai's riposte was 'this is the only witty remark you have ever uttered'.[44]

But were Indira and Mathai lovers? Indira's sexuality is itself a vexed issue. Many men – both those who knew her well and others who were merely acquainted with her – found her extremely feminine, even beautiful, and also warm and appealing. Women, on the other hand, tended to feel that she was cold, aloof, even 'nunlike', and assumed that she did not enjoy sex.[45]

In the seventies Mathai wrote an account in his autobiography of what he claimed was a twelve-year affair with Indira Gandhi in a chapter entitled 'She' – a chapter that Mathai himself suppressed when the book was about to be published, even though Indira Gandhi was out of power at the time. This chapter was widely believed to have been destroyed – and some people doubted it had ever existed – but in the early eighties, some five years after Mathai's death, it surfaced when Indira's estranged daughter-in-law, Maneka Gandhi, circulated it among a small group of Indira's enemies. The 'She' chapter contains such explicit material that even if Mathai had not suppressed it, it is doubtful whether his publishers would have taken the risk and proceeded to publish it. Mathai describes Indira as 'highly sexed' and includes, among other salacious details, the claim that she became pregnant by him and had an abortion. At the time that Mathai wrote the chapter – long after the events he maintains happened – he was a disillusioned man eager to have the last destructive word against Indira, her husband and her father, all of whom he felt had wronged him. So he had a strong motive to lie. Nevertheless, people who knew Indira and Mathai well, including B.K. Nehru, who is a reliable source and no enemy of his cousin, feel that the 'She' chapter contains more fact than fiction.[46]

Nehru apparently never suspected that there was anything afoot between his secretary and daughter, though Mathai claims in the 'She' chapter that he was constantly fearful that Indira's careless behaviour would alert her father to their relationship. But if Nehru remained ignorant of the alleged affair, very few others did. The rest of Delhi buzzed with rumours. One day in the hall of Parliament, Feroze – who had long been known as 'the nation's son-in-law' – was enraged when someone referred to Mathai as 'the Prime Minister's *real* son-in-law'. Indira, significantly, did nothing to quell the rumours of the alleged liaison.

In fact, the rumours may have been the whole point of the 'affair' –

whether actual or phantom – for her. For years she had been debased by Feroze's chronic unfaithfulness, especially since he had recently moved to Delhi and openly flaunted his affairs. Infidelity had now become a weapon they used against one another. Now it was Feroze's turn to be humiliated. And he was – deeply. He determined to ruin Mathai and enlisted the help of his journalist friend, Nikhil Chakravartty.[47]

In 1958 Feroze ceased living at Teen Murti altogether; he moved his belongings into his bungalow on Queen Victoria Road and only went to the Prime Minister's residence during the day in order to visit his sons when they were home from boarding school. Feroze made no secret of his estrangement from Indira. He announced to his friend, the journalist Inder Malhotra one day, 'Look here, before you hear a doctored version of it, let me tell you that I have stopped going to the Prime Minister's house completely.'[48]

In addition to moving out of Teen Murti, Feroze found a way of striking back at Indira where she was most vulnerable: through her father. In February he made one of his blistering speeches in Parliament, this time exposing the fraudulent dealings of officials employed in the government-owned Life Insurance Corporation with a private business-man named Haridas Mundhra. Mundhra had long been a generous contributor to Congress, and when he got into financial difficulties in the late fifties, he persuaded the Finance Minister T.T. Krishnamachari, and the principal Finance Secretary, H.M. Patel, to 'bail him out' by persuading the Life Insurance Corporation to purchase 15 million rupees worth of shares in his companies. He argued that the stock market would be hard hit if the government did not intervene. The transaction was irregular and furthermore, the value of the stocks fell sharply soon after the sale. Feroze Gandhi stood up in Parliament and declared: 'I hope I have established collusion between the Life Insurance Corporation of India and Mr Mundhra. I have, I hope, established a conspiracy in which public funds were wrongfully employed for financing the interests of an individual at the cost of the insured.'[49] The Life Insurance Corporation was under the remit of the Finance Ministry and therefore Krishnamachari – popularly known at TTK and a close friend and associate of Nehru – was held officially responsible.

Nehru was forced to set up a commission of inquiry into what quickly became known as 'the Mundhra Scandal', and when the commission issued its report stating that the Finance Minister was 'constitutionally

... responsible' for the shares transaction, TTK was forced to resign, even though Nehru remained convinced he was innocent of any wrong-doing.[50] Morarji Desai replaced TTK as Finance Minister.

As a result of the scandal Feroze's reputation as a crusader grew into that of a giant killer. He now gained national stature and attracted his own coterie of followers and hangers-on. The central hall of Parliament where Feroze's men gathered to meet with their idol became known as 'Feroze's corner'. 'Red, rotund and Pickwickian', Feroze would preside here and also at the salon at his bungalow on Queen Victoria Road.[51] In effect, he had become a kind of unofficial opposition to the Prime Minister.

Not surprisingly, Indira wrote to Dorothy Norman at this time complaining that she was feeling 'very unsettled'. And also trapped. 'Ever since I was a small girl, there seemed to be some force driving me on – as if there were a debt to pay. But suddenly the debt seems to be paid – anyhow I get a tremendous urge to leave everything and retire to a far place high in the mountains. Not caring if I ever did a stroke of work again.'[52] This 'dream of escape' would lace Indira's letters to Dorothy Norman over the next few years.

Indira also told Dorothy that she had now taken up yoga seriously. 'I get up early these days to do a special set of exercises. It is a system ... of Yoga ... taught us by an exceedingly good-looking Yogi. In fact, it was his looks, especially his magnificent body, which attracted everyone to his system ... He is, however, exasperating to talk to – so full of superstition.'[53] Indira's yoga teacher, Dhirendra Brahmachari, was to become an important and mysterious figure in her life. Mathai, who had reason to view Brahmachari's advent and growing influence at Teen Murti with alarm, described him as 'a bearded, semi-literate Swami' though Mathai conceded that Brahmachari was also 'tall and attractive'. Brahmachari's superb physique, enhanced by the fact that he wore few clothes even in cold weather, his long raven-black hair and beard and his penetrating eyes struck everyone, men and women alike.

In 1958 Brahmachari (whose name means 'one who is celibate') had only recently arrived in Delhi, penniless it was said because he had been expelled from Kashmir for making sexual advances towards his female yoga students. According to Mathai, soon after Indira fell under Brahmachari's spell, Nehru too began to take yoga lessons from Brahmachari. Other prominent politicians soon became followers of the *swami*, including Lal Bahadur Shastri, Jayaprakash Narayan, Morarji Desai and the Indian President, Dr Rajendra Prasad. In 1959 Brahmachari established his Vishwayatan Yoga Ashram and Trust for the Promotion of Yoga in Delhi, which was inaugurated by Nehru. The ashram was given a hefty annual grant by the Ministry of Education and Brahmachari himself was allotted a government bungalow on Jantar Mantar Road by the Housing Ministry. And so began Brahmachari's remarkable rise in the world of power politics in Delhi.

Indira was not the only one at Teen Murti harbouring a dream of escape at this time. In late April 1958 Nehru made a serious attempt to resign as Prime Minister. He had already tried three times before to give up his burdensome position – in 1954, 1956 and 1957 – but the speech he made on 29 April 1958 was more earnest and heartfelt than his previous bids for freedom. Nehru was exhausted; he felt 'stale'. On 1 May, following a long, private conversation with her father, Indira wrote and delivered a letter to him by hand, urging him to act on his desire to resign. Though they were both at home at Teen Murti at the time, Indira wanted to commit her thoughts to paper as she had in the past when she tried to advise her father. Recently she had warned him that 'some very ugly things are happening right around you. It is of course the familiar green-eyed monster jealousy.'[54] Now in her letter she said that since Nehru had publicly raised the issue of resignation 'is it wise to go back to the *status quo*? . . . So much is rotten in our politics that everybody sees things through his own avaricious myopic eyes and is quite unable to understand nobility or greatness. There will therefore be a feeling that you had no intention of giving up the P.M.ship and were only bluffing. Let them try to manage by themselves, otherwise they will drag you down with their own rottenness. If you are outside, it may at least reassure the general public that you were not responsible for all the wrongdoing.'[55]

It is a naive but revealing letter. At this stage in her political life, Indira was peculiarly sensitive to 'rottenness' – she used the word as if holding it with a pair of tongs. She did not want her father to be tainted by the corruption she sensed was closing in on both of them. She even felt that he needed to be protected from it. In this she underestimated Nehru; he may have been a poor judge of character when it came to people like M.O. Mathai or even Krishna Menon, but Nehru was politically extremely astute. Whereas it was Indira who was politically unsophisticated. (In time, of course, she would become adept at and would far surpass her father in tolerating and handling corruption.) This letter also reveals Indira's capacity for distrust, even paranoia: she is fearful of those she considers Nehru's 'enemies' – the forces of evil ranged against her father's 'nobility' and 'greatness'. She thinks that a corrupt coterie – 'they' – are out to trap her father and bring him down and he must dissociate himself from 'them', particularly in the eyes of 'the general public'.

In the event, Nehru did not resign. But he was badly in need of a rest and so a long sabbatical was discussed and planned. During the summer of 1958 Indira attended a meeting of the International Union for Child Welfare in Brussels. When she returned to Delhi in August, she discovered that Nehru's sabbatical had been reduced to a holiday in Tibet and Bhutan. She insisted that she must accompany him and they left for the Himalayas in early September.

There they trekked by pony and by foot on rough bridle paths through regions with no roads and no telecommunications, crossed passes of 15,000 feet, and spent their nights in sleeping bags in tents rather than Dak bungalows. They were completely cut off from Delhi and from politics in a way that would be unthinkable for a Prime Minister in a later age of faxes and satellite telephones. It was if they had been transported to another world. As Nehru himself said of the Himalayas, they 'give one a sense not only of peace but of permanence, and of something above and away from the follies of human beings. In Hindu mythology the gods had their abodes in these mountains; they chose well ... the peace of Buddha still prevails here.'[56]

But they were unable to bask in the Buddha's peace for long. While Indira and Nehru were negotiating a pass in the Greater Himalayas in northern Bhutan, a message finally caught up with them that back in Delhi Feroze had suffered a serious heart attack and was in hospital. In fact, he had had two heart attacks in rapid succession on 22 and 24 September. Indira immediately set off for home – a tortuous journey by horseback, jeep and aeroplane. Arriving at Delhi's Palam airport on 2 October, she drove straight to Willingdon Hospital where Feroze was by now out of danger.

Feroze was discharged on the 11th, after which Indira, Feroze and their children embarked on their own holiday to Kashmir, renting a houseboat in Srinagar. Despite the bitterness that had grown between them in recent years, they somehow managed to put the past behind them and to find forgiveness for one another. Feroze's heart attack, and the shadow of mortality cast by it, had seemed to work a true reconciliation.

But it was fleeting. Things began to fall apart again almost as soon as they returned to the hubbub of Delhi. For one thing Delhi was abuzz with rumours of the imminent downfall of M.O. Mathai, which Feroze had been plotting for some time. His friend, the journalist Nikhil Chakravartty, had uncovered some potentially damaging information. In 1952 Mathai had bought an opulent house and large orchard in Kulu from two Scottish sisters and then sold it for a profit; Mathai also owned a house near Claridge's Hotel in an exclusive area of New Delhi, and he had set up a dubious trust in memory of his mother. Chakravartty also claimed that Mathai had large sums of money secreted away in foreign bank accounts.[57] Where had the Prime Minister's secretary got the money from to buy these properties? Mathai's financial dealings were raised in Parliament and a commission of inquiry was appointed. Mathai, of course, protested his innocence and no conclusive evidence was found against him. But he was forced to offer his resignation to Nehru, who publicly exonerated his secretary but agreed that it would be best if he depart. But Mathai's exodus was not without repercussions. He left Teen Murti filled with animus against Nehru, Indira and Feroze. And it would be Indira who would later feel the full brunt of this.

The Mathai scandal, and Feroze's continued infidelities, quickly undid the peace Indira and Feroze had found together in Kashmir. When Mathai's financial dealings were questioned in Parliament, everyone grasped that it had been part of Feroze's personal vendetta. The gossip in Delhi was that the marriage of Indira and Feroze was finally over. Indira herself told her friend Pupul Jayakar that she wanted a divorce. One day Indira scribbled a memo to herself on a scrap of paper that she dated and put away in a drawer: 'But your thoughts they will not rest. They flutter like bats in ghostly confusion. Round and round the exhausted brain. They gnaw and nibble their way like rats through your leaden weariness.'[58] This was the note on which the year 1958 closed.

* * *

1959 opened with the annual session of Congress held in Nagpur. U.N. Dhebar, the Congress President, was due to retire before the end of his two-year term, and he and other party leaders pressed Indira to succeed him. According to Indira's account, it was G.B. Pant, the Union Home Minister, who first broached the subject. Her immediate, instinctive response was, in her own words, 'that I couldn't manage it. I did not have doubts. I was absolutely certain that I wouldn't be able to handle it.' Pant overruled, saying, 'it's not a question of your decision. We have decided and you have to do it. This is your duty.'

Indira then said she felt she must consult her father. Pant, who was well aware of Nehru's reluctance to promote his daughter, replied: 'It has nothing to do with your father. It is for you to decide.'

Indira, nevertheless, went to Nehru. Later she learned that Pant had already spoken to her father and that Nehru had tried to dissuade Pant from encouraging Indira further. But to Indira Nehru merely said, 'It must be your decision. I am not going to enter into it.' She sensed, however, that he did not want her to accept the post.

Nehru's cool response might have been the end of the matter but for Pant's and Dhebar's grim determination. After a good deal of harassment from them, Indira caved in and agreed to become Congress President. But almost as soon as she had accepted she changed her mind and rang Pant to say, 'No Pantji, I have thought about it, I can't do it.' He then played his trump card. He told Indira that the news had already been released to the press. The next day a series of editorials and columns appeared in the national papers arguing that Indira was not up to the job. These stung. But Indira still insisted to U.N. Dhebar that 'I simply cannot do it. It is not fair either to me or the organization.' Dhebar and Pant now, in one voice, asked Indira if she was willing to let the press 'get away with this?' Indira realized she would face humiliation if she refused. Her answer to Dhebar and Pant was now a simple 'all right'.[59]

On 2 February Indira was formally elected President of the Indian National Congress. Because Dhebar had resigned mid-term, she was elected for the remaining eleven months only, though she would be able to seek re-election if she wanted to. She took office six days later at a simple ceremony at the All-India Congress Committee headquarters in Delhi. The occasion was far removed from her grandfather Motilal Nehru's grand presidential cavalcade through Calcutta in 1928 and from her father's procession on a white charger through the streets of Lahore in 1929. Partly this was because since independence Congress had lost much of its importance as a mass mobilizing organization and thus the status of Congress President had changed significantly. After 1947, real power lay with the Prime Minister and the parliamentary wing of the party rather than with the Congress President and the organizational wing and it was now the party in the legislatures that formulated policy.

But as Congress President Indira was more than a figurehead. Nehru himself had been both Congress President and Prime Minister between 1951 and 1954. Indira also followed in the footsteps of distinguished female Congress Presidents: Annie Besant (1917), Sarojini Naidu (1925), and Nellie Sen Gupta (1933). Although avowedly not a feminist, Indira chose to quote from a popular Hindi film song in her presidential inauguration speech:

> We are the women of India
> Don't imagine us as flower-maidens
> We are the sparks in the fire.

Years later Indira was asked by an interviewer if her political rise might have been easier if she had been her father's son rather than his daughter and she replied that on the contrary, 'I think there would probably have been more difficulties, because ... I could not really have remained with him and helped him in the way I have. I would have had to make a living ... I think the political world also would have been much more sensitive to the situation and wary of it.'[60]

This had indeed been the case in 1955 when Indira joined the CWC. The party leadership assumed Indira would be malleable; a pawn who would act at her father's and their behest. And Indira had yet to prove them wrong. Capable, industrious and responsible though she had shown herself to be, Indira had not given any strong indications that she possessed a political mind or will of her own.

Nehru was mildly disapproving about his daughter becoming Congress President. He viewed her as an adjunct to himself – not as a politically independent being, and whilst correctly grasping her indifference to parliamentary procedure and legal rules, he underestimated her intelligence. He also feared the impression Indira's promotion might give. He stated that he 'would not like to appear to encourage some sort of dynastic arrangement. That would be wholly undemocratic and an undesirable thing', and he insisted that he was 'not grooming her for anything'.[61] Indeed Nehru had always gone to great lengths to avoid any behaviour that could be interpreted as nepotism. When TTK urged Nehru to make either Nan Pandit or Indira a member of the Cabinet, Nehru had shot back that neither his sister nor daughter would ever be in the Cabinet as long as he was Prime Minister.

If Nehru was unenthusiastic about Indira's leadership of Congress, Feroze was positively hostile. He saw Indira's presidency 'as the final assault on their relationship'.[62] After her election Indira wrote to Dorothy Norman: 'a veritable sea of trouble is engulfing me. On the domestic front, F[eroze] . . . has always resented my very existence, but since I have become President he exudes such hostility that it seems to poison the air. Just to make things difficult for me, he is leaning more and more towards the communists and is sabotaging my efforts to strengthen the Congress. Unfortunately, he and his friends are friendly with some of our ministers and an impossible situation is being created.'[63]

Indira felt, in fact, that Feroze had become her chief political foe. But her sense of allies and her own loyalties were becoming confused. She had allowed the Congress old guard to pressurize her into the presidency. But at the same time – January 1959 – Indira aligned herself with the Congress Socialist Forum, a radical ginger group which opposed Congress' leadership and Nehru's toleration of them. Feroze was a leading member of the Forum and despite severely strained relations with his wife, he apparently persuaded Indira to sign their manifesto attacking party policy for deviating from socialist lines. For many years to come Indira would style herself as – and was generally perceived to be – a leftist. But within months of her election as Congress President she aligned herself with right-wing and communal forces in Kerala.

Situated at the extreme south-western tip of India, Kerala was – and still is – a unique Indian state due to its high literacy rate, and balanced population of Christians, Muslims and Hindus (which in turn means that the Church, Muslim League and the Nair and Ezhava castes are all powerful in the state). Kerala also has a large Communist party that, in 1957, was voted into power. This new administration, headed by Chief Minister E.M.S. Namboodiripad, proceeded to pass radical and potentially destabilizing legislation including an agrarian reform bill to promote reform in land ownership and protect tenant farmers, and an education bill to regulate private education. The Church, Muslim League and Nair Service Society, whose agricultural interest and privately-run schools were threatened by the acts, joined together with Kerala's Congress to agitate against the state government.

Indira visited Kerala in April 1959 in her new role as Congress President. Even before her visit, she was aware that Kerala's Congress had joined forces with non-secular forces – including the old Congress enemy, the Muslim League. Despite her ostensible left-wing stance Indira chose to overlook these alliances. She launched a stinging attack against the Communist government, which she also accused of being agents of the Chinese.

Civil disobedience intensified in the months after Indira's visit. In June she told a newspaper correspondent, 'As Congress President I intend to fight them [the Communists] and throw them out.'[64]

Throughout the uproar over Kerala – which was widely covered in the press – Feroze agitated in Delhi, publicly and vehemently denouncing the national Congress leadership – headed, of course, by his wife – for aligning itself with right-wing forces. At a Congress meeting he demanded, 'Where are the principles of the Congress? . . . Has the Congress . . . fallen so low that we are going to be dictated [to] by communal elements, by leaders of caste? . . . in Kerala you have forged the instrument of your own destruction.'[65]

In July 1959 the democratically-elected Communist government of Kerala was dismissed by Nehru and the state was put under direct rule from Delhi. In this Feroze and others saw Indira's hand; they accused her of bullying her father into taking this action.

But such accusations belied a more subtle chain of events. In January 1958 – a year before Indira became Congress President – Nehru's trusted adviser Krishna Menon reported that 'sinister trends' were developing in Kerala and that conditions would probably only get worse. In May 1958 Nehru stated in an interview in the British *Daily Telegraph* that 'in my opinion the Communists have to have a great deal of luck to be able to stay in power in Kerala much longer'.[66] At this time, Nehru was becoming increasingly alienated from communism and the Soviet Union, especially in the wake of communist policies in Hungary and Yugoslavia. Nehru, like Indira, came to believe that under the Communist control Kerala was slipping into violence and anarchy. Krishna

Menon made a second tour of Kerala in September 1958 and gave a gloomy report confirming Nehru's fears. In October 1958 Nehru asked his Home Minister to secure more information from local Kerala sources and began considering whether or not the Indian army would have to be sent in to restore order.

On 22 June 1959 Nehru went to the Kerala capital, Trivandrum, and was shocked by what he saw. Not even Indira's account of her April trip had prepared him for an atmosphere of 'near hysteria with "thick walls of group hatred"'.[67] Nehru urged Kerala's Chief Minister Namboodiripad to call for fresh elections – arguing these would test the opposition's claim that the government had lost all its popular support. But Namboodiripad refused. On 31 July 1959 Nehru ordered that the Communist government of Kerala be dismissed.

This was the first time in independent India's history that a federated state government had been dissolved, and it set a dangerous precedent. The following year, when new state elections were held, Kerala's Congress party came to power on the back of its opportunistic alliance with the Muslim League and other right-wing forces.

Indira's critics, with hindsight, view the dismissal of the Kerala government as prophetic: the first display of her 'ruthlessness', her authoritarian tendencies and her indifference to democratic norms. But although Indira clearly supported – and may have expedited – her father's dismissal of Kerala's government, she did not orchestrate it.[68]

What is significant about Indira's response to the unrest in Kerala is that it touched a raw nerve in her – her fear of disorder and loss of control. It was Indira's overreaction to political instability – rather than an innate authoritarianism – which makes Kerala a revealing episode in her political development. Indira did not share Nehru's faith that democratic institutions would survive unstable circumstances. In the face of conflict and instability, her instinct was to choose order above democracy.

Though she felt she had been right in her reaction to the Kerala crisis – and her involvement, however belated, in the dismissal of the state government – the affair took its toll on Indira. Just ten months into her presidency she decided that she did not want to serve another full, two-year term as Congress President. She explained to Dorothy Norman that 'all sections in India, with the solitary exception of the Communists, feel that I have done a good job and there is tremendous pressure on me to continue for another term. It has been tough work – sometimes exhausting . . . I have gained tremendously in self-confidence. But I do not wish to continue for many reasons. The routine part of the work takes too much time and is too confining. I have felt like a bird in a too-small cage.'[69]

On the night of 30 October Indira could not sleep. She tossed and turned for hours; finally she rose at 3.45 a.m. and started to write a letter to Nehru – even though he was sleeping in his room in the opposite wing of the house. She was agitated she said and felt she must tell him 'the real reason' why she did not feel she could serve a second term as Congress President.

> Since earliest childhood I have been surrounded by exceptional people and have participated in exceptional events . . . The circumstances in which I passed my girlhood – both domestic and public spheres – were not easy. The world is a cruel place for the best of us and specially so for the sensitive.

She had always felt a 'debt' and 'burden' and 'these last eight years or so I have worked harder and longer . . . always feeling that I could never do enough'. But now she felt the debt

> has been paid off . . . I have felt like a bird in a very small cage, my wings hitting against the bars whichever way I move. The time has come for me to live my own life. What will it be? I don't know at all. For the moment, I just want to be free . . . and find my own direction. The experience of being President of the Congress has been exhilarating at times, depressing at times, but certainly worthwhile. But . . . I can only be warped & unhappy if I have to continue.[70]

It was a crucial, in-the-dead-of-night confession that could not have been uttered face to face to her father during the day. Though there is nothing accusatory in the letter, Indira made it clear that the 'debt' or 'burden' she had always borne – and the choices she had made – were not her own. Her life had never been of her own making. From the very beginning, her family and historical events had determined her fate. Of course she *had* chosen her husband, in the face of strenuous opposition, and that choice had been a bid for freedom, but the bid had failed. Now she was estranged from her husband and her children were growing up and away at school. She was middle-aged – nearly forty-two.

If she was ever going to create a life of her own, she had to start now before it was too late.

Thus, to the dismay of the Congress leaders, Indira made a public announcement that she would be stepping down as Congress President. Once the decision had been made, she expected to feel liberated. In the face of considerable opposition, she was breaking out of her cage. But instead Indira fell into a deep depression. She wrote to Dorothy Norman that 'apart from the mental depression there was a physical one too. I lost a lot of weight and have been quite shaky on my feet, fainting off a couple of times'. She thanked Dorothy for some phonograph records she had sent to Indira: 'all through this dark period, the only thing that seemed to help was music and poetry'.[71] A month later Indira wrote again, 'I am far from well.' But this time it was not the 'old trouble'. The TB cure had worked. Indira now had a kidney stone that was giving her pain and sleepless nights. 'I am afraid,' she confessed to Dorothy Norman, that 'I am not looking at all radiant just now.'[72]

Despite posting her resignation as President of Congress, Indira's term of office did not finish until January 1960, so she had to carry on with her party duties, despite depression and illness, until the end of 1959. In November, when serious sectarian rioting broke out in Bombay, she visited and toured the state. Three years earlier the old state system in India had been reorganized and individual states redefined on the basis of their dominant language. Two states, however, had escaped this reorganization scheme: the bilingual states of Bombay (known as the Bombay Presidency under British rule) and the Punjab. Nehru wanted the bilingual states to survive, but ever since the 1957 elections there had been agitation to create two separate states out of Bombay: Maharashtra and Gujarat. The unrest that now greeted Indira was over the fate of the city of Bombay and the issue of which state it would go to if and when separate Marathi-speaking and Gujarati-speaking states were created.

Indira had only been in Bombay a short time before she was convinced that – contrary to her father's wishes – the state should be divided. In addition to accepting the arguments of those who wanted two states, Indira was responding to what she perceived as a 'law and order' situation – just as she had in Kerala. Unless the proponents of Gujarat and Maharashtra were given their states, she argued, she could see no end to the trouble and unrest engulfing Bombay. In her last month as Congress

President Indira appointed a committee of inquiry. On 4 December it recommended that the state be bifurcated and that the city of Bombay be given to Maharashtra. In due course the old Bombay Presidency was divided in two and the new states of Gujarat and Maharashtra became part of the Indian union.

Throughout her Bombay tour Indira had been suffering severe stomach and back pains because of her kidney ailment. When she returned to Delhi she consulted a specialist physician who said she must have surgery to remove her kidney stone. When Feroze heard of the impending surgery, he came to see Indira immediately at Teen Murti. Once again they were reconciled, just as they had been after Feroze's heart attack the previous year. Illness – and behind it, the unspoken possibility of death – was the one thing that could still bring them together. On 17 February, shortly after her term as Congress President expired, Indira was operated on. Feroze was with her at the hospital and after she was discharged, he moved back into Teen Murti to nurse her during her convalescence.

In June 1960, when Indira was fully recovered, she, Feroze and the children returned to Kashmir for a holiday. They stayed on a houseboat on Nagin Lake, Srinagar. Feroze and the boys swam, boated and took photographs. Indira tutored the children in English and tried, without a great deal of success, to teach herself Spanish. Nearly tame kingfishers and swifts flew about the houseboat to the delight of the children and one flew inside and perched on Rajiv's shoulder. For several days they went to Daksun – a place of pine and fir forests and trout streams. They walked and fished. Back in Srinagar, Sanjay and Rajiv learned how to water-ski. Feroze told Indira that he had just bought a piece of land in Mehrauli, near Delhi, and they spoke of building a house there for themselves – their *own* house rather than Teen Murti or Feroze's government bungalow.

They had been through so much; there had been so many quarrels and betrayals and humiliations – much of it occurring in the glare of public knowledge or rumour. But up in the shadow of the Himalayas they escaped the wounds of the past. They planned a future together, rediscovered joy in each other and dwelt for a short but precious time in 'the peace of Buddha'.

Years later, Indira confided to one of her biographers that she decided during this interlude in Kashmir that after her father died she would devote herself to Feroze's political career – that 'she would commit herself totally to him'.[73]

Scarcely two months later, on the night of 7 September, Indira was in an Air India plane flying home from Trivandrum in Kerala where she had been speaking at a Congress women's conference. When she landed at Delhi's Palam airport, long past midnight, she was told that Feroze had suffered another heart attack. As she had two years before, she went directly from the airport to his bedside at Willingdon Hospital. There she found her assistant, Usha Bhagat, among others. All night, Usha told her, Feroze had been drifting in and out of consciousness, rousing himself periodically to ask, 'Where's Indu?'[74]

A week earlier, Feroze had begun having acute chest pains. On the afternoon of 7 September he rang his doctor and friend, Dr H.L. Khosla, who told him to come into hospital immediately. Feroze drove himself there and collapsed while Khosla was examining him. At about 4.30 a.m. on the morning of the 8th, he opened his eyes. Indira was sitting beside him. She had not slept or eaten all night and seeing her pale, gaunt face, Feroze told her she must go get some breakfast. She refused. Feroze lost consciousness again. Indira was with him when he stopped breathing at 7.45 a.m. It was just four days short of what would have been Feroze's forty-eighth birthday.

Indira rode with Feroze's body when it was taken from the hospital to Teen Murti. She insisted upon washing it herself and preparing it for cremation. She refused to allow anyone else to help her or even be present while she did this. She had all the furniture cleared out of the ground-floor rooms of Teen Murti and clean white sheets spread over the carpets. Then crowds of visitors – hundreds of them – arrived to pay their last respects. Sanjay and Rajiv sat cross-legged on the white-sheeted floor, stone-faced, next to their father's body. Nayantara Sahgal found Nehru alone in his room in a stunned state. He was amazed at the number of mourners descending on the house and said over and over that he never expected Feroze to die so young. Indira herself was almost preternaturally controlled, but her face was ashen and her eyes full of anguish.[75]

The next day Feroze's body, draped in the Indian tricolour, was put on an open truck and with Indira, Rajiv, Sanjay and his sister Tehmina beside it, the truck slowly travelled the crowd-lined two miles to the Nigambodh Ghat of the Jumna where sixteen-year-old Rajiv lit the funeral pyre. Feroze's last rites were a Hindu cremation. After his first heart attack, he had told friends that this is what he wanted because he hated the thought of his body exposed to vultures in the Parsi Towers of Silence. Nevertheless Indira had seen to it that Parsi rites were performed over her husband's body before it was taken to the cremation ground. Two days later the urn containing Feroze's mortal remains was carried by train to Allahabad where a portion of the ashes was submerged at the Sangam and the remainder buried in the Allahabad Parsi cemetery.

Indira remained in control and in charge throughout the immediate aftermath of Feroze's death. But when the boys went back to school in Dehra Dun and life resumed and the old routines kicked in, she broke down. She wrote to sixteen-year-old Rajiv at the Doon School:

> The first . . . days I was quite numb, and although my eyes were aching and burning, I could not really cry – but now I have begun to cry and don't seem to be able to stop. I have never before known such utter desolation and grief. I look at things and people but don't really see them. Everything seems so dark. What am I going to do? This dreadful thing has happened just when I thought everything was going well and that we might all live together as a family again. However, you are young and brave and have many other qualities of which we are proud. Your life lies before you, and I do not wish to burden you with my sorrow. However much one loves one's father, it is not as close a relationship as that of husband and wife. There is one thing about which I want to warn you. You never talk – that is, about what is really in your mind. It was this same trait in Papa which caused him so much mental suffering, and prevented me from doing so many things to help him. If you do not talk, how can I do so? And that is what makes for loneliness.[76]

Feroze's death was physically as well as psychologically wounding. After he died, Indira felt ill – sick at heart. She also stopped menstruating.[77] As she described her state much later, 'My whole mental and physical life changed suddenly, my bodily functions changed . . . I was physically ill. It upset my whole being for years . . . it was not just a mental shock, but it was as though someone had cut me in two.'[78]

At Feroze's cremation, Indira wore a white sari, as Hindu widows always do – for in India white is the colour of mourning. She eschewed the other harsh strictures of Hindu widowhood – shaving her head, breaking her bangles, sleeping on the floor, eating plain, unspiced food. Few women of Indira's class and background embraced this brutal traditional life of Indian widowhood.

Eventually the *illness* of her grief eased, but for a long time after Feroze's death Indira abided by one traditional rule: she wore white exclusively. She did this not because it was enjoined on her as a widow but because, as she later explained, when Feroze died all the colour drained out of her life.[79]

TWELVE

Towards a Hat Trick

INDIRA HAD PLANNED to make an extended two-month tour of Africa, South America, Mexico and the United States in the autumn of 1960. But when Feroze died in early September, all but the unofficial, Mexican and American parts of the trip were hastily cancelled. By the end of September, she was still in Delhi when she wrote to Dorothy Norman, 'I am . . . quite numb with shock and although the burden of sorrow seems heavy enough . . . now, I feel it can only increase.' She felt 'empty and hollow', but also as if there were 'an enormous weight crushing' her. 'Will I ever be free from the burden or be able to touch and see without feeling "the heartbreak in the heart of things"?'[1]

As she predicted, Indira's misery intensified rather than diminished as the weeks passed. When she finally got to Mexico in late October, she was almost perpetually in tears, crying even while visiting the Mayan ruins.[2] Her grief seemed like 'a veil surrounding and covering me from all sides'.[3] She could not take any pleasure in sightseeing. It took an enormous effort merely to keep going.

After Mexico, Indira met Dorothy Norman in Dallas, Texas and they travelled together to Arizona and New Mexico. Indira was still, in her own words, 'enveloped in a black cloud of misery'.[4] They then went on to New York. John F. Kennedy had just been elected president by a narrow margin, and the day after the election Indira wrote to Nehru, 'We had a terrible night of ups & downs & contradictions in the figures but finally Kennedy has won. He is better for India & Asia but most of the vote was anti-Nixon rather than pro-K[ennedy].[5]

By the time Indira reached the east coast, she was exhausted – 'I feel I cannot even stand', she wrote to Nehru – but she staggered on to Yale University in New Haven, Connecticut to lecture and to present a portrait of 'old Elihu Yale', chief benefactor of the university who had worked for the British East India Company and served as Governor of Madras. In Washington she stayed for a few days with her cousin B.K. Nehru, now Indian ambassador. B.K.'s wife, Fori Nehru, 'lectured' Indira on her miserable psychological state, and Indira managed to 'pull herself together' before flying on to Paris for a UNESCO conference, which she reported back to Dorothy was 'deadly dull'.

Back in India, in January 1961, outwardly Indira's life resumed its normal tenor.

Her official period of mourning ended and she became politically active again. She was re-elected to the Congress Working Committee, and also became a member of the Central Election Committee – formed to select candidates for the 1962 general election. In fact, Indira, Lal Bahadur Shastri and Nehru approved each candidate. But depression still clung to her. She wrote to Dorothy Norman in the summer of 1961, 'I have been hesitating to write to you, waiting until I felt better. But now I really don't know if such a time will ever come. I've always thought of myself as a positive person. Now I feel terribly negative. I'm not ill. I'm not well. I just don't feel alive. Nobody seems aware of the difference.' She was still 'in the depths of depression', when she flew to London on 17 October and said she only hoped she would be 'more alive and awake by the time I get to the US'.[6]

Indira and Nehru made their second state visit to the United States in November 1961, twelve years after their first American trip. Everyone – except perhaps Nehru and Indira – had high expectations for this summit because of the newly elected Democratic government, headed by a dynamic, youthful president. Nehru had previously met Kennedy as a young Congressman in India and had been unimpressed, but B.K. Nehru was confident that Nehru would now recognize Kennedy's worth. John Kenneth Galbraith, the American ambassador to India, who accompanied Nehru and Indira to the States, also expected Nehru to be won over by Kennedy.

Indira and Nehru flew on a scheduled Air India flight to New York, and Nehru arrived exhausted. Almost immediately after disembarking, badly jet-lagged, he had to appear on the current affairs television programme, *Meet the Press*. He was subjected to a gruelling interrogation and his lacklustre responses were punctuated with long silences and pauses. Then he and Indira went to Rhode Island to meet the Kennedys at their farm. Driving past the huge mansions of the super rich in Newport, Kennedy jocularly remarked to Nehru that he wanted him to see how the American poor lived. But Nehru did not crack a smile. Over lunch he remained just as impassive and silent. Even Indira failed to make headway with her father. Kennedy pressed Nehru for advice on Vietnam, but Nehru 'said nothing at all'.[7] Indira, B.K. Nehru and Galbraith were acutely embarrassed but there was nothing they could do. The only person Nehru seemed willing to converse with was Jackie Kennedy.

After lunch, they flew to Washington – Nehru sat on his own and stared out the plane window, Indira read a copy of *Vogue* and Jackie Kennedy a Malraux novel.[8] The atmosphere did not improve in the capital. During talks between Nehru and Kennedy, which Galbraith and B.K. Nehru sat in on, Nehru 'simply did not respond. Question after question he answered with monosyllables or a sentence or two at most.' The subjects covered included Berlin, Vietnam, nuclear testing and Indo-Pakistani relations, but only the last provoked any meaningful response from Nehru.[9] Nehru and Kennedy then had a long private meeting, but neither divulged what transpired during it. Probably very little as Kennedy later described Nehru's 1961 visit as 'the worst head-of-state visit I have had', and likened talking to Nehru with trying 'to grab something, only to have it turn out to be just fog'.[10]

B.K. Nehru, who was with Nehru and Indira throughout their time in America, found Nehru 'spiritless, listless, uninterested in his surroundings and uncommunicative – the very reverse of Jawaharlal as he usually was.' He ascribed Nehru's behaviour to jet lag and fatigue and speculated that Nehru might be physically unwell. But Galbraith does not recall Nehru being below par. Nehru's tepid response to Kennedy – which amounted to a thinly disguised antipathy – reflected his opinion of the American president. B.K. Nehru and Galbraith were typical in their assessment of Kennedy as 'intellectual, articulate, sophisticated'. But Nehru was not convinced. He distrusted Kennedy's charisma and doubted his political vision. For her part, Indira was less than charmed by the glamorous Jackie Kennedy.[11]

After Washington Indira and Nehru flew to Los Angeles where they revived somewhat, visiting Disneyland and a film studio and meeting with Marlon Brando, the writer Aldous Huxley and the historian Will Durrant before returning to India. The only tangible outcome of the

1961 visit to the United States in fact was Jackie Kennedy's highly successful and much publicized return visit to India the following March.

Indira, inevitably, was much involved in the American First Lady's 1962 visit to India. But because Jackie had twice postponed her trip, Indira was able to escape on a prior commitment to a lecture tour in America while Jackie and her sister Lee Radziwill were still in India. During this American lecture tour, Indira wrote home to her father. Like Nehru, she did not have a high regard for Americans and complained at how 'extraordinarily rightist' and ignorant she found people. 'Speaking is rather a bore because of the lack of knowledge; one has to say the same thing over & over & to say it in words of one syllable.'[12]

In New York she met up with Dorothy Norman and then wrote Dorothy complaining, dispirited letters as she travelled around the country. From Washington DC, for example, Indira wrote on 26 March that she was depressed and utterly exhausted and did not know '*how* I am going to survive this trip!'[13] She needed great draughts of sleep every night just to keep going. She seems to have sleepwalked, in fact, through most of the tour, delivering anodyne (and reportedly ghost-written) speeches on uncontroversial cultural and political topics. From California, she wrote to Dorothy again, 'nothing is lacking except me – I just don't know *where* I am. The body is there – grinning, talking, but it's just a shell. The real me is non-existent. Is it dead or dormant? It's *most* depressing.' She said she felt 'like a string instrument that's out of tune – the very sound of it grating to the ears'.[14]

Indira felt swamped now by symptoms that she rightly suspected signalled the onset of menopause.[15] When Feroze died, her periods abruptly stopped altogether. After about a year, Indira began to menstruate again, but erratically and unpredictably. She confided to Dorothy Norman that her irregular 'cycle . . . jerks me sharply out of focus . . . bringing acute depression and physical exhaustion'.[16] She was not ill; she was not grief-stricken, but she was out of tune with her own body as well as her environment. And occasionally she was assailed by a sense of the futility of all things. The following year Indira wrote to Dorothy more explicitly that 'at a time of life which is difficult . . . I have been under tremendous physical and emotional strain, struggling with hormone imbalance'.[17] Despite this imbalance, she was not prescribed newly available hormone replacement medication. It was only the passage of time that restored her vitality, resilience, sense of physical well-being and emotional self-possession.

In April 1962, while Indira was still touring America, Nehru, who was now almost seventy-three, fell seriously ill with a kidney infection. Running a high fever and in pain, he had to be confined to bed. Krishna Hutheesing, who was staying at Teen Murti during Indira's absence, was frantic with worry. But by the time Indira reached home, Nehru was on the mend.

And he seemed completely recovered by early September when he and Indira travelled to London for the Commonwealth Prime Ministers' Conference. But Indira was still not herself. Dorothy met her in London and found her looking exhausted and depressed. They went to see the just-released film *Lolita* based on Nabokov's novel. Then Indira spent 'two heavenly days' in Cambridge with Rajiv who had just entered Nehru's old college, Trinity. But even seeing her son failed to cheer Indira. Rajiv was now eighteen – he had 'new friendships, new attachments, new loves. My heart aches.'[18]

Back in India, in the autumn of 1962, serious trouble was brewing on the border with China. For centuries the Himalayas – *the abode of snow* in Sanskrit – had provided a natural barrier for India against invasion from the north. Despite ominous signs, Nehru had never anticipated that the Chinese would mount an offensive from those remote mountains. 1954 – the year that Chou-En-lai visited India and Indira and Nehru went to China – had marked the beginning of *Chini Hindi Bhai Bhai* – or 'Chinese Indians, Brother Brother' – the year India and China signed a treaty based on the fie principles – *Panch Sheel* – of peaceful co-existence and non-aggression, that had became the focus of the 1955 Bandung Conference.

In 1956, however, China had clandestinely begun to build a road through the remote Aksai Chin region of Ladakh in Kashmir. In 1959 it consolidated its domination of Tibet. The Dalai Lama, the spiritual and political ruler of Tibet, fled to India where Nehru gave him asylum, a move supported by Indira who helped establish a Central Relief Committee for the thousands of Tibetan refugees who followed the Dalai Lama into exile. India, of course, was condemned by Peking for harbouring the Dalai Lama and his followers.

In September 1962, whilst Indira and Nehru were in Europe, Chinese troops began to cross the British-established Sino-Indian border – the McMahon Line – in the Northeast Frontier Agency (now the state of Arunachal Pradesh), at the junction where India joins Tibet and Bhutan. A second area of penetration was the 16,000-square-mile Aksai Chin region in Ladakh in Kashmir, through which the Chinese had secretly constructed their 750-mile road in 1956/57. Far away in Paris Nehru dismissed these incursions, as 'a number of petty conflicts between patrols'.

Indira and Nehru were back in Delhi by early October. On the 12th they left for a state visit to Ceylon, Nehru having agreed to send two divisions of soldiers to the northeast just before leaving. On the 20th, after they had returned, the Chinese launched their first full-scale invasion into Indian territory with heavy mortars and mountain artillery, and in some places, tanks. On 22 October a state of emergency was imposed and India urgently requested arms from the United States and Britain.

Up to the eve of the Chinese invasion in October 1962, India's Defence Minister, Krishna Menon, had refused to take the Chinese threat seriously, with the result that the country and the army were woefully unprepared for the assault. When it came, voices rose in a chorus demanding Menon's head. Whilst the Chinese had been amassing their forces and building the Aksai Chin Road, Menon had set the Indian defence industry to producing pressure cookers and coffee percolators.

Even before this episode Menon was a far from popular man in India. In the forties, when he was High Commissioner in London, he had become embroiled in a dubious contract for buying several thousand jeeps for India of which only a fraction were ever delivered. In the fifties he headed the Indian delegation at the United Nations and managed to alienate American goodwill by, among other things, condoning the Soviet invasion of Hungary. As far as Indians were concerned, the only thing Menon had done right at the UN was to deliver a blistering nine-hour tirade defending India's policy in Kashmir at the UN Security Council. In 1956 Nehru asked Menon to return to India and initially made him Minister without Portfolio and then Defence Minister. Menon had been away from India for the better part of thirty-two years and he came back to his native land a foreigner, unable to speak any language other than English (he had forgotten his mother tongue Malayalam and he never knew Hindi); his digestive system was no longer able to tolerate spicy food; his tall lanky frame was accustomed only to tweed jackets and flannel trousers rather than a *dhoti* and *angavastram*.

Though Menon was an old friend and mentor of Indira's, her voice was among those who called for his resignation as Defence Minister in late October 1962 – not because she held Menon responsible, but because she wanted to deflect the blame for the Chinese debacle away from her father. Indira had once observed to a friend, 'it does not matter who they are, if people do not function, they must go. No one is indispensable', a remark that showed that Indira was 'a great deal sharper than her father.'[19] Or less bound by emotional ties – what Indira's enemies would later refer to as her 'ruthlessness'. Unlike Indira, the last thing Nehru wanted to do was make a scapegoat of Menon, but, amidst rumours of a possible military coup, on 31 October he bowed to pressure and relieved Menon of the defence portfolio. It was effectively the end of Menon's political career and the greatest blow of his life.

19 November was Indira's forty-fifth birthday. Her aunt, Krishna Hutheesing, who was staying at Teen Murti, came down to breakfast to find the atmosphere positively glacial. News had just come through that the Chinese had broken through the Se La Pass, which was supposed to be impregnable. Beyond the pass lay Assam – and the rest of India. The Chinese, in fact, had come down the Himalayas in the northeast 'in a human avalanche', and besieged the under-equipped and badly outnumbered Indian troops.

Tezpur, the major town in Assam, just thirty miles from the Chinese lines, was threatened, and by midday on the 19th Indira had decided she would go there. She flew to Tezpur in a plane laden with Indian Red Cross supplies. The Chinese now occupied some 50,000 square miles of Indian territory. Indira returned to Delhi for exactly eight hours, displaying 'a flaming confidence because the tribal people had refused to leave Tezpur'. She made a brief radio broadcast, had the aircraft refilled with supplies and returned to Assam for another forty-eight hours.

The 1962 Chinese invasion of India came out of the blue and ended as abruptly as it began. On 21 November, the Chinese unexpectedly announced a unilateral cease-fire and withdrew in the eastern sector to a position fifteen miles north of the McMahon Line, and to the 'line of actual control' in the other sectors. The war was over. India had been completely humiliated. Nehru was crushed.

For Indira, the period following the war with China was one of personal turmoil. Nehru now seemed politically vulnerable, physically old and psychologically depressed. As a consequence, he was more dependent on his daughter than ever. And for the first time, Indira began to resent his dependence. She felt a compulsion to break off the shackles of duty and responsibility that had gripped her for so long. And in secret, she devised a plan to leave her father and India and create a new, independent life for herself abroad.

On 13 October 1963, Indira wrote to Dorothy Norman, 'My need for privacy and anonymity has been growing steadily these last three years until now I feel I cannot ignore it without risking some kind of self-annihilation. Privacy, unfortunately, is not possible for me even in the remotest corner of this subcontinent. I have had people presenting their cards and their problems even at the foot of the Kolahoi glacier (16,000 feet high)! It's not just meeting people but that they come only to get or ask something. And not even a few moments are left for thinking or relaxing or just being oneself.'

Indira told Dorothy that she had fallen in love with a small house that she had seen for sale in London the previous spring. She had very little money and no foreign exchange, but nevertheless 'spent much time figuring out ways and means'. She hoped to raise enough money to get a mortgage, buy the house, live in a small part of it and rent out the remaining rooms. She was sure she could live frugally on her own in London, and saw no incongruity in a transformation from Prime Minister's daughter to London landlady. Then she heard the house had been bought by someone else and 'it was as if a door had been slammed in my face'. In part she wanted to be abroad to be close to Rajiv and also to Sanjay who would shortly go to England too. But most of all Indira wanted to 'be on my own. Free to work or to rest. It doesn't sound much to ask of life yet it seems to be out of my reach.'

It was not, Indira insisted, that she wanted to run away from anybody or anything. 'I can claim to have done my duty to my country and my family all these long years. I don't for an instant regret it, because whatever I am today has been shaped by these years. But now I want another life. It may not work out. I may not like it or be good at it.

But at least it deserves a trial. There is a compulsion within me which is driving me always from the old life.'[20]

At the age of nearly forty-six Indira was going through a crisis, but it was actually closer to an adolescent identity crisis than a mid-life one. What life should she choose, *could* she choose? What would freedom be like? Indira had never really had the chance to ask these questions. First she had been Jawaharlal Nehru's daughter, then Feroze Gandhi's wife and Rajiv and Sanjay Gandhi's mother. It was only after Feroze died, the boys had become teenagers and her father an old man, that she had begun to consider what she herself might be and made an effort to find out.

Dorothy Norman proved an eager collaborator. If Indira lived abroad she would need an income. The previous year, on her American lecture tour, she had been approached by two American publishers, Simon & Schuster and Doubleday, who suggested she write a book. But as Indira told Dorothy at that time, 'I just cannot see WHEN anything can get written.' Now, with the end of her father's career looming, the book idea took hold, and Dorothy Norman brokered a deal with another New York publisher, Morrow, who offered what Indira described as 'attractive' terms.[21] Exactly what the book was to be about was unclear – most probably a memoir of her father's life and Indira's role in it. Indira, who was a fluent writer, was tempted by the prospect of writing a book, but even more the money she would get for it which would be a ticket out of India. 'The book', however, never went beyond the talking stage, and the Morrow contract never materialized.

The irony of Indira's secret dreams and plans in the autumn of 1963 – dreams of escape not only from politics but from India as well and above all the dream of 'finding herself' – was that she was nurturing them at precisely the time that many others assumed she was manoeuvring to take over power from her father. In the summer of 1963 Congress had lost three crucial by-elections. After the humiliating Chinese invasion of the previous year, Nehru's power and stature had shrunk. His days now appeared numbered. The question of who would succeed him, which had been tacit for a long time, began to be openly asked.

In fact, in 1963 a thirty-three-year-old American journalist, named Welles Hangen, who headed the National Broadcasting Corporation bureau in India, published a book entitled *After Nehru, Who?* It consisted of profile interviews with the likely (and some unlikely) aspirants to the prime ministership 'after Nehru': Morarji Desai, Krishna Menon, Lal Bahadur Shastri, Y.B. Chavan, Jayaprakash Narayan, S.K. Patil, Brij Mohan Kaul – and the sole woman Welles interviewed – Indira Gandhi. *After Nehru, Who?* raised a storm of controversy in India, including at Teen Murti where Nehru 'testily' asked Indira why she had allowed herself to be questioned by Hangen and 'dragged into' his book.[22]

Soon, however, the debate aroused by Hangen was eclipsed by the announcement of a new Congress initiative called the Kamaraj Plan. Ostensibly formulated by the Chief Minister of Madras, K. Kamaraj, this was designed to 'cleanse' and revitalize the moribund Congress party. Kamaraj first discussed the plan with Nehru in early August, 1963. The idea was that senior Congressmen – both cabinet ministers and chief ministers – would resign their positions in order to take up full-time organizational work for the party. All holders of government office were liable to be 'Kamarajed' – relieved of office – with the exception of the Prime Minister. Although the rationale was to give new vigour to the party, its immediate effect was a purge at the highest levels of leadership in the run-up to Nehru's succession. It neatly dispensed with some of the 'less desirable' candidates such as the right-wing Desai, while obscuring this fact by also sending a more attractive contender like Shastri into the wilderness.

This, at any rate, was Desai's own sour view of the Kamaraj Plan. Desai maintained that the plan was not Kamaraj's idea at all, but rather Nehru's plot to install Indira Gandhi as his successor.[23] Nehru's reaction to this charge was that it showed 'the most fantastic kind of motive hunting I ... It arises from something like a dynastic concept of succession which is altogether foreign to a parliamentary democracy ... besides being repulsive to my own mind.'[24] Indira herself pointed out that if her father had wanted her to succeed him 'surely he would have wanted me to be elected to Parliament', but during the run-up to the 1962 general elections and earlier he, as well as Indira, 'agreed that I should not go into Parliament'.[25]

The Kamaraj Plan was activated on 24 August 1963 and widely acclaimed. Nehru chose six cabinet ministers to resign (including Desai and Shastri – both leading candidates to succeed him) and six chief ministers (including Kamaraj himself who soon became President of the Congress Party). Kamaraj was given credit for the Plan but he was acting in league with a small cabal of Congress leaders who came to be known as the Syndicate. This included, besides Kamaraj himself, Atulya Ghosh of West Bengal, S.K. Patil from Bombay, Sanjiva Reddy, the Chief Minister of Andhra Pradesh and S. Nijalingappa, the Chief Minister of Mysore. In October 1963 they met in the temple town of Tirupati in South India and decided that a collective leadership, headed by Lal Bahadur Shastri, should succeed Nehru and that the rigid, doctrinaire and right-wing Morarji Desai must be stymied.

In November 1963 Marie Seton, a British film critic and writer who had come to know Nehru and Indira through Krishna Menon, told Nehru she wanted to write a book about him. But she said she would not if he had objections. Nehru told Marie to discuss it with Indira and said, 'You and Indu must work it out.' Marie promised to, but she also asked him to mention to Indira that he had no objections.

'If I can remember to tell her,' Nehru said, 'I will. I hardly see her to talk to these days. She is so busy.'[26] Indira, in fact, was scheduled to leave shortly for a twenty-three-day tour of East Africa – her first solo official trip abroad – to attend the independence celebrations in Kenya, and to visit Zambia, Uganda, Ethiopia and Tanzania. Nevertheless she and Marie spoke briefly in late November (it was the day before Kennedy was assassinated), and Marie asked Indira not only about Nehru but also about her own ambitions and her reaction to Welles Hangen's book. Indira's response to Marie's question of whether she wanted to succeed her father was: 'before there is any likelihood of that coming up, they'll kill me off.' Seton was taken aback, but interpreted this to mean that Indira thought that those who opposed her would destroy her politically, not literally. Whichever way one takes Indira's remark, it reflects her enduring sense that others were 'out to get' her.[27]

While writing her Nehru book, *Panditji*, Marie Seton spent weeks and months at a time at Teen Murti and became Indira's confidante, but Indira also continued to turn to Dorothy Norman. On 4 January 1964, when she had just got back from Africa, she wrote to Dorothy reiterating her by now familiar escape theme: 'How I wish I could make a clean break with Indian or any other politics – I shall certainly try to.'[28] But two days later she was at the annual Congress session at Bhubaneshwar in the eastern state of Orissa. So was Seton, who continued to shadow Nehru during the last months of his life. On the morning of 8 January, Nehru rose to speak and then suddenly pitched forward. Indira jumped up from her seat on the dais, rushed forward to her father and caught him under his arms before aides and security men got to the podium. Nehru had had a stroke.

It was serious and the prognosis uncertain: Nehru was partially paralysed on his left side and greatly weakened. Congress leaders like Biju Patnaik, the former Chief Minister of Orissa, urged Indira to take over as Deputy Prime Minister immediately despite the fact that not only was she not a member of the cabinet, she did not even hold an elected position in the government. Indira refused.

For the next few days she went back and forth between the Congress session and her father's bedside at Raj Bhawan, the Governor's residence. Nehru rallied, but not enough to appear in public again at the Congress session. Indira told Marie Seton that she tried to persuade Nehru to name a successor – she herself was being besieged by would-be candidates – but he refused. 'He's been arguing all these days!' Then Indira took Marie to her room and showed her two beautiful, vibrantly coloured Orissan saris which she had bought just before Nehru was struck down. '"I feel I want to wear colours," she said. "Just now, after three years, I feel I've ceased to mourn Feroze."'[29]

By 12 January Indira and Nehru were back in Delhi where Nehru continued to convalesce. His working hours were reduced from seventeen to twelve a day and he was coerced into taking a nap in the afternoons. The public, however, was not informed of how dangerously ill he had been or how precarious his condition still was. Nehru had recovered sufficiently by the end of January to make an appearance at the annual Republic Day parade on the 26th, and he was present for the opening of Parliament in February, though he had to speak sitting down.

There were rumours that Indira would shortly enter the Cabinet as Minister of Foreign Affairs, but when nothing came of it, they died down. Gossip in Delhi persisted, however, that Indira was now running things behind the scenes – as had the American President Woodrow Wilson's wife earlier in the century. The journalist Inder Malhotra, who had been a close friend of Feroze, went to see her, and she told him that it was 'absurd' to compare her to Mrs Wilson. She obviously was helping her father more than ever, but she was far from being in charge of the government.

Malhotra believed her, but he also sensed that Indira was not unhappy about being perceived as 'the power behind the throne'.[30] It was actually the Home Minister, Gulzarilal Nanda and the Finance Minister TTK, who jointly looked after the Prime Minister's day-to-day work. Then on 22 January Lal Bahadur Shastri was brought in from the cold of the 'Kamarajed' and rejoined the Cabinet as Minister without Portfolio and assumed major responsibilities.

Nehru was now seventy-four and the great question mark of his successor did not go away even though rumours were denied and his recovery was misleadingly spoken of as complete. An Indian Institute of Public Opinion survey carried out at this time on the question 'After Nehru, who?' placed Shastri as first choice, Kamaraj second, Indira third and Morarji Desai fourth.

In early April Indira slipped a disc and had to encase her neck in 'an unlovely plastic collar which is terribly uncomfortable and hot'.[31] Her father's illness and the atmosphere of uncertainty and intrigue it fuelled in Delhi had put her under terrific psychological strain. The left-wing journalist, Romesh Thapar, spoke to her round about this time and found her 'so overwrought with keeping what was left of Panditji together, pasting up the ends, which kept coming apart at the seams, that she just broke down and wept'.[32]

Despite her slipped disc and shaky psychological state, Indira flew to New York on 15 April for the inauguration of the World Fair. The sort of large crowd of sycophants and hangers-on that usually saw off the Prime Minister when he left India congregated for Indira's departure at Palam airport – a clear indication that talk of her succeeding her father was rampant. Bizarrely, Tarakeshwari Sinha, Feroze Gandhi's former mistress and a disciple of Morarji Desai, was amongst the crowd. Sinha, like many others, foresaw where power in the future might lie, and she sought help from Indira at the airport to prevent the Attorney General from examining papers connected with her dubious acquisition of some valuable real estate. Marie Seton observed the two women: Indira remained perfectly controlled and impassive while Sinha vainly petitioned her.[33]

Indira flew to New York via Hong Kong where, during a brief stop–over, she told reporters that she had no intention of succeeding her father and that she had resisted all efforts to manoeuvre her into the cabinet as Foreign Minister. When she arrived in America she appeared on *Meet the Press* and when asked: 'Would you like to be Prime Minister of India?' she replied without hesitating, 'I would not.' But the panel of reporters and commentators continued to grill her.

> Q. Would you refuse to run if you were nominated and if elected, would you refuse to serve?
> A. Well, I am not a member of Parliament and in India you cannot be in the government without being a member of Parliament.
> Q. If the will of the people of India were such that you were clearly the wish of the majority, would you serve as Prime Minister?
> A. I find it very difficult to believe there would be such an overwhelming demand.
> Q. But you aren't going to say that you would refuse to serve?
> A. Well, shall I say that 90 per cent I would refuse.[34]

In Washington Indira delivered a letter from Nehru to President Johnson concerning Kashmir and the information that Nehru planned to hold talks with Sheikh Abdullah (who was finally released from detention on 8 April 1963) and Pakistan's Ayub Khan in Delhi.

Indira returned from New York at 5.40 a.m. on 29 April, the same day that the newly released Sheikh Abdullah arrived, at Nehru's invitation, in Delhi. That afternoon, she went back to Palam airport to receive the Sheikh. He embraced Indira and Nehru – whom he had not seen in eleven years – at Teen Murti. Abdullah was shocked by Nehru's physical state, and it was an emotional reunion. But an inconclusive one, though Nehru urged Abdullah to visit Pakistan and Nehru himself agreed to meet with Ayub Khan if the Pakistani President would come to Delhi. It was obvious to Abdullah that Nehru was not well enough to go to Pakistan himself. For the first time since independence there was real hope that the open wound of Kashmir might be healed.[35]

Indira's trip to America had been a respite. Back in Delhi, by early May the toll of her father's illness and the continuing 'After Nehru who?' speculation had reached the point where again she was desperate to escape. She wrote to Dorothy Norman on 8 May, 'The whole question of my future is bothering me. I feel I must settle outside India at least for a year or so and this involves earning a living and especially foreign currency ... The desire to be out of India and the malice, jealousies and envy, with which one is surrounded, are now overwhelming. Also the fact that there isn't one single person to whom one can talk or ask advice.'[36]

On 13 May she and Nehru went to Bombay for the annual AICC meeting. On the 18th an interview conducted in Delhi with Nehru and Indira was televised in New York in which Nehru said that it was very unlikely that his daughter would succeed him, and Indira answered a query about the likelihood of the prime ministership being 'thrust' on her with: 'It can't be thrust upon me if I do not want it.'[37] On 22 May Nehru held his first press conference in seven months. It was attended by more than two hundred correspondents and lasted forty minutes. The question, 'After Nehru, Who?' was raised in one form or another repeatedly and finally an exasperated Nehru said, 'My life is not ending so very soon!' His response provoked a standing ovation.

The following day, 23 May, Indira and her father went to Dehra Dun by helicopter for a three-day holiday, returning to Teen Murti on the afternoon of the 26th. That night Nehru went to bed early. He awoke several times in the night and was given a sedative by his servant, Nathu Ram, who slept in a chair beside the Prime Minister's bed.

Before dawn on 27 May, Nehru woke again. He was in pain, but he did not rouse Nathu Ram for two more hours. At 6.30 the servant sent a security man to get Indira and Nehru's physician, Dr Bedi, who had been staying in the house since Nehru had his first stroke in January. When Indira and the doctor appeared in his room, Nehru seemed disoriented and asked, 'What is the matter?' A few moments later he fell back unconscious. Dr Bedi examined Nehru and realized his aorta had burst. Indira belonged to the same blood group as her father and Dr Bedi immediately drew blood from her so that he could perform a transfusion. But it was of no help and Nehru fell into a coma.

He remained unconscious all morning while Indira cabled Rajiv in England and sent messages to Kashmir, where Sanjay was on holiday. Then she rang her two aunts, both of whom were in Bombay. The only other person she telephoned was Krishna Menon who immediately rushed over from his house across the street from Teen Murti.

Nehru died at 1.44 p.m. on Wednesday afternoon, 27 May 1964, without ever having regained consciousness. Indira and Krishna Menon were with him. Throughout that long, hot afternoon and early evening they remained next to Nehru's body, like obelisks, sitting on the floor, Menon with his hacked-out, gaunt visage, Indira with 'her face, all drained of colour'.[38]

But they were not alone for long. Within minutes of Nehru's passing, the corridors, rooms and stairways of Teen Murti were swarming with people. TTK and Jagjivan Ram were the first to arrive, both in tears. Other cabinet members soon followed, and an emergency committee of the Cabinet met in a downstairs room between 2 and 3 p.m. and decided to recommend that the Home Minister, Gulzarilal Nanda, who held the number two cabinet position, be appointed acting Prime Minister. Everyone who milled about the house was stunned, except for two figures who appeared more watchful than grief-stricken: Kamaraj and Morarji Desai – in close proximity to each other but in no sense together. Both stood for hours in the passageway outside Nehru's room while groups of mourners swirled about them. Desai, in fact, openly greeted people coming up the stairs to pay their last respects as if he were 'a host at a diplomatic reception'.

After darkness fell, Nehru's body, covered with lilies, marigolds and roses and draped in the Indian flag, was brought downstairs on a bier and placed in the foyer of Teen Murti so that the public could pay their last respects to him throughout the night. It was still terrifically hot and electric fans blew over huge blocks of ice to forestall decomposition as the endless stream of people filed past. Indira hovered nearby with her aunt, Vijayalakshmi Pandit, who had arrived from Bombay with her sister Krishna Hutheesing, and Padmaja Naidu who had flown in from Calcutta. No one slept and the gates of Teen Murti remained open all night to visitors except for an hour between 3.30 and 4.30 a.m.

Sanjay Gandhi arrived from Kashmir early on the 28th, the day of the funeral. Indira scrupulously saw to all the arrangements, down to the appearance of the servants. They were disconsolate and had scarcely eaten or bathed since Nehru's death. She told them gently to go home, wash, shave and change. 'My father always liked neatness; there will be no slovenliness around him today.'[39]

Nehru's body was placed on a gun carriage that left Teen Murti at noon and slowly wound its way through the hot, dusty, crowd-lined streets of New and Old Delhi to the Jumna. Indira and Sanjay (Rajiv had not yet arrived from England) followed in an open car, both in white *khadi*, both sweating profusely under the blazing sun. It took more than three hours to cover the five miles to the river. Two to three million people lined the way, standing ten to twenty deep. At the river more crowds – including royalty, heads of state and foreign dignitaries from all over the world – congregated at the cremation site and surged forward to get a last glimpse of their leader. Over 8,000 special police and 6,000 troops maintained order.

Despite Nehru's explicit injunction against religious rites in his will, the funeral was a Hindu cremation. This was Indira's decision and it cost her considerable pain (and considerable criticism), knowing that she was defying her father's wishes. Her motives are obscure, but immediately after her father's death, religious leaders and some politicians placed enormous pressure on her, and they probably convinced her that the people of India would not accept a secular funeral. Nehru's body was placed on a sandalwood pyre; priests intoned Vedic prayers, the honour guard fired three volleys and bugles played *The Last Post*. Seventeen-year-old Sanjay Gandhi lit the funeral pyre.

Thirteen days after the cremation Indira made the five-hundred-mile pilgrimage by train to Allahabad, bearing an urn full of her father's ashes. All along the way, crowds lined the rail track, and the train stopped at every town and village so that the normal ten-hour journey took twenty-five hours. At Allahabad, a small portion of Nehru's ashes was submerged at the Sangam, along with some of Kamala's ashes which Nehru had brought back from Switzerland nearly three decades earlier and kept at his bedside – in prison cells, at Anand Bhawan, the York Road bungalow and Teen Murti – over all the intervening years. Nehru, however, had stipulated in his will that he wished most of his ashes to be strewn by air over every state in India. Indira herself took possession of those destined for Kashmir. She went to Srinagar, boarded a small plane and scattered her father's ashes over the land he had loved and from whence he had sprung.

After Nehru died, Indira sank into a deep depression – less acute and debilitating than what she went through when Feroze died, but more intractable and confused. Despite his age, it seemed inconceivable, somehow, that her father was gone. But what Indira felt now was more complicated than grief. Her feelings for her father had been profound but ambivalent, and their relationship had undergone periods of estrangement as well as intimacy. They had actually been closer in the early years when they lived apart – when Indira was at school and Nehru in jail, or while Indira was in Europe and Nehru in India. Over distances they could speak to each other in long, revealing letters.

In the fifties all this changed. Life became too crowded and too exhausting. Confined together in Teen Murti, it was difficult to talk to each other freely and frankly, even had there been time, which there was not, and even when they were alone, which they rarely were. Thus at crucial junctures, such as when Indira felt her father should stick to his resolve to resign and when she decided not to stand for re-election as Congress President, she again reverted to the old pattern of writing to her father even though they were under the same roof.

In Nehru's last years Indira was devoted to but not emotionally close to him. In the closing months of his life she had actually been secretly planning to leave him and India. Guilt and anger, as well as pain, were woven into her grief as a consequence. In the aftermath of Nehru's death Indira may also have felt that she had failed her father in some fundamental way. He had undoubtedly been proud of her during all the years she had lived with him at Teen Murti. Certainly he had relied on her heavily. But there was no disguising the fact that Indira had not lived up to the promise he had envisioned and articulated to her so long ago – as 'a child of storm and trouble', the participant in a new revolution.

Something in their relationship had died when Indira insisted upon marrying Feroze Gandhi, a decision that brought both her and her father pain. Nehru had interpreted her marriage as a retreat from larger challenges and responsibilities. In addition, beginning in the late forties, he seems to have looked at his daughter more realistically and come to the conclusion that she lacked the intelligence and vision to play a major role in India's future. Indira was undoubtedly aware of her father's assessment of her. And belatedly – after his death – she rebelled against it.

But throughout the summer and autumn of 1964 what oppressed her most was loneliness. Indira now felt isolated as she never had before. Her father had been the dominant presence and force in her life. Now she was not only a widow but an orphan. Of course, she was still a mother, but her sons were in their late teens, and the bond between a mother and her adolescent sons is rarely close. Rajiv and Sanjay had not lived at home for the past ten years. Indira's relationship with them was also disturbed after Feroze's death. According to several people close to Indira, including Pupul Jayakar, after Feroze died, Sanjay accused his mother of neglecting Feroze, implying that she was responsible for his premature death.[40]

Quite apart from this, in 1964 both Rajiv and Sanjay were in England, far away from Indira. Rajiv was struggling with his studies at Cambridge and in the autumn of 1964 Sanjay began what was supposed to be a three-year apprenticeship with Rolls-Royce. Even if they had been nearer to Indira, she had little in common with her sons now. Neither was interested in books, art or the theatre. They were mediocre students, and never bothered – as boys or men – to read their grandfather's books.[41] Nor were they interested in politics, and Indira was determined at this point to keep them far away from the political world. Instead, Rajiv and Sanjay were both obsessed, as Feroze had been, with mechanical things, especially aeroplanes and cars. Rajiv studied engineering at Cambridge and Imperial College. He failed his exams and never got a degree. Sanjay did not attempt to go to university and instead embarked on the Rolls-Royce apprentice programme in Crewe where he also took evening classes at the local technical college.

The succession battle to determine the second prime minister of India began, as Krishna Menon later bitterly remarked, practically over Nehru's body, and it intensified in the days after the funeral. On 30 May, just three days after Nehru died, Shastri called on Indira at Teen Murti and urged her to take on the leadership of the country. The precise words he reportedly used were, '*ab aap mulk ko sambhal leejiye*' (you should now assume responsibility for the country). But without hesitating, Indira refused, saying she was too grief-stricken to contest an election or assume power.[42] Other Congress leaders also approached Indira but she remained steadfast in her refusal. Whether or not these appeals were seriously made is questionable. Indira was, after all, Nehru's daughter. She had to be consulted and the issue of her candidacy had to be clarified before the real succession conflict – between Lal Bahadur Shastri and Morarji Desai – got underway. If Indira *had* wanted to succeed her father now, the Congress leaders might have had to acquiesce, but almost no one doubted that at this time she genuinely did not feel capable of assuming power.

Kamaraj, the Congress President, and the Syndicate backed Shastri and after a good deal of manoeuvring, Desai reluctantly withdrew from the field. By 1 June Shastri was the unanimous choice of the party. That evening, after visiting Nehru's cremation site, he called on Indira at Teen Murti and again suggested to her that she become Prime Minister. But this was, in fact, an empty gesture. Even if Indira had not refused again – which, of course, she did – Shastri was in no position to offer the prime ministership to her. The next morning in Parliament acting Prime Minister Nanda proposed Shastri as Party Leader. Desai seconded the motion and it was carried.[43]

When the diminutive Shastri (a sparrow of a man at barely five feet) stood up to speak in Parliament, he praised Indira's fortitude and said he looked forward to her 'continued association with us'. He realized that it was imperative to 'have a Nehru in the Cabinet to maintain stability' and in fact he almost immediately offered Indira a cabinet post. She later claimed that Shastri had offered her the post of Minister of Foreign Affairs but that she turned it down in favour of a lighter portfolio.[44] But Indira's claim is disputed by others.

Indira's explanation for turning down Foreign Affairs was that she was too overcome with grief and wanted to devote herself to a memorial to her father. Certainly this was very important to her. Shastri had already indicated that he had no wish to move into Teen Murti and it had been decided that the former Commander-in-Chief's house would be turned into the Nehru Memorial Museum and Library. Indira would oversee every aspect of its establishment – a huge enterprise – and so she reportedly turned down the taxing office of Foreign Minister – *if* it had been offered to her – and took on the less demanding post of Minister of Information and Broadcasting. The crucial point, however, is that she did agree to join Shastri's government.

Why? Less than two months earlier Indira had written to Dorothy Norman of how desperate she was to escape India and politics. Indeed this had been the major theme of her correspondence for the past two years. Why then accept Shastri's offer? It was largely, no doubt, out of a sense of duty, to carry on her father's work, to make a gesture towards continuity. But there is also the very salient fact that Indira needed a job. When Nehru died, she was left with very little other than Anand Bhawan, which in itself was a huge financial drain. Nehru had never made any financial provision for his daughter's future. Apart from her father's possessions and the family home, Indira inherited only her father's royalties and these fluctuated and were never lucrative. Nor did she now have a home in Delhi. In fact, she was given notice to leave Teen Murti with what she felt was indecent haste. A place in Shastri's Cabinet provided her with both a salary and a roof over her head in the form of a government bungalow. She was assigned a typical specimen: 1 Safdarjung Road where she would spend the next twenty years except for a three-year period in the late seventies.

In order to be a member of the Cabinet Indira had, of course, to become an MP. The logical step would have been for her to stand in the upcoming by-election in her father's constituency, Phulpur, but Nehru's sister, Vijaya Lakshmi Pandit, coveted this seat, though Mrs Pandit made it clear to her niece that she would step aside if Indira wished her to. Indira, however, felt unable to face a by-election for a seat in the Lok Sabha and instead chose to be appointed a member of the upper house, the Rajya Sabha, by the President of India.

Indira was ranked number four in Shastri's Cabinet after Shastri himself, the Home Minister, Gulzarilal Nanda, and the Finance Minister, TTK. But her ranking did not reflect the role she initially chose to play which was minimal. Indira rarely spoke in Parliament or in cabinet meetings. Shastri, however, realized she could be useful. In October 1964 he sent her to London to represent India at the 1964 Commonwealth Prime Ministers' Conference. Inder Malhotra visited her at Claridge's Hotel on the day that it was announced in the papers that Shastri had chosen Swaran Singh to be Minister of Foreign Affairs. Indira was irate and though she told Malhotra she herself did not want the job, she felt that Shastri should have consulted her over the appointment.[45] She felt slighted, and her dissatisfaction under Shastri can be dated from this point. She realized now that he wanted her in the Cabinet but not in a position of power. In order to assert herself and emphasize her considerable experience in foreign affairs (experience which, in comparison to her, both Shastri and Swaran Singh lacked), Indira went from London on to Belgrade and met Tito and then on to Moscow where she conferred with the new Soviet Premier, Alexei Kosygin. Their talks were reported to be 'very friendly, fruitful, frank, warm and cordial'.[46] Later Indira went to France, the United States, Yugoslavia, Canada, Mongolia, Burma and to the Soviet Union again, on the government's behalf.

As Minister of Information and Broadcasting Indira's tenure was moderately productive but scarcely impressive. She regarded both television and radio as educative media. She sponsored an Urdu service, a general overseas service, extended broadcasting hours, and encouraged more controversy on the air. But as a member of government, Indira made more of an impact in areas outside her ministry's jurisdiction.

For example in the case of the language riots that broke out in Madras in March 1965. This was the year when the constitution had stipulated that Hindi would become the official language of India, replacing English. Unrest broke out also in Tamil-speaking South India where some opponents of Hindi went as far as publicly immolating themselves. Shastri and Kamaraj, both in Delhi, decided to wait out the crisis. Indira, however, immediately hopped on a plane to Madras where she gave assurances to the protesters against Hindi and helped restore peace. Shastri was extremely annoyed at the way she had 'jumped over his head'. Inder Malhotra discussed the situation with Indira who told him she did not consider herself merely the Minister of Information and Broadcasting but 'one of the leaders of the country', and asserted, 'Do you think this government can survive if I resign today? I am telling you it won't. Yes, I have jumped over the Prime Minister's head and I would do it again whenever the need arises.'[47]

Indira was in the midst of another crisis, in Kashmir, in August 1965. Ostensibly she flew to Srinagar on 8 August for a holiday, but she was aware that the situation there was volatile. No sooner had she landed than she learned that Pakistani troops, disguised as civilian volunteers, were poised to capture Srinagar and foment a pro-Pakistan uprising in Kashmir. Indira was urged to take the next flight back to Delhi but she refused. Not only did she stay; she flew to the front when hostilities broke out. The press hailed her as 'the only man in a cabinet of old women'. Indira returned to Delhi and then went back to Kashmir again when hostilities erupted in full force in September. She told a huge crowd in Srinagar, 'We shall not give an inch of our territory to the aggressor.' She inspected bombed-out areas on the Punjab border, visited military hospitals in Ferozepur, carried on to Abohar, Fazilka, Ambala, Amritsar and Gurdaspur. According to correspondents' reports, 'wherever she went, Mrs Gandhi was greeted by enthusiastic crowds'.

As in Madras, Shastri was completely upstaged. But not for long. The Pakistan army was defeated and India imposed a cease-fire on 23 September. Kashmir remained part of India and with peace Kashmir was once again securely Indian; Shastri – the little man who had been the butt of newsreel jokes – became a hero overnight. According to Inder Malhotra, 'Indira was furious.' Shastri reportedly had had enough of Indira by this time too and planned now to get her out of his hair by sending her to Britain as High Commissioner.[48]

But by now Indira had gathered a protective ring of friends and advisers around herself – a coterie, in fact, which believed she rather than Shastri was the future. This inner circle included Dinesh Singh, a handsome prince who was Minister of State for Foreign Affairs; Asoka Mehta, the Deputy Chairman of the Planning Commission; Inder Gujral, who had come to know Indira well through his brother, the painter Satish Gujral who had painted both Indira and Nehru; and the journalist Romesh Thapar. 'Dinesh and Inder were the bidding boys.'[49] Certainly they all egged Indira on and fed her hostility toward Shastri.

Largely due to the influence of her coterie, it was really only at this late juncture – in 1964 and 1965 – that Indira's political ambition was truly ignited. Less than a year earlier she had been dreaming of a private life in England. Now she was insisting she was 'a national leader' and could overrule the Prime Minister whenever she pleased. By this time 'her contempt for the [Shastri] Government was apparent'. She was openly critical of Shastri, telling the newspaper correspondent, Kuldip Nayar, in a November 1965 interview, that Shastri had 'swerved from the right path' and that socialism and nonalignment were being forgotten.[50] While her father was alive, Indira had been the object of assiduous political courting and treated with almost as much deference and respect as Nehru himself. Now she felt herself overlooked and ignored. It was as if she were asserting her hereditary rights.

And yet this is not the full explanation. Indira had lived in the limelight for virtually her whole life and at the heart of political power for nearly twenty years. Intermittently she longed for a normal, private life, but in a way this was a fantasy. She was no closer to having a normal, private life now, but she was distanced from the seat of power. She maintained that her father's policies and plans were being ignored. But what motivated her just as much in her struggle with Shastri was wounded pride. She was not about to recede into the shadows, as number four in the Cabinet.

And yet Indira still claimed, as late as December 1965, to have no political ambition. Vijaya Lakshmi Pandit had heard rumours that

Indira, on reflection, wanted her father's old constituency, Phulpur, after all, and resented her aunt's representing it in Parliament. Mrs Pandit wrote to Indira on the 6th, offering to relinquish the seat. But Indira replied emphatically by return of post:

> I don't know who has been talking to you but there is absolutely no foundation in the remark that I am not happy at your being in Phulpur ... It may seen strange that a person in politics should be wholly without political ambition but I am afraid that I am that sort of a freak ... I did not want to come either to Parliament or to be in Government. However, there were certain compelling reasons at the time for my acceptance of this portfolio. Now there are so many crises one after another that every time seems to be the wrong time for getting out.[51]

Of course, Indira had never been open or candid with her aunt. But soon after writing to Nan Pandit that she had no political ambitions, she said much the same thing to others, including the very group of advisers who wished her to supplant Shastri. It was in December 1965 that Indira dined for the first time at the home of one member of her inner circle – the left-wing journalist Romesh Thapar. Thapar and his wife Raj were a dynamic, intellectual couple and Indira's eagerness to become part of their set became apparent when Raj Thapar came in her car to collect Indira. When Raj arrived at 1 Safdarjung Road, Indira was shouting for her driver who had suddenly disappeared. Raj pointed out that Indira did not need the driver because Raj, herself, would bring her back home, but Indira insisted he be found: 'He must know where you live because this is not going to be the last time.' She enjoyed the evening and regaled the Thapars with funny anecdotes about Congress leaders, especially Shastri, lamented the state the party was in and 'seriously discussed the possibility of retiring from political life altogether. She saw no future in it for her ... She seemed genuine in her decision to withdraw, to be an "ordinary citizen."'[52]

On 3 January 1966 Shastri flew to Tashkent in Soviet Central Asia, for peace talks with Ayub Khan of Pakistan, mediated by Alexei Kosygin. On the 10th a settlement was finally agreed. After he went to bed in the early hours of the 11th, Shastri had a fatal heart attack. He was sixty-one and had served as Prime Minister for only nineteen months.

Indira was at home at 1 Safdarjung Road at 1.30 a.m. on the 11th of January when her telephone rang. It was her secretary, N. K. Seshan, calling to say that Shastri had died in Tashkent half an hour earlier. Seshan told Indira that the Home Minister, Gulzarilal Nanda, had been informed of Shastri's death and gone directly to the President's house. Indira called for a car and went to Rashtrapati Bhawan, the President's residence. She and the Finance Minister were the only ones present when the President swore in Nanda as acting Prime Minister at 3.15 a.m.

When Indira returned from the President's house at about 4 a.m., she rang Romesh Thapar and asked him to come over right away. He found her in an almost hectic mood as she vividly described the swearing-in ceremony at Rashtrapati Bhawan: the *dhoti*-clad President facing the *dhoti*-clad Gulzarilal Nanda, surrounded by liveried attendants in red and gold braid. Then Indira got down to the 'gut question' she wanted to ask Thapar. Some of her advisers had already been in touch with Indira and they were urging her to 'make a bid for power'. She wanted Thapar's advice.

'What do you feel like doing?' Thapar asked her.

'"Nothing,"' she replied.

But of course, the fact that Indira had summoned Thapar to her house in the middle of the night to discuss the issue meant that her reply was at best half-hearted. She was testing the waters with Thapar, a man she trusted. She wanted to be persuaded out of – or into – the future that now beckoned. And it beckoned unexpectedly, because the third man in a triumvirate of 'obstacles' – Feroze Gandhi, Jawaharlal Nehru and Lal Bahadur Shastri – had suddenly died. Indira could never have come to power if any one of these men had not disappeared from the scene. Feroze because she would have put her marriage and husband's career before her own; Nehru because she was a dutiful daughter and Shastri because the power brokers and king makers in the Congress Party favoured him.

When the plane bearing Shastri's body descended through the thick winter clouds blanketing Delhi on the afternoon of 11 January, it was met by a sea of mourners thronging Palam airport and its runways. Amongst the crowd waiting to receive the remains of the Prime Minister, was a well-known astrologer, clad – despite the extreme cold – in thin white *khadi* and *chappals*. He was a holy man much consulted in political circles and when a high-ranking Congress leader espied the astrologer, he hastened up him to ask, 'What do the stars foretell?'

'A hat trick' was the reply.

Both Nehru and Shastri were from Allahabad. It was now prophesied that the next Prime Minister of India would be too.

PART THREE

Prime Minister Gandhi

The valley of flowers was about to burst into flames.

Sheikh Abdullah, *Flames of the Chinar*

THIRTEEN

I am the Issue

DESPITE THE ASTROLOGER'S PREDICTION, for a number of days the question of who would be India's third prime minister remained uncertain. Indira herself may, as she indicated to Romesh Thapar, have been undecided. Morarji Desai, however, was not. Having lost the prize in 1964 he was determined to win it now. Nor was Desai the only contender. Gulzarilal Nanda sought Indira's support for his candidacy the morning after he was sworn in as acting Prime Minister. By the evening of Tuesday 11 January 1966 – within twenty-four hours of Shastri's death – the Defence Minister Y.B. Chavan had also put himself forward. Two days later the number of aspirants for the prime ministership had risen to seven: Desai, Indira, Nanda, Chavan, S.K. Patil, Sanjiva Reddy and Kamaraj himself. But Kamaraj, although a highly skilled politician, lacked a national following. To those who prevailed on him to succeed Shastri, he responded, 'No English, no Hindi. How?'[1]

Kamaraj's refusal cleared the way for Indira, especially in view of the general election to be held the following year – the first since Nehru's death. Indira *was* a national leader; she spoke English and Hindi; she was not identified with any caste, region, religion or faction; she was popular among Muslims, Harijans and other minorities and with the poor. Above all, she was a Nehru. For all these reasons, she emerged as the choice of the Syndicate who had anointed Shastri and now turned to her.

Desai's ambition and obduracy, however, guaranteed a fight after the other contenders dropped out of the race. Nineteen months earlier, 'after Nehru', a unanimous consensus, orchestrated by Kamaraj, had been arrived at behind the scenes. 'After Shastri' there was going to be an open and heated battle in the Congress parliamentary party. The problem with Desai, in the eyes of the Syndicate, was that he was his own man – and a rigid, doctrinaire one at that. Desai had all of Gandhi's fads and none of his virtues. His actions were dictated solely by his own inflexible principles and political convictions. Personally as well as politically, he was conservative. A strict Hindu, teetotaller and vegetarian, he had renounced sex at the age of twenty-seven. He shunned Western science and medicine in favour of a traditional regime that included drinking a glass of his own urine every morning.

Indira was everything Desai was not, but for the Congress bosses, her greatest asset was her weakness, or more accurately, their perception that she was weak. The choice of Indira was actually 'a negative decision', provoked by her political 'indistinctness and ambiguity'. Kamaraj persuaded his followers that Indira would do their bidding, that they could run the show, as it were, by remote control. They would thereby enjoy 'that rarest form of political power' which gives 'the privileges of decision without its responsibilities'.[2] They believed this possible not only because Indira lacked administrative experience, but also because she was a woman. The idea was for her to perform as a figurehead, much as Sucheta Kripalani, the woman Chief Minister of Uttar Pradesh, did. Kamaraj and the Syndicate assumed that Indira would be 'pliable, weak . . . a lump of clay they could mould and remould according to need'.[3] As a Nehru, she would also, crucially, help win the 1967 election for Congress after which a suitable replacement could be brought in to succeed her. In the words of another future Prime Minister, Narasimha Rao, Indira was merely a 'vote-catching device'. After the elections 'she would take or they would make her take a back seat [and] . . . a more experienced leader [would] . . . take over and run the country'.[4]

Indira was the choice not only of Kamaraj but also of the powerful Madhya Pradesh Chief Minister, D.P. Mishra, who was a key player in this second succession because of his influence with other chief ministers. Indira, in fact, had rung Mishra in Bhopal at 5.30 a.m. on 11 January, just hours after Shastri's death, and asked him to come to Delhi immediately because she felt he would be a powerful ally.[5] She was right: Mishra was able to persuade eight chief ministers to back Indira and on 15 January they issued a statement of support. Four more chief ministers jumped on Indira's bandwagon the same day so that she had a total of twelve out of fourteen chief ministers. That evening large crowds gathered outside her house at 1 Safdarjung Road to congratulate her.

Another important ally was the President of India, Sarvepalli Radha-krishnan. Outwardly Radhakrishnan remained aloof and impartial in the struggle between Desai and Indira, but he favoured Indira and actively 'coached her on how to manoeuvre'. Radhakrishnan's position as presi-dent was supposed to be non-partisan, but he absolved himself of impro-priety and justified his pro-Indira stance as an old friend of Nehru and 'a much needed counsellor to this hesitant and inexperienced woman'. According to Radhakrishnan's son, S. Gopal, Radhakrishnan actually went beyond advising Indira on 'the timing of crucial moves'. The President also spoke privately to key Congress leaders and informed Indira of those who supported her.[6]

Indira, then, emerged as a coalition candidate by 'a process of elimin-ation' – not because she was a strong one but because of the various shortcomings and drawbacks of the other contenders and the need for the Syndicate and the Chief Ministers to agree on someone who could beat Desai.[7] She was perfectly aware of this. In her own words, 'they were not so much for me as against him'.[8] She never formally declared herself a candidate. Instead she waited for 'the call'. She owed her triumph to Kamaraj, Mishra and Radhakrishnan for putting her forward, to her father for giving her the 'name and mantle' and to Desai for insisting on a secret ballot. She was, quite simply, the only person certain to win.[9]

It was rumoured that Indira's aunt, Vijaya Lakshmi Pandit, supported Desai, but when it became clear that the balance was tilting towards Indira, Mrs Pandit released a statement of support for her niece, though it was a barbed one: 'It is a certainty that Indira Gandhi will be India's next Prime Minister. We Nehrus are very proud of our family. When a Nehru is chosen as Prime Minister, the people will rejoice. Mrs Gandhi has the qualities, now she needs the experience. With a little experience she will make a fine Prime Minister . . . She is in very frail health, but with the help of her colleagues she will manage.'[10]

19 January 1966, the day of the Congress parliamentary party election, dawned a cold misty day. Indira awoke very early and dressed with care, putting on a white *khadi* sari (the same one she had worn when she became Congress President), a plain Kashmiri shawl, and a string of dark brown beads, which she habitually wore as a kind of talisman in

critical situations. The beads had been given to her by one of Kamala Nehru's spiritual gurus, Anandamayi, the Bengali female 'saint'. Before Delhi came to life, Indira went by car through its empty streets to Rajghat and Shanti Vana on the Jumna and stood silently before Mahatma Gandhi's and her father's cremation sites. Then she went to Teen Murti, now a national museum dedicated to Nehru, walked through the silent corridors and stood before her father's portrait.[11]

From Teen Murti, Indira proceeded to Parliament accompanied by acting Prime Minister Nanda and the woman MP Subhadra Joshi with whom, years before, Indira had worked in the Delhi refugee camps at the time of Partition. At the entrance to Parliament someone presented Indira with a bouquet. Subhadra plucked a rose out of it and pinned it to Indira's shawl.[12] Thus adorned, Indira entered Parliament as Nehru invariably had done in the past when he sported a fresh rose in the buttonhole of his *sherwani*.

The Congress parliamentary party election meeting began at 11 a.m., and the secret ballot dragged on for four-and-a-half hours. Five hundred and twenty-six Congress MPs were present. One by one, each cast his ballot in a concealed, closed booth. Then the votes were laboriously counted. Outside a huge crowd gathered round the circular Central Hall of Parliament. When the Congress chief whip finally appeared on the balcony to announce the results, someone in the crowd shouted, 'Is it a boy or a girl?' 'A girl' was the answer and the crowd roared with approval. Indira had beaten Desai, 355 votes to 169. (Both Indira and Desai abstained from voting themselves.)

Inside, when a party official announced the results, Indira walked to the podium and uttered her first words as Prime Minister. 'My heart is full,' she said in Hindi, 'and I do not know how to thank you ... As I stand before you my thoughts go back to the great leaders: Mahatma Gandhi, at whose feet I grew up, Panditji, my father, and Lal Bahadur Shastri. These leaders have shown the way, and I want to go along the same path.'[13] Before leaving the oak-panelled central hall, she performed another act of homage when she approached the seat of her opponent, Morarji Desai, with hands raised palm to palm in the *namaste* greeting.

'Will you bless my success?' she asked Desai.

'I give you my blessing,' was the laconic reply.

Then Indira emerged from Parliament to be greeted and garlanded by the jubilant crowd awaiting her. 'Indira Gandhi *Zindabad!*' filled the air along with '*Lal Gulab Zindabad!*' (Long live the red rose). From her first moments as Prime Minister Indira was perceived as her father's inheritor, even as his reincarnation.

Five days later, on 24 January, Indira was sworn in as Prime Minister by the President. When she took the oath, she raised her right hand and 'solemnly affirmed' rather than 'swore in the name of God', underlining her modern, secular image.

Indira was the Syndicate's choice and thus beholden to them. This meant that Kamaraj was able to insist that she retain most of Shastri's Cabinet. She wanted to drop the Home Minister, Gulzarilal Nanda, who had twice performed as acting Prime Minister, but was forced to keep him. The new cabinet members she was able to induct were Asoka Mehta, an intellectual and socialist, who was given the new post of Minister of Planning, G.S. Pathak, who was given the Law portfolio, Fakhruddin Ali Ahmed from Assam who took on Irrigation and Power and Jagjivan Ram, the Harijan leader, who was given the Ministry of Labour. Desai, of course, was not invited to join the Cabinet, as he admitted in his autobiography, though he claimed that, 'even if I had been, I would not have accepted'.[14]

In America, five days after Indira was sworn in, she appeared on the cover of *Time* magazine in full colour, complete with red rose and white-streaked hair, under the banner 'Troubled India in a Woman's Hands'. Betty Friedan, the best-selling author of *The Feminine Mystique*, packed her bags to fly to India to write a long profile article on how 'Mrs Gandhi Shattered the Feminine Mystique' for the American *Ladies Home Journal*. In London John Grigg wrote in the *Guardian*: 'Probably no woman in history has assumed a heavier burden of responsibility and certainly no country of India's importance has ever before entrusted so much power to a woman under democratic conditions . . . If she makes a success of the job she will deal what may be a knockout blow to lingering notions of male superiority.'[15]

Indira's emergence as Prime Minister coincided with the burgeoning women's movement in the West, and though she denied being a feminist and was always impatient with questions about her role as a female politician, the women's movement intensified public interest in her. Feminists like Friedan hoped that Indira's powerful position as a woman leader might become the norm rather than remain an anomaly. And despite the fact that Indira continued to disassociate herself from feminism, she was particularly forthcoming and revealing with women writers like Friedan and the Italian journalist Oriana Fallaci, as well as her early biographer Uma Vasudev and the American academic Mary Carras.

Within India, however, Indira was not viewed as a harbinger of the women's movement. Instead, reflecting the Syndicate's motive for installing her as Prime Minister, her gender was generally seen only as a liability. Shortly after Indira was elected by the Congress parliamentary party, the Bombay *Economic and Political Weekly* remarked with considerable prescience that 'a woman ruler is under a social handicap until she has been able to consolidate her position. In the beginning every group leader wants to advise and control her and so faction fights start among them. Either the ruler is able to satisfy everyone that she is not too close to anyone in particular, as Queen Elizabeth I did, and enjoy a long tenure of office, or fails to survive the initial period of uncertainty.'[16]

In the early months of Indira's prime ministership, the idea took hold that there must be male power behind the throne. Dinesh Singh, the handsome and urbane former Raja of Kalakankar, in particular, cultivated this role. He was made a minister of state in Indira's first cabinet and from the early months of her term as Prime Minister, she relied on him heavily. Singh's influence did not go unnoticed. A presidential order was issued to the effect that the Prime Minister assigned to him 'such functions as she may', and in February 1966, just a month after Indira became Prime Minister, she was accused in Parliament of making Dinesh Singh 'a virtual *de facto* Prime Minister'.[17] When the historian V. N. Datta told Krishna Menon that he had presented a copy of Datta's book on Syed Mahmud to the Prime Minister, Krishna Menon replied, 'Ah, you mean to Dinesh Singh?' According to the journalist Kuldip Nayar, until 1967 'every important paper received by Mrs Gandhi or sent by her was routed through Dinesh Singh'.[18]

Indira relied on Singh and conferred with him at all hours. Inevitably, there were rumours that he was her lover, rumours which Singh himself encouraged. When Indira became more confident and when she learned that Singh used his closeness to her for his own purposes, he was at first subtly and then not so subtly marginalized. By this time Indira's secretary, P. N. Haksar, whom she trusted completely, had supplanted Dinesh Singh as her principal adviser. In 1969 Singh threatened to resign from the Cabinet, but Indira pre-empted him by moving him to the Ministry of Foreign Affairs against his wishes.

India in January 1966 was in a worse shape than it had ever been under either Nehru or Shastri. Severe droughts had led to food shortages and famine conditions in large parts of the country. This generated unrest, especially in Kerala where there were rice riots. The economy was flagging with rampant inflation and a shortage of foreign exchange. There was agitation in the Punjab for a separate Punjabi-speaking state. The Naga people of the northeast were threatening secession. Internationally, India's relations with the United States had been strained since the American provision of arms to Pakistan during the 1965 war and they grew worse with the US involvement in Vietnam.

Just a month after becoming Prime Minister, Indira addressed the All-India Congress Committee meeting in Jaipur. The food crisis was the most pressing issue. Indira theatrically announced that she would not eat rice until there were adequate supplies of rice available in Kerala. Congressmen demanded that the established food zones (within, but not between which, food could be moved) be abolished so that food could be transported from surplus to famine-stricken areas of the country. Indira handled this demand ineptly, and in the midst of much tumult, she rather desperately called for the withdrawal of the proposed amendment banning food zones and promised to review the government's food policy. Kamaraj was forced to take over the floor and restore order.

Back in Delhi, Indira was mortified at her poor performance at Jaipur. 'With hurt and bitterness', she told her friend Pupul Jayakar how her aunt, Vijaya Lakshmi Pandit, had undermined her self-confidence in childhood by calling her ugly and stupid. 'This shattered something within me,' Indira told Jayakar, 'faced with hostility, however well prepared I am, I get tongue-tied and withdraw.' She confessed she was 'scared of the coming Parliament session'.[19]

Justifiably as it turned out, for Indira cut a sorry figure on the floor when Parliament opened. Apart from her American lecture tour (when she appears to have delivered ghost-written lectures), Indira's experience as a public speaker was principally as an election campaigner. She proved a weak parliamentary performer who lapsed into silences and could not think on her feet. The opposition heckled her; colleagues tried to come to her rescue by passing her slips of paper but still she faltered. The socialist Ram Manohar Lohia called her *goongi gudiya* – (the dumb doll) – a label that stuck even after Indira began to find her voice. This bad start engendered in her both anxiety towards and a contempt for Parliament. As time passed, she attended Parliament less and less and increasingly overruled or circumvented it.

As far as the Punjab was concerned, Indira supported dividing it as she had Bombay five years earlier, this time into the states of Haryana, Himachal Pradesh and a greatly reduced Punjab. This, however, was only partly done on the basis of language. Haryana and Himachal Pradesh had very small Sikh populations (5 per cent and 2 per cent in 1966); while in the new Punjab 52 per cent were Sikhs. Although the division of the Punjab into three new states could be rationalized on the basis of language, a far more explosive political, communal issue was at stake which would later have disastrous consequences.

In late March 1966 Indira visited the United States – her first foreign visit as Prime Minister. She insisted that her trip was a goodwill visit only and that she was not going with a begging bowl. Privately, however, she told the journalist Inder Malhotra that her 'main mission is to get both food and foreign exchange without appearing to ask for them'.[20] The United States had suspended aid to India (and also to Pakistan) in 1965 at the time of the Indo-Pak war and it now stipulated conditions before aid would be restored. So, too, were the World Bank and the International Monetary Fund, both of which demanded that the rupee be devalued. Indira appointed a committee to consider the issue. It included the Finance Minister Sachin Chaudhuri, the Planning Minister, Asoka Mehta, and the Food Minister, C. Subramaniam, all of whom supported devaluation, as did B.K. Nehru, Indira's cousin – the Indian ambassador to America. Before Indira left for the States the committee produced a report for the IMF indicating India's intention to devalue the rupee, without specifying its timing or scope. The plan, however, was not made public.[21]

At the time, Indira's 1966 trip to America was regarded as an enormous success, primarily because President Lyndon Johnson, a huge, strapping Texan, found Indira irresistible. Indira turned on her subtle charm, and looked glamorous with a new, bouffant hairstyle, full make-up and jewellery. (In contrast to her tousled hair and the plain cotton saris she wore in India.) Johnson was so entranced with Indira that after a private meeting at the home of the B.K. Nehrus, he stayed on, and on, downing tumblers of bourbon on the rocks whilst the evening's banquet guests arrived. When the meal could be postponed no longer, Fori Nehru and Indira politely suggested to Johnson that he join them, and ignoring protocol, he agreed, even though the Vice-President, Hubert Humphrey, was supposed to be the guest of honour.[22]

Most of the speeches Indira made during her trip to the States were unimpressive and unremarkable, consisting largely of strings of clichés. Her speech to the National Press Club in Washington became newsworthy only because she insisted that women should be allowed to join the all-male bastion. In New York, however, she tackled the thorny issue of Kashmir and flatly rejected the idea of a plebiscite. 'It is now too late to talk of a plebiscite. The second invasion of Kashmir by Pakistan last autumn has destroyed whatever marginal or academic value the old United Nations resolution might have had. Kashmir is also vital now to the defence of India in Ladakh against China. Any plebiscite now would definitely amount to questioning the integrity of India. It would raise the issue of secession – an issue on which the United States fought a civil war ... we cannot and will not tolerate a second partition of India on religious grounds.'[23] Indira may have claimed not to be seeking aid during her visit, but she agreed to key American demands in order to secure it: the devaluation of the rupee and the establishment of an Indo-American educational foundation. The vast rupee funds that the US had accumulated in India, as a result of massive shipments of wheat, would be used to further education and research. Indira's agreement to the latter was actually 'a subterfuge', in B.K. Nehru's words, 'to get the American Congress to supply us with the colossal amount of wheat we needed'.[24] Indira also issued a statement that 'India understood America's agony over Vietnam'. About the only thing she refused to do was whirl around the dance floor with the American President at a White House banquet, explaining to Johnson that this would make her unpopular back in India. Johnson, for his part, said that he wanted to see that 'no harm comes to this girl', and promised three million tons of food and $9 million in aid.

Delighted with the outcome of her visit, on the return flight to India Indira stopped off in the Soviet Union where she had talks with Alexei Kosygin, and Britain where she conferred with Prime Minister Harold Wilson. But Indira's satisfaction with her American trip soon evaporated; shortly after she arrived back in India her bargains with Johnson were decried. She was denounced for even discussing devaluation, for agreeing to the Indo-American educational foundation (which critics said would grant America far too much influence over Indian higher education), and for condoning US involvement in Vietnam. Krishna Menon – anti-American to his bones – was particularly incensed and led the chorus of criticism against Indira. Indira rounded on her old friend and accused him of 'rank misrepresentation and distortion of facts'.

Although Indira was deeply disturbed by such negative reaction, she went ahead and devalued the rupee by a whopping 57.5 per cent. The official announcement of devaluation was made at 11 p.m. on the night of 6 June, after receiving the IMF's approval. On 12 June Indira broadcast to the nation on All India Radio:

> Let me be frank with you. The decision to devalue the rupee was not an easy one ... There are times in the history of every nation when its will is tested and its future depends on its capacity for resolute action and bold decision. This is such a time in India ... A combination of circumstances, aggravated by war and drought, has temporarily slowed down, and almost halted economic growth. There is scarcity. The balance of payments crisis has rendered industrial capacity idle and compelled retrenchment. Small industry has been particularly hard hit. Exports have come to a rest. Prices have moved up steeply. There is frustration, agitation, and uncertainty. Above all people are in distress. We tried various remedies. But these first-aid measures proved ineffective. Stronger medicine was necessary to restore the nation to economic health.[25]

Indira did not consult Kamaraj, the Congress President, about the 'strong medicine' of devaluation, knowing that he was vehemently opposed to it. As were a number of cabinet ministers when the matter was finally raised at a cabinet meeting on 6 July. Indira argued that there could be no foreign aid without devaluation. Her insistence on devaluation, in the face of such opposition, revealed two crucial elements in her emerging political character: she was capable of taking an unpopular decision, and she felt beholden to no one.

Devaluation was attacked in every quarter – on the right and the left, among the press, the public and Indira's Congress colleagues. The CWC itself passed a resolution denouncing it and Kamaraj, who had ensured that Indira rather than Desai became Prime Minister, reportedly moaned, 'a big man's daughter, a small man's mistake'. Embarrassingly for Indira, the promised American aid was slow to materialize and when it did, food shipments were erratic.

Within months of becoming Prime Minister, Indira had managed to make herself far more unpopular than Shastri had ever been. Her closest advisers – the 'kitchen cabinet' comprising Dinesh Singh, Inder Gujral, Nandini Satpathi, a young woman MP from Orissa, Umar Shankar Dikshit, D.P. Mishra, the powerful Chief Minister of Madhya Pradesh, and three men who were also members of Indira's official Cabinet, C. Subramaniam, Asoka Mehta and Fakhruddin Ali Ahmed – urged a leftist ideological line on her and a repudiation of her friendliness with the United States. Such a policy shift would also distance Indira from the old guard bosses in the Syndicate.

Indira responded swiftly. As an opening salvo she issued a statement on 1 July 1966 'deploring' the American bombing of Hanoi and Haiphong. Then, during a further visit to the Soviet Union she signed a joint statement with Kosygin condemning 'imperialist aggression' in Vietnam. Lyndon Johnson was furious and deliberately delayed food shipments to India. Chester Bowles, the US ambassador to India, pointed out to Johnson that the UN Secretary General U Thant and the Pope had also condemned American policy in Vietnam; but Johnson retorted that the Pope and U Thant 'do not want our wheat'.[26] Unperturbed, Indira continued to denounce America's involvement in Vietnam. She also agreed to scrap the Indo-American education foundation. Her cosy relations with Lyndon Johnson were now in a shambles.

Closer to home, there were further troubles for the Prime Minister. In November 1966 a mob of thousands of trident-bearing, naked holy men called *sadhus* staged a demonstration in front of Parliament calling for an end to cow slaughter. India was a secular democracy and beef was a cheap source of protein for non-Hindus. Nevertheless, Hindu chauvinists demanded a ban on killing cows throughout the country. The cow slaughter demonstration swiftly deteriorated into looting and violence. Six people were killed when police fired into the crowd; shops were stripped; cars and buildings were torched. Indira told the *Times of India* that she would not be 'cowed down by the cow-savers'. And she stood firm. She also astutely used the agitation to rid herself of her Home Minister, Gulzarilal Nanda – a 'superstitious cow-saver' who had twice served as acting Prime Minister and was a particular thorn in Indira's side and he was now peremptorily dropped from the Cabinet.

Having begun to realign herself ideologically to the left, Indira girded herself to take on the Syndicate – to whom she owed her position as Prime Minister. Her relations with Kamaraj had been severely strained since the devaluation of the rupee. He and the rest of the group now grasped the extent to which Indira was able to exercise her own power in the run-up to the forthcoming 1967 general election.

On Christmas Day 1966 Indira made a highly significant statement to the press. Referring to Kamaraj and Desai – who, though not yet allies, both wanted her out – she said: 'Here is a question of whom the party wants and whom the people want. My position among the people is uncontested.'[27] This was perhaps the first blatant indication of Indira's key strategy in the years to come. She was asserting a direct, personal relationship with the electorate which bypassed the party organization, its rules and its norms.

1967 – the twentieth anniversary of Indian independence – was also the year that Indira turned fifty. The previous year Indira had been angered when her aunt, Vijaya Lakshmi Pandit, publicly referred to her niece's 'frail health'. Soon afterwards, when the writer Ved Mehta interviewed Indira and questioned her about her health, she replied: 'Here [in India], if you don't look well fed, people think you are ill. A little while ago I put on some extra weight and, with great effort, I lost it again. Everyone said, "Indu, you look ill. What's the matter?" I am very fit. I keep fit by holding to a daily regime. The first thing in the morning, at five o'clock, I do my yoga exercises for fifteen or twenty minutes.'[28]

Most prime ministers and presidents age dramatically in office, but Indira actually thrived. In 1967, in fact, she was in better health than she had ever been. The sickly child was now a mature, robust woman with remarkable stamina. Tuberculosis had been banished a decade earlier; Indira's last serious illness was the troublesome kidney stone that was surgically removed in 1959. By her late forties all her menopausal symptoms had subsided. She was safely through 'the change' and now felt an unprecedented sense of wellbeing and vitality. She ate healthily and sparingly and kept fit with yoga. The only tablets she ever took were multivitamins. She continued to eschew alcohol (according to B.K. Nehru, at banquets Indira drank toasts of 'innocuous coloured water'). She rarely managed to get more than five or six hours of sleep a night – and often less – but she had the capacity to drop off immediately and also to catnap on planes and during car journeys.

In addition to a sensible, healthy lifestyle, Indira had developed the gift of withdrawing psychologically into herself. She had deliberately trained herself not to agonize or brood over matters. She asked an interviewer once if he had read in the papers about the 'large voids in the universe' which scientists had recently reported and went on to explain, 'I have always felt that within you, within a person, you have such voids, and you can retire into them without disrupting yourself. You may be doing anything. You may be having a conversation or you may be in a crowd. But if you want to retire into yourself, you can retire and you can do almost anything you like . . . that is why you can't get tired because you are automatically relaxing yourself.'[29] Indira's oft-noted aloofness in the midst of others was a symptom of this strategy of withdrawal.

It was a device that she employed, however, only in certain situations. In large crowds, making speeches or campaigning, Indira was manifestly present and in small groups, in her family or small circle of close friends, she was seldom distant or detached. Instead, it was with groups in the middle ground – especially officials or groups of politicians – that Indira would 'remove' herself while in the midst of others. In such situations, too, Indira was cautious, restrained and on her guard. As a consequence she could appear, variously, impassive and remote, cold or indifferent. Also intimidating and imperious: hence the sobriquet, 'the Empress of India', that began to appear in newspaper columns once Indira's diffidence as Prime Minister subsided.

By withdrawing into herself Indira was able to shore up reserves of her remarkable stamina and energy, which she then released to great effect at critical times – such as in the run-up to the 1967 general election. As a campaigner she proved to be the most charismatic leader since Gandhi. It was during the 1967 campaign that Indira fully demonstrated her intangible but powerful connection with the Indian people. In the first two months of the year, she campaigned relentlessly, covering 15,000 miles and speaking at hundreds of public meetings. All over the country, she drew enormous crowds – larger even than those who had come to see Nehru. Like many charismatic leaders before her, she claimed in the words of one analyst, 'to give voice to the frustrations of the dispossessed and downtrodden and . . . to dent the existing structures of domination and privilege'.[30] But Indira's political style was also imbued with her aristocratic heritage: she was the scion of the Nehru family, *and* 'one of us', speaking to village people in homely metaphors and in terms of family relationships. Her approach and her language were populist; she spoke in the regional language; she wore her sari as the local women did and ate their food with her fingers. But at the same time, Indira appeared lofty and awesome, copiously garlanded, immaculate in a sea of whirling dust as her prime ministerial car roared to a halt before a huge crowd. It was an unbeatable combination.

Not that she was always revered. In Jaipur, the Maharani of Jaipur's right-wing Swatantra followers tried to break up one of Indira's public meetings and Indira rounded on them with words calculated to rouse her audience:

> I am not going to be cowed down. I know who [the Maharani] is behind these demonstrations and I know how to make myself heard. I am going to do some plain speaking today. Go and ask the Maharajas how many wells they dug for the people in their States when they [the princes] ruled them, how many roads they constructed, what they did to fight the slavery of the British. If you look at the account of their achievements before Independence, it is a big zero there.[31]

It was at this late date, in 1967, that Indira stood for Parliament for the first time. Not, however, for Nehru's constituency (though her aunt, Vijaya Lakshmi Pandit, said that she was still willing to give up the Phulpur seat), but instead for Feroze Gandhi's constituency, Rae Bareilly. Indira's decision to stand for her husband's former seat was a product of sentimental, pragmatic and political considerations. Rae Bareilly would in some sense restore Feroze to her; she could tell herself that she would carry on his work. The place was saturated with memories of their marriage and that first 1952 campaign in particular, when they had worked so hard together to get Feroze elected. Indira had canvassed strenuously for her husband who had been enormously popular in his constituency and she was well known and loved there. In addition, taking up Feroze's banner, Indira would inherit as well the image of her husband's crusading radicalism.

But she was more than Nehru's daughter and Feroze Gandhi's wife. Indira needed her own particular relationship with the Indian electorate and this she articulated during an emotional speech at Rae Bareilly in early 1967. Up until now most people had regarded her gender as a weakness. Lyndon Johnson wanted to protect 'this girl'. Indira was the 'dumb doll' in Parliament. Indira's antagonist Morarji Desai once referred to her as 'this mere *chokri*' (slip of a girl). Journalists called her 'the little woman'. The public said that at least they now had a pretty face to look at on the front page of the newspaper. Indira turned such dismissive remarks on their head, and now invoked her womanhood as a source of strength and compassion:

> My family is not confined to a few individuals. It consists of crores of people. Your burdens are comparatively light, because your families are limited and viable. But my burden is manifold because crores of my family members are poverty-stricken and I have to look after them. Since they belong to different castes and creeds, they sometimes fight among themselves, and I have to intervene, especially to look after the weaker members of my family, so that the stronger ones do not take advantage of them.[32]

Thus was born the myth of 'Mother Indira'. Two weeks later she was hailed as such 2,000 miles away from Rae Bareilly while campaigning in Cochin.

The crucial point is that during the 1967 campaign Indira failed to adopt an issue-oriented, ideological stance. She presented herself as the great provider and reconciler. Her relationship to 'the people' was intimate, parental – both maternal and paternal – and unconnected to political institutions. Children do not choose their parents; parents, both good and bad, possess a natural authority over their children. To what extent was Indira conscious of her strategy and its implications? Undoubtedly she saw it as a means of political survival, but it is unlikely that at this point she fully grasped its subversive and undemocratic overtones.

During the strenuous 1967 campaign Indira encountered hostility in Bhubaneshwar in Orissa, another right-wing, Swatantra Party stronghold. Shortly after she began to address the crowd, hecklers started to stone the speakers' platform. A guard was hit in the forehead and a journalist in the leg. Two security men then stood on either side of Indira; she refused, despite their pleas, to wind up her speech. Stones continued to sail through the air. Ignoring them, Indira finally got to the end of her speech and sat down. When she finished, the local Congress candidate rose to speak and the stoning resumed. Indira jumped up and went to the podium again, grabbed the microphone and cried angrily to the crowd, 'What insolence is this! Is this the way you're going to build the country? . . . are these the sort of people [referring to the hecklers and stone-throwers] you're going to vote for?' Several stones were then hurled at once and one hit Indira full in the face. She took the blow silently, but bent over and covered her face with her hands, trying to staunch the blood. The stone had fractured her nose.[33]

The assault on Indira at Bhubaneshwar was unprecedented and made headlines the next day across the country. From early on, Indira generated intense hatred among those who opposed her. But her physical courage was equally admired, especially when she continued to campaign across the country with her nose and top half of her face swathed in white bandages that made her, she joked, look like a white-masked version of Batman.

When she returned to Delhi, Indira had minor surgery to realign her nose. She wrote to her old friend Dorothy Norman that she had tried to take advantage of this to have 'something done' to her prominent nose, something she had wanted, she confessed, 'ever since plastic surgery was heard of'. Indira had even put some money aside for an operation and 'thought the only way it could be done without the usual hoo-ha was first to have some slight accident'.[34] But the Delhi doctors who repaired her nose fracture were not trained in plastic surgery and Indira was persuaded to forego her dream of a svelte new nose.

India's fourth general election was held in February 1967 and although Congress remained in power, the results were dismaying. Congress lost 95 seats, winning only 282 out of a house of 520, leaving it with a precarious overall majority of 44. It also lost its majority in seven states: Kerala, Madras, Orissa, West Bengal, Bihar, Uttar Pradesh and

Rajasthan. The *Times* headline in London read: 'After the broken nose, a slap in the face.'

Kamaraj lost his parliamentary seat to a twenty-six-year-old student leader of the regional Dravida Munnetra Kazagham Party in Madras. But the defeat of Kamaraj indicated that Congress losses might prove Indira's gain, because he was not the only Syndicate member to lose office. S.K. Patil in Bombay, Atulya Ghosh in Bengal and Biju Patnaik in Orissa were all thrown out. For Indira these were 'sweet defeats': she had secured her own Rae Bareilly constituency by a large majority. At the meeting of the Parliamentary Board on 27 February she remarked, to the discomfort of the high command, that 'the elections showed a triumph of youth over age'.[35] This triumph meant that those who had been biding their time until the elections were over to oust Indira were, in some cases, no longer around to do so.

Indira's nemesis, Morarji Desai, however, had been returned handsomely and he was still intent on becoming Prime Minister. Another battle between them for the leadership of the parliamentary party looked inevitable. Kamaraj (who, though no longer an MP, was still President of Congress) was determined to avoid this. In early March he began tortuous negotiations with Indira and Desai. For several days various compromise formulas were discussed, but Indira and Desai vetoed them all.

On Friday 10 March, the two antagonists – Indira and Desai – met twice, in the morning and the late afternoon. At midday Desai announced that he intended to contest the party leadership and 'the decision was in the hands of God'.[36] More accurately, however, it was in Kamaraj's rather than divine hands. Kamaraj, along with D.P. Mishra and C.B. Gupta, an MP from Uttar Pradesh, stepped up their intricate negotiations. Desai finally indicated that he would give up the contest if he were made both Home Minister and deputy Prime Minister – a post that had not existed since the death of Sardar Patel in 1950. Indira responded that she was willing to make Desai number two in her Cabinet, but not deputy Prime Minister, nor was she willing to drop Chavan in order to give the Home Ministry to Desai.

Despite this deadlock, the bargaining reached fever pitch by the afternoon, as the small Indian-manufactured cars, appropriately called 'Ambassadors', crisscrossed New Delhi ferrying Kamaraj and his emissaries. A particularly well-worn path was beaten between Indira's and

Desai's homes. On Saturday 11 March, Desai and Indira had 'a final confrontation'. Desai told Indira that he could only be 'useful' to her in the post of deputy Prime Minister. And with his characteristic arrogance, he warned her that there were now some very strong people in opposition, that 'they are very good speakers. As I have more experience [than you],' he argued, 'I can meet their arguments better than you. You have not got much experience [as a parliamentarian] . . . I can reply more effectively to the opposition.'[37]

Despite such tactlessness, Indira reluctantly agreed to make Desai deputy Prime Minister, but with the Finance Ministry rather than the Home Ministry he coveted. Previously, when Kamaraj made this same offer Desai had turned it down; this time he did not. However, Indira felt immediately she had made a terrible mistake and tried to withdraw her offer. But both Kamaraj and Mishra argued that it was too late: she was 'the prisoner of her own commitment'.[38]

Thus after the 1967 general election Indira remained at the helm as Prime Minister, but with the prickly and ambitious Desai elevated to her deputy. In order to assert her independence, and to demonstrate that her authority would remain 'unfettered', Indira chose her cabinet without consulting either Desai or Kamaraj. Her supporters and allies were given key posts: Y. B. Chavan (Home), the Harijan leader, Jagjivan Ram (Food and Agriculture), Fakhruddin Ali Ahmed (Industrial Development) and Dinesh Singh (Commerce). She also stated publicly that the post of deputy Prime Minister did not imply 'any duality of authority', and reported that Desai had pledged 'full and unqualified support' to her.[39] Indira dispensed with the system of ranking cabinet members. Henceforth, she would rely on simple alphabetical order rendering cabinet positions meaningless as indicators of future power line-ups.[40]

Desai may have been Indira's deputy, but as her senior – in both age and political experience – his position would prove to be untenable to both of them. As D. P. Mishra observed, Desai 'continued to think of [Indira], a woman fifty years old and occupying the office of Prime Minister, as a chit of a girl'. Indeed, Desai complained of her to Mishra *'Chhokari sunti nahin hai'* (the girl does not listen).[41] Desai and Indira came into conflict on a series of issues such as the continuation of English as the official language, but the greatest area of contention was the nationalization of commercial banks, which Desai vehemently opposed and Indira's left-wing followers supported. Desai's high-handedness and rigidity galled Indira as much as his patronizing behaviour. For example, at a meeting of the Planning Commission in May 1967 he interrupted her at one point, saying, 'Indiraben (Indira, my sister), you don't understand this matter. Let me deal with it.' Indira was 'livid with anger but let him have his say'.[42]

Indira, however, was able to assert her will over Desai in the choice of the new President, when her candidate, Zakir Husain, was elected. She also demonstrated that her knowledge and experience of foreign affairs was superior to Desai's. In fact, Indira, like her father, would hold the positions of both Prime Minister and Minister for Foreign Affairs (from September 1967 to January 1969), just as her father had.

Between September and November 1967 Indira completed an exhausting itinerary of state visits to Ceylon, the Soviet Union, Poland, Yugoslavia, Bulgaria, Romania and the United Arab Republic. In May the following year she toured Singapore, Malaysia, Australia and New Zealand. In September 1968 she travelled through Latin America, visiting Brazil, Argentina, Chile, Venezuela, Uruguay, Colombia, Trinidad and Guyana. In New York she addressed the UN General Assembly. On her homeward journey she made her customary stop in the Soviet Union. In 1969 she visited Burma, Afghanistan, Japan and Indonesia.

Indira's extensive travels, her uniqueness as a female Prime Minister, her elegance and charm, all made her one of the most famous and recognizable political figures in the world. She communicated well not only with other leaders and crowds but also with journalists and intellectuals. Her English and French were impeccable. To foreigners she seemed exotic but also modern and progressive.

Back at home, the continuing enmity of Indira and Desai reflected the ever-deepening fissure in the Congress Party between its radical and conservative wings. Desai – whose principal cheerleader was none other than Feroze Gandhi's former mistress, Tarakeshwari Sinha – was the clear leader of the conservatives. The radicals, or 'Young Turks', were somewhat misleadingly equated with Indira who was considerably less ideologically committed than they.

In May 1967, pursuing her leftist image, Indira had announced a ten-point programme which included social control of banking, a check on monopolies, the nationalization of general insurance, curbs on property, the state control of exports and food grains, and the abolition of the former princes' privileges and privy purses in the Princely States.

In addition, various agrarian reforms, begun in the 1950s under the rubric of 'the Green Revolution', had started to pay off. In the later years of Nehru's final term and during the Shastri interregnum, agricultural reform had shifted from institutional and structural reform of land use and ownership to a variety of technological developments. Among the most important of these was the introduction of hybrid, high-yielding varieties of seeds for wheat and rice, crops that increased production dramatically, especially in the Punjab, Haryana and Uttar Pradesh. Indira made the Green Revolution a key government priority and along with the new hybrid seeds, initiated state subsidies, the provision of electrical power, water and fertilizers and credit to farmers. Agricultural income was not taxable. The result was that India became self-sufficient in food – a heartfelt aim for Indira after President Johnson's erratic and condition-laden food aid. In addition, the country was able to build up buffer grain stocks to survive several seasons of drought and even became a modest food exporter. The Green Revolution in India was of a piece with the rest of Indira's radical programme in the mid and late sixties.[43]

By the beginning of 1968 both Desai and Kamaraj (who had won a by-election and returned to Parliament, like Banquo's ghost, to haunt Indira) wanted to oust Indira; but they first needed to persuade S. Nijalingappa, who had succeeded Kamaraj as Congress President, to come over to their side. Opposition to Indira had now brought the Syndicate, still headed by Kamaraj, and Desai together as allies. Indira's opponents made much of the dismissal of non-Congress governments and the imposition of President's rule in West Bengal, Uttar Pradesh, Bihar and the Punjab, following the example of Kerala in 1959.

In the midst of the struggle between the two factions of Congress Indira was briefly distracted by the marriage of her son, Rajiv, to a beautiful young Italian named Sonia Maino on 25 February 1968. Rajiv and Sonia had met three years earlier, in Cambridge, when Rajiv was still struggling with his degree course at Trinity College and Sonia was studying English at a language school for foreign students. They first saw each other at a local restaurant, the Varsity. Rajiv was instantly attracted to Sonia, a slender girl with long golden hair and dark eyes, and he asked a mutual friend to introduce them. It was a classic case of love at first sight for both of them. Rajiv, in fact, was so certain of the relationship, that he wrote to Indira within weeks of meeting Sonia, 'You're always asking me about girls, whether I have a special girl and so forth. Well, I've met a special girl. I haven't proposed yet, but she's the girl I want to marry.'[44]

Sonia Maino was the eighteen-year-old daughter of a prosperous builder from Turin named Stefano Maino who had been a supporter of Mussolini during the war and who remained a fascist sympathizer. The Mainos were strict Roman Catholics and Sonia was an obedient, dutiful daughter. Before Cambridge she had never been outside of Italy. When she met Rajiv she knew nothing of India except that it 'existed somewhere in the world with its snakes, elephants and jungles, but exactly where it was and what it was really all about, I was not sure'.[45]

Both Sonia and Rajiv were untouched by the students' and women's movements in Cambridge and London in the sixties. The only unconventional thing they ever did, either then or later, was to fall in love with a foreigner. This was unacceptable to Sonia's father who wanted all three of his daughters to marry Italian Catholics. Not only was Rajiv not a Catholic, he was an Indian, and it made no difference to Signor Maino who Rajiv's mother or grandfather were.

Indira Gandhi had no such prejudices, but in her own muted way, she was disconcerted at the thought of a foreign daughter-in-law. But most of Indira's reservations evaporated when she first met Sonia in London, early in 1966. Sonia was terrified by the prospect of meeting Indira, then still a minister in Shastri's government, but Indira chatted with her in French (which Sonia spoke more fluently than English) and put her completely at ease by saying 'she herself had been young, extremely shy and in love, and she understood' Sonia perfectly.[46]

Signor Maino, however, remained obdurately opposed to the relationship, and it was difficult for Rajiv to understand Sonia's inability to defy her father. He wrote to Indira that 'Sonia does not seem to be able to talk to her parents . . . She just does whatever her father says.'[47] In 1966, after an inconclusive stint at Imperial College, London and without a degree, Rajiv returned to India and began to train as an airline pilot in Hyderabad. Sonia dutifully went home to Turin. But in her own quiet way, she remained determined to marry Rajiv. She bided her time in Italy for a year, until she legally came of age at twenty-one.

In January 1968 – exactly three years after she first met him – Sonia flew to India to marry Rajiv. Indira arranged for her to stay at the home of old family friends, the Bachchans (whose son, Amitabh Bachchan, was a rising film star). Sonia was eager to adapt to the Indian way of life – or at least to the rather Westernized version of it she would lead with Rajiv – and did so quickly. On 25 February, a month after Sonia's arrival in India, she and Rajiv were married in a civil ceremony, and Sonia moved into her mother-in-law's house at 1 Safdarjung Road where she and Rajiv were to live for the next sixteen years.

Indira was not one to form close emotional bonds quickly or easily. At the age of fifty-one, she had only three intimate friends: Dorothy Norman, Marie Seton (both of whom she rarely saw) and Pupul Jayakar. But in a remarkably short period of time, Indira became extremely fond of her daughter-in-law, Sonia. In part, this was because Sonia seemed to be docile, accommodating and quietly affectionate. She was also intensely interested in the domestic arrangements of the household and an excellent cook. Indira was, too, but she had no time for such matters and for some years the house had been more or less run by her assistant Usha Bhagat. Now Sonia took over this job. In addition, she quickly grasped Indira's tastes and preferences. In time, she even bought her mother-in-law's saris and looked after her wardrobe. The one thing Sonia did not share with Indira was politics, which she neither attempted to understand or take an interest in. It was only later, however, that Sonia came to positively loathe politics and view it as the enemy of her own and Rajiv's personal happiness.

By the time Sonia and Rajiv married, Sanjay was back in India and living at home. Indira's bungalow at 1 Safdarjung Road was now bursting at the seams, so that some members of her clerical staff were forced to work in sheds in the garden. There was talk around this time of Indira moving back to Teen Murti House and re-establishing it as the official residence of the Prime Minister. The Cabinet approved the plan, but several members of the Nehru Trust objected and after a great deal of discussion, Indira decided to remain at the overcrowded 1 Safdarjung Road house. Soon afterwards, the government allocated the adjoining bungalow at 1 Akbar Road to her for her offices.

On 3 May 1969, the Indian President Zakir Husain, (Indira's choice to succeed Sarvepalli Radhakrishnan in 1967) died suddenly. The President, whose position in India is analogous to that of the monarch in the British constitutional monarchy, acts on the advice of the Prime

Minister. However, he has the scope to act as a check on the Prime Minister – or a rubber stamp. It is conceivable that a situation might arise when a President's actions could be decisive: if, say, a ruling party was weak or there was a constitutional crisis.[48]

Indira's enemies in Congress wanted the Speaker of Parliament, Sanjiva Reddy, to be their next President. This Indira feared because she knew Reddy, as President, could lever her from office and install Desai as Prime Minister. To safeguard her position Indira sought to transform her struggle for political survival into an ideological contest by considerably intensifying her leftist image. The most transparent area in which to demonstrate her leftist credentials was the economy. Thus at the July meeting of the All-India Congress Committee, where the Indian presidency was to be decided, Indira, who was not present ostensibly because she was ill, had a loyal cabinet colleague read out 'some stray thoughts' on economic policy. These reiterated the ten-point programme formulated in May 1967, but focussed in particular on the radical measure of bank nationalization which the 'Young Turks' in the Congress had been agitating for and which Desai, as Finance Minister, would never countenance.

Indira's reasons for having her 'stray thoughts' on bank nationaliz-ation aired at the AICC meeting were clearly motivated by her drive for self-preservation as Prime Minister. But this did not necessarily mean that Indira 'had no interest in bank nationalization' itself, and was merely 'using this [issue] to safeguard her position on the question of selecting'. It is easy, with hindsight, to insist that 'ideology was [Indira's] . . . weapon; she was not its weapon'. For years to come, commentators would argue that Indira's leftist policies were 'largely a defensive strategy born out of pragmatism . . . [she] realized that she would lose ground to leftist forces unless [she] moved to the left . . . so she often made use of left slogans to discredit the opposition and to contain her enemies within the party by representing the party conflict as a fight between forces of progress and reaction'.[49]

Frequently in Indira's political life, ideological and self-preserving initiatives overlapped. For her biographer, once Indira is established as Prime Minister, her behaviour – both political and personal – becomes increasingly ambiguous and open to interpretation. She appears, at times, impenetrable. Most of the photographs of Indira dating from this time are flat and unrevealing, posed, official pictures – glossy, but without depth. In addition, after the mid-sixties, the sources that have most intimately revealed her inner thoughts do not exist. Her father is dead so there are no further letters to him. She was now writing less frequently and less openly to Dorothy Norman and other friends. Indira's personal letters were rarely private at this stage because, like her official correspondence, most of them were dictated and typed up by secretaries. Nor are there any autobiographical reflections: Indira Gandhi never kept a diary because, as she once told an interviewer, 'When would I write it? I go to bed very late. I get up very early . . . if I have a free moment, I really don't want to spend it on myself.'[50]

Indira Gandhi's precise motives for her intensified leftist stance in July 1969 are, then, far from clear and her own words are often contradictory. She espoused radical change but also took pains to assure the propertied classes that reforms would not threaten their interests. Politicians, as someone very close to Indira observed, wear masks.[51] They are performers and play a part or role. They are also, in T.S. Eliot's phrase, 'hollow men', personae who are put together, taken apart, fashioned and refashioned day in and day out, not only by themselves but also by those who surround them. They are briefed; they are advised. Like vessels, they are filled. And emptied. By 1969 Indira's metamorphosis into an adroit politician was complete.

Indira Gandhi now gathered round her a gifted, astute, primarily leftist and in some cases highly principled group of people – all of them men, many of them Kashmiris like herself. Some she chose; others chose her. Most were quite young – of her own rather than her father's or Desai's generation. They had been followers of Nehru who saw her as her father's inheritor. They invested her with their ideology and values. Not cynically like Dhebar, Kamaraj and the Syndicate who had tried to use Indira as a tool. Indira's inner circle knew her weaknesses; they grasped that she was her father's daughter not her father incarnate. But to them she was still young, dynamic, left-leaning and genuinely committed to the future of India. Despite her inexperience in many areas, they believed she possessed within herself what it took to lead the country – with their help.[52]

The most important of these men, the epicentre of what came to be called Indira's 'Kashmiri mafia' was not a cabinet minister or any other elected office-holder, but rather a senior civil servant, the head of the Prime Minister's Secretariat, the author of her 'stray thoughts' on economics and her main policy formulator. This person was none other than Parmeshwar Narain Haksar who fifty years earlier had, as a ten-year-old boy, first seen Indira perched on a servant's shoulder in an Old Delhi courtyard while everyone cooed 'poor thing' at the child with the huge eyes.

P. N. Haksar became Indira's Principal Private Secretary in the Secretariat in May 1967 when he was fifty-four. After completing a degree at Allahabad University, he had gone to England in the late thirties, studied anthropology at the LSE under Bronislaw Malinowski, was called to the bar at Lincoln's Inn, became a friend and Hampstead neighbour of Feroze Gandhi, and had cooked delicious Kashmiri meals for Feroze and Indira during the Blitz. In the forties Haksar practised law in Allahabad until Nehru persuaded him to enter the Indian Foreign Service shortly after independence. Haksar first worked as a diplomat under Krishna Menon at the London High Commission; later he was India's first ambassador to Nigeria and also ambassador to Austria before serving as deputy and acting High Commissioner in London in the sixties from whence Indira Gandhi summoned him to be her right-hand man – and more.

Indira, in fact, deliberately handpicked Haksar to replace L.K. Jha, the Secretary she had inherited from Shastri, whom she felt was too conservative. Haksar's leftist credentials were impeccable and long-standing as Indira well knew from her own and Feroze's friendship with him in the thirties. In 1966 Haksar had accompanied her to America when he was deputy High Commissioner in London and adroitly advised her in her tricky dealings with President Johnson. Haksar's opinion of Indira at this time was that she was intelligent but out of her depth. He felt that 'basically she was not a political person, that she didn't grasp the complexities and problems of political situations'. In short, she needed guidance, but she had real potential. Her most valuable gift in Haksar's eyes was her ability to connect with the people, an extraordinary bond he always believed to be genuine.[53]

Within a short time of becoming Indira Gandhi's Principal Private Secretary, Haksar was the dominant policy maker in the government and the possessor of enormous power. A socialist, an intellectual, and a man of unimpeachable integrity, he formulated the 1967 ten-point programme of reforms and pushed for bank nationalization and the removal of the princes' privy purses. Above all, Haksar's was the hand that guided Indira through the 1969 split of the Congress Party. In the late sixties, in fact, he was guiding most government policy. While Indira has repeatedly been accused of hollow populism and sham radicalism during this period, and her actions attributed solely to self-interested political survival, few have questioned the instincts of her key adviser and policy maker, P. N. Haksar.

Personally Haksar was a magnetic figure: handsome, witty, erudite and cosmopolitan, but also, like Nehru, he had a deep sense of consciousness of his Indian identity. He had worshipped Nehru as a boy and young man and much of his thinking and policy were informed by Nehruvian principles. But Haksar was also the protégé of Krishna Menon. Haksar's dedication to the Indian government and country was profound, but it is no secret that he was largely responsible for the momentous growth in power and influence of the Prime Minister's Secretariat in the late sixties and its corollary: the weakening of the Cabinet and Cabinet Secretariat. He was behind, for example, the transfer of the intelligence network and revenue intelligence to the Prime Minister's Secretariat in 1969. By this time, in fact, the Prime Minister's Secretariat, headed by Haksar, 'had acquired both direct and indirect control of most governmental organs and emerged as the main centre of power and authority'.[54]

Indira trusted Haksar's intelligence and judgement implicitly and completely. From 1967 to 1973, he was probably the most influential and powerful person in the government. It was also Haksar rather than the Cabinet Secretary who was the most important civil servant in the country. Haksar initiated the controversial and unprecedented reality of a 'committed bureaucracy' – a civil service that was ideologically oriented rather than politically neutral. At the time and later in speech and in print, Haksar insisted that 'commitment was not a dirty word' and argued that the notion of an uncommitted bureaucracy was a myth. But he must also have realized that with the sacrifice of political neutrality, a democratic institution would inevitably be sacrificed in order to achieve certain ideological ends. And once the damage was done, it could not be contained. The whole balance of power in government was irreparably compromised. The Prime Minister's Secretariat became 'an all-powerful body which eclipsed not only the Cabinet Secretariat but also the Cabinet and the individual ministries and departments'.[55]

Haksar's role was also crucial in the events of the summer of 1969 when the issue of bank nationalization was mooted at the July meeting of the AICC in Bangalore. Indira arrived at the AICC meeting on 10 July when the decisive issue of the presidential candidacy was raised. Indira suggested Jagjivan Ram, the Harijan leader, invoking Mahatma Gandhi's dream of raising a Harijan to high office. The Syndicate remained solidly behind Sanjiva Reddy and two days later, on 12 July, the Congress Parliamentary duly nominated Reddy for President by four votes to two. By now Indira was convinced, with good reason, that the Syndicate wanted Reddy to be President principally in order to force her out. She was furious. Tarakeshwari Sinha, Feroze's erstwhile girlfriend and a staunch Desai supporter, drafted a statement: 'If the Prime Minister feels distressed over the party's decision [to elect Reddy as President] . . . she can refuse to lead the party in Parliament,' which at the last minute Sinha changed to read, 'she can appeal for reconsideration'.[56] Meanwhile, the vice-president V.V. Giri announced that he would also run for the presidency.

After the AICC meeting, Indira, advised by Haksar and others, acted swiftly and decisively. On 16 July she 'relieved' Desai of the Finance portfolio and took it over herself, justifying her move on the grounds of Desai's opposition to bank nationalization. She explained to the press that Desai had to go because she could not implement her 'progressive programme' with him as Finance Minister. Technically, Desai was not removed from his post as deputy Prime Minister, but Indira wanted him to resign and predictably, he did.

Four days later Indira nationalized fourteen commercial banks by presidential ordinance, even though Parliament was shortly due to convene. Nationalization by ordinance emphasized that it was a 'personal act' of the Prime Minister. Announcing the measure on All India Radio, Indira invoked an Indian proverb: 'A man said, "I complained that I had no shoes until I met the man who had no feet." We have to look at the problems of the country from that angle. Nobody wants to deny the rights of any person unless these rights are impinging on far more valid rights of a far larger number.'[57] Bank nationalization was a populist move and predictably it was greeted with public euphoria: 'Low-paid government and other employees, taxi and auto-rickshaw drivers . . . [the] unemployed and others who had never seen the interior of a bank . . . danced in the streets' and held rallies outside Indira's bungalow on

Safdarjung Road.[58] It also endeared Indira to the Communist Party of India (CPI).

The Syndicate and the President of Congress Nijalingappa now needed allies, but they made what would prove to be a fatal blunder when they established contact with the right-wing Jan Sangh and Swatantra parties. Indira signed Reddy's presidential nomination papers and he became the official Congress Party candidate, but she did not issue a whip instructing Congress legislators to vote for Reddy. Indira's followers urged her to call for 'a vote of conscience' because of the possible right-wing Jan Sangh and Swatantra support for Reddy.

Nijalingappa proceeded to compound this tactical error when he assured Indira that her government would not be toppled if Reddy became President, to which Indira responded with delicious moral authority: 'I must record a strong protest at this attempt to inject power politics into a discussion involving fundamental issues. I need no personal assurance, nor do I seek to retain office at all cost.'[59]

Finally on 20 August the presidential election results were announced. V.V. Giri, the former vice-president – not Reddy – won, but narrowly and with the help of various opposition groups such as the Communists, the Sikh party, the Akali Dal, and the regional DMK Party of Tamil Nadu. As one observer put it, 'Giri won . . . but it was difficult to say that Sanjiva Reddy lost.'[60] In fact, only a third of Congress MPs and a quarter of Congress MLAs voted for Giri. The eighty-four-year-old Congress Party, which Nehru had called 'the mirror of the nation' because it encompassed such a diversity of ideologies and factions, was about to split wide open.

Throughout the autumn 'unity talks' and meetings were held between the warring Congress factions – the Syndicate old guard and Indira's followers. But to no avail. On 28 October, the Congress President Nijalingappa wrote an open letter to Indira charging her with having created a 'personality cult' that threatened the democratic working of Congress, and concluded by chiding her for having made 'personal loyalty to you the test of loyalty to the Congress and the country'.[61] In October 1969, however, Nijalingappa's voice was considered a lonely reactionary rather than prophetic one.

On 1 November an unprecedented two Congress Working Committee meetings took place at the same time in two different locations in New Delhi: at the All-India Congress Committee headquarters on

Photograph of Indira taken by Feroze Gandhi during their courtship.

ABOVE Feroze and Indira on shipboard on their way back to India from England in early 1941.

LEFT The wedding of Indira Nehru and Feroze Gandhi. Jawaharlal Nehru is standing on the far left and Sarojini Naidu on the far right.

Indira, the radiant bride, at her wedding.

LEFT Indira with Sanjay, aged one, in 1948.

Indira and Nehru shortly after Independence.

Indira and Nehru during their trek through Bhutan, September 1958.

BELOW Indira, Nehru and President and Jacqueline Kennedy in Washington DC, November 1961. When she travelled abroad Indira dressed far more elaborately than she did in India. Here she wears a mink stole, a silk sari, jewellery and full make-up while her hair is carefully coifed in a bouffant style.

ABOVE Indira making her acceptance speech as President of Congress, 13 February, 1959.

BELOW Indira beside Nehru's body as it lies in state, May 1964.

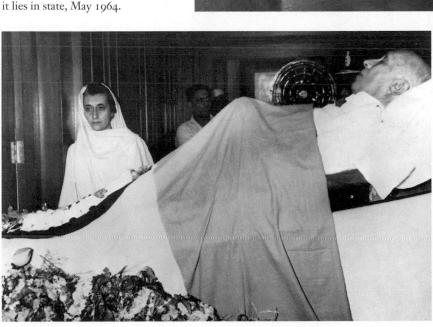

'Troubled India in a Woman's Hands.'
Time magazine cover after Indira was
elected Prime Minister in January 1966.

ABOVE Indira meets President Lyndon Johnson
on her first prime ministerial visit to the United
States during India's 1966 food crisis. The two
leaders established an immediate rapport.

ABOVE Indira with a bandaged nose – looking
in her own words 'like Batman' – after a rock
was thrown at her in Orissa during the 1967
election campaign. President Radhakrishnan
stands next to her.

RIGHT Indira with her sons, Rajiv and Sanjay,
at their home, 1 Safdarjung Road, in 1967.

Jantar Mantar Road and at Indira Gandhi's home at 1 Safdarjung Road. Each meeting was attended by ten members. A week later Indira released a 'Letter to Congressmen' in which she unconvincingly insisted:

> What we witness .... is not a mere clash of personalities and certainly not a fight for power. It is not as simple as a conflict between the parliamentary and organizational wings. It is a conflict between two outlooks and attitudes in regard to the objectives of the Congress and the methods in which Congress itself should function. It is a conflict between those who are for socialism, for change and for the fullest internal democracy and debate in the organization, on the one hand, and those who are for the status quo, for conformism and for less than full discussion inside the Congress, on the other.[62]

On 12 November the Syndicate held an inquisition: Indira Gandhi was tried *in absentia* and found guilty of indiscipline and defiance of party leadership. It was even hinted that she intended to 'sell' India to the Soviet Union, and that P. N. Haksar was her direct link with the Soviet Embassy and Moscow. The next day Congress President Nijalingappa announced that Indira had been expelled from the party.

Seething with indignation and rage, Indira called a meeting of the Cabinet which (with a few exceptions) pledged its loyalty to her. She also issued a statement: 'It is presumptuous on the part of this handful of men to take disciplinary action against the democratically elected leader of the people. Are we to submit to them [the party bosses] or clean the organization of these undemocratic and Fascist persons?'

Intense lobbying followed in order to ascertain who would hold onto the majority of the Congress. Describing this period, Narasimha Rao later said, 'Indira Gandhi ... constituted a dangerous choice, albeit a compelling one.'[63] Predictably, more Congressmen were compelled than frightened: Indira won, with a total of 297 Congress MPs, 220 of them from the Lok Sabha. Thereon Indira's Congress took on the title Congress (R) – for Requisitionist and the Syndicate clique became Congress (O) – for Organization, (though Congress R was commonly taken to stand for the ruling Congress and Congress (O) for the old Congress).

Writing of the Congress split in the *Sunday Standard*, Indira's cousin Nayantara Sahgal, now a writer and journalist, said, 'the government has put on a performance worthy of the best gangster tradition in politics

. . . it has launched a new unprincipled era in Indian politics. The word "leader" has assumed menacing proportion [sic] . . . It denotes personal rule with all the dangers inherent therein.'64 Sahgal's mother, Vijaya Lakshmi Pandit, who had ostensibly retired from politics the previous year, also made her unhappiness known. Indira repaid her when Anand Bhawan was given to the nation at the end of the year and – in defiance of Nehru's provision in his will that his sisters should always have access to their family home – Indira refused to allow her aunt to stay overnight at Anand Bhawan the night before the memorial ceremony.

As a result of the Congress Party split, Indira lost her majority in both houses of Parliament, but her position was not essentially threatened because she still had the support of the Communist Party of India, some independents and several regional parties. When the Congress (O) called for a vote of no-confidence in Parliament, it was soundly defeated. At an All-India Congress Committee meeting held in New Delhi at the end of November, Indira spoke emotionally of her family's role in Congress and tearfully of her expulsion from the party by the Syndicate. Like all members of Congress, she explained, she had to wait until she was twenty-one before officially joining the party. But Congress membership had been her birthright and she felt she had been irrevocably born a Congressman, all those years ago in Anand Bhawan. 'Nobody,' Indira declared, fifty-two years on 'can throw me out of the Congress. It is not a legal question, nor one of passing a resolution to pronounce an expulsion order. It is a question of the very fibre of one's heart and being.'65

Indira showed no compunction about splitting Congress. Some three years earlier she had told the writer Ved Mehta in an interview that 'I am not afraid to say that the Congress Party has become moribund. It has scarcely a single leader with a modern mind . . . Congress has never succeeded in evolving into a modern political party.' Even more ominously (and prophetically), she went on to say: 'Sometimes I feel that even our parliamentary system is moribund. Everything is debated and debated and nothing gets done. Everything that can be exploited for political purposes is exploited. On top of all this, the inertia of our civil service is incredible.'66

The 'Great Split' of Congress in 1969 marked a milestone in Indira's development as well as Indian political history. She had come into her own. As the *New York Times* commented, 'she has proved herself a courageous, tough-minded politician as well as an exceedingly skilful tactician – a Prime Minister in her own right and not a transitional figure, trading on her legacy as the daughter of Nehru.'[67] As a result of this new independence and authority, six months after the Congress split, Indira reshuffled her Cabinet, removing Chavan (who had backed Reddy in the presidential struggle) and taking over the Home Ministry herself. This move enabled her to reorganize the Intelligence Bureau, which until then had been responsible for both internal and external intelligence. Indira split the bureau into two, with internal intelligence and counter-espionage in one wing; for external intelligence she created the Research and Analysis Wing. She put both branches under the Prime Minister's direct control.

The Great Split irrevocably transformed the Congress Party. It marked an abrupt end to decades as a coalition, 'loose organization with groups ideologically stretched across a spectrum from extreme right to mild radicalism'.[68] Hitherto opposition forces had often been contained *within* Congress. Now they were driven out into the cold. In addition, the split marked the triumph of the parliamentary over the organiz-ational wing of the party, which would henceforth rapidly atrophy. In order to prevent her position and authority being jeopardized again, Indira needed to centralize her power, and she now sought to control not merely the Indian President, but also the Cabinet, the President of Congress, the Congress Working Committee, the Parliamentary Board and the Central Election Committee.

Indira also needed to extend her control to the states beyond New Delhi. Over the next few years, she tactically 'eased out' state leaders who had failed to support her against the Syndicate, including, in time, the Chief Ministers of Rajasthan, Andhra Pradesh, Madhya Pradesh and Maharashtra. She then replaced them with her own people by 'nominating' candidates for chief minister who were then ratified in office by the dominant Congress legislative party. She made sure the candidates were men personally loyal to her but who lacked their own power bases.

The consequences of the split thus radiated from Delhi – the centre – to provincial, local and lower levels in the political order 'disrupting the filaments of patronage and dissolving the vote banks they com-manded'. The end result, in the words of Sunil Khilnani, was that 'the party . . . degenerated into an unaudited company for winning elections'.

It became 'a simple mechanism for collecting funds, distributing "tickets" or nominations for seats, conducting campaigns.'[69]

Indira's motives at this time are oblique. Can we attribute her dismantling of the Congress Party and the erosion of India's democratic system purely to 'the logic of political survival'?[70] Indira's strategy had been formulated largely by her gifted, committed coterie of personal advisers – in particular P.N. Haksar. And Haksar, D.P. Dhar, I.K. Gujral and the others close to Indira were all ideologically motivated. But like Indira, they were less fastidious than Nehru had been about interfering with the democratic system and structure of government to attain their ideological ends. Indira, at this stage, did not possess the political guile so often attributed to her, though she had undoubtedly acquired a good deal of political acumen during her first three turbulent years as Prime Minister. The real danger to India lurking within Indira Gandhi's psyche in the late sixties was not ruthlessness or hypocrisy – the gestural radicalism or sham populism her critics invariably accuse her of – but rather her growing belief that only she could lead the country. This conviction came from her sense of her personal legacy. Indeed it was, in her father's words, 'the burden' of her past and the Nehru familial past. It derived from her family's participation in India's history that Nehru had so passionately tried to inculcate in his daughter. Indira was 'born' to a 'world of storm and trouble', as Nehru had told her all those years ago in *Glimpses of World History*.

Indira felt not only the burden of the past, but a responsibility to India's present and future. But she misconstrued her obligation and responsibility as a necessity. Worse, she became increasingly indifferent to the means by which she discharged her duties. The split of 1969 revealed her ignorance of the structural integrity of democracy. And because she did not properly grasp, much less have confidence in, the democratic system, she had no faith that it – and India – could or would survive without her.

At this time, however, she looked no further than her own personal tenure. She did not yet envisage a family dynasty. Indira, in fact, repeatedly stated in interviews that her sons had no interest in politics and that she would do everything in her power to see that they remained outside of the political world. She had no wish to pass the family 'burden' on to them. Nor did she share it with her friends. As I.K. Gujral noted, Indira never mixed the political and the personal; a definite *cordon sanitaire* separated the two. Political colleagues were not friends. And friends like Dorothy Norman, Marie Seton and Pupul Jayakar had scant access to Indira's political life.

Indira's demarcation between family and country, between private and public, however, began to crumble on 13 November 1968 when it was announced in the Lok Sabha that her twenty-two-year-old son, Sanjay Gandhi, had applied for a licence to produce a small, efficient, indigenous Indian car. According to the Minister of State for Industrial Development, the car would cost 6,000 rupees to buy, have a maximum speed of 53 miles per hour and fuel consumption of 56 miles to the gallon. The idea of an 'Indian Volkswagen'– a cheap, mass-produced 'people's car' – had been discussed in government committees for more than a decade, but it was only in 1968 that it was decided that it should be produced in the private sector. There were fourteen applications in addition to Sanjay's, including ones from such well-established manufacturers as Renault, Citroen, Toyota, Mazda and Morris.[71]

Sanjay, with his uncompleted Rolls-Royce apprenticeship, was obviously no car manufacturer or businessman. But he had a well established reputation as a hell-raiser. As a teenager he and one of his friends, Adil Sharyar (the son of the Nehru family friend, Mohammed Yunus), used to steal cars, joyride and then abandon them in Delhi. Sanjay also had a history of scrapes with cars in England. While abroad, Sanjay had been a constant headache for the Indian High Commission when he was repeatedly arrested for speeding in his Jaguar. In December 1966, still in England, he was arrested for driving without a valid licence.

When Sanjay returned to India in 1967, he made gestures to set himself up as the Henry Ford of India. He opened up a car workshop with his friend Arjun Das in Gulabi Bagh in Delhi. Here, 'surrounded by garbage dumps and overflowing sewers', the workshop 'crowded with bits and pieces of twisted metal [and] rusting parts' Sanjay's dream of an Indian car – called the 'Maruti', the name of the son of the Hindu wind god – was born.[72]

Despite Sanjay's incxperience, in November 1970 a letter of intent was given to him by Dinesh Singh, the Minister of Industries, after a cabinet discussion at which Indira, of course, had presided. Sanjay was granted a licence to produce 50,000 'low-priced' cars per year made entirely of indigenous materials. Maruti – the car of the nation – was launched. Not surprisingly, there was a general outcry after Sanjay was awarded the contract. George Feranandes, a Socialist Party MP, accused Indira in the press of 'practising nepotism of the worst type'. Another MP, Raj Narain, called it 'a disgrace to democracy and socialism'. A.B. Vajpayee, an MP (and future Prime Minister), spoke of 'corruption unlimited'. Jyoti Basu, the Bengali Communist Party MP, also denounced what he saw as Indira's 'corruption and nepotism'. In response to this deluge of criticism, Indira lamely responded: 'my son has shown enterprise . . . if he is not encouraged, how can I ask other young men to take risks?'[73]

It is unclear what Indira's attitude was towards Sanjay's receiving the Maruti contract. Most likely she felt torn. Sanjay had no qualifications, no achievements, and if he had been anyone other than the Prime Minister's son, an inauspicious future. Maruti was a golden opportunity for Sanjay to prove himself. But at the same time, Indira must have realized that it would also bring him into public life. Sanjay, himself, was aggressive in his pursuit of the contract. Ever since Feroze's death, he had wielded a peculiar psychological power over his mother, and predictably he now applied intense pressure on her to facilitate granting him the licence. Although this was not the first time she had proved unable to say no to Sanjay, Indira's acquiescence over the car licence would have fatal consequences. She continued to insist that she did not want either of her sons to become involved in politics, but the Maruti contract opened a door into that world for Sanjay.

In the spring of 1970 Indira passed a personal milestone when she became a grandmother. Sonia Gandhi had suffered a miscarriage the previous year, but in April 1970 she gave birth to a healthy baby boy who was named Rahul. In August, Indira reported in a letter to Dorothy Norman, 'My grandson Rahul is a darling. He has got rid of his wrinkles and still has his double chin!'[74]

Indira doted on the baby, but had scarcely any free time to spend with him. Later, when her grandchildren were toddlers, they sometimes came with her to her morning *darshans* when she greeted the hordes of admirers and supplicants who swarmed round her garden to speak to her before she went to her office. There are also photographs of Indira

Gandhi talking to crowds of journalists on her lawn with Rahul or one of the other children playing in the background. Even later, when they were three or four and older, Indira often had her grandchildren sleep in her room at night. At least then there was time to be together, even though they were asleep.

But Indira's principal activities in 1970 were scarcely the stuff of most grandmothers' lives. Under Haksar's and her other advisers' influence, she continued to implement a range of radical measures, the most dramatic and controversial of which was her proposed abolition of the privy purses and privileges that had been guaranteed to the Indian princes at independence by the Indian constitution. In 1970 there were 278 princes in India, and the amount they received annually from the government ranged from $350,000 which went to the largest (both in terms of principality size and, appropriately, the huge bulk of the Prince himself), the Maharaja of Mysore, familiarly known as 'His Heaviness', to the Talukdar of Katodia who received an annual gift of just $25. All privy purses were tax-free. Indira engineered an amendment to rescind the privy purses and put it before Parliament in September 1970. The Lok Sabha passed the amendment, 339 to 154. But the bill was defeated by one vote in the upper house, the Rajya Sabha. Indira then proceeded to have a presidential proclamation issued by the obliging President V.V. Giri to 'derecognize' the princes, stripping them not only of their privileges and purses, but also of their titles. Over $6 million dollars was added to the national exchequer. As had been the case with bank nationalization, the abolition of the privy purses was greeted with great public acclaim.

Despite the popularity of her middle-leftist measures at this time, Indira's was a minority government and thus vulnerable. The Supreme Court overturned the government's bank nationalization legislation and in early December 1970 delivered a verdict invalidating the proclamation abolishing the princes' privy purses. Mutterings could now be heard in inner government circles of the need for 'a committed judiciary' as well as a 'committed bureaucracy' in order to achieve 'social justice'. Indira needed popular endorsement and Haksar urged her to call a mid-term poll as a referendum on her policies. Thus on 27 December Indira broadcast to the nation that elections would be held a year early, in February 1971. 'Time will not wait for us,' she said. 'The millions who demand food, shelter and jobs are pressing for action. Power in a democracy resides with the people. That is why we have decided to go to our people and seek a fresh mandate from them.'[75]

Soon after her announcement a *Newsweek* reporter asked Indira what the issues were in the up-coming election. She answered without a pause: 'I am the issue.'[76]

FOURTEEN

Seeing Red

THE OPPOSITION TO INDIRA – the 'Grand Alliance' consisting of the Congress (O), the Jan Sangh, Swatantra and Samyukta socialist parties – all knew that she was the issue in 1971, and they made the mistake of choosing a personalized campaign slogan to reflect this: 'Indira *Hatao*' (Remove Indira). Indira retaliated with the simplistic but effective battle cry of '*Garibi Hatao*' (Remove Poverty). '*Garibi Hatao*' was a call for the eradication of India's worst evil. And as a vote-winner it worked. *Garibi Hatao* 'was a thunderbolt ... a revelation ... a revolution'. Its impact was 'instant and electric'.[1] The poor, who were the vast majority of the electorate, now saw Indira as their saviour.

Throughout January and February Indira campaigned even more strenuously and relentlessly than she had in 1967. Now that there was no party organization to speak of and no other leaders of her stature, she was the star performer as well as 'the issue' in the campaign. In addition, by calling for an early mid-term poll, Indira had separated the parliamentary from the state assembly elections (to be held on schedule the following year), so that the focus was squarely on national issues and the central government in New Delhi.

This election would be a referendum on Indira Gandhi herself. Raj Thapar, the wife of Indira's adviser Romesh Thapar, later recorded a commonplace experience that reflected Indira's pre-eminence in 1971. In a Delhi taxi one day, Raj asked the driver who he planned to vote for:

'Oh we taxi drivers have ... decided to vote for Indira,' he answered immediately.

'That means the Congress?' Raj inquired.

'No, of course not. We wouldn't vote for the Congress. We are voting specifically for her.'

When Raj asked, 'Why Indira?' the taxi driver said it was because she had 'shown guts' by nationalizing the banks. And when Raj then pointed out that surely he did not have enough money to put in a bank account, he retorted, 'You don't understand. I don't have the money. But she has shown that she is willing to give the money boys a bit of her mind. That means she has courage. And that again means that she [will] . . . do something for all of us.'[2]

During the eight-week campaign, Indira's stamina was tested to the limit; but she was indefatigable, rising before dawn and seldom going to bed before one or two o'clock in the morning. Between early January and the elections in early March she covered over 30,000 miles by air and 3,000 by road and rail. She addressed 410 election meetings attended by 20 million people, many of whom had trekked miles to see and hear her. She explained this marathon campaign and her appeal, which surpassed even Nehru's heyday, to an interviewer. It was, she said, 'exhilarating . . . a sort of movement – a people's movement. It is true that I like being with the people. I shed my fatigue when I am with them . . . I don't see the people as a mass, I see them as so many individuals . . . Each person really feels that I am communicating with him.'[3]

Never had attention been so focussed on one individual candidate. Huge, garishly painted billboards with Indira's image appeared in the middle of city roundabouts. Villagers in even remote areas wore badges bearing her face pinned to their *dhotis* and saris – especially saris, for Indira captured virtually the entire female vote. The other Congress candidates – many of whom were handpicked by her – remained in her shadow as she crisscrossed the country, taking her radical *Garibi Hatao* message to the people.

By this time Indira was a forceful, dynamic speaker and she no longer resorted to invoking her Congress heritage – and the legacy of her father and Mahatma Gandhi – as she had so often done in the past. As one journalist put it, 'instead of the hesitant, shrill-voiced jumble of irrelevancies, we have forthright, impassioned oratory. She fires her audience.' The great theme with which Indira fired them was her heroic crusade 'against the forces of reaction . . . and her selfless commitment to the war on poverty and social injustice'. At the same time, however, she promised stability and economic growth to the prosperous middle classes. Indira's ambiguous manifesto called for the 'advance of socialism ... [while giving] scope to the private sector to play its proper role in the economy'. The future, Indira maintained, held something for everybody or, as one of her biographers later put it, she 'was able to ride both horses, convincing the rich and the poor that she would protect each from the other'.[4]

The 1971 Indian general election was the biggest democratic poll in history: 150 million people voted in 520 constituencies. The result was a Congress landslide – a tremendous mandate for Indira. Her Congress (R) won a two-thirds majority in the Lok Sabha: 325 seats in all, which was seventy more than an undivided Congress had won in 1967. Indira was in Calcutta on the last day of the polls when P.N. Haksar rang her with the news of her impending victory. Soon after she got back to Delhi, Raj Thapar and Pupul Jayakar went to congratulate her at 1 Safdarjung Road and found her surrounded by a mob of devotees, paying homage and touching her feet. Her face beaming, Indira beckoned to Raj and Pupul. Overcome with emotion, Raj began to stutter out her incoherent congratulations. Indira interrupted and said, 'Aren't you going to show a little more warmth than that?' and Raj gave her a big hug. As Raj remarked years later in her autobiography, they were 'so caught up in the euphoria of turning the corner and finding all our dreams waiting for us, that we pushed [this atmosphere of sycophancy and power politics] ... to the back of our minds'.[5]

Indira was re-elected leader of the Congress parliamentary party, uncontested, on 17 March. The general election had virtually annihilated the old guard, Congress (O). Among the many casualties was Indira's own opponent in Rae Bareilly – an eccentric, clownish Congress (O) politician named Raj Narain who seemed noteworthy in 1971, only for having come up with the disastrous 'Indira *Hatao*' slogan.

Immediately after the elections Indira appeared unassailable. She had become the most powerful Indian prime minister since independence. And India's political system had dramatically changed. Indira, the woman – rather than Congress, the party – was the victor in 1971. Prime ministerial power and authority were hugely strengthened. Indira's leadership was indispensable to Congress; she was the only person in India 'with a personal following transcending regional, communal and caste lines . . . Her paramountcy' derived from her enormous popular support rather than the strength of the Congress Party organization or state party bosses.[6]

In March 1971 few seemed aware of the dangers inherent in this concentration of power at the top. The left-wing Indian magazine *Link* described the 'Indira wave' of the elections as a 'mandate for radical reforms . . . [and] against the forces of reaction and the Right parties . . . It will now be easy to push through the Lok Sabha any constitutional amendment.'[7] Indira's government did embark on a reform programme after the elections, but it was only radical in parts – such as in the nationalization of the general insurance and coal industries. And in the passing of the twenty-sixth amendment, which deprived the rulers of the Princely States of their privy purses and privileges once and for all. But in other respects – such as the Maintenance of Internal Security Act (MISA), which sanctioned the arrest and imprisonment of individuals without trial for up to a year – the reforms were blatantly repressive.

Most crucially, in August and December 1971, the twenty-fourth and twenty-fifth amendments to the constitution were passed. These empowered the government to alter the fundamental rights enshrined in the Indian constitution, and to protect such changes from judicial review. The previous year the Supreme Court had invalidated the government's attempt to seize the princes' privy purses and power; now the way had been paved to weaken the judiciary's independence. The underlying premises of the amendments were, as Indira told the Lok Sabha, that the constitution was neither sacrosanct nor static, and that Parliament, rather than the constitution, should have the authority to determine fundamental rights. As Indira put it, amidst much tumult on the floor, 'the constitution has been changed in other countries, it has been changed in our country too and if it is necessary to change it in the people's interest certainly we should do so . . . This is obvious – democracy must mean the right of the largest number of the people.'[8] Indira hailed the twenty-fourth and twenty-fifth amendments as 'milestones in the progress of democracy', but her opponents and critics claimed the amendments had 'reduced the constitution to tatters'.[9]

Indira's programme of constitutional change was officially defended by Mohan Kumaramangalam – an old Marxist friend of Feroze Gandhi and P. N. Haksar from their London days in the thirties. Kumaramanga-lam had left the Communist Party to join Congress in 1966, and after Indira's 1971 election victory, she appointed him Minister of Steel and Heavy Engineering. He soon became one of her key strategists and the vocal spokesman for a leftist group within Congress called the Congress Forum for Socialist Action. A primary aim of the Forum was to alter the Indian constitution 'so that the relationship between Fundamental Rights and the Directive Principles of State Policy was reversed, and the larger social good placed above the good of the individual . . . [because] there was no reason why individual rights should be considered more fundamental than society's rights'.[10] Kumaramangalam also called for a 'committed judiciary' just as Haksar had defended the idea of 'a committed bureaucracy'.

In a report entitled 'constitutional Amendments: The Reason Why', Kumaramangalam explained that the 'clear object' of the amendments was 'to subordinate the rights of the individual as expressed in the Fundamental Rights [provision in the constitution] . . . to the urgent needs of society.'[11] In other words, to make it possible for the ends to justify the means. All well and good if those determining the ends were men of principle like Kumaramangalam or P. N. Haksar. But these men and Indira were still – with the best of intentions – tampering with the machinery of government. What would happen if less principled – or 'progressive' – individuals were in a position to decide when 'to subordi-nate the rights of individuals', to the 'good of the community' – rights which included not only the right to own property (the prime target of the 1971 amendments), but also equality before the law, freedom of speech, assembly, association and movement?

Constitutional change – and its implications – did not, however, seem the most pressing issue in the spring of 1971. What dominated Indira's and the country's attention immediately after the general election was the plight of East Pakistan. The notion of Pakistan – a country with two wings separated by a vast stretch of 1,200 miles of Indian territory – had seemed untenable at the time of Partition and now, some twenty-four years later, Jinnah's Muslim homeland was about to self-destruct. Bengali East Pakistan had the larger population (approximately 60 per cent), but it was geographically smaller than West Pakistan, which had dominated it politically and economically since 1947. In her autobiogra-phy, Benazir Bhutto, later Prime Minister of Pakistan, conceded that in this bifurcated Pakistan 'the majority province of East Pakistan was basically being treated as a colony by the minority West. From revenues of more than thirty-one billion rupees from East Pakistan's exports, the minority in West Pakistan had built roads, schools, universities and hospitals for themselves, but had developed little in the East. The army, the largest employer in our very poor country, drew 90 per cent of its forces from West Pakistan. 80 per cent of government jobs were filled by people from the West.'[12] There was racial and cultural conflict too. It was not difficult to distinguish between the generally smaller, darker Bengali-speaking East Pakistanis and their Urdu, Punjabi and Sindhi-speaking 'countrymen' in West Pakistan. Language, in fact, was a major cause of dispute between the two wings when Urdu – rather than, or in addition to, Bengali – was declared the sole official language of the state.

In contrast to India, where democracy survived political unrest, famine, war and other vicissitudes, in Pakistan it collapsed a little more than a decade after independence, and the army took over. In 1971 the country had been under military rule for nearly thirteen years. The movement for self-determination in East Pakistan that emerged in the late sixties was pro-democratic, and it was led by a figure as charismatic as Sheikh Abdullah in Kashmir: Sheikh Mujibur Rahman, a man with whom Indira was to develop a rare personal as well as political rapport.

The crisis that would ultimately give birth to Bangladesh began in December 1970 when a general election was held for the first time in many years in Pakistan. Sheikh Mujibur Rahman's party, the Awami League, campaigned for regional autonomy for the eastern wing, and it was overwhelmingly victorious, winning all but two seats in East Pakistan which in turn gave the League a decisive majority in Pakistan's National Assembly. In accordance with the election results, Sheikh 'Mujib' should have assumed office as President. But the *in situ* military leader, General Yahya Khan, and Zulfikar Ali Bhutto, the leader of West Pakistan's People's Party which had less dramatically won in the western wing, collaborated to prevent Sheikh Mujib from taking power. In response, the Awami League launched a massive civil disobedience movement in East Pakistan.

On 25 March 1971 General Yahya Khan imposed a brutal regime of repression to crush the political unrest in East Pakistan. The Pakistani army descended on East Pakistan, looted and burned down homes and businesses, raped women and murdered thousands of innocent people. Any and everyone suspected of dissidence was hounded down and slaughtered, including students, university lecturers, writers, journalists, professionals and intellectuals. Mujib himself was arrested and flown to prison in West Pakistan. The East Bengali Police, the East Pakistan Rifles and the only Bengali regiment in the Pakistani army all mutinied. East Pakistan – now renamed Bangladesh – declared itself independent and those Awami League leaders who had escaped to Calcutta set up a government in exile. Back in what was still East Pakistan, the slaughter of Bengalis by West Pakistanis escalated into genocide. By the end of the year an estimated three million people had been killed.

On 31 March, six days after General Khan unleashed his reign of terror in East Pakistan, Indira stood up in the Lok Sabha and delivered an impassioned resolution:

> This House expresses its profound sympathy for and solidarity with the people of East Bengal in their struggle for a democratic way of life. Bearing in mind the permanent interests which India has in peace, committed as we are to uphold and defend human rights, this House demands immediate cessation of the use of force and the massacre of defenceless people. This House calls upon all peoples and governments of the world to take urgent and constructive steps to prevail upon the Government of Pakistan to put an end immediately to the systematic decimation of the people which amounts to genocide. This House records its profound conviction that the historic upsurge of the 75 million people of East Bengal will triumph. The House wishes to assure them that their struggle and sacrifices will receive the wholehearted sympathy and support of the people of India.[13]

Soon refugees from East Pakistan were pouring over the borders into India. At its height, up to 150,000 a day flowed in, totalling ten million over the next nine months. They came by truck, bullock cart, rickshaw and by foot, seeking refuge in hastily-constructed camps similar to the camps that had been built in Delhi at the time of Partition.

A month after the refugees began to flood into West Bengal, Indira visited a number of the camps scattered around Calcutta. She thought that after her experience of refugee camps in Delhi twenty-four years earlier she would be prepared for what would confront her. But she was not. P. N. Dhar, who accompanied Indira, described the scene that confronted them: 'What we saw in the camps defied description. More than the stories of what had happened to them, it was their physical and mental state that assaulted our moral sensibility. In our offices in Delhi we had been preoccupied with their number, with the political fall-out of their presence, with the calculations of the financial cost of maintaining them.' On the outskirts of Calcutta they heard the refugees' accounts of rape, torture and murder. Even more, they were brought face to face with the stink and sight of terror-stricken, traumatized, displaced and homeless people. Dhar and the other aides expected Indira to 'say a few words of solace and sympathy', but she was 'so overwhelmed by the scale of human misery that she could hardly speak'.[14]

This tremendous influx of Bengali refugees aroused a strong reaction in India and many voices demanded that immediate and hawk-like action be taken against West Pakistan. The refugees were also creating an enormous financial burden for India – more than 360 *crores* rupees by December 1971 – a price that India simply could not afford to pay. Nevertheless, two thirds of the refugees were housed in camps where they were fed, sheltered, clothed and received medical treatment. In addition, India helped train and arm Bangladesh's liberation army, the *Mukti Bahini*.

In the midst of this burgeoning crisis with Pakistan, India was briefly distracted by a bizarre – and not wholly unrelated – scandal in late May. The chief cashier at the State Bank of India, a man named Ved Prakesh Malhotra, received a phone call one morning from someone who identified herself as the Prime Minister. Malhotra was instructed to withdraw 60 million rupees in one-hundred rupee notes and deliver this stash of money to '*Bangladesh ka Babu*' (a gentleman from Bangladesh) who would meet Malhotra at a designated spot in Delhi. Malhotra did as he was told; he rendezvoused with the 'man from Bangladesh' who turned out to be a Parsi former army captain named Rustom Sohrab Nagarwala who worked for the Research and Analysis Wing of Indian intelligence.

After handing over the cash, Malhotra hurried to Indira's office to report to P. N. Haksar that he had done as he had been instructed. A stunned Haksar told him that Indira had authorized no such transaction. Haksar urged Malhotra to go directly to the police. Nagarwala was arrested almost immediately and confessed to impersonating the Prime Minister on the telephone in order to acquire the money to finance the freedom movement in Bangladesh.

But Nagarwala's confession did not quieten the public furore over the caper. Nor did his trial, conviction and imprisonment, all accomplished within a record three days of his arrest. 'The Nagarwala affair' was raised in Parliament and dominated the press. In jail, Nagarwala retracted his confession and demanded a retrial. But he died in prison – ostensibly of heart disease – in March 1972. The police officer who had been in charge of the Nagarwala case also conveniently died, in a car accident. Malhotra was sacked from the State Bank of India. After this, the case was closed. To the end, Malhotra maintained the official version of the Nagarwala affair. But it was a murky business; rumours circulated that it had indeed been Indira who first demanded the 60 million rupees and then had Nagarwala silenced. Years later, however, it was alleged that far from being Indira's henchman, Nagarwala was in the pay of the CIA who sought to use him to smear Indira.[15]

By the time the Nagarwala scandal faded from the headlines, hostilities between India and Pakistan had intensified even further. Indira, as always in a crisis, remained in complete control. Despite the nearly hysterical political clamour that surrounded her, she acted neither impulsively or rashly. Her actions over the coming months were largely determined and orchestrated by the trusty P. N. Haksar and they proved virtually flawless and exquisitely timed. Indira took the regional struggle between West and East Pakistan to the world stage and did everything in her power to make West Pakistan's reign of terror in the East a global issue – one that had at its heart human rights, including those of basic democratic freedoms and self-determination. Her hope was that international pressure would secure a peaceful settlement, and though Indian military preparations began at an early stage of the crisis, Indira was determined not to go to war unless forced to do so.

There was another, strategic reason for not rushing into armed conflict. The chief of staff of the Indian armed forces was an amiable Parsi general with a nose (as he later quipped), even longer than the Prime Minister's, named Sam Manekshaw. Manekshaw told Indira early on that it would be foolhardy to get involved militarily until the rainy season had ended. He was also worried about the threat of China coming to West Pakistan's aid. If India could desist from hostilities until the winter, it would be difficult, if not impossible, for the Chinese army to get over the snowbound passes of the Himalayas.

On 7 July 1971 Henry Kissinger, President Richard Nixon's national security adviser, arrived in Delhi for a brief visit in the course of an extended tour of Asia. Kissinger was actually bound for China, his mission to prepare for Nixon's historic detente with a country the United States did not even recognize. Kissinger's ultimate destination, however, was a closely guarded secret. Only in retrospect did Haksar reflect how appropriate it had been that the Indian government had arranged a lavish Chinese banquet in Kissinger's honour at Delhi's Ashok Hotel.

Before leaving Delhi, Kissinger make it clear to Indira and Haksar that if India and Pakistan went to war over Bangladesh, the United States would not be prepared to help India.[16] Then he flew to Pakistan where it was announced that Kissinger had succumbed to the heat and a bout of 'Delhi belly', and had been forced to retire to a remote hill station to recuperate. In reality, the Pakistanis had put Kissinger on a military plane in the dead of night, which flew to China where he met with the Chinese leaders Chou En-lai and Chairman Mao.

Indira and Haksar did not discover this until later. But in light of Kissinger's plain talking in India, and of the good relations between the United States and Pakistan, Indira now took up the offer of a 'treaty of peace, friendship and cooperation' with the Soviet Union that had first been broached three years earlier by Leonid Brezhnev. Haksar formulated the careful terms of the treaty, including article nine, which guaranteed that both the Soviet Union and India agreed 'to abstain from providing any assistance to any third party that engages in armed conflict with the other party'. Haksar also added a clause restating India's commitment to non-alignment, though ironically, the pact served to bury this Nehruvian principle once and for all. Indira's other close adviser and head of the Policy Planning Committee, D. P. Dhar – often described in the press as 'India's Kissinger' – negotiated the agreement in Moscow. On 9 August 1971, barely a month after Kissinger's Chinese banquet, the Soviet Foreign Minister Andrei Gromyko arrived in Delhi and the treaty was signed, with considerable fanfare.

A few days later General Khan announced the imminent military trial of Sheikh Mujib in Pakistan. He was to be tried by a special military court *in camera* and the court proceedings would remain secret. Indira

immediately wrote to heads of government around the world warning
that 'this so-called trial will be used only as a cover to execute Sheikh
Mujibur Rahman' with disastrous consequences in East Pakistan and
also India. She appealed to the world leaders 'to exercise your influence
with President Yahya Khan . . . in the larger interests of the peace and
stability of the region'.[17] When this plea failed to provoke a strong
response, Indira decided to go abroad and personally present her case
before the international community.

In September 1971 Indira, accompanied by Haksar, travelled to the
Soviet Union. In a speech in Moscow Indira insisted that 'what has
happened in Bangladesh can no longer be regarded as Pakistan's domestic affair. More than nine million East Bengalis have come into our
country. Do they not have the right to live and work in their country?
We cannot be expected to absorb them. This is not an India-Pakistan
dispute. The problem is an international one. But the weight of it has
fallen on India. It is surely the duty of the world not to delay in creating
conditions in which these refugees . . . can return without fear.'[18] After
talks with Brezhnev and Premier Kosygin, Indira left with a promise of
Soviet military aid should India go to war with Pakistan over Bangladesh.

Scarcely a month later, on 24 October, Indira, Haksar and the Indian
Foreign Secretary, T.N. Kaul, embarked on a twenty-one-day tour of
Europe and America in an attempt to galvanize world opinion. They
visited Belgium, France, Austria, West Germany, Britain and the United
States. India's case was listened to sympathetically everywhere except
in the US where Indira and Haksar arrived in early November 1971.

President Richard Nixon and Indira instinctively recoiled from one
another, or as Henry Kissinger delicately put it, they 'were not intended
by fate to be personally congenial'. Three years earlier, in 1969, Nixon
had visited India on a round-the-world trip and had been dismayed by
the restrained reception in Delhi in contrast to the crowds who had
cheered Eisenhower in 1956. Since this low-key visit, it seemed he had
held a grudge against Indira. Moreover, she intimidated him. According
to Kissinger, Indira 'brought out all of Nixon's latent insecurities'.[19]

Not surprisingly, the atmosphere of their discussions was steeped in
antipathy and distrust. They met on two successive days, 4 and 5 November, in the White House Oval Office where Indira and Nixon sat in
two wing chairs on either side of the fireplace, while Haksar and Kissinger, like seconds in a duel, sat on sofas adjoining their principals.

After the press photographers left, Indira opened up the discussion by commending Nixon's policy in Vietnam and China 'in the manner of a professor praising a slightly backward student'. She did not improve her position by then going on to point out how, with regard to China, 'Nixon had consummated what India had recommended for more than a decade'. Nixon controlled his anger with 'glassy-eyed politeness'. Haksar and Kissinger sat 'dumbly' on their sofas.[20]

Kissinger later described the talks between Indira and Nixon as 'a classic dialogue of the deaf' and reported that Nixon's comments afterwards 'were not always printable'.[21] Nixon would do nothing to help facilitate Sheikh Mujibur Rahman's release, nor would he do anything to persuade General Khan to open a dialogue with the leaders of the Awami League. Nixon wanted to give the military government in West Pakistan two years to come to terms with the situation in the East. Indira countered that 'the situation was explosive and could not be defused until Mujibur was released and a dialogue started with the already elected leaders of East Pakistan'. She also told Nixon 'in no uncertain terms that India would be forced to retaliate if Pakistan continued its provocations across [India's] border'.[22]

Having reached deadlock on the first day the two heads of state did not even attempt to go through the motions of discussing the Indo-Pak crisis on the second, when Nixon kept Indira waiting forty-five minutes in an anteroom before arriving at the Oval Office. She was livid and repaid his rudeness with finesse, by making no reference to Pakistan at all during the ensuing discussion. Instead, Indira asked Nixon 'penetrating questions about [American] . . . foreign policy elsewhere, as if the subcontinent were the one corner of peace and stability on the globe'. As Kissinger put it, 'she gave us honor grades everywhere except there'.[23]

During this second meeting – when nothing of substance transpired – Haksar found himself closely observing Nixon and Kissinger. The President, he decided, 'lacked moral principles', whereas Kissinger, a more subtle and self-assured character, was 'an egomaniac who fancied himself another Metternich'.[24]

Haksar was transfixed by Nixon's face and felt an almost irresistible urge to touch it; it seemed 'mask-like' and 'unreal' with its jerky mechanical smile and bushy-eyebrowed scowl. Although Indira could be cold, aloof, haughty and remote, compared to the automaton Nixon, Haksar felt, she still remained deeply human. The only indication that any sort of emotion flickered inside Nixon was his tendency to perspire profusely, especially under pressure.[25] The plight of the East Pakistani refugees, and the financial burden under which India was struggling, left both men unmoved. The American 'tilt' towards Pakistan was now confirmed.

In keeping with her practice in India, Indira now took her case to the masses and appealed directly to the American public, over President Nixon's head. In an emotive speech she described how she was 'haunted by the tormented faces in our overcrowded refugee camps reflecting the grim events which have compelled the exodus of these millions from East Pakistan. I have come here looking for a deeper understanding of the situation in our part of the world.'[26] When she spoke at the National Press Club in Washington she explained why any sort of understanding with General Yahya was out of the question. It was impossible, she said, to 'shake hands with a clenched fist'. Indira regarded Yahya as her polar opposite: a hard-drinking, crude bully. He had publicly referred to Indira as 'that woman' and vowed not to be 'cowed down' by her. Indira took the opportunity of a *Newsweek* interview to express her restrained contempt for his comments: 'I am not concerned with the remark, but it shows the mentality of the person.'[27]

Though she was sorely pressed for time in America, Indira managed to snatch a couple of days in New York with Dorothy Norman who had organized an informal gathering at her home of well-known intellectuals such as Hannah Arendt, Edward Albee, Erik Erikson and the musician John Cage. But even in this context, India's troubles with Pakistan dominated the conversation. On this visit, it was simply impossible for Indira to relax and enjoy the sort of cultural activities that she and Dorothy had always shared. They did go to a performance of the New York Philharmonic Orchestra, conducted by Leonard Bernstein, but the next evening when they had tickets for a new Stravinksy ballet choreographed by George Balanchine, Indira suddenly pulled out. 'I can't go,' she told Dorothy. 'It will be too wonderful. I won't be able to bear it.' She was on the verge of tears, and Dorothy was worried. But by the next morning Indira 'had regained her equilibrium'.[28]

When Indira and Haksar got back to India in mid-November they found that their futile negotiations in America had been widely reported and had fuelled pro-Bangladesh, anti-Pakistan, and anti-American feeling. 'Nixon and Kissinger became names to curse . . . followed by hawking and spitting.' Their faces were plastered over the newspapers, so that even the 'illiterate . . . learned to recognize the two villains' pictures: the scowling one with rat's eyes [Nixon] and the bespectacled one with the face of a constipated ox [Kissinger].'[29] Meanwhile, Indira further enhanced her own reputation by once again visiting refugee camps and military outposts. She spoke to ordinary soldiers and to the sick and wounded in the camps. Her presence and words of encouragement – widely reported with photographs in the press – buoyed India's armed forces, the refugees and the country at large.

During her foreign tour Indira had addressed an audience at the India League in London. She told them she felt as though she were 'sitting on top of a volcano and I honestly do not know when it is going to erupt.'[30] Less than a month after she and Haksar returned from the United States, the volcano exploded. Just before darkness fell, on 3 December 1971, the Pakistani air force bombed nine Indian air bases in the north and west, including those at Amritsar, Agra and Srinagar in Kashmir. The third Indo-Pak war was ignited. With this air strike Pakistan was named as the formal aggressor. But the conflict had been inevitable. Two weeks earlier Indian forces had moved into defensive positions on the Pakistan border and established operational bases inside Pakistan in preparation for an assault on Dhaka scheduled for 4 December, timed to take advantage of the full moon.

Indira was actually in Calcutta, addressing a huge rally of half-a-million people at the Calcutta Brigade Grounds, when the Pakistani planes made their raid. Just as she was saying, 'India stands for peace. But if a war is thrust on us we are prepared to fight, for the issues involved are our ideals as much as our security,' an aide rushed to the podium and handed her a slip of paper on which was scrawled the news of the Pakistani attack. She made no announcement, but hurriedly wound up her talk. Privately, she said to those with her, 'Thank God, they've attacked us.' She had not wanted to be seen as the aggressor, but had approved General Manekshaw's secret plans for India to strike the next day.[31] Now Indira's strategy of deferred action and her exquisite sense of timing had been vindicated.[32]

That evening Indira flew back to Delhi, encircled by an escort of Indian air force planes. When they approached Delhi, there was nothing but darkness below: the capital was shrouded in a blackout. Indira went directly to her office in Parliament's South Block and called an emergency meeting of the Cabinet. Then she met with leaders of the opposition. She remained completely self-possessed, 'calm, cool and confident'.[33] At midnight she broadcast to the nation that India was once again locked in battle with Pakistan and called for an Indian victory to this 'war forced on us'. She stayed up through the night monitoring the escalating military situation. The next morning she told a packed Lok Sahba:

> For over nine months the military regime of West Pakistan has barbarously trampled upon freedom and basic human rights in Bangladesh. The army of occupation has committed heinous crimes unmatched for their vindictive ferocity. Many millions have been uprooted, ten millions have been pushed into our country. We repeatedly drew the attention of the world to this annihilation of a whole people, to this menace to our security. Everywhere the people showed sympathy and understanding for the economic and other burdens and danger to India. But Governments seemed morally and politically paralysed . . . West Pakistan has escalated and enlarged the aggression against Bangladesh into full war against India. . . . We should be prepared for a long struggle.[34]

Two days later, on 6 December, Indira stood up in Parliament and announced Indian recognition of independent Bangladesh to wild acclaim. She also explained that combined Indian and Bangladeshi *Mukti Bahini* forces were fighting the war in East Pakistan.

Meanwhile, on 9 December, Nixon dispatched a task force of the US Seventh Fleet, led by a nuclear warship, the *Enterprise*, to the Bay of Bengal. Undeterred, at a midnight meeting, Indira, D. P. Dhar, Haksar and General Manekshaw decided to proceed with the war and attempt to take Dhaka before the US fleet arrived in Indian waters. China was making sabre-rattling noises, but it showed no signs as yet of intervening. D. P. Dhar rushed off to Moscow to secure Soviet support in the event of American or Chinese involvement. A Soviet fleet was duly dispatched to the Bay of Bengal close on the heels of the Americans.

With the situation thus approaching boiling point, Nixon vociferously denounced India's 'aggression' against Pakistan. In response, on 14 December Haksar drafted an open letter for Indira to send to Nixon setting forth her position. The letter was intended, of course, not merely for the President but as a robust defence of India's actions before the world. It began by saying that it was written 'at a moment of deep anguish' – a moment akin to that when the American Declaration of Independence was formulated with its assertion that 'whenever any form of government becomes destructive of man's inalienable rights to life, liberty, and the pursuit of happiness, it was the right of the people to alter or abolish it'. The letter continued:

> This tragic war [in East Pakistan] . . . could have been averted if . . . the power, influence and authority of all the states, and above all of the United States, had got Sheikh Mujibur Rahman released . . . Lip service was paid to the need for a political solution but not a single worthwhile step was taken to bring this about . . . We seek nothing for ourselves. We do not want any territory of what was East Pakistan and now constitutes Bangladesh. We do not want any territory of West Pakistan. We do want lasting peace with Pakistan . . . But will Pakistan give up its ceaseless and yet pointless agitation of the last 24 years over Kashmir? Are they willing to give up their hate campaign and posture of perpetual hostility towards India? How many times in the last 24 years have my father and I offered a Pact of Non-Aggression to Pakistan? It is a matter of recorded history that each time such an offer was made, Pakistan rejected it out of hand. We are deeply hurt by the innuendoes and insinuations that it was we who have precipitated the crisis and have in any way thwarted the emergence of solutions . . . During my visit to the United States, United Kingdom, France, Germany, Austria and Belgium, the point I emphasized, publicly as well as privately, was the immediate need for a political settlement. We waited nine months for it. When Dr Kissinger came [to India] on July 7 1971, I had emphasized to him the importance of seeking an early political settlement. But we have not received, even to this day, the barest framework of a settlement which would take into account the facts . . . it is my sincere and earnest hope that . . . you . . . will at least let me know where precisely we have gone wrong before your representatives or spokesmen deal with us with such harshness of language.[35]

It was a provocative, indignant but forthright letter, guaranteed to infuriate Nixon. Knowing this, Indira vacillated for a whole day, deciding whether or not to send it and release it to the press. In the end, she did.[36]

Throughout this period Indira was in an unusually heightened state of mind – her perceptions razor-sharp and vivid. Her innate sensitivity to colour was intensified and she wore saris with vivid borders – often in shades of red – the colour of battle, passion and bloodshed, a colour that it was traditionally taboo for widows to wear. In fact, Indira told her friend Pupul Jayakar later that she seemed to see things through a red filter and that 'the colour red suffused me throughout the war'.[37]

The Indo-Pak war, whose outbreak Indira and Haksar had stalled for so many months, lasted only fourteen days. The Pakistani army was both outnumbered and underequipped. Late in the afternoon of 16 December, before the US fleet reached the Bay of Bengal, Indo-Bangladeshi forces liberated Dhaka and Pakistan surrendered unconditionally. General Manekshaw rang Indira with the news at about 5 p.m., when she was in the middle an interview with a Swedish television team. She excused herself politely, went directly to Parliament and, barely containing her emotion, announced to the assembled MPs:

> I have an announcement to make, which I think the House has been waiting for, for some time. The West Pakistan forces have unconditionally surrendered in Bangladesh . . . Dacca is now the free capital of a free country. This House and the entire nation rejoice in this historic event. We hail the people of Bangladesh in their hour of triumph. We hail the brave young men and boys of the *Mukti Bahini* for their valour and dedication. We are proud of our own Army, Navy, Air Force and Border Security Force . . . Our objectives were limited – to assist the gallant people of Bangladesh and their *Mukti Bahini* to liberate their country from a reign of terror and to resist aggression on our land . . . We hope and trust that the Father of this new nation, Sheikh Mujibur Rahman, will take his rightful place among his own people and lead Bangladesh to peace, progress and prosperity. . . . The triumph is not theirs alone. All nations who value the human spirit will recognize it as a significant milestone in man's quest for liberty.[38]

Indira's announcement was greeted by thunderous cheering from both Congress and Opposition MPs who heaped her with garlands of flowers. For once, she made no attempt to disguise her joy in public.

Indira knew, however, that she had to contain her own and the country's jubilation. On her way to Parliament, she told her aide and speech-writer, Sharada Prasad, 'I must order a cease-fire on the western front also. For if I don't do so today, I shall not be able to do it tomorrow.'[39] Indira and her advisers, principally Haksar and Dhar, anticipated a loud demand for India not to stop with the liberation of Bangladesh and to pursue retribution against Yahya and West Pakistan. This would be highly risky because the Soviets opposed the idea and if India went after Pakistan, it was likely China and the United States would become involved.

Haksar, in particular, urged an immediate cease-fire on the western front. He reasoned that now that India held the moral as well as the military high ground, it should not seek to humiliate and further damage West Pakistan. Manekshaw concurred that a unilateral cease-fire was the 'right thing to do'.[40] After the disgruntled Defence Minister, Jagjivan Ram (whom Indira had largely ignored throughout the whole crisis, deal-ing directly with Manekshaw and the army herself), had been silenced, the Cabinet endorsed the idea of restraint and Indira publicly announced an immediate cease-fire on the western front. Responding to rumours that it was the superpowers and the threat of Nixon's Seventh Fleet bearing down on India that had dictated the cease-fire, Indira loftily told a *Time* magazine interviewer, 'The decision was made right here [in India] . . . I am not a person to be pressured – by anybody or any nations.'[41]

The war was over and Indira was its heroine. She had accomplished what neither Nehru nor Shastri had been able to pull off: a military victory. The effect was even more profound than that enjoyed by Prime Minister Margaret Thatcher 's victory in the Falkland Islands, a decade later. Indira was now elevated to god-like stature. She was praised in Parliament as a new *Durga*, the Hindu goddess of war, and likened to *Shakti*, who represents female energy and power. Even the foreign press viewed her in grandiose terms as the new 'Empress of India'.[42] In a 1971 American Gallup poll Indira was rated the most admired person in the world.

Sheikh Mujibur Rahman was released from prison in Pakistan in early January 1972. On 10 January, Indira, most of her cabinet ministers and an honour guard, were on the tarmac of Delhi's Palam airport when he arrived for a brief stopover on his way home to Bangladesh. Together Indira and Sheikh Mujib addressed a huge public rally, speaking with great emotion. She said of Sheikh Mujib that 'his body might have been imprisoned, but none could imprison his spirit. He inspired the people of Bangladesh to fight, and today he is free.' Rahman responded by saying that he felt he had to stop off in India in order 'to pay [his] personal tribute to the best friends of my people, the people of India, and to your Government under the leadership of your magnificent Prime Minister, Mrs Indira Gandhi, who is not only a leader of men but also of mankind'.[43]

In the coming days and weeks, thousands of female babies born all over India were named Indira. One, however, born the day after Sheikh Mujibur's triumphant visit to Delhi, was not. This was the second child of Rajiv and Sonia Gandhi, Indira's granddaughter, Priyanka Gandhi.

In March Indira visited the new country of Bangladesh. She and Sheikh Mujib jointly addressed a huge crowd of close to a million people in Dhaka. Most of these were too far away to hear the words spoken by the Prime Minister of India, but they could clearly see that she was wearing a Bengali-style yellow, raw silk sari with a bright red border. Mujib spoke with great emotion and turning to Indira on the podium, he quoted Rabindranath Tagore to her, 'I am a pauper. I have nothing to give. I have only love to give you.'

On her second day in Dhaka, Indira, Sheikh Mujib, the Foreign Minister Swaran Singh, the Foreign Secretary T.N. Kaul and P.N. Haksar took a day-long trip on a river steamer during which they discussed a treaty of friendship between India and Bangladesh. Kaul and the Bangladeshi Foreign Secretary drafted the treaty that evening after they returned from their river outing. It was signed by Mujib and Indira at nine the next morning.

Indira's triumph in the war with Pakistan was confirmed in the March 1972 state assembly elections when Congress captured 70 per cent of the seats contested. Once again, she campaigned strenuously and while invoking the war with Pakistan, she emphasized even more in her speeches 'the bigger war against poverty'. And to persuade doubters this was more than mere rhetoric she promised to better the lot of the rural poor with legislation that would impose lower ceilings on land ownership.

*　　*　　*

On 28 June 1972 a peace summit between India and Pakistan – the outcome of the war, which India had won six months earlier – commenced at the hill station of Simla, that favourite site of colonial conclaves in the past. After its defeat, the military government in Pakistan had collapsed, and Zulfikar Ali Bhutto had taken over as civilian president from General Khan.

Indira arrived at Simla a day early to oversee the preparation of Bhutto's and his daughter Benazir's rooms at the Governor's residence, Raj Niwas. She had brought furniture and wall hangings with her from Delhi for this purpose. According to P. N. Dhar who was part of her entourage, Indira 'threw a tantrum when she saw a large portrait of herself [hanging up] in what was going to be Bhutto's sitting room'. She ordered that it be removed immediately so that the Pakistani President would not be subjected to her gaze. Then she checked on the toiletries in the bathroom and was 'mollified' when she found them to be acceptable and of Indian origin, commenting to Dhar, 'let him [Bhutto] see that the Indian economy is catering to civilian needs'.[44]

Despite Indira's thoughtful arrangement of Bhutto's quarters, from the moment the Pakistani President and Benazir (who had just turned nineteen and was about to enter her final year at Radcliffe College, the sister college of Harvard) arrived, the antipathy between the two leaders was palpable. It almost equalled that between Indira and Nixon. It was all that press photographers could do to get them to shake hands properly on the Simla football pitch where Bhutto's helicopter landed. Indira, however, gave a warm *namaste* welcome and smile to Benazir Bhutto who was struck by how tiny and elegant the Indian Prime Minister was.

The *froideur* that accompanied their first meeting in person was hardly surprising. Three months earlier, in an interview with the Italian journalist Oriana Fallaci, Indira had described President Bhutto as 'unbalanced'. Bhutto was so enraged by this that he summoned Fallaci to Karachi in April and denigrated those involved in the fourteen-day Indo-Pak war. Bhutto branded Mujib Rahman 'a congenital liar' with 'a sick mind'. As for Indira Gandhi, she was 'a mediocre woman with mediocre intelligence. There's nothing great about her ... it's that throne that makes her seem tall ... And also the name she bears.'[45]

Indira and Bhutto found one another repellent. But in addition to personal antagonism, they clashed on their objectives. Indira wanted to use the Simla conference to settle the Kashmir question once and for all. Bhutto wanted the return of 93,000 Pakistani prisoners of war and 5,000 square miles of territory now occupied by India. Indira was willing to relinquish all of the territory that was not in Kashmir, but she felt that the prisoners of war could not be released without the consent of Bangladesh which wanted to try them for war crimes.

The talks between the Pakistani and Indian delegations dragged on for five days with no sign of resolution. The Pakistani core group consisted of Bhutto, his Foreign Secretary, Aziz Ahmed, and General Zia ul Haq (later the President of Pakistan), whom the army had insisted accompany Bhutto to Simla. Indira's delegation included her principal advisers, the stalwart Dhar and Haksar, and her Foreign Secretary T. N. Kaul – the cream of her 'Kashmiri mafia' – all urbane, intelligent, principled and shrewd men. When Dhar suffered a minor heart attack on the third day of the summit, Haksar took over at the helm.

The main objective, in Haksar's eyes, was not to humiliate Pakistan but rather to create trust and confidence between it and India. He said to Indira 'you must not forget the Versailles Treaty [of the First World War]. You don't trample a man who is down and out. We have a vested interest in seeing there is democracy in Pakistan.'[46] Haksar then drafted and redrafted various treaties calling for bilateralism, the exclusion of third parties including the United Nations, the renunciation of force, the conversion of the Kashmir cease-fire line into an international boundary and the resolution of the Kashmir issue.

But the Pakistani delegation refused to accept any of Haksar's proposals. At the heart of their rejection lay the issue of Kashmir, and in particular India's demand that the Kashmiri cease-fire line be transformed into a formal line of control that would evolve into a recognized international boundary. Bhutto would only go as far as saying 'let there be a line of peace; let people come and go; let us not fight over it'.[47] But this vague hope was not enough for the Indian delegation. Indira continued to push for a resolution of Kashmir. In turn Bhutto and his party amended or flatly rejected each proposed draft treaty that the Indian delegation presented to them.

After the last meeting of the two delegations on the afternoon of 2 July, the Indian Foreign Minister, T. N. Kaul, came out to meet reporters and told them despairingly that they were stuck: 'everything is finished'. The media rushed off to announce the failure of the summit.

T. N. Kaul packed his bags and left for Delhi before the closing banquet, convinced that there would be no resolution and no treaty.[48]

However, just before the closing banquet began at the Governor's residence Bhutto suggested that he and Indira meet privately – without their respective delegations – one last time. Indira agreed and before they retired to a small sitting room, Bhutto told Haksar and P. N. Dhar, 'you officials give up too easily'.[49] While Indira and Bhutto talked, Haksar and Dhar waited impatiently in the billiard room; the Pakistani contingent was in an adjoining reception foyer. From time to time Indira and Bhutto would emerge from the sitting room, hastily consult their advisers and then dart back to continue their private meeting.

In the course of their discussion, both Bhutto and Indira made crucial concessions. Indira agreed to withdraw Indian troops from Pakistani territory, but she reiterated that she could not promise the return of Pakistani prisoners of war without the consent of Bangladesh. Bhutto verbally promised to recognize Bangladesh in due course and he and Indira agreed not to resort to force regarding Kashmir. They also agreed to negotiate over Kashmir bilaterally – without foreign interference, and specifically without the interference of the United Nations. The December 1971 cease-fire line would be recognized by Pakistan and renamed the 'line of control' – the implication being that it would evolve into an international boundary, thus deciding the issue of Kashmir once and for all.[50]

The wording of the accord stipulated that 'the line of control resulting from the cease-fire of December 17, 1971 shall be *respected* by both sides without prejudice to the *recognized* position of either side'.[51] But respect and recognition are not legally binding and this meant that the ultimate fate of Kashmir remained dangling. Haksar suggested – and Bhutto and Indira agreed – that they all undertook to meet again 'at a mutually convenient time in the future' to discuss 'a final settlement of Jammu and Kashmir and the resumption of diplomatic relations'. It had been a real achievement for the Indian delegation to get this past Bhutto without any mention of a plebiscite in Kashmir.[52]

After midnight, the final version of the treaty was hastily typed up. Indira and Bhutto signed it in the billiard room at 12.40 a.m. on 3 July. When they emerged, they were met by a small group of aides and a couple of journalists. Indira's assistant, Usha Bhagat, called out to her in Hindi: 'Is it a boy or a girl?' ('A boy' would indicate an agreement had been reached, that the negotiations had finally yielded a success, while 'a girl' would mean they were still deadlocked.) Haksar answered cheerfully in English, 'Not only is it a boy, but a well-brought up, fully educated boy.'[53]

Indira and Bhutto left Simla – the site of futile summits between Britain and India in the past – satisfied and hopeful. But beyond Simla there was criticism. Voices in 1972 – and later – said that Indira Gandhi had made a fatal blunder by failing to force Bhutto's hand on Kashmir. Rumours circulated that the accommodations had only been achieved because both principals had agreed to some 'secret clause'. More convincing, however, is the view that Bhutto hinted to Indira that he could not survive politically if he came back from Simla having lost both East Pakistan and Kashmir. As Haksar argued, India had 'a vested interest' in seeing the continuation of democratic rather than military rule in Pakistan. Although Indira still thought Bhutto untrustworthy, she felt that he had spoken honestly about his own precarious situation and believed that he wanted peace with India.[54]

The fatal problem of the Simla Accord was, in P. N. Dhar's words, 'that it was dependent upon a continued occupation of their positions of power by the two leaders who had signed it ... there was also the presumption that Bhutto would stand by the verbal assurance [that the Kashmiri line of control would evolve into an international boundary] he had given Indira Gandhi ... The possibility that his political will might weaken, or that he might lose power did not seem to bother the Indian side,' and no one at this point imagined a day when Indira Gandhi would not be in power.[55]

In fact, after victory in the Indo-Pak war, independence for Bangladesh and the signing of the Simla Accord, Indira's position in the summer of 1972 seemed unassailable. Her unprecedented strength as India's Prime Minister had depended on a unique combination of patriotism and radicalism that won the admiration – even adoration – of the right, the centre and the left. The journalist, Kuldip Nayar, who had always been a fierce critic of Indira, conceded that she had 'won the war and appeared to have also won the peace. She was the undisputed leader of the country; the cynicism of the intellectuals had given way to admiration; the masses were even more worshipful ... She was hailed as the greatest leader India had ever had.'[56]

From this pinnacle of power, fame and popularity, Indira had nowhere to go but down.

FIFTEEN

No Further Growing

DURING THE LONG, HOT SUMMER MONTHS OF 1972, India dried up. Fields parched; crops shrivelled. A cloud of dust choked Delhi. After six years of good monsoons, the rains had failed. The result was a poor harvest, food scarcity – especially of the basic grains, rice and wheat – and rising prices all over the country. Food riots broke out in Nagpur, Bombay, Mysore and Kerala. As famine loomed in rural India, Indira's slogan *Garibi Hatao* – Remove Poverty! came back to haunt her. She told her growing chorus of critics that poverty could not be eradicated overnight. They said she was not removing poverty; she was removing the poor.

Inflation soared by 20 per cent and the price of oil escalated. In response, the government drastically cut expenditure and imposed programmes of compulsory savings on salaries and incomes. But these economic measures could not quell the industrial unrest that began to spread through the country. All over India, factories closed. Strikes became commonplace. In Bombay alone, the industrial capital of the country, there were more than 12,000 strikes during 1972 and 1973.

The weather and the monsoon were beyond Indira's control, but she could do something about the growing social turbulence. Her instinct was to impose order – to take charge without being fastidious about the means. Indira's policy of controlling the state governments by handpicking chief ministers had now become the rule. 'Unfriendly' state leaders were disposed of through recourse to 'President's rule', under which states were run directly from Delhi. In addition, Indira began to suspend rather than dissolve state legislatures, in order to paralyse opposition to the Congress Party in the states.

At the centre, Indira surrounded herself with unswervingly loyal cabinet ministers. Cabinet meetings had become forums to rubber stamp – rather than formulate – policy. Congress' organizational party structure had by this time fallen into decay. Party elections were a thing of the past. The Congress President and members of the Congress Working Committee were all now nominated by Indira herself.

Corruption thrived. That, of course, was not new. Both Nehru and Shastri's governments had been tainted by it. But it was only under Indira that corruption became endemic to the workings of government at every level.

The bizarre Nagarwala scandal had been just one manifestation of this all-pervasive phenomenon. Power lay among Indira's 'chosen'; they in turn acquired unprecedented amounts of patronage to dispense. Ironically, the state machinery set up to regulate and control economic activity for the 1967 ten-point socialist economic programme now aided the rapid spread of corruption. With the passing of the Monopolies and Restrictive Trade Practices Act in 1970 and the Foreign Exchange Regulations Act in 1973, licences, permits and clearances were required to establish every new business venture, to modify and expand existing ones and to import equipment and spare parts. Foreign exchange was also regulated. Such measures gave bureaucrats and politicians enormous scope for exploitation.

Corruption also permeated Congress Party fundraising, now directly controlled from the Prime Minister's office. Party contributions were collected in the untraceable and unaccountable form of cash which was delivered to Indira's offices at 1 Akbar Road. After Sanjay Gandhi began dabbling in politics cash donations went directly to Indira's home at 1 Safdarjung Road. Such practices extended beyond the capital; when state chief ministers were allocated quotas for party contributions, they competed to see who could most dramatically exceed them in order to impress those at the top.

Congress fundraising had become a chronic necessity as a direct result of Indira's centralization of power. Because she had dismantled the party structure and crippled its hierarchy Indira could no longer draw upon the teams of dedicated regional and local party workers to canvass for and deliver votes. Instead she communicated directly with the electorate. A huge amount of party funds was spent on organizing and transporting crowds to rallies in the states, which Indira would address. Party workers themselves were now rarely motivated by political ideals; many entered politics simply to become rich and powerful. Although Congress politicians continued to dress in white homespun *khadi* and *chappals*, as their founding fathers Gandhi and Nehru had before them, their wives and daughters now displayed the trappings of party corruption, wearing imported silk saris, diamonds and Italian leather shoes.

Indira, however, still chose to live frugally, austerely even. She owned few jewels and her most precious saris were still those made of the cotton thread spun by Nehru in prison. Though she had a highly developed aesthetic sense, Indira was neither materialistic nor extravagant. Her only real indulgence was her rare map collection. Neither Rajiv nor Sanjay, however, shared their mother's asceticism, and Indira was not inclined to deny her sons anything – Sanjay in particular.

Indira was fully aware of the power and influence money held over those around her. By the early 1970s she was surrounded by an atmosphere of unquestioning sycophancy, which she demanded and exploited. She was well aware of the corruption close to her, but she left the details to individuals such as her private secretaries Yashpal Kapoor and R.K. Dhawan, and the serious wheeling-dealing to others. Indira's principal fundraiser was an MP from Bihar named Lalit Narayan Mishra – an old friend of Feroze's from the fifties, before Mishra had gained his reputation as a consummate back-room operator and horse trader. After the 1969 Congress Party split, Mishra had become a government minister, holding at various times the Defence, Production, Trade and now the Railway portfolio. While Minister of Trade he brought into being the infamous 'licence raj' under which businessmen and industrialists were granted government contracts or export and import licences in exchange for large gifts of money to the Congress party. Short and squat with multiple chins, Mishra looked the part he played – that of the classic corrupt politician.

So too did Sanjay Gandhi's personal benefactor, a bespectacled, hefty Jat named Bansi Lal. Lal was Chief Minister of Haryana, the state that had been carved out of the Punjab, adjacent to Delhi. Two years after Sanjay Gandhi had been awarded the government contract for the Maruti project, his company had failed to manufacture a single vehicle. Bansi Lal wanted to ingratiate himself with the Prime Minister, so he sold Sanjay more than 400 acres of choice Haryana farm land on the outskirts of Delhi for the Maruti factory – land from which more than a thousand villagers were hastily 'relocated'. Not only was the price at which the land was sold suspect, its location next to an army ammunition dump violated government regulations against building an industrial plant within a thousand metres of a defence installation.

Many other politicians clamoured to help Sanjay with his languishing car company. Prominent businessmen, including K.K. Birla (the head of the Birla family in whose house Mahatma Gandhi had died) invested large sums in Maruti. Birla was also the proprietor of the *Hindustan Times* and he sacked its editor, B.G. Verghese, in 1973 after a number of articles criticizing Sanjay's company appeared in the paper.

Despite assistance from Birla, Bansi Lal and others, Sanjay's business did not take off. All the Maruti prototypes developed faults, including steering, suspension and overheating problems. In 1972, Sanjay exhibited a sample model at the Asia Trade Fair, but it proved to be only a shell with no engine. The following year the journalist Uma Vasudev, who had recently published a biography of Indira, decided she would interview Sanjay about Maruti for her magazine *Surge*. He agreed and they met at the car plant in Haryana on 5 May 1973, by which time another prototype had been produced.

Sanjay offered to take Vasudev for a drive on the test track that ran round the perimeter of the Maruti factory. With Sanjay at the wheel and Vasudev sitting next to him, they roared off 'at break-neck speed . . . across a country patch and over bushes, ditches and boulders at a speed of 100 kilometres an hour'. Vasudev was terrified. She also realized that the Maruti was a disaster. The car overheated and leaked oil. The suspension was appalling and the engine deafening. The steering was light and the car doors would not close securely. Back in the Maruti factory, Vasudev saw only five, unpainted specimens of the 'finished' car. Another fifteen more were in the process of being built. Engines were cast by hand and there was no sign of an assembly line in operation. Rather than the cheap, mass-produced car the government had contracted Sanjay to develop, Vasudev realized with horror that the Maruti was actually a custom-built product.[1]

Sanjay was tireless in his efforts to raise funds for Maruti. In 1973 he appointed seventy-five Maruti car dealerships and collected a deposit of 500,000 rupees from each in return for a promise (that was not fulfilled) to deliver cars to sell within six months. Sanjay then turned to the banks. The recently nationalized Central Bank of India and the Punjab National Bank granted him unsecured loans totalling 7.5 million rupees. The Central Bank even opened a branch with an accommodating manager at the Maruti factory site. Still the Maruti car failed to materialize.

Eventually the Reserve Bank of India intervened and sent a circular to all the nationalized banks, warning that further loans to Maruti would undermine the basis of the country's credit policy. D.V. Taneja, the chairman of the Central Bank, who had been appointed in part because he had helped Maruti in the past, now had to tell Sanjay that he could no longer bypass the bank's regulations and release 2.5 rupee *crores* to him. Taneja was summoned to 1 Safdarjung Road for an acrimonious meeting with Sanjay who threatened to have him dismissed. Taneja refused to back down. Shortly afterwards Taneja was informed that the government had decided not to renew his chairmanship of the Central Bank.[2]

Many of the people around Indira were troubled by Sanjay's activities, but few spoke out openly against him. Three years earlier, Indira's chief adviser P. N. Haksar had been one of the few prepared to point out to her the impropriety of granting a lucrative government contract to her son. Haksar warned Indira that it would make her vulnerable to criticism, and he continued to voice his concerns in the hope that he could put a halt to the Maruti folly. Haksar queried the Bansi Lal land deal and the feasibility of the Maruti prototype model. Finally, he frankly advised Indira to send Sanjay away from Delhi and the political sphere – to Europe, or at least to Kashmir – to give the scandal time to die down.[3]

This was the first time during all his years of working closely with the Prime Minister that Haksar had miscalculated Indira; and it would be the last. Like many others, Haksar could see the influence Sanjay had over his mother. He hoped Indira would respond to the rationality of his argument, that she would see how damaging the Maruti affair could be to the Prime Minister's Secretariat. But Indira merely remained silent. Her answer would come obliquely, later. In September 1973, Haksar's post as Principal Private Secretary was due to be renewed, a process which had been automatic since his appointment in 1967. Despite the massive contribution Haksar had made to her prime ministership, Indira was now prepared to jettison him. Instead of automatically renewing Haksar's contract, she just allowed it to expire. Haksar had by this time reached the official retirement age, and he retired gracefully, surrendering his post without fuss. The following year Indira gave him the deputy chairmanship of the Planning Commission – a significant body under Nehru, but now it had been reduced, in the words of one commentator, to 'a sophisticated accounts office and a retirement home for the socially benevolent'.[4]

P.N. Dhar then moved up to replace Haksar as Principal Private Secretary. He would remain in that post, working alongside Indira, despite some misgivings, for the next four years. Like Haksar, Dhar was a Kashmiri, a gifted economist and an astute adviser; but according to Haksar, if Dhar found himself on a collision course with Indira, he could be 'spineless'. Haksar was the last of Indira's coterie prepared to question or stand up to her. No one did now – except Sanjay Gandhi himself.

The Maruti controversy was briefly eclipsed in the spring of 1973 by the Supreme Court's findings on the government's constitutional amendments of 1971. The Court endorsed the idea that Parliament had the power to amend the constitution, as long as it did not alter its 'essential features' – namely that India was a democratic, republican, federal state. But what precisely constituted an 'essential feature' would be left to the discretion of the courts. In other words, legislation affecting the basic structure of the constitution would still be subject to judicial review. Indira and her supporters interpreted the judgement as a defeat because it denied Parliament and the executive untrammelled power.

On 25 April, the day after the Supreme Court announced its judgement, the Chief Justice, S.M. Sikri, retired. Normal procedures would have seen the next senior justice on the bench – in this case J.M. Shelat – succeed the Chief Justice. But Shelat had been among the six judges who had voted to put a brake on Parliament's power to reform the constitution. As had the next two senior judges, K.S. Hegde and A.N. Grover. Instead of appointing one of these three men, Indira instructed the President to name her choice, A.N. Ray, as Chief Justice of the Supreme Court. All three of the superseded judges immediately resigned.

This provoked a public outcry against Indira who was accused of suborning judges in her drive for 'a committed judiciary'. A group of six distinguished jurists issued a joint statement on 26 April branding the supersession of judges 'a manifest attempt to undermine the Court's independence'. It was, once more, the Minister of Steel and Heavy Engineering, Mohan Kumaramangalam, rather than the Minister of Law, H. R. Gokhale, who came to Indira's defence on the floor of Parliament, on 2 May: 'We had to take into account what was the Judge's basic outlook,' Kumaramangalam argued. 'Was it not right to think in terms of a more suitable relationship between the Court and the Government? Was it not good . . . to put an end to a period of confrontation and ensure stability? In appointing a . . . Chief Justice, I think we have to take into consideration . . . his attitude to life, his politics.'[5]

Four weeks later, on 31 May 1973, Kumaramangalam died in a plane crash. His loss would intensify the shift in power from the Cabinet to the Prime Minister's Secretariat (PMS) located at 1 Akbar Road. Later, power would shift again, to the Prime Minister's house next door at 1 Safdarjung Road, popularly referred to as 'the Palace', where increasingly Sanjay Gandhi presided over his mother's court.

Kumaramangalam's death was a personal blow and left Indira depressed. He had been close to Feroze Gandhi in London in the late thirties and remained so until Feroze's death. Kumaramangalam also seemed to Indira to be one of her few colleagues not driven by his ego and a desire for power. As she told Dorothy Norman in a letter, 'except for an intense concern for people and a desire to give, he wasn't a political person'.[6]

Indira, however, had irrevocably become 'a political person', and now for the second time in her life she felt trapped and oppressed by her position. In this same letter to Dorothy Norman, Indira confessed, 'I have been very moody these days. Except in the early years there has hardly ever been a moment free and available for introspection . . . Always just ahead was a task to be done which brooked no delay . . . I am feeling imprisoned – by the security people who think they can hide their utter incompetence by sheer numbers and a tighter closing in, but also and perhaps more so by the realization that I have come to an end, that there's no further growing in this direction.'[7]

* * *

What was the nature of the routine – personal and political – that Indira felt imprisoned her? In interviews, she had always insisted that she made no division between her public and private lives, an assertion she dramatized by having her toddler grandchildren wandering about the garden while she held outdoor press conferences. By this time, however, politics had taken over Indira's life; she had very little time for her family, friends, for reading or any other activities unrelated to her six-teen-hour, or longer, working day.

She rose at 6 a.m., and did yoga exercises for twenty minutes. Then she bathed and dressed quickly, in five minutes if necessary, which, as Indira commented 'very few men can do'. She scanned the newspapers while eating breakfast on a tray in her bedroom. Then, before 8 a.m. she met with her private secretary to run through the day's schedule of appointments and discuss any other matters. Initially this was a man named Yashpal Kapoor, but in the early seventies he was replaced by his younger cousin, also from the Punjab, R. K. Dhawan. These men were not civil servants. They were of an altogether different, lower order and their position more amorphous than that of P. N. Haksar and P. N. Dhar. Nor did they see to Indira's personal needs as Usha Bhagat and Sonia Gandhi did.

Both Kapoor and Dhawan had had secretarial training and then worked for Nehru as typists and stenographers. Kapoor was assigned to Indira when she became Congress President in 1959. After Nehru's and Shastri's deaths, he remained with her and came to hold consider-able unofficial power. Kapoor, and then Dhawan, both looked to Nehru's former secretary, M.O. Mathai, as their role model in terms of their professional responsibilities. They devoted themselves entirely to the Prime Minister and although neither of them actually lived with Indira at 1 Safdarjung Road (as Mathai had lived at Teen Murti House) they were invariably there every day, all day. Whilst never the complete filter Mathai had been, Kapoor and Dhawan made decisions on the Prime Minister's behalf, screened visits and calls, and wielded an inap-propriate amount of power. It was said of Kapoor, for example, that he had 'more authority than a state Chief Minister . . . he was in a position to make or mar the image of a politician' in Indira's eyes.[8] Kapoor, for example, had hastened the marginalization of Indira's friend and confidante, Dinesh Singh, when Kapoor told the Prime Minister that Singh hinted far and wide that he was Indira's lover.

Before the 1966 and 1971 general elections, Kapoor also served as Indira's election agent and 'fixer' in her constituency, Rae Bareilly – a fact that would start a chain of events leading to Indira's fall from power four years later. By this time, however, Kapoor had prospered financially and become a member of the Rajya Sabha as a consequence of his powerful position close to the Prime Minister.

R. K. Dhawan – with slicked-down black hair and a Colgate smile – was even more ambitious to serve Indira than his cousin Kapoor had been. And he did so unwaveringly until 1984. Dhawan remained a bachelor and had no private life of his own. As he told a journalist in the late seventies, he was 'with the Prime Minister from eight in the morning every day to the time she retires, all the 365 days of the year. I have not taken even one day's casual leave since 1963. No casual leave, no earned leave, no [holidays] . . . I am always with the Prime Minister.' At home, travelling in India and abroad, Dhawan was Indira's 'shadow'.[9]

After meeting with her Private Secretary, Indira would always hold her morning *darshan* for one hour in the garden of 1 Akbar Road. In the seventies security for the Prime Minister was lax; anyone could drop in at these morning gatherings. Amongst the daily throng of visitors were party workers, labour activists, factory workers, peasants, students, newly-weds, mothers with babies, and foreign tourists. By 10 a.m. Indira was behind her desk at 1 Akbar Road, one of her three offices, or South Block in the Parliament building. She would come home for lunch at 1 o'clock and then return to her office to work, staying until seven or eight in the evening. Dinner at 1 Safdarjung Road would always be a family gathering, sometimes with family friends; politics was never discussed. After dinner, Indira would continue working on files or see people until midnight or later. Sundays she would try to keep clear for her grandchildren and friends. This was her routine on 'normal' working days. But there were also incessant visitors – political and state – to meet with and entertain. And Indira, of course, spent a great deal of the time travelling herself – in India or on state visits abroad.

It was a work-driven life, with no time for reflection, personal or idle conversation or relaxation. There was scant time, too, for correspondence. With rare exceptions, by this time, Indira's long, confessional letters to Dorothy Norman had been reduced to hasty notes or hurriedly dictated, typed letters. Indira had seen her father live thus. She was even more efficient than Nehru. She dispensed with convoluted greetings, made visitors come to the point in a matter of seconds, listened attentively and usually made up her mind quickly.

Rumours persisted regarding the Prime Minister's love affairs, despite her lack of time or privacy, even if she had had the inclination. Indira's yoga teacher, the charismatic, handsome holy man, Dhirendra Brahmachari, was still a frequent visitor to 1 Safdarjung Road. In the seventies Brahmachari became close to Sanjay Gandhi and in time he was virtually a member of the household. Brahmachari was the only man to see Indira alone in her room while giving her yoga instruction, and he was the only male with whom she could have had a relationship during this period.

But Indira was now in her mid-fifties, a widow and a grandmother with a pronounced grey streak in her hair. In traditional societies, widows and grandmothers, and indeed all women past menopause, are assumed to be sexually inactive. Indira was not a traditional Indian woman but the vast majority of her countrywomen were. Indira was also, by nature, cautious, and it would have been out of character for her to flout convention and risk her reputation and position for fleeting self-gratification.

And by 1973, with those surrounding her increasingly tainted by corruption, Indira was especially concerned about her reputation. She, in fact, was already vulnerable. Though it was scarcely covered in the media, at about the same time as the controversial appointment of A.N. Ray as Chief Justice, Indira's opponent during the 1971 general election, Raj Narain, filed a petition with the Allahabad High Court accusing her of electoral irregularities. Narain – popularly known as 'the Clown Prince of India' – was a colourful figure who sported a bandanna and behaved like a buffoon. Those who noticed his petition thought it just another of his stunts. It certainly lacked substance. The list of corrupt practices he accused Indira of included using Yashpal Kapoor as her election agent when he was still employed by the government as her Private Secretary. Another charge against Indira was that she had illegally used government employees such as public works men to erect platforms and set up loudspeakers when she made campaign speeches during the run-up to the 1971 election.

The monsoon failed for the third year in a row in 1974 with the result that drought and food shortages continued. So did the soaring inflation.

Indira was forced to approach the World Bank and International Monetary Fund. The IMF obliged with a loan but attached rigid conditions, which required wholesale back-pedalling on Indira's socialist economic policy, including curtailing government expenditure. Unemployment escalated. Even grants from the World Bank and IMF could not stem India's tide of growing industrial and social unrest. The country was crippled by yet more strikes and marches which often led to violence and police intervention. In January 1974 students in Gujarat protested against the high price of basic commodities. Their discontent quickly spread to the population at large, and the state was reduced to near anarchy. Shops and houses were looted, buses and cars burned and government property destroyed. The police could not contain the situation and were often the subject of attacks. In one month over 103 people were killed in riots, 300 were injured and 8,000 arrested. As in the rest of the country, protest focussed on high prices and government corruption, but in Gujarat, protesters went further and called for *nav nirman* or political regeneration. They wanted their corrupt Chief Minister, Chimanbhai Patel, to resign, the state assembly to be dissolved and fresh state elections held. Patel was one of the few remaining state leaders not of Indira's own choosing, so she was not loath to see him go when he was forced to resign in early February. Indira initially balked at dissolving the state assembly since Congress held a two-thirds majority there. She capitulated, however, and President's rule was imposed on Gujarat on 9 February 1974. Indira hinted darkly of a conspiracy behind the unrest, which she maintained (as she had on so many other occasions) was backed by 'foreign elements' – namely the CIA.

Such was the background and the context for the emergence of the former freedom fighter and long-standing friend of the Nehru family, Jayaprakash Narayan, and the juggernaut of a movement that he now organized and led. Narayan – or JP as he was popularly known – had been an early disciple of Gandhi's, and during the Quit India movement he had become a hero of the underground movement, sabotaging railway lines and British installations. After independence, Narayan left Congress for the Socialist Party, and then retired from mainstream politics altogether. During these years, he led an austere, selfless existence devoted to social improvement and the welfare of the most oppressed sectors of Indian society.

Appalled at how much had gone drastically awry in India in the seventies, Narayan decided to re-enter the political world. Despite being in his seventies, suffering from kidney disease and other ailments, he threw himself into the agitation against Indira's government. Because of his moral stature he was able to unify Indira's disparate opponents on both the left and the right. With the exception of the Communist Party of India, opposition forces rallied to JP and his call for a 'total revolution' to bring down Indira's government. As Indira put it in a letter to Dorothy Norman, Narayan's 'theme is that I am the "world's greatest dictator". This is Morarji Desai's bandwagon [too], now supported by the Jan Sangh on the one hand and the Communist Extremists (Marxist-Leninists) on the other.'[10] The JP movement drew together under its umbrella a wide range of groups covering the whole political spectrum, from the right-wing Hindu party, the Jan Sangh, and its militant cadres in the Rashtriya Swayamsevak Sangh (RSS) on the one hand, to far left-wing organizations such as the Naxalites on the other. The only objective these disparate groups shared was the extra-constitutional overthrow of Indira Gandhi's government.

The JP movement began in Narayan's home state of Bihar in early 1974, and as was the case in Gujarat, its immediate goal was to oust the Chief Minister, dissolve the state assembly and hold fresh elections. One significant difference between the situations in Gujarat and Bihar was that in Gujarat left-wing students were the standard-bearers while in Bihar, Narayan tried to bring farmers, landless labourers and other poor sections of society into the movement. In Bihar JP called for a week-long *bandh* or general strike. And also for a *gherao* – an encircle-ment of the Bihar parliament which Indira refused to dissolve. *Gheraos* – the word literally means 'encircle and besiege' – were a new tactic of dissent and even more successful than the passive withdrawal of labour brought about by a strike.

With the situation approaching boiling point in Bihar, the socialist trade union leader George Fernandes launched a nationwide railway strike in May.[11] The 1.4 million railway workers – 10 per cent of the total number of people employed in the public sector – demanded an eight-hour working day and a 75 per cent increase in their wages to bring their salaries in line with other workers in nationalized industries. The government made some concessions but these were rejected. Invok-ing the Defence of India Rules, Indira declared the strike illegal and on

2 May Fernandes and other labour leaders were arrested. Five days later a million railway workers went on strike. Their aim, in Fernandes' words, was nothing less than to 'change the whole history of India and bring down the Indira Gandhi government ... by paralysing the railway transport to a dead stop'.[12] The country's rail network ground to a halt.

With the railways paralysed, food shortages became acute bringing famine to parts of the country. Utilizing the new Maintenance of Security Act (MISA), which allowed for 'preventive' detention, Indira determined to break the strike at any cost. And the cost was great. During the first few days of government action over 20,000 railway workers were arrested and jailed. The number later rose to something between thirty and forty thousand. The jailed railway workers' families were thrown out of their government-owned houses and reduced to destitution. The arrests were often violent and the strikers wounded, sometimes mortally. Indira's government managed to crush the strike after twenty days. Despite widespread condemnation of the government's ruthless tactics, many Indians – especially those in the middle and upper classes – praised Indira's measures. Like the British before them, they wanted the trains to run on time.

Indira may have won this round, but the brutal suppression of the railway strike was uniting and galvanizing her opposition.

On 18 May 1974, with the railway strike still on, at Pokharan in Rajasthan, India detonated an underground nuclear device to great acclaim. This 'peaceful nuclear experiment' had been kept a closely guarded secret. Not even Indira's Cabinet knew – and they were not informed until four hours after the explosion. India had become the sixth nuclear power in the world, and for a day or two the public celebrated this fact and the railway strike was forgotten. Internationally, however, there was considerable criticism of the nuclear test, especially from Pakistan and nations with established nuclear powers. Indira responded emotively to such criticism in Parliament: 'No technology is evil in itself: it is the use that nations make of technology which determines its character. India does not accept the principle of apartheid in any matter and technology is no exception.'[13]

President V.V. Giri's term expired at about the same time as the nuclear test. Though Giri had been Indira's choice in 1969 and her backing of him rather than the Syndicate's candidate had precipitated the Congress Party split, their relationship had been difficult at times. The President, for example, had objected to the supersession of Supreme Court judges the previous year. Instead of encouraging Giri to serve another term, Indira nominated Fakhruddin Ali Ahmed, a seventy-year-old Muslim, to replace him as the next President. She knew that Ahmed would be unquestionably loyal and malleable. By 1974 Indira herself controlled Congress' organization party – including the Congress President, Dev Kanta Barooah, most of the state chief ministers, and of course her own cabinet ministers. With Ahmed as President, her position would be virtually unassailable. This was neatly summed up by the telling slogan coined by Barooah, the Congress President – 'Indira is India, India is Indira.'

As the hot turbulent summer of 1974 wore on, Indira was briefly distracted by the plans for her younger son's marriage. On 29 September 1974 Sanjay Gandhi, now nearly twenty-eight, married Maneka Anand, a seventeen-year-old Sikh girl, in a civil ceremony at the home of the old Nehru family friend, Mohammed Yunus. It had also been at Yunus' home, at another wedding party, that Sanjay met Maneka the previous December. She was the daughter of a Sikh army officer named Colonel T. S. Anand and his flamboyant, aggressive wife, Amteshwar. More than ten years Sanjay's junior, Maneka was a beautiful, vivacious, assertive woman who in some ways took after her mother. When she first met Sanjay, she had just dropped out of a political science course at Lady Sri Ram College in Delhi, and she now had ambitions to become a journalist.

Sanjay and Maneka's marriage took everyone except the principals and their families by surprise. Since setting up Maruti, Sanjay had led a workaholic existence with little time for women. He would arrive at his car plant early in the morning, getting home at seven or eight in the evening. Fixated on Maruti, and balding at twenty-seven, Sanjay was no longer the playboy he had reportedly been in England. Since returning from England he had had only two serious relationships – one with a Muslim and the other with a European woman. He had turned into a serious, driven young man with little time or taste for social activities. Maneka, however, was keen to go out and to be seen. She was garrulous and uninhibited. At that time, despite the Sikh prohibition on tobacco, she smoked, which Sanjay disliked intensely. They were temperamentally polar opposites and they had no common interests or friends. In addition, Maneka was greatly influenced by her domineering mother, Amteshwar, who from the beginning saw that there was much to be gained from an alliance with the Gandhi family. Sanjay and Maneka's relationship had all the ingredients for a disastrous marriage.

Indira, herself, was far from pleased with her son's choice, but she tried not to interfere. When the couple became engaged in July 1974, she gave Maneka her mother Kamala's engagement ring (designed by Motilal Nehru all those years ago). And when they married, Indira showed great generosity to her new *bahu* (daughter-in-law). She gave Maneka twenty-one exquisite saris, two sets of gold jewellery and most precious of all to Indira, a *khadi* sari made of yarn spun by her father when he was in jail.

Immediately after the marriage, Maneka joined Indira's household at 1 Safdarjung Road just as Sonia Maino had done when she married Rajiv six years earlier. Indira personally decorated and arranged the newlyweds' bedroom. She wrote to Dorothy Norman that 'the wedding was quiet. I had some misapprehensions about the whole thing as Maneka is so very young . . . and I could not guess whether she knew her own mind. However, she seems to have fitted in and is a gay and joyous person to have around.'[14]

But not for long. It was soon apparent that Maneka, unlike her sister-in-law, Sonia, could or would not adapt to the Gandhi household and its routine. She was loud, boisterous and uninhibited. From the beginning she clashed with her easy-going brother-in-law, Rajiv, and his wife. Maneka could also be disrespectful of her mother-in-law. Indira was far from the stereotypical, domineering Indian mother-in-law, but she found Maneka's behaviour inappropriate and grating. Maneka herself later confessed that she 'was young, immature and easily bored. I didn't know housework and didn't want to learn cooking . . . In my own home we were . . . informal and often brash. The Gandhis observe decorum . . . with each other.'[15] With Maneka's arrival at 1 Safdarjung Road, a highly discordant presence had come into the household and disrupted the rare haven of peace it provided for Indira.

*　　*　　*

During 1974, India's relations with the tiny neighbouring state of Sikkim were deteriorating. Tucked away in the midst of perpetually snow-covered mountains, with a population of only 200,000 and occupying just 2,800 square miles, Sikkim's importance lay in its strategic location, wedged in between Nepal to the west, Chinese-occupied Tibet to the north, Bhutan to the east, and West Bengal to the south. Under British rule, Sikkim had been a remote outpost of British India. Although technically it had been granted sovereign status, it was run, much like the Princely States, by a resident British political officer. Unlike the Indian princes, however, the King or *Chogyal* of Sikkim did not have to swear an oath of loyalty to the British Crown. After independence, Sikkim was made a protectorate of India rather than one of its constituent states. This protectorate status meant that Sikkim retained control over its internal affairs while India was responsible for its defence and territorial integrity.

In the seventies, the *Chogyal* – best known in the West for having taken as his second wife a young American woman named Hope Cooke – was resisting the demands of the Sikkim National Congress and other parties for parliamentary democracy. Hope Cooke, like Grace Kelly, had been transformed by marriage into a royal personage and she eagerly embraced her new status. According to one commentator, 'Hope's dreams of queening it in the Himalayas cut off [her husband] from his throne's traditional supporters and isolated him from Sikkimese society.'[16] Her royal ambitions and revival of regal titles, forms and rituals strengthened the *Chogyal*'s resistance to Sikkim's growing pro-democracy movement. Inspired by his wife, the *Chogyal* began a drive for the transformation of Sikkim from an Indian protectorate into an independent, sovereign state.

Delhi was alarmed by the *Chogyal*'s secessionist movement. P. N. Dhar later wrote of the situation, 'the defence of Sikkim was a strategic compulsion for India' because it provided a buffer zone on the Tibet border in between India and China.[17] But the *Chogyal* also needed the Indian government's support against the Sikkimese pro-democracy movement, which he soon received from India's intelligence bureau, the Research and Analysis Wing.

In 1974 elections were held in Sikkim. A chief minister and council of ministers took charge and the *Chogyal*'s position was reduced from spiritual and temporal ruler to constitutional monarch. At the end of

August 1974, a constitutional amendment bill was formulated to convert the kingdom into an associate state of India. In India the media had portrayed the *Chogyal* as a 'monster and his objections to the bill as . . . a device to perpetuate royal absolutism'.[18] Clearly he was a serious obstacle. But as one journalist put it, 'a kingdom in association with a republic was . . . a constitutional absurdity'.[19] By this time, 'Queen Hope' had tired of Sikkim and returned home to America, leaving the abandoned *Chogyal* a melancholy, late middle-aged anachronism.

In an attempt to save his position, the *Chogyal* flew to Delhi to appeal to Indira personally. They, in fact, already knew each other well. Nehru had been a close friend of the *Chogyal*'s father and thought the son 'a potentially dynamic leader who would lead Sikkim out of its medieval thraldom'.[20] Not only had Indira met the *Chogyal* in 1952 and 1958 when she accompanied Nehru on visits to Sikkim, as a young man the *Chogyal* had also stayed with the Nehrus at Teen Murti House. But when he flew to Delhi in 1974, seeking Indira's support, she treated him almost as a stranger. According to P. N. Dhar, who sat in on their meeting, 'she was brief, even curt'. She pointed out that 'the politicians [he, the *Chogyal*] was running down were the chosen representatives of the people and advised him not to go against their wishes. He wanted the discussion to continue but Mrs Gandhi fell silent and looked aloof'. As Dhar notes, Indira had 'perfected the use of silence as a negative response. After an oppressive moment in which nothing was said, the *Chogyal* stood up to leave. Mrs Gandhi bade him farewell with folded hands and an enigmatic smile, still without saying anything.'[21]

The *Chogyal* did, however, find support among India's foes. In Pakistan Zulfikar Ali Bhutto accused India of swallowing up Sikkim. There were protests in Nepal against India's 'policy of colonialism and imperialism', and China compared India's designs on Sikkim with the Soviet Union's 1968 invasion of Czechoslovakia. Indira Gandhi scathingly reminded China of its own invasion of Tibet.

On 8 April 1975, the Indian army struck. Over 5,000 soldiers invaded the Sikkimese capital, Gangtok. The following day they closed in on the *Chogyal*'s twenty-room palace. Delhi's representative tried to buy time by reassuring the King that this was only 'a military exercise', and there was no cause for alarm. But he was not taken in by the ruse. An amateur radio operator, he broadcast news of the Indian invasion from a transmitter in his palace; the message was picked up by, among others, an elderly, retired coroner in a village in Kent and two other radio hams, one in Sweden and one in Japan.[22] No one responded, however, to the *Chogyal*'s message of distress. His own Imperial Guard was easily overcome by the Indian troops and the *Chogyal* was put under house arrest in his palace.

A referendum was hastily arranged for 14 April to decide the fates of the *Chogyal* and Sikkim. As a result the institutions of the *Chogyal* and his family's 333-year-old dynasty were abolished and the kingdom of Sikkim was 'integrated' into the Indian Union as its twenty-second state. In some quarters, there was an outcry against the forced 'annexation' of Sikkim, which was described as a 'smash and grab' operation. The official view from Delhi, however, was that the 'integration' of Sikkim into India was yet another triumph for democracy.

Sikkim had been much easier to settle than the on-going problems in Kashmir. A clause in the 1972 Simla Accord had stated that representatives from India and Pakistan would meet again 'at a mutually convenient time in the future' to discuss 'a final settlement of Jammu and Kashmir', but three years on it had yet to be acted on. In May 1973, a bizarre incident in Anantnag, south of Srinagar, re-ignited unrest in Kashmir. A student at Anantnag College discovered a drawing of the Prophet Mohammed with the Archangel Gabriel dictating the Holy Koran to him in a copy of the classic British imperial encyclopaedia for children, *The Book of Knowledge* by Arthur Mee. The multi-volume work had originally been owned by the Mission School in Anantnag, whose library the college inherited when the school closed down some thirty years earlier. The picture was brought to the notice of the Islamic authorities, who denounced it as blasphemy – since Islam forbids all representations of the Prophet Mohammed. The college students at Anantnag went on strike. Two days later there were large protest marches in Srinagar with marchers waving placards reading 'Hang the Author' – a vain demand since Arthur Mee had died in England in 1943.

The unrest spread and intensified. Shops in Kashmir closed, public transport ground to a halt, police opened fire on demonstrators and at least four were killed in Srinagar. Hundreds more were arrested. The government of India banned sale or possession of Mee's encyclopaedia.

The Book of Knowledge was, of course, only a spark – not the cause – of the trouble that once again engulfed Kashmir. In Pakistan Bhutto used the situation to criticize India for not allowing a plebiscite to be held in the state. He called for the people of Kashmir to stage a two-day *hartal* to demonstrate their desire for self-determination. It was an opportune moment for Kashmir's former leader Sheikh Abdullah (whose political exile had ended in the spring of 1972), to re-enter politics. He condemned Bhutto for meddling in the internal affairs of Kashmir. Indira recognized that she now had the opportunity to secure Abdullah as an ally, and in early 1974, she began a protracted series of negotiations with him.

Whilst Indira spoke with Abdullah in Delhi, her principal adviser on Kashmir, a gifted negotiator named G. Parthasarathi, who had been Indian High Commissioner in Pakistan, had extensive discussions with his Kashmiri counterpart Mirza Afzal Beg. Sheikh Abdullah pressed Indira to dissolve the Kashmir state assembly and to hold fresh elections. This she refused to do, but, as had become her practice, she offered him the post of Chief Minister. Eventually Parthasarathi and Beg and Indira and Abdullah hammered out a framework for an agreement, ratified in the Kashmir Accord.

Indira announced the six-point Kashmir Accord in Parliament on 24 February 1975. The previous day the Chief Minister of Kashmir had obediently resigned. This cleared the way for Sheikh Abdullah to be elected Chief Minister – an office he had last held in 1953 – by the Congress Party in the state legislature. Under the 1975 Accord, Kashmir was described as a 'constituent unit of the Union of India', but its special status, as guaranteed by Article 370 of the Indian constitution, was retained. Its autonomy, however, had been whittled down over the years, and it was now further compromised by a crucial clause of the accord which stated that the Indian government was free to 'make laws relating to the prevention of activities directed towards disclaiming, questioning or disrupting the sovereignty and territorial integrity of India or secession of a part of the territory from the Union'.[23]

Bhutto called the Kashmir Accord a 'sellout' and maintained that it violated the 1972 Simla Accord. From Indira's point of view, the agreement with Abdullah had laid to rest the idea of a plebiscite; it confirmed the irrevocable accession of the state to India and thereby put a halt to the movement for Kashmiri self-determination. In his autobiography,

Sheikh Abdullah explained that he had only agreed to cooperate in order to regain power, 'but soon had to regret my decision'.[24]

For the time being the Kashmir question appeared to be settled. Much closer to home, the JP movement led by Jayaprakesh Narayan had spread from Bihar throughout India and evolved into a moral and political crusade against Indira and her government. Narayan called for Indira to be removed, for 'total revolution – political, economic, social, educational, moral and cultural' and 'a partyless democracy'. He travelled across India with his message and was received by huge crowds as a saviour.

Narayan and his movement now posed a real threat. Indira viewed Narayan's exhortation to the Indian people that the constitution and its laws had integrity *independent* of elected ministers, including the Prime Minister, as a threat to democracy itself. A general election was due to be held only a year and a half hence. But Narayan was unwilling to wait until then, arguing that the election would be rigged.

Indira could no longer afford to ignore Narayan. Reluctantly, she agreed to meet with him in November 1974. Instead of any sort of reconciliation, the result was an explosive confrontation. Indira accused Narayan of being backed and financed by the United States through the CIA. He said she wanted to establish a Soviet-backed dictatorship in India. After exchanging these bitter words, Narayan asked Indira if he could see her privately (two ministers as well as aides had sat in on their discussion). When everyone else had left the room, Narayan gave Indira a folder of old, yellowed letters that Kamala Nehru had written to his wife, Prabha Devi, some forty and fifty years earlier, in the midst of the freedom struggle. Kamala and Prabha Devi had been close friends and Narayan had discovered Kamala's letters only recently, after the death of his wife in 1973. They graphically described Kamala's great unhappiness in the Nehru household and her persecution by the other Nehru women. Indira was profoundly moved by the bundle of faded letters and also grateful to Narayan for giving them to her.

But this act of personal kindness had no impact on the political enmity between Indira and Narayan. Their meeting came to nothing and Narayan vowed to escalate his crusade against Indira. As a Gandhian and old freedom fighter, he knew what tactics to use when Indira did not yield: civil disobedience. The *bandhs* and *gheraos* proliferated and spread from the provinces into Delhi.

At 5.50 p.m. on the afternoon of 2 January 1975 Lalit Narayan Mishra, the Railway Minister and Indira's chief fundraiser, was blown up in his home state of Bihar by a bomb planted under the platform of the Samastipur railway station where he was inaugurating a broad-gauge railway line. He died the next morning in hospital. Mishra had told colleagues that he feared an assassination attempt by trade unionists after the government's brutal suppression of the 1974 railway strike. Despite his fears, however, Mishra's security protection remained sketchy and his medical treatment unaccountably delayed. Suspicion over his death immediately fell on Indira's government because Mishra's rampant corruption had become an embarrassing liability. The journalist Nikhil Chakravartty had no doubts that Mishra's death was arranged by Yashpal Kapoor and that Indira was aware of the plot. Indira, however, blamed Narayan's 'cult of violence', aided and abetted by 'foreign elements'. Then Indira went further and claimed that Mishra's assassination was 'a dress rehearsal' of a larger plot in which she was 'the real target'. With passion, she declared that 'When I am murdered, they will say I arranged it for myself.'[25]

Mishra's murder heralded more disturbing events. On 15 February Narayan addressed government employees in New Delhi and exhorted the army and police 'not to obey orders that are illegal ... or unjust'.[26] Civil servants, police officers and soldiers were all obliged, he said, to abide by the constitution, not the will of the government and its leaders, including the Prime Minister. Narayan was asking the forces of authority and law and order to join in a coup d'état by paralysing the state and central governments.

Then on 6 March Narayan led a five-mile long march through Delhi to Parliament where he presented a charter of demands to the Speaker of the Lok Sahba. At a rally afterwards, he openly called for Indira's resignation. The vast band of people who followed Narayan through the streets of Old and New Delhi was the largest demonstration the city had ever witnessed and the procession was compared in the press to Gandhi's famous 1930 salt march.

Meanwhile, on 11 March, Indira's old foe, Morarji Desai, now aged seventy-nine, embarked on a Gandhian 'fast unto death' in protest against the government's failure to allow state assembly elections to go ahead in Gujarat. But Desai's underlying motive, as he confessed in an interview with the Italian journalist, Oriana Fallaci, was to start 'the battle [with Indira Gandhi] I had been dreaming of ever since 1969 [the year of the Congress Party split and ascendancy of Indira Gandhi]'.[27] Indira wanted to delay the Gujarat elections until the harvest – which she claimed a poll would disrupt – but Desai, now warmly supported by Narayan, persisted in his fast. For five days he refused all nourishment and Indira did nothing to intervene. But Desai was a frail, old man and Indira finally caved in, dissolved the Gujarat state assembly and agreed to new elections in early June. Her opponents were jubilant.

One hot morning in late April, Padmaja Naidu was found cold and unconscious in her cottage in the grounds of Teen Murti House where she had lived since the early sixties. She had been ill and reclusive for some time, refusing to see anyone or even to answer the telephone. It had been months since Indira had last seen her. Padmaja was taken in a coma to the hospital where she died, with only Indira's assistant Usha Bhagat beside her. Hearing of Padmaja's death, Vijaya Lakshmi Pandit took a taxi all the way from Dehra Dun. Indira was in Jamaica when she got word of Padmaja's death, and she hurriedly made arrangements to return to Delhi in time for the funeral. Padmaja – almost the last link with Nehru and the world of Indira's childhood – was cremated on 4 May 1975 in a 'saffron, red-bordered sari, bedecked with . . . flowers, looking like a grand African queen'.[28]

After Padmaja's death, summer descended on Delhi. The sun burned in a cloudless sky. The days got longer, hotter and dustier. The Lodi Gardens' lush greenery turned ashen-coloured. City streets at noon were all but deserted. But despite the paralysing heat, the usual torpor of the pre-monsoon period did not set in. Instead, the government and Indira moved through the long days of May in a state of expectancy and suppressed anxiety.

Much hung in the balance. In Gujarat, people were about to go to the polls and deliver their verdict on Indira's Congress. That seemed the primary threat. But Indira knew that greater danger actually lay elsewhere, in Uttar Pradesh. She was worried about a situation of which the public at large was barely aware. In March, she had gone to Allahabad and given evidence for five hours as the star witness in the High Court case brought against her by Raj Narain, charging her with electoral malpractice during the 1971 general election. Some time in June the High Court was expected to deliver its decision.

SIXTEEN

Drastic, Emergent Action

POLITICAL LIGHTNING STRUCK THREE TIMES on 12 June 1975. While Indira was still having breakfast on a tray in her room, R.K. Dhawan knocked on the door with news that her adviser and friend, D.P. Dhar, had just died in hospital where he had been admitted to have a pacemaker fitted that day. A heart attack had killed him before the procedure could be done. Dhar was one of the dwindling number of Indira's 'Kashmiri mafia' – the gifted coterie of experts and aides, which had been diminished by Haksar's retirement, and the departure (or banishment) of others. He had been a cabinet minister and at the time of his death was ambassador to the Soviet Union. Indira immediately went to the hospital where Dhar had died to see his bereaved family and help with the funeral arrangements.

By the time Indira returned home to 1 Safdarjung Road, at around noon, the results of the Gujarat state assembly elections, held the previous day, had come in. The Janata Front – a five-party coalition that included the followers of J.P. Narayan and Morarji Desai – had defeated Congress.

The third fork of lightning was the most shattering. At three that afternoon, N.K. Seshan, one of Indira's secretaries, received the news off the ticker tape machine at Safdarjung Road that the Allahabad High Court Justice, Jagmohan Lal Sinha, had ruled that Indira Gandhi was guilty of electoral malpractices during the 1971 general election campaign. Seshan informed Rajiv, who went into Indira's study and told his mother in private. The verdict had invalidated Indira's election as MP for Rae Bareilly and would debar her from holding elective office for six years.

The charges of which Indira had been found guilty were relatively trivial but still illegal. All candidates were prohibited from using 'a government servant for the furtherance of [their] prospects'. The Court found that Indira's former Private Secretary, Yashpal Kapoor, had submitted his government resignation papers on 13 January, but had begun working as Indira's agent on 7 January. The papers themselves were not formally processed and signed by P. N. Haksar (with whom Kapoor did not get on) until 25 January. In addition, Indira had used Uttar Pradesh officials to build rostrums and set up loudspeakers for her rallies in the state. In the 1971 election Raj Narain lost to Indira by a margin of more than 100,000 votes. Kapoor's electioneering and the rostrums and loudspeakers clearly did not contribute to his defeat. Nevertheless, the High Court ruled that the Prime Minister should be unseated and gave the Congress Party twenty days to make 'alternative arrangements' for running the government. As the *Times* in London put it, 'it was like dismissing a prime minister for a traffic offence'. Indira Gandhi had been Prime Minister for nearly a decade and had been active in Indian politics all her life. Now she was being thrown out in the cold.

The judiciary – whose power Indira's government had systematically attempted to undermine – had taken its revenge. Or so it seemed. But like any other citizen, Indira had the right of appeal. An appeal, however, could take months and who would lead the government during this period? 'Indira was India and India Indira,' as the Congress party slogan had it. She had personalized politics to such a degree that it was virtually impossible to imagine another member of Congress – Jagjivan Ram, say, or Swaran Singh or Y. B. Chavan, all of whom were cabinet ministers – leading the country.

For at least a day, no one knew what Indira would do. She herself may not have known. When she saw the Chief Minister of West Bengal, her old friend Siddhartha Shankar Ray, on the afternoon of 12 June, Indira said to him, 'I must resign.' He disagreed and advised her not to decide hastily. A flurry of meetings and discussions followed. Should Indira step down? None of the obvious candidates to take over as Prime Minister urged her to. Her colleagues and supporters beseeched her in one voice to remain in office and fight the decision. Indira listened to their arguments, but kept her own counsel. She discussed the situation with her son Sanjay, but not with other members of her family. In the end, it was agreed that Indira's lawyer, Frank Anthony, would ask the Supreme Court for an unconditional stay against the Allahabad verdict until her appeal was decided. This would enable her to continue as Prime Minister.

In the days following the Allahabad High Court decision, Sanjay and R.K. Dhawan orchestrated a series of pro-Indira demonstrations and marches. Government employees were ordered to attend if they did not want to be marked absent from duty and their pay docked. Between 12 and 25 June, 1,761 Delhi Transport Corporation buses were requisitioned by Congress to transport Indira's supporters to rallies. On 13 June alone, the entire fleet of municipal buses plying the Delhi routes was withdrawn from public use and diverted to converge on the Prime Minister's house. In addition, large numbers of people from Haryana, Punjab, Rajasthan and Uttar Pradesh were bussed into Delhi in vehicles commandeered by the state authorities.[1] Special express trains packed with Indira supporters were sent from Varanasi, Lucknow and Kanpur. These crowds were deposited at scheduled rallies at the Delhi parade grounds or at 'spontaneous' demonstrations at the front of 1 Safdarjung. The crowds were given milk and hot snacks at round-the-clock political *mela*s or festivals. At least once daily, Indira would emerge from the house to address her supporters amidst shouts of *'Indira Zindabad!'* – Long Live Indira!

On 20 June Indira addressed a solidarity rally of around 50,000 people at the Boat Club in New Delhi. Sanjay, Rajiv and Sonia stood on the podium with her. Indira told the vast crowd that service was the Nehru-Gandhi family tradition, and she vowed to continue to serve the people 'till her last breath'. The rally was a huge success and not merely because of Sanjay's 'rent-a-crowd' tactics. Indira still had considerable popular support.

Four days later, on 24 June, Supreme Court Justice Krishna Iyer announced in Delhi that Indira could remain in office but not vote in Parliament until her appeal was settled, which could be many months hence. This would reduce her to the lamest of lame duck Prime Ministers. Iyer's compromise of a conditional stay satisfied no one and sealed the opposition's determination to oust Indira. J.P. Narayan called for a mass rally to be held the next day at New Delhi's vast Ramlila Grounds, to be followed by daily anti-government demonstrations throughout India.

Indira's intelligence advisers warned her that at the rally of 25 June, Narayan intended to call upon the police and army of Delhi to mutiny.

In addition, on the eve of the rally, Morarji Desai told the journalist, Oriana Fallaci, that Indira's opposition planned to stage a *gherao* around 1 Safdarjung Road, reducing Indira to a prisoner in her own house and preventing anyone else from entering it. 'We'll camp there night and day,' Desai boasted. 'We intend to overthrow her, to force her to resign. For good. The lady won't survive this movement of ours.'[2]

Unwittingly, Narayan and Desai had set their own trap. By threatening to reduce the government to chaos and stage a non-military coup, they handed to Indira the justification she required to suspend Parliament and impose a state of emergency. The tactics of the 1942 Quit India movement simply would not work in 1975. Civil disobedience could only succeed under a regime where the people had no vote or voice. India – despite all of Indira's constitutional amendments and ordinances – was still a democracy. If the government was unsatisfactory, then, Indira reasoned, the people could vote it out of power in the upcoming March 1976 election.

On the morning of 25 June, the Chief Minister of West Bengal, Siddhartha Shankar Ray, who happened to be in New Delhi rather than at home in Calcutta, was in bed when the phone rang. It was Indira's secretary R.K. Dhawan summoning Ray to the Prime Minister's house. Ray rushed over to 1 Safdarjung Road and found Indira in her study, sitting at a desk piled high with intelligence reports. For the next two hours they discussed the situation in private. Indira described the chaos she felt was engulfing the country. She told Ray 'we're in serious trouble. Some drastic action is needed. The Gujarat Assembly is dissolved. Bihar is dissolved. There will be no end. Democracy will come to a grinding halt.' Then with great emphasis and far from spontaneously, she repeated, 'Some drastic, *emergent* action is needed.' Ray was struck both by the adjective '*emergent*' and by the fact that grammatically Indira used the passive rather than active voice – she said action *is needed* rather than they must take action.[3]

Indira then read aloud from the intelligence reports on her desk. They outlined the rally to be held that evening at which Narayan would call for the police and army to mutiny. She also told Ray that Indian intelligence had implicated the CIA. She knew she was high up on Richard Nixon's hate list, and she was genuinely afraid that she would be overthrown and destroyed in the same way Chile's CIA-backed General Augusto Pinochet had staged a coup against Salvador Allende in 1973.

Indira felt personally threatened, but even more she believed that if Narayan succeeded in ousting her, it would be a disaster for the country. She was convinced that India would self-destruct if she relinquished power. 'We can't carry on like this,' Indira told Ray. 'When a baby is stillborn, you shake it to make it come to life. India needs to be shaken up.'[4] Later, in an interview, Indira said the country needed 'a shock treatment'. It had to be resuscitated – violently jolted back to life.

The meeting between Indira and Ray continued for some time in this vein. She had summoned Ray because he was a legal expert on the constitution. She did not, however, confer that day with her Minister of Law, H. R. Gokhale. Indira did not want advice; she needed an imprimatur for a course of action that had already been set in motion the previous day by Sanjay Gandhi, Om Mehta, the second-in-command at the Home Ministry, and Sanjay's patron, Bansi Lal, the Chief Minister of Haryana. In fact, before Dhawan even rang Siddhartha Shankar Ray on the morning of 25 June, this trio – with Indira's knowledge – was busy in R. K. Dhawan's office drawing up a preliminary list of people to be arrested and detained. At the top of the list were Narayan and Desai.

Ray was a man of integrity as well as legal acumen, but he had authoritarian leanings. In addition, unlike many of Indira's associates, he had not yet alienated Sanjay. Twelve days earlier, when the Allahabad High Court decision was announced, Ray had urged Indira not to resign. It was unlikely that he would go back on this advice now.

And he did not. But neither did he pick up his cue immediately. When Indira asked 'What shall we do?' Ray said he must go and study the constitutional position. Indira agreed but asked him to come back 'as soon as possible'. Ray left and spent several hours examining the text of not only the Indian but also the American constitution. He reported back to 1 Safdarjung Road at 3.30 in the afternoon, and explained to Indira that under Article 352 of the Indian constitution the government could impose a state of emergency in the face of, or in anticipation of, external aggression or internal disturbance. Ray drew a careful distinction between an external and internal threat and maintained that the emergency declared in 1971, at the time of the war with Pakistan over Bangladesh – which was still in effect – was 'an external emergency' and was inadequate in the present crisis.

Article 352 of the Indian constitution states that the President of India is empowered to declare a national emergency if the country is threatened 'by war or external aggression or by armed rebellion'. War was obviously an external threat while 'armed rebellion' Ray interpreted as an internal menace to the state. Hence the importance to him, and to Indira, of Narayan's call for the police and army not to obey orders which they considered an *incitement* to 'armed rebellion'. Indira listened attentively as Ray explained the difference between an external and internal emergency. Then she told Ray that she did not want to discuss the Emergency with the Cabinet until *after* it had been imposed. Now that she had made up her mind to introduce the Emergency, Indira did not want any objections raised to it. Ray had already considered this angle, and he told her they could tell the President, Fakhruddin Ali Ahmed, that there was insufficient time to call a cabinet meeting. He also proffered the legalistic explanation that not all presidential proclamations needed to be formulated with the prior knowledge of the Cabinet. Ray told Indira that the President could impose an internal emergency, which the Cabinet could then endorse retroactively.

Indira then asked Ray 'to go to the President'. Ray protested that he was the Chief Minister of West Bengal, not the Prime Minister, but he agreed to accompany Indira to see the President.

They went to the President's residence, Rashtrapati Bhawan, at 5.30 p.m. President Ahmed proved himself the loyal servant Indira had counted on him to be when she pushed for his appointment the previous year. Nevertheless, Indira and Ray spent some time describing the necessity for imposing a state of emergency given the 'near anarchy' they claimed the country was in. Ray then explained the legal position and Article 352. Ahmed asked whether Indira had consulted the Cabinet and she said the matter was too urgent, and that the Cabinet could approve the Emergency retrospectively. After several other questions, the President told her to 'send the Emergency order'.

Indira and Ray drove back to 1 Safdarjung Road as night was falling. On the way they passed a group of schoolgirls who waved enthusiastically at the Prime Minister and she waved back, commenting to Ray, 'I still have that constituency.' She spoke emotionally, as if the children's safety lay in her hands.[4] Back at home P. N. Dhar was briefed by Ray. Dhar then dictated to a typist an 'Emergency Order Proclamation' to send to the President for him to sign. He also dictated an accompanying letter from Indira to the President.

As soon as these documents were ready, they were entrusted to R.K. Dhawan who set off with them to Rashtrapati Bhawan. Indira gave instructions that all cabinet ministers should be telephoned at five the next morning and told that a Cabinet meeting would be held promptly an hour later. In her letter to the President, Indira had said that the security situation 'was extremely urgent', and therefore the Emergency should be imposed immediately. She went on to explain, 'I would have liked to have taken this to the Cabinet, but unfortunately this is not possible tonight . . . I shall mention the matter to the Cabinet first thing tomorrow morning.'[5] Later, Indira gave 'the maintenance of law and order' as her rationale for not consulting the Cabinet. She said that she had to act secretly in order to prevent information of the state of emergency being leaked. She wanted to take the opposition by surprise and arrest its leaders before morning.

Dhawan returned from the President's residence. Midnight came and went, but Siddhartha Shankar Ray stayed on at 1 Safdarjung Road for several more hours, helping Indira draft the speech she would broadcast to the nation the next morning after the Cabinet meeting. While they worked together at her desk, Sanjay Gandhi kept popping in and out of the room. Sanjay also called Indira out several times and she left at his behest for periods of ten or fifteen minutes.

In R.K. Dhawan's office Sanjay and Om Mehta were finalizing the list of the opposition members to be arrested and they needed Indira's authorization. By this time, Bansi Lal had returned to Haryana but he was in constant contact with Sanjay by phone regarding the list of detainees. These arrests – to be carried out under the provisions of the Maintenance of Internal Security Act (MISA) – had been in the offing even before the Emergency was discussed. Sanjay had apparently broached the subject shortly after the 12 June Allahabad High Court decision went against Indira, when the opposition began demanding that she step down. Preventive detention, of course, had been a widely used tactic under British rule, which had left it as a legacy to independent India. But Indira had significantly enhanced detention powers through MISA and the related Defence of India legislation, enacted during the 1971 war with Pakistan.

The cabal in Dhawan's office was also making plans for massive censorship of the media beginning with cutting the electricity supplies to the Delhi newspapers so that papers would not appear the next morning. Indira endorsed censorship while letting Sanjay and Dhawan work out the mechanics of imposing it.

When Indira and Ray had finished drafting her speech, she retired. By now it was 3 a.m., but Ray stayed on and chatted with the other key players still in the house, including the Home Minister, Brahmananda Reddy, and Kishan Chand, the Lieutenant Governor of Delhi. Ray had already told Indira that she must also inform the Congress President, Dev Kanta Barooah, and R. K. Dhawan rang Barooah. No one questioned the course of action now set in motion, though Reddy at one point said to Siddhartha Shankar Ray 'but we already have an emergency'. Ray explained that the external emergency in effect was inadequate for the current situation and the need to contain it.

After discussing the situation with Reddy, Ray finally rose to leave, but on the way out he ran into Om Mehta who told him that the electricity to the city's newspapers was going to be cut and all the law courts locked up. Ray protested to Mehta that 'this is absurd. This is not what we discussed. This is not on.' He turned around and went back and told R.K. Dhawan that he wanted to see Indira. Dhawan said the Prime Minister had gone to bed. Ray insisted, 'I want to see Indiraji. I must see her.'

Reluctantly, Dhawan left. He returned soon with Indira. According to Ray, she was shocked by what he told her about the plans to cut the electricity and shut the courts. Indira instructed Ray to wait and hurried out of the room. She was gone for fifteen or twenty minutes. Meanwhile, in Dhawan's office, Sanjay rang Bansi Lal in Haryana and told him that Ray was causing trouble over the electricity cut. Bansi Lal's response was, 'Throw him out, he is spoiling the game . . . He thinks too much of himself as a lawyer although he knows next to nothing.'[6]

While Ray was waiting for Indira to come back, Om Mehta explained to him that though Indira supported censorship, she had not been aware of the orders to cut the electricity and close the courts. These had come from Sanjay. When Indira finally returned to Ray, her eyes were red and she had obviously been crying. She said, 'Siddhartha, it's alright; there will be electricity and no courts will be closed.' Ray took her at her word and finally departed for home – falsely reassured.[7]

*   *   *

By the time Indira finally retired to bed in the early hours of 26 June, police in Delhi and elsewhere in India were already out in force, waking people up and carting them off to jail. At the top of the list of the thousands arrested were Narayan and Desai. So was Raj Narain, the original source of all Indira's woes. At the same time, just as the Delhi-based newspaper presses were about to roll, electricity supplies suddenly stopped. Of the dozen or so daily papers, only the *Statesman* and the *Hindustan Times* (whose electricity was supplied by the New Delhi rather than Delhi municipality) were on sale in the capital the next day to report the imposition of the Emergency and the arrests made in its name.

Indira got little if any sleep that night, but she looked neither tired nor haggard the next morning when she met with her Cabinet at six. Because of the unusually early hour, the meeting was held at her office at 1 Akbar Road, next door to her house, rather than in her South Bank office. Eight cabinet ministers (the other nine were not in Delhi) and five ministers of state attended. As they filed into the room, they were each given a copy of the Emergency Proclamation Order and a list of the prominent members of the opposition who had been arrested. The ministers seated themselves, as usual, in alphabetical order at the round cabinet table. This meant that Karan Singh, the Minister of Health and Family Planning, was directly opposite Indira. Her Principal Secretary P.N. Dhar sat next to her. Sanjay, contrary to later rumours, was not present at this or any other cabinet meeting.

Indira opened with an abrupt announcement of the Emergency and then went on to explain why conditions in the country had necessitated this 'drastic' action. The news of the Emergency had not been leaked and most of those present were dumbstruck, both by the fact of the Emergency and the long list of detainees. The atmosphere was strained and Indira was tense and taciturn. Cabinet meetings had long since ceased to be a forum of policy-making or debate, but the one held shortly after dawn on 26 June 1975 was particularly fraught. The only person to ask a question was the Defence Minister, Swaran Singh, who said 'under what law were the arrests made?'[8] Indira gave him a brief, barely audible, response.

Though the cabinet meeting had ostensibly been called to approve the Emergency, no vote was taken. This, however, was not unusual. Votes were not taken in cabinet meetings because that would make it possible for the Prime Minister to be overruled by her ministers. Instead, a 'consensus' was reached and the Emergency Proclamation 'approved'. No discussion, however nominal and perfunctory, preceded this approval. Not only did 'no one say no' to the Emergency, as P. N. Dhar later put it, there was no real discussion of why this extreme measure had been taken in the dead of night. The cabinet meeting to ratify the Emergency was over in less than half an hour.[9]

Immediately after it was adjourned, I. K. Gujral, the Minister of Information and Broadcasting, was accosted by Sanjay Gandhi in the reception room outside Indira's office. Sanjay ordered Gujral from now on to submit all news bulletins to him before they were broadcast. Gujral told Sanjay that this was 'not possible'. Indira was standing in the doorway and heard the exchange between Sanjay and Gujral but said nothing. Later in the morning, when Indira was not present, Sanjay accused Gujral to his face of not running his ministry properly. As Gujral described his response, he 'took exception to [Sanjay's] . . . remarks'. In fact, Gujral told Sanjay that if he had something to say to him he had better be 'civil and polite', and added that his own 'association with the Prime Minister and the Congress had started before [Sanjay] . . . was born', and that Sanjay 'had no business to interfere in the work of my ministry'.[10]

The following day Indira's old friend Mohammed Yunus rang Gujral from Indira's Akbar Road office and told him to close down the BBC office in Delhi and arrest its correspondent Mark Tully because the BBC had broadcast news that Jagjivan Ram and Swaran Singh had been placed under house arrest. Yunus ordered Gujral to 'send for Mark Tully, pull down his trousers, give him a few lashes and send him to jail'. Gujral told Yunus that arresting foreign correspondents was not 'the function of the Ministry of Information and Broadcasting'. When he got off the phone, Gujral sent for the monitoring report of the BBC and learned that it had not, in fact, broadcast that Ram or Singh were under house arrest. He communicated this information to Indira but that same evening she nevertheless sent for Gujral and informed him that she was relieving him of his portfolio because the Information Ministry needed 'a different and firmer handling in the circumstances'.[11]

On the morning of 26 June, Indira broadcast to the nation on All India Radio. She opened by saying, 'The President has proclaimed an

Emergency. This is nothing to panic about.' She then went on to speak of the 'deep and widespread conspiracy' that had 'been brewing ever since I began to introduce certain progressive measures of benefit to the common man and woman of India'. The Emergency was necessary to re-establish stability, peace and order and to safeguard democracy and national unity. She explained that certain 'precautionary arrests' had been made, but quickly went on to reassure her listeners that those detained were 'being extended all courtesy and consideration'. The press regrettably had to be restrained because it had been guilty of 'irresponsible writing' in a situation of grave disturbance. 'The purpose of censorship,' Indira told her countrymen, 'is to restore a climate of trust.'[12]

Contrary to her usual practice of reworking a text supplied by her principal speechwriter, Sharada Prasad, Indira drafted the speech announcing the Emergency herself (but with the help of Siddhartha Shankar Ray) the night before. However Prasad and P. N. Dhar revised the announcement before Indira went on the air. They added, in particular, the closing statement, 'I am sure that internal conditions will speedily improve to enable us to dispense with this proclamation [the Emergency] as soon as possible.'[13]

In her radio speech, at press conferences, in interviews and during a lengthy debate in Parliament, Indira insisted again and again that the government was being assailed and threatened and that she had no option but to declare a state of emergency. On the evening of 27 June, two days after it was imposed, Indira broadcast to the nation again and explained how

> a climate of violence and hatred had been created . . . The Opposition parties had chalked out a programme of countrywide *gheraos*, agitation, disruption and incitement to industrial workers, police and defence forces in an attempt to paralyse totally the Central Government. One of them [J P Narayan] went to the extent of saying that armed forces should not carry out orders . . . This programme was to begin from the 29th of this month. We had no doubt that such a programme would have resulted in a grave threat to public order and damage to the economy beyond repair. This had to be prevented.[14]

Indira claimed that she had been besieged on all sides. The right, the left, Hindu extremists, Naxalite terrorists and a myriad of other 'elements' were all hellbent on destroying the law of the land. The enemy was diverse, but it was led by the 'fascist' JP movement, backed, Indira maintained, by 'a foreign hand'. She paradoxically argued that the only way to safeguard and preserve Indian democracy was through the Emergency's suspension of democratic institutions, procedures and norms. The Emergency was an extreme remedy – an authoritarian vaccine to protect the country against a virulent anti-democratic virus.

What Indira did not publicly acknowledge was that she also had serious 'enemies within' – the dissidents in her own Congress Party. At least fifty Congress members on the left had defected to J.P. Narayan and his movement, and on the right, another sixty or seventy, who deplored her socialist stance, wanted to replace Indira with Jagjivan Ram, a Harijan and the Minister of Irrigation and Agriculture. Indira's hold on Congress, in fact, had not been so weak since she caused its split in 1969.

The voices that could have protested against the Emergency had mostly been stifled. Opposition leaders and Indira's foes were either in jail or under house arrest. Men of integrity such as I.K. Gujral – who had stood up to Sanjay Gandhi – did not publicly speak out against the Emergency, probably because they realized the futility of doing so. For a while, at least, these silent dissenters thought they might be able to manoeuvre against the Emergency from within. Meanwhile, newspapers were censored. Twenty-six anti-Congress – or more accurately anti-Indira – political organizations were banned, including the Hindu extremist RSS on the right and the Communist Party Marxist and the underground Naxalite Marxist-Leninist branch of the Communist Party on the left. (The CPI or Communist Party of India, which had strong links with Moscow, warmly endorsed the Emergency.)

In the coming days, the public's experience of the Emergency was that daily life seemed less erratic and stressful. Suddenly there were no strikes, no protest marches and no street skirmishes with police. Prices fell and shortages of essential commodities diminished. The throngs of beggars on the streets of Delhi disappeared. So did most of the stray cows. No one seemed to worry about where the beggars and cows had gone. Government officials, civil servants and clerks turned up at work punctually and remained there until closing time. Taxis and auto-rickshaws drove on the correct side of the road. People queued for buses. Trains ran on time.

In the early months, at least, the Emergency was widely popular. Indira had restored peace and order to the land. Hoardings displaying her gigantic image sprouted again on city roundabouts with slogans such as 'The Leader's right, the Future's bright', and 'She stands between Chaos and Order'. Billboards proliferated, emblazoned with the Prime Minister's inspirational words – homilies such as 'Discipline is the watchword of the hour' and exhortations such as 'Don't indulge in rumour and loose talks [sic]'. The windows of buses and shops were adorned with bromides: 'The only magic to remove poverty – hard work, clear vision, iron will, strict discipline.'

Although intellectuals at home and abroad denounced the Emergency, outwardly at least it seemed to be a success. A front-page story in the *New York Times*, headlined 'Authoritarian Rule Gains Wide Acceptance in India' went on to describe the country as 'almost completely at peace'. The artist M. F. Husain celebrated the new order by painting a huge triptych of Indira as the goddess Durga, triumphantly riding a tiger after conquering her foes.

A number of intelligent people of good will, including Indira's cousin, B.K. Nehru (now Indian High Commissioner in London), Michael Foot – Secretary of State for Employment in the Callaghan Labour government, and his Labour colleague Jennie Lee, all warmly supported the Emergency. B.K. Nehru later stated that it had been his 'duty' to defend it. But he did not find this a burden because he 'wholeheartedly approved of it'. B.K, in fact, urged Indira to use the 'breathing space' of the Emergency to change the constitution from a parliamentary to a presidential form of democracy so that more power would be concentrated with the Executive. It was widely rumoured at the time that this is precisely what Indira had in mind. But according to B.K. Nehru, she actually vetoed the proposal saying 'she did not approve . . . without really giving me any cogent reason for her disapproval'. Others that Nehru spoke to, however, were enthusiastic, including Jagjivan Ram, Swaran Singh and Y. B. Chavan. Bansi Lal went even further and said to Nehru, 'Nehru saheb, get rid of all this election nonsense. If you ask me, just make our sister President for life and there's no need to do anything else.'[15]

Indira was eager to secure international approval for the Emergency so she invited a number of foreign politicians and journalists to come to India and see it in action. The British journalist John Grigg, among others, turned her down.[16] The British Conservative Party leader, Margaret Thatcher, however, accepted and made her first trip to India in September 1976. This was also the first encounter between Indira Gandhi and Margaret Thatcher, and these two notoriously 'difficult' women hit it off from the start. As Thatcher's biographer, Hugo Young, put it, Indira 'was one of the few women by whom [Mrs Thatcher] has ever allowed herself to be impressed'. They had 'from the beginning a uniquely easy relationship, based not on ideological sympathy' – though Mrs Thatcher voiced no qualms about the Emergency – 'so much as on the shared experience of being a woman leader'. Indira and Margaret Thatcher were aberrations in the predominantly male world of politics. Although they both repudiated feminism, their loneliness as women leaders led them to form a bond that would endure until Indira's death.[17]

Another prominent visitor during the Emergency was Michael Foot who was destined to become Mrs Thatcher's opponent as leader of the Labour Party. During his visit Foot was not as uncritical as Mrs Thatcher had been. He was concerned about the plight of the socialist leader George Fernandes (who had recently been jailed by Indira) and asked Indira 'when will democracy be restored?' She assured him that she would hold elections as soon as the country had stabilized and confided, as she had to Siddhartha Shankar Ray earlier, that she did not 'want to suffer the fate of [Salvador] Allende'.

Foot's impression at the time was that, despite heightened fears of a coup or an assassination attempt, Indira seemed remarkably cavalier about her own security. To the dismay of her bodyguards, she would habitually plunge into crowds. She was determined to remain close to the masses and 'would allow nothing to sever that connection'. Despite some misgivings, when Foot returned to England, he publicly defended Indira and the Emergency. He also wrote a report on his visit which he circulated to the Cabinet in which he urged the British government to have 'an imaginative understanding of what has been achieved during the Emergency and why these achievements invoke so much popular support [in India]'.[18]

Few people who knew Indira challenged or criticized the Emergency to her face. Two who did were Fori Nehru, who did not share her husband B.K.'s views, and Indira's friend Pupul Jayakar. Jayakar had been in New York staying with Indira's American friend, Dorothy Norman when she heard about the imposition of the Emergency. Both women were appalled at the news. Dorothy Norman, in fact, along with the New York based writer Ved Mehta, drew up a petition denouncing the Emergency which was signed by over eighty prominent Americans including Noam Chomsky, Arthur Ashe, Allen Ginsberg, Lewis Mumford, Linus Pauling, Benjamin Spock and John Updike. The petition was then released to the press and the media. Dorothy also felt compelled to write directly to Indira, but in reply she merely received a gift accompanied by a short note saying, 'If you can bear to accept a gift from the "Great Dictator", here is something . . . for you . . . from Bhutan.'[19] Four years would pass before Indira and Norman made contact again.

Jayakar, in contrast, remained close to Indira throughout the Emergency. She confronted her when she returned from the States in July 1975: 'How can you, the daughter of Jawaharlal Nehru, permit this?' Jayakar asked. Indira was 'taken aback' and shocked. No one else had dared to challenge her openly. The degree of Indira's suspicion – grown now to something close to paranoia – was obvious in her defence to Jayakar. 'You do not know the gravity of what was happening. You do not know the plots against me. Jayaprakash and Morarjibhai have always hated me. They were determined to see that I was destroyed . . . Jayaprakash's wife Prabha was very close to my mother but with her death relationships have altered. Jayaprakash has always resented my being Prime Minister . . . He has never discovered his true role. Does he want to be a saint or a martyr? Why does he refuse to accept that he has never ceased to be a politician and desires to be the Prime Minister?'[20]

It was during this tense conversation that Jayakar first noticed that Indira had developed a pronounced tic in her right eye – a quirk that remained with her from this time and was particularly noticeable when she was under stress. Jayakar realized also that there was no point trying to persuade Indira that she was in the wrong. She decided that all she could do was listen for the time being so that Indira would feel free to speak to her without 'the wariness which by now had become her habitual response'.[21]

Less than a month after the Emergency was imposed, Parliament was convened. On 21 July, both houses endorsed the Emergency by a large majority – 336 votes to 39 in the Lok Sabha, and 136 to 33 in the Rajya Sabha. Dissent in Parliament was curbed by a resolution suspending the daily question hour. Only 'urgent and important government business' was now to be transacted on the floor.

Foremost among the 'urgent and important government business' was a series of bills introduced to amend the constitution. The primary purpose of these amendments was to make the Emergency and Indira invulnerable to the judiciary. On 1 August, the thirty-eighth amendment was passed which safeguarded the declaration of an internal emergency, President's rule in the states and the promulgation of ordinances to put them beyond the reach of the courts. Indira also strengthened her new regime by eliminating the remaining opposition in the states. She used the President's rule to dismiss the non-Congress government that had just come to power in Gujarat, and did the same in Tamil Nadu, which had been under the regional DMK Party.

The thirty-ninth amendment, which swiftly followed, invalidated the Allahabad High Court judgement against Indira and for extra measure retroactively nullified the specific 'corrupt practices' in the election law of which she had been found guilty. Subsequent amendments prevented judicial review of election results involving the Prime Minister, and granted the Prime Minister immunity from criminal and civil proceedings for offences committed before and during his or her term of office. All these were quickly passed in Parliament where Congress still held a two-thirds majority.

Overshadowing them all, however, was the gargantuan, fifty-nine-clause forty-second amendment enacted in November 1976. Its most crucial point was that it gave Parliament the power to amend the previously unamendable basic structure of the constitution, thus undermining, in the words of one analyst, 'the very foundations of the political order established at independence'.[22] Parliament was now authorized to change any feature of the government. The 'fundamental rights' provision of the constitution was subordinated to 'the Directive Principles of State Policy'. Other clauses of the forty-second amendment consolidated the supreme power of the Executive. It could now prevent or prohibit 'anti-national' activities even if doing so infringed on the fundamental rights of political freedom and equality under the law. The forty-second amendment also extended the terms of the Lok Sabha and state assemblies from five to six years, made it mandatory for the President to act only on the advice of the Cabinet and empowered the central government – in the event of a breakdown of law and order in a state – to send in armed forces without consulting state governments.

The forty-second amendment was justified on the grounds that it secured 'the welfare of the people' and 'to usher in a new social revolution'. But this ladder of consitutional amendments served only to strengthen the centre's coercive powers and provide a 'legal rationale for depriving dissidents of their political rights'.[23]

After the amendments were passed, the Emergency was further consolidated by a series of ordinances or 'extraordinary laws'. These were measures issued in the name of the President to be endorsed by Parliament within a narrow time frame. During the Emergency, although much of the opposition was in jail, Indira increasingly resorted to ordinances to shortcut parliamentary delays. She would wait for Parliament to recess and then instruct the President to act. In the year before the Emergency, he issued fourteen ordinances. In the six months after the Emergency began in June 1975, he promulgated no less than twenty-five. These included stringent censorship measures, and one repealed the 1956 law – introduced by Feroze Gandhi – that gave immunity to journalists reporting on parliamentary debates.

Censorship was, in fact, a key feature of the Emergency. The Press Council – an independent body – was abolished. The government banned 'publication of objectionable matter' and issued strict press guidelines that only 'positive' information and news should be stressed. The government now controlled the media. Many of the major newspaper owners were wealthy industrialists who needed government licences and permits to operate, and so they quickly fell into line. The government also 'restructured' the four national news agencies into one public sector corporation. Called Samachar, this became a propaganda machine similar to Tass in the Soviet Union. Independent news magazines such as Nikhil Chakravartty's *Mainstream* and Romesh Thapar's monthly *Seminar* ceased publication rather than submit to censorship. During the course of the Emergency, 253 Indian journalists were jailed, including one of Indira's most forthright critics, Kuldip Nayar.

In addition more than forty foreign correspondents were asked to leave India, their accreditation withdrawn on the flimsiest of pretexts. Among those forced out were British and American journalists – from the *Guardian, Baltimore Sun* and *Washington Post* – and also Mark Tully of the BBC, who had been covering India for years.

On the surface many people felt better off and their lives seemed to run more smoothly under the Emergency. But they had lost significant constitutional freedoms, including freedom of speech and assembly and the right of *habeas corpus*. In addition, the Maintenance of Internal Security Act and the Prevention of Smuggling Activities Act were strengthened so that people could be arrested and detained for two years without recourse to a court of law or without their being told the grounds on which they were being held. For a time, however, these retrograde measures were eclipsed by the government's propaganda acclaiming the progressive gains brought about by the Emergency. Black marketeers, smugglers and tax evaders were hunted down; landlords' and money-lenders' powers were drastically curbed; bonded peasants were released; the poor were given employment on public projects; inflation fell from 30 to 10 per cent in less than a year.

Then, in August 1975, just as everything seemed to be moving forward unhindered, the Bangladeshi leader, Sheikh Mujibur Rahman, was toppled in a coup in Dhaka. Indira, of course, had been the architect of the creation of Bangladesh and Sheikh Mujib's release from a Pakistani prison to become its first Prime Minister. The two leaders were not only allies but also close friends.

But in the three-and-a-half years since the birth of Bangladesh, Mujib had systematically undermined the four declared principles of 'Mujibism' – nationalism, secularism, democracy and socialism. In December 1974 he set an example for Indira when he assumed emergency powers and suspended civil liberties. He went on to amend Bangladesh's constitution and inaugurate a presidential system under which he became President. In June 1975 – at approximately the same time as Indira cracked down with her own emergency – Mujib turned Bangladesh into a one-party state which gave him virtually absolute power. Not only was democracy eroded in Bangladesh; Mujib's regime was riddled with corruption and notorious for nepotism as he appointed members of his large extended family to powerful positions from which they derived enormous financial benefits.

On 14 August – the eve of the anniversary of India's independence – junior army officers arrived in tanks at Mujib's house and quickly surrounded it. The leader of the coup, a man called Major Huda, presented the President with a resignation document to sign. Mujib angrily refused. One of Mujib's sons entered the room with a pistol, then another son burst in shouting for help from Mujib's personal guard.

Major Huda aimed his Sten gun at Mujib and his sons and shot all three of them. The soldiers then searched the house and systematically killed Mujib's wife, his ten-year-old son, Mujib's two daughters-in-law, his brother, and two servants. The entire clan was wiped out with the exception of Mujib's twenty-eight-year-old daughter, Sheikh Hasina, who was not at home and would survive to become Prime Minister of Bangladesh twenty-one years later.

Indira was devastated by the news of the assassination of Mujib and his family. And for once her belief that the CIA was implicated in their deaths was probably correct. But she failed to grasp the logic of Mujib's end and why it had come about. Instead, she interpreted his assassination as an omen of what could happen to her and her own family. She was haunted, above all, by the murder of Mujib's wife and young son. This seems to have been the first time that it occurred to Indira that her position as Prime Minister made a target not only of herself, but also of her sons, daughters-in-law and grandchildren. Instinctively, she now took action to protect herself, her family and position by intensifying intelligence activity and detentions without trial.

Indira's fears also affected the household arrangements at 1 Safdarjung Road. Sanjay left the bedroom he shared with his wife, Maneka, and installed himself just down the corridor from Indira's room. They kept their doors ajar at night. Indira confided the new sleeping arrangements to the chief of the Research and Intelligence Wing, a man she trusted named R.N. Kao, who regularly reported various plots against her. Indira still felt perfectly secure out in public, in the midst of crowds – with whom she freely mixed. But in her own heavily guarded house, she felt endangered. Instinctively, she turned to her son for protection when, in fact, he was the very person who was, in many ways, her greatest threat.

SEVENTEEN

The Rising Son

FROM THE START the Emergency was touted as a programme of national regeneration. Not only would democracy be saved, India would be reborn. To achieve this Indira announced a twenty-point economic plan that included initiatives making bonded labour illegal, cancelling all debts owed by the rural poor to moneylenders, limiting land ownership among the wealthy, cracking down on smugglers and tax evaders, providing income tax relief to the middle classes and controlling the price of essential commodities. All these measures looked good on paper. But the programme's 'assault on poverty' – especially among the rural poor – could not succeed on a wide scale because states now lacked the administrative machinery and infrastructure to implement reform.

Real gains were achieved, however, in the campaigns against income tax evasion and smuggling. After a voluntary disclosure scheme was introduced, 250,000 people came forward and reported their wealth and income yielding revenue of 249 rupees *crores*. During the first year of the Emergency the amount collected by taxation increased by 27 per cent. More than 2,000 smugglers were jailed and over 60,000 raids on black marketeers resulted in the seizure of goods worth tens of *crores* of rupees. The difference between the official and black market exchange rates diminished. Prices stabilized and shortages of essential commodities eased.[1]

But it was Sanjay's five-point plan – rather than Indira's complex twenty-point programme – that captured the public imagination. Sanjay was still running his car company, Maruti, but during the past several years he had begun to interfere in politics. Various politicians had contributed to Maruti as a way of gaining favour with Indira, and contact with these benefactors had whetted Sanjay's appetite for political power.

Although Sanjay had entered politics by the back door – without authority, experience, or an electoral mandate – no one questioned the propriety of his formulating government policy as he vigorously promulgated his five-point plan. The government spent more than 800,000 rupees publicizing it, and it caught on like wildfire.

Sanjay's five aims were to increase adult literacy (pushed with the slogan 'each one teach one'), abolish bride dowry, end the caste system, 'beautify' the environment (which included slum clearance and tree planting) and finally – and most controversially – to initiate a radical programme of family planning. Most of these were valid enough goals. But the five-point plan, like the Emergency itself, became more a vehicle for Sanjay Gandhi's personal aggrandizement than for social improvement in India.

From its declaration the Emergency gave Sanjay Gandhi open sesame to power and money. And he used it to settle old scores. P. N. Haksar – who had tried to persuade Indira to curb Sanjay's power – became one of his first targets. Sanjay could not touch Haksar himself, but Haksar's family owned a large store in Connaught Place in Delhi called Pandit Brothers that sold fabrics, handloom furnishings and household linen. The firm's directors were Haksar's eighty-four-year-old uncle R. N. Haksar and his seventy-five-year-old brother-in-law, K. P. Mushran.

On 10 July Pandit Brothers was raided on grounds of tax evasion. The order for the raid originated with Sanjay Gandhi and was passed down the line of command from R.K. Dhawan to the Lieutenant Governor of Delhi's office. But after searching the premises for more than two hours, the tax inspectors were unable to produce any incriminating evidence. Unhappy with this outcome, Sanjay accused the inspectors of colluding with the Pandit Brothers. On 14 July a second raid was carried out in the name of the Delhi Essential Articles Rules, legislation that required all items for sale in stores to be clearly priced. In the course of this second 'price tag raid' goods were found that did not have their price clearly marked and R. N. Haksar and K. P. Mushran were arrested. When Indira found out about this from her old friend Aruna Asaf Ali, she intervened to have Haksar's elderly uncle and brother-in-law released immediately.[2]

Many people believed that it had been Sanjay who had first proposed the idea of a national emergency after the Allahabad High Court announced its decision against Indira. But it is more likely that the option was mooted by an adviser – such as Bansi Lal, the Chief Minister of Haryana – and then seized upon and pushed by Sanjay, who in turn persuaded his mother to summon Siddhartha Shankar Ray and insist on the need for 'some drastic, emergent action'. Even if the idea of the Emergency did not originate with Sanjay, he was its most vehement proponent. His power grew in tandem with it and over the next eighteen months India would become the 'land of the Rising Son'.

Though most of Sanjay's energies were now channelled into political activities, his company Maruti still existed, at least in name. The 'people's car' remained moribund but Maruti had diversified with the creation of Maruti Technical Services (MTS), a private consultancy firm which ostensibly existed to 'supply . . . expertise for [the] design, manufacture and assembly of cars'.

Initially Indira knew nothing about MTS; nor did Rajiv Gandhi, now a pilot with Indian Airlines. Whilst Rajiv was out of Delhi, Sanjay persuaded his wife, Sonia, to sign several documents relating to the new company, appointing her its managing director and her toddler son and infant daughter shareholders. This entitled Sonia – who of course possessed no managerial or motor industry experience – to a monthly salary of 2,500 rupees, 1 per cent commission on net profits, bonuses, gratuities, medical insurance, travel expenses, a house allowance, a telephone, car and driver. Sonia apparently failed to grasp the significance of what her brother-in-law had asked her to sign. When Rajiv discovered that his brother had embroiled his family in MTS he, reportedly, was furious. He complained to Siddhartha Shankar Ray about it but he did not ask his wife to disengage herself from the new company.[3]

MTS was a front. According to Sanjay's biographer, Vinod Mehta, 'there was hardly any consultancy rendered [and] . . . hardly any company to render it'.[4] MTS's only purpose was to milk its parent company, the larger and financially stronger Maruti Limited, into which various banks and industrialists beholden to Indira and Sanjay were pouring money. By June 1975 MTS had extracted 10 rupee *lakhs* from Maruti Limited and Sanjay was spurred to set up another company – Maruti Heavy Vehicles (MHV), 'a small-scale enterprise' to produce roadrollers, which paid 2 per cent of its net sales to MTS for 'consultancy services'. Like MTS, Maruti Heavy Vehicles was a dubious operation. Sanjay purchased Ford engines from companies which had import licences (and whose directors generously contributed to Congress Party coffers), put them into old, scrap roadrollers, gave them a lick of paint and sold them as new rollers. Compliant state governments and corporations snapped them up despite their exorbitant price tag.

During 1976 Maruti enterprises, and Sanjay's personal wealth, mushroomed. Maruti became involved in banking, civil, criminal and company law, import licensing, marketing, producing bus bodies and selling chemicals and, of course, through Maruti's benefactors, politics. Maruti also became the agent for various foreign multinationals including International Harvester and Piper Aircraft.

On 6 August 1975 Uma Vasudev, who had published a biography of Indira two years earlier and also interviewed Sanjay about Maruti, interviewed him again for her magazine *Surge*. Vasudev tape-recorded the interview. The huge-reeled machine, which whirred noisily as they talked, should have put the normally cautious Sanjay on his guard. Instead, he was remarkably indiscreet, exposing himself as hostile to many of his mother's policies and most of her political allies. He denounced nationalization, praised big business and multinational corporations and said he favoured removing all economic controls. The public sector, he said, should be allowed to die 'a natural death'. Of the Communist Party of India (CPI) – which had given the government crucial support during the early months of the Emergency – Sanjay said 'I don't think you'd find a richer or more corrupt people anywhere.'[5]

During the interview Vasudev could barely contain her excitement. Sanjay was spilling, as she later put it, 'explosive material'. Before publishing it, she gave out the interview to Reuters and several other news agencies. Sanjay himself saw that the censors passed it on 27 August.

Indira did not see the interview – or even know that Sanjay had given it – until the following day when lengthy extracts were splashed across the front pages of the Indian newspapers. It was also covered by ninety American newspapers and the British press. Indira was furious and summoned her Principal Secretary, P. N. Dhar. Dhar happened to be at a family gathering on the other side of Delhi and it took him nearly an hour to get to 1 Safdarjung Road. When he arrived, even though they were to have a lengthy conversation about Sanjay's interview, Indira gave him a handwritten note which she had scribbled while waiting for him:

> Troubles never cease. Sanjay has made an exceedingly stupid statement about the Communists. I knew nothing about the interview until I saw the papers and even then I did not read it. It is only this evening that the headlines in the Evening News struck me like a sledgehammer. At a most crucial and delicate time, we have not only grievously hurt those [the CPI] who have helped us and are now supporting us within the country, [but also] created serious problems with the entire Socialist Bloc. It is already so late, but Dhawan is trying his best to prevent any further printing. But what has already been printed cannot be taken back. What are we to do? I am terribly worried – it is the first time in years that I am really upset. How do we inform the USSR and others? . . . What excuse do we find or concoct? Should I issue a statement? Should we get Sanjay to say something – he will not, I am sure (though I have not spoken to him). I do not wish to put the blame on the interviewer or anyone else. I'm quite frantic. Can you think up something? There is absolutely no time to lose.[6]

Dhar spent more than an hour discussing with Indira what they could do in the way of damage control. The obvious person for them to turn to was the new Minister of Information and Broadcasting, V.C. Shukla. But Shukla now took his orders from Sanjay and both Dhar and Indira knew they could not trust him. In the end it was decided that Dhar would have the interview withdrawn from *Surge* and other papers and magazines where it had not yet appeared in print, and that Sanjay would be persuaded to publish a 'clarification' of his statements regarding the CPI.

Privately Dhar was appalled by the interview – not just for what it revealed about Sanjay, but because the present situation exposed how little control Indira had over her son. Dhar already knew that Sanjay was a great liability – that he modelled himself on President Ferdinand Marcos, whose *The Democratic Revolution in the Philippines* was one of the few books Sanjay owned; that Sanjay made irreverent comments about his grandfather and described his mother's cabinet ministers as a bunch of 'ignorant buffoons'. While Dhar and Indira sought to calm the storm of controversy Sanjay's interview had unleashed, the offices of *Surge* were besieged with phone calls from embassies, high commissions and international newspapers. So, too, were Indira's offices at her Akbar Road office. The CPI was outraged and demanded an explanation. On the evening of 28 August Dhar had the interview withdrawn from all the Indian media. *Surge* itself had not yet reached the newsstands and Uma Vasudev got a curt telephone call from the Prime Minister's office telling her that it could not be released.[7]

The next day the Indian papers published Sanjay's own 'clarification' of his remarks about the CPI. How Dhar and Indira managed to wring it out of him is unrecorded. But Sanjay's statement read like a recantation: 'I did not mean to make such a sweeping statement about an entire party [the CPI],' he said. 'Obviously in some [other] parties like the Swatantra [and] the Jan Sangh . . . there are far more wealthy people and . . . more corruption . . . I do not agree with the Communists but . . . their workers are dedicated to their cause and . . . the CPI has supported and worked wholeheartedly for progressive politics, specially those affecting the poor people.'[8]

P. N. Dhar viewed Sanjay's *Surge* interview as 'a daring attempt to bypass the Prime Minister'.[9] Despite his retraction statement it was now public knowledge that Sanjay repudiated his mother's political views and was not prepared even to give lip service to the traditional Congress ideals of democracy, socialism and 'progressive programmes'. He was clearly pro-capitalist, conservative and authoritarian.

Sanjay had built up a power base – the headquarters of which was his home, the Prime Minister's house – to rival the Prime Minister's Secretariat. Through a policy of positioning his own men as ministerial seconds-in-command, Sanjay now had access to and control over certain key ministries. Thus he ran the Home Ministry not through the Home Minister, Brahmananda Reddy, a member of Indira's Cabinet, but through the Home Minister of State, Om Mehta (soon known as Home Mehta). He manoeuvred Pranab Mukherjee into Finance and A. P. Sharma to Industry. By December 1975 Bansi Lal, Sanjay's Maruti benefactor and the Chief Minister of Haryana, had become Minister of State for Defence.

Sanjay was also courted beyond Delhi, by the state chief ministers. They vied for the attention of 'the son', welcomed him to their states with VIP receptions and feted him at mass rallies. In Uttar Pradesh, however, Yashpal Kapoor reported back that the Chief Minister, H. N.

Bahuguna, had hired four tantric priests to pray for the annihilation of Sanjay and the Prime Minister. Sanjay gave orders that the priests be tracked down and arrested. Bahuguna was dismissed and replaced by N. D. Tiwari (soon known as New Delhi Tiwari, because of his loyalty to the centre where he spent most of his time).

In Sanjay's cabal at the Prime Minister's house, or PMH as Dhar refers to it, the criteria of merit and integrity were dispensed with and replaced with the new *sine qua non* of loyalty. As one of Dhar's colleagues would later put it, the Prime Minister's Secretariat 'was the waterworks [of government] while the PMH was the sewage system'.[10] The PMH by now also included Kishan Chand, the new Lieutenant Governor of Delhi, and Indira's indefatigable Private Secretary and factotum, R.K. Dhawan. This gang functioned 'like a well-oiled extra-constitutional authority'. They began giving orders – via Dhawan – to officials in Indira's Secretariat, most of which, in Dhar's words, 'were of a kind which could not be entertained'.[11]

At the annual Congress Party session held in late December 1975 at Chandigarh – the joint capital of the Punjab and Haryana – Sanjay was publicly anointed as his mother's heir when he was made a member of the Executive Committee of the Congress Party Youth Wing. Sanjay's aim was to resurrect the previously defunct Youth Congress and use it as a platform from which he could 'influence' members of the Congress Party with whom he was in conflict. The Youth Congress would be a rival centre of power to the parent Congress Party, just as Sanjay's PMH at Indira's house now opposed her Secretariat. A thirty-five-year-old woman and Sanjay-devotee named Ambika Soni was installed as the body's president. The Youth Congress proposed policies of urban renewal, family planning, literacy, legal aid to the poor and the removal of stray dogs from the streets of Delhi. But under Sanjay's influence it also degenerated into 'an umbrella organization which sheltered a variety of . . . thugs . . . [and] criminals . . . "bad characters" and "anti-social elements"'.[12]

'Youth Congress boys' harassed Delhi shopkeepers, and extorted 'donations' from them for non-existent adult literacy or family planning centres. A merchant from Connaught Place spoke for many when he recalled 'whenever I saw these ruffians, I thought my God how much will I have to give this time . . . I always gave. My only interest was to get rid of them.'[13]

Sanjay's boys did not stop at collecting donations. Under the Emergency it was mandatory for shopkeepers to display stock lists, reduce prices by 10 per cent and attach price tags to every item. Youth Congress members – and sometimes thugs posing as members – roamed the city's commercial establishments and levied instant fines on any merchant infringing Emergency regulations. Sometimes the fines were pocketed by those who extorted them. By and large, however, they were conveyed directly to Sanjay and 'his people'.

Lurid rumours also abounded of how Sanjay's 'hit men' liquidated human targets on his orders. Some of these rumours were true. During 1976 Sanjay arranged for an underworld figure named Sunderlal to be 'eliminated'. One evening two years later Sanjay and his wife Maneka called on Sanjay's close friend, Navin Chawla, who was secretary to the Lieutenant Governor of Delhi. Evidence had come to light implicating Sanjay in Sunderlal's death. Sanjay and Maneka asked Chawla if he would 'do the small favour' of taking out 'anticipatory bail' – for his own arrest on charges of murdering Sunderlal. Sanjay was asking Chawla to take the rap for the murder. Understandably, Chawla refused.[14]

Romesh Thapar – Indira's friend and adviser in the sixties from whom she was now estranged – claims that Sanjay had another enemy murdered (a Delhi underground figure like Sunderlal) with whose girlfriend Sanjay was having an affair. When this man challenged Sanjay about his appropriation of his girlfriend, Sanjay had him arrested by Delhi's Chief of Police, P.S. Bhinder. The mafioso's body was later found dumped in a large plastic bag at the bottom of the Jumna river. This incident was no secret and served as an effective warning to any others who might want to cross Sanjay.[15]

In late 1975 B.K. Nehru visited Delhi as Indian High Commissioner and was appalled to find that 'the rule of law was being replaced by the rule of Sanjay Gandhi'. He told his close friend P.N. Haksar that he 'was going to talk to Indira about what Sanjay was doing', but Haksar persuaded Nehru that this would be a great mistake because Nehru would be marginalized as he, Haksar, had been. Haksar told Nehru that Indira 'was absolutely blind as far as the boy was concerned; she regarded him as perfect, he could do no wrong. The slightest expression of doubt' would result in Nehru's banishment. Nehru, Haksar pointed out, was one of the few members of Indira's old guard who still had unlimited access to her. 'What little good [Nehru] could do and was doing ... would no longer be possible' if he openly criticized Sanjay. Reluctantly, Nehru held his peace.[16]

Indira occasionally expressed doubts about her son; she intimated to one worried Congress leader: 'you know his views are different than ours ... He's not a thinker, he's a doer.'[17] And yet, despite his political views, his bullyboy tactics, his gradual usurping of her prime ministerial position and emasculation of her Secretariat, Sanjay was undoubtedly, at this time, the most important person in Indira's life – the only person whom she trusted, confided in, and believed in. Why?

In and of himself, Sanjay – like his mother before him – could never have made it on his own in politics. Apart from his hereditary connection with Nehru and Indira, he had no assets other than youth, energy and ambition. He was crafty and cunning but not particularly intelligent. He read little other than motor magazines and technical manuals. He had no real understanding of the structures or procedures of government. Sanjay even lacked the social skills possessed by most politicians. He was brash, outspoken and rude. He had never formed close emotional attachments – not even with his parents, brother or wife. His friends were sycophants or *chamchas* – the Hindi word for spoon, meaning someone who curls up to you, as spoons cup each other. Sanjay's *chamchas* were poorly-educated young men like himself – an assortment of politicians, cronies and thugs.

Over the years, Indira had become increasingly isolated emotionally. Padmaja Naidu had died. Pupul Jayakar was never as close to Indira, as she later claimed. Dorothy Norman had broken off contact with Indira over the Emergency. Marie Seton was far away and Indira saw her infrequently. Indira was not as close to her elder son, Rajiv, as she was to Sanjay. Rajiv was also essentially apolitical, though he made it clear that aspects of the Emergency made him uneasy. Indira was fond of her daughter-in-law, Sonia, and relied on her, but Sonia was not a confidante and she had no experience of or interest in politics. Indira had by this time distanced most of her 'Kashmiri mafia', and in any case, men like Haksar, the late D.P. Dhar and T.N. Kaul had never been personal friends.

This left only one intimate relationship in Indira's life – that with her younger son. The sway Sanjay held over his mother was obvious, and those who had known her when Feroze Gandhi was still alive felt that Sanjay's hold derived from his connection in Indira's mind with Feroze. Whilst her older son, Rajiv, bore an uncanny physical resemblance to his father, he was quiet, diffident and unambitious. It was Sanjay who took after Feroze in character and temperament. He had Feroze's dynamism, his 'go', his bull-headedness, his drive, but he lacked Feroze's principles and political insight. Sanjay was an altogether darker version of his father, with Feroze's flaws writ large and none of his virtues. He was also the same type of man as Indira's putative lover – her father's secretary, M.O. Mathai. Both Mathai and Sanjay were aggressive, dominant men on the make. They possessed none of Nehru's refinement – or his moral strength.

In her reaction to her son's 'exceedingly stupid [*Surge*] statement' P.N. Dhar saw that 'in some ways [Indira was] afraid of her son, at least to the extent of fearing his displeasure'. Dhar could not tell 'whether she was simply unwilling or plainly unable to restrain him'.[18] Dhar was not the only person who believed Indira was frightened of Sanjay. Pupul Jayakar and Nayantara Sahgal also sensed this. Indira feared few people in her life. But she had been intimidated by both her father and her husband even though she had, on occasion, stood up to and defied both men. Sanjay, however, could frighten and paralyse his mother. The *Washington Post* correspondent, Lewis Simons, reported that someone who dined with the Gandhis in the summer of 1975 said that in the midst of an argument, Sanjay slapped his mother across the face six times. According to the anonymous dinner guest, 'She did not do a thing . . . she just stood there and took it. She's scared to death of him.' Rejecting the veracity of this story, another family friend told the writer Ved Mehta, 'not even God could slap Mrs Gandhi across the face six times'.[19]

Most people, including those working closely with Indira and Sanjay such as P.N. Haksar, P.N. Dhar and B.K. Nehru, found Indira's fear of her son inexplicable. Jayakar ascribed it to Indira's confession to her after Feroze's death that Sanjay had accused his mother of causing his father's death by neglecting him. In her heart, Indira may have felt this was true. Long years ago she had chosen Feroze against her father's wishes – she had put love before duty. But the marriage had foundered and she had left Feroze and ended up in her father's house; she may have believed Feroze died alone and estranged even though she was at his deathbed. For as long as she lived, Indira's relationships with Feroze and Sanjay were her two vulnerabilities. Even in the early eighties, after both were dead, when Salman Rushdie in his novel *Midnight's Children* resurrected Sanjay's accusation that Indira had caused Feroze's death, Indira was stung. She successfully sued Rushdie for libel even though the book was a work of fiction.[20]

Undoubtedly it was Sanjay's emotional grip on his mother that was the source of his power. But Uma Vasudev speculates that Indira actually advanced her son because it was politically expedient to do so, that despite her repeated articulation of traditional Congress ideals, Indira had developed a system and style of 'parallel politics'. This involved dividing the opposition while presenting herself as all things to all people. Sanjay, Vasudev believes, had utility for Indira as a 'symbol of the right' while she herself still tried to cultivate her own image as a radical. The two of them together, Indira calculated, covered the political spectrum.[21] Inexorably, Sanjay emerged as Indira's heir. The Emergency, Indira's foes claimed, was jettisoning democracy and replacing it with dynasty.

In February 1976, Indira postponed the upcoming general election and extended the Emergency. Democracy remained suspended, because, she said, the government needed more time to 'consolidate the gains' of the Emergency. The term of the current Lok Sabha was prolonged by a vote of 180 to 34 in Parliament. Only a few, mildly dissenting voices, including P. N. Dhar's, opposed the postponement. Dhar tried to persuade Indira to go ahead and hold the election with the argument that the Emergency had become counterproductive and if it were prolonged, Dhar predicted economic difficulties would worsen.[22]

But Indira rejected Dhar's advice. Sanjay wanted to postpone the elections indefinitely and so the Emergency continued. According to Amnesty International, during the first year of the Emergency more than 110,000 people were arrested and detained without trial in India. Morarji Desai and J. P. Narayan, like Mahatma Gandhi during the Quit India movement, were jailed in fairly pleasant surroundings, in guesthouses. Then soon after his arrest, Narayan was transferred to a Bombay hospital because of his failing health. Other high-profile prisoners did not fare as well. Rajmata Gayatri Devi of Jaipur and the

Rajmata of Gwalior (the wives of the former Princes of Jaipur and Gwalior) were both held in Delhi's Tihar jail in cells alongside prostitutes and criminals. Gayatri Devi complained that it was 'like living in a bazaar with squabbling women', and asked a friend to send her some wax earplugs. She was released on parole after writing to Indira that she agreed entirely with the twenty-point economic programme.

Ordinary prisoners – who were the vast majority – endured horrendous conditions. In part this was simply because the prisons were so overcrowded. In Tihar jail, for example, 4,000 prisoners occupied cells intended for only 1,200. Twenty-two Emergency prisoners died in jail.

The socialist leader, George Fernandes, was one of Indira's few critics who escaped the first wave of arrests of June 1975. He went underground where he led a sabotage operation similar to that Feroze Gandhi conducted during the 1942 Quit India movement. Under his leadership, railway lines were blown up and bombs set off in Bombay, Bihar and Karnataka. Indira was convinced that Fernandes and his followers were plotting to assassinate her. She told Fori Nehru that when she gave a public speech in Benares, 'Fernandes intended to blow me up.'[23] When the police could not track him down, they arrested and tortured his brother Lawrence. Eventually, in June 1976, George Fernandes was caught in Calcutta and jailed.

But the most numerous victims of the Emergency were not Indira's political opponents but the poor whom she claimed the Emergency was intended to help and protect. And it was the urban and rural poor – menial labourers, beggars, the homeless and peasant farmers – who suffered most grievously under the two most controversial of Sanjay's five points: slum clearance and sterilization programmes. Both drives went drastically wrong.

By the time the Emergency was declared Sanjay already had two of his men in key positions of civic power in Delhi. Kishan Chand, a malleable man, had been selected as the new Lieutenant Governor of Delhi by Sanjay's friend Navin Chawla, a high-ranking civil servant in the Indian Administrative Service. Chawla in turn became Chand's secretary and a powerful administrator in his own right, running the Delhi Development Authority on Sanjay's orders. The vice-chairman of the Development Authority, a man called Jagmohan – he possessed only the one name – became the leader of what became known as 'Sanjay's Action Brigade'.

In contrast to most of Sanjay's other associates Jagmohan was a man of integrity and a hard-working, dedicated, civil servant. Entirely self-taught, he had developed a high level of technical expertise in the fields of architecture, planning, urban infrastructures and the environment. Jagmohan had a mission to 'save Delhi', to regenerate the capital.

Jagmohan also seems to have truly believed that Sanjay Gandhi was the man to make his dream for Delhi possible. To this day, Jagmohan remains utterly loyal to him.[24] In early April 1976, by which time the Delhi Development Agency's slum clearance and beautification programmes were well underway, Jagmohan accompanied Sanjay on an inspection tour of Old Delhi. Much of the old city was a congested warren of lanes and streets, lined with ancient, tumbledown houses and makeshift shacks. The whole area was an insanitary, overcrowded and polluted environment for its inhabitants, the majority of whom were Muslims.

Sanjay and Jagmohan stopped at an entrance to the old city, Turkman Gate, which overlooked a maze of teeming tenements. Sanjay announced 'I want to see the Jama Masjid [the old main mosque] from Turkman Gate.' Jagmohan, all but saluting, took these words as an order. Everything obstructing the view of Jama Masjid from Turkman Gate would have to go.

In a matter of days it was decreed that tens of thousands of people in this area would be 'relocated' to vacant land twenty miles away, across the Jumna, on the outskirts of the city. On 13 April demolition teams with bulldozers arrived to level stores, pukka houses, shacks, and stalls. Shop owners, traders and food sellers were given forty-five minutes to clear their premises. Householders were granted slightly longer. By 19 April, after six days of destruction, an uprising broke out. A large crowd of women marched on and surrounded the local family planning clinic (another of Sanjay's controversial measures) shouting threatening slogans. Their menfolk meanwhile formed a mob that proceeded to stone, throw bricks and Molotov cocktails at the demolition squads.

The police swiftly descended and tried to disperse the crowds with tear gas. Women and children retreated indoors. But men and boys climbed to roof and wall tops and continued their barrage. At this point the police opened fire. Police records report that only fourteen rounds were fired at Turkman Gate on 19 April. But witnesses who later testified before the Shah Commission (set up to inquire into abuses committed during the Emergency) maintained the shooting continued sporadically for three hours. Hundreds of people were injured and somewhere between six and 150 (depending on whether your source of information is the official police report, Jagmohan, the *Shah Commission Report*, rumour or the international press) were killed, including a thirteen-year-old boy who was watching the riot. At least one man was shot in the back as he tried to flee. Later it was found that there were glaring discrepancies between the police and medical reports of the shootings. A twenty-four-hour curfew was imposed on the entire area which lasted until 13 May 1976, allowing the demolitions to continue.

According to the *Times of India*, 150,000 *jhuggis* (shacks inhabited by the urban poor), shops, houses and other structures were demolished. Their inhabitants – more than 70,000 people – were bundled off in vans at gunpoint and driven to their new homes – barbed-wire-fenced plots of farmland. Families were given twenty-five square yards of land, bricks to build their own shelters and ration cards to buy food at the 'development site' shop.

Two years later Jagmohan published a book entitled *Island of Truth* about his work for the Delhi Development Authority during the Emergency in which he dealt with the Turkman Gate episode in some detail. Defending the demolition squads, he said, 'Bulldozers were used as a labour-saving technique and for clearing the debris speedily . . . This practice has been in vogue for the last one or two decades. Free transport was provided to the families effected [sic] for carrying their belongings. . . . There have [sic] been absolutely no wilful demolition.' Regarding the speed of the operation, he conceded, 'it undoubtedly increased. There were valid reasons for it. Even otherwise, was it wrong to shake off lethargy, eliminate "gossip cafés", from our offices, relieve the tyranny of Kafkaesque world of papers, full of sound and furry [sic], signifying nothing?'[25]

Turkman Gate and other areas of Delhi were not the only areas to undergo 'beautification' during the Emergency. Cities targeted for 'urban improvement' included Bombay, Agra – the home of the Taj Mahal – and the holy city of Varanasi. When Pupul Jayakar visited Varanasi she was horrified to see that bulldozers had widened a road in the area of Vishwanath Gali, slicing through seventeenth-century houses, 'leaving sitting rooms with half the door space cut away; rooms . . . open to the road, verandas smashed'. Jayakar took photographs of this devastation, which 'looked as if a bomb had fallen on it', and showed them to Indira in Delhi. Indira 'hit the ceiling'. She telephoned the Chief Minister of Uttar Pradesh, N. D. Tiwari and 'exploded' at him long distance. Tiwari went into a panic, promised to investigate and eventually reported back that the Varanasi demolitions had been based on an inaccurate 1920 map of the city.[26]

The second major assault of Sanjay's five-point plan was a radical programme of sterilization designed to halt India's population explosion. When Indira was a child India's population growth was kept in check by diseases, epidemics, high rates of infant mortality, drought, floods, earthquakes and famines. In 1922 the birth rate was 48.1 per 1,000 and the death rate, 47.2. But by the early seventies, after decades of advances in medical care, nutrition and improved hygiene, the death rate had plummeted to an all-time low of 17.4. The population of India was increasing by 12 million people a year.

In the late sixties the government had tried to stem the tide. But it encountered both practical and cultural obstacles to family planning. The pill was not yet widely available in India; diaphragms were impractical for those who lived communally, without privacy and they had to be supplied and fitted by a medical practitioner. The loop had its own drawbacks.

For a while, condoms seemed to be the answer. In his book on family planning, *A Matter of People*, Dom Moraes describes how in the late sixties an elephant roamed about certain Indian villages carrying a load of condoms which were freely distributed to the populace. The children instantly saw the practical value of the condoms, and blew them up into small balloons which they tied to sticks. There was a popular government slogan at this time to the effect that family planning made for happy children, which the condom-dispensing elephants certainly illustrated.[27] The birth rate, however, did not go down.

The safest, cheapest and most efficient method of controlling the size of the population was sterilization – usually of men (vasectomy), occasionally of women (tubectomy). Vasectomies could be done under a local anaesthetic, in a few minutes, with no recovery period and usually no side effects. But in a culture where fertility was crucial to both men and women's sense of self-worth and where children were a source of income and insurance against destitution in old age, sterilization would never be embraced willingly. Thus it was an electoral liability for any political party to adopt.

To succeed, sterilization had to be imposed from above, and it was only when the Emergency itself was imposed and democratic norms suspended that this became possible. Sanjay, who had previously expressed no interest in family planning, quickly realized its potential as the central issue and goal of the 'New India'. A popular jingle of the day went, 'Come, have yourself vasectomized, make your family systemized.' But sterilization would not merely 'systemize' families. In Sanjay's eyes, it would be a history-making panacea that would transform the country.

In April 1976 the government initiated a new 'National Population Policy' to lower the annual birth rate from 35 to 25 per 1,000 by 1984. In its original form, the programme consisted of incentives and 'disincentives' to limit family size to three children. The minimum age of marriage was raised and benefits such as subsidized housing and free medical care were withheld from those who did not undergo sterilization after the birth of their third child. But when these measures did not produce dramatic results, Sanjay Gandhi ensured that harsher ones were introduced.

The Emergency sterilization drive became, in fact, Sanjay's cause célèbre. He, rather than the Health Minister, Karan Singh, directed it, though the Health Minister countenanced what went on. Today, Singh insists he was only vaguely aware of the means used in Sanjay Gandhi's family planning programme, that he and Sanjay never sat on the same platform – much less discussed the issue.[28] According to B.K. Nehru, however, in 1976 he quizzed Singh about the sterilization excesses, and Singh's blunt response was: 'you couldn't make an omelette without breaking eggs'.[29] The vasectomy tents in cities and the sterilization vans that roamed the countryside were, however, Sanjay's – rather than Karan Singh's – doing; as were the army of family planning 'motivators', the rewards given to those who submitted to sterilization, and the quota system imposed on government employees who had to produce a certain number of people to be sterilized in order to be paid.

Sanjay also formed a controversial 'task force' of glamorous young women 'family planning workers' who ran assembly-line sterilization clinics in the depressed areas of Delhi. One of these, Rukhsana Sultana, was a socialite jewellery designer, who wore sunglasses and chiffon saris, had scarlet varnished fingernails and dark, kohl-smudged eyes. Rukhsana – popularly known as the 'queen of the walled city' – held no official position, but she cut an arresting figure in the Delhi slums where the Muslim women moved about shrouded from head to foot in black *burkhas*. Looking more like a Bombay film star than a social worker, Rukhsana toured these congested areas with a police escort and oversaw the sidewalk vasectomy clinics in hastily set-up tents. Later she established and ran her own vasectomy clinic in Old Delhi. But perhaps her most dramatic family planning feat was to persuade two Muslim *imams* to undergo vasectomies. The press was on hand to witness Sanjay Gandhi personally award them 'Motivation Cards'.

Ordinary vasectomy patients were variously rewarded with 120 rupees, a tin of cooking oil or – most notoriously – a transistor radio. Not surprisingly, some enterprising and needy men underwent the procedure more than once in order to get more than one reward. The average number of sterilizations per day in Delhi rose sharply from 331 to 5,644, peaking at 6,000.

But many men – both in Delhi and remote, rural villages – resisted. There was confusion over how the operation would affect potency. In addition, some men simply did not want the size of their families to be dictated to them. To poor peasant farmers, labourers and homeless urban beggars, children were a valuable resource. Children provided income; they worked for their parents in the fields or begged for them in the streets.

To counter this resistance government employees such as policemen, inspectors, doctors, nurses and teachers were paid their salaries only after they successfully 'motivated' a certain quota of men to undergo vasectomies or (more rarely) women, tubectomies. Again, the primary victims were the helpless and the poor, especially Muslims, Harijans and tribal peoples. In the six months between April and September 1976, two million Indians were sterilized.

Those who did not have government jobs were 'encouraged' by other means to submit to sterilization. When a man had undergone sterilization, he was given an official sterilization certificate. These had to be produced in a variety of situations. Motor rickshaw drivers, for example, had to show theirs in order to get their driving licences renewed. Sterilization certificates became passports necessary to negotiate daily life for people in all walks of life, and forgers who had previously produced bogus educational certificates did a brisk trade now in sterilization ones.

Some people were simply coerced – rather than motivated or bribed – to be sterilized. In Delhi, Calcutta, Bombay and other Indian cities, tens of thousands of homeless people lived on the streets. During the Emergency, thousands were arrested for 'vagrancy' and taken off to sterilization camps where they had no choice but to undergo vasectomies.[30]

Fori Nehru reported back to Indira that young boys and old men were being forcibly sterilized in Chandigarh through which the Nehrus passed to reach their summer home in the hills at Kasauli. Indira apparently broke down with Fori and wailed, 'What am I to do? What am I to do? They tell me nothing.' But then she pulled herself together and insisted 'that most of these allegations were lies'.[31]

For a long time, in fact, Indira refused to give any credence to the reports of forced and brutal sterilizations. She would ask 'her people' to look into these reports and then be reassured when they told her they were unsubstantiated rumours. When P.N. Dhar brought to Indira's attention the case of a forcibly sterilized village schoolteacher who had somehow travelled to Delhi and made it into Dhar's office in the Prime Minister's Akbar Road office, Indira finally reacted. She was appalled at the details the schoolteacher recounted. She was also shocked by irrefutable evidence that Dhar produced indicating that other schoolteachers had been physically assaulted when they failed to produce their quota of vasectomy volunteers. Indira confessed to Dhar that she had been uneasy about the family-planning programme for some time, but had lacked hard evidence when Sanjay's people insisted that the reports, which alarmed her, were bogus. Now – very late in the day – she sent a stern message to all state chief ministers that 'anyone engaged in harassment while propagating family planning will be punished'.[32]

In the first five months of the Emergency, 3.7 million Indians were sterilized. By the time it ended, the target of sterilizing 23 million people in three years was well on the way to being over-fulfilled. The sterilization programme turned out to be harmful not only to its victims, but to Indira also. The programme 'undermined [Indira's] credibility among her strongest supporters' – the minorities such as Muslims, Harijans and other oppressed castes.

*   *   *

Meanwhile, Sanjay's public image grew and even began to eclipse that of his mother. In August 1976 he appeared on the cover of the Independence Day issue of the *Illustrated Weekly*, a popular magazine edited by the well-known Indian journalist Khushwant Singh, who himself interviewed Sanjay for the cover story. Singh was an enthusiastic supporter of the Emergency. He described Sanjay as 'the hope of the future . . . an incredibly handsome young man' with 'fiercely intense and honest eyes'. But as Singh himself described it, the interview was 'not a success':

'Do you remember much of your grandfather? . . . Were you close to him?'

'As close as other people are to their grandfathers.'

'Did he influence your thinking in any way?'

'I cannot recall any specific way in which he influenced me.'

'What about your father? Were you close to him?'

'Yes – like any son is to his father.'

'I suppose it is the same with your mother and your brother?'

'Yes, my relationship is no different than that of anyone else with his mother or brother.'

'What about books? Has any book influenced you particularly?'

'I can't think of any.'

'What is your favourite reading? Poetry? Fiction? History? Biography?'

'No, none of those.'

'What do you feel about the proposed amendments to the Constitution?'

'I don't know enough about the Constitution.'

Sanjay was just as unforthcoming when Singh tried to question him on the subjects of his role in determining government policy, nationalization, and the Congress Party's methods of collecting funds.[33]

Despite its banality, Khushwant Singh's interview with Sanjay reflected the growing media cult that had grown up round him. Soon other large-circulation English-language weeklies such as *Blitz* and *Current* also ran Sanjay cover stories. Of the five national English-language newspapers, only the *Indian Express* criticized Sanjay, the government and the Emergency. The *Times of India*, in contrast, was soon referred to as the *Times of Indira*.

All this was largely the doing of V.C. Shukla, the Minister of Broadcasting and Information who had replaced I. K. Gujral. From the beginning of the Emergency, Shukla ran a veritable Indira-Sanjay propaganda machine, monitoring and stage-managing all the media. He made sure that 'positive' news dominated the headlines and these good tidings invariably sprang from the activities and words of the Prime Minister and her son.

Shukla's ministry was responsible, for example, for the fact that in the first two weeks of January 1976 no less than 192 news items were broadcast about Sanjay as main news bulletins on the state-owned All India Radio. Newspapers were dominated with such headlines as: 'Sanjay Storms Kanpur' and 'Sanjay and the Youth Congress', 'Sanjay in Delhi', 'Sanjay on tour' and 'Sanjay's Five Point Programme'. As the politician and long-time foe of Indira, L.K. Advani, put it, during the Emergency journalists 'crawled when they were asked merely to bend'.[34]

V.C. Shukla also presided over the 1976 celebrations of the first year of the Emergency – 'A Year of Fulfilment' – which involved numerous activities, including a documentary film called *A Day with the Prime Minister*. Even more spectacular were the festivities Shukla orchestrated in honour of Indira's ten-year tenure as Prime Minister – a 'Dynamic Decade in Power'. A book of laudatory essays about Indira was published entitled *A Decade of Achievement 1966–75* and an exhibition organized with the same title. At one of the many functions organized to commemorate Indira's glorious decade, Shukla claimed that she had done more for India in the past ten years than had been accomplished in the previous one thousand years.

In November 1976 Indira postponed the general election again – this time for a full twelve months. Both this and the earlier postponement announced the previous February would prove to be strategic mistakes. If Indira had held the elections on schedule in early 1976, when the Emergency still had many supporters, she and Congress almost surely would have won. And their victory would have legitimized the Emergency and all the draconian laws, ordinances and constitutional amendments made in its name. But Sanjay convinced his mother to postpone the elections not once but twice. Those close to 'the son' had no doubt that his plan was to keep on postponing them indefinitely.

According to P.N. Dhar, however, Indira was 'uncomfortable about the second postponement . . . She thought [it] . . . gave out the wrong signal – that she was afraid to face the people.' When Dhar again urged Indira to go ahead with the elections, she became 'nostalgic about the way people reacted to her in the 1971 election campaign and she longed to hear again the applause of the multitudes. She wanted to regain her ability to reach the people at an emotional level.'[35]

And thus Sanjay was foiled. On 18 January 1977 Indira did a U-turn, defied Sanjay, and stunned the nation by announcing that a general election would be held – not the following November as she had previously announced – but in a mere two months' time. 'Every election is an act of faith,' she said in her broadcast announcement: 'It is an opportunity to cleanse public life of confusion. So let us go to the polls with the resolve to reaffirm the power of the people.'

Indira had consulted no one but Dhar and Sanjay about her decision to proceed with the election. Unfortunately, there is no report or record of the showdown with her son. The Cabinet, the Chief Ministers, the Home Minister, even President Fakhruddin Ali Ahmed, were not informed of Indira's decision, and they were all as shocked by it as the country at large. It was a brave move, and the first time on record that Indira had directly overruled Sanjay. She then defied him again by ordering the release of most of the well-known political prisoners and suspended the censorship press guidelines.

Indira's confidants were dumbfounded when she called for elections. It was widely held at the time (and later) that she did so because intelligence reports assured her of an overwhelming victory. Pupul Jayakar, however, later learned from the intelligence chief, R. N. Kao, that he had told Indira that she ran a risk of losing if she released imprisoned members of the opposition. Indira herself told a journalist several years later, 'I was by no means sure that I would win. I was sure that we would not get a big majority. I thought that we would just get through perhaps.'[36]

It is possible that Indira also had genuine qualms about extending the Emergency and violating any longer the constitution and the form of government her father had devoted his life to creating. For Indira, the Emergency had been a means to an end. But she was no Bhutto or Mujib. For all her failings and despite her irrational belief that only she could lead and control the country, on some level she remained committed to democracy. She was guilty of hubris but not megalomania.

It was also shrewd to announce elections at this juncture. The opposition was weak and fragmented. Many of its leaders had spent the past two years in jail; their parties had been silenced and their funding had all but dried up. J. P. Narayan's movement was made up out of a discordant collection of parties, including left-wing socialists, militant Hindu chauvinists and right-wing capitalists. In addition, Indira had given them only two months to prepare for the elections.

In the early weeks of 1977 Indira campaigned vigorously. She visited every one of the twenty-two states and spoke at 224 public meetings. But compared with past elections the crowds who came to hear her speak were smaller and, not infrequently, hostile. At one rally witnessed by Mark Tully, a number of women in the audience turned their backs on Indira. This infuriated her. To the consternation of her security men, she left the platform, went down to the front rows and physically tried to turn the women around.[37]

For much of the campaign Indira felt unwell: she developed shingles on her face; she was in pain and ran a fever. This did not slow her down but she sometimes had to swathe half of her face in a scarf to conceal the small herpes blisters.

On 1 February – in the middle of the campaign – President Fakhruddin Ali Ahmed died suddenly. Rumours circulated that he had suffered a heart attack after a heated argument with Indira during which she had demanded he cancel the upcoming election. But Ahmed had a history of heart disease and there is no evidence that Indira asked him to postpone the poll.

The day after Ahmed died, there was another shock. Jagjivan Ram, the powerful Harijan Minister of Irrigation and Agriculture, resigned from the Cabinet, defected from Congress and founded a new party, the Congress for Democracy, which immediately joined the fold of the Janata Party. It was an opportunistic move. Ram surmised Indira would lose the election. He felt that his hour had arrived and he planned to seize power. In making his announcement, Ram took the high moral ground and denounced both Indira and the Emergency. At a press conference he called upon his fellow Congressmen to join him in his move to end the 'totalitarian and authoritarian trends . . . in the nation's politics'. In his resignation letter to Indira, Ram said that 'the coming general elections provide perhaps the last opportunity for preventing the total reversal of the nation's cherished policies, and for correcting the illegitimacy that predominates in our national life'.

Publicly Indira responded, 'It is strange you should have remained silent all these months, but should make these baseless charges now.'[38]

Privately she observed to friends that Jagjivan Ram just wanted to be Prime Minister himself and thought Janata would hand it to him on a plate.

A host of Congress defectors followed in Ram's wake including H. N. Bahuguna, the former Chief Minister of Uttar Pradesh. Worse, even Indira's own flesh and blood turned against her. Ten days after Ram's dramatic defection, her aunt, Vijaya Lakshmi Pandit, came out of political retirement and theatrically bestowed her support on the Janata Front. In her public statement Mrs Pandit said that Indira and the Emergency had 'smothered and destroyed' democratic institutions, 'undermined' the rule of law and the independence of the judiciary. This 'erosion of our cherished values,' she argued, 'must be stopped and we must go back to the ideals to which we are pledged'.[39] What Mrs Pandit did not mention was that she hoped to make a political comeback after Indira's defeat. In fact, she appeared to be counting on a Janata Prime Minister – who would probably be Morarji Desai – to make her President of India.[40]

As the strength of the opposition mounted, Sanjay urged his mother to cancel the election – but to no avail. Meanwhile, a general election was held in Pakistan on 7 March 1977. Zulfikar Ali Bhutto and his Pakistan People's Party won, although the elections were rigged to ensure a landslide victory. As his biographer put it, 'in the excess of his "victory" lay the time bomb of defeat'.[41] Immediately riots broke out all over Pakistan, and that was just the beginning.

When Sanjay realized that the Indian elections were going ahead, he filed papers to stand for Parliament for the first time from the 'safe' Uttar Pradesh constituency of Amethi, next door to Indira's constituency, Rae Bareilly. Both Amethi and Rae Bareilly were regarded as Congress strongholds because the whole of Uttar Pradesh had long been the traditional power base of the Nehrus and the Gandhis. Sanjay campaigned energetically, but he foolishly and fatally pushed the deeply unpopular 'gains' of his sterilization programme. When his wife, Maneka, spoke at a reception, she was verbally attacked by angry women who accused Sanjay of reducing them to *bewas* (widows) because sterilization had made their husbands 'no longer men'.[42]

On 14 March 1977, two days before the beginning of the general election, Sanjay wound up a long day of campaigning in Amethi when he left at about 9.30 at night to join Maneka in Gauriganj, an hour's drive away. Around 10 o'clock, as Sanjay's jeep negotiated a crossing, a volley of bullets showered the vehicle. Sanjay, who was sitting in the front next to the driver, just happened to be leaning back to talk to an aide in the rear seat when the bullets hit the car – and missed him. The would-be assassins escaped in their car. As soon as Sanjay arrived in Gauriganj he reported the attempt on his life to the police. The next day Indira, who was in Patna, the capital of the neighbouring state of Bihar, made a strangely subdued statement: 'I am always against violence and I condemn this incident.'[43]

Despite its high drama, the assassination attempt on Sanjay received surprisingly little press coverage. Inevitably, its authenticity has been questioned. The assailants were never caught; an investigation report was never published. The attack occurred just two days before the poll was to begin, when Sanjay belatedly realized that voters were up in arms against him because of sterilization. Indira's understated reaction is also peculiar; she may have suspected that Sanjay had staged his own narrow escape from death. If the assassination attempt was bogus, however, it was also pointless. It failed entirely to gain Sanjay a sympathy vote.

On 16 March 1977, India's sixth general election commenced. The Congress Party had a new ideograph printed on the ballot papers – a cow and a calf which many people felt was an unfortunate choice given Sanjay's enormous influence on his mother.

After five days of polling, 60 per cent of the electorate had voted – about 194 million people. (Again, this was the 'largest democratic election' ever – just as previous and successive Indian elections were, for the simple reason that India was, and remains, the world's largest democracy.) Janata received a staggering 40 per cent of the vote to Congress' 35 per cent. Janata (including Jagjivan Ram's Congress for Democracy) captured 299 seats and Congress only 153. The Communist Party (CPI) deserted Congress and together with the smaller, regional parties took the remaining number of seats in the Lok Sabha.

Indira herself was humiliatingly defeated in the Rae Bareilly constituency by her erstwhile opponent, Raj Narain. Sanjay lost also in Amethi. In the former Nehru family stronghold of Uttar Pradesh, Congress failed to win a single one of the 84 seats. Most of Indira's followers in the Cabinet and Parliament were also routed.

On the night of 20 March, India rejoiced as it had not done since the eve of independence from the British thirty years earlier. Far into the night, drums beat, people danced in the streets, fireworks lit up the sky in celebration of Indira Gandhi's downfall. At about 8 p.m., Pupul Jayakar visited Indira at her home. The house was preternaturally quiet and still – without the usual swarm of people and hubbub of noise. Indira was alone in the sitting room. When Jayakar entered, she rose and said, 'Pupul, I have lost.' They sat in silence for a while.

Finally at 10.30 Indira ordered dinner and sent for Rajiv and Sonia. Sanjay was still in Amethi. After the meal, they retired to the sitting room. It was past midnight when Jayakar took her leave. Rajiv walked her to the door where he said, 'I will never forgive Sanjay for having brought Mummy to this position.'[44]

In the middle of the night, Indira met with the Cabinet at her Akbar Road office. It was twenty-one months since the cabinet meeting at which she had inaugurated the Emergency. This cabinet meeting – to undo what was done at the first – was just as short and perfunctory. But this time the Prime Minister consulted the Cabinet *before* going to the President. At 4 a.m. Indira was driven to the home of the acting President, B.D. Jatti where she instructed him to end the Emergency. Then she resigned.

For the first time in her life, at the age of fifty-nine, Indira Gandhi found herself without a job, an income or a roof over her head.

EIGHTEEN

Witch-Hunt

A ROOF – a home for herself and her family – was Indira's most pressing need. She had lived at 1 Safdarjung Road for thirteen years, ever since Shastri had appointed her Minister of Information and Broadcasting in 1964. But now that she was out of power Indira had to vacate her government bungalow. Nehru had left the family home, Anand Bhawan in Allahabad, to Indira in his will. But she had given Anand Bhawan to the nation in 1970, and like Teen Murti House, it was now a museum. Even had it still been hers, Indira would not have been able to afford to run and maintain Anand Bhawan.

She still owned the land in Mehrauli, outside Delhi, that Feroze bought in 1959. With his savings, Rajiv had begun to build a family house there, but his money had run out and the house remained half-built. In any case, Indira had no desire to retire to the country. Many years earlier, shortly before her father's death, she had wanted to leave India and politics, buy a flat in London and live abroad. In 1977, however, in the aftermath of her electoral disgrace, though she thought briefly of taking a break in Kashmir, she did not consider a retreat from public life. Her intention was to stay not only in India, but in New Delhi, at the hub of things.

But where were she and her family to live? Mohammed Yunus, their old family friend, came to the rescue and vacated his bungalow at 12 Willingdon Crescent for Indira. This was the house where Sanjay and Maneka had been married three years earlier. It was smaller than 1 Safdarjung Road (which had been extended to accommodate Rajiv and Sanjay and their families). Thirteen years' worth of possessions, the belongings of five adults and two small children, five dogs, boxes of books and papers all had to be crammed into it.

Out of power, Indira lost her staff – her secretaries, assistants and domestic servants – along with her government bungalow. Her long-time assistant, Usha Bhagat, had been unhappy since the onset of the Emergency, and she left now with a sigh of relief. Indira's Private Secretary, R.K. Dhawan, however, remained steadfastly loyal and continued to work for her without any salary.[1] Sonia Gandhi took on all the cooking and shopping as well as most of the housekeeping. Indira, of course, pitched in. Maneka did nothing.[2]

On 23 March 1977 Morarji Desai was sworn in as the fourth – and first non-Congress – Prime Minister of India. He had waited thirteen years for his place in the sun, having come close to achieving it in both 1964 and 1967. Now, at the age of eighty-one, Desai had finally won that place, and he was determined to humiliate as well as usurp Indira. He insisted on moving into 1 Safdarjung Road, which was not the official Prime Minister's residence but merely one of the standard government bungalows allotted to senior government officials and MPs. Desai and his family took over Indira's house with unseemly haste, and did not change a thing except for having the Western-style bathroom ripped out and replaced with an Indian toilet and shower area for bucket baths.

Desai's personal humiliation of his predecessor did not stop with taking over her house. As a former Prime Minister, Indira was entitled to continued security protection, but Desai was intent on paring it down to a bare minimum. P. N. Dhar delayed resigning until Desai had chosen his replacement. In the meantime Desai summoned Dhar and complained that Indira had too much security. 'What is she afraid of?' he asked Dhar, adding 'It is not good for her to be surrounded by so many policemen.' Dhar began to explain that Indira's security 'had been beefed up because of the hostile atmosphere against her and Sanjay,' but Desai cut him off with 'No, it is her vanity.' Then Desai launched into the general subject of women in power from Cleopatra and Catherine the Great to the present. All of them, according to Desai, had not only been vain but also disastrous as rulers.[3]

Indira's situation now – financially, politically and emotionally – was precarious. She had no income and few resources. Mohammed Yunus had put a roof over her head, but she still had to feed and maintain her family. No money was forthcoming from Sanjay. He had never been open with his mother about his finances and he did not offer to help her now. Indira knew that Sanjay had profited during the Emergency. But she did not ask him for assistance.[4]

The money she lived on came in uncertainly and irregularly from various sources. Though the number of her rich and influential friends plummeted after she lost the 1977 election, several industrialists – both in Delhi and abroad – did not desert her. One of these was a young man who owned a soft drinks company in Delhi and was a great friend of Sanjay. Over the next three years he and several of Indira's own friends in the business world sustained her on the understanding that their loyalty would be rewarded if she ever regained power.[5] Not that anyone – including Indira herself – expected this. When the old Nehru family friend, Aruna Asaf Ali, tried to reassure her that the people would 'surely bring her back', Indira despairingly asked, 'When? After I am dead?'[6]

Janata's campaign promise had been to repair the damage done to the country during the Emergency. The new government did, in fact, repeal a number of the amendments and ordinances enacted during the previous two years. But it had too many partisan factions and would-be prime ministers jockeying for power to function properly. Ideology and ambition kept Janata fractured.

The new Foreign Minister, A.B. Vajpayee, said Janata would 'consign Indira Gandhi to the dustbin of history', but far from forgetting her, she was their only consensus issue. Men as diverse as Desai, Jagjivan Ram, Vajpayee and Charan Singh could only agree on the need to hunt Indira down and bring her to justice, along with her son Sanjay. Instead of tackling what to do about India, Janata focussed on what to do about Indira.

As soon as Janata gained power, it embarked on a programme of harassment. The Central Bureau of Intelligence tailed Indira, Sanjay, Rajiv, Sonia and Maneka and bugged their private telephones. The CBI also descended on Indira's half-built Mehrauli farm with metal detectors in the vain hope of discovering Sanjay's buried loot. The income tax department unsuccessfully pursued Rajiv for tax evasion.[7] The entire family had their passports impounded, presumably because Janata thought they would attempt to flee the country. Sanjay's pilot's licence was revoked to prevent him from flying Indira to safety in his Cessna.

Indira wrote to Fori Nehru of the government's 'vindictiveness' and how her 'own people are turning against me to save their own skins. The wildest stories are being circulated about Sanjay . . . I am accused of causing the deaths of all kinds of people. Because of surveillance, people are hesitant to come [to see me], because of phone tapping the phone has become virtually useless . . . Do I sound grouchy? I am deeply worried though I realize that the warfare is psychological and I must keep my chin up.'[8]

The press and the media joined in the persecution. After Indira lost the election, chequebook journalism flourished. 'Indiragate' was hot copy and Indira became the new Nixon – the politician everyone loved to hate. Renegade Congressmen now 'told all' in exclusive interviews in the national newspapers. Magazines vied with each other to publish fresh exposés on Indira and Sanjay. In America Ved Mehta – one of Indira's most acerbic and intelligent critics – published long, damning essays on her in the *New Yorker*.

A spate of anti-Indira books was also rushed into print. Many of these quickies were written by the same people who had previously published adulatory works. Indira Gandhi bashing was now not only safe but also intellectually fashionable. These books ran the gamut from barely literate innuendo and gossip to polished intellectual assaults. Among the most controversial were Janardan Thakur's *All the Prime Minister's Men* and *Indira Gandhi and Her Power Game*, Kuldip Nayar's *The Judgement*, Uma Vasudev's *The Two Faces of Indira Gandhi* and Nayantara Sahgal's *Indira Gandhi: Her Road to Power*. The poet and writer, Dom Moraes, who had been writing a semi-authorized biography of Indira, remained loyal to his subject, but his was a lonely voice of defence. Khushwant Singh would wait until the political weathervane had spun round again before he published his admiring *Indira Gandhi Returns* in 1979. Meanwhile, during the three years immediately after Indira's defeat, the only lasting work inspired by the Emergency was being written in London by an obscure novelist named Salman Rushdie. *Midnight's Children* made a fine art out of demonizing Indira, depicting her as a monstrous, devouring widow. It went on to win the Booker Prize in 1980.

Indira always claimed that she never read articles and books about her, but she was remarkably familiar with their tenor and content. Although she had successfully sued Rushdie after *Midnight's Children* was published, the press and media were not Indira's principal worries.

It was Desai and his government she feared. On 23 May the Janata Home Minister, Charan Singh, stood up in Parliament and claimed that Indira had 'planned or thought of killing all opposition leaders in jail during the Emergency'.[9] Five days later a commission headed by the former Supreme Court Justice, J.C. Shah, was appointed to inquire into 'subversion of lawful processes and well-established conventions, administrative procedures and practices, abuse of authority, misuse of powers, excesses and/or malpractices committed during' the Emergency.[10] Sanjay too fell under the purview of the Shah Commission. In addition the Khanna Commission was created specifically to probe into Maruti Limited, while the Reddy Commission was set up to investigate the activities of Bansi Lal. Indira, however, remained Janata's primary target and it was the Shah Commission that dominated public attention. The hearings were scheduled to begin in the autumn of 1977.

In late May, Maneka Gandhi's father, Colonel T.C. Anand, was found dead, lying in an open field. A pistol lay beside him and also a note that read: 'Sanjay worry unbearable.' Anand's death was not a complete shock to his family and friends. He had a history of mental instability and had previously made an attempt on his life by taking a drug overdose.[11] Still, rumours quickly spread that his death was actually a murder staged to look like a suicide. Stories circulated that Anand planned 'to tell all' about his son-in-law Sanjay Gandhi if he was summoned by the Shah Commission, and so had to be disposed of. But once the media attention died down, the case was quickly forgotten.

Throughout the summer of 1977 Indira kept a low profile in Delhi, meeting daily with her lawyers in preparation for the Shah Commission inquiry. Then in July, in a remote village in Bihar called Belchi, upper-caste landowners massacred a large number of Harijans. Belchi had no telecommunications, and it took several days for news of this atrocity to reach Delhi. When it did, the Janata government failed to take action. Indira, in contrast, immediately set off for Belchi with a group of loyal Congressmen. It was a risky undertaking because Bihar was a state notorious for roaming bands of dacoits who robbed and often killed travellers, and Indira no longer had security men to protect her.

She began the journey to Belchi in a jeep, but when it started to rain and the roads became impassable, she switched to a farmer's tractor.

On the last leg of the journey, she had to cross a flooded river on an elephant. Indira finally reached Belchi after dark. The frightened villagers, carrying flame torches to see by, approached her with trepidation. Then, when they recognized Indira, they welcomed her like a saviour and threw themselves at her feet. She had come to Belchi knowing full well that it would be a public relations opportunity and a chance to test the feasibility of a political comeback. But once there, Indira was profoundly moved by the dirt-poor, grief-stricken villagers and the ashes of the communal funeral pyre where they had burned the bodies of their murdered kin and neighbours.

The next morning Indira went to Patna, the capital of Bihar, where her old antagonist, J.P. Narayan, had retired and was slowly dying. Now that Indira had been defeated and scorned, Narayan forgave her. After a fifty-minute tête-à-tête, they posed for photographers. Making peace with Narayan was a politically astute move, but it was also for both of them an emotional reunion and brought back the days when Nehru was still alive, and Narayan's wife and Kamala Nehru were the closest of friends.

Buoyed by her reception in Belchi and her reconciliation with Narayan in Patna, when Indira returned to Delhi she decided to visit her former constituency, Rae Bareilly. She had not been back since the voters had so decisively rejected her. It was a gamble, but Indira's reception in Rae Bareilly was, if possible, even more enthusiastic than it had been in Belchi. Thousands of people flocked to see her under a blazing sun. Indira went to all the surrounding villages, and again and again great crowds gathered to hear her apologize for the Emergency and then launch into an attack on Janata. By the end of the day, she was still going strong, unwilted by the heat, though coated in dust and soaked with sweat. The Delhi papers falsely reported that Indira's former constituency had met her with black flags. Rae Bareilly had taken back its *bahu* or daughter-in-law – the wife of their first MP, Feroze Gandhi – and their 'Mother', as she called herself years before in her 1967 campaign speech. As the *Guardian* in England reported, Indira's former constituents forgave her 'in ten minutes flat'.[12]

After Indira's triumphant visits to Belchi and Rae Bareilly, Janata became alarmed. The Shah Commission, which was about to get underway, was meant to indict Indira, but here the masses were starting to worship her again. Something had to be done. On 15 August 1977 –

Indian Independence Day – Indira's man Friday, R.K. Dhawan, was arrested. So too were Indira's former campaign manager, Yashpal Kapoor, the treasurer of the Congress Party, P.C. Sethi, and the Defence Minister and Sanjay's crony, Bansi Lal. Before the end of the month, the Law Minister, H.R. Gokhale and two other former cabinet members were also arrested. The net was closing in on Indira.

The Shah Commission hearings began in Delhi on 29 September 1977. The Commission's stated purpose was to inquire into 'excesses, malpractices and misdeeds during the Emergency or in the days immediately preceding [it] . . . by the political authorities, public servants, their friends and/or relatives and in particular allegations of gross misuse of powers of arrest or detention, maltreatment of and atrocities on detenus [sic] . . . compulsion and use of force in the implementation of the family planning programme and indiscriminate and high-handed demolition of houses, flats, shops, buildings . . . and destruction of property in the name of slum clearance . . . resulting . . . in [a] large number of people becoming homeless'.[13]

From the beginning, Justice Shah ran his one-man show like a Chinese people's court. The ambience at Patiala House, where the hearings were held, was vociferously hostile. A filled-to-capacity audience of over two hundred loudly cheered allegations and accusations and booed all attempts at defence. Loudspeakers broadcast the testimony and tumult to those outside the hall. The proceedings were also tape-recorded.

Though she was eventually summoned to appear before Justice Shah, for several months Indira evaded the hearings. But Sanjay could not escape giving testimony and his frequent appearances became a theatrical spectacle. When he entered Patiala House he was greeted with catcalls and other verbal abuse. On several occasions hostile spectators and Sanjay's supporters hurled steel chairs across the courtroom and physically assaulted each other.

The hearings went on throughout the autumn and winter, and hundreds of people testified. Key protagonists in the Emergency such as Siddhartha Shankar Ray submitted written depositions. Though the Shah Commission hearings were not televised, as the Watergate ones had been three years earlier, like Watergate, they had a high entertainment value and gripped the public.

One of the first people to testify was Jagmohan, the man on the ground at Turkman Gate and other demolition sites during the Emergency. Congenitally verbose, Jagmohan put on a tedious and exasperating performance when he took the stand. In response to Shah's interrogation, he embarked on 'humble submissions' and long-winded explanations in a hopeless attempt to give what he called the 'correct picture' of all the good that had been done in Delhi during the Emergency. Justice Shah had to warn him repeatedly to be precise.

Navin Chawla, in contrast, performed like a matinee idol – smooth, convincing, articulate – but utterly implausible. Like many of those who testified before Shah, Chawla pleaded ignorance. He claimed that he had no hand in the demolition operations and that Jagmohan and those under Jagmohan acted independently of Chawla's boss, the Lieutenant Governor of Delhi, Kishan Chand. Chawla also insisted that his own long-standing, personal relationship with Sanjay Gandhi did not in any way impinge on his official actions as Chand's secretary. With heavy irony, Shah congratulated Chawla on his 'compartmentalized mind'.

Predictably, nothing in Chawla's testimony was self-incriminating. Others, however, gave evidence that revealed the enormous and sinister power Chawla wielded during the Emergency. He was Sanjay's henchman and carried out his orders, but he also used the Emergency to settle his own scores. Particularly shocking was the way Chawla, in the words of the *Shah Commission Report*, exercised 'extra statutory control in jail matters' including 'the treatment of detenus [sic]'. Chawla not only specified who should be arrested and jailed but also how they were to be treated in prison. His orders included 'the construction of [special] . . . cells with asbestos roofs to "bake"' certain prisoners.[14]

The performance of Chawla's boss, the former Lieutenant Governor Kishan Chand, was far from impressive. Chand's testimony not only incriminated himself but also revealed that he had been the spineless and often witless puppet of Sanjay Gandhi, who operated him by remote control through Navin Chawla. Certain files 'signed' by Chand were discovered to have been forged and backdated. Demolition orders of which he had no knowledge were dispatched in his name. Those that he did personally authorize, he gave, he said, 'under compulsion' from 'the Prime Minister's House'. The assessment of the *Shah Commission Report* was that Chand 'by his various actions and inactions [sic] with regard to important and vital matters appears to have abdicated his legitimate functions in favour of an over-ambitious group of officers like ... Bhinder, Bajwa and Navin Chawla with disastrous consequences to the people. He betrayed his trust and committed a serious breach of faith with the citizens of Delhi and failed to administer the affairs of the territory honestly and justly.'[15]

In the end, Chand passed judgement on himself. Shortly after the *Shah Commission Report* was published, he committed suicide by jumping into a well near his home. He left a note saying that death was better than 'a life of humiliation'. Even though Chand's death was clearly self-inflicted, people maintained that he had been 'eliminated' at Sanjay Gandhi's behest.[16]

Throughout the Shah Commission hearings, Justice Shah tried hard to nail the figure at the centre of this high drama – Indira Gandhi. Shah wanted to question Indira on eleven specific points, including the appointments of certain bank governors and judges, the events that transpired between 12 and 22 June 1975, and the arrests made on the night of 25/26 June 1976.

Guided by her lawyer, Frank Anthony, Indira initially postponed appearing before the Shah Commission. She argued that the Commission was unconstitutional and illegal and pointed out that it denied her the opportunity to cross-examine witnesses who had deposed against her. Then she issued a public statement saying that she would appear before Shah only 'in accordance with the law', and only if she were given the freedom to produce evidence, call upon her lawyers and cross-examine those who made allegations against her. For the time being she escaped Shah's net.

But not Janata's. Within days of the beginning of the Shah Commission hearings, on the afternoon of 3 October 1977, a police van drove up to 12 Willingdon Crescent. Sanjay and Maneka were playing badminton on the front lawn. Two officers got out of the van and when Indira came to the door, they informed her that she was under arrest. She had been expecting this – as indeed had the rest of the country. She told the police she needed time to pack and left them standing on the doorstep. At 8 p.m. she re-emerged in an immaculate white sari with a green border. A large crowd surged forward and many people garlanded her. During the five hours while the police waited for Indira, telephone calls had been made to the press, friends and supporters, all of whom flocked to the house. It was also later rumoured that while

Indira 'packed', Sonia Gandhi's pasta maker was put to use as a paper shredder.[17] Before consenting to go with the police, Indira insisted that they handcuff her. Reluctantly, the police complied while press photographers snapped pictures.

This photo opportunity over, Indira got into the police van which drove off followed by a flotilla of cars carrying Indira's two sons and their wives, her lawyers, numerous supporters and journalists. The police proceeded to drive towards the neighbouring state of Haryana, but when they reached a railway crossing on the outskirts of Delhi, two long mail trains were lumbering past which meant an enforced wait of at least thirty minutes. Indira was allowed to leave the van during this halt. She sat down on the ground, encircled by a crowd, while her lawyers advised her that she should refuse to cross the city limits. A loud argument ensued among the policemen, lawyers and Indira's supporters while Indira sat quietly on the ground and the press photographers took more pictures. When the mail trains finally passed she was driven to Delhi's Police Lines where the policeman on duty saluted her smartly and then locked her up. She refused the food offered to her, read a novel she had brought along for an hour or so, and then slept soundly through the night.

The next morning Indira was driven to the magistrate's court. The charges brought against her were that during the March 1977 elections, jeeps had been donated to Congress that were later sold to the army, and also that Indira's government had given a contract to a French oil company whose bid was several million dollars higher than an American company's bid. But the magistrate before whom Indira appeared released her unconditionally, saying that 'there was [sic] no grounds for believing [either] . . . accusation is well founded'. Janata was foiled. By arresting Indira and locking her up they had now made a martyr of her and put her on the road to political recovery. As Rajiv said to a foreign correspondent, 'Even Mummy could not have thought out a better scenario.'[18]

After the fiasco of her arrest, Indira's popularity increased. She made a triumphant tour of Gujarat where she was enthusiastically greeted everywhere, especially in the tribal areas. Back in Delhi, her Willingdon Crescent garden filled up every morning with admirers – most of them poor. A visiting American said to Indira that this loyalty meant she must have done something for them when she was in power. But Indira contradicted him, saying, 'No, those for whom something was done are nowhere to be seen.'[19]

Among those 'nowhere to be seen' was a sizeable proportion of the Congress leadership. Indira's old admirer Dev Kanta Barooah (the man who had coined 'Indira is India and India Indira') had abandoned her after her defeat. The new Congress Party president, Brahmanda Reddy, kept his distance. Others also decided the future did not lie with Indira. On New Year's Day 1978, the Congress Party split for the second time. As in 1969, this second bifurcation was instigated by Indira. She and her followers now formed the Congress (I) party, the 'I' standing for Indira herself. Faced with the prospect of formally deserting her, seventy MPs followed Indira into Congress (I), leaving seventy-six MPs in the old rump party now led by Swaran Singh and known as Congress (S). Among those who defected from Indira were her former Health Minister, Karan Singh, and Indira's co-worker in the Partition refugee camps, Subhadra Joshi. Both Congresses tussled over who would keep the party symbol of the cow and her calf. With hindsight, this was one battle Indira was lucky to lose, given the comparisons her critics had drawn between the symbol and the Prime Minister and her son. Congress (S) retained the cow and calf icon, while Indira's Congress took the more fortunate ideograph of a raised, open palm.

It was only on 9 January 1978 – more than three months after the Shah Commission hearings began – that Indira was forced by a summons to come face to face with her inquisitor, J.C. Shah, at Patiala House in Delhi. She may have been physically present, but her lips remained sealed. Frank Anthony stood up and protested to Shah that Indira was the 'prime target of attack', rather than a witness, and that she refused to be questioned or to make a written statement. Shah ordered Indira to appear the following day.

Indira and her lawyer duly returned to Patiala House the next day. Anthony again spoke on his client's behalf and made the following points to Shah:

1. The appointment of Shah's commission was vitiated.
2. Newspapers had published garbled accounts of the hearings.
3. The terms of reference of the Commission were vague.
4. The Commission could not inquire into circumstances which preceded the declaration of the Emergency or into the manner in which the President was advised to declare it.

5. Mrs Gandhi had been denied knowledge of the demeanour of witnesses and to that extent the proceedings were vitiated.
6. The investigating officers should be available for cross-examination.

Shah rejected all of these points and instructed Frank Anthony and his client to appear again the next day.

On 11 January Indira persisted in her non-cooperation. Anthony reiterated his points of the previous day. Shah finally lost patience and addressed Indira directly:

'Mrs Gandhi, would you please come here.'

Indira walked to where Anthony was standing in front of a microphone.

Shah said, 'I want to know whether you are willing to make a statement.'

Indira answered, 'I have just said I am not legally bound.'

Shah got sterner. 'Are you willing?'

Indira (softly), 'I decline.'

She paused and then added, 'I am bound by my oath of secrecy not to make any statement.' Then she walked back to her seat and before sitting down, added, 'I am not constitutionally bound either.'

Shah raised his voice. 'Tell that to the magistrate.' Then he began dictating an order to lodge a formal complaint with a magistrate to proceed against Indira.

At this point Indira brought up what seemed an extraneous issue. She told Shah that when she raised the matter of bank nationalization in 1969 her action had been branded unconstitutional in certain quarters and a demand was made that all bankers and bank shareholders be amply compensated. This, Indira reminded Shah, had created a furore and a petition was then drawn up alleging that certain members of the judiciary would suffer if banks were nationalized and that they were behind the drive against nationalization. The petition called for an investigation which Indira refused to authorize.

Indira now said to Shah, 'As Prime Minister, I stopped it [the petition] to uphold the dignity of the judiciary. Two hundred MPs, including some who are now ministers in the Janata government, sent in a memorandum demanding impeachment action against the judges. Again I stopped it.'

Few in the crowded hearing room would have grasped what Indira was driving at if Shah had not interrupted her with, 'I never was a shareholder of any bank ... Some people made that allegation. It is a false allegation.'

'I am not mentioning you at all,' Indira calmly replied.

Shah – the head of the Commission hearings – foolishly persisted in defending himself before his star 'culprit'. 'Some of my brother judges,' he said, 'had shares. I told them that I did not hold any shares. I had an account in a certain bank ... [but] I personally held no shares in any of the fourteen banks at the time they were taken over.'[20]

After this triumph, when Indira appeared for the last time before Shah, on 19 January, it was an anti-climax. She again refused to go to the witness box and insisted that she was not legally and constitutionally bound to do so. The Shah Commission hearings finally drew to a close a month later on 20 February 1978.

After her appearances before the Shah Commission Indira took to the road to promote herself and her new Congress (I). She made a pilgrimage to see the ascetic, Vinoba Bhave – one of the last remaining Gandhians – at his ashram in Wardha in Maharashtra. Bhave had supported J.P. Narayan and his total revolution movement before the Emergency. During the Emergency his ashram had been raided. Bhave's warm reception of Indira was, therefore, a dramatic indication of her growing rehabilitation.

In April 1978 there was a violent confrontation at an agricultural college in Pantnagar in Uttar Pradesh over higher wages for the workers. The police opened fire on the demonstration and eighty-one people were killed. Indira, accompanied by the British writer and journalist Bruce Chatwin and the photographer Eve Arnold, travelled to Pantnagar. When they arrived, they were invited to view a coagulated pool of blood and brains which has been carefully left for Indira's inspection. Indira responded with appropriate horror and then met with and comforted the widows of those killed. After this, according to Dom Moraes, who also went along, Indira, 'as usual, sped around in her sandals like Hermes', pausing only to address the agricultural students and staff.[21] Indira confided to Chatwin that her secret was 'her stamina. Physically,' she said, 'she could outpace every other Indian politician.'[22]

Chatwin and Eve Arnold also accompanied Indira on a tour of South India. In Cochin, Kerala, Indira spoke from a balcony, after which she sat on a chair perched on top of a table. When it grew dark 'she jammed a torch between her knees, directing the beam upwards to light her face and arms . . . [which] she rotated' while observing to Chatwin, 'you've no idea how tiring it is to be a goddess'. It began to rain, but 'a downpour did not prevent about a quarter of a million drenched figures from filing past to pay their respects'.[23]

By the time they reached Calicut, both Chatwin and Arnold were going 'through alternative phases of "Love Indira" or "Loathe Indira"'. They had come to India expecting only to hate her, but Indira had taken them aback. When a hostile person threw a glass bottle at their cavalcade of cars, Chatwin got hit on the nose. Indira, who had been in another car, only realized this when they arrived at a rally that she was to address. 'Good Heavens, Mr Chatwin,' she said. 'Whatever happened to you?' Chatwin explained and Indira responded with, 'That's what comes of following me around.'

After they had returned to their hotel later in the day, Indira sought out Chatwin and asked, 'Are you sure you're all right? Have they got all the glass out? Well, thank Heaven for that! Do you want to lie down?' Chatwin did not want to, but Eve Arnold, who was 'wilting in the heat', did. Indira had an air-conditioned room, and as Chatwin described it, 'Mrs G sized up the situation and led Eve into her own bedroom where her briefcase was open and papers were strewn about. She laid her down on the bed and let her sleep for two hours. She then returned with the eternal cup of tea and said she needed the room to change.'[24]

On 6 August 1978, six months after the Shah Commission hearings ended, the Ministry of Information and Broadcasting published the third volume of the *Shah Commission Report* – 'The Final Report'. Two interim reports had been previously published in March and April. In his three-volume report, Justice J.C. Shah declared that the proclamation of the Emergency was unconstitutional and fraudulent because there was 'no evidence of any breakdown of law and order in any part of the country – nor any apprehension in that behalf'. Shah's verdict was that Indira had resorted to Emergency powers in 'a desperate endeavour to save herself from the legitimate compulsion of a judicial verdict against her'. Among the evils Shah said Indira's government had perpetrated between 1975 and early 1977, were the detention of thousands of innocent people and 'a series of totally illegal and unwarranted actions involving untold human misery and suffering'.[25]

The *Shah Commission Report* was a comprehensive indictment of Indira Gandhi, her younger son and the Emergency. No matter was too great or too small to be investigated. In addition to illegally detaining more than a thousand people, killing at least six at Turkman Gate and forcibly sterilizing thousands, Indira's regime was found guilty of 'misuse of powers and miscarriage of justice in saving Shri Sudarshan Kumar Verma, a clerk in the Railways, from legal punishment by the CBI officials', and of 'misuse of power and abuse of authority by Shri T.R. Tuli, Chairman of the Punjab National Bank, in allowing a clean over-draft to M/s. Associated Journals Ltd'. Only rarely did Shah fail to come up with the goods. Regarding 'concessions by Punjab National Bank in favour of Maruti Ltd', for example, his report stated that 'taking into account the evidence adduced and the arguments advanced, the Commission is of the view that no subversion of administrative procedures or misuse of power or abuse of authority has been established in this case'.[26]

Despite the furore surrounding its publication, the *Shah Commission Report* was a disappointing document. It contained only a fraction of the complete proceedings of the Shah Commission hearings, and its three volumes ran to only 500 double-columned pages in total. Haphazardly constructed and written in a verbose, legalistic English, it is laden with solecisms and strange idioms. It survives, however, as the only official record of the Emergency because the full tape-recorded proceedings of the Commission have vanished.

The publication of Shah's report in three instalments inevitably engendered a false air of expectation. When volume one failed to create a stir, everyone waited for the 'dynamite' of volume two. When it, too, fell flat, hopes were nourished for volume three – the longest of all, but just as dull as the previous two. Rumour and 'scurrilous' allegations had far outstripped the often-banal reality of the Emergency. For every reported crime, violation, detention, act of censorship, violence and death the hearings yielded, three times as many or more had already been alleged in the media or Delhi political gossip.

The Commission's report was, in fact, no more than a dreary and predictable summary of J.C. Shah's foregone conclusions, based on the evidence provided to him in the course of the Commission hearings and padded out with selected extracts from witnesses' testimonies. It was obvious that the *Report* was a highly subjective interpretation of the evidence. The author's bias – and his purpose – were unmistakable. Indeed the report makes it clear that the hearings were not and were never intended to be a proper, objective inquiry into abuses, malpractices and crimes committed during the Emergency. Shah was Janata's man and the Commission and report were primarily Janata propaganda exercises. There are no heroes in the *Shah Commission Report* but a surfeit of fools and villains. The chief villain – Indira Gandhi – however remains intractably elusive as Shah's baying hounds pursue her through its pages.

Despite its serious shortcomings the *Shah Commission Report* survives as a treasure trove of evidence for Sanjay Gandhi's illicit power in the period leading up to and during the Emergency, and of the sycophancy and cowardice of numerous public servants and government officials during the same period. It is not surprising that Indira Gandhi had all copies of the *Report* withdrawn as soon as she regained power in 1980.[27]

In the end, the Shah Commission proved a largely pointless exercise. Despite its extensive and theatrical hearings, it was merely a fact-finding body. The Commission's report itself states clearly that the 'proceedings' were 'neither of the nature of a civil suit nor . . . a criminal trial'.[28] Or as Shah conceded later in an interview, 'my work was purely investigatory'.[29] His report caused a storm of controversy but it had no legal authority. It could not pronounce anyone guilty of anything. All the 'illegal and unwarranted actions' the report enumerated would have to be proved in a court of law. And this could take years.

Prime Minister Desai had been foiled when Indira's arrest backfired. Despite the findings of the Shah Commission, he was not about to risk jailing her again. This meant that for the time being she was legally safe until Janata set up the legal machinery with which to prosecute her. As time passed and Indira travelled about the country and her popularity with the masses grew, the press and the public ignored Janata's witch-hunt.

But unlike Indira, Sanjay was not legally safe. Throughout the spring of 1978 he was pursued in the courts for among other things, intimidating and suborning prosecution witnesses who testified before the Shah Commission. On 5 May the Supreme Court sentenced him to prison for one month and he was locked up in Delhi's notorious Tihar Jail where so many of the Emergency prisoners had languished. Indira was having a rare holiday in Karnataka, visiting temples and monasteries, when she got news of Sanjay's arrest. She took the first plane back to Delhi and went straight from the airport to Tihar Jail where, in front of television film crews and journalists, she embraced her son and told him, 'Don't lose heart. This is going to be your political rebirth.'[30]

Sanjay was released in late June by which time Indira had decided to stand again for Parliament. By now she had travelled extensively in India and with few exceptions, had been received with enthusiasm, especially by the rural poor – the vast majority of the country's voters. The press, the intelligentsia and Janata were still out to ruin her, but she had already gone a long ways towards political resurrection in the hearts of the masses. Their long-term memories of her and her father were warm and strong while the recent events of the twenty-one-month-long Emergency now seemed an aberration.

One evening when the journalist Inder Malhotra was dining at a friend's house and the dinner guests began to speak critically of Indira, the servant who was serving the food interjected: 'Indiraji did bad things [during the Emergency, but] . . . she did good things in the past.' Uma Vasudev's cook told her that though he had voted against Indira in 1977, now that that 'Indiraji' was about to stand for election again, he would enthusiastically vote for her. When Vasudev asked why, the cook responded: Indira 'cares about us' – the poor – while Janata did not.[31] Workers were declaring their belief in Indira to their employers all over the country. Rickshaw drivers, sidewalk traders and sweepers were also speaking out. Eventually even the intelligentsia could see that a real pro-Indira wave was underway.

Janata helped it along with its own poor performance. Many people in fact harked back nostalgically to the 'good old days' and 'discipline' of the Emergency. Janata had opened the jails and released smugglers, horders and racketeers who had been locked up during the Emergency. Prices rose and communal violence – especially against Harijans – increased. In the midst of all this, the Janata coalition government was coming apart at the seams. At the top, Desai struggled with Charan Singh, the Home Minister, who wanted to replace him as Prime Minister. An ailing and dying J. P. Narayan – in retirement now in Patna – could no longer hold Janata together.

Matters came to a head in June 1978 when Charan Singh – Indira's most vehement foe – accused Desai and the other cabinet ministers of being 'a collection of impotent men' because they had failed to bring Indira Gandhi to justice.[32] Desai dropped Charan Singh from the Cabinet and also Singh's disciple, Raj Narain, the Health Minister, who had filed the Rae Bareilly election malpractice case against Indira in 1971 and then defeated her in 1977. Eventually Desai was forced to take Charan Singh back as Defence Minister and Deputy Prime Minister (a post shared with Jagjivan Ram), but the fatal cracks in Janata were now clear to everyone.

As Janata self-destructed, Indira polished her own position. In July 1978 she gave a long interview to an American academic named Mary Carras who was writing a political biography of her. By this time Indira had perfected her line on the Emergency and her 1977 electoral defeat, and she realized Carras was an opportune mouthpiece.

For the most part, the interview rehearsed familiar territory. Indira explained that she had imposed the Emergency to save the country from chaos; that she did not consult the Cabinet in advance because she feared the announcement would be leaked; that admittedly some things 'did get a little out of hand' during the Emergency, but the reports of abuses, especially concerning sterilization, were grossly exaggerated. She lost the 1977 election because she had 'annoyed' certain segments of the society and also because Janata 'had a lot of foreign help . . . the movement against us was engineered by outside forces'.

Indira's occasional admissions of errors – things 'getting a little out of hand' and 'annoying certain segments of society' – were quite calculated. Indira knew that she would be rehabilitated sooner if she took a portion of the blame. She had already publicly apologized for certain 'aspects' of the Emergency. Now she also admitted that muzzling the press 'may have been too strong a step', and also that 'some of our chief ministers arrested people for no reason at all, I mean just personal enmity'. But she also claimed that 'except for the detention of political persons and press censorship, there was not much abnormal . . . At the Turkman Gate incident, six people died, all from outside the area'. Carras' scathing response was 'so basically, it was sort of run-of-the-mill violence?' Indira stood her ground and replied with a blatant lie: 'There was no violence . . . just one or two isolated cases.'

During the interview, Indira fielded most of the questions about the Emergency with ease. But when Carras strayed beyond it and asked her why literacy rates in India had remained so low, Indira gave an ill-considered response: 'I don't know how important literacy is. What has it done for the West? Are people happier or more alive to problems? On the contrary, I think they have become more superficial.'[33]

The interview with Carras defined Indira's retrospective, public analysis of the Emergency. Shortly after it, Carras had the opportunity to see Indira present it to the masses when she travelled with her to Madras and Madurai. Carras, who was small and dark like Gandhi, was wearing a sari rather than her normal American clothes. She and Indira got separated in the crush of people entering a temple near Madurai and Carras, who walked ahead of Indira, suddenly found herself surrounded by a mob. Men and women garlanded Carras with flowers, prostrated themselves at her feet, and nearly yanked her hands and arms out of their sockets. In vain, the local Congress leaders tried to tell the crowd that Carras was not 'the Mother' – Indira – whom they had come to adore. For Carras it was an alarming but enlightening experience. For the first time she realized that the public adulation of Indira Gandhi was unassailable no matter how many Shah commissions and special courts Janata created to destroy her.[34]

In November 1978, Indira formally re-entered politics when she stood in a by-election in the rural constituency of Chikmaglur in the southern state of Karnataka. It was an ideal constituency for her: 50 per cent of the voters were women; 45 per cent belonged to scheduled or backward castes or minorities and nearly half of the population lived below the poverty line. Chikmaglur was also a Congress stronghold; the incumbent, who stepped down for Indira, was Deve Gowda, a longtime Congress leader in Karnataka. Janata sent George Fernandes, the Minister of Industry, to take charge of the fight against Indira. Fernandes, a popular Janata leader and one of the few with left-wing credentials, campaigned vigorously on behalf of Indira's opponent, Veerendra Patil, a former Chief Minister of Karnataka. Everyone expected Patil to win. But the crowds that came to hear Indira were enthusiastic, even reverential, and they far outnumbered those who came to see Patil and Fernandes. It was Mother Indira all over again. Despite press predictions, Indira won by a large margin of 70,000 votes.

* * *

On 12 November 1978, just four days after her victory in Chikmaglur, Indira flew to London. All the Gandhis' passports had been impounded after Indira's defeat in 1977. Because of international criticism of Janata's persecution of Indira, the government now issued her a diplomatic passport though it was valid for travel only to Britain. This was a mistake, however, because Indira's primary motive for going abroad was to refurbish her international reputation. At Heathrow Airport she got off to a good start. A crowd of journalists awaited her and their first question was, 'Have you come to Britain to make your comeback?' Indira answered with a big smile, 'But where had I gone?'[35]

Officially this was a private visit. Indira stayed at Claridge's Hotel, and in the same suite she had occupied when she had been Prime Minister. But in 1978 she was the guest of a wealthy Indian industrialist, established in Britain, named Swraj Paul who paid all her expenses. Indira brought $250 in traveller's cheques with her – the limit allowed by the Indian government. She asked Paul – for whom $250 would cover a dinner or two out – to change the cheques for her. He laughed and insisted she was his guest, but Indira was adamant that he take the travellers' cheques which she signed and thrust on him.[36]

Indira's friendship with Swraj Paul went back to 1966 when his young daughter was being treated for leukaemia in London. Though he had established himself as an international businessman by then, Paul's other children were still in India and he wanted them to visit their sister. In the mid-sixties it was necessary to obtain government permission for foreign travel. This had not been forthcoming and so Paul wrote to Indira for assistance, even though he had met her only once or twice. Within two days Swraj Paul had the necessary clearance for his children's air tickets.

Paul's daughter died, but he did not forget Indira's intervention. In the mid-seventies he proved himself an invaluable Congress fundraiser in England, and when Indira lost power in 1977, Paul remained loyal and financially helpful. As soon as he heard the election results, he rang Indira from London and told her, 'Indiraji, as long as I have something to eat, you will eat first.' During the two-and-a-half years she was out of power, Paul did not waver in his friendship, a fact that made his position with the Janata government difficult. In his own words, between 1977 and 1980, he 'went through hell for' Indira.[37]

In November 1978 it was Swraj Paul who orchestrated Indira's political rehabilitation in Britain. On this 'private visit', he organized numerous support rallies for her which were attended largely by Indians. He arranged for her to meet the Prime Minister, James Callaghan, and to address a large gathering of both Labour and Conservative MPs. Indira admitted freely to Callaghan and the other MPs that she and Congress had lost the election because they had managed to 'annoy all sections of society at the same time'. Indira's friend, the Conservative Party leader, Margaret Thatcher, was, of course, also present and entirely sympathetic.[38]

While in England, Indira had dinner with her old friend Michael Foot and his wife, Jill Craigie.[39] She also had lunch with the romantic novelist, Barbara Cartland. Indira had wanted to meet Cartland for some time, not because (as is sometimes claimed) she admired her fiction, but because Cartland followed a complicated dietary regime that involved vitamin supplements and organic foods and Indira was interested in the health benefits Cartland claimed for her system.[40] While in London Indira also went to the theatre, saw several films and shopped at Woolworth's and Foyle's bookshop. For every day that Indira was in London Paul sent her roses from Harrods, but Indira did not shop there herself.

Throughout her visit, the Indian High Commission made disgruntled noises, especially when Indira met with political figures. Back in New Delhi Morarji Desai and the Janata government were becoming increasingly agitated by Indira's high-profile welcome.

While Indira was repairing her international image from London, back in India Janata was making a last-ditch effort to bring her down again. Shortly after Indira returned to Delhi in December 1978, the Privileges Committee in Parliament found her guilty of obstructing four officials who were investigating Maruti Limited. On 19 December a resolution was passed in Parliament demanding that Indira 'be committed to jail till the prorogation of the House and also expelled from membership of the House for the serious breach of privilege and contempt of the House committed by her'.

On the floor of the Lok Sabha, Indira responded to this sentence with dignified rage. 'I am a small person, but I have stood for certain values and objectives. Every insult hurled at me will rebound, every punishment inflicted on me will be a source of strength to me ... My voice will not be hushed for it is not a lone voice. It speaks not for myself, a frail woman and unimportant person.' Then she paused and when she resumed her tone had shifted from martyrdom to a mocking defiance. 'The atmosphere in the House [is like] . . . Alice in Wonderland when all the cards rise up in the air and shout "off with her head!" My head is yours. My box has been packed these several months; we had only to put in the winter things.'[41]

After her speech, Indira rose to leave the Lok Sabha. She walked slowly down the aisle that separated the rows of seats, her back to the other members present. But when she reached the door, Indira turned round and raised her arm, palm outwards, and said, 'I will be back.'[42]

By the time Indira was expelled from Parliament, Desai had managed to pass legislation to set up special courts to try Indira and Sanjay Gandhi. Soon after her expulsion and dramatic exit from Parliament, Indira was arrested and taken to Tihar Jail where she was put in a barracks on her own – in the same cell complex that George Fernandes had occupied during the Emergency. Sonia Gandhi brought all Indira's meals to her from home. But on 26 December, after just one week in jail, Indira was released.

Once again, Janata had blundered. Incarcerating Indira had resurrected her 'from the ashes of the Emergency' and made her more popular than ever.[43] By the time she was released, Indira was a heroine and martyr. She made a triumphant return to Karnataka and told the people of Chikmaglur that her arrest and imprisonment had been illegal. After a rapturous reception, Indira then went on to Madras for a short break with Pupul Jayakar and the spiritual leader, Krishnamurti, of whom Jayakar was an ardent follower. According to Jayakar, Krishnamurti met with Indira alone and counselled her to leave politics altogether. But Indira told him that there was no question of leaving: she either had to fight her enemies or be destroyed by them.[44]

By early 1979, however, the enemy was fighting and destroying itself with a vengeance. Desai and Charan Singh had fallen out again. Desai's son, Kantilal, was found guilty of crooked business deals and other corrupt practices. Jagjivan Ram's son – a married man of forty – was photographed having sex with a college girl in her teens. This, of course, made the Janata persecution of Sanjay Gandhi look ridiculous. Maneka Gandhi got hold of some of the photographs of Ram's son *in flagrante delicto* with his young girlfriend and published them in her magazine, *Surya*, which she had set up and edited with the help of the journalist and Gandhi friend, Khushwant Singh.

But despite the misdeeds of Desai's and Ram's sons, Sanjay was still in a precarious position and Indira was extremely fearful of what Janata would do to him. The Janata government, in fact, filed no less than thirty-five criminal cases against Sanjay during its two-and-a-half years in power. On 27 February 1979, Sanjay and V.C. Shukla were sentenced to two years imprisonment and given hefty fines for destroying the film *Kissa Kursi Ka*, (the title means the 'chair' or 'throne') – a savage political satire on the Emergency. Sanjay and Shukla were released on bail and could, of course, appeal, but this was likely to be a lengthy process in the Indian courts.

For some time domestic discord at 12 Willingdon Crescent had been brewing and as Sanjay grew more embroiled in legal battles, it became nearly intolerable. It was rumoured that Rajiv and Sonia were about to leave the household and move to Italy. This was untrue; they were not about to abandon Indira, but relations between Rajiv and Sanjay were chilly and between Sonia and Maneka frigid. Indira's two daughters-in-law were not on speaking terms and avoided being in the same room together except when absolutely necessary. One morning B.K. and Fori Nehru were breakfasting with the family and Sanjay went into a rage and threw his plate across the room when Sonia failed to cook his eggs in the precise way he had ordered. Indira did not utter a word of criticism to Sanjay but she was clearly embarrassed.[45]

The situation at home was made worse by Maneka's erratic, uncontrolled behaviour. She responded to the pervasive atmosphere of uncertainty and anxiety with wild outbursts and tantrums against nearly everyone, including her husband. Their volatile marriage became even more explosive. Indira admitted to Pupul Jayakar that the household was in chaos, but she exonerated her daughter-in-law's behaviour: 'Maneka is barely twenty-one . . . Long jail sentences threaten Sanjay . . . Maneka is under great strain. People should understand and forgive her hysteria.'[46]

In the early hours of 4 April 1979, at Rawalpindi Central Jail in Pakistan, Zulfikar Ali Bhutto was executed by hanging. Back in December 1971, in the wake of Pakistan's defeat by India, the Pakistani army and US State Department had handpicked Bhutto – the leader of the Pakistan

People's Party (PPP) – to be the country's civilian leader. The army had long been 'the spinal cord of the state apparatus' in Pakistan and they intended to remain in control during Bhutto's civilian regime. For six years they put up with Bhutto's increasingly demagogic populism because he did not fundamentally alter the power of the military, civil service or Pakistani landlord system. But when Bhutto refused wholly to be the army's tool and then when he rigged the 1977 elections, the generals overthrew him.[47]

General Zia-ul-Haq – whom Bhutto had believed would pose no threat to him – took over in July 1977 and declared martial law. On 3 September Bhutto was arrested and charged with 'conspiracy to murder' one of his political opponents, Ahmed Raza Kasuri. A nineteen-month trial – a 'judicial farce' – ensued, at the end of which Bhutto was sentenced to death and hanged – not because he was guilty of conspiring to murder Kasuri so much as 'Bhutto alive represented a permanent potential alternative to military rule'. The army feared that like Indira Gandhi, Bhutto would plot his political resurrection.[48]

Though Indira had never liked Bhutto (or he Indira), when he was sentenced to death, Indira publicly condemned the sentence and telegraphed Zia-ul-Haq urging him to grant Bhutto clemency. She also wrote to a number of other heads of state asking them to apply pressure on Zia not to execute Bhutto. Janata, foolishly, did not raise a finger to save him.[49]

On 31 May 1979 Sanjay and several of his associates in Maruti Limited were indicted for irregular business dealings. But before further legal action could be taken against him and Indira, on 11 July, the warring factions in Janata gave up all pretence of cooperation. Y.B. Chavan moved a no-confidence motion against Morarji Desai. The government fell. Desai resigned as Prime Minister on 15 July and Charan Singh formed a new government. Amazingly, he assumed power with the support of Congress (I) which, despite his relentless vendetta against Indira, Charan Singh had been wooing since falling out with Desai. Indira's support of Charan Singh was negotiated by Sanjay Gandhi who urged Indira to league with the enemy and let bygones be bygones in order to achieve her political resurrection.

Before he could become Prime Minister, Charan Singh had to submit to a vote of confidence in the Lok Sabha. The crunch came when Indira made her continued support of him conditional on Charan Singh withdrawing the Special Courts Act – the legislation enacted by Desai in order to try Indira of 'Emergency crimes'. Singh refused to bury the Special Courts Act whereupon Indira withdrew Congress (I)'s support for Charan Singh's unstable embryonic government.

Without Congress (I), Charan Singh could never survive a vote of confidence. The game was up for Janata. On 22 August 1979 the President dissolved Parliament and ordered new elections be held during the first week of January 1980. In the interim Charan Singh would remain as caretaker Prime Minister 'without taking any major policy decision'.

Indira Gandhi was poised to return.

NINETEEN

Fault Lines

AT THE BEGINNING OF THE 1980s India was threatening to deconstruct. Political upheavals rumbled in Assam, the Punjab and Kashmir. Throughout the country upper castes turned on Harijans, Hindus on Muslims, Sikhs on Hindus, Hindus and Muslims on Christians, and everyone on Tribals. The inclusive, accommodating nation that Nehru celebrated in all his books – especially in *The Discovery of India*, which Indira proofread when her father was in prison – seemed to be falling apart. Nehru's monolithic India had, of course, always been part myth – as evidenced by Partition and Pakistan. But for nearly thirty years the myth survived. By the time the Janata government fell in 1979 and Indira's political comeback looked likely, 'the idea of India' as well as its reality was cracking up.[1]

The fault lines with which India was now riven were a direct product of Indira Gandhi's eleven-year tenure in office between 1966 and 1977. Her centralization of power had severely undermined state and local autonomy and fuelled regional and communal discontent as a consequence. Ironically, the more she sought to control matters from Delhi, the more divisions grew. By the late seventies, aggrieved regional and religious minorities all over the country were clamouring for power and self-determination. But although Indira Gandhi was the source of the crisis India now faced, she was also perceived as its saviour. As she campaigned her way across the country in the closing weeks and days of 1979, many people felt – what she herself believed – that Indira was the only person who could hold India together.

In the run-up to the January 1980 general election, Indira spent sixty-two days on the road (and in the air), covering 40,000 miles and addressing up to twenty meetings a day. An estimated 90 million people

– or one in every four of the Indian electorate – throughout the country saw and heard Indira Gandhi in the course of her last and most arduous campaign.

Indira stood not only for her old constituency, Rae Bareilly in Uttar Pradesh, but also for a new one, Medak, in Andhra Pradesh, (Indian electoral rules do not prohibit a candidate from standing for more than one constituency). She won both contests by a large margin. And she carried her party with her all over the country – Congress captured 351 out of 542 Lok Sabha seats. As the *Times of India* headline put it, 'It's Indira All the Way'. Reluctantly, Indira decided to resign from Rae Bareilly, allowing Sanjay who was elected as the MP for the neighbouring constituency of Amethi to look after Uttar Pradesh. Indira handpicked a young family member named Arun Nehru – a successful businessman and precocious political manipulator – to take over in Rae Bareilly. In time he would become Rajiv Gandhi's key adviser and right-hand man.

Shortly after she was sworn in as Prime Minister for the fourth time, on 14 January 1980, Indira moved back into her old house at 1 Safdarjung Road. Before she returned, however, she sent in a dozen Hindu priests to 'purify' the house and also workmen to tear out the Desais' traditional Indian bathroom and replace it with the original Western-style one. By the time Indira and her family settled in, it was almost as if they had never been gone.

In fact, immediately after the election, when a Scandinavian journalist asked Indira how it felt to be India's leader again, she replied angrily, 'I have always been India's leader.'[2] It seemed as if the country, too, was suffering from amnesia and that the Emergency and Indira's spell in the wilderness after her 1977 defeat had been erased from history. The justices appointed by Desai to prosecute Indira and Sanjay Gandhi for Emergency crimes conveniently dissolved their special courts, pronouncing them unconstitutional. Cases pending against Sanjay were hastily dropped, including the *Kissa Kursi Ka* case in which Sanjay and V.C. Shukla had been found guilty of destroying the film satirizing the Emergency. Indira needed a clean slate in the states too and she erased the past there by dismissing the nine Janata state governments, imposing President's rule and calling for fresh state assembly elections. Congress won all but one of them.

As an elected MP Sanjay Gandhi finally possessed political legitimacy.

He came into his own and so did a large number of his cronies and associates who ran for office for the first time in 1980. Of the 351 Congress MPs elected, 234 were new to Parliament and at least 150 were ardent Sanjay followers. As the journalist Inder Malhotra described them, they were an entirely new breed of Congressman, 'lumpen young men . . . innocent of . . . parliamentary proprieties, unencumbered by ideology or idealism, short on cerebration and long on . . . muscle power, Sanjay's acolytes looked upon their membership of Parliament and proximity to the centre of power as a short-cut to making the maximum amount of money in the shortest possible time.'[3]

Everyone expected Indira to make Sanjay a minister in her Cabinet, but wisely she did not. She knew that Sanjay's power should appear earned and derived from others rather than herself. There was also a drive to make him Chief Minister of Uttar Pradesh, but Sanjay wanted to be at the centre, in New Delhi, where the action was. In the end, Indira consented to his appointment as General Secretary of the All-India Congress Committee.

Indira had been back in power for a month on 16 February when there was a solar eclipse – the first in India in eighty-four years. She took the day off (a rare occurrence) and invited her friend Pupul Jayakar to 1 Safdarjung Road to view the event with her. Rajiv and his children were out in the garden during the afternoon where he had set up a telescope and equipped everyone with dark glasses. Sanjay was too busy to bother about the eclipse. Maneka, his wife, was eight months pregnant and to Jayakar's surprise, Indira told Maneka to stay in her room and not view the eclipse with the rest of the family because traditional belief held that a solar eclipse 'was a direct threat to the unborn child', and that no pregnant woman should 'expose herself to [the eclipse's] . . . baleful influence'.

While they waited for the eclipse to begin, Indira and Jayakar watched a video of Thomas Hardy's *Far from the Madding Crowd*. Outside traffic noises receded. The sky got dimmer and the air colder. Birds fell silent. A dark blue light spread over the city, erasing shadows. Suddenly, Indira rose up, left Jayakar and went to her room where she remained, alone, until the eclipse was over. She was clearly unnerved by the obscuring of the sun, but she wanted to conceal her fear. Jayakar was dismayed at her friend's susceptibility to 'ritual and superstition' and wondered what had happened to 'the robust Indira' of former days.[4]

Jayakar was also disturbed by the ubiquitous presence of Dhirendra Brahmachari – the handsome, forceful swami who had hovered in the background of Indira's life and been her yoga teacher for more than twenty years. Since the Emergency Brahmachari's influence had seemed to grow in relation to Indira's increasing distrust and fear of others. Brahmachari, indeed, fed Indira's paranoia by regularly informing her of people he claimed wanted to harm her and Sanjay. Brahmachari's strategy with Indira was twofold. First he alarmed her with reports of plots – often supernatural ones – hatched against her by her enemies. Then he apparently got her to agree to 'counter rituals' – various rites and mantras that he performed to protect her and to annul the harmful forces unleashed by those seeking her destruction.[5]

Indira not only gave credence to Brahmachari's occult prognostications, she also heeded his political advice, and ignored the possibility that his counsel might be motivated by self-interest. One of the major findings of the Shah Commission was the extent to which Brahmachari exploited his power over Indira Gandhi and leagued with her son Sanjay to further his own fortunes. Brahmachari had established a yoga centre, Vishwayatan Yoga Ashram in Delhi, with government backing in the late fifties when Nehru was still Prime Minister. His influence had been muted as long as Indira was guided by P. N. Haksar and the 'Kashmiri mafia'. But now it grew alongside Sanjay's rise to power. In 1973 Brahmachari founded Aparna Agro Private Limited to sell and buy aircraft – a passion he shared with Sanjay who was one of the company's directors. That same year the swami also established another yoga centre in Mantalai in Kashmir, called the Aparna Ashram.

In 1976 – at the height of the Emergency – Brahmachari applied for and received government permission to accept a four-seater M-5 aircraft donated by the Maule Aircraft Company in the United States. The ostensible function of the plane, according to Brahmachari's application, was 'agricultural spraying', though when it was discovered that the plane was not equipped for this purpose, he amended the application to read that it would be used 'for the furthering of the activities of the Aparna Ashram'. The plane was exempted from customs duty and the value of its import permit was unaccountably raised to $67,356 when in fact it was worth much less. Despite Brahmachari's claims, the plane was not a gift; he had paid $40,585 for it in cash when he visited the United States in 1976. Shortly after he returned to India, he was granted permission to construct a private airstrip at Mantalai in Kashmir although this violated security regulations because of the site's proximity to the Pakistan border.

This information only came to light during the course of the Shah Commission hearings, as did the true nature of Brahmachari's 'charitable' ashram in Kashmir. Tax inspectors visited Aparna Ashram after Indira's 1977 defeat and found 'a palatial building . . . superb and marvellous . . . lavishly furnished with marble floors . . . colour-glazed tiles in the bathrooms, four bathtubs, ten telephones, a washing machine, cooking range, movie camera, cassettes, tape recorder, telescope . . . electric kettle, hair drier and [intriguingly] a vibrator'. In the words of *The Shah Commission Report*, the ashram complex was 'equipped to provide a luxurious living and all sorts of comforts and amenities . . . It is indeed difficult to understand that such a costly and luxurious complex was meant to impart Yoga education and training.' The books and documents at the ashram which were seized by the tax inspectors did 'not show any evidence of either . . . yoga disciple or yoga instructor ever living at Mantalai'. Instead, it was obvious that the ashram was 'furnished and equipped . . . to be a holiday home for the rich and affluent class of people'.[6]

The findings of the Shah Commission should have ruined Brahmachari. But when Indira, and Sanjay, returned to power in 1980, the 'flying swami', as he was now called because of the plane business, returned with them. In fact, Brahmachari had by now become an integral part of the Prime Minister's daily life – continually in and out of the house at all hours, often present at meals, where he behaved like one of the family – except his table manners were cruder and his appetite voracious.[7] Because he was omnipresent and had instant access to Indira, it continued to be rumoured that Brahmachari was her lover. Now in his sixties, Brahmachari was still an attractive, magnetic man with raven-black hair and beard, his lean, six-foot tall body draped in spotless white muslin. But in 1980, when Brahmachari's power over Indira was at its height, his role in her life was both more insidious and dangerous than that of a lover.

Less than a month after the solar eclipse, on 13 March, Maneka Gandhi gave birth to a baby boy who was named Feroze Varun after

...aksar, Indira's Principal
...ry and most important adviser.

Indira at talks with Premier Kosygin and Leonid Brezhnev
in Moscow during which she secured the promise of Soviet
military aid in the event of India going to war with Pakistan
over Bangladesh, September 1971.

...nd the Pakistani leader Zufikar Ali Bhutto, looking
...er than they actually were, during the Simla summit
...nce following the Indo-Pak war of December 1981.

Indira with Siddhartha Shankar
Ray and Sheikh Mujibur
Rahman at Delhi airport.
Sheikh 'Mujib' had just been
released from prison in Pakistan
and was en route to Dacca where
he would become the first Prime
Minister of the newly created
Bangladesh.

LEFT Formal family portrait of
Indira and her family in 1974.
Rajiv and Sanjay Gandhi stand
behind Sonia, Rahul, Indira,
Priyanka and Maneka.

BELOW Indira with Sanjay, an
elected MP, in Rae Bareilly after
she was returned to power as
Prime Minister, 1980.

LEFT Indira, her one-year-old
grandson Varun, and Maneka
Gandhi on the first anniversary
remembrance ceremony of
Sanjay Gandhi's death, 1981.

RIGHT Margaret Thatcher and Indira in front of 10 Downing Street, 22 March 1982.

BELOW Indira surrounded by Sikhs during a campaign tour in the 1980s.

BELOW RIGHT Indira photographed with her Sikh bodyguard Beant Singh in London in 1980. Four years later, Singh would be one of her two assassins.

Indira in Kashmir shortly before her death.

The funeral pyre of Indira Gandhi with her family, Rajiv, Priyanka, Sonia and Rahul Gandhi looking on, 3 November 1984.

his maternal grandfather. Most of its care fell to Sonia Gandhi. Indira, however, doted on the child and soon took him into her own bedroom to sleep with her.

On the morning of 23 June 1980, when the baby was just three months old, Sanjay Gandhi decided to take his new Pitts S-2A two-seater plane for an early morning flight above Delhi.

The Pitts was Sanjay's newest toy, an American acquisition brokered by Brahmachari. Sanjay left 1 Safdarjung Road early and drove to the nearby Delhi Flying Club where he invited one of the instructors at the club, Captain Subhash Saxena, to go up with him and try out some aerobatic stunts. Saxena was reluctant because he knew Sanjay lacked experience flying the Pitts S-2A. But after some persuasion, he agreed to go up, and soon Sanjay and Saxena were soaring in great swoops above New Delhi. Then, according to eyewitnesses on the ground, Sanjay made a steep dive, apparently with the intention of pulling up and doing an aerobatic loop. But he lost control. The plane ploughed nose first into the ground, killing both Sanjay and Saxena on impact.

It was already scorching hot at 8.15 a.m. when V. P. Singh, the new Chief Minister of Uttar Pradesh, arrived at Indira's office at 1 Akbar Road for an appointment with the Prime Minister. At 8.20 he was waiting in the reception room when R.K. Dhawan suddenly rushed past into Indira's office. Singh overheard Dhawan tell her 'something terrible has happened'. Indira and Dhawan then ran out of the office, straight past Singh, and out the front door where an Ambassador car was waiting. They leapt in and the car roared off. Singh followed them outside, jumped into his own car and pursued them at high speed. Two minutes later they screeched to a halt at the crash site which by now was swarming with police.

The fire brigade, army and an ambulance were also on the scene, and medics had extricated Sanjay's body from the wreck and carried it into an army truck. Singh watched Indira climb into the truck. She bent over her son and pulled back the red blanket covering his face. For a moment she seemed to swoon; then she grabbed the handrail and steadied herself. She looked again at Sanjay, then covered her own face with both her hands. After what seemed a long time, she came out of the truck, followed by the army people.[8]

Though it was obvious Sanjay and Saxena were dead, the ambulance took them to the nearby Ram Manohar Lohia Hospital. Indira rode in the ambulance next to her son. At the hospital Sanjay's shattered corpse was stitched together by surgeons – an operation that took more than three hours. While they were still working on Sanjay's body, Maneka arrived at the hospital, in a hysterical state. Indira took charge of her, explaining that 'there had been an accident', and that 'the doctors were fixing' Sanjay. When the surgeons had finished, Indira went into the operating theatre and asked everyone else in the room to leave her alone with her son. When she came out several minutes later, her face was ashen-coloured, but she had regained complete control.[9]

Sanjay's body was taken back to 1 Safdarjung Road and laid out on huge blocks of ice. Indira spent most of the day at home receiving mourners. But she also went out. As if under some sort of compulsion, she insisted on revisiting the crash site. Later it was rumoured that she did so to retrieve Sanjay's watch and keys. On the key ring, it was alleged, there was a key to a safe deposit box or perhaps a safe, containing Sanjay's hoarded wealth. On the back of the watch, it was said, were engraved the numbers of Sanjay's secret Swiss bank accounts.

Indira did indeed revisit the place where Sanjay met his death, but not because she was level-headed enough to secure incriminating evidence. She went back to the crash site not once, but twice, on 23 June in order to fix the scene in her mind and carefully inspect the mangled aircraft. Her compulsion was part of the primitive searching behaviour of those who have been suddenly and violently bereaved. She was drawn back to the spot where her son had last been alive because she was looking for him, trying to recover him, not his personal effects. Gazing on the hideous scene, Indira began to comprehend the enormity of her loss.

The day that Sanjay piloted himself into oblivion found Rajiv and Sonia and their children far away, visiting Sonia's family in Italy. When the news of Sanjay's death reached them, they caught the next plane back to Delhi. The funeral was held on 24 June. Indira planned it, as she had her husband's and father's funerals, meticulously. Despite Rajiv's objections, it was a public affair, paid for with government funds. Sanjay's body was carried on an open truck through the streets of Delhi – as Mahatma Gandhi's, Feroze Gandhi's and Nehru's had been before him. Indira and Maneka sat on either side of the corpse, soaked in sweat under a burning sun. Large dark glasses hid Indira's swollen, red eyes.

Sanjay had been sewn up in the hospital and his face was exposed above the mountain of flowers that covered his corpse. But he had been mutilated as well as fatally injured in the crash – one eye and his nose were crushed and disfigured. Stitched together, his corpse looked like an Indian Frankenstein's monster. No surgeon or undertaker's skill could make him seamless and whole and anything less than what he now was: a grotesque, bloodless husk of a human being.

Sanjay was cremated at Shantivana, on the banks of the Jumna, near the spot where Nehru had been cremated. Brahmachari oversaw the obsequies. Indira and Maneka sat on the ground in front of the pyre. Behind them gathered friends, family and political figures, with thousands of mourners ranged beyond them, almost as far as the eye could see. Though women do not normally participate in Hindu funeral rites, Indira herself removed the Indian flag draped over her son's body before Rajiv lit the sandalwood pyre with a torch. As the nearest male relative of the deceased, Rajiv performed the funeral rites as tradition prescribed, circumnavigating his brother's body under a blazing sun, following the directions of Brahmachari and the chanting Hindu priests.

Within days of Sanjay's death, instant monuments sprang up all over India – everything from statues to public paths to park benches commemorated the life of 'the Son'. In death Sanjay was elevated to martyrdom, his personality cult burgeoned, and the nation indulged in a frenzy of grieving, renaming hydro-electric stations, train and bus terminals, bridges, dams, streets, schools, hospitals and perhaps most incongruously, a string of animal homes, established by his widow.[10]

The day after Sanjay's funeral, B.K. Nehru asked Rajiv about all the money Sanjay had amassed during the Emergency and where it was. Rajiv told him that only twenty *lakhs* of rupees had been found in the central Congress office in Delhi. But Rajiv also confided to Nehru that Sanjay had possessed 'crores and unaccounted crores' of wealth at the time of his death. This money did not disappear when Sanjay crashed. A small group of people were substantially enriched when he died – some of them in New Delhi, others – who had looked after his money abroad – in London.[11]

Dhirendra Brahmachari also prospered after Sanjay was killed because their business dealings had been intertwined for several years. The swami went from strength to strength after Sanjay's death – dealing in arms, acquiring his own television show, dispensing licences and permits to the highest bidders. His influence over Indira was now greater than ever. Before Sanjay's death, Brahmachari had warned Indira that her enemies were engaging in tantric rites to bring down a calamity on her family. To avert harm, Brahmachari told Indira she must visit a specific number of shrines and perform certain rituals. She had not been able to complete all these shrine visits – and so not fully placated hostile forces – when Sanjay crashed his plane. Indira told Pupul Jayakar that his death could have been prevented and that it was her fault. Brahmachari exploited her fears and nursed her sense of guilt.[12]

Though she presented a secular façade and claimed to have only the vaguest of spiritual beliefs, Indira had always been superstitious – a legacy no doubt of her maternal grandmother, Swarup Rani Nehru, as well as her mother. Indira had irritated Nehru, for example, by refusing to move to Teen Murti House until the exact auspicious time and date. For years the only jewellery Indira wore was a string of wooden beads given to her by her mother's spiritual adviser, Anandamayi, and these beads were a talisman rather than personal adornment.

In 1980, in the wake of Sanjay's death, Indira's personal world was in ruins, and she turned to 'higher' powers as mediated to her by and through Brahmachari. Her behaviour was not unusual. Many of her countrymen, including politicians and Westernized intellectuals, put their faith in high-profile gurus. These celebrity 'godmen' are not cosmetic spiritual advisers – the Indian equivalent, say, of Billy Graham and his prayer breakfasts with Richard Nixon. Indian politicians' reliance on their gurus is played down, even hidden, rather than publicized. They turn to them for reassurance, counsel, or to forecast the future, particularly at times of crisis. After losing her husband, Sanjay's death was the greatest crisis of Indira's life, and in the period immediately following it, she relied heavily upon Brahmachari.

It took weeks, even months, for Indira to recover some semblance of normality when Feroze and Nehru died. But after Sanjay's death, she returned to work almost immediately. According to R.K. Dhawan, 'not one file was delayed'.[13] Not that this indicated that Indira had regained her balance. As Sonia Gandhi put it many years later, after the 'disaster' of Sanjay's death, Indira 'for all her courage and composure was broken in spirit'.[14]

Nevertheless, on 27 June, just four days after Sanjay's fatal crash and on the day that Rajiv, Sonia and Maneka took his ashes to be submerged in the Sangam at Allahabad, Indira was back in her office. On 28 June an American professor named Francine Frankel had a scheduled appointment with Indira. Frankel was writing a biographical essay on Indira for the new edition of the *Encyclopaedia Britannica*, and she was certain her scheduled meeting with the Prime Minister – scarcely an urgent one – would be cancelled in the wake of Sanjay's death. But it was not. Frankel saw Indira – whom she had met several times before – at her Akbar Road office. Indira was poker-faced and taciturn, but not uncooperative. Frankel was unnerved by her chilliness, the chronic tic in Indira's right eye and the patent absurdity of the interview under the circumstances. It was obvious that Indira was grief-stricken and drained, but she remained completely composed until the end of the interview when Frankel asked 'what one thing' Indira most wanted to be remembered for? Indira glared at Frankel for a moment, and then said bitterly: 'I do not want to be remembered for anything.'[15]

It was a prophetically accurate retort. For history was not going to remember Indira Gandhi for any one thing – for a coherent strategy, ideology, policy or vision. In the late sixties and early seventies Indira had been guided by the left. But when Sanjay emerged on the political scene, all adherence to a political vision was dropped. Though it scarcely seemed possible, when Sanjay died, Indira's life took a turn for the worse. Indira was not just heartbroken. She also lost her confidence. She had for a long time – from the beginning of her political career in fact – reacted rather than acted. But her habitual ad hoc behaviour became desperate in the wake of Sanjay's death. In the coming months and years, she would play various castes, religious, regional and political groups off against each other in an increasingly doomed attempt to safeguard her position.

The immediate personal aftermath of Sanjay's death, however, was positive. Family and friends – even those who had been estranged from Indira – now flocked to her in sympathy. And vulnerable and shattered as she was, Indira was glad to be reconciled with them. For days the house at 1 Safdarjung Road was full of women who had been close to Indira in the course of her life. Now they came to stay with her in her grief: Fori Nehru, Pupul Jayakar, Shanta Gandhi, Subhadra Joshi. Indira's aunt, Vijaya Lakshmi Pandit – with whom Indira had had a rocky relationship all her life and who had campaigned against Indira in the 1977 election – rushed down from Dehra Dun to come to her niece's succour. More than thirty years earlier, Indira and her husband Feroze had sustained Nan Pandit when her husband died in prison. Now the ill will and suspicion that had separated them for so long was wiped away.

Dorothy Norman also overcame estrangement. When she heard of Sanjay's death, she wrote to Indira immediately, breaking a silence of more than four years. Swraj Paul – who had supported Indira through the dark period after the Emergency – flew in from London. But despite all this outpouring of feeling – public and private – an odd, ambiguous mood gripped Delhi. As Raj Thapar wrote, people wept 'at the tragedy of it all ... because a tragedy it certainly was'. But at the same time, when Sanjay died 'a wave of indefinable relief blew right across the country'.[16] Years later B.K. Nehru expressed what so many felt but could not say in June 1980 – that Sanjay's death far from being a catastrophe was actually 'the best thing that could happen to India'.[17]

With Sanjay dead, Indira could have implemented fundamental changes in her government and shed Sanjay's unsavoury legacy and associates. It was still possible at this stage to win back the support of some of the intelligent men who had been her advisers in the past – P. N. Haksar, above all, but also Romesh Thapar, I. K. Gujral and those segments of the intelligentsia who were willing to forgive Indira for the 'aberration' of the Emergency.

But apart from making unsuccessful overtures to Thapar, Indira did not attempt to woo back these people or to break free from Sanjay's dubious inheritance. When Inder Malhotra arranged a meeting between Indira, her press adviser, Sharada Prasad, and six prominent newspaper editors, Indira told them that her intellectual critics were all under either American or Soviet influence. She also explained why she mistrusted the bureaucracy and let her 'own people' manage things. She could not rely on senior bureaucrats, she said, who had never 'lifted a finger to help me. In the circumstances, am I to blame if I entrust sensitive jobs to men who may not be very bright but on whom I can rely?'[18]

By this time, Indira, in fact, did not trust anyone who was not her kith or kin. Though free to form bonds with figures of stature and integrity, she chose to rely on 'men who may not be very bright but on whom I can rely'. Foremost among these was her remaining son Rajiv, who was the obvious choice to replace Sanjay.

Within days of Sanjay's death, Rajiv was being variously urged, exhorted and begged to enter politics. Not by Indira herself, but by her loyalists in Congress, including members of the old guard who had not fallen from grace, such as T. N. Kaul. It took Rajiv nearly a year to make up his mind, and the pressures on him during this period were intense. Above all, there was his mother's tacit need and the vehement opposition of his wife, Sonia, who in her own words 'fought like a tigress' to prevent Rajiv from entering politics. Indeed, according to Sonia, Rajiv was 'tormented by the conflict'. 'There stood his mother, crushed and alone.' At the same time, Sonia invoked the 'life we had made together', which she knew would be sacrificed to a political 'system . . . [that] would crush and destroy him'.[19]

As always in the Nehru-Gandhi family history, a sense of duty won this battle. On 5 May 1981, Rajiv finally announced that he would stand in a June by-election for Amethi, Sanjay's old constituency. Amethi had waited patiently for this announcement, for Sanjay's seat should have been filled within six months of his death. Rajiv ran for office despite the fact that he had never been interested in politics and was not even a card-carrying member of Congress. For him, it was like entering a prison. But after ten months of indecision, enter Rajiv did because as he put it, 'someone had to help Mummy'.[20] He resigned from his job with Indian Airlines, shed his shirt, jacket and tie and took to wearing the Congress white *khadi*.

Predictably, there was an outcry among intellectuals. As his critics pointed out, Rajiv had no political base, no constituency, no experience and no knowledge of politics. The only qualifications he possessed were his genes. In India and abroad, the majority of intellectuals remained hostile to Indira. Especially when it became clear that she planned to anoint Rajiv as her heir. Ved Mehta's scathing attacks in the *New Yorker* were published in book form. There were few writers or journalists – Trevor Fishlock was one exception – willing to publish anything dispassionate about Indira.

But the masses did not see things this way. As one of Indira's biographers later put it, 'Indian history . . . is an unbroken saga of rule by hereditary monarchs. Family connection is also of the utmost importance in every Indian's life ... tradition enjoins that a man ... follow the vocation of his forefathers. For centuries, master craftsmen and maestros of music have taught their skills to their progeny ... In grooming her son as her successor' Indira was merely following a well-established pattern.[21]

To no one's surprise, Rajiv won the Amethi by-election by over a quarter of a million votes in June. He was sworn in as an MP on 17 August 1981, three days before his thirty-seventh birthday. It would be nearly a year before he made his maiden speech in Parliament, but long before then he had become extremely popular. He was handsome and personable, without shady contacts and associations. He appeared to be a good-hearted, kind man. Indeed, Rajiv was soon dubbed 'Mr Clean'. And for extra measure, he had a beautiful, photogenic family.

Once Rajiv had made the decision to enter politics, Sonia Gandhi supported her husband – just as she had always supported Indira – entirely. Rajiv's sister-in-law, Maneka Gandhi, however, remained hostile to his new political commitment, even after Rajiv won the Amethi election, because Maneka herself wanted to take on Sanjay's mantle. At twenty-three, Maneka was still too young to stand for Parliament, but she would be old enough in two years. She began to be noisily critical of her brother-in-law and, more discreetly, of her mother-in-law as well.

Maneka had long been a major irritant in the household and this only increased after Sanjay's death. At first Indira was sympathetic to her young widowed daughter-in-law. She even offered Maneka the post of her personal assistant. But Sonia Gandhi – who remained on bad terms with Maneka despite the fact that Sonia was primarily responsible for the care of Maneka's baby, Varun – objected strenuously. Sonia had become very close to Indira emotionally and in deference to her feelings, Indira withdrew her offer to Maneka.[22]

Troubles in the Punjab and Kashmir would dominate Indira's last term in office, but throughout 1980 and 1981, she was more worried about Assam in the northeast. The problem in Assam came from outside, with a large number of Bengali immigrants – most of them Muslims – who had settled in the state after leaving Bangladesh during the 1971 war. So large was the influx that they threatened to reduce the Assamese to a minority in their own state. In response, the largely Hindu Assamese made four demands regarding the 'foreigners', known as the four 'd's: they wanted the central government to *detect* the Bengali immigrants, *disenfranchise* and *deport* them to Bangladesh or *disperse* them in other Indian states. A student organization, the All-Assam Students Union, mobilized and led anti-Bengali demonstrations in the state. When the unrest became critical in April 1980, Assam was declared 'a disturbed area'. Law and order broke down and Delhi had to send in paramilitary forces to secure the oil pipeline by which Assam supplied a third of India's oil.

But it was not only Bengalis who were viewed as causing trouble in Assam. The indigenous tribal peoples also rose up at this time against high-caste Assamese domination, and demanded that 'unauthorized occupants' be thrown out of their tribal areas. Despite the legitimate grievances of the various Assamese inhabitants, Indira – as had become her habit – blamed a 'foreign hand' for fomenting trouble in the state. Her new Home Minister, Zail Singh, specifically denounced the United States and China in Parliament for interfering in Assam.

Despite growing instability at home – or perhaps in part because of it – Indira spent a good deal of 1981 making high-profile visits abroad. This gave her a good press in India as well as a reprieve from domestic tribulations. In May she went to Switzerland, Kuwait and the United Arab Emirates, and while in Switzerland she visited her old school at Bex. L'École Nouvelle was now a convent whose nuns enthusiastically welcomed her. (Indira did not, however, make a sentimental pilgrimage to Rollier's sanatorium in Leysin – or rather to the block of luxury apartments into which it had been turned.) In August she went to Kenya with Sonia, Rahul, Priyanka and a surly Maneka who complained that everyone in the family but herself travelled on a special diplomatic passport. A long tour of Southeast Asia – Jakarta, Fiji, Tonga, Australia and the Philippines – followed in late September and early October. The rest of October was taken up with a visit to Romania and then the North-South summit of heads of state in Cancun, Mexico. All this meant that Indira was away from India for the better part of the summer and autumn of 1981.

Troubles back home continued to mount in her absence. Communal riots engulfed both Assam and Punjab. The upheaval in the Punjab had been building up since the 1977 elections when Congress lost all nine of the Lok Sahba seats in the Punjab to the Sikh Akali Dal party. But the conflict in the Punjab actually dated from much earlier. It went back, indeed, to Partition when the region was split down the middle between India and Pakistan.

In 1966, soon after Indira became Prime Minister, she had done what her father, Nehru, had refused to countenance. She acceded to the creation of a separate Punjabi-speaking state and Haryana and Himachal Pradesh were carved out of the already mutilated Punjab, which had been created at Partition. Indira's government, however, insisted that the new Punjab, like the other states established as a result of the States Reorganization Act of 1956, was the product of *linguistic* – not religious – considerations, despite the fact that 56 per cent of the population in the Punjab were Sikhs. (In contrast to this slim majority in the state, Sikhs are a tiny minority of only 2 per cent in the rest of India where the majority of people – 80 per cent – are Hindus.)

Since the foundation of the Sikh religion some five hundred years earlier, Sikhs in the Punjab had for the most part lived in harmony with their Hindu neighbours and often intermarried with them. In its monotheism and rejection of the caste system, however, Sikhism diverged radically from Hindu belief. And the Sikhs themselves deliberately accentuated their separateness by adhering to five practices that set them apart from their neighbours. The Sikh 'Khalsa' or pure ones do not cut their hair or shave their beards, always carry a comb, wear a steel bangle, short breeches and arm themselves with a dagger. It is the males' long hair, invariably wrapped up in a turban, that most obviously distinguishes them as Sikhs.

After the creation of the Punjab in 1966, certain issues concerning land distribution, access to rivers and the capital Chandigarh, which the Punjab shared with Haryana, all remained unresolved and a source of Sikh grievances. In 1973 the Sikh party, the Akali Dal, formally articulated their demands at a meeting in Anandpur Sahib in a report that became known as the Anandpur Sahib Resolution. The Sikhs wanted sole possession of the state capital of Chandigarh, to retain Hindu Punjabi-speaking regions and control over the river waters essential to agriculture in the state.

Delhi dragged its heels on meeting Sikh demands. The Sikh majority in the Punjab became more assertive and their political party, the Akali Dal, began to pose a political challenge to Congress. Then in 1977 the

Akali Dal defeated Congress in the elections. Although Indira was out of power, Sanjay Gandhi, with an eye to the future, decided to damage Akali Dal dominance in the state. The former Chief Minister of the Punjab, a Sikh Congressman named Zail Singh, advised him to split Sikh feeling by backing a newcomer who would defy the established Akali leadership.

Sanjay sent some of his loyalists to the Punjab to find a new *sant* or Sikh holy man who could divide Sikhs and break up the Akali Dal. They produced a demagogue named Jarnail Singh Bhindranwale, a thirty-year-old, orthodox preacher with penetrating dark eyes and a long, silken black beard. Bhindranwale was a fundamentalist who wanted to 'purify' Sikhism and return it to its orthodox, uncontaminated state. He quickly acquired a large number of die-hard followers. Covertly, Sanjay and Zail Singh supported them and their leader.

But as Bhindranwale's strength grew so did his ambition and autonomy. In 1980 he campaigned actively for Congress in three Punjabi constituencies and the Janata candidate in one even alleged that Indira appeared on the same platform as Bhindranwale. But soon after the elections, Bhindranwale declared his independence and refused to be the tool of Congress. In time he and his followers would come to represent the demand not just for a special status for the Punjab but the creation of a sovereign Sikh state called 'Khalistan'.

On 9 September 1981 Lala Jagat Narain, the owner of a Punjabi chain of newspapers whose editorial pages denounced Bhindranwale, was shot dead. His assassination had been masterminded by Bhindranwale and the charismatic *sant* was arrested on 20 September. Angry protest demonstrations against his imprisonment broke out all over the Punjab. The central government intervened and Zail Singh, now the Home Minister, saw to it that Bhindranwale was released on 14 October. As was so often the case in Indian history, jail was a turning point in Bhindranwale's career. He entered prison a provincial charlatan but emerged a national hero. He did not feel beholden to Delhi for his deliverance and upon his release, he made triumphal tours of the capital and Bombay, demonstrating his huge popularity among the Sikhs who live outside the Punjab.

When he returned to the Punjab, Bhindranwale stepped up his disruptive activities. Random violence in the state escalated. Hindus were murdered. Cows were decapitated and the cows' heads thrown into

Hindu temples. Bhindranwale had hit lists published in the newspapers of those targeted for assassination. Panic spread and Hindus began migrating to Haryana and Delhi. Exactly a year after the murder of Lala Jagat Narain, his son – also a journalist – was killed, dramatically reinforcing Bhindranwale's message that anyone who spoke ill of his movement would be eliminated. Prominent Sikhs critical of Bhindranwale as well as Hindus were murdered. By the end of 1982, he had got rid of a large number of his opponents.

By the time Indira and Zail Singh realized that the Frankenstein Singh and Sanjay had created was out of their control it was too late. After his release from prison, Bhindranwale and his army of followers moved into the complex of buildings that comprise the holiest of Sikh shrines, the Golden Temple in Amritsar. From this sanctuary, Bhindranwale continued to run his terrorist squads – who went out and desecrated Hindu temples, murdered, looted and set fire to villages. Delhi now had a secessionist challenge on its hands in the Punjab. Meanwhile, international television crews and journalists descended on Amritsar to cover Bhindranwale who had become a media star.

In the late months of 1981 and throughout 1982, as the Punjab burned, Indira played 'the Hindu card' by refusing to clamp down in the state, thereby allowing Bhindranwale's army to run amuck. She did this not only to keep the Akali Dal Party divided, but also to increase her support among the Hindu majority in the rest of the country. It was a desperate manoeuvre and it did not work for long. But it was only when the Punjab had descended into complete chaos and the violence became uncontainable that Indira realized she was not going to be able to retrieve the situation. At this point she tried to negotiate with the Akali Dal and Bhindranwale's people. She met with them twice, though it is unlikely, as has been alleged, that she met with Bhindranwale himself. Nothing came of these negotiations, and soon Rajiv Gandhi and his advisers, particularly his second cousin, Arun Nehru, took over the sticky and increasingly dangerous job of dealing with the Punjab, Bhindranwale, and the Akali Dal.

The 1982 session of Parliament opened with the announcement that in the past two years 960 Harijans had been killed in the country. Hindu-Muslim riots flared up in the major cities. The communal situation was further exacerbated by a wave of Harijan conversions to Islam or Christianity – the only way an 'untouchable' could escape his fate of caste. Only he did not because discrimination continued after conversion. In South India, for example, Harijan-born Christians were not allowed to sit near non-Harijan Christians in church and sometimes were barred from even entering the church. The mass conversion of Harijans sparked off yet more atrocities against them. Hindu zealots demanded that the government ban conversions. Indira refused, insisting that India was a secular state and that banning conversion was 'incompatible with the religious freedom guaranteed by the Constitution'. Nevertheless, Indira became drawn into the vortex and as had by now become her strategy, she played various communal groups off against each other.

Indeed there seemed to be troubles everywhere Indira turned, including her own household. For the problems with Maneka did not go away either. After the trip to Kenya in the summer of 1981, it was clear to everyone that Indira favoured Sonia and that Maneka irritated her intensely. Increasingly, Maneka was sidelined. At formal dinners, she was seated at a separate table with members of staff such as R.K. Dhawan, because Indira feared Maneka would say something offensive or embarrassing to guests. Nor was Maneka just a source of friction in the family. There were all sorts of unusual rumours in Delhi – none fully substantiated – about Maneka and her mother. In despair, Indira asked Khushwant Singh to speak to Maneka about the trouble she was causing the Prime Minister. When he did, Maneka told Singh that she was being treated like 'dirt' by the Gandhis and called Indira an 'old bag'.[23]

Feeling herself increasingly marginalized at 1 Safdarjung Road, resenting Indira, vying with Rajiv and loathing Sonia, in February 1982, Maneka decided to get revenge by selling her picture magazine, *Surya*, to a group of Indira's political foes who were right-wing Hindu fundamentalists. She also leaked sensitive information from the Prime Minister's household, including family letters. The strife in the household waxed and waned. Much of the time the occupants refused to speak to each other. Maneka's sister, Ambika, and her mother, Amteshwar Anand, were closely involved in the on-going battle.

Things finally came to a head in March 1982 when Maneka agreed to address a convention of Sanjay Gandhi's supporters – all of whom were enemies of Rajiv Gandhi – at Lucknow. Indira was in London at the time, attending the Festival of India, meeting Prime Minister Margaret

Thatcher and the Queen. From afar, Indira communicated to Maneka that she was not to attend the Lucknow convention, which Indira perceived as an anti-Congress (I) and an anti-Rajiv event. Indira flew back to Delhi on 27 March. When she landed at Palam airport she learned that Maneka had just departed for Lucknow in order to address the conference. Indira sent a letter in hot pursuit, reiterating her command that Maneka not speak before the delegates. If she did, Indira warned, Maneka would have to leave the Gandhi household. Undeterred, Maneka went ahead and made her speech and then returned to Delhi to face the music.

Indira was furious and 'girded for battle'. The inevitable explosion with her daughter-in-law swiftly followed. Indira lost control and became like 'one possessed'.[24] After a shouting match, Indira wrote an intemperate letter to Maneka accusing her of using bad language, suggesting that Sanjay had become fed up with his wayward wife, and criticizing Maneka's very different background and family. Though Maneka accused Indira of writing the letter 'for posterity and the press', it was not made public and its contents had to be inferred from Maneka's stinging reply published in the *Indian Express* on 31 March.

In her own public letter, Maneka accused Indira of 'physical and mental abuse' and 'literally torturing' her 'in every conceivable way'. She also maintained that she had gone to the Lucknow conference as a guest and that while there she 'spoke & will always speak for you'.[25] Maneka's letter caused such a sensation that Indira's press adviser, Sharada Prasad, released a statement to the press agency, the United News of India, which was carried in most of the national papers. It stated that

> the differences between Mrs Gandhi and her daughter-in-law arose when the latter entered into a secret deal with the RSS leader, Sardar Angre, for the sale of the *Surya* magazine. Mrs Maneka Gandhi ... did not breathe a word of this to Mrs Gandhi, who felt that the step constituted a total betrayal of all the ideals and values Sanjay Gandhi had stood for. [Maneka's] ... subsequent actions were all designed to bolster up elements and forces hostile to ... the Prime Minister ... although Mrs Maneka Gandhi had a different family background, Mrs Gandhi and other members of the household had accepted her without reservations as a life-partner of Sanjay Gandhi.[26]

It was left to R.K. Dhawan to orchestrate Maneka's inevitable eviction from 1 Safdarjung Road on 29 March. But she did not go quietly. In the afternoon Indira and Maneka had a face-to-face showdown in the presence of Dhawan and Dhirendra Brahmachari. Maneka was told to pack her bags and leave. This took the better part of what was left of the day. Maneka called a friend of Sanjay's and told him to tell her family, friends and the press that she was being thrown out of the house. Maneka's sister, Ambika, soon arrived to help her pack and ended up shouting abuse at Indira. Maneka and Ambika then watched a video for several hours and only prepared to leave when the crowd of journalists that had been summoned had arrived to witness Maneka's exit.

With the press looking on, Dhawan and Brahmachari unsuccessfully tried to search Maneka's luggage. Then Indira tried to prevent Maneka from taking her two-year-old son away with her. Ever since Sanjay's death, little Varun had slept in Indira's bedroom at night, while Sonia took care of him during the day. Maneka had had little to do with the child, but she insisted on taking him with her and legally there was nothing Indira could do to keep him. The young widow and child finally drove off in a blaze of publicity at 11 p.m. Car loads of toys, dogs and possessions followed in a caravan across Delhi.[27]

Indira was distraught over Maneka's departure and especially pained by the loss of her youngest grandchild. Indira's secretary, P.C. Alexander, tried to calm her down after they had left, reminding her that she had weathered many crises during her life, including political turmoil and the deaths of those she loved. Indira's response was that 'this girl' had taken 'Varun from me. You know my relationship to Sanjay's son. He is my grandson. He is being taken away.'[28] Nothing could console Indira. But she had no legal right to keep Varun and he effectively disappeared out of Indira's life at the end of March 1982.

Maneka out of sight, however, was not Maneka out of mind. She continued to taunt her in-laws and argue that she – not they – carried Sanjay's torch now. Since she was no longer a member of the household at 1 Safdarjung Road, Maneka could afford to be more daring in her revenge. She obtained and distributed copies of the censored and explicit 'She' chapter of the (now deceased) M.O. Mathai's autobiography. Maneka also had copied and circulated family letters that were critical of Rajiv. In a speech Maneka compared Indira to the goddess Kali, 'who drinks blood'. Indira's response was that Sanjay's marriage to Maneka was 'a conspiracy to plant' an enemy 'in the inner circles'. She maintained that she had always opposed the marriage and said that 'latterly her son, too, had discovered the truth' about his wife. Maneka's put-down to this was that Indira's 'mind was affected by age and that she wished her a happy and speedy retirement'.[29]

The often unhappy relationship between mothers-in-law and daughters-in-law was a staple of Indian film, fiction and soap opera. But this was taking things too far. Nor did Maneka limit herself to crude verbal attacks on Indira. After the Lucknow convention, she founded a political party ostensibly committed to Sanjay Gandhi's legacy – the Rashtria Sanjay Vichar Manch (National Forum of Sanjay Thought) – with which she intended to fight both Indira and Rajiv Gandhi. But though the public closely followed the feud between Maneka and Indira, they did not flock to her new party. Nobody was convinced that Maneka – rather than Rajiv Gandhi – was the true inheritor of the Nehru-Gandhi dynasty.

In late July 1982, Indira went to Washington to confer with President Ronald Reagan whom she had met for the first time the previous year at the North-South heads of state summit in Mexico. Their meetings were cordial, though Indira was far from impressed with the President's intellect. Reagan and his wife Nancy, Indira noted, enjoyed the sort of American westerns and television programmes the President used to star in. Later Indira obliquely referred to Reagan's cultural tastes when the French President Mitterand visited Delhi. Mitterand, Indira wrote to Dorothy Norman, 'is different from most other Heads whom I have met, and especially your own President. Have you read his [Mitterand's book] *Wheat and Chaff*?' Mitterand, according to Indira, was a personal friend of the Colombian author and Nobel Prize winner Gabriel Garcia Marquez, whom Indira greatly admired.[30]

Indira's 1982 talks with Reagan were meant to repair Indo-American relations. But they were far from productive. In the wake of the 1979 Soviet invasion of Afghanistan, the United States backed Pakistan as strongly as ever. And in American eyes, India was still considered an ally of the Soviets. At a press conference in Washington, a reporter asked Indira why India 'always tilted towards the Soviet Union?' to which she responded: 'We do not tilt on either side . . . we walk upright.'[31]

On her way to Washington, Indira spent several days in New York where she saw Dorothy Norman for the first time in many years. Though Dorothy was apprehensive about the reunion, she and Indira immediately recovered their old closeness. And back in India, Indira began to correspond with Dorothy and confide in her again. In her letters, she admitted that she was 'terribly overworked', and there was 'utter indiscipline and many agitations' all over the country. She also complained of 'the net of protocol and security' that surrounded her and press reports that falsely accused her of financial deals 'when we do not even have the means to finish the building of our small house' in Mehrauli. It seemed to Indira 'that the world is becoming a nastier place'. But above all, she said she was burdened by a sense of loss and decay. 'Is it because of age that one thinks things everywhere are deteriorating? . . . Yeats said that things fall apart, the centre does not hold. What is the centre, and where?'[32]

Pupul Jayakar saw Indira shortly after her return from America. She found her haggard and tired. Indira confessed she had not slept well for several months, had recurrent bad dreams, and habitually woke at 2 a.m. with a 'sense of foreboding'. Then she confided to Jayakar, 'I have been receiving secret reports of tantric rituals and black magic rites being performed to destroy me and my sanity.' Jayakar tried to talk to Indira about the enormous stress she was under, but Indira only wanted to know if Jayakar herself believed that 'malignant forces . . . can be released through tantric rites'.[33] Their conversation left Jayakar feeling helpless. Indira was bordering on paranoia. Clearly there were people who wished Indira ill; but disturbingly Indira now actually seemed to believe they could damage her through supernatural forces.

On 8 September 1982, Sheikh Abdullah, the Chief Minister of Jammu and Kashmir, died after a massive cardiac arrest. He was seventy-seven and had been in poor health since suffering his first heart attack during the 1977 elections. His relations with Indira and her government, after their 1975 accord, had fluctuated. She and many others in Congress never trusted his loyalty to India. In 1981 – at just about the time Rajiv Gandhi was entering politics – Abdullah named his son, Farooq, as his successor. Farooq was sworn in as Chief Minister just ninety minutes after his father's death. But his succession was neither smooth nor secure.

Indira was said to have opposed Farooq following in his father's footsteps, but if she did, she made no indication of this when she attended Sheikh Abdullah's funeral; nor did she give any encouragement to Farooq's brother-in-law, Ghulam Mohammed Shah who wanted to take over as Chief Minister himself. Arun Nehru claims that Indira wanted Sheikh Abdullah's daughter, Khaleda (who was married to Shah), to succeed him, but realized – as the Sheikh had – that conservative Muslim Kashmiris would not accept a woman leader when there was a son to take over.[34]

The son, however, was an unlikely candidate – and in his own way, just as unqualified to enter politics as the Gandhi boys. Trained as a doctor, Farooq spent all his adult life in Britain where he married an English nurse. He was a completely Westernized, ebullient fellow who frequented discos and parties and rode around Srinagar on a motorbike, often with an attractive woman riding pillion.

To his credit, however, though he did little to modify his frivolous lifestyle, Farooq took his new responsibilities seriously. He asked the Governor of Kashmir, Indira's cousin, B.K. Nehru, for direction and advice.[35] He removed suspect individuals from the Cabinet and staved off the political ambitions of his unpleasant brother-in-law G.M. Shah. This quelled to some extent the charges of corruption and incompetence that had dogged his father's government. But when Farooq called for elections the following year, he refused to form an alliance with Indira. He insisted on the independence of his National Conference Party from Congress (I), and this paved the way for dissident communalists in Kashmir to foment trouble in the state. Indira's habit of running states from the centre was by this time inveterate. There was no way she would allow Kashmir, a crucial borderline state that had already been the cause of three wars between India and Pakistan, to be governed by a chief minister who was anything less than totally loyal to her.

But for the time being the situation in the Punjab eclipsed Indira's uneasiness over the future of Kashmir under Farooq. The previous July, Indira had stage-managed the election of Zail Singh, her Home Minister, as President of India. Singh had proved malleable and useful as Home Minister but she realized he could play an even more critical role as President, should the law and order situation in the states and the country deteriorate further. Also, Indira hoped to mollify Sikh feeling by making Singh the first Sikh Indian President. Singh plainly understood the roles expected of him. He even boasted of his sycophancy when he announced that 'if my leader [Indira Gandhi] had said I should pick up a broom and be a sweeper, I would have done that. She chose me to be President.'[36]

What should have been a pleasant diversion from the troubles in Punjab actually exacerbated them and brought them to the heart of government in Delhi. In November 1982 the ninth Asian Games were held in Delhi with over 5,000 athletes competing from thirty-three 'Asian' countries (including the Middle East, as well as the entire Asian region). 'Asiad 82' was the special charge of Rajiv Gandhi – a high-profile, non-controversial, ostensibly foolproof project with which he could gain kudos.

As soon as Rajiv entered politics in 1981 he started preparatory work on the Asian Games. It was a massive endeavour involving the costly construction of six new sports stadia, three five-star government hotels and a village with living quarters for the athletes. Multi-lane motorways, flyovers and overpasses were also built. Delhi, in fact, received a complete facelift in preparation for Asiad 82.

All this activity involved not only huge sums of money – official estimates ran to over 3 billion rupees and unofficial estimates from 6 to 10 billion – but also a vast army of labourers working round the clock as the date of the Games approached. Contractors, licence and permit brokers, cement, brick and steel manufacturers all prospered. But the workers who built the roads, stadia and hotels did not. Most of them were bonded labour from South India or other distant parts of the country who had been hired by contractors' agents and sent by the truckload to Delhi where they toiled all day – 'wasted, half-clad men, women and children covered with dust ... many of them high on scaffolding and weighed down with heavy loads'.[37] They lived in squalid camps, without running water or electricity, next to their construction sites. The lucky ones slept in shacks built of cardboard or other waste material. Others huddled under plastic or canvas mats held up with sticks. The daily wage was 11 rupees.

The ordinary citizens of Delhi suffered from the consequences of Asiad 82 in milder ways. The money, raw materials and electricity poured into the games diverted essential resources. Land needed for hospitals or low-cost housing was co-opted. The strain on the Delhi water supply and electricity was enormous, resulting in chronic shortages all over the city.

Rajiv, Arun Nehru and another of Rajiv's advisers, Arun Singh, took overall responsibility for the games. On the face of things, they had acquitted themselves well and Asiad 82 opened with considerable pomp on 19 November 1982, Indira's sixty-fifth birthday. But inevitably, people lamented the vast expense, and journalists exposed the exploitation of those who built the impressive infrastructure for the games.

More damaging, however, was the fallout in the Punjab. Believing the games to be merely a public relations exercise, Bhindranwale called for them to be disrupted. On 6 November Harchand Singh Longowal, the Akali leader, announced that his party would hold daily demonstrations in Delhi. The government clamped a security ring round the city so that no demonstrator from the Punjab could enter. Roadblocks sprang up all over Haryana, the state through which any Punjabi would have to pass, to reach Delhi. In this climate, every Sikh was viewed as a potential terrorist. The Haryana police were over-zealous in their screening of Sikh travellers and submitted many innocent people to harassment and indignities. More than 1,500 were arrested. Sikhs not only in the Punjab but also all over India were enraged.

In response, Indira again attempted to negotiate and she brought in a former Sikh Maharaja named Amarinder Singh to try to persuade the Akali Dal to settle with her government. By 18 November they had reached an agreement, particularly over the vexed issues of the state capital Chandigarh and the river waters. But then authorities in Haryana and Rajasthan – who did not want to cede Chandigarh or share river access – complained to Indira and she reneged on the agreement at the last minute. Bhindranwale was delighted and said this just proved there was no point negotiating with the 'Brahmin woman' or 'Pandit's daughter', as he scornfully called Indira.

Indira was now left with a political deadlock and a sense of impending disaster.

TWENTY

Another Amritsar

In December 1982, Richard Attenborough's film *Gandhi* opened in Delhi 'with much fanfare', as Indira wrote to Dorothy Norman. She felt ambivalent about the film. She told Dorothy it was 'impressive', but thought it a 'tragedy ... no Indian film maker [had] ... been inspired' to tell Gandhi's story. Indira felt Attenborough's version was 'a spectacle' with Gandhi as a 'super star ... messiah – not more than he was but rather less'. The film, in fact, 'diminished' him.[1]

While the Indian past was being repackaged as mass entertainment, the Indian present was also looking more and more like something on a celluloid screen. The charismatic, wild-eyed Bhindranwale preached Sikh separatism in television interviews, waving his Sten gun before a global audience. In February 1983, the most sought after criminal in India, a woman named Phoolan Devi – known as the 'Bandit Queen' – surrendered to the Indian police before an audience of thousands in a dusty town called Bhind in Madhya Pradesh. In a few years' time her story would be turned into an internationally-acclaimed film, after which Phoolan Devi – despite her criminal record and illiteracy – would be elected as an MP.

Phoolan Devi's transformation from outlaw to film icon to politician reflected the ease with which notoriety could be turned into power in India. The huge, film-going Indian public worships film and television stars. As Tariq Ali puts it, Indian popular films are the 'cinematic opium [and] ... religion of the masses'.[2] An Indian film star who decides to enter politics has a ready-made mass electorate. In 1977, three years before Ronald Reagan became President of the United States, a South Indian movie star named M.G. Ramachandran was elected Chief Minister of Tamil Nadu. MGR, as he was known, specialized in playing larger-than-life mythological and legendary heroes. The assumption was that he would perform in a similar epic vein as a politician. But MGR's film feats were not repeated in office, and the lives of the lower-class and low-caste voters who elected him materially worsened during his ten-year reign. Despite this failure, he continued to be worshipped, and when he died in 1987, his funeral was 'a spectacle of grief', attended by thousands, including thirty-one devotees who publicly committed suicide.[3]

In the January 1983 state assembly elections in Andhra Pradesh, another former film star named N.T. Ramarao – known as NTR – and his new Telugu Desam Party, defeated Congress. NTR had no political experience or connections, but he was a household name, even divinity, was famous for playing Hindu gods on the big screen. Not content with being Chief Minister of Andhra Pradesh, NTR soon made it clear that he had higher ambitions of 'playing God' in Delhi after the next general election.[4]

Congress lost the 1983 state assembly elections not only in Andhra Pradesh but in the neighbouring state of Karnataka as well. These defeats and the continued supremacy of MGR's regional DMK Party in Tamil Nadu disheartened Indira. Hitherto, South India had always voted for her – even in 1977 when the North turned against her with a vengeance. Now Karnataka (the same state that brought Indira back to Parliament in 1978) rejected Indira's Congress and voted for Janata.

Following the rout of Congress in the South, 'a monstrously deadly and destructive election' took place in Assam.[5] The state was in chaos and had been under President's rule for nearly three years. As a result, the basic conditions necessary to hold a poll simply did not exist in Assam. According to the constitution, however, President's rule had to be withdrawn and elections held by mid-February 1983. But the prospect of a poll exacerbated existing strife in the state because a principal Assamese grievance was that the Bengali immigrants, whom they regarded as 'foreigners', were Congress vote banks.

Predictably, the Assamese movement, backed by Janata and the Hindu Bharatiya Janata Party, announced they would boycott the elections. Delhi's response was to go ahead with the poll on 13, 17 and 30 February. The result, inevitably, was yet more violence. The Assamese proceeded to slaughter Bengalis – both Muslims and Hindus – while Bodo tribesman attacked and killed whoever strayed into their territory.

Thousands were killed and millions made homeless throughout the state.

The worst atrocity occurred at a Bengali refugee town called Nellie where 5,000 innocent men, women and children were killed – most of them cut down with machetes or burnt in their homes. Tariq Ali described it as the 'My Lai massacre [of Vietnamese villagers] multiplied by ten'.[6] On 21 February, immediately after news of the Nellie massacre had reached Delhi, Indira flew to Assam. She was horrified by what she found. At a news conference, she struggled for control and told the reporters in a choked voice: 'I cannot find words to describe the horrors.'[7]

The poll boycott had been so successful that overall voting across the state was only 2 per cent. Countless polling stations were burnt down; others reported 'nil voting'. Indira knew the elections had been a grotesque farce, but in Parliament four days later she maintained that the newly-elected government in Assam would 'be better able to handle the situation . . . [and restore] the political process' in the state.[8]

The week after Indira defended the Assam elections in the Lok Sahba, she presided more convincingly over the seventh summit of the Non-Aligned Movement in Delhi. But the Nellie massacre lingered. One of the first things the non-aligned heads of state saw upon their arrival in India, was the news weekly *India Today* colour photographs of murdered and mutilated children on its cover. Soon, however, this gruesome image was supplanted by newspaper and magazine photographs of Indira Gandhi clenched in a bear hug by Fidel Castro, who handed over the chairmanship of the Non-Aligned Movement to his 'sister', as he called her. Throughout the summit Indira ran a tight, admirable ship. She was able to steer the assembled delegates through debates on Kampuchea, Afghanistan and Latin America. This would prove to be a rare interlude of statesmanship for Indira, giving her good press at a time when she felt heavily beleaguered.

In April, in Kashmir, Farooq Abdullah – 'the disco Chief Minister', as he was popularly known because of his flamboyant lifestyle – announced that early state assembly elections would be held in June. Ten months had passed since Farooq inherited the chief ministership from his late father, Sheikh Abdullah. Now he wanted a popular mandate to continue in power. Indira had been edgy about Farooq almost from the moment he took over in Kashmir. She was particularly incensed when he went to Amritsar in November 1982 and met with Akali leaders and – even more controversially – with Bhindranwale himself. By early 1983 Indira was openly denouncing Farooq and his National Conference Party (which refused to ally itself with Congress) for being 'anti-national'. Indira went even further and accused Farooq of allowing Kashmir to be used as a base for Sikh extremists and Pakistani agents backing Kashmiri separatists.

Indira, in short, wanted Farooq out – preferably voted out by the electorate rather than pushed out by President's rule. Thus she personally went to Kashmir and launched a whirlwind campaign for the Congress candidates in the state. This became all the more necessary when Farooq had formed an alliance with the Muslim Awami League which was led by an openly anti-India religious leader named Maulvi Farooq. Using the same communalist rhetoric she had relied on in the Punjab, Indira told the Hindus of Jammu that a National Conference government in Srinagar would be a 'disaster' for them.[9]

Indira dramatically shifted tack, however, as soon as she got to Srinagar, where there was a Muslim majority and all the Congress candidates were Muslim. The selection of Muslim Congressmen to stand was no accident. Congress wanted to convince Kashmiri Muslims that they would be secure under a Congress state government. Indira's old – but now estranged – friends, Romesh and Raj Thapar happened to be on holiday in Srinagar when she 'invaded the valley'. In Raj Thapar's words, Indira was 'on the warpath against Farooq . . . hurling abuse and communal accusations'.[10] The journalist Tavleen Singh was also there and reported that 'there was something shameful and cynical about the Congress Party's approach'.[11]

Indira also exploited her own Kashmiri heritage during the campaign. Wearing the regional garb of *shalwar* and *kameez*, her head demurely covered, she proclaimed herself 'the daughter of Kashmir'. In Srinagar she spoke in Urdu, but she ran into trouble in the countryside because she spoke no Kashmiri with the result that in rural areas and villages, the crowds who came to hear her looked on with incomprehension. Farooq, of course, was fluent in Kashmiri and wherever he 'went he seemed to have a Pied Piper effect. People would come out as if to greet a conquering hero'.[12]

Indira wound up her Kashmir campaign back in Srinagar where she was scheduled to speak at the huge Iqbal Park. A crowd of four to five thousand was expected. But to the amazement of the press and everyone else present, scarcely a hundred turned up to hear the Prime Minister and most of this 'handful of people' were 'Congress workers and policewomen in civvies pretending to be an audience'.[13] As Raj Thapar put it, 'the audience was so thin that you . . . felt that people had been out for a walk and just stopped to listen to the band'.[14]

Scanning her meagre audience, Indira became 'furious, her face visibly twitching with anger'. She tried to brazen it out by attacking the National Conference, which she accused of 'preventing people from coming to her meeting'. 'Wherever there is trouble,' she said, 'you know who gets there first – Indira Gandhi.' For over an hour she harangued the audience, recalling her father's closeness to Sheikh Abdullah one minute, boasting of the success of the recent Non-Aligned Movement summit in Delhi the next. Somebody in the audience began lobbing stones towards the podium. Far from intimidating Indira, this angered her all the more. A scuffle broke out between Congress and National Conference members and, according to press reports, several men indecently 'flashed' themselves at Indira.[15]

After the disastrous Iqbal Park meeting Indira went directly to Srinagar airport to catch a flight back to Delhi. The Governor, B.K. Nehru, and his wife, Fori, among others, were on hand to see her off. But none of the usual civilities were observed. As Nehru described it, Indira was 'in a rage. Her face was flushed with anger, she spoke to nobody' and after glaring at the Nehrus and the officials on the runway, Indira got on the plane without a word of thanks or farewell.[16]

Polling in Kashmir ended on 5 June. As expected, Congress won in the Hindu-dominated Jammu region, but it was overwhelmingly defeated by the National Conference in Kashmir. Having failed to control the election, Congress now tried to discredit it. As soon as the result was known, Indira and Congress made loud accusations that it had been rigged.

It had not – at least not seriously. Congress' claims that the polling had been violent were also untrue.[17] Congress' attempts to discredit Farooq Abdullah were in vain. They were also unnecessary because Farooq was perfectly capable of discrediting himself. He was a loveable man – prone to hopping out of his car and directing traffic if he thought he could improve a constable's technique – but as Tavleen Singh (who knew him well) put it, he was 'too unserious, too much of a political lightweight to have remained popular for very long'.[18] Farooq spent more time in Delhi than Srinagar, had a penchant for movie starlets and continued to frequent discotheques. Left to himself, he would have created his own opposition. But Congress could not leave him alone. By this time Indira had an established history of getting rid of unco-operative chief ministers. Farooq had been earmarked for removal, though it would be some time before this plan could be executed.

During the summer of 1983 – just a month after the Kashmir state assembly elections – ethnic conflict between the majority Sinhalese and minority Tamils of Sri Lanka exploded. Sri Lanka's troubles reached back to 1948 when Ceylon (so called until 1972) gained its independence from the British. The Tamils of Sri Lanka, most of whom are Hindus, live primarily in the north and east of the island. They account for only 18 per cent of the national population and have long suffered at the hands of the Buddhist Sinhalese majority government which imposed Sinhalese as the national language, barred Tamils from educational and employment opportunities and in many other ways marginalized and reduced them to second-class citizens.

In response to this oppression, in the mid-seventies the Tamils formed a militant, secessionist movement called the Liberation Tigers of Tamil Elam (the LTTE). The 'Tamil Tigers' had – and continue to have – sympathizers in India, especially among the Indian Tamils who live in the southern state of Tamil Nadu.[19]

In the early eighties, in the face of growing Tamil unrest, the Sin-halese-dominated Sri Lankan government indicated that they were will-ing to devolve power. But at the same time, they cracked down on the LTTE. In July 1983, to avenge an LTTE ambush that had killed thir-teen Sinhalese soldiers, the Sri Lankan government unleashed a pogrom against the Tamils. In just several days 3,000 were murdered and 150,000 made homeless. Thousands of Tamils fled to India and took refuge in Tamil Nadu – a mass exodus that internationalized the Sri Lankan civil war. India now found the Tamil problem not only on its doorstep to the south, but inside its own borders in Tamil Nadu.

Even before the July 1983 massacre of Tamils, the Indian government had begun to provide the Tigers with money, arms and training. In fact, it was the larger-than-life former film star, the Chief Minister of Tamil Nadu, MGR, who was the LTTE's most visible benefactor. In this, Congress in Delhi was also implicated. With Indira's authorization, the government's Research and Intelligence Wing – which had been so notorious during the Emergency – sent people south to train LTTE refugee soldiers in camps in Tamil Nadu.

Thus in Sri Lanka, Indira's government appeared to be facilitating the same sort of secessionist movement that it was vehemently fighting at home in the Punjab and Kashmir. The obvious explanation for Indian support of the LTTE seemed to be that Indira wanted to placate the huge Tamil population in South India. But there may also have been a very different motive. Although Indian support of the Tigers seemed to contribute to the destabilization of Sri Lanka, Indira could actually have been trying to maintain the status quo there – employing the same insidious strategy she had used in the Punjab. Just as she had secretly built up Bhindranwale and his rabid Sikh followers in order to split the Sikhs of the Punjab, her covert support of the Tamil Tigers may have been intended to divide the Tamils in Sri Lanka. By backing extremists in both Sri Lanka and the Punjab, Indira could neutralize more moderate voices and thus negate the possibility of Tamil and Punjabi separatism.[20]

Publicly, Indira Gandhi refused to invoke the example of Bangladesh for Sri Lanka. Instead, she called only for autonomy and equal status for the Tamils in a *united* Sri Lanka. Thus in August 1983, she stood up in Parliament and declared: 'India stands for the independence, unity and integrity of Sri Lanka. India does not interfere in the internal affairs of other countries. However, because of the historical, cultural and other such close ties between the peoples of the two countries, especially between the Tamil community of Sri Lanka and us, India cannot remain unaffected by events there.'[21]

Whilst Sri Lanka was erupting, rioting and violence escalated in the Punjab. Sewers outside the Golden Temple began to fill up with bodies – victims of Bhindranwale's gang which was holed up inside. On the morning of 23 April the Amritsar Police Chief, a Sikh named A.S. Atwal, was shot dead leaving the temple after worship. He was one of a number of prominent Sikhs killed because they did not support the separatist goal of 'Khalistan' – an independent Punjab.

After Atwal's assassination, the Chief Minister of the Punjab, Darbara Singh, begged Indira to allow him to send the police into the temple complex in order to round up and arrest Bhindranwale and his guerrilla army. Indira, on the advice of Zail Singh – who had his own quarrels with Darbara Singh – refused to authorize this initiative. Though the situation in the Punjab was spiralling out of control, Delhi was still intent on keeping Sikhs in the state divided and also on playing the 'Hindu card' in the rest of the country.

It was a disastrous course of action, practically as well as morally. Among many others, the journalist Inder Malhotra and the historian Bipan Chandra – both of whose political and historical vision was acute – tried to persuade Indira to negotiate with the dissidents in the Punjab. She had repeatedly withdrawn from negotiations in the past because she thought it politically expedient not to reach a settlement. She was wrong. But by now Indira had not only lost her political judgement but also any vestiges of her old uncanny sense of timing and decisiveness. She wavered. She listened to Zail Singh. She wanted Rajiv to take the credit for what transpired in the Punjab. She turned a deaf ear to sound counsel and heeded bad advice.

Inevitably, it became too late to resolve the Punjab crisis, and not merely because Indira had waited too long. The Punjab was itself hopelessly divided and there were too many individuals with whom Delhi had to negotiate, such as the Akali leader, Harchand Singh Longowal, Gurcharan Singh Tohro, who headed the committee which was meant to control all the 'Gurudwaras', including the Golden Temple, and Bhindranwale himself. It was Bhindranwale who was the most intransigent. Belatedly, Indira agreed to the transfer of Chandigarh to the Punjab but there were still quarrels over the Hindu regions of the Punjab that Haryana wanted.

Meanwhile, Bhindranwale moved his headquarters from the outer precincts of the Golden Temple to an internal shrine called the Akal Takht. His fortifications were strengthened and more arms smuggled into the temple under loads of milk and food grains. Every morning Bhindranwale delivered fiery anti-Indian and anti-Hindu harangues from the roof of his sanctuary. Those who could not make it to Amritsar to listen to the *sant* in person, heard his message on tapes sold throughout the state. Bhindranwale also had a message for the Prime Minister. 'Peace and violence are from the same root. We are like a matchstick, that is made of wood and is cold. But when you strike, it flames.'[22]

From the Golden Temple, Bhindranwale continued to send his terror squads out into the countryside. On 5 October they stopped the Amritsar-Delhi bus on the Grand Trunk Road and forced six Hindu passengers to get off and line up on the road. Then they shot them. This provoked outrage throughout India. The next day, Indira dismissed the Chief Minister of the Punjab, Darbara Singh, and placed the state under President's rule. By ousting Singh, she had removed the only Sikh authority in the state prepared to take a hard line with Bhindranwale.

But President's rule could not quell the escalating lawlessness and violence. Two weeks after it was imposed, the Calcutta-Kashmir express train was derailed while passing through the state. Nineteen people were killed and 129 injured. On 18 November another bus was hijacked and four Hindu passengers shot dead.

Meanwhile, back in Delhi, Indira hosted the opening ceremony of the Commonwealth heads of government meeting on 23 November. Like the Non-Aligned summit, this occasion gave Indira a stage on which to perform, an international public relations opportunity and a reprieve from the distressing situation at home. The 1983 Commonwealth meeting was the last international gathering over which Indira presided and she enjoyed it, especially the closing banquet, the menu of which she scrupulously planned herself. The Queen attended in full regalia; Margaret Thatcher wore a stunning evening dress. But Indira – the smallest of them all, dressed in a plain silk sari – looked the most regal and powerful of the three women. Despite outward appearances, Indira, in truth, was losing her grip.

Emotionally, Indira was now isolated. Since Sanjay's death she rarely shared her thoughts or feelings with anyone. She was not close to Rajiv; he had dutifully taken over Sanjay's political role, but he could not occupy the place his brother had held in Indira's heart. In addition the swami, Brahmachari, was being marginalized.

This was Rajiv's doing. By early 1984 Rajiv Gandhi had grown into his political role. He had proved himself a competent General Secretary of the All-India Congress Committee and his office, located on Motilal Nehru Marg, was a model of organization and efficiency, 'complete with newspaper clippings, data banks, documents, books, a computer and a Xerox machine'.[23] Rajiv, indeed, was a paragon of efficiency and integrity compared to the party hacks and sycophants surrounding Indira. Though he inherited several of Sanjay's cronies – most notably Navin Chawla – he had nothing to do with his brother's more unsavoury associates.

Rajiv attracted his own coterie of clean-cut, attaché case-carrying business executives and technocrats. They were the new generation – a modern breed who put their faith in technology, statistics and computers. (Rajiv possessed the first Toshiba laptop computer in India.) They may have donned *khadi* but they still wore their Gucci loafers. Many had attended the elite Doon School and Cambridge University with Rajiv. They were more at home speaking English than Hindi. For them, Mahatma Gandhi was a vague childhood memory, and like Rajiv, most of them had not read Jawaharlal Nehru's books. They lived in the present – busy, pragmatic, unreflective young men – with no time or use for religion, ideology or superstition.

This meant that Brahmachari's days were numbered. Sanjay Gandhi had cultivated a friendship with the swami not because he believed in Brahmachari's occult powers but because he found him useful. Brahmachari could acquire airplanes, traffic in arms, hire hit men and launder money. Rajiv had complained of many of Sanjay's activities when his brother was alive. In contrast to Sanjay, Rajiv was straightforward and direct in his manner and generally honest in his conduct. Arun Singh, for example, once curtly told a friend who wanted him to use his influence with Rajiv to get government accommodation, 'I was forced [by him] to buy my own house. Do you expect him to even listen to this proposal?'[24]

As Rajiv's influence and power flourished, Brahmachari's inevitably waned. Brahmachari was everything Rajiv was not: subtle, wily, dishonest and utterly unWesternized. The swami's presence in the household had annoyed Rajiv for years. Now he was in a position to remove him. Imperceptibly, but surely, Brahmachari's stature at 1 Safdarjung Road was undermined by Rajiv and his advisers, Arun Nehru and Arun Singh. Indira was weaned away from Brahmachari's mysticism to a faith in Rajiv's strategic plans, technology and statistics. First Brahmachari's weekly television programme was axed; then government grants to his ashrams were slashed. He disappeared from the family dinner table. Indira became less and less accessible to him. Finally, he was informed that 'Madame' no longer had the time to see him. Rajiv had seen to it that Brahmachari was all but banished from the Prime Minister's house.

* * *

February – when the natural world comes to life again in India – is the loveliest month in Delhi. Between the cold of winter and the onset of the terrific heat of the Indian summer, for four or five weeks there are warm, balmy days when the foliage is intensely green and gardens come into their full glory. In the past, no matter what situation her life and the country was in, Indira always felt elated by the coming of the spring. But not in 1984; Pupul Jayakar found her 'deeply depressed' and 'isolated ... filled with dark moods'.[25] In this state of mind, Indira felt that she had to take action in Kashmir and topple Farooq Abdullah. This should have been straightforward since Indira's cousin and old friend, B.K. Nehru, was Governor of Kashmir and therefore the person able to impose Governor's rule – the Kashmiri equivalent of President's Rule. Indira did not directly ask her cousin to dismiss Farooq, but she made it unambiguously clear to him that she wanted Farooq out.[26]

B.K Nehru, however, saw no need, justification or constitutional reason for dismissing Farooq. In his eyes Indira was pursuing a personal vendetta. When she pressed her for specific grounds on which to dismiss Farooq, Indira complained that Farooq was 'unreliable ... and incompetent in the administration of the state'. As Nehru put it, 'both these charges I could certify from personal experience were totally correct'. But he also pointed out to Indira that 'unreliability was (and is) not an unusual characteristic among the politicians of India; if Farooq was unreliable ... he was not exceptional. Nor was he the only Chief Minister who maladministered his state; there could be found examples of worse maladministration ... among the states ruled by ... Congress.'[27]

B.K. Nehru was an oddity in Indian politics because in certain respects, he was not really a political animal. He was a vestigial specimen of the by now almost extinct breed of *uncommitted* Indian civil servants. In fact, B.K. Nehru was not even a member of the Congress Party. Inconveniently for Indira, he also had a mind of his own and was a respecter of democratic norms. Nehru was fond of and respected Indira – even when he thought she was wrong – but he was not the least bit intimidated by her.

Indira's secretary, P.C. Alexander – an urbane, intelligent man but not of the same ilk as his predecessors P.N. Haksar or P.N. Dhar – repeatedly rang B.K. Nehru on the unreliable phone link between Delhi and Srinagar and pressed him to dismiss Farooq. Alexander tried to feed Nehru the Congress line that Farooq was a dangerous, pro-Pakistani, anti-India secessionist. Alexander also informed Nehru that a reliable successor, who would not compromise Indian unity, was already in place to take over as Chief Minister. This was none other than Farooq's brother-in-law, G.M. Shah, who was in the process of luring thirteen of Farooq's National Conference Party members away from the fold with cash (supplied by Congress in Delhi) and the promise of a ministership in G.M. Shah's new state government. With these defections, Farooq's National Conference government would be fatally outnumbered and would fall. Shah's renegades could then form a flimsy coalition with the Kashmir Congress Party and take power.

The plan was for Shah and his thirteen defectors to come to B.K. Nehru at the Governor's mansion in the dead of night and for Nehru to swear them all in on the spot. Farooq would then be informed after the fact. But B.K. Nehru refused to carry out this 'act of intrigue', as he referred to it later. He insisted that as Governor he was 'an independent Head of State drawing his authority from the Constitution. He was not concerned with, and was above, political parties and was not subordinate . . . to the Government of India.' Nehru argued that the only legitimate way to handle the defection of Shah and his followers was to call for a vote of no-confidence in the state assembly.[28]

The tussle between Indira and her cousin over Farooq continued for months. As Nehru later put it, 'we went over the same ground again and again quite endlessly. She really did not have any logical answer to my objections; all she wanted was that Farooq should be out.'[29] Nehru argued that Shah would be an even worse Chief Minister than Farooq. Indira was well aware that Shah was of dubious character, but when Fori Nehru asked her, 'Why Shah?' Indira curtly answered, 'We know how to deal with Gul Shah.'[30]

Finally Nehru sent a letter to Indira listing his political and practical – as well as moral – objections to her scheme. A Shah government, he told her, would be unstable and would fall apart. Farooq would 'not sit quiet'; he would probably have to be arrested with the result that he would become a martyr and hero. After Shah's appointment, elections would have to be held and unless there was large-scale rigging, Congress would be 'wiped out'. The secessionist movement in the state would gain strength under Shah. Farooq, Nehru admitted, was a far from ideal Chief Minister, 'but the result of removing him will have such immense short-term and long-term harmful consequences for the entire country that between the two evils his continuance for the present is the better choice'.[31]

Nehru's argument was cogent, but Indira was not listening. Moreover, her Kashmiri advisers – including the ubiquitous Arun Nehru – attempted to undermine Indira's trust in her cousin. They accused Nehru of being an alcoholic and of being far too friendly with Farooq – a bond based, they said, on Nehru and Farooq's shared fondness for drink. When these accusations got back to Nehru, he denied being 'a drunk' but said that he had never made a secret of the fact that he 'enjoyed a glass of whiskey in the evening'. (Indira knew full well that one of the reasons he had never joined Congress was that he refused to take the Party pledge of teetotalism.)[32] Nehru also refuted the charge of being 'soft' on Farooq.

The situation was now irretrievable. When Indira saw that her cousin would not be bullied, she had no option but to relieve him of his governorship and replace him with one of her hardcore loyalists. B.K. Nehru duly tendered his resignation, citing 'purely personal' grounds. P.C. Alexander summoned Nehru to Delhi, opened a bottle of Chivas Regal whisky, and suggested that instead of resigning, Nehru should be transferred from the governorship of Kashmir to that of another state. Nehru's response was that this was a ruse and he would have none of it. Alexander then pointed out that if Nehru resigned no one would believe he had done so for personal reasons; people would guess it had been because he refused to dismiss Farooq, and this 'would cause personal embarrassment to Indira Gandhi'. Surely, Alexander said, Nehru 'had nothing personal against Indira Gandhi; surely [he] ... did not want to embarrass her?'[33]

Nehru gallantly agreed to withdraw his resignation. Indira was his 'sister', as he put it, after all. He was duly transferred to the governorship of Gujarat, a completely dry state, where he languished for the next several years. Indira replaced Nehru with none other than Jagmohan in Kashmir, the slavishly loyal bureaucrat who had run the Delhi District Authority during the Emergency and levelled the slums of the old city in the name of beautification. His victims then had been largely Muslims, as was the population in the Kashmir Valley; to many his appointment therefore made Delhi's plans for Kashmir unambiguously clear. The stage was now set for the removal of Farooq.

Meanwhile, contingency plans were being made for a military routing of Bhindranwale and his army from the Golden Temple in Amritsar. This was the brainchild of Rajiv Gandhi, Arun Nehru and Arun Singh who painstakingly drew up the invasion blueprint. Indira was aware of the plan, but for a long time she hoped it would never have to be implemented. According to Arun Nehru, 'she was scared of attacking a house of God'. And so she 'delayed and resisted'. The plan was top-secret, and during the weeks it was being devised, Indira quietly had *pujas* performed in the hope that some sort of 'miracle' might make the invasion of the Golden Temple unnecessary and resolve the Punjab crisis.[34]

The resort to *pujas* reflected Indira's deep sense of helplessness. Around this time, she talked to Rajiv and Arun Nehru about 'grey areas in history' – her phrase for the irresolvable situations in places such as the Punjab and Kashmir. She said that the only thing to do in a 'grey area' was 'to play for time', to wait and see – and hope. But Rajiv and Arun Nehru were men of action. They opposed Indira's passive approach of watching and waiting – and of hoping for miracles.[35]

In January 1984 Indira stood up in Parliament and accused Pakistan of aiding Sikh terrorists in the Punjab. Then her Home Minister, P.C. Sethi, stood up and reassured the house that force would not be used in Amritsar – a promise made in good faith since Sethi had no inkling of the invasion Rajiv and his team were planning. Though the Home Minister should have been a central figure in the Punjab drama, he was, in fact, deliberately not consulted. Neither was Zail Singh, the Sikh President who hitherto had been so closely involved in policy making in the Punjab. Singh later claimed that he was not informed of the invasion plan until the end of May 1984.[36]

In February, Indira's government embarked on another round of negotiations with the Akali leaders in the Punjab. She was worried about the forthcoming general election – due to be held in less than a year. In order to keep the Hindu vote, Indira knew that the 'Punjab problem' had to be resolved. Despite this pressure, the negotiations came to nothing. Indira was trapped. On the one hand, she did not want to appear soft on the Sikh militants; on the other, if she had to resort to military action, she knew that conditions in the state had to deteriorate further before she would be justified in sending in the army. Faced with a crisis situation in the Punjab and the prospect of the election, Indira became paralysed.

She no longer had skilled advisers and negotiators to assist, as she had ten years earlier when she had hit an impasse with Zulfikar Bhutto at the Simla summit. At one point, Indira asked for advice from Subhadra Joshi who had worked with her during the Partition riots in Delhi. Joshi was a Punjabi herself and a politician with vast experience of communal conflict. She tried to persuade Indira that there were still ways in which a peaceful settlement might be reached. But Indira did not heed Joshi's advice.[37] Instead the inexperienced and far from diplomatic Rajiv, Arun Nehru and Arun Singh continued to guide Indira's policy.

The situation thus remained deadlocked, but the violence increased.[38] During March and April 1984 Bhindranwale's hit squads murdered eighty people and injured 107. This toll included prominent Hindus and pro-Congress Sikhs. Those Hindus who had not already left the Punjab now began to flee the state – including traders, money-lenders and shopkeepers as well as wealthy industrialists. By this time, Bhindranwale had infiltrated the state administration and the police and had also taken control of the state's telephone exchange.

Meanwhile, difficulties of a different sort were mounting in Andhra Pradesh when the movie-star Chief Minister N.T. Ramarao convened a meeting of anti-Congress state leaders in May. NTR's idea was to form an opposition coalition to Indira and Congress in the general election, due in early 1985. The ebullient, over-confident Kashmir Chief Minister, Farooq Abdullah, was among those who attended the Andhra Pradesh meeting, apparently oblivious of the very tenuous hold he had on power in Kashmir. Farooq's appearance at the conference sealed his fate.

Whilst NTR, Farooq and Indira's other enemies were plotting, a last-ditch round of negotiations on the Punjab got underway. Indira entrusted these to her Foreign Affairs Minister, Narasimha Rao, rather than the Home Minister, P.C. Sethi, whom Indira considered weak and incompetent. Indira's secretary, P.C. Alexander, was also a key negotiator. Neither Alexander nor Rao, of course, was a Sikh or a Punjabi. Rajiv Gandhi and his team were stage-managing events from the wings.

The Akali leader, Longowal – who by this time had come into conflict with Bhindranwale and occupied a different part of the Golden Temple – declared that he was willing to meet the Indian government halfway. Bhindranwale, however, was not. Narasimha Rao and company once again offered up Chandigarh. Bhindranwale insisted that *all* the

Anandpur Sahib Resolution demands – including those pertaining to land and access to river waters – must be met, knowing this would not happen. Caught in the middle, Longowal announced that beginning on June 3 – the date of the martyrdom of Guru Arjun, who had built the Golden Temple, grain would cease to flow out of the Punjab. The state was the breadbasket of India; if grain supplies were halted the rest of the country would eventually starve.

At this point the contingency plan of storming the Golden Temple and flushing out Bhindranwale and his followers became an inevitability. Because of the low morale of the Punjabi police force, it would have to be a military operation, and it was essential that Sikh officers and soldiers participate. On 30 May Indian troops began to surround Amritsar. A dusk-to-dawn curfew was imposed, transforming the bustling city into a ghost town by night.

On the morning of 2 June it was announced that Indira would broadcast to the nation that evening at 8.30. She agonized over her speech and made numerous last-minute changes with the result that she did not come on air – on both radio and television – until 9.15 p.m. 'The Punjab,' she said, 'is uppermost in all our minds. The whole country is deeply concerned. The matter has been discussed and spoken about time and again. Yet an impression has been assiduously created that it is not being dealt with.' She went on to say that a commission would be established to decide 'the whole territorial dispute' of Chandigarh, the river waters and Hindu areas of the Punjab. The major problem, she insisted, was not that the government had failed to offer an equable settlement, but rather that the Akalis had surrendered authority to Bhindranwale. She could not 'allow violence and terrorism in the settlement of issues. Those who indulge in such anti-social and anti-national activities should make no mistake about this.' But Indira did not end on this threatening note. Instead, she made an emotional appeal 'to all sections of Punjabis . . . don't shed blood, shed hatred'.[39]

Even as Indira spoke, Indian army troops were closing in on the Golden Temple. The curtain was about to rise on 'Operation Blue Star'. It would be carried out by the 9th Division of the Indian army, commanded by a Sikh army officer, Major General Kuldip Singh Brar. On 3 June, all foreign journalists were expelled from the Punjab. Rail, bus and air movement in the state was halted; telex and telephone lines were cut and the border with Pakistan sealed. 'The Punjab was cut off from the rest of the world in preparation for the final assault.'[40]

By this time, the prospect of an invasion – and of another 'Amritsar' as bloody as that of 1919 – was no secret, although the Indian President, Zail Singh, unconvincingly maintained that as late as 5 June, he had not been given 'even an inkling' of what was about to happen.[41] If he truly remained ignorant, he was one of the very few. From his sanctuary in the Akal Takht, Bhindranwale defiantly told journalists: 'If the authorities enter this temple, we will teach them such a lesson that the throne of Indira will crumble. We will slice them into small pieces . . . They will chew iron lentils . . . Let them come.'[42]

While central government intelligence was poor, Bhindranwale's spies were efficient and their information was 'exact and up-to-the-minute'. The Indian army did not know how many extremists were in the Golden Temple, exactly where they were located in the temple complex and the nature or extent of their arms and defences. On 1 June, Major General Brar – dressed in civilian clothes, ostensibly to worship – entered the temple complex to gather intelligence. To his dismay, he saw well-fortified dugouts, makeshift bunkers and caches of arms. He also observed that some of the Golden Temple's walls and marble trelliswork had been modified in order to support automatic weapons. But General Brar had little time to do a proper reconnaissance. Delhi had already informed him that the mission would start on 6 June.[43]

At 4 p.m. on 5 June, Indian army officers called upon the civilians inside the Golden Temple to come out, and for the armed extremists within to surrender. None of Bhindranwale's people emerged, but 126 others – worshippers, pilgrims and moderate Sikhs – did. That night Indian army commandos forcibly entered the area of the temple where the Akali leaders – but not Bhindranwale – were hiding. Throughout the raid Bhindranwale's gunfire rained down, and more than half of the ninety commandos were killed or seriously injured before they reached their goal. Those who made it found Longowal and a number of other unarmed Akali leaders and brought them out. As he left with his captors, Longowal said bitterly, 'Tell [Bhindranwale] . . . that his guests have arrived.'[44]

Pupul Jayakar visited Indira at home during the evening of 5 June. Indira, suffering from a sore throat, was sipping warm milk and found it difficult to talk. But even if she could have spoken easily, she would not have told Jayakar what was about to be unleashed in Amritsar.

Although it is unlikely she got much sleep that night, 'she showed no strain or anxiety' the next morning when she had a lengthy interview with Andrew Neil, the editor of the London *Sunday Times*. Nor did she give any indication of what was going on in the Punjab even as they spoke. Neil was interviewing Indira because it was obvious the situation in the Punjab was on the verge of erupting, but Indira told him that 'India has lived a long, long time – thousands of years – and my sixty-six years hardly count. India will survive . . . It has been through tremendous vicissitudes in its long history and it has come through.'[45]

It was 100 degrees in Delhi on the morning of 6 June, and even hotter in Amritsar, when the 9th Division made its first assault on the Golden Temple. Official government orders instructed soldiers to use 'minimum force', to inflict 'as little damage as possible', and specifically not to violate or disturb the holiest shrine, the Harmandir Sahib (the dome-shaped sanctum sanctorum where the Sikh holy book, *Guru Granth Sahib*, has been read for the past 200 years). Bhindranwale and his men were barricaded in the Akal Takht, also a holy shrine, but this area was apparently not specified in the 'minimum force' orders.

The Indian soldiers were sitting ducks for Bhindranwale's men, hidden behind their heavily defended and sandbagged positions. More than a hundred soldiers died in the initial attempt to gain entry to the Golden Temple. After their failure tanks and artillery rumbled into the temple complex that afternoon. In order to get at the heavily-armed Bhindranwale and his followers inside, the army had to fire directly on the Akal Takht, inflicting great damage to the shrine. In Sikh eyes, this was tantamount to sending tanks into St Peter's in Rome or the Kaaba at Mecca. In the words of the Sikh Indian President, Zail Singh, 'this was the place built by the fifth Guru, an apostle of peace, as a symbol of love and unity of mankind. This was the temple of God . . . the shrine built on a lower level than the surrounding land in a spirit of humility. It has doors on all four sides proclaiming its accessibility to people of all faiths and creeds.'[46] It had taken an act of desecration to destroy Bhindranwale.

For some hours, however, the *sant*'s fate was unknown. The Akal Takht had scarcely a pillar left standing and its marbled rooms were blackened by fire; but there was still 'the agonizing possibility' that Bhindranwale had escaped.[47] Late on the night of 6 June, however, when the army finally entered the shrine, they found Bhindranwale's body along with those of thirty-one of his men. But no survivors of the assault saw Bhindranwale achieve his martyrdom. In the room where the bodies were strewn, the soldiers found a diary listing all the people Bhindranwale's squads had 'liquidated', and also a huge bag of fan mail written to Bhindranwale not only from Indians, but from people all over the world.

The fighting came to end with Bhindranwale's death. But the cost of exterminating him had been high. It had exceeded all estimates made to Indira by her intelligence sources, by the army and her advisers; it was far higher than she herself imagined. Operation Blue Star was a horrendous debacle. Out of the 1,000 troops sent into the Golden Temple somewhere between 300 and 700 and over half the Special Forces commandos had been killed. The exact death toll of civilians – many of them innocent pilgrims – is unknown, but it is estimated to be well over a thousand. An Indian government white paper later reported 493 were killed, leaving 1,600 unaccounted for. Besides the human loss, the Golden Temple library – which contained all the hand-written manuscripts by the Sikh Gurus – went up in flames; 300 bullet holes riddled the Harmandir Sahib and the Akal Takht was severely damaged.[48]

On 9 June, at Indira's request, the Indian President, Zail Singh, visited the Golden Temple. R.K. Dhawan and Arun Singh accompanied him. It was a brutally hot and sultry day in Amritsar. As Zail Singh, Dhawan and Arun Singh entered the temple complex they could hear the singing of holy hymns. The next thing they were aware of was a foul odour that assailed their nostrils. In Zail Singh's words, though 'efforts [had been] ... made to cleanse the area ... yet [the] stench of human flesh was hanging heavy in the air. No amount of cleansing could have wiped out the strong smell of so many decomposed bodies in that scorching summer heat.'[49]

As they entered the wide promenade surrounding the holy tank and temple, a burst of gunfire rang out. The security man next to Zail Singh was hit in the shoulder, the bullet having just missed its intended target – Indira's emissary, the Indian President. There were still a few desperate extremists active in one of the Temple towers whom the army had been unable to flush out.[50]

This was a warning shot. When the full extent of the carnage and desecration wreaked on the Golden Temple became known, it was obvious that ultimate revenge would be taken – and on whom.

TWENTY-ONE

31 October 1984

SONIA GANDHI LATER DESCRIBED how after Operation Blue Star, 'a shadow entered our lives'.[1] Indira discussed the possibility of assassination with Rajiv and Sonia and wrote out instructions for her funeral. She also talked about the risk to her life with her fourteen-year-old grandson, Rahul. Rahul and Priyanka had been sent to boarding school in 1982, but when the situation in the Punjab exploded, they returned home and were enrolled in day schools in Delhi. After Operation Blue Star, Indira worried obsessively about their safety. She told them not to play beyond the garden gate which led to the path that connected her house to her Akbar Road office next door. 1 Safdarjung Road was now a prison for all its inhabitants.

Everyone around Indira knew that her life was in danger. According to Inder Malhotra, 'the gloom and foreboding in Delhi' were 'palpable'. Yet Indira did not appear to be under any strain – she looked as calm and collected as ever. Her energy levels and appetite were undiminished; she slept soundly. One evening she had B.K. Nehru, Fori, and Fori's brother, Joseph Friedman, to dinner. The food was excellent and Indira was in high spirits and relaxed. No one mentioned Operation Blue Star or the ongoing problems in Kashmir. Joseph Friedman did, however, ask Indira how she managed to remain free of tension in the midst of such trying times. 'Tension,' Indira replied, 'is within. One never wears it on one's sleeve.'[2]

Others, however, worried outwardly, and Indira's security protection was stepped up. The Defence Minister tried to persuade the Prime Minister to transfer her security from the police to the army. But Indira told him not 'even to entertain this idea'. She was the leader of a democratic not a military government.[3] Indira did agree, however, to have commandos from the Indo-Tibetan Border Police added to her protection team. The head of the Intelligence Bureau then ordered that all Sikh security men be removed from duty at 1 Safdarjung Road. Indira immediately vetoed this order. She had played the communal card in the Punjab and Kashmir, but she would not countenance it on her own doorstep. India, she insisted, 'was secular'. The Sikhs stayed.[4]

Despite an enhanced and enlarged security team, Indira remained extremely vulnerable. The intelligence plan to protect her designed only to prevent an attack from the outside. Even after Indira countermanded the order banning Sikh bodyguards, no one guessed there was an enemy within. In the words of one officer who testified later, 'what we did not perceive was that an attempt could be made inside the Prime Minister's house'.[5]

After the Golden Temple debacle in the Punjab, Indira should have proceeded with caution in Kashmir. But just a month after Operation Blue Star, she pushed ahead with her plan to topple the Kashmiri Chief Minister, Farooq Abdullah. She claimed that Farooq had been colluding with Kashmiri dissidents and that he was anti-national and had condoned Pakistani aid to the secessionist movement. Indira was convinced that Pakistan was supplying arms and training to Kashmiri as well as to Punjabi separatists.

Though Jagmohan, the new Governor of Kashmir, had been dispatched to Kashmir to do the Prime Minister's bidding, he was not eager to sack Farooq Abdullah in favour of Indira's choice for Chief Minister, G.M. Shah. Instead, Jagmohan suggested that Indira impose Governor's rule. Constitutionally this was the appropriate course of action. But as Jagmohan put it, this 'legitimate constitutional option . . . was denied to me'. Indira insisted that Jagmohan get rid of Farooq Abdullah forthwith and replace him with Shah.[6]

This could only be done if a sufficient number of Farooq's majority in the state assembly transferred their allegiance to Shah. But according to B.K. Nehru, 'the members of the legislature were no fools; they knew that if they defected to Gul Shah they would be torn to pieces by an angry populace'. A desperate solution was decided on. The government would entice the members away from Farooq with cash and/or the promise of ministerial posts in Shah's new government. Indeed Shah had been working towards this end, courting defectors, for some months. According to B.K. Nehru the necessary funds – 'the standard rate was two lakh rupees' per bought defector – were supplied in cash from the Congress Party in Delhi and transported to Srinagar in the mail pouches of the Intelligence Bureau. By this time 'the use of official machinery for party purposes had . . . become so commonplace that no eyebrows were raised'.[7]

Early in the morning on 2 July, G.M. Shah, accompanied by thirteen deserters from Farooq's National Conference government, arrived at Governor Jagmohan's office. In addition to his band of defectors, Shah produced a letter of support from the Kashmir Congress Party. He demanded that he be sworn in as Chief Minister of a new coalition state government. Jagmohan rang Farooq and asked him to come immediately to his office. Forty-five minutes passed before Farooq arrived in a highly emotional state. Jagmohan asked him to resign. Farooq refused and insisted that the state assembly be convened in order for him to face a vote of confidence.

According to Jagmohan, he once again pressed Delhi to allow him to impose Governor's rule. Only when this route was categorically closed to him, did he proceed to dismiss Farooq and swear in G.M. Shah as Chief Minister of Kashmir. All thirteen defectors were then sworn in as cabinet ministers. As Jagmohan put it, they 'were keen to get into the saddle immediately'.[8] All this took place in Srinagar, but Jagmohan was being operated by remote control by Rajiv Gandhi and Arun Nehru in Delhi, who had been instructed by Indira to 'get rid of Farooq at all costs'.[9]

A month later, in August, Arun Nehru – apparently again on Indira's orders – encouraged the governor of Andhra Pradesh to dismiss the Chief Minister of Andhra Pradesh, the film star N.T. Ramarao.[10] This time there was a national outcry. Indira protested in Parliament that she knew nothing of Ramarao's dismissal, but few people believed her.[11] Instead, it was believed she would now stop at nothing. Rumours swelled that Indira was about to introduce a constitutional amendment to postpone the 1984 general election. It was beginning to feel like the Emergency all over again.

*   *   *

With discontent and discord in the Punjab, Kashmir, Andhra Pradesh and elsewhere, Indira's popularity sunk to an all-time low. Newspapers accused her of 'the rape of democracy'. If the general election was held on schedule, many people thought Indira would be defeated and banished to the political wilderness again. She kept her own counsel, but those close to her felt that psychologically she had retreated and detached herself from the gathering storm. Indira would be sixty-seven in November. She did not feel old; her health remained perfect and she was as energetic as ever; but she was like the eye at the centre of a hurricane – still and calm.

It was in this state of mind in the autumn of 1984 that Indira wrote a document that she mentioned to no one. It was later found among her papers:

> I have never felt less like dying and . . . calm and peace of mind is what prompts me to write what is in the nature of a will. If I die a violent death as some fear and a few are plotting, I know the violence will be in the thought and the action of the assassin, not in my dying – for no hate is dark enough to overshadow the extent of my love for my people and my country; no force is strong enough to divert me from my purpose and my endeavour to take this country forward. A poet has written of love – 'how can I feel humble with the wealth of you beside me.' I can say the same of India. I cannot understand how anyone can be an Indian and not be proud – the richness and infinite variety of our composite heritage, the magnificence of the people's spirit, equal to any disaster or burden, firm in their faith . . . even in poverty and hardship.[12]

This is more a testament of faith – even love – than a will. Indira knew that the end of her life was near, and she guessed it would probably be violent. It had not been the life she had wanted when she was young; it was not the life she would have chosen. But this scrawled note shows that she felt that the choice that had been thrust on her was the right one; it had been better, after all, to take on the family legacy of service rather than seek personal fulfilment. The real poignancy of this document is not Indira's premonition of her assassination, but rather her failure to fulfil her 'purpose and . . . endeavour to take this country forward'. Like her father, she loved India, but she knew full well that the country was in chaos.

On 11 October, Indira's sense of foreboding was heightened when she heard that Margaret Thatcher had narrowly escaped being blown up by an IRA bomb attack during the Conservative Party conference in Brighton. Although Mrs Thatcher escaped unharmed, five others were killed and two of her Cabinet were seriously injured. As Thatcher's biographer put it, 'nothing like it had ever happened before in Britain'. Publicly Mrs Thatcher retained her sangfroid, but privately she was as shaken as any human being would be.[13]

Indira, unlike Margaret Thatcher, was no stranger to assassination and violent death. Too many people close to her had already died thus – Gandhi, Sheikh Mujib Rahman and Sanjay, among others. Indira rang Mrs Thatcher and perhaps more than any other person who consoled the British leader, Indira understood Thatcher's acute vulnerability. The difference between these two women Prime Ministers – who had been friends for eight years – is that for Mrs Thatcher the IRA assassination attempt was a revelation. Assassination had always been theoretically possible, of course, especially after the terrorist murder of 'Dickie' Mountbatten five years earlier. But now it had become a terrifying reality. For Indira, in contrast, assassination had long been an occupational hazard. Now it felt like an inevitability.

In late October, Indira suddenly decided she wanted to visit Kashmir and see the chinar trees in their autumn blaze of colour. Politically, the state was still troubled – the situation had not settled down after Farooq was removed and Gul Shah installed as Chief Minister. Governor Jagmohan told Indira there had been unrest in Srinagar and advised her not to visit. But she insisted. On the morning of 27 October she flew to Srinagar, taking her grandchildren, Rahul and Priyanka, with her. They were met at the airport by Jagmohan and Gul Shah and driven to the Chasma Shahi guesthouse, across the road from the Governor's house.

It was a fleeting visit – only thirty-six hours, with Indira departing the following afternoon – but according to Jagmohan, it was a busy, upbeat one. Indira was briefed by both Jagmohan and Shah. Despite the security situation, she insisted upon taking the children to the Srinagar market. According to Jagmohan, Indira was in exceptionally good spirits – animated, jovial, eating heartily, including chocolates, which she usually refused because she watched her weight. Jagmohan remembers as well that Indira made a number of references to future events. She told him he must come to Delhi in early November for a meeting with her and the Cabinet Secretary; she said that she wanted to bring the children back to go to Leh in July. For several hours, Indira walked in the woods and Jagmohan was aware that she visited a holy man as well as looked at the chinar trees – now saturated in shades of vermilion, amber, and burnt sienna. But in Jagmohan's memory, the visit was a happy, hopeful one. Indira, to him, had never seemed more alive.[14]

Her friend Pupul Jayakar – who was not with Indira in Srinagar in late October 1984 but who later traced her journey – tells a different story. Jayakar saw Indira in Delhi the night before she flew to Srinagar. Though Indira mentioned upcoming events, including a meeting with the Dalai Lama in November, her thoughts seemed 'entangled with death', and she told Jayakar that she had instructed Rajiv 'to scatter my ashes over the Himalayas'. This information came out of the blue, and Jayakar asked her why she spoke of death. Indira replied, 'Isn't it inevitable?'[15]

Jayakar did not question Jagmohan about Indira's visit to Kashmir in October 1984, so there is nothing in her account of Indira's briefings with the Governor and Chief Minister, or her high spirits and good appetite. In fact, Jayakar mistakenly says that Indira 'saw very few people [and] attended to no official business'. But she did reconstruct Indira's movements on the morning of 28 October. Indira climbed Shankaracharya, a sacred hill nearby, to visit the temple, and then went to visit a sage named Lakshmanjoo who had an ashram in the Nishat gardens.

The anchorite told Jayakar that Indira came to him early on the morning of 28 October, and that she 'spoke of death. Indira said that she felt her time was over and death was near.' He, too, 'felt death was very close to her'. Nevertheless, the sage was not one to let an opportunity pass. He pointed out a small building in the ashram to Indira and asked if she would return and preside at its inauguration. She said, 'I will come if I am still alive.' Then she left the ashram to go on and visit the nearby temple of Sharika, the patron goddess of the Kashmiri Brahmin community. Here Indira performed the ritual of *puja* while the priests chanted. Before she left, they put the vermilion *tilak* of the sun on Indira's forehead – a mark to show that the Goddess had touched her.[16]

This pilgrimage accomplished, Indira returned to the guesthouse, gathered her grandchildren, left immediately for the airport and flew back to Delhi.

The next day, 29 October, Indira flew to Bhubaneshwar, the capital of the eastern state of Orissa, for a whirlwind election tour. For the next thirty-six hours, she travelled by helicopter to meetings all over the state. It was a punishing schedule, and Indira was exhausted by the time she made her last speech, back in Bhubaneshwar, on the evening of 30 October. Bhubaneshwar was a place saturated with memories for Indira. It was here that her father suffered his first stroke – and his protracted dying began – in January 1963. It was in Bhubaneshwar that Indira had been stoned – and her nose broken – while campaigning for the general election of 1967.

The speech that she gave in Bhubaneshwar on the night of 30 October 1984, like most of her speeches, had been drafted by her principal speechwriter, Sharada Prasad. It was emotive, interlaced with historical references, eloquent and stirring. It was, in fact, a typical campaign speech. It resurrected great moments in India's history from ancient times to the freedom struggle; it invoked high-sounding phrases such as 'eternal vigilance is the price of freedom'; it asked rhetorical questions such as 'What is the meaning of freedom if somebody is hungry?' It made the usual large campaign speech claims and promises.

And then it suddenly shifted tone. Indira's voice drowned out her speechwriter's:

> I am here today, I may not be here tomorrow . . . Nobody knows how many attempts have been made to shoot me . . . I do not care whether I live or die. I have lived a long life and I am proud that I spent the whole of my life in the service of my people. I am only proud of this and of nothing else. I shall continue to serve until my last breath and when I die, I can say, that every drop of my blood will invigorate India and strengthen it.[17]

This valediction, like so much else in Indira Gandhi's life, was both sincere and deluded.

After the speech, she returned to the Governor's house where she was staying. The Governor, B.N. Pandey, told Indira he had been shocked by her allusion to a violent death. Indira explained that she was simply being realistic and honest: she had watched her grandfather and mother die slowly and painfully, and as a consequence, she not only expected but wanted to 'die on her two feet'.

This discussion was interrupted by news from Delhi that Indira's grandchildren, Rahul and Priyanka, had been involved in a car accident while being driven home from school. Since Operation Blue Star Indira had been terrified that her grandchildren would be kidnapped or harmed. The car accident was a minor one, and no one was hurt, but Indira insisted upon cutting short her Orissa visit and flying back to Delhi immediately.

She arrived at 1 Safdarjung Road late that same night. The children had gone to bed, and Sonia reassured Indira that they were fine. Before retiring, Indira spoke with her secretary, P.C. Alexander, who felt she looked unusually tired and worried. He tried to cut short their meeting, but she insisted on discussing Kashmir and the Punjab before letting him go. She confessed she was exhausted, and then called in R.K. Dhawan whom she told to cancel all but the most pressing of the next day's appointments.[18]

It was well past midnight by the time Indira went to bed. That night she probably slept little if at all. Sonia Gandhi, in the room next door, woke up at 4 a.m. and went to the bathroom for her asthma medication. Indira, 'obviously . . . wide awake' came in, helped her find the pills and told Sonia to call out if she felt ill again.[19]

Two hours later, at 6 a.m., Indira was up and dressed as usual. Perhaps in remembrance of the strong autumnal colours of Kashmir, she chose a vibrant saffron-coloured sari with a hand-woven black border. She scanned the newspapers while eating her breakfast off a tray in her bedroom. Then R.K. Dhawan popped in and they reviewed the pared-down schedule for Wednesday 31 October 1984. Indira's first appointment was a television interview with Peter Ustinov who was making a documentary on Indira for the BBC and had been with her in Orissa, filming. In the afternoon, Indira was to meet the former British Prime Minister, James Callaghan, and then a leader from the small state of Mizoram. In the evening, she would host a formal dinner for Princess Anne.

After breakfast, Indira submitted to the attentions of two make-up artists who prepared her for the Ustinov television interview, which would be filmed at Indira's Akbar Road office. Originally it was scheduled for 8.30, but Dhawan came in to say there was some trouble with the equipment and the interview had been put back to 9.20. While the cosmeticians applied powder and blusher, Indira chatted with her personal physician, Dr K.P. Mathur, who looked in on her most mornings. Among other things, Indira joked about Ronald Reagan's heavily made-up face when he appeared on television and they speculated about Reagan's lack of grey hair.

When Indira emerged from her house at 9.10 she was greeted by a crisp, golden day. The trees, flowers and foliage in her garden had been washed clean by the summer monsoon; the air was clear and the sun's heat balmy and warm. She began to walk down the garden path that connected her home with her Akbar Road office. Constable Narain Singh, holding a black umbrella to shield Indira from the sun, walked beside her. R.K. Dhawan followed several steps behind, and behind Dhawan came Indira's personal servant, Nathu Ram. Sub-inspector Rameshwar Dayal brought up the rear of the small group.

At the far end of the bougainvillaea-bordered path, Indira saw her bodyguard, Beant Singh, standing at the wicket gate. Singh was a great bear of a man, a Sikh from the Punjab, who had been one of Indira's security guards since she had returned to office in 1980. Not far away from Beant Singh was a young, new constable named Satwant Singh who had not yet seen Indira at close range. Indira was talking over her shoulder to Dhawan as she approached the gate, but she broke off the conversation to acknowledge her bodyguards, holding her hands up to them, prayer-like, in the *namaste* greeting.

In response, Beant Singh pulled out his revolver and pointed it directly at Indira. There was a second or two when all was silent, save for the birds singing in the trees.

Then Indira said, 'What are you doing?'

At the same moment Beant Singh fired his gun and a bullet hit her in the abdomen. Indira raised her right arm and hand to protect her face. Beant Singh fired four more shots at point-blank range. These bullets entered Indira's armpit, chest and waist.

Five feet away stood Satwant Singh, holding an automatic Sten gun. He was immobilized with fear until Beant Singh shouted at him to shoot. The younger man responded automatically and pumped twenty-five bullets into Indira's body. She spun round like a top from the impact before falling in a crumpled heap on the path.

Twenty-five seconds had passed since Beant Singh fired the first shot. Only Rameshwar Dayal, in the rear, reacted quickly. While Satwant Singh was still emptying his Sten gun, Dayal rushed forward, but before reaching Indira, he was hit in the thigh and leg and himself mown down.

Indira's other companions formed a frozen tableau behind her body. Dhawan, who had narrowly missed the second volley of bullets, stood rooted to the spot. Nathu Ram stared at Indira in horror. Then, slowly Dhawan came out of his trance and crept forward and crouched over Indira. Another security man named Dinesh Kumar Bhatt came running from the Akbar Road office next door. Nathu Ram rushed back to Indira's house to get the physician on duty, Dr R. Opch.

Both Beant Singh and Satwant Singh dropped their guns.

Beant Singh said in Punjabi, 'I have done what I had to do. Now you do what you have to do.'[20]

At this, Narain Singh lunged forward and tackled Beant Singh, bringing him to the ground. Commandos from the Indo-Tibetan Border Police surged out of the nearby guardroom and overpowered Satwant Singh.

By this time Dr Opeh had arrived on the scene and was attempting to give Indira mouth-to-mouth resuscitation. Other security men joined them, as did Indira's political adviser M.L. Fotedar, who had been in the house, and now shouted for a car to take Indira to hospital. A white Ambassador was brought round and R.K. Dhawan and Dinesh Bhatt carried Indira's limp form from the path to the car and laid it in the back seat. Dhawan and Bhatt then got into the front next to the driver. Just as the car was about to depart, Sonia Gandhi came running down the path in her dressing gown, crying 'Mummy! Oh my God, Mummy!' She wrenched open the back seat car door and jumped in with her mother-in-law. The car sped off towards the All-India Institute of Medical Sciences.[21]

The three-mile journey in heavy Delhi traffic was 'nightmarish'. No one spoke. Sonia Gandhi sat in the back cradling Indira's head in her lap. Her dressing gown was soon soaked in blood.[22]

They reached the All-India Institute of Medical Sciences at 9.32 a.m. The Institute had a supply of Indira's blood type, O Rh negative, and also her medical records. But no one back at 1 Safdarjung Road had thought to telephone the hospital to say Indira was being brought in, critically wounded. When she was rolled in, the young house doctors on duty panicked when they recognized it was Indira. One young doctor, however, had the presence of mind to call the Institute's senior cardiologist and within five minutes a dozen of the hospital's top doctors were working on Indira. An endotracheal tube was pushed down her mouth and windpipe to pump oxygen into her lungs, and two intravenous lines inserted to start blood transfusions. An electrocardiogram showed faint traces of a heartbeat and the medical team tried to massage her heart. But they could find no pulse and Indira's eyes were dilated, indicating brain damage.

Though it was clear that she was already lost, Indira was moved up to the operating theatre on the eighth floor. During a four-hour operation a team of surgeons tried to perform a miracle. What they found, though, was that bullets had ruptured Indira's liver, perforated her small and large intestines, penetrated one lung, shattered bones and vertebrae and severed her spinal cord. Only her heart was left intact.

At 2.23 in the afternoon, five hours after being gunned down by men entrusted with protecting her life, Indira Gandhi was pronounced dead.[23]

TWENTY-TWO

After Indira

ON THE MORNING OF 31 OCTOBER 1984, Rajiv Gandhi was in a remote area of West Bengal, travelling from village to village on a whirlwind pre-election tour. More than a hundred miles south of Calcutta, on a dusty rural road in the middle of nowhere, Rajiv's white Ambassador car was intercepted by a police jeep. An officer got out and handed Rajiv a note with the message, 'There has been an accident in the Prime Minister's house. Cancel all appointments and return to Delhi immediately.'[1] Rajiv and his entourage hastily abandoned their Ambassador for the faster Mercedes follow-up car and roared off towards Calcutta. As they sped along the pot-holed road, the driver tuned the car radio to BBC World Service. When the 10 o'clock news bulletin came on, they heard that Indira had been shot by her bodyguards and had been taken to the All-India Institute of Medical Sciences.

After two-and-a-half hours of hard driving, a police helicopter intercepted the Mercedes and transported Rajiv and his companions the remaining thirty miles to Calcutta where a Boeing Indian Airlines plane was waiting to fly them home. Rajiv spent most of the flight in the cockpit with the pilots, who were in continuous radio contact with Delhi. It was here, over the crackling aircraft radio, at 2.30 p.m., that Rajiv learned his mother was dead. When he landed at Delhi's Palam airport, he was met by a large party of Congress politicians, aides and friends. But he already knew what they – in one voice – had come to say. Whether he wanted it or not, Rajiv Gandhi would become the next Prime Minister of India.

No one – or at least no member of Congress and no one who had worked for Indira Gandhi – dissented from this decision. That Rajiv should take over from Indira seemed as inevitable as a law of nature, though there was no precedent for his direct inheritance of power. When Jawaharlal Nehru and Lal Bahadur Shastri died in office, an interim Prime Minister had taken charge before a Prime Minister was elected by the Congress parliamentary party. But no one raised the possibility of an interim leader or party elections on 31 October 1984.

The only thing that delayed Rajiv's immediate assumption of power was that the President of India, Zail Singh, was not in Delhi to appoint and swear him in. On the afternoon of 31 October 1984, Zail Singh was also airborne – flying home from an official visit to Yemen upon hearing of Indira's assassination. He, too, on his flight, 'firmly made up [his] ... mind to appoint Rajiv Gandhi as the new Prime Minister'.[2] Upon arriving at Delhi, Singh was met by R.K. Dhawan and Arun Nehru, who immediately told him Rajiv was prepared to take over. They then drove directly to the All-India Institute of Medical Sciences.

By this time, a huge crowd had gathered at the hospital. The gates and streets outside thronged with thousands of people. Inside there had gathered a large cast of characters who had figured in Indira's life, including a weeping Maneka Gandhi and a distraught Dhirendra Brahmachari, and even Indira's flamboyant beautician, Shanaz Hussain. Huddled groups of cabinet ministers and bureaucrats, aides and secretaries talked and wept together.

While these people milled about the corridors, in the corner of a room off the operating theatre where the surgeons were still stitching up Indira's corpse, stood Rajiv and Sonia Gandhi. Rajiv was standing very close to his wife, gripping both her hands while talking intently in a low voice. Sonia was sobbing as she begged him not to agree to become Prime Minister. She protested that he would be killed if he took office. Rajiv kissed her on the forehead and explained that 'he had no choice ... he would be killed anyway'.[3]

Indira's secretary, P.C. Alexander, witnessed this intimate discussion and with effort, managed to pry Rajiv away from Sonia. They needed to set the wheels of succession in motion without delay. Rajiv told Alexander he would go home to change his clothes, and to expect him at the President's residence, Rashtrapati Bhavan, shortly after 6 p.m. for the swearing in.

Alexander then hastily called a 5 o'clock meeting of the Congress Parliamentary Board at Indira's Akbar Road office. It was necessary to go through the formalities, at least. The Board passed a resolution nominating Rajiv as the leader of the Congress parliamentary party and recommended that he form a new government. The Congress Parliamentary Board consisted of just five members: the most important member – the Prime Minister – was dead; two others were not in Delhi that day. This left just Narasimha Rao, the Home Minister, and Pranab Mukherjee, the Finance Minister, to validate Rajiv Gandhi's nomination.[4]

The swearing-in of Rajiv Gandhi as the sixth Prime Minister of India took place at 6.30 p.m. in the Ashok Hall of Rastrapati Bhavan.[5] Immediately afterwards, Rajiv presided over his first cabinet meeting. Before being sworn in to office, Rajiv had made it clear that he wanted to retain his mother's entire cabinet – with no new members and no reshuffling of portfolios. Most of his first cabinet meeting was devoted to discussing his mother's funeral ceremony, and it was agreed that her body would lie in state at Teen Murti House for two days and that the funeral would be held on 3 November.

A flurry of crisis meetings followed while All India Radio and the national television station, Doordarshan, announced that the new Prime Minister would address the country at 10.30 p.m. In fact, it was well past eleven when Rajiv Gandhi finally appeared on television screens and his voice was heard on radios not merely all over India, but round the world.

Rajiv spoke with dignity as well as anguish, with resolve as well as pain.

> Indira Gandhi has been assassinated. She was mother not only to me but to the whole nation. She served the Indian people to the last drop of her blood. This is a moment of profound grief ... We can and must face this tragic ordeal with fortitude, courage and wisdom. Indira Gandhi is no more but her soul lives. India lives. India is immortal. The spirit of India is immortal.[6]

In its eloquence and emotive power, this speech recalled Nehru's spontaneous broadcast after the death of Mahatma Gandhi: 'The light has gone out of our lives and there is darkness everywhere. I do not know what to tell you and how to say it. Our beloved leader, Bapu as we called him, the Father of the Nation, is no more.' Sharada Prasad, Indira's principal speechwriter, must have had Nehru's words in mind when he drafted Rajiv's first broadcast.

But Rajiv's speech, though shot through with grief, was not despairing, as Nehru's more honest and realistic oration had been. Rajiv exhorted that though Indira was dead, her legacy lived on – and that her violent death had not been in vain because every drop of her blood, as Indira herself had prophesied the night before her death in Orissa, had gone to the service of her country. Just how mistaken Rajiv was, soon became obvious when a holocaust burst on Delhi and other Indian cities in the wake of the assassination.

In fact, the holocaust had already begun even as Rajiv spoke, though he was not yet aware of it. For Rajiv and Indira's family – including the estranged Vijaya Lakshmi Pandit and her daughter Nayantara Sahgal who rushed to Delhi from Dehra Dun – the night of 31 October was endless. Indira's body had been brought home from the hospital to 1 Safdarjung Road for one last night before it would be taken to Teen Murti to lie in state. The sitting room had been cleared of furniture and the floors covered with clean white cloths. Throughout the night mourners sat on the floor round Indira's muslin-draped form. These were all close friends and family, but even so the house was overflowing with people. Servants produced mattresses and bedrolls for those who did not live in Delhi so they could spend Indira's last night at home with her. In addition to Mrs Pandit and Nayantara Sahgal, those who spent the night at Safdarjung Road included B.K and Fori Nehru, who had flown in from Ahmedabad. But no one could sleep that night. They talked and wept.

At about 2 a.m., B.K and Fori went outside for a breath of air. It was a very still night. The sky was cloudless and the garden and its path were bathed in moonlight. They followed the path down to the wicket gate at the end. Here they saw that the pavement was spattered with Indira's blood. It still looked fresh, and round each small pool of blood, the police had drawn a circle in white chalk. Many white circles glimmered in the moonlight.[7]

The following day Indira's body was moved to Teen Murti where it was laid out on a flower-bedecked bier in the front hall. For the next two days, while Hindu priests chanted round the clock, an endless stream of mourners passed the bier: heads of state, political leaders, film stars, friends, family, and thousands upon thousands of Indians who had never met Indira Gandhi but still felt themselves profoundly bereaved.

But it was not only grief that engulfed the country. Some Sikhs rejoiced when Indira was assassinated and communal hatred flared up as virulently as during the days of Partition. Two Sikhs had avenged the storming of the Golden Temple and now mobs of Hindus – some of them hooligans, others Congress party workers – were determined to avenge the murder of Indira Gandhi. They went on the rampage. While Indira lay in state at Teen Murti, with television cameras trained relentlessly on her decomposing body, whole areas of Delhi and other cities in India burned.

Sikh neighbourhoods and areas were surrounded and Sikh-owned shops and businesses looted and torched. Indira's avengers dragged turbaned men and boys out of their houses and hacked them to death in front of their wives and children. Some mobs summarily burnt down houses without giving their occupants – women and children, as well as men – the chance to come out. On the streets, bands of roaming thugs beat Sikhs to death or doused them with petrol and set them alight. Sikhs on trains, buses, taxis and auto-rickshaws were dragged off and butchered.

Where were the police? Often on the scene, looking the other way. Some, however, participated in the massacres.

In the three days following Indira's assassination, at least 3,000 Sikhs were slaughtered, more than 2,000 in Delhi alone. Some of those who survived did so because they cut their hair and beards to pass as Hindus. Over 50,000 Sikhs fled from the capital – mostly to the Punjab. Another 50,000 sought refuge in camps in Delhi, similar to the ones that Indira had worked in after Partition.

On the evening of 2 November, Rajiv Gandhi belatedly told a nation-wide television audience that the violence must stop. He said that 'the incidents which occurred in Delhi and elsewhere since Indira Gandhi's assassination are an affront to everything she stood for'.[8] The next day, Rajiv sent in the army to quell the chaos and slaughter that had engulfed Delhi. By this time, however, it was too late for thousands of Sikhs, though the violence might have burned on even longer had not armoured tanks rumbled into the affected areas of the city on the day of Indira Gandhi's funeral.

*   *   *

On Saturday 3 November, Indira's body, covered with marigolds and white lilies, was loaded on to a gun carriage in front of Teen Murti House. Ninety men from the three armed services slowly pulled the gun carriage through the broad avenues of New Delhi and the narrow, winding streets of the old city to the cremation grounds on the banks of the Jumna. It was the same four-mile route that Mahatma Gandhi, Feroze Gandhi, Jawaharlal Nehru and Sanjay Gandhi had travelled before Indira. But the carnage that engulfed Delhi after Indira's death meant that the crowds along the way were sparse, only one row – or at some places two – deep on each side of the road. As the journalist Mark Tully described it, 'Indians used to flock to see their Prime Minister, but fear kept them away from her last journey.'[9]

A large number of foreign leaders and VIP guests attended Indira's funeral at Shantivana – 'the woods of peace' – on the banks of the Jumna. Among these were Margaret Thatcher, George Bush, Yasser Arafat, the Pakistani President, Zia-ul-Haq, Kenneth Kaunda, the President of Zambia, Milton Obote of Uganda, Ferdinand and Imelda Marcos of the Philippines, the composer Zubin Mehta, Mother Theresa and a collection of film stars, artists and writers, European royalty, business tycoons, eminent scientists and other celebrities. All the Indian chief ministers, as well as other Congress Party and opposition politicians and government bureaucrats and the military were also present. But, like the crowds who lined the procession route, the number of ordinary Indians who watched the two-hour funeral ceremony was paltry compared to the vast carpet of humanity that surged round the cremation grounds when Mahatma Gandhi and Jawaharlal Nehru died.

When the gun carriage bearing Indira's body reached Shantivana, Rajiv Gandhi, Arun Nehru and the armed forces chiefs carried the bier to a plain pallet set on top of the funeral pyre of fragrant sandalwood. While Hindu priests chanted, Rajiv walked around his mother's body seven times – just as forty-two years earlier, Indira and Feroze had walked seven times round their marriage fire. Then, with a torch, Rajiv set the pyre alight.

As the flames took hold, the sun set in the west in a fiery blaze of red, saffron and gold. Indira's close friends and family members stoked the pyre with more sandalwood. Other mourners threw green leaves and incense into the fire. The priests, too, fed the flames with a mixture of honey and ghee while the army and navy buglers played 'The Last

Post'. Before Indira's body was wholly consumed, Rajiv tapped her cranium with a bamboo pole, releasing – according to Hindu belief – her spirit from its prison.

For two days the funeral fire smouldered on the banks of the Jumna. When it was finally cold, the ashes were gathered into heavy brass urns. Thirteen days later, Rajiv flew with them to Kashmir. From an Indian Air Force plane he scattered his mother's ashes over the Himalayas. In her end was her beginning. Indira Gandhi had 'passed into history' – but she had also come home.[10]

EPILOGUE

On the night of 21 May 1991, Rajiv Gandhi was campaigning in Sriperumbudur, a small, dusty town south of Madras, where he was scheduled to address a huge rally. As he approached the dais, among those who surged forward to garland him was a young Tamil woman named Dhanu. After she placed her garland round Rajiv's neck, Dhanu knelt forward to touch his feet. Then, still crouching, she detonated a bomb concealed beneath her orange *salwar kameez*. Rajiv and his assassin, along with eighteen other people, were killed instantaneously by the blast.

After Rajiv's death, his Italian-born widow, Sonia, turned her back on politics. The Nehru-Gandhi saga, it seemed, had finally ended. But six years after Rajiv Gandhi's assassination, under intense Congress Party pressure, Sonia agreed to become President of Congress. The following year she was elected to Parliament from her late husband's constituency, Amethi. Today Sonia Gandhi is the opposition leader in the Lok Sabha while the government is headed by the Bharatiya Janata Party Prime Minister, Atal Vajpayee.

During her 1999 campaign, Sonia reportedly studied videos of her mother-in-law's speeches. She also dramatically adopted Indira's style and mannerisms. Her hair colour deepened from light to dark, nearly black, brown. She wore saris reminiscent of Indira's and took to wearing a man's large wristwatch, just as Indira had.

Sonia's daughter, twenty-seven-year-old Priyanka Gandhi Varda, campaigned vigorously for her mother, and Priyanka (who bears an uncanny resemblance to her grandmother, Indira), is said to harbour political ambitions of her own. When Priyanka gave birth to a baby boy on 29 August 2000, the BBC and other media heralded the event as 'a new addition to the Gandhi dynasty'.

But the truth is that the Gandhi cult and its political vehicle, the Congress Party, are now almost defunct. Indira Gandhi's life was measured out in funeral pyres and political resurrections, but in the twenty-first century, this cycle appears finally to have closed.

When Indira was a child, Nehru wrote in *Glimpses of World History* of the immutable power of India, insisting that it would always survive. Today Indira Gandhi, and those who came before her, are gone. For good and ill, they shaped what India has become. But India is much larger than a single person or a single family. Nehru's vision holds true. Like the mountains of Kashmir which Indira Gandhi loved and from whence her family came, India endures.

NOTES

ONE: *Descent from Kashmir*

1. Pankaj Mishra has suggested that Indian security forces were in fact responsible for this massacre and that its rationale was to discredit Pakistan and Pakistani support of Islamic militants in Kashmir, *Guardian*, 14 October 2000.
2. Author's interview with B.K. Nehru.
3. Bradnock, Robert W., 'Regional Geopolitics in a Globalising World: Kashmir in Geopolitical Perspective', *Geopolitics*, 3, no 2 (Autumn 1998), p. 14.
4. Nehru, Jawaharlal, *Autobiography*, p. 1.
5. Ibid.
6. Harijan (which means 'children of God') was the term chosen by Mohandas Gandhi for 'untouchables' – those outside the ancient Hindu caste system. There are approximately 3,000 Hindu *jatis* or castes which are loosely grouped into four classes or *varnas*: Brahmins (priests and scholars), Kshatriyas (warriors and rulers), Vaisyas (merchants, traders, farmers), Sudras (artisans, labourers, servants). Notions of pollution and purification are central to the caste system; each caste has its own dietary habits, customs, fixed place in the social and religious hierarchy, and traditional occupations. After independence, the Constituent Assembly of India abolished the caste system and made use of the term 'untouchable' and the disabilities associated with it illegal. Caste, however, is still important in traditional and rural life. The sweepers at Anand Bhawan, according to Hindu practice, were segregated from other members of the household. But this was the only instance of caste rules being observed at Anand Bhawan. Motilal and later Jawaharlal Nehru's valet, Hari Lal, was an untouchable and mixed freely with the family, as did various other untouchable servants, including cooks.
7. Nehru, op. cit, p. 25.
8. Ibid p. 20.
9. Gopal, Sarvepalli (ed.), *Selected Works of Jawaharlal Nehru*, I, pp. 92–3, p. 97.
10. Nehru, op. cit, p. 28.
11. The view that Kamala was a cipher and Nehru's marriage to her a disaster is a commonplace of Nehru biography, especially among biographers such as Stanley Wolpert who make much of Nehru's later relationship with Edwina Mountbatten. The idea that Jawaharlal and Kamala were woefully unsuited to each other is also held by many Nehru family members who witnessed the marriage, including B.K. Nehru,

Nayantara Sahgal and her sister Chandralekha Mehta. I, however, have relied on Nehru's own reflections on his wife and marriage. His book *The Discovery of India*, his letters and his prison diaries, all paint a quite different picture of his feelings for Kamala. Though most of these were written after her death and thus tinged with grief, regret and longing, they nevertheless reveal that Nehru loved his wife deeply and that he also respected, admired and was even sometimes awed by her.

12. Nehru, op. cit, p. 37.
13. Ibid p. 38.
14. Ibid.
15. Ibid.
16. Ibid p. 39.

TWO: *'Hua'*

1. Pandit, Vijaya Lakshmi, *The Scope of Happiness*, p. 57.
2. Gandhi, Indira, *Anand Bhawan Memories*, p. 1.
3. Nehru, Jawaharlal, *Glimpses of World History*, p. 2.
4. Gandhi, Sonia (ed.), *Freedom's Daughter*, pp. 268–9.
5. Gandhi, Indira, *My Truth*, p. 13.
6. Gandhi, Indira, *Remembered Moments*, p. 53.
7. Nehru, Jawaharlal, *A Bunch of Old Letters*, p. 1.
8. Author's interview with B.K. Nehru.
9. Gandhi, Indira, *My Truth*, p. 15.
10. Pandit, Vijaya Lakshmi, op. cit, p. 173.
11. Gandhi, Indira, *Remembered Moments*, p. 53.
12. Nehru, Jawaharlal, *Autobiography*, p. 51.
13. Ibid p. 77.

14. Motilal Nehru to Jawaharlal Nehru, 16 September 1920, Nehru Library.
15. Nehru, Jawaharlal, *Autobiography*, p. 80. Author's interview with B.K. Nehru.
16. Gopal, Sarvepalli (ed.), op. cit, I, p. 232.
17. Nehru, Jawaharlal, op. cit, p. 80.
18. Ibid p. 80.
19. Brown, Judith M., *Gandhi*, p. 100.
20. Masani, Zareer, *Indira Gandhi*, p. 17.
21. Kumar, Ravinder and Panigrahi, D.N. (eds.), *Selected Works of Motilal Nehru*, I, p. 221.
22. Gopal, Sarvepalli (ed.), op. cit, I, 1, p. 282.
23. Ibid p. 349.
24. Jawaharlal Nehru to Indira Nehru, 15 November 1922, Nehru Library.
25. Nanda, B.R., *The Nehrus*, p. 201.
26. Gandhi, Indira, *What I Am* p. 14.
27. Gandhi, Indira, *My Truth*, p. 12.
28. Kalhan, Promilla, *Kamala Nehru*, p. 143.
29. Nehru, B.K., *Nice Guys Finish Second*, p. 15, p. 68.
30. Gandhi, Indira, *What I Am*, p. 14.
31. Ibid p. 10.
32. Her husband's family changed her name from Sarup Kumari Nehru to Vijaya Lakshmi Pandit, but family members and friends continued to call her Nan.
33. Author's interview with P.N. Haksar.
34. Gandhi, Indira, *Anand Bhawan Memories*, pp. 2–3.
35. Ibid p. 7.
36. Nehru, Jawaharlal, *Autobiography*, p. 124.
37. Ibid p. 134.
38. Ibid p. 102.
39. Nehru, Jawaharlal, *A Bunch of Old Letters*, p. 42.
40. Anand Bhawan Museum, Allahabad.
41. Gopal, Sarvepalli, *Jawaharlal Nehru* I, p. 87.

THREE: *Breathing with Her Heels*

1. Kumar, Ravinder and Panigrahi, D.N. (eds.), *Selected Works of Motilal Nehru*, V, p. 31.
2. Motilal Nehru to Jawaharlal Nehru, 20 May 1926, Nehru Library.
3. Jawaharlal Nehru was an inept manager of money throughout his life. As a young man in England he was extravagant and ran up debts. From the twenties onwards he led a simple, frugal existence but still managed to live beyond his means. Motilal Nehru threatened to leave all his money to Kamala and Indira because of his son's inability to keep track of and control his finances. (In the event, Motilal died intestate so that Jawaharlal was his heir.) Well into his tenure as Prime Minister Jawaharlal was selling off his father's things in order to remain afloat. Much of his later financial difficulties, however, were due to the great expense of running Anand Bhawan and paying the wages and pensions of its numerous servants.
4. Bryder, Linda, *Below the Magic Mountain*, pp. 191–2.
5. Brecher, Michael, *Nehru: A Political Biography*, p. 105.
6. Kumar, Ravinder and Panigrahi, D.N. (eds.), op. cit, V, p. 64.
7. Ibid p. 109, p. 122.
8. Sahgal, Nayantara (ed.), *Before Freedom: Nehru's Letters to His Sister*, p. 82.
9. Nehru, Jawaharlal, *Autobiography*, p. 149.
10. Author's interview with P.N. Haksar.
11. Gandhi, Indira, *My Truth*, p. 19.
12. Jayakar, Pupul, *Indira Gandhi*, p. 19.
13. Sahgal, Nayantara (ed.), op. cit, p. 52.
14. Gandhi, Sonia (ed.), *Freedom's Daughter*, p. 35.
15. Gopal, Sarvepalli (ed.), *Selected Works of Jawaharlal Nehru* I, 1, pp. 384–5.
16. Ibid.
17. Sahgal, Nayantara (ed.), op. cit, p. 76.
18. Gandhi, Sonia (cd.), op. cit, p. 35.
19. Ibid p. 36.
20. Gandhi, Indira, *Anand Bhawan Memories* , p. 10.
21. Gopal, Sarvepalli, *Jawaharlal Nehru*, II, p. 241.
22. Ibid p. 243.
23. Sahgal, Nayantara (ed.), op. cit, p. 91, p. 94.
24. Thurre, Pascal, *Crans-Montana*, p. 34.
25. Gandhi, Indira, *Anand Bhawan Memories*, p. 13.
26. Ibid.
27. Many of the places Indira visited in Paris, London and Heidelberg in 1926 are mentioned by Nehru in *Letters from a Father to His Daughter*.
28. Gandhi, Indira, *Anand Bhawan Memories*, pp. 8–9.
29. Hutheesing, K.N., *We Nehrus*, p. 57.
30. Gandhi, Indira, *My Truth*, p. 17.
31. Mohan, Anand, *Indira Gandhi*, p. 187.
32. Vasudev, Uma, *Indira Gandhi*, p. 59.
33. Nehru, Jawaharlal, *Autobiography*, p. 15.
34. Ibid p. 25.
35. Datta, V.N., and Cleghorn, B.E., (eds.), *Nationalist Muslim and Indian Politics: Being the Selected Correspondence of the late Dr Syed Mahmud*, p. 74.
36. Ibid p. 77.
37. Ibid p. 32.
38. Hutheesing, K.N., op. cit, p. 74. Sarvepalli Gopal says that Nehru did not meet Krishna Menon until

1936, op. cit, I, p. 202. When Marie Seton first met Krishna Menon in 1932, however, he said to her, 'The only man to lead India into the modern world is Jawaharlal Nehru. Gandhi can't do this. Nehru has a modern scientific mind.' This would seem to indicate that Krishna Menon had met Nehru, as Hutheesing claims, in 1926. Menon came to England in 1924, Marie Seton, *Panditji*, p. 66.

39. Datta, V.N., and Cleghorn, B. E., (eds.), op. cit, p. 70.
40. Ibid.
41. Ibid p. 73.
42. Ibid.
43. Ibid p. 79.
44. Ibid.
45. Ibid p. 81.
46. Gandhi, Sonia (ed.), *Freedom's Daughter*, p. 38.
47. Nehru, Jawaharlal, op. cit, p. 166.

FOUR: *Indu-Boy*

1. Brecher, Michael, *Nehru: A Political Biography*, p. 122.
2. British dominions such as Canada, Australia and New Zealand, were self-ruling, autonomous states, but they remained formally allied to the Empire and recognized the British monarch as their sovereign. In the late 1940s, newly independent states such as India, considered 'dominion status' to be a position of subordination. With the dismantling of the British Empire, former dominions became known as 'members of the British Commonwealth', and were not obligated to swear allegiance to the British Crown. Instead, the King or Queen was recognized as the head of the Commonwealth.
3. In 1997 the Principal of St Mary's, Sister Carola, told me that Indian pupils were not officially admitted to the school until after independence in 1947. Before that, they were unofficially tolerated but were removed during school inspections.
4. Gandhi, Indira, *Anand Bhawan Memories*, p. 13.
5. Gandhi, Indira, *My Truth*, p. 17.
6. Gandhi, Indira, *What I Am*, p. 18.
7. Nehru, B.K., *Nice Guys Finish Second*, pp. 76–7.
8. Ibid.
9. French, Patrick, *Liberty or Death*, p. 50.
10. Nehru, Jawaharlal, *Autobiography*, p. 180.
11. Nehru, B.K., op. cit, p. 76.
12. Ali, Tariq, *The Nehrus and the Gandhis*, p. 136.
13. Jawaharlal Nehru's medical report on Kamala Nehru, Nehru Library.
14. Quoted in Kalhan, Promilla, *Kamala Nehru: An Intimate Biography*, p. 39.
15. Author's interview with B.K. Nehru.
16. Author's interviews with Chandralekha Mehta and Nayantara Sahgal.
17. Gandhi, Sonia (ed.), *Freedom's Daughter*, p. 38.
18. *Letters from a Father to His Daughter* was originally published in English by the Allahabad publisher Kitabistan in 1930. It was soon translated into Hindi and Urdu and read by thousands of school children in India. In 1939 Nehru wrote to Indira that 'the little book . . . has become quite a gold mine, though I am not going to profit by it. It is becoming a textbook in many provinces . . . and vast numbers have been printed.' Nehru discovered that Kitabistan had made

20,000 rupees out of it, of which a mere 2,500 rupees had 'trickled' down to him. But rather than negotiate for a profit, he gave the rights to provincial governments and universities 'on condition that the book was issued at a very low price', Gandhi, Sonia (ed.), *Freedom's Daughter*, p. 448. The book has not been out of print in India since it first appeared in 1930.

19. Nehru, Jawaharlal, *Letters from a Father to His Daughter*, p. 1.

20. Ibid p. 40.

21. Ibid p. 50.

22. Nine years earlier Motilal Nehru had also been elected President of the 1919 Amritsar Congress. The Indian National Congress, founded in 1885, began as a pressure group, petitioning the British government for political and administrative reforms. In the twenties and thirties it spearheaded the movement for independence led by Mahatma Gandhi and the Nehrus. When provincial self-government was introduced in 1935, Congress became the governing political party in most of the states in India. With independence, it emerged as the ruling party of India. The President of Congress is the elected leader of the organizational party consisting of voluntary members. After independence, there was also a parliamentary wing of Congress, consisting of elected Members of Parliament. The parliamentary party elected a leader who then became Prime Minister if Congress was in power or the opposition leader if it was not. It is possible for the same person to be Congress President of the organizational party and leader of the parliamentary party as Nehru was in the early years of his prime ministership.

23. Nanda, B.R., *Jawaharlal Nehru: Rebel and Statesman*, p. 304.

24. Some forty-five years later Siddhartha Shankar Ray would become one of Indira Gandhi's most trusted advisers and an architect of the Emergency declaration of 1975. In 1972, when Siddhartha Shankar Ray was Chief Minister of West Bengal and Indira Gandhi was Prime Minister, another Congress session was held in Calcutta. Ray had a banana tree planted outside the bedroom window of the house Indira stayed in to remind her of her banana-eating feat in 1929. She told him that she had stuffed herself with bananas to counter the poor impression she knew she'd made – to prove her strength. Author's interview with Siddhartha Shankar Ray.

25. Brecher, Michael, op. cit, p. 134.

26. Nehru, B.K., *Nice Guys Finish Second*, p. 79.

27. Nehru, Jawaharlal, *Autobiography*, pp. 194–5.

28. Brecher, Michael, op. cit, p. 138.

29. Nanda, B.R., op. cit, p. 324.

30. Gopal, Sarvepalli (ed.), *Selected Works of Jawaharlal Nehru* I, 4, p. 189.

31. Nehru, Jawaharlal, op. cit, p. 612.

32. Gandhi, Indira, *My Truth*, p. 22.

33. Nehru, Jawaharlal, op. cit, p. 203.

34. Ibid p. 205.

35. Ibid p. 207.

36. Nehru, Jawaharlal, *The Discovery of India*, p. 41.

37. Arnold Michaelis, 'An interview with Indira Gandhi', *McCall's Magazine*, April 1966, p. 187.

38. Pande, B.N., *Indira Gandhi*, p. v, p. 31.

39. Sen, Ela, *Indira Gandhi*, pp. 28–9.

40. Nehru Library; translation in Kalhan, Promilla, op. cit, pp. 27–8.

41. Nehru, Jawaharlal, *Glimpses of World History*, p. 58.
42. Ibid p. 3.
43. Ibid p. 274.
44. Ibid p. 28.
45. Gandhi, Sonia (ed.), op. cit, p. 45.
46. Nehru, Jawaharlal, *Autobiography*, p. 240.
47. Gopal, Sarvepalli (ed.), *Selected Works of Jawaharlal Nehru* I, 4, p. 451.
48. Nehru, Jawaharlal, *Glimpses of World History*, p. 5.
49. Kalhan, Promilla, op. cit, pp. 49–50.
50. Nehru, Jawaharlal, op. cit, p. 18.
51. Ibid p. 39.
52. Kalhan, Promilla, op. cit, p. 69.
53. Nehru, Jawaharlal, *Autobiography*, p. 246.
54. Author's interview with Nayantara Sahgal.
55. Author's interview with P.N. Haksar.
56. Nehru, Jawaharlal, op. cit, p. 247.

FIVE: *Enter Feroze*

1. Gandhi, Indira, *Anand Bhawan Memories*, p. 22. Even Indira Gandhi's severest critics concede her extraordinary physical courage which seems to have had its seed in the humiliation she felt over this early episode.
2. Gandhi, Indira, *My Truth*, p. 22. Sahgal, Nayantara (ed.), *Before Freedom*, p. 21.
3. Nehru, Jawaharlal, *Autobiography*, p. 271.
4. Hutheesing, K.N. (ed.), *Nehru's Letters to His Sister*, pp. 21–2.
5. Nehru, Jawaharlal, *The Discovery of India*, pp. 42–4.
6. Quoted in Aruna Asaf Ali, *Private Face of a Public Person: A Study of Jawaharlal Nehru*, pp. 33–4.
7. Hutheesing, K.N. (ed.), op. cit, p. 25.
8. Gopal, Sarvepalli (ed.), *Selected Works of Jawaharlal Nehru* I, 4, p. 558.
9. Gandhi, Indira, *My Truth*, p. 22.
10. Pupul Jayakar, *Indira Gandhi*, pp. 44–5. Vijaya Lakshmi Pandit's daughters, Nayantara Sahgal and Chandralekha Mehta, maintain that this episode never happened. Their memory is that Indira felt herself ugly and they say that the remark that was most often made of her was not that she was ugly, but that 'she was sickly'. Author's interview with Nayantara Sahgal and Chandralekha Mehta.
11. Coonverbai Vakil remained close to Indira for the rest of her pupil's life and was one of the few people who stood up to her during the Emergency of 1975–6. She outlived Indira by eleven years, dying in 1995 at the age of ninety-nine.
12. Author's interview with Ira Vakil Chaudhuri.
13. Gandhi, Shanta, 'When Indira Was a Student', Parthasarti, G., and Prasad, H.Y. (eds.), *Indira Gandhi: Statesmen, Scholars, Scientists and Friends Remember*, p. 185.
14. Nehru, Jawaharlal, *Glimpses of World History*, p. 327.
15. Gopal, Sarvepalli (ed.), op. cit, I, 5, p. 409.
16. Gandhi, Sonia (ed.), *Freedom's Daughter*, p. 69.
17. The Ramakrishna Order was established by the followers of the nineteenth-century Bengali, Ramakrishna, who was a devotee of the Hindu goddess, Kali. Foremost among Ramakrishna's disciples was Vivekenanda, who was widely known in the West, including America and Europe, where he travelled with his spiritual message.

The mission was active in relief work in India and set up hospitals, schools, dispensaries and libraries all over the country. It continues to thrive today, with its Calcutta headquarters still at Belur Math, which Kamala Nehru and her daughter so often visited.

18. Gandhi, Sonia (ed.), op. cit, p. 52.

19. Ibid p. 59.

20. Gopal, Sarvepalli (ed.), op. cit, I, 5, p. 454.

21. Nehru, Jawaharlal, *Glimpses of World History*, p. 949. Interestingly, though Nehru did not send any of the manuscript *Glimpses* letters to Indira, he did send a number of them to Gandhi who made editorial suggestions and urged Nehru to publish them. Despite its personal origin, the book was never meant solely for Indira; Nehru always had a much larger audience in mind.

22. Mahatma Gandhi to Jawaharlal Nehru, 9 October 1933, Nehru Library.

23. Nehru, Jawaharlal, *Autobiography*, pp. 478–9.

24. Gandhi, Sonia (ed.), op. cit, p. 111.

25. Quoted in Vasudev, Uma, *Indira Gandhi*, p. 97.

26. Gandhi, Indira, *Anand Bhawan Memories*, pp. 21–2.

27. Sahgal, Nayantara (ed.), op. cit, pp. 113–14.

28. Papers of Vijaya Lakshmi Pandit. Also quoted in Pand, B.N., *Nehru*, p. 182.

29. Gandhi, Sonia (ed.), op. cit, p. 116, pp. 119–20.

30. Author's interviews with Nayantara Sahgal and Chandralekha Mehta.

31. Gandhi, Sonia (ed.), op. cit, p. 118.

32. Nehru Papers, Nehru Library.

33. Gopal, Sarvepalli (ed.), op. cit, I, 6, pp. 248–9.

34. Dutta, Krishna and Robinson,

Andrew, *Rabindranath Tagore*, p. 54, p. 323.

35. Gandhi, Indira, 'Reminiscences of Tagore', January 1961, *Women on the March*, published by the Women's All-India Congress Committee, New Delhi.

36. Dutta, Krishna, and Robinson, Andrew, op. cit, p. 332.

37. Gandhi, Sonia (ed.), op. cit, p. 122.

38. Gandhi, Indira, *Remembered Moments*, p. 17.

39. Mohan, Anand, *Indira Gandhi*, p. 120. *Convocation Addresses at Visva-Bharati: The Common Pursuit*, p. 86.

40. Dutta, Krishna, and Robinson, Andrew, op. cit, p. 134, p. 325–6.

41. Indira's room at Sri Bhawan Ashram is now unoccupied and kept as a memorial to her with various photographs of her, both as a student and later as Chancellor of Santiniketan during the years when she was Prime Minister and gave the annual convocation address at Visva-Bharati.

42. Gopal, Sarvepalli (ed.), op. cit, I, 6, p. 267.

43. Gandhi, Sonia (ed.), op. cit, p. 133.

44. Gopal, Sarvepalli (ed.), op. cit, I, 6, pp. 463–4.

45. Ibid p. 267.

46. Nehru, Jawaharlal, op. cit, p. 561.

47. Jayakar, Pupul, *Indira Gandhi*, pp. 61–2.

48. Gandhi, Sonia (ed.), op. cit, pp. 124–5.

49. Sahgal, Nayantara (ed.), op. cit, pp. 120–1.

50. Burrell, L.S.T., *Artificial Pneumothorax*.

51. Gandhi, Sonia (ed.), op. cit, p. 130.

52. Nehru Papers, Nehru Library.

53. Falk, Bertil, unpublished biography of Feroze Gandhi.

54. Ibid.

55. Ibid.

56. Ibid. Author's interview with B.K. Nehru.
57. Mehta, Vinod, *The Sanjay Story*, p. 6. Bertil Falk's interview with S.M. Jaffer, 1993.
58. Gopal, Sarvepalli (ed.), op. cit, I, 6, pp. 306–7, p. 310.
59. Ibid pp. 312–3.
60. Ibid pp. 320–1.
61. Nehru Library, quoted in Jayakar, Pupul, op. cit, p. 69.
62. Jayakar, Pupul, op. cit, p. 63.
63. Nehru's 'Note' on Kamala Nehru, Nehru Library. Quoted also in ibid p. 111.
64. Kalhan, Promilla, *Kamala Nehru*, pp. 112–3.
65. Gandhi, Sonia (ed.), op. cit, p. 151.
66. Nehru, Jawaharlal, *A Bunch of Old Letters*, p. 105. The manuscript letter is in the Santiniketan Archives.
67. Gandhi, Sonia (ed.), op. cit, p. 158, p. 160.
68. Ibid p. 163, p. 166.
69. Gopal, Sarvepalli (ed.), op. cit, I, 6, p. 364.

SIX: *In the Black Forest*

1. Gandhi, Sonia (ed.), *Freedom's Daughter*, p. 168.
2. Ibid p. 169.
3. Ibid p. 175.
4. Ibid p. 173.
5. Ibid p. 169.
6. Ibid p. 176.
7. Gopal, Sarvepalli (ed.), *Selected Works of Jawaharlal Nehru* I, 6, p. 377.
8. Ibid p. 382.
9. Gandhi, Sonia (ed.), op. cit, p. 180.
10. Gandhi, Indira, *My Truth*, p. 28.
11. Gandhi, Sonia (ed.), op. cit, p. 190.
12. Ibid pp. 182–3, p. 193.
13. Ibid p. 198.
14. C.F. Andrews to Jawaharlal Nehru, Nehru Library.
15. Ibid.
16. Gandhi, Sonia (ed.), op. cit, p. 215.
17. Jayakar, Pupul, *Indira Gandhi*, p. 76.
18. Seton, Marie, *Panditji*, pp. 78–9.
19. Agatha Harrison Papers, Friends House Library, London.
20. Ibid.
21. Sahgal, Nayantara (ed.), *Before Freedom*, p. 158.
22. Letter from Agatha Harrison to Mahatma Gandhi, 13 November 1935, Agatha Harrison Papers, Friends House Library, London.
23. Sahgal, Nayantara (ed.), op. cit, p. 173.
24. Nehru, Jawaharlal, *The Discovery of India*, p. 43.
25. Sahgal, Nayantara (ed.), op. cit, p. 192.
26. Education Committee Minute Book, meeting held 6 November 1935, Somerville College Archives, Oxford.
27. La Pelouse Archives, Bex, Switzerland.
28. Brecher, Michael, *Nehru*, p. 210.
29. Nehru, Jawaharlal, *The Discovery of India*, p. 45.
30. The only source for the Wengen reunion of Indira and Feroze Gandhi is Pupul Jayakar who apparently was told about it many years later by Indira. But Jayakar gives a very sketchy and inconclusive account of the episode in her biography, *Indira Gandhi*, pp. 79–80.
31. Mathai, M. O., *Reminiscences of the Nehru Age*, p. 93.
32. A.C.N. Nambiar's account of Kamala's opposition to a marriage between Indira and Feroze contradicts most biographical versions of Kamala's feelings. Usually it is held that Kamala very much wanted Indira and Feroze to

marry and made her wishes clear to them and Nehru before her death. Nambiar's account is published in M.O. Mathai's unreliable *Reminiscences of the Nehru Age*, but Nambiar himself is a trustworthy witness. He was alive when Mathai's book was published in 1978, lived on until 1986, and he never denied the truth of the episode as it is recounted by Mathai.

33. Gandhi, Sonia (ed.), op. cit, pp. 235–6.
34. Nehru, Jawaharlal, op. cit, p. 46.
35. Gandhi, Sonia (ed.), op. cit, p. 239.
36. Ibid p. 240.
37. Agatha Harrison Papers, Friends House Library, London.
38. Nehru, Jawaharlal, op. cit, p. 48.
39. Ibid.

SEVEN: *A Veteran at Parting*

1. Gandhi, Sonia (ed.), *Freedom's Daughter*, pp. 242–3.
2. Ibid p. 246.
3. Ibid p. 253–4.
4. Ibid p. 256.
5. Ibid p. 261.
6. Ibid p. 283.
7. Ibid p. 271.
8. Ibid p. 283.
9. Jayakar, Pupul, *Indira Gandhi*, p. 88.
10. Ibid p. 86.
11. Gandhi, Sonia (ed.), op. cit, pp. 293–4.
12. Ibid p. 301.
13. Ibid pp. 268–9.
14. Quoted in Parthasarthi, G. and Prasad, H. Y. Sharada (eds.), *Indira Gandhi: Statesmen, Scholars, Scientists and Friends Remember*, p. 308.
15. Gandhi, Indira, *Anand Bhawan Memories*, p. 31.
16. Gandhi, Sonia (ed.), op. cit, p. 285, p. 296, p. 298.
17. Ibid pp. 287–8.
18. Ibid p. 309.
19. Ibid p. 326.
20. Seven years later, in 1943, the Latin entrance exam also nearly kept Margaret Roberts (destined to be Margaret Thatcher) out of Somerville College. According to her biographer, Hugo Young, 'She had had to mug up Latin and had failed to reach Somerville's priority list for entrance. Only when someone dropped out was she hoisted off the waiting list and offered' a place at Somerville, Young, Hugo, *One of Us*, p. 14.
21. Vasudev, Uma, *Indira Gandhi*, p. 132.
22. Gopal, Sarvepalli (ed.), *Selected Works of Jawaharlal Nehru* I, 13, p. 680.
23. Ibid p. 684.
24. Ibid p. 682.
25. Gandhi, Sonia (ed.), op. cit, p. 332.
26. Sahgal, Nayantara, *Prison and Chocolate Cakes*, p. 142.
27. Jayakar, Pupul, op. cit, p. 92.
28. Author's interview with Sarvepalli Gopal.
29. Gopal, Sarvepalli (ed.), op. cit, I, 13, p. 662, p. 664.
30. Ibid p. 667.
31. Ibid p. 664.
32. Ibid p. 678.
33. Ibid p. 694.
34. Pande, B.N., *Indira Gandhi*, p. 71.
35. Ibid p. 75.
36. Gandhi, Sonia (ed.), op. cit, p. 332.
37. Norman, Dorothy, (ed.), *Letters to an American Friend*, p. 78.
38. Author's interview with Mary Thompson.
39. Ibid.
40. Interviews with Mary Thompson, Kay Davies and Anne Whiteman. Wayne, Jenifer, *The Purple Dress*, p. 62.
41. Author's interview with Mary

Thompson. Gandhi, Sonia (ed.), op. cit, p. 336.

42. Ibid p. 336, p. 340.

43. Author's interview with Kay Davies. It has been generally held that Indira Nehru was a poor student at Oxford, but Somerville College and Oxford University records contradict this, as do the recollections of classmates such as Kay Davies and the reported judgements of her tutors.

44. Gandhi, Sonia (ed.), op. cit, p. 343, p. 348.

45. Ibid p. 342.

46. Author's interview with Mary Thompson.

47. Adams, Pauline, *Somerville for Women*, p. 225. Vasudev, Uma, *Indira Gandhi*, p. 136.

48. Author's interview with Mary Thompson.

49. Lord Chalfont's interview with Indira Gandhi, BBC television, broadcast 26 October 1971.

50. Falk, Bertil, unpublished biography of Feroze Gandhi. Vasudev, Uma, op. cit, pp. 128–9.

51. Gandhi, Sonia (ed.), op. cit, p. 353.

52. Oxford students were required to pass four subjects in the pass moderations examination, one of which had to be Latin or Greek. Pass mods was a university exam and Oxford University records list only pass marks. The *University Gazette*, however, publishes the candidates for upcoming exams and subsequently those candidates who were successful. Indira Nehru is listed among the candidates for the pass moderations examination in Michaelmas term 1937, but she is not listed among those who passed the examination. Correspondence between Nehru and Agatha Harrison also indicates that Indira failed the first time she took the pass moderations examination, Oxford University Archives, Oxford; Agatha Harrison Papers, Friends House Library, London.

53. Gandhi, Sonia (ed.), op. cit, p. 359.

54. Wayne, Jenifer, op. cit, p. 70.

55. Author's interview with Nikhil Chakravartty.

56. Author's interview with Anne Whiteman.

57. Gopal, Sarvepalli, *Jawaharlal Nehru*, I, p. 234.

58. Gandhi, Sonia (ed.), op. cit, pp. 389–90.

59. Ibid p. 392.

60. Ibid p. 395.

61. Ibid p. 397.

62. Interviews with Mary Thompson and Anne Whiteman. The late Nikhil Chakravartty, who was at Balliol College while Indira was at Somerville, maintained that her illness in the spring of 1938 and later was a convenient fiction to avoid being sent down after she failed the pass mods Latin exam in June 1938. Mary Thompson (but not Kay Davies) was also under the impression that Indira 'had to leave' Somerville because she failed the pass mods exam for a third time. But the Oxford University *Gazette* does not list Indira Nehru on either the candidates or pass list for the pass mods exam in Trinity term (June 1938) or later and this indicates that she did not take the examination a third time.

63. Sahgal, Nayantara (ed.), *Before Freedom*, p. 254.

64. Ibid p. 259.

65. Ibid p. 257.

66. Quoted in Gopal, Sarvepalli, op. cit, I, p. 235.

67. Sahgal, Nayantara (ed.), *Before Freedom*, p. 255.

68. Author's interview with Kay Davies.

69. Gandhi, Indira, *Anand Bhawan Memories*, p. 31.
70. Ibid pp. 29–30.
71. Hangen, Welles, p. 166–7.
72. Nehru, Jawaharlal, *A Bunch of Old Letters*, p. 206.
73. Gopal, Sarvepalli (ed.), op. cit, I, 13, p. 705.
74. Gandhi, Indira, *My Truth*, p. 36, and *Anand Bhawan Memories*, p. 32.
75. Gandhi, Sonia (ed.), op. cit, pp. 399–400.
76. Gopal, Sarvepalli, op. cit, I, p. 238.
77. Gandhi, Sonia (ed.), op. cit, p. 401.
78. Ibid p. 404.
79. Ibid p. 410.
80. Thapar, Raj, *All These Years*, p. 30.
81. Seton, Marie, *Panditji*, p. 65.
82. Ibid. Author's interview with Alice Thorner. Hangen, Welles, op. cit, p. 63. Ram, Janaki, *V.K. Krishna Menon: A Personal Memoir*, pp. 51–4.
83. One of the most revealing and moving letters in Sarvepalli Gopal's *Selected Works of Jawaharlal Nehru* was written to Menon on 15 May 1939, several weeks after Indira returned to Europe. In this letter, headed 'Personal', Nehru describes his mental turmoil and despair in the midst of what amounts to a nervous breakdown: 'I want to tell you briefly the state of my mind. It is bad. I have lost all pep and feel devitalized and my interest in life itself seems to be fading away. Don't be alarmed. I can still function fairly effectively and it may be that I shall recover some of my vitality. For the moment, however, the outlook is not encouraging. Most of the things that I value and for which I have worked seem to be going to pieces, and it is not surprising that I should disintegrate in the process ... many things contribute to it. Events in India, events elsewhere. What has happened in Spain has affected me greatly as a deep personal sorrow. What has happened, and is happening in India, being near to me, affects me continuously. The kind of human material that I see about me, the all-pervading pettiness and vulgarity, the mutual suspicion and back-biting ... distress me beyond measure. Everywhere the wrong type of person is pushing himself to the front, everywhere disruptive forces are growing ... I wrote to you two and a half months ago that I was very ill mentally. I had received a sudden shock which upset me more than almost anything else had ever done. I was afraid of a breakdown ... the after-effects continue. I am sorry to write to you all this and to distress you. I do so to enable you to realize somewhat how I am functioning at present. Partly also to relieve myself ... It is a phase which will pass perhaps.' I, 12, pp. 712–3.
84. Gandhi, Sonia (ed.), op. cit, p. 414. Information on the diploma in social and public administration from conversations with Simon Bailey, Archivist, Oxford University Archives.
85. Ibid. p. 421–2.
86. Nehru Papers, Nehru Library.
87. Agatha Harrison Papers.
88. Gandhi, Sonia (ed.), op. cit, p. 425.
89. Ibid p. 426.
90. Agatha Harrison Papers.
91. Gandhi, Sonia (ed.), op. cit, p. 450.

EIGHT: *The Magic Mountain*

1. In all the accounts that Indira Gandhi gave of her life, including interviews, she never mentioned her

long stay in a Swiss sanatorium. In *My Truth*, her fullest autobiographical statement, she merely says that 'I went to Switzerland' and 'then I returned to London via Spain'. Her biographers likewise omit or hastily dismiss her ten months in Leysin and all repeat Indira's official diagnosis of pleurisy. The patient records for Auguste Rollier's clinics no longer exist, but Rollier's daughter, Suzanne Rollier, whom I interviewed, knew Indira Nehru when she was a patient at Les Frênes.

2. Agatha Harrison Papers.

3. Gandhi, Sonia (ed.), *Freedom's Daughter*, pp. 457–8.

4. Desponds, Liliane, *Leysin: Histoire et Reconversion d'une Ville a la Montagne*. Author's interview with Suzanne Chapuis-Rollier.

5. Hobday, Richard, 'Sunlight Therapy and Solar Architecture', *Medical History*, 1997, p. 455.

6. Smith, F.B., *The Retreat of Tuberculosis*, p. 97.

7. Author's interviews with Dr John Moore-Gillon and Dr Richard Hobday.

8. *Les Cliniques du Dr Rollier a Leysin* (a brochure describing Rollier's sanatoria in Leysin). Les Frênes still exists, though today it is a trendy gym and fitness centre.

9. Smith, F.B., op. cit, p. 97, p. 101.

10. Bryder, Lynda, *Below the Magic Mountain*, p. 223.

11. Author's interview and correspondence with Dr John Moore-Gillon.

12. Author's interview with Maurice André.

13. Author's interviews with Suzanne Chapuis-Rollier and Maurice André.

14. Gandhi, Sonia, (ed.), *Two Alone, Two Together*, pp. 3–4.

15. Ibid p. 15.

16. Ibid p. 38.

17. Rollier, Auguste, *Heliotherapy*, p. 154.

18. Gandhi, Sonia, (ed.), op. cit, p. 14.

19. Author's interview with Suzanne Chapuis-Rollier.

20. Gandhi, Sonia, (ed.), op. cit, pp. 18–19.

21. Ibid p. 18. Three months seems to have been the standard time period doctors gave to TB patients. In A.E. Ellis's novel *The Rack*, about life in a French TB sanatorium in the early 1950s, the narrator reflects, 'They say "three months" here as other doctors say "three days". They've been saying "three months" to me ever since I arrived. The last words I'll hear when I leave … will be: "We'd have cured you if only you could have stayed another three months." There's only one sure thing – I am never well, but I always will be in another three months,' p. 87.

22. Gandhi, Sonia, (ed.), op. cit, pp. 21–2.

23. Author's interview with Maurice André. Ibid p. 29.

24. Ibid pp. 32–3.

25. Bell, P.M.H., *The Origins of the Second World War in Europe* p. 131.

26. Ibid pp. 34–5.

27. Gopal, Sarvepalli (ed.), *Selected Works of Jawaharlal Nehru* I, 13, p. 713.

28. Gandhi, Sonia, (ed.), op. cit, p. 41.

29. Most of Indira Gandhi's personal papers – including her correspondence with her father, husband and son – are closed to researchers. Sonia Gandhi has edited two volumes of the letters written between Nehru and Indira Gandhi, *Freedom's Daughter* (1989) and *Two Alone, Two Together* (1992) and she says that these volumes

contain 'most of their correspondence'. The published letters are an invaluable resource, but there are significant omissions. Indira Gandhi showed a number of crucial letters to Sarvepalli Gopal, who edited Nehru's *Selected Works*, which appear in the book but are not in Sonia Gandhi's edition; nor are they in the Nehru Library catalogue. Sonia Gandhi quotes from several letters written by Indira Gandhi to Feroze and Rajiv Gandhi in her memoir of her husband, *Rajiv*. She has no plans at present to publish any further letters or papers of Indira Gandhi. Author's interview with Sonia Gandhi.

30. Gandhi, Sonia, (ed.), op. cit, p. 41–2.
31. Ibid p. 29.
32. Ibid p. 29, pp. 43–4.
33. Ibid pp. 48–9.
34. Gopal, Sarvepalli (ed.), op. cit, I, 11, p. 457.
35. Ibid p. 469.
36. Ibid pp. 470–1.
37. Ibid pp. 465–6.
38. Gandhi, Sonia, (ed.), op. cit, pp. 58–9.
39. Ibid p. 61.
40. Gandhi, Indira, *Anand Bhawan Memories*, p. 22.
41. Gandhi, Sonia, (ed.), op. cit, pp. 66–8.
42. Gopal, Sarvepalli (ed.), op. cit, I, 11, p. 423.
43. Ibid pp. 86–7.
44. Ibid p. 88.
45. Author's interview with P.N. Haksar.
46. Vasudev, Uma, *Indira Gandhi*, p. 146.
47. Gandhi, Indira, *What I Am*, p. 25.
48. Gandhi, Sonia, (ed.), op. cit, p. 94.
49. Ibid p. 94.
50. Vasudev, Uma, op. cit, p. 146.
51. Gandhi, Indira, *Remembered Moments*, p. 23.
51. Gandhi, Indira, *My Truth*, p. 42.
52. Ibid p. 44.
53. Gandhi, Indira, *Remembered Moments*, p. 27.

NINE: *Not a Normal, Banal, Boring Life*

1. Gandhi, Indira, *What I Am*, p. 24 and *My Truth*, p. 45.
2. Gopal, Sarvepalli (ed.), *Selected Works of Jawaharlal Nehru* I, 11, p. 581.
3. Ibid pp. 589–90.
4. Gandhi, Sonia, (ed.), *Two Alone, Two Together*, pp. 107–9.
5. Gopal, Sarvepalli (ed.), op. cit, I, 11, p. 604. Indira's 'angry, agitated letter' is not included in Sonia Gandhi's edition of the letters nor is it available at the Nehru Library.
6. Ibid p. 641.
7. Gandhi, Sonia, (ed.), op. cit, pp. 107–9.
8. Ibid pp. 112–3.
9. Fallaci, Oriana, *Interview With History*, pp. 107–9.
10. Seton, Marie, *Panditji*, p. 103.
11. Gopal, Sarvepalli (ed.), op. cit, I, 11, pp. 643–5.
12. Ibid pp. 643–8.
13. Ibid p. 740.
14. Jayakar, Pupul, *Indira Gandhi*, p. 117.
15. Mohandas Gandhi to Jawaharlal Nehru, 5 December 1941, Nehru Library.
16. Gandhi, Indira, *What I Am*, p. 25.
17. Hutheesing, K.N., *We Nehrus*, p. 153.
18. Jayakar, Pupul, op. cit, p. 117.
19. Rau, M. Chalapathi, *Journalism and Politics*, p. 76. Masani, Zareer, *Indira Gandhi*, p. 59.

20. Quoted in Masani, Zareer, op. cit, p. 62.
21. Michaelis, Arnold, 'An Interview with Indira Gandhi', p. 189.
22. Sahgal, Nayantara, *Prison and Chocolate Cake*, pp. 99–100.
23. Hutheesing, K.N., op. cit, pp. 154–5.
24. Norvin Hein later became a Professor at Yale Divinity School. His film of Indira and Feroze's wedding runs for about ten minutes and much of the following description is drawn from the highlights of the wedding and wedding dinner that he captured with his movie camera.
25. Soon after the marriage and for some years afterwards, it was rumoured that Indira and Feroze had secretly gone through a civil marriage or got married in a Princely State where marriage was permitted between those of different faiths. In the early seventies Uma Vasudev asked Indira Gandhi about these rumours. Indira categorically denied them, telling Vasudev, 'nothing of the kind [happened]. It just didn't bother me, whether it was legal or not.' Vasudev, op. cit, p. 166. Author's interview with Uma Vasudev.
26. Nehru, B. K., *Nice Guys Finish Second*, p. 111. Gandhi, Sonia, *Rajiv*, p. 20.
27. Sahgal, Nayantara, op. cit, pp. 101–3.
28. Falk, Bertil, unpublished biography of Feroze Gandhi.
29. Correspondence (in Hindi) between Rajpati Kaul and Jawaharlal Nehru, Nehru Library.
30. Falk, Bertil, op. cit.
31. French, Patrick, *Liberty or Death*, p. 140.
32. Ibid p. 146.
33. Gandhi, Sonia, (ed.), *Two Alone, Two Together*, pp. 138–9.
34. Gopal, Sarvepalli (ed.), op. cit., I, 13, pp. 4–5. Hutheesing, K.N., *Dear to Behold*, p. 98.
35. French, Patrick, op. cit, p. 162.
36. Gandhi, Indira, *Remembered Moments*, p. 28.
37. Vasudev, Uma, op. cit, p 187. Falk, Bertil, op. cit.
38. Pandit, Vijaya Lakshmi, *The Scope of Happiness*, p. 165.
39. I visited Naini Jail on 2 April 1997 and was given a tour by the Senior Superintendent, R.N. Upadhyay. Nehru's cell complex at Naini is carefully preserved and contains among other artefacts, his spinning wheel. His weight at various dates is recorded on a painted poster. At the women's barrack there is a memorial pillar to Vijaya Lakshmi Pandit's prison term, but no trace of Indira Gandhi's eight-month sojourn in jail.
40. Michaelis, Arnold, op. cit, p. 188.
41. Author's interview with Chandralekha Mehta.
42. Ibid.
43. Gopal, Sarvepalli (ed.), op. cit, I, 13, p. 34.
44. Gandhi, Sonia, (ed.), op. cit, p. 160.
45. Ibid p. 170.
46. Ibid p. 192.
47. Ibid p. 186.
48. Ibid p. 188.
49. Friedan, Betty, 'How Mrs Gandhi Shattered the Feminine Mystique', p. 165.
50. Gandhi, Sonia, (ed.), op. cit, p. 212.
51. Ibid.
52. Sahgal, Nayantara (ed.), *Before Freedom*, p. 355.
53. Ibid p. 357.
54. Ibid p. 300.
55. Mathai, M, O., *Reminiscences of the Nehru Age*, p. 267.
56. Gopal, Sarvepalli (ed.), op. cit, I, 13, p. 287.

57. Mathai, M. O., *Reminiscences of the Nehru Age*, p. 268.
58. Pandit, Vijaya Lakshmi, op. cit, p. 177.
59. Gandhi, Sonia, (ed.), op. cit, pp. 345–6.
60. Fallaci, Oriana, op. cit, pp. 174–5.
61. Gopal, Sarvepalli (ed.), op. cit, I, 12, pp. 360–1.
62. Gandhi, Sonia, (ed.), op. cit, p. 368.
63. Khilnani, Sunil, *The Idea of India*, p. 168.
64. Nehru, Jawaharlal, *Discovery of India*, p. 159.
65. Gandhi, Sonia, (ed.), op. cit, p. 373, p. 381.

TEN: *Things Fall Apart*

1. Interestingly, Nehru, who was no believer in astrology, wrote to his sister Krishna that 'a proper horoscope made by a competent person' should be drawn up for the baby, *Nehru's Letters to his Sister*, p. 162.
2. Gopal, Sarvepalli (ed.), *Selected Works of Jawaharlal Nehru* I, 13, p. 501.
3. Ibid p. 505.
4. Ibid.
5. Gandhi, Sonia (ed.), *Two Alone, Two Together*, p. 25.
6. Gopal, Sarvepalli (ed.), op. cit, I, 13, p 518; pp. 588–9.
7. Gandhi, Tehmina, 'How We Welcomed Indira into the Family', p. 13.
8. Author's interview with Nayantara Sahgal.
9. Gopal, Sarvepalli (ed.), op. cit, I, 13, p. 602.
10. Gandhi, Sonia (ed.), op. cit, p. 469.
11. Ibid p. 487.
12. Ibid p. 516.
13. In 1975, after they had signed the Kashmir Accord, Indira Gandhi visited Srinagar and Sheikh Abdullah arranged another (peaceful) river procession for her.
14. Sahgal, Nayantara (ed), *Before Freedom*, p. 507–8.
15. Ibid p. 132.
16. Quoted in French, Patrick, *Liberty or Death*, p. 234.
17. Ibid p. 239.
18. M.O. Mathai papers, Nehru Library
19. Gopal, Sarvepalli (ed.), op. cit, II, 3, p. 331.
20. Rau, M. Chalapathi, *Journalism and Politics*, p. 13.
21. Mathai, M.O., *Reminiscences of the Nehru Age*, p. 98.
22. Rau, op. cit, p. 16.
23. Author's interview with Nayantara Sahgal.
24. Moraes, Dom, *Mrs Gandhi*, p. 83.
25. Gupte, Pranay, *Mother India*, p. 219.
26. Gopal, Sarvepalli (ed.), op. cit, II, 3, p. 335.
27. Sahgal, Nayantara, and Rai, E.N. Mangat, *Relationship: Extracts from a Correspondence*, p. 163. Feroze's affair with the daughter of Lucknow politician Ali Zareer is widely known but documented in print only by M.O. Mathai in *Reminiscences of the Nehru Age*, p. 95. Mathai claims Indira Gandhi confided in him about the relationship and Nehru's role in ending it. My account draws on Mathai and the research of Bertil Falk who is working on a biography of Feroze Gandhi.
28. Vasudev, Uma, *Indira Gandhi*, p. 208.
29. Hutheesing, K.N., *We Nehrus*, p. 208.
30. Mathai, M.O., op. cit, p. 1.
31. Gopal, Sarvepalli (ed.), II, p. 311–2.
32. Ibid p. 310.
33. Mathai, M.O., op. cit, p. 8.
34. M.O. Mathai admits as much in his

autobiography, but he explains that he kept 'a spare copy of everything Nehru wrote and also copies of important telegrams and documents' to show to Indira to help 'inform her mind . . . to talk somewhat sensibly to foreign dignitaries who sat on either side of her at social functions. She was extremely good at keeping secrets'. B.K. Nehru and Nehru's biographer, S. Gopal, however, told me that Mathai made copies secretly, without Nehru's or Indira's knowledge. Gopal and others believe Mathai passed some of these copies, as well as other information, on to the CIA. According to B.K. Nehru, Mathai used to boast in his last years of having copies of all Nehru's papers, Mathai, *Reminiscences of the Nehru Age*, p. 249. Author's interviews with S. Gopal and B.K. Nehru

35. Author's interview with S. Gopal. Gill, S.S., *The Pathology of Corruption*, p. 59–60.

36. Author's interview with B.K. Nehru

37. Morgan, Janet, *Edwina Mountbatten: A Life of Her Own*, p. 382.

38. Cannadine, David, *The Pleasures of the Past*, p. 58.

39. Ibid p. 386.

40. Ziegler, Philip, *Mountbatten: The Official Biography*, p. 363.

41. Morgan, Janet, op. cit, p. 403.

42. Ibid p. 408.

43. Most observers agree that Edwina Mountbatten and Nehru fell in love, but whether or not they had a sexual relationship is a matter of dispute. Edwina's daughter, Pamela Hicks – one of the few people who has read the extensive correspondence between her mother and Nehru – told me that the affair was unconsummated but that her mother would have wished it otherwise. (Author's interview with Pamela Hicks.) Edwina Mountbatten's biographer, Janet Morgan, who has also read the correspondence, holds that the relationship was not sexual. Mountbatten's most authoritative biographer, Philip Ziegler is more equivocal when he states, 'If there was any physical element it can only have been of minor importance to either party.' (Ziegler, Philip, op. cit, p. 473.) Nehru's most recent biographer, Stanley Wolpert, not only holds that the couple were lovers, but also claims, (apparently without any evidence since he has not read their letters) that Nehru seriously contemplated leaving India and his position as Prime Minister in order to live with Edwina in Britain. In a similar vein, Andrew Roberts and Akbar Ahmed argue that Nehru exploited his relationship with Edwina in order to influence Mountbatten, (Roberts, Andrew, *Eminent Churchillians*; Ahmed, Akbar S., *Jinnah, Pakistan and Islamic Identity*). In his memoir, M.O. Mathai luridly describes an affair between Edwina Mountbatten and Nehru, along with a string of other liaisons he claims Nehru had over the years. But Mathai is a suspect witness. The letters exchanged between Edwina and Nehru undoubtedly make clear the nature of their relationship. Edwina Mountbatten's letters are held at Broadlands. The Mountbatten family returned Nehru's letters to Delhi and they are in the possession of Sonia Gandhi. Copies of Nehru's letters are also at Broadlands. Both sides of the correspondence are currently closed to researchers, though Janet Morgan and Philip Ziegler were given access to them. Pamela Hicks and her sister, the

Countess Mountbatten, would like the correspondence to be published, but Sonia Gandhi is unwilling to sanction publication.

44. Author's interview with Pamela Hicks.
45. Gopal, Sarvepalli (ed.), I, p. 349.
46. Collins, Larry and Dominque LaPierre, *Freedom at Midnight*, p. 309.
47. Ibid p. 321.
48. Lord Chalfont's interview with Indira Gandhi, BBC television. M.O. Mathai claims that in Nehru's draft of the speech the phrase was 'date with destiny' which was changed to 'tryst' at Mathai's suggestion when he pointed out to Nehru that in American English 'date' means an 'assignation with girls and women'. In his autobiography Mathai says that he has given the draft speech to the Nehru Museum along with 'innumerable documents and photographs'. But the draft speech is not listed in the M.O Mathai Papers at the Nehru Library. Mathai, *Reminiscences of the Nehru Age*, p. 11.
49. Author's interview with Alan Campbell-Johnson.
50. French, Patrick, op. cit, p. 318.
51. Khilnani, Sunil, *The Idea of India*, p. 201.
52. Ibid.
53. Gandhi, Indira, *My Truth*, p. 59.
54. Author's interview with Subhadra Joshi. Gandhi, Indira, *Remembered Moments*, pp. 38–42.
55. Seton, Marie, *Panditji*, p. 137.
56. Much ink has been spilt on the timing of the accession and the legality of the Indian intervention, but as Victoria Schofield notes, whether or not accession preceded intervention, 'the maharaja had agreed to accession in principle . . .

he never [afterwards] suggested that he had not signed an Instrument of Accession before Indian troops landed nor that he had never signed one', Schofield, p. 150.

57. Quoted in Lamb, Alistair, *Kashmir: A Disputed Legacy*, p. 138.
58. Ibid p. 182.
59. Gandhi, Sonia (ed.), op. cit, p. 548.
60. Gandhi, Indira,op. cit, pp. 63–4. Sahgal, Nayantara, *Prison and Chocolate Cake*, p. 225. Hutheesing, K.N., op. cit, pp. 237–8.
61. Hutheesing, K.N., Ibid pp. 241–2.
62. *Hindustan Times*, 31 January 1948.
63. Nehru, Jawaharlal, *Speeches*, I, pp. 42–4.
64. Gandhi, Sonia (ed.), op. cit, pp. 551–2.
65. Ibid p. 556.
66. Gopal, Sarvepalli (ed.), op. cit, II, 7, p. 684.
67. Gandhi, Indira, *My Truth* , pp. 70–1.
68. Masani, Zareer, *Indira Gandhi*, p. 83.
69. Mohan, Anand, *Indira Gandhi*, p. 190.
70. Gandhi, Indira, op. cit, p. 72. Mohan, Anand, *Indira Gandhi*, p. 188.
71. Jayakar, Pupul, op. cit, pp. 142–3.

ELEVEN: *Metamorphosis*

1. Nehru also vetoed this daily allowance.
2. Gopal, Sarvepalli, *Jawaharlal Nehru*, II, p. 60.
3. Ibid p. 61.
4. Norman, Dorothy (ed.), *Letters to an American Friend*, p. 8.
5. Ibid.
6. Ibid pp. 6–7.
7. Ibid p. 10.
8. Ibid p. 35.
9. Author's interview with Dorothy Norman.

10. Their friendship ruptured after Dorothy Norman made a public statement in 1975 condemning the Emergency, but she and Indira were reconciled after Sanjay Gandhi was killed in 1980.

11. Gandhi, Sonia (ed.), *Two Alone, Two Together*, pp. 566–70.

12. Author's interview with Dorothy Norman.

13. Gopal, Sarvepalli (ed.), op. cit., II, 17, p. 36.

14. Ibid p. 635.

15. Jayakar, Pupul, *Indira Gandhi*, pp. 144–5.

16. Gandhi, Sonia (ed.), op. cit, pp. 592–3.

17. Ibid.

18. Ibid p. 594.

19. Ibid pp. 592–4.

20. Gopal, Sarvepalli (ed.), op. cit, II, p. 133, p. 302.

21. Gandhi, Sonia (ed.), op. cit, p. 596.

22. Ibid pp. 596–7.

23. Ibid p. 597.

24. Ibid p. 598.

25. In 1954, when the Gandhi boys were enrolled at the Doon School, the headmaster was J.R. Martyn. Martyn had taught at Nehru's alma mater, Harrow, and then went to India with Arthur Foot of Eton to found the Doon School in Dehra Dun in the late thirties. Rajiv thrived at the Doon School, though he was only an average student; nor did he excel at sports. Sanjay had serious problems there from the beginning, though he was actually academically better than his older brother. But Sanjay got into numerous scrapes, played truant and repeatedly broke school rules. He fought with and bullied other students, and was apparently even cruel to the school pets. Indira withdrew Sanjay from the Doon School in 1960 – possibly to avert his being expelled, and he then attended St Columbus', a day school in Delhi. The Doon School remains today the premier public school in India.

26. Norman, Dorothy, op. cit, p. 26.

27. The Congress Working Committee, which stands at the apex of the Congress Party organizational structure, is composed of the Congress Party President, the party leader in the Lok Sabha and nineteen other members, ten of whom are elected by the All-India Congress Committee and nine who are appointed by the party President.

28. Seton, Marie, *Panditji*, p. 198.

29. Norman, Dorothy (ed.), op. cit, p. 27.

30. Ibid p. 29.

31. Nehru, B.K., *Nice Guys Finish Second*, p. 263.

32. Ibid p. 262.

33. Ibid p. 264.

34. Gandhi, Sonia, *Rajiv*, p. 42.

35. Gandhi, Sonia, (ed.), *Two Alone, Two Together*, p. 614.

36. Indira Gandhi to Padmaja Naidu, January 1947, Nehru Library.

37. Ryan, Frank, *Tuberculosis: The Greatest Story Never Told*, pp. 383–4.

38. Author's interviews with Dr John Moore-Gillon, Dr Vatsala Samant and Dr K.P. Mathur. I am grateful to Dr Moore-Gillon, of the Department of Respiratory Medicine, St Bartholomew's Hospital, London, for discussing Indira Gandhi's tuberculosis with me. Dr Vatsala Samant treated Indira Gandhi in Allahabad and Dr K.P. Mathur was her personal physician after Indira became prime minister.

39. Indira Gandhi to Padmaja Naidu, Nehru Library.

40. Gandhi, Sonia, (ed.), op. cit, p. 616.
41. Author's interview with Nikhil Chakravartty.
42. Sarvepalli, Gopal, (ed.), op. cit, II, pp. 311–2.
43. Mathai, M.O., *My Days with Nehru*, pp. xiii–xiv.
44. Mathai, M.O., *Reminiscences of the Nehru Age*, p. 10.
45. Author's interviews with B. K. Nehru, P. N. Haksar, Khushwant Singh, Trevor Fishlock and Pupul Jayakar.
46. Author's interview with B.K. Nehru. Nehru's biographer, S. Gopal, also believes there was an affair of some sort between Indira and Mathai. Author's interview with S. Gopal.
47. Author's interview with Nikhil Chakravartty.
48. Malhotra, Inder, *Indira Gandhi*, p. 70. Author's interview with Inder Malhotra.
49. Vasudev, Uma, *Indira Gandhi*, p. 246.
50. Gill, S.S., *The Pathology of Corruption*, pp. 50–1.
51. Mohan, Anand, *Indira Gandhi*, pp. 203–5.
52. Norman, Dorothy (ed.), op. cit, p. 47.
53. Ibid p. 48.
54. Gandhi, Sonia, (ed.), op. cit, p. 619.
55. Ibid p. 623.
56. Sarvepalli, Gopal, (ed.), op. cit, III, pp. 81–2.
57. Author's interview with Nikhil Chakravartty.
58. Jayakar, Pupul, op. cit, pp. 154–5.
59. Gandhi, Indira, *My Truth*, p. 115. Lord Chalfont's interview with Indira Gandhi.
60. Michaelis, Arnold, 'An Interview with Indira Gandhi', p. 190.
61. Hutheesing, K.N., *Dear to Behold*, p. 149.
62. Jayakar, Pupul, op. cit, p. 156.
63. Dorothy Norman papers, Beinecke Library, Yale University.
64. Vasudev, Uma, op. cit, p. 276.
65. Bertil Falk unpublished biography of Feroze Gandhi.
66. Sarvepalli, Gopal, op. cit, III, p. 59.
67. Ibid.
68. Jeffrey, Robin, 'Jawaharlal Nehru and the Smoking Gun: Who Pulled the Trigger in Kerala's Communist Government in 1959?', p. 81.
69. Norman, Dorothy (ed.), op. cit, p. 63.
70. Gandhi, Sonia, (ed.), op. cit, pp. 627–8.
71. Norman, Dorothy, op. cit, p. 59.
72. Ibid p. 61.
73. Vasudev, Uma, op. cit, p. 293.
74. Author's interview with Usha Bhagat.
75. Author's interview with Nayantara Sahgal.
76. Gandhi, Sonia, *Rajiv*, pp. 50–1.
77. Dorothy Norman Papers.
78. Moraes, Dom, op. cit, p. 146.
79. Lord Chalfont's interview with Indira.

TWELVE: *Towards a Hat Trick*

1. Dorothy Norman Papers.
2. Author's interview with Usha Bhagat.
3. Norman, Dorothy (ed.), *Letters to an American Friend*, p. 79.
4. Gandhi, Sonia, (ed.), *Two Alone and Two Together*, p. 648.
5. Ibid p. 647.
6. Norman, Dorothy, op. cit, pp. 85–6.
7. Nehru, B.K., *Nice Guys Finish Second*, p. 364.
8. Galbraith, John Kenneth, *Ambassador's Journal*, p. 226.
9. Ibid p. 227.
10. Sarvepalli, Gopal, (ed.), *Selected*

Works of Jawaharlal Nehru, III,
p. 188.

11. Author's interviews with B. K.
Nehru and John Kenneth
Galbraith.

12. Gandhi, Sonia, (ed.), op. cit, p. 672.

13. Norman, Dorothy, op. cit, p. 88.

14. Ibid p. 89.

15. According to Indira's personal
physician, Dr K. P. Mathur, she
went through an 'early' menopause.
Author's interview with Dr K. P.
Mathur.

16. Dorothy Norman Papers.

17. Ibid.

18. Norman, Dorothy, op. cit, p. 95.

19. Seton, Marie, *Panditji*, p. 480.

20. Norman, Dorothy, op. cit,
pp. 96–7.

21. Dorothy Norman Papers.

22. Malhotra, Inder, *Indira Gandhi*,
p. 81. With remarkable prescience,
Welles Hangen ended his book
with the observation that 'the vital
question in India is not "After
Nehru, Who?" but "After Nehru's
successor, who?" . . . [When Nehru
dies] . . . there will be strong
pressure for Congress unity and
maintenance of an effective central
government . . . powerful forces in
Congress and the country will be
working to close the leadership gap
as quickly as possible. To avoid a
prolonged factional struggle, Shastri
might be given the nod . . . The
situation will be entirely different
when Shastri or whoever succeeds
Nehru leaves the scene (probably
not long after Nehru's passing) and
a new prime minister must be
chosen . . . Congress is almost
certainly to have split openly and
officially by that time. At best it will
be a two-way division on Left-Right
factional lines . . . Indira Gandhi
cannot be ignored . . . she is a
strong possibility. (*After Nehru
Who?*, pp. 276–7.) Hangen lived to
see his forecast come true in 1966.
But four years later he was killed by
Viet Cong and Khmer Rouge
guerrillas in Cambodia while
covering the Vietnam War.

23. Desai, Morarji, *The Story of My Life*,
II, p. 204.

24. Quoted in Vasudev, Uma, *Indira
Gandhi*, p. 302.

25. Nayar, Kuldip, *India: The Critical
Years*, p. 20.

26. Seton, Marie, op. cit, p. 373.

27. Ibid p. 374.

28. Norman, Dorothy, op. cit,p. 98.

29. Seton, Marie, op. cit, p. 404. Indira
later told Uma Vasudev: 'I began to
wear white after he [Feroze] died.
Then gradually I felt like wearing
grays and browns and blacks. I was
just beginning to want to wear
colours again when my father died,'
Vasudev, op cit, p. 310.

30. Malhotra, Inder, op. cit, p. 78.

31. Norman, Dorothy (ed.), op. cit,
p. 100.

32. Thapar, Raj, *All These Years*, p. 223.

33. Seton, Marie, op. cit, p. 426.

34. Quoted in Vasudev, Uma, op cit,
p. 305.

35. Abdullah, Sheikh, *Flames of the
Chinar*, pp. 152–3.

36. Norman, Dorothy, op. cit, p. 103.

37. Quoted in Seton, Marie, op. cit,
p. 451.

38. Ibid p. 460.

39. Malhotra, Inder, op. cit, p. 78.

40. Author's interviews with P.N.
Haksar, Nayantara Sahgal and
Pupul Jayakar.

41. Author's interview with Mani
Shankar Ayer.

42. Srivastava, C.P., *Lal Bahadur
Shastri*, p. 85.

43. Brecher, Michael, *Succession in India*,
pp. 65–6.

44. Gandhi, Indira, *My Truth*, p. 101.

45. Malhotra, Inder, op. cit, p. 83.

46. Vasudev, Uma, op cit, p. 324.
47. Malhotra, Inder, op. cit, p. 84.
48. Malhotra, Inder, op. cit, pp. 85–6.
49. Thapar, Raj, op. cit, p. 248.
50. Nayar, Kuldip, *Between the Lines*, p. 14.
51. Sahgal, Nayantara, *Indira Gandhi: Her Road to Power*, p. 5.
52. Thapar, Raj, op. cit, p. 252.

THIRTEEN: *I am the Issue*

1. It was not until 1996 that India had its first non-Hindi, non-English speaking Prime Minister: H.D. Deve Gowda.
2. Kaviraj, Sudipta, 'Indira Gandhi and Indian Politics', p. 1697.
3. Rao, P.V. Narasimha, *The Insider*, p 493.
4. Ibid p. 496.
5. Mishra, D.P., *The Post-Nehru Era: Political Memoirs*, p. 22.
6. Author's interview with S. Gopal. Manor, James, *Nehru to the Nineties*, p. 128. Gopal, S., *Radhakrishnan*, pp. 344–6.
7. Brecher, Michael, *Succession in India*, p. 236.
8. Gandhi, Indira, *My Truth*, p 115.
9. Brecher, Michael, op. cit, pp. 236–7.
10. Masani, Zareer, *Indira Gandhi* p. 140.
11. Vasudev, Uma, *Indira Gandhi: Revolution in Restraint*, pp. 348–9.
12. Ibid p. 346.
13. *Time* magazine, 28 January 1966.
14. Desai, Morarji, *The Story of My Life*, II, p. 229.
15. Author's interview with John Grigg.
16. Quoted in Ali, Tariq, *The Nehrus and the Gandhis*, p. 154.
17. Mishra, D.P., op. cit, pp. 34–5.
18. Nayar, Kuldip, *India: The Critical Years*, p. 30.
19. Jayakar, Pupul, *Indira Gandhi*, p. 187.
20. Malhotra, Inder, *Indira Gandhi*, p. 95.
21. Frankel, Francine R., *India's Political Economy*, pp. 296–7.
22. Author's interview with B.K. Nehru.
23. Malhotra, Inder, op. cit, p. 95.
24. Author's interview with B. K. Nehru.
25. Gupte, Pranay, *Mother India*, pp. 293–4.
26. Nehru, B.K., *Nice Guys Finish Second*, pp 459–60.
27. Gandhi, Indira, *Selected Speeches and Writings of Indira Gandhi*, I, p. 93.
28. Mehta, Ved, *Portrait of India*, p. 498.
29. Gandhi, Indira, *Remembered Moments*, pp. 67–8.
30. Jalal, Ayesha, *Democracy and Authoritarianism in South Asia*, p. 66.
31. *Times of India*, 26 December 1966.
32. Ibid 20 January 1967.
33. Masani, Zareer, op. cit, p. 171. Author's interview with Inder Kapur.
34. Norman, Dorothy, *Letters to an American Friend*, p. 117.
35. Quoted in Brecher, Michael, 'Succession in India: 1967', p. 426.
36. Ibid p. 432.
37. Desai, Morarji, op. cit, 2, p. 237.
38. Brecher, Michael, op. cit, p. 434.
39. Nayar, Kuldip, *Between the Lines*, p. 28.
40. Sahgal, Nayantara, *Indira Gandhi: Her Road To Power*, p. 12.
41. Quoted in Mishra, D.P., op. cit, p 80.
42. Quoted in Malhotra, Inder, op. cit, p 107.
43. The Green Revolution in India was far from an unalloyed blessing. Francine Frankel's *India's Green Revolution: Economic Gains and Political Costs* and Vandana Shiva's

The Violence of the Green Revolution discuss the social, economic and political consequences of the technology of the Green Revolution.

44. Fallaci, Oriana, *Interview with History*, p. 176.
45. Gandhi, Sonia, *Rajiv*, p 1.
46. Ibid p. 2.
47. Malhotra, Inder, op. cit, p. 117.
48. The Indian President is indirectly elected by members of Parliament and state legislators. He is the constitutional head of the country and possesses no executive power. Nevertheless, governmental decisions are issued in the President's name; the President is commander-in-chief; he 'appoints' the Prime Minister, ministers, Supreme Court and High Court justices and state governors.
49. Hasan, Zoya, 'The Prime Minister and the Left', in Manor, James, *Nehru to the Nineties*, p. 216.
50. Gandhi, Indira, op. cit, pp. 71–2.
51. Author's interview with P.N. Haksar.
52. Author's interviews with P.N. Haksar and P.N. Dhar.
53. Author's interview with P.N. Haksar.
54. Panandiker, V.A. and Mehra, Ajay K. (eds.), *The Indian Cabinet*, p. 227.
55. Ibid p. 230.
56. Nayar, Kuldip, *India: The Critical Years*, p. 33.
57. Gandhi, Indira, *Selected Speeches*, II, p. 133.
58. Malhotra, Inder, op. cit, p. 119.
59. Gill, S.S., *The Dynasty*, p. 245.
60. Rao, P.V. Narasimha, op. cit, p. 599.
61. Malhotra, Inder, op. cit, p 122.
62. Nayar, Kuldip, op. cit, pp. 2–3.
63. Rao, P.V. Narasimha, op. cit, p. 610.
64. Sahgal, Nayantara, *Indira Gandhi: Her Road to Power*, pp. 52–3.

65. Masani, Zareer, op. cit, p. 211.
66. Mehta, Ved, *Portrait of India*, p. 501.
67. Masani, Zareer, op. cit, p. 211.
68. Kaviraj, Sudipta, 'Indira Gandhi and Indian Politics', p. 1698.
69. Sahgal, Nayantara, op cit, p 66.
70. Kaviraj, among others, use this phrase.
71. Mehta, Vinod, *The Sanjay Story*, p. 56.
72. Ibid. p. 41.
73. Quoted in Merchant, Minhaz, *Rajiv Gandhi: The End of a Dream*, p. 46.
74. Norman, Dorothy, op. cit, p. 128.
75. Gandhi, Indira, op. cit, 2, II, p. 76.
76. Malhotra, Inder, op. cit, p. 128.

FOURTEEN: *Seeing Red*

1. Rao, P.V. Narasimha, *The Insider*, pp. 621–2. Malhotra, Inder, *Indira Gandhi*, p. 128.
2. Thapar, Raj, *All These Years*, p. 322.
3. Gandhi, Indira, *My Truth*, p. 148.
4. Gill, S.S., *The Dynasty*, p. 252. Masani, Zareer, *Indira Gandhi*, pp. 230–1.
5. Thapar, Raj, op. cit, p. 325, p. 342.
6. Frankel, Francine R., *India's Political Economy*, p. 460.
7. Quoted in Abbas, K.A., *That Woman*, p. 90.
8. Gandhi, Indira, *Speeches in Parliament*, p. 540.
9. Frankel, Francine R., op. cit, pp. 466–7.
10. Gill, S.S., op. cit, p. 263.
11. Frankel, Francine R., op. cit, p. 468.
12. Bhutto, Benazir, *Daughter of the East*, p. 53.
13. Abbas, K.A., op. cit, p. 101.
14. Dhar, P.N., *Indira Gandhi, The Emergency and Indian Democracy*, p. 156.

15. *The Hindustan Times*, 11 and 12 November, 1986.
16. Author's interview with P.N. Haksar.
17. Abbas, K.A., op. cit, p. 118.
18. Sarkar, Bidyut (ed.), *P.N. Haksar: Our Times and the Man*, p. 181.
19. Kissinger, Henry, *White House Years*, p. 848.
20. Ibid pp. 878–9. Author's interview with P.N. Haksar.
21. Kissinger, Henry, op. cit, pp. 880–1, p. 848.
22. Author's interview with T.N. Kaul. Kaul, T.N., *Diplomacy in Peace and War*, pp. 182–3.
23. Kissinger, Henry, op. cit, p. 882.
24. Author's interview with P.N. Haksar.
25. Ibid.
26. Masani, Zareer, *Indira Gandhi*, p. 241.
27. Ibid p. 242.
28. Norman, Dorothy (ed.), *Letters to an American Friend*, p. 135.
29. Mistry, Rohinton, *Such a Long Journey*, p. 298.
30. Masani, Zareer, op. cit, p. 240.
31. Sisson, Richard and Rose, Leo E., op. cit, pp. 213–14.
32. Author's interview with P.N. Haksar.
33. Sisson, Richard and Rose, Leo E., *War and Succession: Pakistan, India, and the Creation of Pakistan*, pp. 213–14.
34. Gandhi, Indira, *Speeches in Parliament*, pp. 808–9.
35. Gandhi, Indira, *Selected Speeches*, vol II, pp. 611–13.
36. Author's interview with P.N. Haksar.
37. Jayakar, Pupul, *Indira Gandhi*, p. 245.
38. Gandhi, Indira, *Speeches in Parliament*, pp. 812–13.
39. Malhotra, Inder, *Indira Gandhi*, p. 140.

40. Ibid.
41. Masani, Zareer, op. cit, p. 248. In *White House Years* (p. 913), Henry Kissinger says there was 'no doubt' in his mind that Indira was forced into calling a cease-fire by 'Soviet pressure, which in turn grew out of American insistence, including the fleet movement'. P.N. Haksar, however, vehemently denies this was reason for agreeing to a cease-fire, (author's interview P.N. Haksar).
42. *Economist*, quoted in Malhotra, Inder, *Indira Gandhi*, p. 141.
43. Abbas, K.A., op. cit, pp. 161–2.
44. Dhar, P.N., op. cit, p. 202.
45. Fallaci, Oriana, *Interview with History*, p. 188, p. 190, p. 199.
46. Author's interview with P.N. Haksar.
47. Dhar, P.N., op. cit, p. 192.
48. Author's interview with T.N. Kaul.
49. Dhar, P.N., op. cit, p. 192.
50. Author's interview with P.N. Haksar. Dhar, P.N., op. cit, pp. 193–4.
51. Lamb, Alistair, *Kashmir: A Disputed Legacy*, p. 211, but author's emphasis.
52. Author's interview with P.N. Haksar.
53. Ibid. Benazir Bhutto gives a different account of this episode in her autobiography, *Daughter of the East*.
54. Author's interview with P.N. Haksar.
55. Dhar, P.N., op. cit, p. 210.
56. Nayar, Kuldip, *India After Nehru*, p. 208.

FIFTEEN: *No Further Growing*

1. Vasudev, Uma, *Two Faces of Indira Gandhi*, pp. 106–7. Author's

interview with Uma Vasudev. Birla,
K.K., *Indira Gandhi: Reminiscences*,
p. 39.

2. Nayar, Kuldip, *The Judgement*,
p. 197. Thapar, Raj, *All These Years*,
pp. 397–8. Abbas, K.A., *Indira
Gandhi: The Last Post*, p. 15.

3. Author's interview with P.N.
Haksar.

4. Khilnani, Sunil, *The Idea of India*,
p. 89.

5. Nayar, Kuldip, *Supersession of Judges*,
p. 35.

6. Norman, Dorothy (ed.), *Letters to
an American Friend*, p. 145.

7. Ibid.

8. Vasudev, Uma, op. cit, p. 13.

9. Thakur, Janardan, *All The Prime
Minister's Men*, p. 101.

10. Norman, Dorothy (ed.), op. cit,
p. 138.

11. George Fernandes had originally
planned to be a Roman Catholic
priest, but after a short spell in a
seminary he entered radical politics
and the trade union movement. His
later career was erratic. In 1977 he
joined forces with Morarji Desai's
Janata Party. After Desai made him
Industry Minister, Fernandes
ejected the multi-nationals, Coca-
Cola and IBM, from India. Twenty
years later, in 1998, Fernandes – a
long-time campaigner for nuclear
disarmament – warmly defended
India's nuclear testing initiative
while serving as Minister of
Defence in the BJP government
headed by A.B. Vajpayee. In the
spring of 1999 he was instrumental
in preventing Sonia Gandhi from
forming a Congress coalition
government. During the 1999
conflict with Pakistan in Kashmir
he repeatedly visited the troops on
the frontline in order to boost
morale.

12. Vasudev, Uma, op. cit, p. 71.

13. Gandhi, Indira, *Speeches in
Parliament*, p. 511.

14. Dorothy Norman Papers.

15. Gill, S.S., *The Dynasty*, p. 246.

16. Datta-Ray, Sunanda K., *Smash and
Grab: The Annexation of Sikkim*,
p. 73.

17. Dhar, P.N., *Indira Gandhi, The
Emergency and Indian Democracy*,
p. 273.

18. Ibid p. 249.

19. Ibid p. 269.

20. Ibid p. 289.

21. Ibid p. 292.

22. Ibid pp. 298–9.

23. Gandhi, Indira, *Selected Speeches III*,
p. 129.

24. Abdullah, Sheikh, *Flames of the
Chinar*, p. 165.

25. Malhotra, Inder, *Indira Gandhi*,
p. 163.

26. Carras, Mary, *Indira Gandhi in the
Crucible of Leadership*, p. 184.

27. *New Republic*, 25 June 1975.

28. Thapar, Raj, op. cit, p. 400.

SIXTEEN: *Drastic, Emergent Action*

1. *Shah Commission Report*, I,
pp. 17–18.

2. Oriani Fallaci interview with
Morarji Desai, *The New Republic*,
July 1975.

3. Author's interview with Siddhartha
Shankar Ray.

4. Ibid.

5. *Shah Commission Report*, I, p. 25.

6. Kapur, Jagga, *What Price Perjury:
Facts of the Shah Commission*,
pp. 51–2.

7. This account of the events during
the twenty-four hours leading up to
the declaration of the Emergency is
based on an interview with
Siddhartha Shankar Ray and on
testimony made before and

depositions submitted to the Shah Commission and published in the *Shah Commission Report*. The Ministry of Information and Broadcasting published the Shah Commission 'Interim Report' on 1 March 1978, a second 'Interim Report' on 26 April 1978 and a 'Third and Final Report' on 6 August 1978. When Indira Gandhi returned to power in 1980 she invalidated the report and had it withdrawn from circulation. The only existing copies of the three volumes that I am aware of are at the School of Oriental and African Studies, University of London.

8. Author's interview with P.N. Dhar. Later that day Swaran Singh told a friend that Indira's 'crude resort to police powers' would not work. When this remark got back to her, Indira dropped Swaran Singh from the Cabinet and replaced him with Bansi Lal.

9. This account of the 26 June 1976 cabinet meeting is based on the *Shah Commission Report* and the author's interviews with Karan Singh and P.N. Dhar.

10. Kapur, Jagga, op. cit, p. 67.

11. Tully, Mark, *From Raj to Rajiv*, p. 119.

12. Gandhi, Indira, *Selected Speeches*, 3, pp. 177–9.

13. Dhar, P.N., op. cit, p. 304. Author's interview with P.N. Dhar.

14. Gandhi, Indira, *My Truth*, p. 161.

15. Nehru, B.K., *Nice Guys Finish Second*, pp. 557–9. Author's interview with B.K. Nehru.

16. Author's interview with John Grigg.

17. Young, Hugo, *One of Us*, p. 120.

18. Author's interview with Michael Foot.

19. Norman, Dorothy (ed.), *Letters to an American Friend*, pp. 148–50.

20. Jayakar, Pupul, *Indira Gandhi*, p. 286.

21. Ibid p. 287.

22. Frankel, Francine R., *India's Political Economy*, p. 570.

23. Ibid.

SEVENTEEN: *The Rising Son*

1. Frankel, Francine R., *India's Political Economy*, pp. 550–6. For a discussion of the modest gains and fundamental failure of the twenty-point programme, see chapter 13.

2. Author's interview with P.N. Haksar. *Shah Commission Report*, I, pp. 72–3.

3. Mehta, Vinod, *The Sanjay Story*, pp. 66–7. Author's interview with Siddhartha Shankar Ray. Rajiv Gandhi later claimed that his wife had never drawn her salary or visited the Maruti office or factory, (Merchant, Minhaz, *Rajiv Gandhi: The End of a Dream*, p. 73).

4. Mehta, Vinod, op. cit, p. 67.

5. Vasudev, Uma, *Two Faces of Indira Gandhi*, pp. 206–7.

6. Dhar, P.N., *Indira Gandhi, The Emergency and Indian Democracy*, p. 326–8. P.N. Dhar reproduces a photograph of Indira's 'frantic', three-page hand-written note in his book.

7. Author's interview with Uma Vasudev.

8. Vasudev, Uma, op. cit, p. 110.

9. Author's interview with P.N. Dhar.

10. Dhar, P.N., op. cit, p. 328.

11. Ibid p. 311.

12. Malhotra, Inder, *Indira Gandhi*, p. 177.

13. Mehta, Vinod, op. cit, p. 85.

14. Author's interview with Rupika Chawla.

15. Author's interview with James

Manor who cites Romesh Thapar.

16. Author's interview with B.K. Nehru.
17. Vasudev, Uma, op. cit, p. 115.
18. Dhar, P.N., op. cit, p. 305.
19. Mehta, Ved, *The New India*, p. 98.
20. For a full account of this libel case see Frank, Katherine, 'Mr Rushdie and Mrs Gandhi', *Biography*, 19, no 3 (Summer 1996).
21. Author's interview with Uma Vasudev.
22. Author's interview with P.N. Dhar.
23. Author's interview with Fori Nehru.
24. Author's interview with Jagmohan. Jagmohan continues to believe that 'Sanjay's instincts were always right,' that 'there were many false accusations against him,' and that Sanjay was morally committed to 'essential environmental work and family planning.'
25. Jagmohan, *Island of Truth* , p. 127, p. 111.
26. Jayakar, Pupul, *Indira Gandhi*, p. 306.
27. Moraes, Dom, *A Matter of People*, p. 162.
28. Author's interview with Karan Singh.
29. Author's interview with B.K. Nehru.
30. Rohinton Mistry's novel, *A Fine Balance*, vividly portrays daily life during the Emergency.
31. Author's interview with Fori Nehru.
32. Dhar, P.N., op. cit, p. 341.
33. Singh, Khushwant, *Indira Ghandi Returns*, pp. 78–86.
34. Nayar, Kuldip, *The Judgement*, p. 64.
35. Ibid. Dhar, P.N., op. cit, p. 344.
36. Jayakar, Pupul, op. cit., p. 313. Gandhi, Indira, *My Truth*, p. 166.
37. Author's interview with J.V. Kapur.
38. Moraes, Dom, *Mrs Gandhi*, p. 264–5.
39. Typescript of Vijaya Lakshmi Pandit's statement from Uma Vasudev. Extracts from it are included in Vijaya Lakshmi Pandit's autobiography, *The Scope of Happiness*, pp. 4–15.
40. Author's interview with Nayantara Sahgal.
41. Wolpert, Stanley, *Zulfi Bhutto of Pakistan: His Life and Times*, p. 283.
42. Mehta, Vinod, op. cit, pp. 108–9.
43. Ibid p. 111.
44. Jayakar, Pupul, op. cit, p. 321.

EIGHTEEN: *Witch-Hunt*

1. Interviews with Usha Bhagat and R.K. Dhawan.
2. Nehru, B.K., *Nice Guys Finish Second*, p. 579. Author's interview with B.K. Nehru.
3. Dhar, P.N., *Indira Gandhi, The Emergency and Indian Democracy*, p. 359.
4. Various people, including Nayantara Sahgal and Uma Vasudev, claim that vans or cars loaded with money left 1 Safdarjung Road under cover of darkness when it became clear that Indira had lost the 1977 election. There is no evidence that money was clandestinely smuggled out of the household and it seems unlikely that Sanjay would have kept very much of the money he had amassed during the Emergency in his mother's house. Sanjay had friends both in India and abroad who could safeguard money for him.
5. Author's interviews with B.K. Nehru and Swraj Paul.
6. Ali, Aruna Asif, *Private Face of a Public Person*, p. 281.
7. Sonia Gandhi, *Rajiv*, p. 76.
8. Jayakar, Pupul, *Indira Gandhi*, pp. 329–30.
9. *Times of India*, 24 May 1977.

10. *Shah Commission Report*, I, p. 1.
11. Author's interview with Khushwant Singh.
12. Moraes, Dom, *Mrs Gandhi*, p. 277.
13. *Shah Commission Report*, I, p. 1.
14. Ibid III, p. 246.
15. Ibid p. 247.
16. The rumour that Chand was killed persists to this day. Rupika Chawla, the wife of Navin Chawla, told me in 1997 that Chand was murdered on Sanjay's orders.
17. Moraes, Dom, op. cit, p. 283.
18. Jayakar, Pupul, op. cit, p. 344.
19. Ali, Tariq, *The Nehrus and the Gandhis*, p. 202.
20. Gangadharan, K., *The Inquisition*, pp. 242–56.
21. Moraes, op cit, p. 296.
22. Chatwin, Bruce, 'On the Road with Mrs G', in *What Am I Doing Here?* , p. 330.
23. Ibid p. 326.
24. Ibid p. 329.
25. *Shah Commission Report*, III, p. 262.
26. Ibid p. 241.
27. To my knowledge, the only extant copy of the full *Shah Commission Report* is at the School of Oriental and African Studies, University of London. Jagga Kapur's *What Price Perjury* and K. Gangadharan's *The Inquisition*, both contain lengthy extracts from the report as well as eyewitness accounts of the Shah Commission hearings.
28. *Shah Commission Report*, III, p. 234.
29. *Sunday*, 23–29 June 1985, p. 22.
30. Malhotra, Inder, *Indira Gandhi*, p. 208.
31. Ibid. p. 198. Author's interview with Uma Vasudev.
32. *Times of India*, 6 June 1978.
33. Carras, Mary, *Indira Gandhi in the Crucible of Leadership*, pp. 231–54.
34. Ibid pp. xiv–xv.
35. Abbas, K.A., *Indira Gandhi: The Last Post*, p. 56.
36. Swraj Paul has kept Indira's signed travellers' cheques as a memento. Author's interview with Swraj Paul.
37. Ibid.
38. Ibid.
39. Author's interview with Michael Foot.
40. Author's interviews with Swraj Paul and Fori Nehru.
41. Kidwai, Anser, *Indira Gandhi: Charisma and Crisis*, p. 33.
42. Author's interview with Karan Singh.
43. Mehta, Ved, *A Family Affair*, p. 343.
44. Jayakar, Pupul, *Indira Gandhi*, p. 376.
45. Author's interview with B.K. Nehru.
46. Jayakar, Pupul, op. cit, p. 380.
47. Ali, Tariq, *Can Pakistan Survive?* Chapter 5.
48. Ibid p. 136.
49. Ali, Tariq, *The Nehrus and the Gandhis*, p. 203.

NINETEEN: *Fault Lines*

1. The phrase is taken from Sunil Khilnani's 1997 book *The Idea of India* in which he describes Nehru's *Discovery of India* as 'an epic of India's past in which it appeared neither as a meaningless dust-storm nor as a glorified Hindu pageant, but as moved by a logic of accommodation and acceptance', (p. 169).
2. Manor, James, *Nehru to the Nineties*, p. 8.
3. Malhotra, Inder, *Indira Gandhi*, p. 215.
4. Jayakar, Pupul, *Indira Gandhi*, p. 403.
5. Ibid pp. 405–6.
6. *Shah Commission Report*, II, pp. 30–1.

7. Author's interview with Rustom Gandhi.

8. Author's interviews with V.P. Singh and R.K. Dhawan.

9. Author's interview with V.P. Singh.

10. Most of these names were later changed back or changed again. However the animal homes bearing Sanjay Gandhi's name still exist today; they were established by Sanjay's widow Maneka Gandhi, an animal lover.

11. Author's interview with B.K. Nehru.

12. Jayakar, Pupul, op. cit, p. 418. Author's interview with James Manor.

13. Author's interview with R.K. Dhawan.

14. Sonia Gandhi, *Rajiv*, p. 6.

15. Author's interview with Francine Frankel.

16. Thapar, Raj, *All These Years*, p. 461.

17. Author's interview with B.K. Nehru.

18. Malhotra, Inder, op. cit, p. 228.

19. Sonia Gandhi, op, cit, pp. 6–7.

20. Author's interview with Trevor Fishlock.

21. Malhotra, Inder, op. cit, p. 238.

22. Singh, Khushwant, 'Of Love and Loathing', *India Today*, 31 October 1995, p. 127.

23. Ibid p. 128.

24. Jayakar, Pupul, op. cit, p. 435.

25. Mehta, Ved, *Rajiv Gandhi and Rama's Kingdom*, p. 10.

26. Ibid p. 11.

27. Ibid p. 2. Singh, Khushwant, op. cit, pp. 129–31.

28. Jayakar, Pupul, op. cit, p. 436.

29. Malhotra, Inder, op. cit, p. 241.

30. Norman, Dorothy (ed.), *Letters to an American Friend*, p. 169.

31. Malhotra, Inder, op. cit, pp. 264–5.

32. Norman, Dorothy (ed.), op. cit, pp. 162–4. In the manuscript letter at the Beinecke Library at Yale, Indira actually attributes the 'things fall apart' quotation to T.S. Eliot. Dorothy Norman silently corrected this when she published Indira's letters. It is one of the few alterations Norman made, though she did cut personal material such as Indira's accounts of her pre-menstrual tension and her experience of menopause.

33. Jayakar, Pupul, op. cit, p. 440.

34. Author's interview with Arun Nehru.

35. Author's interview with B.K. Nehru.

36. Mehta, Ved, *Rajiv Gandhi and Rama's Kingdom*, p. 43.

37. Ibid p. 27.

TWENTY: *Another Amritsar*

1. Norman, Dorothy (ed.), *Letters to an American Friend*, p. 168. In an interview in the London *Daily Express*, Indira said that Gandhi 'was a good film for the West and for those in India who did not know' or remember the man, but she criticized the film's historical inaccuracy and said that it failed to capture the real Gandhi, *Selected Speeches and Writings of Indira Gandhi*, 5, p. 462.

2. Ali, Tariq, *The Nehrus and the Gandhis*, p. 231.

3. Pandian, M.S.S., 'Culture and Subaltern Consciousness: An Aspect of the MGR Phenomenon', in Chatterjee, Partha (ed.), *State and Politics in India*, p. 369.

4. N.T. Ramarao was a colourful figure. It was generally known that he dressed up in a sari in the privacy of his home because his astrologers had told him that this would hasten his bid to replace

Indira. Indira herself was aware of NTR's 'cross-dressing' and mentioned it in an interview with Tariq Ali, insisting that Ali should interview NTR in order to 'get a real flavour of the opposition', *The Nehrus and the Gandhis*, p. 231–2.

5. Malhotra, Inder, *Indira Gandhi*, p. 279.
6. Ali, Tariq, op, cit, p. 226.
7. Malhotra, Inder, op, cit, p. 280.
8. Ibid pp. 280–1.
9. Singh, Tavleen, *Kashmir: A Tragedy of Errors*, p. 25.
10. Thapar, Raj, *All These Years*, p. 470.
11. Singh, Tavleen, op. cit, p. 28.
12. Ibid p. 29.
13. Ibid p. 35.
14. Thapar, Raj, *All These Years*, op. cit, p. 471.
15. Ibid. Singh, Tavleen, op. cit, pp. 35–6. Both Raj Thapar and Tavleen Singh were in the audience at the Iqbal Park rally. Thapar claimed the flashing incident was a lie; Singh reported that it did occur but 'none of us saw it happen'.
16. Author's interview with B.K. Nehru.
17. According to B.K. Nehru, who at the time of the 1983 Kashmir state assembly elections was the state's governor, 'there was definitely a certain, but not great, amount of rigging . . . There was, of course, a hue and cry about the rigging. I accepted the fact that there was rigging. I did not accept the contention that but for the rigging the result would have been different. I told [Congress] not to appear angelic about rigging: did they not rig elections themselves in the states where they were in power?' *Nice Guys Finish Second*, p. 611.
18. Singh, Tavleen, op. cit, p. 37.
19. The founder and leader of the movement is a highly charismatic figure named Velupillai Prabhakaran who runs his revolutionary guerrilla army like a religious cult. Tiger recruits, both male and female, are young, passionate and committed. Their average age is eighteen, but there are guerrillas as young as thirteen. They are fanatically devoted to Prabhakaran and his messianic goal of Tamil liberation. At the end of their rigorous training, when they become full combatants, Tiger guerrillas wear capsules of cyanide suspended from string round their necks. The cyanide is used to commit suicide rather than be taken alive by the enemy. Female tigers resort to their cyanide capsules not only when faced with capture but also when their honour is threatened. For the Tamil Tigers subscribe to a rigid code that proscribes sex, alcohol, drugs and tobacco. All Tigers aspire to martyrdom, and they vie with each other to join the elite Black Tiger squads who carry out suicide bomber missions.

20. This reasoned speculation was suggested to me by Robert Bradnock.
21. Wilson, A. Jeyaratnam, *The Break-Up of Sri Lanka*, p. 203.
22. Jayakar, Pupul, *Indira Gandhi*, p. 464.
23. Merchant, Minhaz, *Rajiv Gandhi: The End of a Dream*, p. 97.
24. Ibid.
25. Jayakar, Pupul, op. cit, p. 459.
26. Author's interview with B.K. Nehru.
27. Nehru, B.K., *Nice Guys Finish Second*, pp. 611–12.
28. Ibid p. 622.
29. Ibid p. 625.
30. Ibid.

31. Ibid p. 622–3.
32. Ibid p. 614.
33. Ibid p. 638.
34. Author's interview with Arun Nehru.
35. Ibid.
36. In his autobiography Zail Singh says: 'Towards the end of May 1984, Mrs Indira Gandhi mentioned nonchalantly that some people suggested to her to send the police into the Golden Temple complex to flush out the militants . . . she said she could not see any alternative.' Singh maintains that he told her such action would not be 'proper' and 'tried to persuade her not to take any provocative step . . . but [she] did not disclose how her mind was actually working', Singh, Zail, *Memoirs of Giani Zail Singh*, p. 177.
37. Author's interview with Subhadra Joshi.
38. The following account of the events leading up to and during Operation Blue Star draws heavily on Tully, Mark and Satish, Jacob's *Amritsar: Mrs Gandhi's Last Battle* and Nayar, Kuldip and Singh, Khushwant's *Tragedy of Punjab*.
39. Tully, Mark and Satish, Jacob, op. cit, p. 143.
40. Ibid p. 154.
41. Singh, Zail, op. cit, p. 178.
42. Nayar, Kuldip and Singh, Khushwant, op. cit, p. 92.
43. Ibid.
44. Ibid.
45. Jayakar, Pupul, op. cit, p. 467.
46. Singh, Zail, op. cit, p. 181.
47. Tully, Mark and Satish, Jacob, op. cit, p. 167.
48. The number of bullet holes in the Harmandiv Sahib is a matter of some dispute. Officially, the Indian army claimed it was not damaged at all.
49. Singh, Zail, op. cit, p. 181.
50. Ibid.

TWENTY-ONE: *31 October 1984*

1. Sonia Gandhi, *Rajiv*, p. 8.
2. Author's interview with B.K. Nehru. Malhotra, Inder, *Indira Gandhi*, p. 294.
3. Ibid p. 303.
4. Ibid pp. 18–19.
5. Sarin, Ritu, *The Assassination of Indira Gandhi*, p. 19. Sarin's is a detailed account of the Sikh plotters who conspired to kill Indira Gandhi in revenge for Operation Blue Star.
6. Jagmohan, *My Frozen Turbulence in Kashmir*, p. 261.
7. Author's interview with B.K. Nehru. Nehru, B.K., *Nice Guys Finish Second*, p. 627.
8. Jagmohan, op. cit, p. 486.
9. Author's interview with Arun Nehru.
10. Malhotra, Inder, *Indira Gandhi*, p. 300.
11. The new Chief Minister of Andhra Pradesh did not survive a vote of confidence in the state assembly and N.T. Ramarao was reinstated in September 1984.
12. Gandhi, Indira, *Remembered Moments*, p. 79.
13. Young, Hugo, *One of Us*, pp. 372–3.
14. Author's interview with Jagmohan.
15. Jayakar, Pupul, *Indira Gandhi*, p. 481. Author's interview with Pupul Jayakar.
16. Ibid pp. 482–3.
17. Gandhi, Indira, *Selected Speeches*, 5, p. 495.
18. Alexander, P.C., *My Years With Indira Gandhi*, pp. 147–8.
19. Sonia Gandhi, op. cit, p. 8.
20. Tully, Mark and Satish, Jacob, *Amritsar*, p. 2.

21. Author's interview with R.K.
    Dhawan. Sarin, Ritu, op. cit, pp. 1–4.
22. Gandhi, Sonia, op. cit, p. 9.
23. One of Indira's assassins, Beant
    Singh, died several hours before his
    victim was pronounced dead on the
    operating table at the All-India
    Institute of Medical Sciences. After
    overpowering both Beant and
    Satwant Singh, the commandos of
    the Indo-Tibetan Border Police
    hustled them into the nearby
    guardroom and proceeded to assault
    both men. Instead of manacling the
    assassins, the commandos abused
    and beat them, and then, in a rage,
    pulled out their guns and opened
    fire. In this frenzied attempt to
    mete out justice, Beant Singh was
    shot dead and Satwant Singh
    critically wounded. Though no one
    present wished him alive, Satwant
    Singh was nevertheless rushed by
    ambulance to Ram Manohar Lohia
    Hospital where he eventually
    recovered. More than four years
    later, on 6 January 1989, after a
    protracted trial, numerous appeals,
    and an unsuccessful plea to the
    Indian President for clemency,
    Satwant Singh and a co-conspirator,
    Kehar Singh, were hanged at Tihar
    Jail in Delhi.

TWENTY-TWO: *After Indira*

1. Merchant, Minhaz, *Rajiv Gandhi:
   The End of a Dream*, p. 135.
2. Singh, Zail, *Memoirs of Giani Zail
   Singh*, p. 204.
3. Gandhi, Sonia, *Rajiv*, p. 9.
4. On 5 November 1984, the
   Congress parliamentary party, with
   a record attendance of 497 MPs,
   'ratified' the decision the two-man
   Congress Parliamentary Board
   made on 31 October.
5. Rajiv had five predecessors:
   Jawaharlal Nehru, Lal Bahadur
   Shastri, Indira Gandhi, Morarji
   Desai and Charan Singh. Indira, of
   course, 'came back' in 1980, so
   technically Rajiv could be said to
   have been the seventh Prime
   Minister of India.
6. Merchant, Minhaz, op. cit,
   pp. 148–9.
7. Author's interviews with B.K. and
   Fori Nehru.
8. Sarin, Ritu, *The Assassination of
   Indira Gandhi*, p. 41.
9. Tully, Mark and Satish, Jacob,
   Amritsar, p. 9.
10. Eliot, T.S., 'East Coker' from *Four
    Quartets*, Malhotra, Inder, *Indira
    Gandhi*, p. 24.

SELECT BIBLIOGRAPHY

Abbas, K.A., *Indira Gandhi: Return of the Red Rose*, Popular Praskashan, Bombay, 1966
—— *That Woman*, Indian Book Company, Delhi, 1973
—— *Indira Gandhi: The Last Post*, Popular Prakashan, Bombay, 1985
Abdullah, Farooq, *My Dismissal*, Vikas, New Delhi, 1985
Abdullah, Sheikh, *Flames of the Chinar*, Penguin Books, New Delhi, 1993
Adams, Jad, and Whitehead, Phillip, *The Dynasty: The Nehru-Gandhi Story*, Penguin Books, London, 1997
Adams, Pauline, *Somerville for Women: An Oxford College 1879–1993*, Oxford University Press, Oxford 1996
Ahluwalia, B.K., and Ahluwalia, Shashi, *Martyrdom of Indira Gandhi*, Manas Publications, New Delhi, 1984
Ahmed, Akbar S., *Jinnah, Pakistan and Islamic Identity*, Routledge, London, 1997
Akbar, M.J., *Nehru: The Making of India*, Viking, London, 1988
—— *The Siege Within: Challenges to a Nation's Unity*, Penguin, London, 1985
Alexander, P.C., *My Years with Indira Gandhi*, Vision Books, New Delhi, 1991
Ali, Aruna Asif, *Private Face of a Public Person: A Study of Jawaharlal Nehru*, Radiant Publishers, New Delhi, 1989
Ali, Tariq, *Can Pakistan Survive?* Penguin, London, 1983
—— *The Nehrus and the Gandhis: An Indian Dynasty*, Picador, London, 1991
Attwood, William, 'A Frank Talk with a Powerful Woman', *Look*, April 30 1968
Baig, Tara Ali, *Portraits of an Era*, Roli Books, New Delhi, 1986
Banerjee, Sumanta, 'Contradictions with a Purpose', *Economic and Political Weekly*, 19, part 48, 1984
Basu, Aparna, *Mridula Sarabhai: Rebel with a Cause*, Oxford University Press, Delhi, 1996
Baxter, Craig, Malik, Yogendra K., Kennedy, Charles H., and Oberst, Robert C., *Government and Politics in South Asia*, Westview Press, Boulder, Colorado, 1993
Bhargava, Onkar Nath, 'Feroze Gandhi: A Biographical Sketch', *Feroze Gandhi College*, Rae Bareilly Degree College Trust, 1971
Bhatia, Krishna, *Indira: A Biography of Prime Minister Gandhi*, Angus and Wilson, London, 1974
Bhushan, Shashi, *Feroze Gandhi: A Political Biography*, Progressive People's Sector Publications, New Delhi, 1977
Bhutto, Benazir, *Daughter of the East*, Hamish Hamilton, London, 1988
Birla, K.K., *Indira Gandhi: Reminiscences*, Vikas, Delhi, 1987
Bobb, Dilip, and Raina, Asoka, *The Great Betrayal: The Assassination of Indira Gandhi*, Vikas, Delhi, 1985
Bose, Sumantra, *States, Nations, Sovereignty: Sri Lanka, India and the Tamil Elam Movement*, Sage, New Delhi, 1994

Brass, Paul, *The Politics of India since Independence*, Cambridge University Press, Cambridge, 1994
—— 'The Punjab Crisis and the Unity of India', in Kohli, Atul (ed.), *India's Democracy: An Analysis of Changing State-Society Relations*, Princeton University Press, Princeton, 1988
Brecher, Michael, *Nehru: A Political Biography*, Oxford University Press, London, 1959
—— *Succession in India: A Study in Decision-Making*, Oxford University Press, London, 1966
—— 'Succession in India: 1967', *Asian Survey*, Volume XVII, no. 7, 1967
Bright, J.S., *Indira Gandhi*, New Light Publishers, Delhi, 1984
Brown, Judith M., *Gandhi: Prisoner of Hope*, Yale University Press, New Haven and London, 1989
—— *Modern India: The Origins of Asian Democracy*, Oxford University Press, Oxford, 1994
Bryder, Linda, *Below the Magic Mountain: A Social History of Tuberculosis in Twentieth-Century Britain*, Oxford University Press, Oxford, 1988
Buchan, James, 'Kashmir', *Granta*, 57, Spring 1997, Granta, London
Burrell, L.S.T., *Artificial Pneumothorax*, Heinemann, London, 1932
Cameron, James, 'India's First Lady: Indira', *Envoy*, London, June 1966
Campbell, John, *Margaret Thatcher: The Grocer's Daughter*, Jonathan Cape, London, 2000
Carras, Mary, *Indira Gandhi in the Crucible of Leadership*, Beacon Press, Boston, 1979
Chalfont, Lord, 'Indira Gandhi of India', interview broadcast on BBC television, 26 November 1971
Chandra, Bipan, Mukherjee, Mridula, Mukherjee, Aditya, Panikkar, K.N., and Mahajan, Sucheta, *India's Struggle for Independence*, Penguin Books, New Delhi, 1988
Chatwin, Bruce, 'On the Road with Mrs G', in *What Am I Doing Here?* Cape, London, 1989
Chisholm, Anne, *Rumer Godden*, Macmillan, London, 1998
Christian, Henry M. (ed.), *Indira Gandhi Speaks on Democracy, Socialism and Third World Non-Alignment*, Taplinger Publishing Co., New York, 1975
Convocation Addresses at Visva-Bharati, Santiniketan 1952–1993: The Common Pursuit, Visva-Bharati, Calcutta, 1995
Curie, Marie, *Journey among Warriors*, Heinemann, London, 1943
Datta, V.N., and Cleghorn, B.E., (eds.), *A Nationalist Muslim and Indian Politics: Being the Selected Correspondence of the late Dr Syed Mahmud*, Macmillan India, Delhi, 1974
Datta-Ray, Sunanda K., *Smash and Grab: The Annexation of Sikkim*, Vikas, New Delhi, 1985
Davies, H. Morriston, *Surgery of the Lung and Pleura*, Oxford University Press, London, 1930
Desai, Morarji, *The Story of My Life*, Volume II, Macmillan India, Delhi, 1974
Dhar, P.N., *Indira Gandhi, The Emergency and Indian Democracy*, Oxford University Press, New Delhi, 2000
—— 'The Kashmir Problem and Simla Solution', *Mainstream*, 15 April 1995
Drieberg, Trevor, *Indira Gandhi*, Vikas, Delhi, 1972
Durrani, Tehmina, *My Feudal Lord*, Bantam Press, London, 1994
Evans, Alexander, 'Kashmir: The Past Ten Years', *Asian Affairs* 30, no. 1 (February 1999)
—— 'The Kashmir Insurgency: As Bad as it Gets', *Small Wars and Insurgencies* 11, no. 1, (spring 2000)
Everett, Jana, 'Indira Gandhi and the Exercise of Power', in Genovese, Michael A. (ed.), *Women as National Leaders*, Sage, London, 1993

Select Bibliography

Fallaci, Oriana, *Interview With History*, Houghton Mifflin, Boston, 1976

Farnell, Vera, *A Somervillian Looks Back*, Oxford University Press, Oxford, 1948

Feroze Gandhi Commemorative Volume, Rae Bareilly Degree College Education Trust, 1970

Fishlock, Trevor, *India File*, John Murray, London, 1983

Forbes, Geraldine, *Women in Modern India*, Cambridge University Press, Cambridge, 1996, Volume IV, 2, in Johnson, Gordon (ed.), *The New Cambridge History of India*

Frankel, Francine R., *India's Green Revolution: Economic Gains and Political Costs*, Princeton University Press, Princeton, 1971

—— *India's Political Economy: 1947–77*, Princeton University Press, Princeton, 1978

Fraser, Antonia, *The Warrior Queens*, 1988, Mandarin, London, 1995

French, Patrick, *Liberty or Death: India's Journey to Independence and Division*, Harper-Collins, London, 1997

Friedan, Betty, 'How Mrs Gandhi Shattered the Feminine Mystique', *Ladies Home Journal*, May 1966

Galbraith, John Kenneth, *Ambassador's Journal*, Houghton Mifflin, Boston, 1969

Gangadharan, K., *The Inquisition: Revelations before the Shah Commission*, Path Publishers, New Delhi, 1978

Gandhi, Arun, *Daughter of Midnight: The Child Bride of Gandhi*, Blacks Publishing, London, 1998

Gandhi, D.V. (ed.), *Era of Discipline (Documents of Contemporary Reality)*, Samachar Bharati, New Delhi, 1976

Gandhi, Indira, *Selected Speeches and Writings of Indira Gandhi*, Volumes I–V, Publications Division, Ministry of Information and Broadcasting, New Delhi, 1971–86

—— *Speeches in Parliament*, Jainco Art India, published for Lok Sabha Secretariat, New Delhi, 1996

—— *India: The Speeches and Reminiscences of Indira Gandhi*, Rupa, Delhi, 1975

—— *India and Bangladesh: Selected Speeches and Statements of Indira Gandhi*, Orient and Longman, Delhi, 1972

—— *My Truth*, Vikas, Delhi, 1981

—— *Of People and Problems*, Hodder, London, 1983

—— *Anand Bhawan Memories and Other Personal Essays*, Indira Gandhi Memorial Trust, 1989

—— *Remembered Moments: Some Autobiographical Writings of Indira Gandhi*, Indira Gandhi Memorial Trust, 1987

—— *Indira Gandhi in Conversation with Pupul Jayakar: What I Am*, Indira Gandhi Memorial Trust, 1986

—— 'The Story of Swaraj Bhawan', *Motilal Nehru Centenary Souvenir*, 1961

—— 'My Reminiscences of Bapu', *Gandhi Marg*, Volume I, no. 3, July 1959

—— 'A Page From the Book of Memory', *Women on the March*, September 1963

—— 'On Being a Hostess at Teen Murti', *The International*, August 1957

—— 'My Sixteenth Year', *Roshni*, 4 November 1959

—— 'Reminiscences of Tagore', *Women on the March*, January 1961

—— 'Design For Living', *Women on the March*, January 1959

Gandhi, M.K., *An Autobiography or The Story of My Experiments With Truth*, 1927, 1929, Penguin Books, 1982

Gandhi, Sonia, *Rajiv*, Viking/Penguin India, Delhi, 1992

—— (ed.), *Freedom's Daughter: Letters between Indira Gandhi and Jawaharlal Nehru 1922–39*, Hodder, London, 1989

—— (ed.), *Two Alone, Two Together: Letters between Indira Gandhi and Jawaharlal Nehru 1940–1964*, Hodder, London, 1992

Gandhi, Tehmina Kershasp, 'How We Welcomed Indira into the Family', in *The Spirit of India*, Volume I, Asia Publishing House, Bombay, 1975

Genovese, Michael A., *Women as National Leaders*, Sage, London, 1993

Gill, S.S., *The Dynasty: A Political Biography of the Premier Ruling Family of Modern India*, HarperCollins India, Delhi, 1996

—— *The Pathology of Corruption*, HarperCollins India, New Delhi, 1998

Godden, Rumer, *Kingfishers Catch Fire*, Macmillan, London, 1953

—— *A Time to Dance, No Time to Weep*, Macmillan, London, 1987

Gopal, Sarvepalli, *Jawaharlal Nehru: A Biography. Volume One: 1889–1947*, Oxford University Press, Delhi, 1975; *Volume Two: 1947–1956*, OUP, Delhi, 1979; *Volume Three: 1956–1964*, OUP, Delhi, 1984

—— (ed.), *An Anthology*, Oxford University Press, Delhi, 1980

—— (ed.), *Selected Works of Jawaharlal Nehru* (First Series) vols. 1–15, Orient Longman, NMML, Delhi, 1972

—— (ed.), *Selected Works of Jawaharlal Nehru* (Second Series) vols. 1–15, Orient Longman, NMML, Delhi, 1984

Grigg, John, 'A Woman with a Heart of a King', *Sunday Times*, 7 March 1971

Grover, Verinder and Arora, Ranjana (eds.), *Great Women of Modern India, Volume 7: Indira Gandhi*, Deep & Deep, New Delhi, 1993

Gujral, Satish, *A Brush with Life: An Autobiography*, Viking, New Delhi, 1997

Gupte, Pranay, *Mother India*, Scribner's, New York, 1992

Haksar, P.N., *One More Life*, Oxford University Press, Delhi, 1990

—— *Premonitions*, Bombay Interpress, 1979

Hangen, Welles, *After Nehru, Who?* Rupert Hart-Davis, London, 1963

Hardgrave, Robert L. Jr., 'India in 1984: Confrontation, Assassination and Succession', *Asian Survey*, 25, part 2 (1985)

Harrison, Irene, *Agatha Harrison*, George Allen & Unwin, London, 1956

Hart, Henry, (ed.), *Indira Gandhi's India: A Political System Reappraised*, Westview Press, Boulder, Colorado, 1976

—— 'Political Leadership in India: Dimensions and Limits', in Kohli, Atul, (ed.), *India's Democracy: An Analysis of Changing State-Society Relations*, Princeton University Press, Princeton, 1988

Hasan, Zoya, 'The Prime Minister and the Left', in Manor, James (ed.), *Nehru to the Nineties*.

Hollis, Patricia, *Jennie Lee: A Life*, Oxford University Press, Oxford, 1997

Hutheesing, K.N., *With No Regrets*, Lindsay Drummond Ltd, London, 1946

—— *We Nehrus*, Macmillan, New York, 1965

—— *Dear to Behold: An Intimate Portrait of Indira Gandhi*, Macmillan, New York, 1969

Hutheesing, Krishna (ed.), *Nehru's Letters to His Sister*, Faber & Faber, London, 1963

Jagmohan, *Island of Truth*, Vikas, New Delhi, 1978

—— *My Frozen Turbulence in Kashmir*, Allied Publishers, New Delhi, 1991

Jahan, Rounaq, 'Women in South Asian Politics', *Third World Quarterly*, July 1987

Jain, C.K., *The Union and State Legislatures in India*, Allied Publishers, New Delhi, 1993

Jalal, Ayesha, *Democracy and Authoritarianism in South Asia*, Cambridge University Press, Cambridge, 1995

Jayakar, Pupul, *Indira Gandhi*, Penguin Books India, New Delhi, 1992

Jeffrey, Robin, 'Jawaharlal Nehru and the Smoking Gun: Who Pulled the Trigger on Kerala's Communist Government in 1959?', *The Journal of Commonwealth & Comparative Politics*, XXIX (March 1991), 1, pp. 72–85

Jones, Mervyn, *Michael Foot*, Gollancz, London, 1994

Select Bibliography

Kalhan, Promilla, *Kamala Nehru: An Intimate Biography*, NIB Publishers, New Delhi, 1990 (second, revised edition; originally published 1973 by Vikas)

Kapur, Jagga, *What Price Perjury: Facts of the Shah Commission*, Arnold-Heinemann, New Delhi, 1978

Kashyap, Subhash C., *Parliament of India: Myth and Realities*, National Publishing House, New Delhi, 1988

Kaul, T.N., *Diplomacy in Peace and War*, Vikas, New Delhi, 1979

—— *My Years Through Raj to Swaraj*, Vikas, New Delhi, 1995

—— *The Kissinger Years*, Arnold Heinemann, New Delhi, 1980

Kaviraj, Sudipta , 'Crisis of Political Institutions in India', *Contributions to Indian Sociology*, no. 2 (1984)

—— 'Indira Gandhi and Indian Politics', *Economic and Political Weekly*, Volume 21 (1986)

Katzenstein, Mary Fainsod, 'Towards Equality: Cause and Consequence of the Political Prominence of Women in India', *Asian Survey*, 18, part 5 (1978)

Khilnani, Sunil, *The Idea of India*, Hamish Hamilton, London, 1997

Kidwai, Anser, *Indira Gandhi: Charisma and Crisis*, Siddhi Books/Cosmo Publications, New Delhi, 1996

Kissinger, Henry, *White House Years*, Weidenfeld & Nicolson, London, 1979

Kochanek, Stanley A., 'Mrs Gandhi's Pyramid: The New Congress', in Hart, Henry (ed.), *Indira Gandhi's India: A Political System Reappraised*

Kohli, Atul,(ed.), *India's Democracy: An Analysis of Changing State-Society Relations*, Princeton University Press, Princeton, 1988

Kothari, Rajni, 'Integration and Exclusion in Indian Politics', *Economic and Political Weekly*, 23, part 43 (1988)

Kumar, Ravinder and Panigrahi, D.N. (eds.), *Selected Works of Motilal Nehru*, 6 Volumes, Vikas, New Delhi, 1982–1995

Lamb, Alistair, *Kashmir: A Disputed Legacy*, Roxford Books, Hertfordshire, 1991

Lukas, J. Anthony, 'She Stands Remarkably Alone', *New York Times*, May 27, 1966

Malhotra, Inder, *Indira Gandhi*, Hodder, London, 1989

Manor, James, 'Innovative Leadership in Modern India: M.K. Gandhi, Nehru and I. Gandhi', in Sheffer, Gabriel (ed.), *Innovative Leaders in International Politics*, Albany: State University of New York Press, 1993

—— 'Parties and the Party System', in Kohli, Atul, (ed.), *India's Democracy: An Analysis of Changing State-Society Relations*, Princeton University Press, Princeton, 1988

—— (ed.), *Nehru to the Nineties*, Hurst & Company, London, 1994

Marwah, Ved, *Uncivil Wars: Pathology of Terrorism in India*, HarperCollins India, New Delhi, 1995

Masani, Zareer, *Indira Gandhi*, Hamish Hamilton, London, 1975

Mathai, M.O., *My Days With Nehru*, Vikas, New Delhi,1979

—— *Reminiscences of the Nehru Age*, Vikas, New Delhi,1978

Mayer, Peter, 'Congress (I), Emergency (I): Interpreting Indira Gandhi's India', *The Journal of Commonwealth & Comparative Politics*, Vol XXII, no. 2 (1984), pp. 128–150

Mehta, Ved, *A Family Affair*, Oxford University Press, Oxford, 1982

—— *Portrait of India*, Farrar, Straus and Giroux, New York, 1970

—— *Rajiv Gandhi and Rama's Kingdom*, Yale, New Haven, 1994

—— *The New India*, Penguin, London, 1978

Mehta, Vinod, *The Sanjay Story*, Jaico Publishing Company, Bombay, 1978

Menen, Aubrey, 'Indira Gandhi is Sort of the De Gaulle of India', *New York Times Magazine*, December 31, 1972

Merchant, Minhaz, *Rajiv Gandhi: The End of a Dream*, Viking/Penguin India, Delhi, 1991

Michaelis, Arnold, 'An Interview with Indira Gandhi', *McCalls*, April 1966

Mishra, D.P., *The Post-Nehru Era: Political Memoirs*, Har-Anand Publications, New Delhi, 1993

Mistry, Rohinton, *A Fine Balance*, Faber, London, 1996

—— *Such a Long Journey*, Faber, London, 1991

Mitra, S. K., 'India: Dynastic Rule or the Democratization of Power?', *Third World Quarterly*, Volume 10, no. 1 (January 1988)

Mohan, Anand, *Indira Gandhi*, Hawthorn Books, New York, 1967

Moodgal, H.M.K., Majumdar, S. and Sharma, R.K., (eds.), *Indira Gandhi: A Select Bibliography*, Gitanjali Prakashan, New Delhi, 1976

Moraes, Dom, *Mrs. Gandhi*, Cape, London, 1980

—— *Never at Home*. New Delhi: Penguin, 1992

Moraes, Frank, *Indira Gandhi*, Directorate of Advertising and Visual Publicity, Delhi, 1966

Morgan, Janet, *Edwina Mountbatten: A Life of Her Own*, HarperCollins, London, 1991

Mukhopadhyay, Tarun Kumar, *Feroze Gandhi: A Crusader in Parliament*, Allied Publishers, New Delhi, 1992

Nanda, B.R., *Jawaharlal Nehru: Rebel and Statesman*. Oxford University Press, Delhi, 1995

—— *The Nehrus: Motilal and Jawaharlal*, Allen & Unwin, London, 1962

Nandy, Ashis, 'Indira Gandhi and the Culture of Indian Politics', *At the Edge of Psychology*, Oxford University Press, Delhi, 1980

Narasimhan, Sakuntala, *Sati: Widow Burning in India*, Anchor Books, New York, 1990

Nayar, Kuldip, *Between the Lines*, Allied Publishers, Bombay, 1969

—— *India: The Critical Years*, Vikas, Delhi, 1971

—— *India After Nehru*, Vikas, Delhi, 1975

—— *The Judgment: The Inside Story of the Emergency in India*, Vikas, Delhi, 1977

—— *In Jail*, Vikas, Delhi, 1978

—— *Supersession of Judges*, Hind Pocket Books, Delhi, 1973

Nayar, Kuldip and Singh, Khushwant, *Tragedy of Punjab: Operation Blue Star and After*, Vision Books, Delhi, 1984

Nelson, Barbara J. and Chowdhury, Jajma, *Women and Politics Worldwide*, Yale University Press, New Haven, 1994

Nehru, B.K., *Nice Guys Finish Second*, Viking Penguin, Delhi, 1997

Nehru, Jawaharlal, *Autobiography*, The Bodley Head, London, 1936

—— *The Discovery of India*, Signet Press, Calcutta, 1946

—— *Glimpses of World History*, Kitabistan, Allahabad, 1934–35; reprinted John Day, New York, 1960

—— *Letters from a Father to His Daughter*, Kitabistan, Allahabad, 1938

—— (ed.), *A Bunch of Old Letters*, Asia Publishing House, Bombay, 1958

Nissan, Elizabeth, *Sri Lanka: A Bitter Harvest*, Minority Rights Group Report, London, 1996

Norman, Dorothy, *Encounters: A Memoir*, Harcourt Jovanovich, San Diego, 1987

—— (ed.), *Indira Gandhi: Letters to an American Friend, 1950–1984*, Harcourt Jovanovich, New York, 1985

—— *Intimate Visions: The Photographs of Dorothy Norman*, Chronicle Books, San Francisco, 1993

Omvedt, Gail, *Reinventing Revolution: New Social Movements and the Socialist Tradition in India*, M.E. Sharpe, Armonk, New York, 1993

—— *We Will Smash This Prison*, Zed Press, London, 1980

Panandiker, V.A. and Mehra, Ajay K. (eds.), *The Indian Cabinet: A Study in Governance*, Konark Publishers, Delhi, 1996

Pande, B.N., *Indira Gandhi*, Government of India, Ministry of Information and Broadcasting, New Delhi, 1989

Pandey, B.N., *Nehru*, Macmillan, London, 1976

Pandit, Vijaya Lakshmi, *Prison Days*, Signet, Calcutta, 1945

—— *The Scope of Happiness: A Personal Memoir*, Crown, New York, 1979

Paul, Swraj, *Indira Gandhi*, Robert Royce, London, 1985

Parthasarthi, G. and Prasad, H. Y. Sharada (eds.), *Indira Gandhi: Statesmen, Scholars, Scientists and Friends Remember*, Indira Gandhi Memorial Trust and Vikas, Delhi, 1985

Pimlott, Ben, *Frustrate Their Knavish Tricks: Writings on Biography, History and Politics*, HarperCollins, London, 1994

Prasad, H.Y. Sharada and Pandey, P.N. (eds.), *The Spirit of India*, 4 volumes, Asia Publishing House, Bombay, 1975

Puri, Bajraj, 'Era of Indira Gandhi', *Economic and Political Weekly*, 20, part 4 (1988)

Rajan, Rajeswari Sunder, *Real and Imagined Women*, Routledge, London, 1993

Ram, Janaki, *V.K. Krishna Menon: A Personal Memoir*, Delhi, Oxford University Press, 1997

Rao, P.V. Narasimha, *The Insider*, Viking/Penguin Books India, New Delhi, 1998

Rau, M. Chalapathi, *Journalism and Politics*, Vikas, Delhi, 1984

Richter, Linda K., 'Exploring Theories of Female Leadership in South and Southeast Asia', *Pacific Affairs*, 63 (1990)

Roberts, Andrew, *Eminent Churchillians*, Weidenfeld & Nicolson, London, 1994

Robinson, Andrew, and Dutta, Krishna, *Rabindranath Tagore: The Myriad Minded Man*, Bloomsbury, London, 1995

Rollier, Auguste, *Heliotherapy*, (translated by G. de Swietochowski), Oxford University Press, Oxford, 1927

Rushdie, Salman, *Imaginary Homelands*, Granta, London, 1991

—— *Midnight's Children*, Cape, London, 1981

Ryan, Frank, *Tuberculosis: The Greatest Story Never Told*, Swift Publishers, Bromsgrove, Worcestershire, 1992

Sahgal, Manmohini Zutshi, 'An Indian Freedom Fighter Recalls Her Life', in Forbes, Geraldine, *Women in Modern India*, M.E. Sharpe, Inc., New York, 1994

Sahgal, Nayantara, *Prison and Chocolate Cake*, HarperCollins India, New Delhi, 1997; Gollancz, London, 1954

—— *From Fear Set Free*, Gollancz, London, 1962

—— *Indira Gandhi: Her Road to Power*, Frederick Ungar, New York, 1982

—— *Rich Like Us*, Heinemann, London, 1985

—— (ed.), *Before Freedom: Nehru's Letters to His Sister*, HarperCollins India, New Delhi, 2000

Sahgal, Nayantara, and Rai, E.N. Mangat, *Relationship: Extracts from a Correspondence*, Kali for Women, New Delhi, 1994

Sarin, Ritu, *The Assassination of Indira Gandhi*, Penguin, New Delhi, 1990

Sarkar, Bidyut (ed.), *P.N. Haksar: Our Times and the Man*, Allied Publishers, New Delhi, 1989

Schofield, Victoria, *Kashmir in the Crossfire*, I.B. Tauris, London, 1996

Sen, Ela, *Indira Gandhi: A Biography*, Peter Owen, London, 1973

Sen, Mala, *India's Bandit Queen: The True Story of Phoolan Devi*, Pandora, London, 1993

Sender, Henny, *The Kashmiri Pandits: A Study of Cultural Choice in North India*, Oxford University Press, Delhi, 1988

Seton, Marie, *Panditji: A Portrait of Jawaharlal Nehru*, Dennis Dobson, London, 1967; Rupa, Delhi, 1967

—— Interview with Ian Jack on Indira Gandhi in *Sunday Times*, 4 November 1984

Shah Commission of Inquiry: Interim Report I, II. Third and Final Report, Volumes I–III, Ministry of Information and Broadcasting, New Delhi, 1978

Shiva, Vandana, *The Violence of the Green Revolution*, Zed Books, London, 1991

Shourie, Arun, *Mrs Gandhi's Second Reign*, Vikas, Delhi, 1983

—— 'Indira Gandhi as Commerce', *Indian Express*, 1982

Singh, Karan, *Autobiography*, Oxford University Press, Delhi, 1994

Singh, Khushwant, 'Indira Gandhi', *Illustrated Weekly of India*, 14 March 1971

—— *Indira Gandhi Returns*, Vision Books, New Delhi, 1979

—— 'Of Love and Loathing: Khushwant Singh's Autobiography', *India Today*, 13 October 1995, pp. 126–31

Khushwant Singh and Nayar, Kuldip, *Tragedy of Punjab: Operation Blue Star and After*. Vision Books, Delhi, 1984

Singh, K. Natwar, *Count Your Blessings*, Har-and Publications, New Delhi, 1993

Singh, Patwant, *India and the Future of Asia*, Faber & Faber, London, 1966

—— *Of Dreams and Demons: An Indian Memoir*. Duckworth, London, 1994; Rupa, New Delhi, 1994

—— *The Sikhs*, John Murray, London, 1999

Singh, Patwant and Malik, Harji (eds.), *Punjab: The Fatal Miscalculation*, Published by Patwant Singh, New Delhi, 1985

Singh, Tavleen, *Kashmir: A Tragedy of Errors*, Penguin, New Delhi, 1996

Singh, Zail, *Memoirs of Giani Zail Singh*, Har-Anand Publications, New Delhi, 1997

Sinha, Aditya, *Farooq Abdullah: The Prodigal Son*, UBSPD, Delhi, 1995

Sisson, Richard and Rose, Leo E., *War and Secession: Pakistan, India, and the Creation of Bangladesh*, University of California Press, Berkeley, 1990

Smith, F.B., *The Retreat of Tuberculosis: 1850–1950*, Croom Helm, London, 1988

Srivastava, C.P., *Lal Bahadur Shastri: A Life of Truth in Politics*, Oxford University Press, Delhi, 1995

Taylor, Anne, *Annie Besant*, Oxford University Press, Oxford, 1992

Thapar, Raj, *All These Years*, Seminar Publications, New Delhi, 1991

Thakur, Janardan, *All The Prime Minister's Men*, Vikas, New Delhi, 1977

—— *Indira Gandhi and Her Power Game*, Vikas, New Delhi, 1979

Thakur, Ramesh, *The Government and Politics of India*, Macmillan, London, 1995

Thurre, Pascal, *Crans-Montana: Un Autre Regard*, Crans-Montana, 1992

Tully, Mark, *No Full Stops in India*, Viking, London, 1991

Tully, Mark and Satish, Jacob, *Amritsar: Mrs. Gandhi's Last Battle*, Cape, London, 1985

Tully, Mark and Masani, Zareer, *From Raj to Rajiv: Forty Years of Indian Independence*, BBC Books, London, 1988

Vasudev, Uma, *Indira Gandhi: Revolution in Restraint*, Vikas, New Delhi, 1973

—— *Two Faces of Indira Gandhi*, Vikas, Delhi, 1977

Wayne, Jenifer, *The Purple Dress: Growing Up in the Thirties*, Gollancz, London, 1979

Wilson, Jeyaratnam A., *The Break-Up of Sri Lanka: The Sinhalese-Tamil Conflict*, Hurst, London, 1988

Wolpert, Stanley, *Nehru: A Tryst with Destiny*, Oxford University Press, New York, 1996

—— *Zulfi Bhutto of Pakistan: His Life and Times*, Oxford University Press, Oxford, 1993

Willcoxen, Harriet, *First Lady of India: The Story of Indira Gandhi*, Doubleday, New York, 1969

Young, Hugo, *One of Us: A Biography of Margaret Thatcher*, Pan, London, 1993

Yunus, Mohammad, *Persons, Passions, Politics*, Vikas, Delhi, 1980

Ziegler, Philip, *Mountbatten: The Official Biography*, Fontana/Collins, London, 1986

INDEX

Shelat, J.M. 353
Shirodkar, Dr Vithal Nagesh 192
Shukla, V.C. 394, 408–9, 437, 441
Sicily (1936) 115–16
Sikhs/Sikhism 3–4, 296, 316, 454–5,
    464, 465, 468, 471; and Indira's
    assassination 485, 492–3, 498–9; *see*
    'Operation Blue Star'
Sikkim, invasion of (1974–5) 363–5
Sikri, S.M. 353
Simla Accord (1972) 344–7, 365, 366
Simla Conference (1945) 197
Simon, Sir John 53
Simon & Schuster (publisher) 268
Simon Commission 53, 196
Simons, Lewis 399
Sinclair, Upton 185
Sindhi, Vimla 213
Singh, Amarinder 464
Singh, Arun 464, 474, 479, 483
Singh, Beant 492–3
Singh, Charan 417, 419, 431–2, 436,
    438–9
Singh, Darbara 471–2, 473
Singh, Dinesh 282, 294–5, 299, 306,
    321, 355
Singh, Maharajah Hari 197, 198, 215,
    216
Singh, Karan 216, 234, 379, 405, 425
Singh, Khushwant 408, 436, 457; *Indira
    Gandhi Returns* 418
Singh, Lady Maharaj 156
Singh, Narain 492, 493
Singh, Maharajah Pratap 201, 202
Singh, Satwant 492–3
Singh, Swaran 280, 343, 372, 379, 383,
    425
Singh, Tavleen 468, 469–70
Singh, V.P. 445
Singh, Zail 453, 455, 456, 462–3, 472,
    478, 481, 482, 483, 496
Sinha, Jagmohan Lal 371
Sinha, Tarakeshwari 242, 272, 307, 315
Sitaramayya, Pattabhi 182
Smuts, General Jan 163
Somerville College, Oxford 105, 108,
    109, 116, 118, 121, 125–31, 133,
    136, 141–2, 143

Soni, Ambika 396
Sorenson, Reginald 135
Soviet Union: World War II 154–5;
    (1953) 233–4; (1955) 238; (1964)
    280; (1966) 298, 299; (1971) 335;
    invasion of Afghanistan 460
Spaghlinger, Henri 35
Spanish Civil War (1936) 116, 117, 119,
    129, 133
Spirit of St Louis (monoplane) 44
Spock, Benjamin 385
Sri Lanka/Ceylon (1931) 72–4; and
    Bandung Conference (1955) 238;
    (1962) 265; ethnic conflict (1983)
    470–1
Srinagar, Kashmir (1934) 85; (1945)
    195–6; (1948) 220–1; (1958) 248;
    (1960) 256–7; (1965) 281; (1973)
    365; (1983) 468–9; (1984) 488–9;
    (2000) 3–4
Stalin, Joseph 154, 155
State Bank of India 332–3
States Reorganisation Act (1956) 454
Statesman (Delhi) 379
Steffan, Dr 103, 106, 107, 108
Stephani, Dr Theodore 40, 42
sterilization programme (1976) 404–7,
    413
Stevenson, Adlai 227, 234
Stieglitz, Dorothy 227
Stravinsky, Igor 337
Subramaniam, C. 296, 299
Sultana, Mahmuna 242
Sultana, Rukhsana 405–6
Sunday Times 482
Surge (magazine) 351, 393, 394, 395
Surya (magazine) 436, 457, 458
Sutherland, Lucy 121, 141
Swaraj Bhawan *see* Anand Bhawan
Swaraj Party 25, 30, 31, 57
Swatantra Party 95, 302, 304, 316, 325,
    395
Switzerland (1926) 34–41; (1935) 104–5;
    (1936) 120; (1939) 142; (1953)
    234–5; *see also* Bex; Leysin

Tagore, Rabrindanath 78, 87, 88, 97,
    98, 172, 343; school *see* Santiniketan